Lecture Notes in Computer Science 4468

Commenced Publication in 1973
Founding and Former Series Editors:
Gerhard Goos, Juris Hartmanis, and Jan van Leeuwen

W0090906

Marcello M. Bonsangue
Einar Broch Johnsen (Eds.)

Formal Methods for Open Object-Based Distributed Systems

9th IFIP WG 6.1
International Conference FMOODS 2007
Paphos, Cyprus, June 6-8, 2007
Proceedings

 Springer

Volume Editors

Marcello M. Bonsangue
Leiden University
Leiden Institute of Advanced Computer Science
2300 RA Leiden, The Netherlands
E-mail: marcello@liacs.nl

Einar Broch Johnsen
University of Oslo
Department of Informatics
PO Box 1080 Blindern, 0316 Oslo, Norway
E-mail: einarj@ifi.uio.no

Library of Congress Control Number: 2007927619

CR Subject Classification (1998): C.2.4, D.1.3, D.2, D.3, F.3, D.4

LNCS Sublibrary: SL 2 – Programming and Software Engineering

ISSN   0302-9743
ISBN-10   3-540-72919-4 Springer Berlin Heidelberg New York
ISBN-13   978-3-540-72919-8 Springer Berlin Heidelberg New York

Springer is a part of Springer Science+Business Media

springer.com

© IFIP International Federation for Information Processing 2007

Typesetting: Camera-ready by author, data conversion by Scientific Publishing Services, Chennai, India
Printed on acid-free paper   SPIN: 12072873   06/3180   5 4 3 2 1 0

Preface

This volume contains the proceedings of the Ninth IFIP WG 6.1 International Conference on Formal Methods for Open Object-Based Distributed Systems (FMOODS 2007). The conference is part of the federated conferences on Distributed Computing Techniques (DisCoTec), together with the Ninth International Conference on Coordination Models and Languages (COORDINATION 2007) and the Seventh IFIP International Conference on Distributed Applications and Interoperable Systems (DAIS 2007). It was organized by the Department of Computer Science of the University of Cyprus, and it was held in Paphos, Cyprus during June, 6-8, 2007. The event was the third federated DisCoTec conference series, initiated in Athens in June 2005 and continued in Bologna in June 2006.

The goal of the FMOODS conferences is to bring together researchers and practitioners whose work encompasses three important and related fields:

- Formal methods
- Distributed systems and
- Object-based technology

The 17 papers presented at FMOODS 2007 and included in this volume were selected by the Programme Committee among 45 submissions. Each submission was reviewed by at least three Programme Committee members. They all reflect the scope of the conference and cover the following topics: semantics of object-oriented programming; formal techniques for specification, analysis, and refinement; model checking; theorem proving and deductive verification; type systems and behavioral typing; formal methods for service-oriented computing; integration of quality of service requirements into formal models; formal approaches to component-based design; and applications of formal methods.

The two invited speakers of FMOODS 2007, who also contributed to the proceedings in this volume, were:

- Mariangiola Dezani-Ciancaglini of the University of Torino, Italy, who is well known for her work on intersection-type assignment systems, which were largely used as finitary descriptions of lambda-models. More recently, she is interested in type systems for object-oriented languages and ambient calculi. In this volume she contributed with a paper introducing session types for object-oriented languages.
- Wolfgang Ahrend of the Chalmers Technical University, Sweden, who is known for his involvement in the KeY project, which aims at a formal methods tool that integrates design, implementation, formal specification, and formal verification of object-oriented software.

The conference was supported by IFIP, in particular by TC 6 and the working group WG 6.1. Thanks are due to John Derrick, Elie Najm, and George

Papadopoulos for their efforts in this respect. We are also grateful to the University of Cyprus and George Papadopoulos for organizing the event, the European project IST-33826 CREDO (`http://credo.cwi.nl`) for sponsoring one invited speaker, and the ITEA project Trust4All for sponsoring the participation of one of the Programme Committee Chairs.

Finally we thank all authors for the high quality of their contributions, and the Programme Committee members and the external reviewers for their help in selecting the papers for this volume. The use of EasyChair as a conference system was very helpful for organizing the technical programme and proceedings of FMOODS 2007.

June 2007   Marcello Bonsangue
                                                                                    Einar Broch Johnsen

Conference Organization

Programme Chairs

Marcello Bonsangue
Einar Broch Johnsen

Programme Committee

Bernhard Aichernig
Alessandro Aldini
Frank de Boer
Eerke Boiten
John Derrick
Robert France
Reiko Heckel
Naoki Kobayashi
Zhiming Liu
Elie Najm
David Naumann
Uwe Nestmann
Erik Poll
Antonio Ravara
Arend Rensink
Ralf Reussner
Grigore Roşu
Bernhard Rumpe
Martin Steffen
Carolyn Talcott
Heike Wehrheim
Martin Wirsing
Wang Yi
Gianluigi Zavattaro
Elena Zucca

Local Organization

George Papadopoulos

External Reviewers

Lacramioara Astefanoaei
Khaled Barbaria
Steffen Becker
Dénes Bisztray
Laura Bocchi
Mario Bravetti
Jan Broersen
Marzia Buscemi
Nadia Busi
Maura Cerioli
Feng Chen
Hung Dang Van
Alessandra Di Pierro
Sonia Fagorzi
Boris Gajanovic
Hans Groenniger
Claudio Guidi
Christian Haack
Christoph Herrmann
Mark Hills
Mohammad Mahdi Jaghoori
Jens Happe
Klaus Krogmann
Ruurd Kuiper

Marcel Kyas
Giovanni Lagorio
Xiaoshan Li
Francisco Martins
Björn Metzler
Roland Meyer
Yasuhiko Minamide
Kazuhiro Ogata
Luca Padovani
Razvan Popescu
Jaime Ramos
Gianna Reggio
Dirk Reiss
Birna van Riemsdijk
Ismael Rodriguez
Martin Schindler
Rudolf Schlatte
Marvin Schulze-Quester
Traian Florin Şerbănuţă
Frank Stomp
Sameer Sundresh
Vasco T. Vasconcelos
Naijun Zhan

Table of Contents

Algebraic Calculi

Specification, Verfication and Refinenment

Quality of Service

Asynchronous Session Types and Progress for Object Oriented Languages⋆

Mario Coppo[1], Mariangiola Dezani-Ciancaglini[1], and Nobuko Yoshida[2]

[1] Dipartimento di Informatica, Università di Torino
{coppo,dezani}@di.unito.it
[2] Department of Computing, Imperial College London
yoshida@doc.ic.ac.uk

Abstract. A session type is an abstraction of a sequence of heterogeneous values sent over one channel between two communicating processes. Session types have been introduced to guarantee consistency of the exchanged data and, more recently, *progress* of the session, i.e. the property that once a communication has been established, well-formed programs will never starve at communication points. A relevant feature which influences progress is whether the communication is synchronous or asynchronous. In this paper, we first formulate a typed asynchronous multi-threaded object-oriented language with thread spawning, iterative and higher order sessions. Then we study its progress through a new effect system. As far as we know, ours is the first session type system which assures progress in asynchronous communication.

1 Introduction

Distributed and concurrent programming paradigms are increasingly interesting, owing to the huge amount of distributed applications and services spread on the Internet. This gives a strong motivation to the study of specifications and implementations of these programs together with techniques for the formal verification of their properties. One of the crucial aspects is that of protocol specification: this consists in checking the coherence and safety of sequences of message interchanges that take place between a number of parties cooperating in carrying out some specific task. The use of type systems to formalise this kind of protocols has interested many researchers: in particular, *session types* [25,16] are recently focussed as a promising type discipline for structuring hand-shake communications. Interaction between processes is achieved by specifying corresponding sequences of messages through private channels. Such sequences are associated with session types, that assures that the two parties at each end of a channel perform consistent and complementary actions. Session types are assigned to communication channels and are shared among processes. For example, the session type `begin .?int.!bool.end` expresses that, after beginning the session, (`begin`), an integer will be received (`?int`), then a boolean value will be sent (`!bool`), and finally it is closed (`end`).

⋆ This work was partly funded by FP6-2004-510996 Coordination Action TYPES, EPSRC GR/T03208, EPSRC GR/S55538, EPSRC GR/T04724, EPSRC GR/S68071, and EU IST–2005–015905 MOBIUS project.

M.M. Bonsangue and E.B. Johnsen (Eds.): FMOODS 2007, LNCS 4468, pp. 1–31, 2007.

Session types have been studied for several different settings, *i.e.*, for π-calculus-based formalisms [14,25,11,16,2], for CORBA [26], for functional languages [13,27], for boxed ambients [10], and recently, for CDL, a W3C standard description language for Web Services [4,28,3,24,17]. In [6] the notion of session types was investigated in the framework of object oriented languages. Such an integration has been attempted before only in [7,26] and more recently in [5].

The integration of type-safe communication patterns with object-oriented programming idioms is done in [6] via the language MOOSE, a multi-threaded object-oriented core language augmented with session types. The type system of MOOSE has been designed not only to assure the type safety of the communication protocols, but also the *progress* property, i.e. that a communication session, when started, is executed without risk that processes in a session are blocked in a deadlock state. The first property is a consequence of the *subject reduction* property, which has been shown to be a critical one for calculi involving session types. A recent article [29] analyses this issue in details, comparing different reduction rules and typing systems appeared in the literature [16,27,2,11].

The progress property, which also is an essential requirement for all kinds of applications, does not seem to have been considered before [6,7] in the literature. The operational semantics of MOOSE, however, requires communications on a channel to be synchronous, i.e. they can take place only when both processes involved in a communication are ready to perform the corresponding action. This is a strong requirement that can sometime generate deadlocks. Take for instance the parallel of the following processes:

```
1   connect c0 begin.?int.end{
2       connect c1 begin.!int.end{
3           c0.send(3);
4           c1.receive
5       }
6   }
```
$$Q_0$$

```
1   connect c0 begin.!int.end{
2       connect c1 begin.?int.end{
3           c1.send(5)
4           };
5       c0.receive
6   }
```
$$Q_1$$

Here connect c0 opens the session over channel c0, c0.send(3) sends value 3 via c0, and c0.receive receives a value via c0. These two processes in parallel, after having opened one connection on channel c0 and one on channel c1, cannot mutually exchange an integer on these channels. The resulting process would be stuck with the reduction rules of [6], since Q_0 and Q_1 are both waiting for a receiving action to synchronise.

In this paper we consider an *asynchronous* version of MOOSE, named AMOOSE: channels are buffered and can perform input and output actions at different times. This extension allows *the senders to send messages without being blocked*, reducing an overhead waiting for heavy synchronisation which the original synchronous session types require. Session types with asynchronous communication over buffered channels have been considered in [22,12] for functional languages, and in [9] for operating system services, to enforce efficient and safe message exchanges. These papers do not consider the progress property. In Java, this asynchronous semantics is found in many communication APIs such as Socket [19] and NIO [20]. Further, with the asynchrony, we naturally

(type)	$t ::= C \mid$ bool $\mid s \mid (s,\bar{s})$
(class)	$class ::=$ class C extends $C \{ \tilde{f}\tilde{t} \ \tilde{meth} \}$
(method)	$meth ::= t\,m\,(\tilde{t}\,\tilde{x},\tilde{\rho}\,\tilde{y})\,\{e\}$
(expression)	$e ::= x \mid v \mid$ this $\mid e;e \mid e.f := e \mid e.f \mid e.m(\tilde{e}) \mid$ new C
	$\mid$ new $(s,\bar{s}) \mid$ NullExc $\mid$ spawn $\{e\} \mid$ connect a $s\{e\}$
	$\mid u$.receive $\mid u$.send$(e) \mid u$.receiveS$(x)\{e\} \mid u$.sendS(u)
	$\mid u$.receiveIf$\{e\}\{e\} \mid u$.sendIf$(e)\{e\}\{e\}$
	$\mid u$.receiveWhile$\{e\} \mid u$.sendWhile$(e)\{e\}$
(identifier)	$a ::= c \mid x$
(channel)	$u ::= a \mid k^+ \mid k^-$
(value)	$v ::= c \mid$ null $\mid$ true $\mid$ false $\mid o \mid k^+ \mid k^-$
(thread)	$P ::= e \mid P \mid P$
(heap)	$h ::= [\,] \mid h :: [o \mapsto (C,\tilde{f}:\tilde{v})] \mid h :: c \mid h :: [k^p \mapsto \tilde{v}]$

Fig. 1. Syntax, where syntax occurring only at runtime appears shaded

obtain more programs with progress: in the above example, for instance, the sending actions transmit the output values to the buffered channels and running of Q_0 and Q_1 in parallel can progress and reach safely its natural end.

In [6] a single type system was defined to assure both type safety and progress. These two properties, however, are rather orthogonal: there seems to be no strong connection between them. In this paper we have chosen to define a type system for type safety and an effect system for progress. This de-coupling results in simpler systems and it allows a better understanding of the conditions needed to assure each property.

Structure of the paper. The syntax and operational semantics of AMOOSE will be introduced in Section 2, the typing system and the main definitions to formulate the subject reduction property will be introduced in Section 3. Progress properties will be discussed in Section 4. The complete proof of the subject reduction theorem is given in the Appendix.

2   Syntax and Operational Semantics

2.1   Syntax

In Fig. 1 we describe the syntax of AMOOSE, which is essentially that of the language MOOSE [6]; AMOOSE and MOOSE differ in the operational semantics, since in AMOOSE output is asynchronous, and the exchange of data between processes is realised via buffers in the queues associated to channels. We distinguish *user syntax*, *i.e.*, source level code, and *runtime syntax*, which includes null pointer exceptions, threads and heaps.

Channels. We distinguish *shared channels* and *live channels*. They both can be parameters of procedures. We deviate from [6] introducing polarised live channels [11,29]. Shared channels are only used to decide if two threads can communicate. After a connection is established the shared channel is replaced by a couple of fresh *live* channels having a different *polarity*, + or −, one for each of the communicating threads. We denote by k^p in the same thread both the receiving channel of polarity p and the sending channel of opposite polarity $\bar{p}$: this will be clear from the operational semantics. Note that the meaning of polarities is different from that in [11], where polarities simply represent the two ends of a (unique) session channel. As a notational convention we will always use $c, \ldots$ to denote shared channels and $k^p, k_0^p, k_1^p, \ldots$ to denote polarised live channels.

User syntax. The metavariable t ranges over types for expressions, ρ ranges over running session types, C ranges over class names and s ranges over shared session types. Each session type s has one corresponding *dual*, denoted $\bar{s}$, which is obtained by replacing each ! (output) by ? (input) and vice versa. We introduce the full syntax of types in § 3. Class and method declarations are as usual.

The syntax of user expressions e, e′ is standard but for the channel constructor new (s, s̄), which builds a fresh shared channel used to establish a private session, and the *communication expressions*, *i.e.*, connect u s {e} and all the expressions in the last three lines.

The first line gives parameter, value, the self identifier this, sequence of expressions, assignment to fields, field access, method call, and object creation. The values are channels, null, and the literals true and false. Thread creation is declared using spawn { e }, in which the expression e is called the *thread body*. The expression connect u s {e} starts a session: the channel u appears within the term {e} in session communications that agree with session type s. The remaining eight expressions, which realise the exchanges of data, are called *session expressions*, and start with "u._"; we call u the *subject* of such expressions. In the below explanation session expressions are pairwise coupled: we say that expressions in the same pair and with the same subject are *dual* to each other.

The first pair is for exchange of values (which can be shared channels): u.receive receives a value via u, while u.send (e) evaluates e and sends the result over u. The second pair expresses live channel exchange: in u.receiveS (x){e} the received channel will be bound to x within e, in which x is used for communications. The expression u.sendS (u′) sends the channel u′ over u. The third pair is for *conditional* communication: u.receiveIf {e}{e′} receives a boolean value via channel u, and if it is true continues with e, otherwise with e′; the expression u.sendIf (e){e′}{e″} first evaluates the boolean expression e, then sends the result via channel u and if the result was true continues with e′, otherwise with e″. The fourth is for *iterative* communication: the expression u.receiveWhile {e} receives a boolean value via channel u, and if it is true continues with e and iterates, otherwise ends; the expression u.sendWhile (e){e′} first evaluates the boolean expression e, then it sends its result via channel u and if the result was true continues with e′ and iterates, otherwise it ends.

Runtime syntax. The runtime syntax (shown shaded in Fig. 1) extends the user syntax: it adds NullExc to expressions, denoting the null pointer error; includes polarised live channels; extends values to allow for object identifiers o, which denote references to instances of classes; finally, introduces threads running in parallel. Single and multiple *threads* are ranged over by P, P'. The expression $P \mid P'$ says that P and P' are running in parallel.

Heaps, ranged over h, are built inductively using the heap composition operator '::', and contain mappings of object identifiers to instances of classes, shared channels and mappings of polarised channels to queues of values. In particular, a heap will contain the set of objects and *fresh* channels, both shared and live, that have been created since the beginning of execution. The heap produced by composing $h :: [o \mapsto (C, \tilde{f} : \tilde{v})]$ will map o to the object $(C, \tilde{f} : \tilde{v})$, where C is the class name and $\tilde{f} : \tilde{v}$ is a representation for the vector of distinct mappings from field names to their values for this instance. The heap produced by composing $h :: c$ will contain the fresh shared channel c. The heap produced by composing $h :: [k^p \mapsto \tilde{v}]$ will map the live channel k^p to the queue $\tilde{v}$. Heap membership for object identifiers and channels is checked using standard set notation, we therefore write it as $o \in h$, $c \in h$, and $k^p \in h$. Heap update for objects is written $h[o \mapsto (C, \tilde{f} : \tilde{v})]$, for polarised channels $h[k^p \mapsto \tilde{v}]$, and field update is written $(C, \tilde{f} : \tilde{v})[f \mapsto v]$. We assume that the heap is unordered, i.e. satisfying equivalences like

$$\upsilon :: \upsilon' \equiv \upsilon' :: \upsilon, \qquad h_1 \equiv h_1', h_2 \equiv h_2' \Rightarrow h_1 :: h_2 \equiv h_1' :: h_2'$$

where υ denotes generic heap elements. With some abuse of notation the operator " :: " denotes heap concatenation without making distinction between heaps and heap elements.

2.2 Operational Semantics

This subsection presents the operational semantics of AMOOSE: the main difference with respect to [6] is that in AMOOSE output is asynchronous and the values are exchanged through queues associated to live channels in the heap. In the reduction rules then the heap plays an essential role also in communications.

We only discuss the more interesting rules. First we list the evaluation contexts.

$$E ::= \quad [-] \mid E.f \mid E;e \mid E.f := e \mid o.f := E \mid E.m(\tilde{e}) \mid o.m(\tilde{v}, E, \tilde{e})$$
$$\mid \quad k^p.\text{send}(E) \mid k^p.\text{sendIf}(E)\{e\}\{e'\}$$

Since heaps associate queues only to live channels, we can reduce only session expressions whose subjects are live channels. Moreover shared channels are sent by send, while live channels are sent by sendS. For this reason there are no evaluation contexts of the shapes $E.\text{send}(e)$, $k^p.\text{sendS}(E)$ etc.

Fig. 2 defines auxiliary functions used in the operational semantics and typing rules. We assume a fixed, global class table CT, which as usual contains *Object* as topmost class.

Expressions. Fig. 3 shows the rules for execution of expressions which correspond to the sequential part of the language. The rules not involving communications are standard [18,1,8], but for the addition of a fresh shared channel to the heap (rule **NewS$^{\rightharpoonup}$**).

Field lookup

$$\mathsf{fields}(\mathit{Object}) = \bullet \qquad \frac{\mathsf{fields}(D) = \bar{\mathsf{f}}'\bar{\tau}' \qquad \mathsf{class}\ C\ \mathsf{extends}\ D\ \{\bar{\mathsf{f}}\,\bar{\mathsf{t}}\ \tilde{M}\} \in \mathrm{CT}}{\mathsf{fields}(C) = \bar{\mathsf{f}}'\bar{\tau}', \bar{\mathsf{f}}\bar{\mathsf{t}}}$$

Method lookup

$$\mathsf{methods}(\mathit{Object}) = \bullet \qquad \frac{\mathsf{methods}(D) = \tilde{M}' \qquad \mathsf{class}\ C\ \mathsf{extends}\ D\ \{\bar{\mathsf{f}}\,\bar{\mathsf{t}}\ \tilde{M}\} \in \mathrm{CT}}{\mathsf{methods}(C) = \tilde{M}', \tilde{M}}$$

Method type lookup

$$\frac{\mathsf{class}\ C\ \mathsf{extends}\ D\ \{\bar{\mathsf{f}}\bar{\mathsf{t}}\ \tilde{M}\} \in \mathrm{CT} \qquad \mathsf{t}\,\mathsf{m}\ (\bar{\tau}\bar{\mathsf{x}})\ \{\mathsf{e}\} \in \tilde{M}}{\mathsf{mtype}(\mathsf{m},C) = \bar{\tau} \to \mathsf{t}}$$

$$\frac{\mathsf{class}\ C\ \mathsf{extends}\ D\ \{\bar{\mathsf{f}}\bar{\mathsf{t}}\ \tilde{M}\} \in \mathrm{CT} \qquad \mathsf{m} \notin \tilde{M}}{\mathsf{mtype}(\mathsf{m},C) = \mathsf{mtype}(\mathsf{m},D)}$$

Method body lookup

$$\frac{\mathsf{class}\ C\ \mathsf{extends}\ D\ \{\bar{\mathsf{f}}\bar{\mathsf{t}}\ \tilde{M}\} \in \mathrm{CT} \qquad \mathsf{t}\,\mathsf{m}\ (\bar{\tau}\bar{\mathsf{x}})\ \{\mathsf{e}\} \in \tilde{M}}{\mathsf{mbody}(\mathsf{m},C) = (\bar{\mathsf{x}},\mathsf{e})}$$

$$\frac{\mathsf{class}\ C\ \mathsf{extends}\ D\ \{\bar{\mathsf{f}}\bar{\mathsf{t}}\ \tilde{M}\} \in \mathrm{CT} \qquad \mathsf{m} \notin \tilde{M}}{\mathsf{mbody}(\mathsf{m},C) = \mathsf{mbody}(\mathsf{m},D)}$$

τ is either t or ρ.

Fig. 2. Lookup Functions

In rule **NewC**$^{\to}$ the auxiliary function $\mathsf{fields}(C)$ examines the class table and returns the field declarations for C. The method invocation rule is **Meth**$^{\to}$; the auxiliary function $\mathsf{mbody}(\mathsf{m},C)$ looks up m in the class C, and returns a pair consisting of the formal parameter names and the method's code. The result is the method body where the keyword this is replaced by the object identifier o, and the formal parameters $\bar{\mathsf{x}}$ are replaced by the actual parameters $\tilde{\mathsf{v}}$.

The operator ":" denotes queue concatenation without making distinction between elements and queues. Thus $\mathsf{v} : \tilde{\mathsf{v}}'$ denotes a queue beginning with v and $\tilde{\mathsf{v}}' : \mathsf{v}$ a queue ending with v.

The send communication rules put values in the queues associated to the live channels with the same names and opposite polarity of the expression subjects. The receive communication rules instead take values in the queues associated to the expression subjects. In rules **SendS**$^{\to}$ and **ReceiveS**$^{\to}$ standard values are exchanged from expressions to queues. Rule **SendSS**$^{\to}$ puts a live channel in the queue: the opposite rule **ReceiveSS**$^{\to}$ (see Fig. 4) is discussed below since it spawns a new thread. In the conditional rules (**SendSIf-true**$^{\to}$, **SendSIf-false**$^{\to}$, **ReceiveSIf-true**$^{\to}$, **ReceiveSIf-false**$^{\to}$) depending on the value of the boolean, the execution proceeds with either the first or

Standard Reduction

Fld$^\rightarrow$
$$\frac{h(\mathsf{o}) = (C, \tilde{\mathsf{f}} : \tilde{\mathsf{v}})}{\mathsf{o}\,.\mathsf{f}_i\,, h \longrightarrow \mathsf{v}_i, h}$$

Seq$^\rightarrow$
$$\mathsf{v}\,; e, h \longrightarrow e, h$$

FldAss$^\rightarrow$
$$\frac{h' = h[\mathsf{o} \mapsto h(\mathsf{o})[\mathsf{f} \mapsto \mathsf{v}]]}{\mathsf{o}\,.\mathsf{f} := \mathsf{v}, h \longrightarrow \mathsf{v}, h'}$$

NewC$^\rightarrow$
$$\frac{\mathsf{fields}(C) = \tilde{\mathsf{f}}\,\tilde{\mathsf{t}} \quad \mathsf{o} \notin h}{\mathsf{new}\ C, h \longrightarrow \mathsf{o}, h :: [\mathsf{o} \mapsto (C, \tilde{\mathsf{f}} : \widetilde{\mathsf{init}(\mathsf{t})})]}$$

NewS$^\rightarrow$
$$\frac{\mathsf{c} \notin h}{\mathsf{new}\ (\mathsf{s}, \bar{\mathsf{s}}), h \longrightarrow \mathsf{c}, h :: \mathsf{c}}$$

Cong$^\rightarrow$
$$\frac{e, h \longrightarrow e', h'}{E[e], h \longrightarrow E[e'], h'}$$

Meth$^\rightarrow$
$$\frac{h(\mathsf{o}) = (C, \ldots) \quad \mathsf{mbody}(m, C) = (\tilde{\mathsf{x}}, e)}{\mathsf{o}.m(\tilde{\mathsf{v}}), h \longrightarrow e\,[\mathsf{o}/\mathtt{this}][\tilde{\mathsf{v}}/\tilde{\mathsf{x}}], h}$$

NullProp$^\rightarrow$
$$E[\mathsf{NullExc}], h \longrightarrow \mathsf{NullExc}, h$$

NullFldAss$^\rightarrow$
$\mathsf{null}.\mathsf{f} := \mathsf{v}, h \longrightarrow \mathsf{NullExc}, h$

NullFld$^\rightarrow$
$\mathsf{null}.\mathsf{f}\,, h \longrightarrow \mathsf{NullExc}, h$

NullMeth$^\rightarrow$
$\mathsf{null}.m(\tilde{\mathsf{v}}), h \longrightarrow \mathsf{NullExc}, h$

In NewC$^\rightarrow$, $\mathsf{init}(\mathsf{bool}) = \mathsf{false}$ **otherwise** $\mathsf{init}(\mathsf{t}) = \mathsf{null}$.

Asynchronous Communication Reduction

SendS$^\rightarrow$
$k^p.\mathsf{send}(\mathsf{v}), h :: [k^{\bar{p}} \mapsto \tilde{\mathsf{v}}'] \longrightarrow \mathsf{null}, h :: [k^{\bar{p}} \mapsto \tilde{\mathsf{v}}' : \mathsf{v}]$

ReceiveS$^\rightarrow$
$k^p.\mathsf{receive}, h :: [k^p \mapsto \mathsf{v} : \tilde{\mathsf{v}}'] \longrightarrow \mathsf{v}, h :: [k^p \mapsto \tilde{\mathsf{v}}']$

SendSS$^\rightarrow$
$k^p.\mathsf{sendS}(k_0^q), h :: [k^{\bar{p}} \mapsto \tilde{\mathsf{v}}'] \longrightarrow \mathsf{null}, h :: [k^{\bar{p}} \mapsto \tilde{\mathsf{v}}' : k_0^q]$

SendSIf-true$^\rightarrow$
$k^p.\mathsf{sendIf}(\mathsf{true})\{e_1\}\{e_2\}, h :: [k^{\bar{p}} \mapsto \tilde{\mathsf{v}}] \longrightarrow e_1, h :: [k^{\bar{p}} \mapsto \tilde{\mathsf{v}} : \mathsf{true}]$

SendSIf-false$^\rightarrow$
$k^p.\mathsf{sendIf}(\mathsf{false})\{e_1\}\{e_2\}, h :: [k^{\bar{p}} \mapsto \tilde{\mathsf{v}}] \longrightarrow e_2, h :: [k^{\bar{p}} \mapsto \tilde{\mathsf{v}} : \mathsf{false}]$

ReceiveSIf-true$^\rightarrow$
$k^p.\mathsf{receiveIf}\{e_1\}\{e_2\}, h :: [k^p \mapsto \mathsf{true} : \tilde{\mathsf{v}}] \longrightarrow e_1, h :: [k^p \mapsto \tilde{\mathsf{v}}]$

ReceiveSIf-false$^\rightarrow$
$k^p.\mathsf{receiveIf}\{e_1\}\{e_2\}, h :: [k^p \mapsto \mathsf{false} : \tilde{\mathsf{v}}] \longrightarrow e_2, h :: [k^p \mapsto \tilde{\mathsf{v}}]$

SendSWhile$^\rightarrow$
$k^p.\mathsf{sendWhile}(e)\{e_1\}, h \longrightarrow k^p.\mathsf{sendIf}(e)\{e_1; k^p.\mathsf{sendWhile}(e)\{e_1\}\}\{\mathsf{null}\}, h$

ReceiveSWhile$^\rightarrow$
$k^p.\mathsf{receiveWhile}\{e\}, h \longrightarrow k^p.\mathsf{receiveIf}\{e; k^p.\mathsf{receiveWhile}\{e\}\}\{\mathsf{null}\}, h$

Fig. 3. Expression Reduction

Struct

$P \mid \text{null} \equiv P \quad P \mid P_1 \equiv P_1 \mid P \quad P \mid (P_1 \mid P_2) \equiv (P \mid P_1) \mid P_2 \quad P \equiv P' \Rightarrow P \mid P_1 \equiv P' \mid P_1$

Spawn$^{\rightarrow}$

$E[\text{spawn}\{e\}], h \longrightarrow E[\text{null}] \mid e, h$

Par$^{\rightarrow}$

$$\dfrac{P, h \longrightarrow P', h'}{P \mid P_0, h \longrightarrow P' \mid P_0, h'}$$

Str$^{\rightarrow}$

$$\dfrac{P_1' \equiv P_1 \quad P_1, h \longrightarrow P_2, h' \quad P_2 \equiv P_2'}{P_1', h \longrightarrow P_2', h'}$$

Connect$^{\rightarrow}$

$E_1[\text{connect c s}\{e_1\}] \mid E_2[\text{connect c } \bar{\text{s}}\{e_2\}], h$

$\quad \longrightarrow E_1[e_1[^{k^+}\!/c]] \mid E_2[e_2[^{k^-}\!/c]], h :: [k^+ \mapsto \varepsilon] :: [k^- \mapsto \varepsilon] \quad k^+, k^- \notin h$

ReceiveSS$^{\rightarrow}$

$E[k^p.\text{receiveS}(x)\{e\}], h :: [k^p \mapsto k_0^q : \tilde{v}] \longrightarrow e[^{k_0^q}\!/x] \mid E[\text{null}], h :: [k^p \mapsto \tilde{v}]$

Fig. 4. Thread Reduction

the second branch. The iterative rules (**SendSWhile$^{\rightarrow}$**, **ReceiveSWhile$^{\rightarrow}$**) simply express the iteration by means of the conditional.

An *elementary* expression reduction is a reduction defined by any of the expression reduction rules except rule **Cong$^{\rightarrow}$**.

Threads. The reduction rules for threads, shown in Fig. 4, are given modulo the standard structural equivalence rules of the π-calculus [21], written $\equiv$. We define *multi-step* reduction as: $\longrightarrow\!\!\!\rightarrow \overset{\text{def}}{=} (\longrightarrow \cup \equiv)^*$.

When spawn$\{e\}$ is the active redex within an arbitrary evaluation context, the *thread body* e becomes a new thread, and the original spawn expression is replaced by null in the context. This is expressed by rule **Spawn$^{\rightarrow}$**.

Rule **Connect$^{\rightarrow}$** describes the opening of sessions: if two threads require a session on the same shared channel name c with dual session types, then two new fresh live channels k^+ and k^- with the same name but opposite polarities are created and added to the heap with empty queues. The freshness of the name k guarantees privacy and bilinearity of the session communication between the two threads. Finally, the two connect expressions are replaced by their respective session bodies, where the shared channel c has been substituted by the live channels k^+ and k^-, respectively.

In rule **ReceiveSS$^{\rightarrow}$** one thread awaits to receive a live channel, which will be bound to the variable x within the expression e. Notice that the receiver spawns a new thread to handle the consumption of the delegated session. This strategy avoids deadlocks in the presence of circular paths of session delegation [6].

We say that a heap h is *balanced* if $k^p \in h$ implies $k^{\bar{p}} \in h$. We only consider balanced heaps: it is easy to verify that reduction rules preserve balance of heaps.

Proposition 2.1. *If* $P, h \longrightarrow P', h'$ *and h is balanced, then h' is balanced too.*

3 The Type Assignment System and Its Properties

The type system discussed in this section is designed to guarantee linearity of live channels and communication error freedom. These properties are consequences of the Subject Reduction Theorem. Instead this system does not assure progress, which we will consider in next section.

3.1 Types

The full syntax of types is given in Fig. 5.

$\dagger ::= \ ! \ \mid \ ?$	direction
$\pi ::= \varepsilon \mid \pi.\pi \mid \dagger t \mid \dagger\langle\pi,\pi\rangle \mid \dagger\langle\pi\rangle^* \mid \dagger(\eta)$	partial session type
$\eta ::= \pi.\text{end} \mid \dagger\langle\eta,\eta\rangle \mid \pi.\eta$	ended session type
$\rho ::= \pi \mid \eta$	running session type
$s ::= \text{begin}.\eta$	shared session type
$\theta ::= s \mid \rho$	session type
$t ::= C \mid \text{bool} \mid s \mid (s,\bar{s})$	standard type

---

Fig. 5. Syntax of types

Partial session types, ranged over by π, represent sequences of communications, where ε is the empty communication, and $\pi_1.\pi_2$ consists of the communications in π_1 followed by those in π_2. We use $\dagger$ as a convenient abbreviation that ranges over $\{!,?\}$. The partial session types $!t$ and $?t$ express respectively the sending and reception of a value of type t.

The *conditional* partial session type has the shape $\dagger\langle\pi_1,\pi_2\rangle$. When $\dagger$ is $!$, $\dagger\langle\pi_1,\pi_2\rangle$ describes sessions which send a boolean value and proceed with π_1 if the value is true, or π_2 if the value is false; when $\dagger$ is $?$, the behaviour is the same, except that the boolean that determines the branch is to be received instead. The *iterative* partial session type $\dagger\langle\pi\rangle^*$ describes sessions that respectively send or receive a boolean value, and if that value is true continue with π, *iterating*, while if the value is false, do nothing.

The partial session types $!(\eta)$ and $?(\eta)$ represent the exchange of a live channel, and therefore of an active session, with remaining communications determined by the ended session type η. Note that typing the live channel by η instead of π ensures that this channel is no longer used in the sending thread.

An *ended session type*, η, is a partial session type concatenated either with end or with a conditional whose branches in turn are both ended session types. It expresses a sequence of communications with its termination, *i.e.*, no further communications on that channel are allowed at the end. A conditional ended session type allows to type spawns or connects in the branches.

We use ρ to range over both partial session types and ended session types: we call it a *running session type*.

A *shared session type*, s, starts with the keyword begin and has one or more endpoints, denoted by end. Between the start and each ending point, a sequence of session parts describe the communication protocol.

A *session type* θ is a running session type or a shared session type.

Standard types, t, are either class identifiers (C), or booleans (bool), or shared session types (s), or pairs of shared session types with their duals (*i.e.*, $(s,\bar{s})$).

Each session type θ has a corresponding *dual*, denoted $\bar{\theta}$, which is obtained as follows

- $\bar{?}=!$ $\bar{!}=?$
- $\overline{begin.\rho} = begin.\bar{\rho}$
- $\overline{\pi.end} = \bar{\pi}.end$ $\overline{\pi.\dagger\langle\eta_1,\eta_2\rangle} = \bar{\pi}.\overline{\dagger}\langle\bar{\eta_1},\bar{\eta_2}\rangle$
- $\bar{\varepsilon}=\varepsilon$ $\overline{\dagger t} = \overline{\dagger}t$ $\overline{\dagger\langle\eta\rangle} = \overline{\dagger}\langle\eta\rangle$ $\overline{\dagger\langle\pi_1,\pi_2\rangle} = \overline{\dagger}\langle\bar{\pi_1},\bar{\pi_2}\rangle$ $\overline{\dagger\langle\pi\rangle^*} = \overline{\dagger}\langle\bar{\pi}\rangle^*$ $\overline{\pi_1.\pi_2} = \bar{\pi_1}.\bar{\pi_2}$

Note that $\theta = \bar{\theta'}$ if and only if $\theta' = \bar{\theta}$.

We type expressions and threads with respect to the global class table CT, as reflected in the rules of Fig. 6 which define well-formed standard types. By dom(CT) we denote the domain of the class table CT, *i.e.*, the set of classes declared in CT. In Fig. 6 we also define subtyping, $<:$, on class names: we assume that the subclassing is acyclic as in [18]. In addition, we have $(s,\bar{s}) <: s$ and $(s,\bar{s}) <: \bar{s}$, as in standard π-calculus channel subtyping rules [15]: a channel on which both communication directions are allowed may also transmit data following only one of the two directions.

3.2 Typing Rules

The typing judgements for expressions and threads have two environments, *i.e.*, they have the shape:

$$\Gamma;\Sigma \vdash e : t \qquad\qquad \Gamma;\Sigma \vdash P : thread$$

where the *standard environment* Γ associates standard types to this, parameters and objects, while the *session environment* Σ contains only judgements for channel names and variables. Fig. 6 defines well-formedness of standard and session environments, where the domain of an environment is defined as usual and denoted by dom().

In Fig. 7, Fig. 8 and Fig. 9 we give the typing rules for expressions and threads. In the typing rules for expressions the session environments of the conclusions are obtained from those of the premises and possibly other session environments using the *concatenation* operator, $\circ$, defined below. We consider different cases for the concatenation of running session types since we want to avoid to have meaningless ε. As usual, $\bot$ stands for undefined.

- $\rho \circ \rho' = \begin{cases} \rho & \text{if } \rho' = \varepsilon \\ \rho' & \text{if } \rho = \varepsilon \\ \rho.end & \text{if } \rho' = \varepsilon.end \text{ and } \rho \text{ is a partial session type} \\ \rho.\rho' & \text{if } \rho \text{ is a partial session type} \\ \bot & \text{otherwise.} \end{cases}$

- $\Sigma \setminus \Sigma' = \{u : \Sigma(u) \mid u \in dom(\Sigma) \setminus dom(\Sigma')\}$

- $\Sigma \circ \Sigma' = \begin{cases} \Sigma \setminus \Sigma' \cup \Sigma' \setminus \Sigma \cup \{u : \Sigma(u) \circ \Sigma'(u) \mid u \in dom(\Sigma) \cap dom(\Sigma')\} \\ \qquad \text{if } \forall u \in dom(\Sigma) \cap dom(\Sigma') : \Sigma(u) \circ \Sigma'(u) \neq \bot; \\ \bot \quad \text{otherwise.} \end{cases}$

Well-formed Standard Types

Class	**Wf-Session**	**Pair**	**Bool**
$C \in \mathrm{dom}(\mathrm{CT})$			
$\vdash C : \mathsf{tp}$	$\vdash \mathsf{s} : \mathsf{tp}$	$\vdash (\mathsf{s}, \bar{\mathsf{s}}) : \mathsf{tp}$	$\vdash \mathsf{bool} : \mathsf{tp}$

Subtyping

$$\frac{}{(\mathsf{s},\bar{\mathsf{s}}) <: \mathsf{s}} \qquad \frac{}{(\mathsf{s},\bar{\mathsf{s}}) <: \bar{\mathsf{s}}} \qquad \frac{C \in \mathrm{dom}(\mathrm{CT})}{C <: C} \qquad \frac{C <: D \;\; D <: E}{C <: E} \qquad \frac{\text{class } C \text{ extends } D\, \{\tilde{\mathsf{f}}\,\tilde{\mathsf{t}}\,\tilde{M}\} \in \mathrm{CT}}{C <: D}$$

Standard Environments and Well-formed Standard Environments

$$\Gamma ::= \emptyset \mid \Gamma, \mathsf{x} : \mathsf{t} \mid \Gamma, \mathsf{this} : C \mid \Gamma, \mathsf{o} : C$$

Emp

EVar

EOid

Ethis

$$\frac{}{\emptyset \vdash \mathsf{ok}} \qquad \frac{\vdash \mathsf{t} : \mathsf{tp} \quad \mathsf{x} \notin \mathrm{dom}(\Gamma)}{\Gamma, \mathsf{x} : \mathsf{t} \vdash \mathsf{ok}} \qquad \frac{C \in \mathrm{dom}(\mathrm{CT}) \quad \mathsf{o} \notin \mathrm{dom}(\Gamma)}{\Gamma, \mathsf{o} : C \vdash \mathsf{ok}} \qquad \frac{C \in \mathrm{dom}(\mathrm{CT}) \quad \mathsf{this} \notin \mathrm{dom}(\Gamma)}{\Gamma, \mathsf{this} : C \vdash \mathsf{ok}}$$

Session Environments and Well-formed Session Environments

SEmp

SERC

$$\Sigma ::= \emptyset \mid \Sigma, \mathsf{u} : \rho \qquad\qquad \frac{}{\emptyset \vdash \mathsf{ok}} \qquad \frac{\mathsf{u} \notin \mathrm{dom}(\Sigma)}{\Sigma, \mathsf{u} : \rho \vdash \mathsf{ok}}$$

Fig. 6. Standard Types, Subtyping, and Environments

The concatenation of two running session types ρ and ρ' is the unique running session type (if it exists) which prescribes all the communications of ρ followed by all those of ρ'. The concatenation only exists if ρ is a partial session type. The extension to session environments is straightforward. The typing rules concatenate the session environments to take into account the order of execution of expressions. We adopt the convention that typing rules are applicable only when the session environments in the conclusions are defined.

In the following we discuss the most interesting typing rules for expressions.

Rule **Spawn** requires that all sessions used by the spawned thread are finally consumed, *i.e.*, they are all ended session types. This is necessary in order to avoid configurations that break the bilinearity condition. The consumption is guaranteed by the condition *ended*(Σ), since we define:

$$\mathit{ended}(\Sigma) = \forall \mathsf{u} : \rho \in \Sigma. \; \rho \text{ is an ended session type.}$$

Rule **Meth** retrieves the type of the method m from the class table using the auxiliary function $\mathrm{mtype}(\mathsf{m}, C)$, defined in Fig. 2. The session environments of the premises are concatenated with $\{\mathsf{u}_1 : \rho_1, \ldots, \mathsf{u}_m : \rho_m\}$, which represents the communication protocols of the live channels $\mathsf{u}_1, \ldots, \mathsf{u}_m$ during the execution of the method body.

Typing Rules for Values

Null	Oid	True	False	Chan
$\Gamma \vdash ok \quad \vdash t : tp$	$\Gamma, o : C \vdash ok$	$\Gamma \vdash ok$	$\Gamma \vdash ok$	$\Gamma \vdash ok$
$\Gamma ; \emptyset \vdash null : t$	$\Gamma, o : C ; \emptyset \vdash o : C$	$\Gamma ; \emptyset \vdash true : bool$	$\Gamma ; \emptyset \vdash false : bool$	$\Gamma ; \emptyset \vdash c : s$

Typing Rules for Standard Expressions

Var
$$\frac{\Gamma, x : t \vdash ok}{\Gamma, x : t \vdash x : t}$$

This
$$\frac{\Gamma, this : C \vdash ok}{\Gamma, this : C \vdash this : C}$$

Fld
$$\frac{\Gamma ; \Sigma \vdash e : C \quad ft \in fields(C)}{\Gamma ; \Sigma \vdash e.f : t}$$

Seq
$$\frac{\Gamma ; \Sigma \vdash e : t \quad \Gamma ; \Sigma' \vdash e' : t'}{\Gamma ; \Sigma \circ \Sigma' \vdash e ; e' : t'}$$

FldAss
$$\frac{\Gamma ; \Sigma \vdash e : C \quad \Gamma ; \Sigma' \vdash e' : t \quad ft \in fields(C)}{\Gamma ; \Sigma \circ \Sigma' \vdash e.f := e' : t}$$

NewC
$$\frac{\Gamma \vdash ok \quad C \in dom(CT)}{\Gamma ; \emptyset \vdash new \ C : C}$$

NewS
$$\frac{\Gamma \vdash ok}{\Gamma ; \emptyset \vdash new \ (s, \bar{s}) : (s, \bar{s})}$$

Spawn
$$\frac{\Gamma ; \Sigma \vdash e : t \quad ended(\Sigma)}{\Gamma ; \Sigma \vdash spawn \{ \ e \ \} : Object}$$

NullPE
$$\frac{\Gamma \vdash ok \quad \vdash t : tp}{\Gamma ; \emptyset \vdash NullExc : t}$$

Meth
$$\frac{\Gamma ; \Sigma_0 \vdash e : C \quad \Gamma ; \Sigma_i \vdash e_i : t_i \quad i \in \{1 \ldots n\} \quad mtype(m, C) = t_1, \ldots, t_n, \rho_1, \ldots, \rho_m \to t}{\Gamma ; \Sigma_0 \circ \Sigma_1 \ldots \circ \Sigma_n \circ \{u_1 : \rho_1, \ldots, u_m : \rho_m\} \vdash e.m(e_1, \ldots, e_n, u_1, \ldots, u_m) : t}$$

Fig. 7. Typing Rules for Expressions I

Rule **Conn** ensures that a session body properly uses its shared channel according to the required session type. The first premise says that the channel identifier used for the session (a) can be typed with the appropriate shared session type (begin.η). The second premise ensures that the session body can be typed in the restricted environment $\Gamma \setminus a$ with session environment containing a : η.

In rules **ReceiveIF** and **SendIF** *both* ρ_1 and ρ_2 are either partial session types or ended session types – this is guaranteed by the syntax of conditional session types.

The rule **WeakES**, where **ES** stands for empty session, is necessary to type a branch of a conditional expression, where the channel which is the subject of the conditional is not used. Rule **WeakE**, where **E** stands for end, allows us to obtain ended session types as predicates of session environments in order to apply rules **Conn**, **Spawn** and **ReceiveS**.

Fig. 10 defines well-formed class tables. Rule **M-ok** type-checks the method bodies with respect to a class C taking as environments the association between formal parameters and their types and the association between this and C.

3.3 Subject Reduction

We will consider only reductions of well-typed expressions and threads. We define types of run time entities in the standard way. The judgment is defined in Fig. 11. The judgment $h \vdash v : t$ guarantees that the runtime value v has type t; for objects we take

Typing Rules for Communication Expressions

Conn

$$\frac{\Gamma \vdash a : \text{begin}.\eta \quad \Gamma \backslash a \; ; \Sigma, a : \eta \vdash e : t}{\Gamma; \Sigma \vdash \text{connect } a \text{ begin}.\eta \{e\} : t}$$

Send

$$\frac{\Gamma; \Sigma \vdash e : t}{\Gamma; \Sigma \circ \{u : !t\} \vdash u.\text{send}(e) : Object}$$

Receive

$$\frac{\Gamma \vdash ok \quad \vdash t : tp}{\Gamma; \{u : ?t\} \vdash u.\text{receive} : t}$$

SendS

$$\frac{\Gamma \vdash ok \quad \eta \neq \varepsilon.\text{end}}{\Gamma; \{u' : \eta, u : !(\eta)\} \vdash u.\text{sendS}(u') : Object}$$

ReceiveS

$$\frac{\Gamma \backslash x \; ; \Sigma, x : \eta \vdash e : t \quad \eta \neq \varepsilon.\text{end} \quad ended(\Sigma)}{\Gamma; \{u : ?(\eta)\} \circ \Sigma \vdash u.\text{receiveS}(x)\{e\} : Object}$$

SendIf

$$\frac{\Gamma; \Sigma_0 \vdash e : bool \quad \Gamma; \Sigma, u : \rho_i \vdash e_i : t \quad i \in \{1,2\}}{\Gamma; \Sigma_0 \circ \Sigma, u : !\langle \rho_1, \rho_2 \rangle \vdash u.\text{sendIf}(e)\{e_1\}\{e_2\} : t}$$

ReceiveIf

$$\frac{\Gamma; \Sigma, u : \rho_i \vdash e_i : t \quad i \in \{1,2\}}{\Gamma; \Sigma, u : ?\langle \rho_1, \rho_2 \rangle \vdash u.\text{receiveIf}\{e_1\}\{e_2\} : t}$$

SendWhile

$$\frac{\Gamma; \emptyset \vdash e : bool \quad \Gamma; \{u : \pi\} \vdash e' : t}{\Gamma; \{u : !\langle \pi \rangle^*\} \vdash u.\text{sendWhile}(e)\{e'\} : t}$$

ReceiveWhile

$$\frac{\Gamma; \{u : \pi\} \vdash e : t}{\Gamma; \{u : ?\langle \pi \rangle^*\} \vdash u.\text{receiveWhile}\{e\} : t}$$

Non-structural Typing Rules for Expressions

WeakES

$$\frac{\Gamma; \Sigma \vdash e : t \quad u \notin dom(\Sigma)}{\Gamma; \Sigma, u : \varepsilon \vdash e : t}$$

WeakE

$$\frac{\Gamma; \Sigma, u : \pi \vdash e : t}{\Gamma; \Sigma, u : \pi.\text{end} \vdash e : t}$$

Sub

$$\frac{\Gamma; \Sigma \vdash e : t \quad t <: t'}{\Gamma; \Sigma \vdash e : t'}$$

Fig. 8. Typing Rules for Expressions II

Start

$$\frac{\Gamma; \Sigma \vdash e : t}{\Gamma; \Sigma \vdash e : thread}$$

Par

$$\frac{\Gamma; \Sigma_i \vdash P_i : thread \quad (i = 1, 2)}{\Gamma; \Sigma_1 \cup \Sigma_2 \vdash P_1 | P_2 : thread}$$

Fig. 9. Typing Rules for Threads

subclasses into consideration in rule **HObjSubs**. The judgment $h \vdash o$ guarantees that the object o is well-formed, *i.e.*, that its fields contain values according to the declared field types in C, the class of that object. Note that in rule **HObjSubs** the equality in the first premise simply asserts that there is an object o in the heap h, while the conclusion asserts that o is well-formed.

In order to formalise agreement between session environments and heaps, it is handy to introduce some definitions. We start by determining the initial and the final parts of a running session type.

M-ok

$$\frac{\{\text{this}:C,\tilde{x}:\tilde{t}\};\ \{\tilde{y}:\tilde{\rho}\}\vdash e:t}{\mathsf{t}\,\mathsf{m}\ (\tilde{t}\,\tilde{x},\tilde{\rho}\,\tilde{y})\ \{e\}:\text{ok in }C}$$

C-ok

$$\frac{\tilde{M}:\text{ok in }C}{\text{class }C\text{ extends }D\ \{\tilde{f}\,\tilde{t}\,\tilde{M}\}:\text{ok}}$$

CT-ok

$$\frac{\text{class }C\text{ extends }D\ \{\tilde{f}\,\tilde{t}\,\tilde{M}\}:\text{ok}\qquad CT:\text{ok}}{CT,\text{class }C\text{ extends }D\ \{\tilde{f}\,\tilde{t}\,\tilde{M}\}:\text{ok}}$$

Fig. 10. Well-formed Class Tables

HTrue

$$\frac{}{h\vdash\text{true}:\text{bool}}$$

HFalse

$$\frac{}{h\vdash\text{false}:\text{bool}}$$

HNull

$$\frac{C\in\text{dom}(CT)}{h\vdash\text{null}:C}$$

HObj

$$\frac{h(\mathsf{o})=(C,\dots)}{h\vdash\mathsf{o}:C}$$

HObjSubs

$$\frac{h\vdash\mathsf{o}:C'\qquad C'<:C}{h\vdash\mathsf{o}:C}$$

WfObj

$$\frac{h(\mathsf{o})=(C,\tilde{f}:\tilde{v})\qquad\text{fields}(C)=\tilde{f}\,\tilde{t}\qquad h\vdash v_i:t_i}{h\vdash\mathsf{o}}$$

Fig. 11. Types of Runtime Entities

A *basic session type* (s-basic type for short) is a session type of the form $\dagger t$ or $\dagger(\eta)$ or $\dagger\langle\rho_1,\rho_2\rangle$ or $\dagger\langle\pi\rangle^*$. Let β be a s-basic type. We denote with $\beta\psi$ a session type which begins with β and has the form $\beta.\rho$ or $\beta.\text{end}$ or β. In these cases let us call ψ the *continuation* of $\beta\psi$. If $\beta\psi$ stands for β or $\beta.\text{end}$ we say that the continuation ψ is *light*. Further let us define

$$\psi^\circ=\begin{cases}\rho & \text{if }\psi\text{ stands for }.\rho,\\ \varepsilon.\text{end} & \text{if }\psi\text{ stands for }.\text{end}\\ \varepsilon & \text{otherwise.}\end{cases}$$

The *core domain* of a session environment Σ (notation cored(Σ)) is the set of subjects in Σ whose predicates do not belong to $\{\varepsilon,\varepsilon.\text{end}\}$.

The *channel range* of an heap h (notation $\text{ran}_c(h)$) is the set of live channels which occur in h inside value queues:

$$\text{ran}_c(h)=\{k^p\mid h(k_0^q)=\tilde{v}:k^p:\tilde{v}'\text{ for some }k_0^q,\tilde{v},\tilde{v}'\}.$$

A heap h agrees with a session environment Σ if each value which is in the queue associated to a live channel k^p in h has the type expected by $\Sigma(k^p)$. We formalise this by means of an inductive definition on the (sum of) the sizes of the queues associated by h to the live channels in the core domain of Σ. The base step is when all these live channels are associated to empty queues and there are no channels in the heap waiting to be activated by receiveS expressions. In the induction cases each top value of a queue associated to a channel is checked against the running session type of that channel in the environment. If this check fails the heap and the session environment do not agree, otherwise both the queue and the environment are updated and the check is inductively applied to the resulting heap and session environment. The induction terminates since at each step a top value in a queue is popped out. Note that, when the considered value is a channel k_0^q of type η, we add the statement $k_0^q : \eta$ to the session environment: this is necessary to type the expression receiving the channel k_0^q. Clearly the order in which the live channels in the heap are considered is not influential.

Definition 3.1. *Fig. 12 defines the* agreement $A(\Sigma; h)$ *of a session environment* Σ *with a heap h.*

$$A(\Sigma;h) = \begin{cases} \text{true} & \text{if } \operatorname{dom}(\Sigma) \cap \operatorname{ran}_c(h) = \emptyset \\ & \text{and } \forall k^p \in \operatorname{cored}(\Sigma).h(k^p) = \varepsilon \\ A(\Sigma[k^p \mapsto \psi^\circ]; h[k^p \mapsto \tilde{v}']) & \text{if } h(k^p) = v:\tilde{v}', v \in \{\text{true, false}\} \\ & \text{and } \Sigma(k^p) = ?\text{bool}\,\psi \\ A(\Sigma[k^p \mapsto \psi^\circ]; h[k^p \mapsto \tilde{v}']) & \text{if } h(k^p) = o:\tilde{v}', h(o) = (C', \tilde{f}), C' <: C \\ & \text{and } \Sigma(k^p) = ?C\psi \\ A(\Sigma[k^p \mapsto \psi^\circ]; h[k^p \mapsto \tilde{v}']) & \text{if } h(k^p) = c:\tilde{v}', t \in \{s,(s,\bar{s})\} \text{ and } \Sigma(k^p) = ?t\,\psi \\ A(\Sigma[k^p \mapsto \psi^\circ], k_0^q : \eta; h[k^p \mapsto \tilde{v}']) & \text{if } h(k^p) = k_0^q:\tilde{v}', \Sigma(k^p) = ?(\eta)\psi \text{ and } k_0^q \notin \operatorname{dom}(\Sigma) \\ A(\Sigma[k^p \mapsto \rho_1\psi^\circ]; h[k^p \mapsto \tilde{v}']) & \text{if } h(k^p) = \text{true}:\tilde{v}' \text{ and } \Sigma(k^p) = ?\langle\rho_1,\rho_2\rangle\psi \\ A(\Sigma[k^p \mapsto \rho_2\psi^\circ]; h[k^p \mapsto \tilde{v}']) & \text{if } h(k^p) = \text{false}:\tilde{v}' \text{ and } \Sigma(k^p) = ?\langle\rho_1,\rho_2\rangle\psi \\ A(\Sigma[k^p \mapsto \pi.!\langle\pi\rangle^*\psi^\circ]; h[k^p \mapsto \tilde{v}']) & \text{if } h(k^p) = \text{true}:\tilde{v}' \text{ and } \Sigma(k^p) = ?\langle\pi\rangle^*\psi \\ A(\Sigma[k^p \mapsto \psi^\circ]; h[k^p \mapsto \tilde{v}']) & \text{if } h(k^p) = \text{false}:\tilde{v}' \text{ and } \Sigma(k^p) = ?\langle\pi\rangle^*\psi \\ \text{false} & \text{otherwise} \end{cases}$$

Fig. 12. Agreement between Session Environments and Heaps

We are now able to formulate the agreement between environments and heaps though the following rule:

WfHeap
$$\frac{\forall o \in \operatorname{dom}(h): \ h \vdash o \qquad \forall o \in \operatorname{dom}(\Gamma): \ h \vdash o : \Gamma(o) \qquad A(\Sigma;h)}{\Gamma;\Sigma \vdash h}$$

In the remaining of this section we outline the proof of subject reduction, while we give full details and proofs in the Appendix.

Standard ingredients of Subject Reduction proofs are Generation Lemmas. The Generation Lemmas in this work are somewhat unusual, because, due to the non-structural rules, when an expression is typed, the session environment used in the typing can be augmented by ending partial session types or by introducing ε-predicates. For example, $\Gamma;\Sigma \vdash x:t$ does *not* imply that $\Sigma = \emptyset$; instead, it implies that $\operatorname{cored}(\Sigma) = \emptyset$.

In order to express the Generation Lemmas, we define the partial order $\preceq$ among session environments, which basically reflects the differences introduced through the application of nonstructural rules.

Definition 3.2 (Weakening Order $\preceq$). $\Sigma \preceq \Sigma'$ *is the smallest partial order such that:* (1) *if* $u \notin dom(\Sigma)$, $\Sigma \preceq \Sigma, u : \varepsilon$; *and* (2) $\Sigma, u : \pi \preceq \Sigma, u : \pi$.end.

Note that $\preceq$ is defined in such a way that, if Σ is well-formed and $\Sigma \preceq \Sigma'$, then also Σ' is well-formed.

Generation Lemmas for standard expressions, communication expressions, and processes are given in the Appendix (see Lemmas A.2, A.3 and A.4) and make use of the relation $\preceq$. For example, $\Gamma; \Sigma \vdash$ u .send (e):t implies t $= Object$ and $\Gamma; \Sigma' \vdash$ e :t' and $\Sigma' \circ \{u : !t\} \preceq \Sigma$ for some Σ', t'.

The following lemma states that the ordering relation $\preceq$ preserves the types of expressions and threads, and its proof is easy using the non structural typing rules and Generation Lemmas.

Lemma 3.3 (Weakening). *Let* $\Sigma \preceq \Sigma'$, *then*

1. $\Gamma; \Sigma \vdash$ e :t *implies* $\Gamma; \Sigma' \vdash$ e :t;
2. $\Gamma; \Sigma \vdash P$:thread *implies* $\Gamma; \Sigma' \vdash P$:thread.

Using the above lemma and the Generation Lemmas one can show that structural equivalence preserves typing.

Lemma 3.4 (Preservation of Typing under Structural Equivalence). *If* $\Gamma; \Sigma \vdash P$: thread *and* $P \equiv P'$, *then* $\Gamma; \Sigma \vdash P'$:thread.

Lemma 3.5 states that the typing derivation of $E[e]$ can be obtained by composing the subderivation of a typing for e, with a typing derivation for $E[x]$. Furthermore, Σ, the environment used to type $E[x]$, can be broken down into two environments, $\Sigma = \Sigma_1 \circ \Sigma_2$, where Σ_1 is used to type e and Σ_2 is used to type $E[x]$.

Lemma 3.5 (Subderivations). *If* $\Gamma; \Sigma \vdash E[e]$:t, *then there exist* Σ_1, Σ_2 *and* t' *such that* $\Sigma = \Sigma_1 \circ \Sigma_2$, *and* $\Gamma; \Sigma_1 \vdash$ e :t' *and* $\Gamma, x : t'; \Sigma_2 \vdash E[x]$:t, *where* x *is a fresh variable in* $E[-]$ *and* Γ.

On the other hand, Lemma 3.6 allows the combination of the typing of $E[x]$ and the typing of e, provided that the contexts Σ_1 and Σ_2 used for the two typings can be composed through $\circ$, and that the type of e is the same as that of x in the first typing.

Lemma 3.6 (Context Substitution). *If* $\Gamma; \Sigma_1 \vdash$ e :t', *and* $\Gamma, x : t'; \Sigma_2 \vdash E[x]$:t, *and* $\Sigma_1 \circ \Sigma_2$ *is defined, then* $\Gamma; \Sigma_1 \circ \Sigma_2 \vdash E[e]$:t.

For stating the Subject Reduction Theorem we need to introduce a partial order (called *evaluation order*) between running session types which takes into account that session types are consumed by reducing terms (Point 1). This evaluation order is also extended to pairs of session environments and heaps in two ways. The first order (Point 2) requires the types for the same live channels in the session environments are consistent through an expression reduction, i.e. that they take into account the consumed actions (first case) and, in the case that a live channel is transmitted or received, that this is correctly registered in the environment and in the heap (the other two cases). The second order (Point 3) extends the first one taking into account that new live channels can be created in a heap via evaluation of connect expressions.

Definition 3.7 (Evaluation Order)

1. $\sqsubseteq$ *is defined as the smallest partial order on running session types such that:* $\varepsilon \sqsubseteq \rho$; $\varepsilon.\text{end} \sqsubseteq \eta$; $\pi_i \sqsubseteq \dagger\langle \pi_1, \pi_2 \rangle$ $(i \in \{1,2\})$; $\eta_i \sqsubseteq \dagger\langle \eta_1, \eta_2 \rangle$ $(i \in \{1,2\})$; $\dagger\langle \pi.\langle \pi \rangle^*, \varepsilon \rangle \sqsubseteq \dagger\langle \pi \rangle^*$; *and* $\pi \sqsubseteq \pi'$ *implies* $\pi \circ \rho \sqsubseteq \pi' \circ \rho$.
2. *We define* $\langle \Sigma'; h' \rangle \sqsubseteq \langle \Sigma; h \rangle$ *if whenever* $k^p, k^{\bar{p}} \in h'$ *we have* $k^p, k^{\bar{p}} \in h$ *and moreover one of the following conditions is satisfied:*
   (a) $k^p : \rho' \in \Sigma'$ *and* $k^p : \rho \in \Sigma$ *and* $\rho' \sqsubseteq \rho$;
   (b) $k^p \in \text{cored}(\Sigma')$ *and* $k^p \notin \text{cored}(\Sigma)$ *and* $k^p \notin \text{ran}_c(h')$ *and* $k^p \in \text{ran}_c(h)$;
   (c) $k^p \notin \text{cored}(\Sigma')$ *and* $k^p \in \text{cored}(\Sigma)$ *and* $k^p \in \text{ran}_c(h')$ *and* $k^p \notin \text{ran}_c(h)$.
3. *We define* $\langle \Sigma'; h' \rangle \sqsubseteq^{\flat} \langle \Sigma; h \rangle$ *if whenever* $k^p, k^{\bar{p}} \in h'$ *we have:*
   – *either* $k^p, k^{\bar{p}} \in h$ *and one of the conditions (2a), (2b), (2c) is satisfied;*
   – *or* $k^p, k^{\bar{p}} \notin h$ *and* $k^p, k^{\bar{p}} \notin \text{dom}(\Sigma)$ *and* $k^p : \rho, k^{\bar{p}} : \bar{\rho} \in \Sigma'$ *for some* ρ.

Note that $\sqsubseteq$ and $\sqsubseteq^{\flat}$ as defined above are partial order relations.

We can now state the Subject Reduction theorem:

Theorem 3.8 (Subject Reduction)

1. $\Gamma; \Sigma \vdash e : t$ *and* $\Gamma; \Sigma \vdash h$ *and* $e, h \longrightarrow e', h'$ *via an expression reduction imply* $\Gamma'; \Sigma' \vdash e' : t$ *and* $\Gamma'; \Sigma' \vdash h'$, *where* $\Gamma \subseteq \Gamma'$ *and* $\langle \Sigma'; h' \rangle \sqsubseteq \langle \Sigma; h \rangle$.
2. $\Gamma; \Sigma \vdash e : t$ *and* $\Gamma; \Sigma \vdash h$ *and* $e, h \longrightarrow e_1 | e_2, h'$ *via a thread reduction imply* $\Gamma; \Sigma \vdash e_1 | e_2 : \text{thread}$ *and* $\Gamma'; \Sigma' \vdash h'$ *where* $\langle \Sigma'; h' \rangle \sqsubseteq \langle \Sigma; h \rangle$.
3. $\Gamma; \Sigma \vdash P : \text{thread}$ *and* $\Gamma; \Sigma \vdash h$ *and* $P, h \longrightarrow P', h'$ *imply* $\Gamma'; \Sigma' \vdash P' : \text{thread}$ *and* $\Gamma'; \Sigma' \vdash h'$ *where* $\Gamma \subseteq \Gamma'$ *and* $\langle \Sigma'; h' \rangle \sqsubseteq^{\flat} \langle \Sigma; h \rangle$.

The proof, given in the Appendix, is by induction on the derivation $e, h \longrightarrow e', h'$ or $P, h \longrightarrow P', h'$. It uses the Generation Lemmas, the Subderivations Lemma, and the Context Substitution Lemma, as well as further lemmas, stated and proven in the Appendix, and which deal with properties of the relation $\preceq$, of the operation $\circ$, weakening, and substitutions.

4   Progress Properties

The Subject Reduction Theorem assures that, in well-typed processes, when a receiving expression is executed, the input value is consistent with the type of receiving channel. This does not guarantee that once a session started, all required communications will be really executed: a process could be stuck in a deadlock even if it is well-typed. The deadlock freedom is usually called *progress* in the literature, see e.g. [23]. Progress has not been considered in most previous works on synchronous and asynchronous session type systems [2,9,11,12,16,22,27]. Also in our system well typing does not guarantees progress, as the following example shows.

Example 4.1. Take the following processes P_0 and P_1:

$$P_0 = \text{connect } c_0 \, s_0 \{\text{connect } c_1 \, s_1 \{c_1.\text{receive} ; c_0.\text{send} (3)\}\}$$
$$P_1 = \text{connect } c_0 \, \bar{s}_0 \{\text{connect } c_1 \, \bar{s}_1 \{c_0.\text{receive} ; c_1.\text{send} (5)\}\}$$

where $s_0 = \text{begin.?int.end}$ and $s_1 = \text{begin.!int.end}$.

The process $P_0 \,|\, P_1$ running from an empty heap reduces to:

$$k_1^+.\text{receive} ; k_0^+.\text{send} (3) \,|\, k_0^-.\text{receive} ; k_1^-.\text{send} (5), \quad [\,]$$

which is stuck even if it is well-typed.

Following essentially ideas from [6] we propose an effect system which assures progress of AMOOSE processes.

We consider a process being stuck if all its non terminated threads are waiting for a communication on channels whose associated queues are empty, and which cannot be fed by any sending expression. More formally we have the following notion.

Definition 4.2. *A process P_0 has the* progress *property if $P_0, [\,] \longrightarrow\!\!\!\!\rightarrow P, h$ implies that one of the following holds.*

- *In P, all expressions are values, i.e., $P \equiv \prod_{0 \leq i < n} v_i$;*
- *$P, h \longrightarrow P', h'$;*
- *P throws a null pointer exception, i.e., $P \equiv \text{NullExc} \,|\, Q$;*
- *P stops with a connect waiting for its dual instruction, i.e., $P \equiv E[\text{connect } c \, s \{e\}] \,|\, Q$.*

A process with the progress property can stop only if its component threads either have terminated their associated computation leading to values or at least one of them either throws an exception or it is waiting for a connection through the execution of a connect statement. In this last case a new process entering the system can restart the computation opening a new channel via the execution of the connect expression.

We now give a set of inference rules that assures that all processes satisfying them have the progress property. A difference with [6,7] is that there the type system itself was assuring the progress property, while here we separated the two goals. More interestingly the asynchronicity of output allows more permissive requirements.

With the output being asynchronous, processes can only stop on receiving expressions. For this reason we require that in the body of a session opened on channel c all receiving expressions have c as a subject. In Example 4.1 we see that the expression $c_0.\text{receive}$ is in the body of the session opened on channel c_1. It is easy to verify that if this expression is moved past the end of the session opened on c_1, the resulting process has the progress property. Note that swapping the sending and receiving expressions in both P_0 and P_1 the resulting process would be stuck in the system of [6].

Output expressions can always be reduced, but they can in some cases produce deadlocks by sending channels whose session expressions cannot be executed by the receiving process (see Example 4.4). For this reason we require that in the body of a session opened on channel c all expressions sending channels have c as subject.

A method call must respect the same conditions, and this is assured by the new rules for well-formed methods of Fig. 13.

We will define formally in Definition 4.5 the notion of *critical expression:* for now a critical expression is an expression which can produce deadlock if its use is not disciplined. Critical expressions are mostly session expressions, but also a method call can be critical. The set containing the subject of a critical expression (this notion will be generalised to method calls too) is said to be the *hot set* of the expression. As motivated below, we will force all critical expressions occurring in the body a session to have the same hot set containing only the channel on which the session has been opened. The notion of hot set can be naturally propagated through composition and spawning.

A channel is *used* in an expression if it occurs in the expression as subject of a session expression, or as a channel communicated by a sendS expression, or as actual parameter with a running session type of a procedure call.

The judgements of our effect system have the form

$$e \triangleright \mathcal{U}; \mathcal{H}$$

where $\mathcal{U}$ (the *used channel set*) is the set of used channels in e and $\mathcal{H}$ is the hot set of e. The set of used channels is motivated essentially by rule **ReceiveS$^\triangleright$** (see Fig. 14).

We define the *singleton-union* of two hot sets $\mathcal{H}_1$ and $\mathcal{H}_2$ (notation $\mathcal{H}_1 \uplus \mathcal{H}_2$) as:

$$\mathcal{H}_1 \uplus \mathcal{H}_2 = \begin{cases} \mathcal{H}_1 \cup \mathcal{H}_2 \text{ if } \mathcal{H}_1 = \mathcal{H}_2 \text{ or } \mathcal{H}_1 = \emptyset \text{ or } \mathcal{H}_2 = \emptyset, \\ \text{undefined otherwise.} \end{cases}$$

The used channels and the hot set of an expression are derived by the set of inference rules given in Fig. 13 and 14. The key observations are:

- a channel which is subject of a critical subexpression of an expression must be used in the whole expression (*i.e.*, if $e \triangleright \mathcal{U}; \mathcal{H}$, then $\mathcal{H} \subseteq \mathcal{U}$);
- a channel which is used in a typed expression must be the subject of an assumption in the session environment which types that expression (*i.e.*, if $e \triangleright \mathcal{U}; \mathcal{H}$ and $\Gamma; \Sigma \vdash e : t$, then $\mathcal{U} \subseteq \text{dom}(\Sigma)$).

The rules in Fig. 13 are quite natural, except for those concerning method calls that will be discussed later. Rule **Seq$^\triangleright$** takes the union of the two used channel sets and the singleton-union of the two hot sets.

As for the rules for communication expressions, note that a send expression can stay everywhere, its hot set is then the hot set of the expression which is sent (rule **Send$^\triangleright$**), while the hot set of a receive expression is forced to be the set containing the subject of the expression (rule **Receive$^\triangleright$**).

We have two rules for the receiveS expressions. If the body of the receiveS expression has an empty hot set, then there are no restrictions on the possible channels used in it (rule **ReceiveSA$^\triangleright$**). Instead, if $\{x\}$ is the hot set of the body of a receiveS(x), then we must require that no other channel is used in this body (rule **ReceiveS$^\triangleright$**), as the following example shows.

Example 4.3. Take the following processes P_2 and P_3:

$$P_2 = \text{connect } c_0 s_0 \{\text{connect } c_1 s_1 \{c_1.\text{sendS}(c_0)\}\}$$
$$P_3 = \text{connect } c_0 \bar{s}_0 \{\text{connect } c_1 \bar{s}_1 \{c_1.\text{receiveS}(x)\{x.\text{receive};$$
$$\text{connect } c_2 s_2 \{c_2.\text{sendS}(c_0)\}\}\}\}$$

Well-Formed Methods

$$\textbf{MCold}^{\triangleright}$$
$$\frac{e \triangleright \mathcal{U}; \emptyset \qquad \mathcal{U} \subseteq \{\tilde{y}\}}{\mathsf{tm}\,(\tilde{t}\,\tilde{x},\tilde{\rho}\,\tilde{y})\,\{e\}\ \text{ is ok in } C}$$

$$\textbf{MHot}^{\triangleright}$$
$$\frac{e \triangleright \mathcal{U}; \{y_1\} \qquad \mathcal{U} \subseteq \{y_1\} \cup \{\tilde{y}\}}{\mathsf{tm}\,(\tilde{t}\,\tilde{x},\rho_1 y_1,\tilde{\rho}\,\tilde{y})\,\{e\}\ \text{ is ok in } C}$$

Progress Inference Rules for Values

$$\textbf{Null}^{\triangleright} \qquad \textbf{Oid}^{\triangleright} \qquad \textbf{True}^{\triangleright} \qquad \textbf{False}^{\triangleright} \qquad \textbf{Chan}^{\triangleright}$$
$$\mathsf{null} \triangleright \emptyset; \emptyset \qquad o \triangleright \emptyset; \emptyset \qquad \mathsf{true} \triangleright \emptyset; \emptyset \qquad \mathsf{false} \triangleright \emptyset; \emptyset \qquad c \triangleright \emptyset; \emptyset$$

Progress Inference Rules for Standard Expressions

$$\textbf{Var}^{\triangleright} \qquad\qquad \textbf{This}^{\triangleright}$$
$$x \triangleright \emptyset; \emptyset \qquad\qquad \mathsf{this} \triangleright \emptyset; \emptyset$$

$$\textbf{Fld}^{\triangleright}$$
$$\frac{e \triangleright \mathcal{U}; \mathcal{H}}{e.f \triangleright \mathcal{U}; \mathcal{H}}$$

$$\textbf{Seq}^{\triangleright}$$
$$\frac{e \triangleright \mathcal{U}; \mathcal{H} \qquad e' \triangleright \mathcal{U}'; \mathcal{H}'}{e;e' \triangleright \mathcal{U} \cup \mathcal{U}'; \mathcal{H} \uplus \mathcal{H}'}$$

$$\textbf{FldAss}^{\triangleright}$$
$$\frac{e \triangleright \mathcal{U}; \mathcal{H} \qquad e' \triangleright \mathcal{U}'; \mathcal{H}'}{e.f := e' \triangleright \mathcal{U} \cup \mathcal{U}'; \mathcal{H} \uplus \mathcal{H}'}$$

$$\textbf{NewC}^{\triangleright} \qquad \textbf{NewS}^{\triangleright}$$
$$\mathsf{new}\,C \triangleright \emptyset; \emptyset \qquad \mathsf{new}\,(s,\bar{s}) \triangleright \emptyset; \emptyset$$

$$\textbf{Spawn}^{\triangleright}$$
$$\frac{e \triangleright \mathcal{U}; \mathcal{H}}{\mathsf{spawn}\,\{\,e\,\} \triangleright \mathcal{U}; \mathcal{H}}$$

$$\textbf{NullPE}^{\triangleright}$$
$$\mathsf{NullExc} \triangleright \emptyset; \emptyset$$

$$\textbf{MethCold}^{\triangleright}$$
$$\frac{e \triangleright \mathcal{U}; \mathcal{H} \quad e_i \triangleright \mathcal{U}_i; \mathcal{H}_i \quad i \in \{1 \dots n\} \qquad \mathsf{mtype}(m,C) = t_1,\dots,t_n,\rho_1,\dots,\rho_m \xrightarrow{\ominus} t}{e.m\,(e_1,\dots,e_n,u_1,\dots,u_m) \triangleright \mathcal{U} \cup \mathcal{U}_1 \dots \cup \mathcal{U}_n \cup \{u_1,\dots,u_m\}; \mathcal{H} \uplus \mathcal{H}_1 \dots \uplus \mathcal{H}_n}$$

$$\textbf{MethHot}^{\triangleright}$$
$$\frac{e \triangleright \mathcal{U}; \mathcal{H} \quad e_i \triangleright \mathcal{U}_i; \mathcal{H}_i \quad i \in \{1 \dots n\} \qquad \mathsf{mtype}(m,C) = t_1,\dots,t_n,\rho_1,\dots,\rho_m \xrightarrow{\oplus} t}{e.m\,(e_1,\dots,e_n,u_1,\dots,u_m) \triangleright \mathcal{U} \cup \mathcal{U}_1 \dots \cup \mathcal{U}_n \cup \{u_1,\dots,u_m\}; \mathcal{H} \uplus \mathcal{H}_1 \dots \uplus \mathcal{H}_n \uplus \{u_1\}}$$

Fig. 13. Well-Formed Methods and Progress Inference Rules for Values & Standard Expressions

where $s_0 = \mathsf{begin}.?\mathsf{int}.\mathsf{end}$ and $s_1 = \mathsf{begin}.!(?\mathsf{int}.\mathsf{end}).\mathsf{end}$ and $s_2 = \mathsf{begin}.!(!\mathsf{int}.\mathsf{end}).\mathsf{end}$.
The process $P_2 \mid P_3$ starting from an empty heap reduces to:

$$k_0^+.\mathsf{receive};\mathsf{connect}\ c_2 s_2\{c_2.\mathsf{sendS}\,(k_0^-)\},\ [k_0^+ \mapsto \varepsilon,\ k_0^- \mapsto \varepsilon]$$

which is stuck. But also the original program does agree neither with rule **ReceiveS**$^{\triangleright}$ nor with rule **ReceiveSA**$^{\triangleright}$. In fact in this case $\{x\}$ and $\{c_0\}$ are respectively the hot set and the set of used channels of the receiveS expression body.

This example shows also that two live channels with the same name and opposite polarities can occur in the same thread.

The following example shows that some care must be taken also in handling the sendS expressions, that can as well destroy progress. We avoid this by forcing the hot sets of sendS expressions to contain their subjects.

Progress Inference Rules for Communication Expressions

Conn$^{\triangleright}$
$$\frac{e \triangleright \mathcal{U};\ \mathcal{H} \quad \mathcal{H} \subseteq \{a\}}{\mathsf{connect}\ a\ s\ \{e\} \triangleright \mathcal{U} \setminus \{a\}; \emptyset}$$

Send$^{\triangleright}$
$$\frac{e \triangleright \mathcal{U};\ \mathcal{H}}{u.\mathsf{send}\ (\ e\ ) \triangleright \mathcal{U} \cup \{u\};\ \mathcal{H}}$$

Receive$^{\triangleright}$
$$u.\mathsf{receive} \triangleright \{u\};\ \{u\}$$

SendS$^{\triangleright}$
$$u.\mathsf{sendS}\ (u') \triangleright \{u, u'\};\ \{u\}$$

ReceiveS$^{\triangleright}$
$$\frac{e \triangleright \{x\};\ \{x\}}{u.\mathsf{receiveS}\ (x)\{e\} \triangleright \{u\};\ \{u\}}$$

ReceiveSA$^{\triangleright}$
$$\frac{e \triangleright \mathcal{U};\ \emptyset}{u.\mathsf{receiveS}\ (x)\{e\} \triangleright \mathcal{U} \setminus \{x\} \cup \{u\};\ \{u\}}$$

SendIf$^{\triangleright}$
$$\frac{e \triangleright \mathcal{U};\ \mathcal{H} \quad e_i \triangleright \mathcal{U}_i;\ \mathcal{H}_i \quad i \in \{1,2\}}{u.\mathsf{sendIf}\ (e)\{e_1\}\{e_2\} \triangleright \mathcal{U} \cup \mathcal{U}_1 \cup \mathcal{U}_2 \cup \{u\};\ \mathcal{H} \uplus \mathcal{H}_1 \uplus \mathcal{H}_2}$$

ReceiveIf$^{\triangleright}$
$$\frac{e_i \triangleright \mathcal{U}_i;\ \mathcal{H}_i \quad i \in \{1,2\}}{u.\mathsf{receiveIf}\ \{e_1\}\{e_2\} \triangleright \mathcal{U}_1 \cup \mathcal{U}_2 \cup \{u\};\ \mathcal{H}_1 \uplus \mathcal{H}_2 \uplus \{u\}}$$

SendWhile$^{\triangleright}$
$$\frac{e \triangleright \emptyset; \emptyset \quad e' \triangleright \mathcal{U};\ \mathcal{H} \quad \mathcal{U} \subseteq \{u\}}{u.\mathsf{sendWhile}\ (e)\{e'\} \triangleright \{u\};\ \mathcal{H}}$$

ReceiveWhile$^{\triangleright}$
$$\frac{e \triangleright \mathcal{U};\ \mathcal{H} \quad \mathcal{U} \subseteq \{u\}}{u.\mathsf{receiveWhile}\ \{e\} \triangleright \{u\};\ \{u\}}$$

Fig. 14. Progress Inference Rules for Communication Expressions

Example 4.4. Let's consider the following processes P_4 and P_5:

$$P_4 = \mathsf{connect}\ c_0 s_0 \{\mathsf{connect}\ c_1 s_1 \{c_0.\mathsf{sendS}\ (c_1)\}\}$$
$$P_5 = \mathsf{connect}\ c_0 \bar{s}_0 \{\mathsf{connect}\ c_1 \bar{s}_1 \{c_1.\mathsf{receive}\};c_0.\mathsf{receiveS}\ (x)\{x.\mathsf{send}\ (3)\}\}$$

where $s_0 = \mathsf{begin}.!(!\mathsf{int}.\mathsf{end}).\mathsf{end}$ and $s_1 = \mathsf{begin}.!\mathsf{int}.\mathsf{end}$. Then $P_4 \mid P_5$, starting from an empty heap, reduces to

$$k_1^-.\mathsf{receive};k_0^-.\mathsf{receiveS}\ (x)\{x.\mathsf{send}\ (3)\}, [k_0^+ \mapsto k_1^+,\ k_0^- \mapsto \varepsilon,\ k_1^+ \mapsto \varepsilon,\ k_1^- \mapsto \varepsilon]$$

which is stuck. Note that P_4 cannot be typed since **SendS$^{\triangleright}$** requires c_0 as hot set.

The rules **SendWhile$^{\triangleright}$** and **ReceiveWhile$^{\triangleright}$** are justified by comparing them with the typing rules **SendWhile** and **ReceiveWhile** (see Fig. 8) and taking into account that the set of used channels must be a subset of the domain of the session environment.

According to the reduction rule **Meth$^{\to}$** a method call corresponds to the replacement of the method body for the call statement. So the used channels of the call can be identified with its live channel parameters. A method can have a non-empty hot set if its body contains critical expressions: in this case we convene the hot channel to be the first channel parameter. A method $t\,m\ (\tilde{t}\,\tilde{x},\tilde{\rho}\,\tilde{y})\ \{e\}$ is *cold* if it is well-formed according to rule **MCold**$^{\triangleright}$ (i.e. if the hot set of its body is empty) and *hot* if it is well-formed according rule **MHot**$^{\triangleright}$, i.e. if the hot set of its body is $\{y_1\}$. We add this information to the method type by decorating the arrow respectively by $\ominus$ and $\oplus$, i.e. we get $\tilde{t},\tilde{\rho}\ \overset{\ominus}{\to}\ t$ and $\tilde{t},\tilde{\rho}\ \overset{\oplus}{\to}\ t$. The *subject of a hot method call* is the actual parameter which replaces the formal parameter y_1.

A last remark concerns rule **Spawn**$^{\triangleright}$, in which we require the hot set be preserved in the spawned expression. Referring to Example 4.1, let P_1' be the process obtained by replacing $c_0.\text{receive};c_1.\text{send}\,(3)$ with $\text{spawn}\,\{c_0.\text{receive};c_1.\text{send}\,(3)\}$ in P_1. Then P_1' could be typed if in rule **Spawn**$^{\triangleright}$ the hot set of the conclusion would be the empty set, but also $P_0\,|\,P_1'$ leads to a deadlock.

We can now formally define the notion of critical expression.

Definition 4.5. *We say that an expression* e *is* critical *if it is either a* receive, receiveS, receiveIf, sendS, receiveWhile *expression or it is a hot method call. If* e *is a critical expression, we denote by* $\text{sub}(e)$ *its subject. A critical expression is* live *if its subject is a live channel.*

In the remaining of the present section we will show that the above rules assure the progress property. Obviously we must consider computations whose starting process is well-typed and closed.

We say that a process P is *initial* if $P = \prod_{1\leq i\leq n} e_i$, all e_i are user expressions and $\emptyset;\emptyset \vdash P,[\,]$ and $e_i \triangleright \emptyset;\emptyset\ (1 \leq i \leq n)$.

The following two lemmas can be easily proved by induction on derivations.

A *direct* subexpression of e is a subexpression of e which does not occur in the body of a connect or receiveS.

Lemma 4.6. *Let* $e \triangleright \mathcal{U};\mathcal{H}$.

1. *If* $\mathcal{H} = \emptyset$, *then there are no critical direct subexpressions of* e.
2. *If* $\mathcal{H} = \{u\}$, *then all critical direct subexpressions of* e *have* u *as subject.*
3. *All critical and live subexpressions of* e *are direct subexpressions of* e.

We use φ to range over t, (η), $\langle\rho,\rho'\rangle$, and $\langle\pi\rangle^*$ and we define:

$$\hat{\varphi} = \begin{cases} t & \text{if } \varphi = t, \\ \eta & \text{if } \varphi = (\eta), \\ \text{bool} & \text{otherwise.} \end{cases}$$

By $|\rho|$ we denote the number of symbols which occur in ρ.

Lemma 4.7. *Assume* $\emptyset;\emptyset \vdash P,[\,]$ *and* $P_0,[\,] \twoheadrightarrow P,h$. *Then there are* Γ, Σ *such that* $\Gamma;\Sigma \vdash P:\text{thread}$, *and* $\Gamma;\Sigma \vdash h$, *and*

1. $\text{ended}(\Sigma)$ *and*
2. *if* $k^p \in \text{cored}(\Sigma)$, *then one of the following conditions holds:*
   - $\Sigma(k^p) = \Sigma(k^{\bar{p}})$;
   - $|\Sigma(k^p)| > |\Sigma(k^{\bar{p}})|$ *and* $\Sigma(k^p) = ?\varphi\psi$ *and* $h = h' :: [k^p \mapsto v : \tilde{v}]$ *and* $\Gamma;\emptyset \vdash v : \hat{\varphi}$;

- $|\Sigma(\mathsf{k}^{\bar{p}})| > |\Sigma(\mathsf{k}^p)|$ and $\Sigma(\mathsf{k}^{\bar{p}}) = ?\varphi\psi$ and $h = h' :: [\mathsf{k}^{\bar{p}} \mapsto \mathsf{v} : \tilde{\mathsf{v}}]$ and $\Gamma; \emptyset \vdash \mathsf{v} : \hat{\varphi};$
- $\mathsf{k}^{\bar{p}} \notin \mathrm{dom}(\Sigma)$ and $\mathsf{k}^{\bar{p}} \in \mathrm{ran}_c(h)$.

A last definition is handy for taking into account the order in which expressions are reduced.

Definition 4.8. *Let* e *be an expression and* e_1, e_2 *be two subexpressions of* e*. We say that* e_1 *precedes* e_2 *in* e *if, for some contexts* $C[-], E[-]$ *and* $C'[-]$ *we have* $e = C[e']$ *and* $e' = E[e_1] = C'[e_2]$.

Notice that the each expression precedes itself since we can choose all contexts as the empty one.

Recall that, according to our notational conventions, live channels are denoted by k^p. In the following we convene that the fresh live channels created reducing a thread take successive numbers according to the order of creation, i.e. they are named $\mathsf{k}_0, \mathsf{k}_1, \ldots$. This means that if $P, h \longrightarrow\!\!\!\rightarrow Q, h' \longrightarrow\!\!\!\rightarrow R, h''$ and k_i is a channel created in the reduction $P, h \longrightarrow\!\!\!\rightarrow Q, h'$, and k_j is a channel created in the reduction $Q, h' \longrightarrow\!\!\!\rightarrow R, h''$, then $i < j$.

The following lemma relating the order of channel creation with their occurrences as hot sets is the key of our progress proof.

Lemma 4.9. *Let* P_0 *be initial and* $P_0, [\ ] \longrightarrow\!\!\!\rightarrow P, h$. *Then*

1. *If* e_1 *precedes* e_2 *in* P *and* e_1 *is a live critical expression and* $sub(e_1) = \mathsf{k}_i^p$, *then for all live channels* k_j^q *occurring in* e_2 *either* $i > j$ *or* $i = j$ *and* $p = q$.
2. *If a live channel* k_j^p *is in the queue associated to a channel* k_i^q *in* h, *then* $i > j$.

Proof. By induction on the reduction. The induction step is by cases on the last reduction rule. We give the most interesting cases.

Case Connect$^\rightarrow$: If the last applied rule was **Connect$^\rightarrow$**, then the last step of the reduction was of the form:

$$E_1[\mathsf{connect}\ \mathsf{c}\ \mathsf{s}\{e_1\}] \,|\, E_2[\mathsf{connect}\ \mathsf{c}\ \bar{\mathsf{s}}\{e_2\}] \,|\, P', h$$
$$\longrightarrow E_1[e_1[\mathsf{k}_i^+/\mathsf{c}]] \,|\, E_2[e_2[\mathsf{k}_i^-/\mathsf{c}]] \,|\, P', h :: [\mathsf{k}_i \mapsto \varepsilon]$$

for some P', where i is the highest index among those occurring in P, h. The only new channels in P are k_i^p, where i is now the highest index and occurs only in subexpressions of $e_l[\mathsf{k}_i^p/\mathsf{c}]$ $(l = 1, 2)$. All expressions that were preceded by e_l are now preceded by subexpressions of $e_l[\mathsf{k}_i^p/\mathsf{c}]$ $(l = 1, 2)$. Since the hot set of the connect expression has been inferred by rule **Conn$^\triangleright$**, then by Lemmas 4.6(2) and 4.6(3), all live critical expressions inside $e_l[\mathsf{k}_i^p/\mathsf{c}]$ must have k_i^p as subject. From this, and induction hypothesis, Point (1) follows immediately. Point (2) is trivial by induction hypothesis.

Case ReceiveSS$^\rightarrow$: If the last applied rule was **ReceiveSS$^\rightarrow$**, then the last step of the reduction was of the form:

$$E[\mathsf{k}_i^p.\mathsf{receiveS}\,(x)\{e\}], h :: [\mathsf{k}_i^p \mapsto \mathsf{k}_j^q : \tilde{\mathsf{v}}] \longrightarrow e[\mathsf{k}_j^q/x] \,|\, E[\mathsf{null}], h :: [\mathsf{k}_i^p \mapsto \tilde{\mathsf{v}}].$$

Note that Point (1) holds between subexpressions of $E[\mathsf{null}]$ by induction hypothesis. As for $e[\mathsf{k}_j^q/x]$ we distinguish two cases.

(a) If the hot set of receiveS expression has been inferred by rule **ReceiveSA**$^\triangleright$, then by Lemma 4.6(1) in $e\,[k_j^p/x]$ there are no live and critical subexpressions and Point (1) holds trivially.

(b) If the hot set of receiveS expression has been inferred by rule **ReceiveS**$^\triangleright$, then only the channel k_j^p can be live in $e\,[k_j^p/x]$. Thus Point (1) follows immediately.

In both cases Point (2) is trivial by induction hypothesis.

Case Meth$^\rightarrow$: If the last applied rule was **Meth$^\rightarrow$** and the method has at least one live channel has parameter, then the last step in the reduction was of the form:

$$E\,[\mathsf{o.m}\,(\tilde{v},k_i^p,\tilde{k})]\,|\,P',h \longrightarrow E\,[e\,[\mathsf{o}/\mathtt{this}][\tilde{v}/\tilde{x}][k_i^p/y_1][\tilde{k}/\tilde{y}]]\,|\,P',h$$

where $h(\mathsf{o}) = (C,\dots)$ and $mbody(m,C) = (\tilde{x},y_1,\tilde{y},e)$. The more interesting case is when the hot set was inferred by rule **MHot**$^\triangleright$. By definition $\mathsf{o.m}\,(\tilde{v},k_i^p,\tilde{k})$ precedes all expressions in $E[-]$ and therefore, by induction hypothesis, the index i of its subject is greater than the index of all live channels occurring in expressions in $E[-]$. By Lemma 4.6(2) and rule **MHot**$^\triangleright$ all critical expressions in e have y_1 as subject, that is replaced by k_i^p. Moreover note that all live channels k_j^q with $i \neq j$ replacing the formal parameters in $e\,[\mathsf{o}/\mathtt{this}][\tilde{v}/\tilde{x}][k_i^p/y_1][\tilde{k}/\tilde{y}]$ occur in the hot method call and then, by induction hypothesis, $j \leq i$. Point (1) follows then immediately. Point (2) is trivial.

Case Spawn$^\rightarrow$: If the last applied rule was **Spawn$^\rightarrow$**, then the last step in the reduction was of the form:

$$E[\mathsf{spawn}\{\,e\,\}],h \longrightarrow E[\mathsf{null}]\,|\,e,h$$

and Points (1) and (2) follow immediately by induction hypothesis.

We conclude now with the desired progress theorem.

Theorem 4.10 (Progress). *Assume P_0 is initial and it satisfies the progress inference rules. Then P_0 has the progress property.*

Proof. If P_0 is initial we have $\emptyset;\emptyset \vdash P_0;[\,]$. Assume now that $P_0,[\,] \twoheadrightarrow P,h$. By the subject reduction property we have $\Gamma;\Sigma \vdash P:\mathtt{thread}$ and $\Gamma;\Sigma \vdash h$ for some Γ,Σ.

Suppose $P \equiv \mathsf{NullExc}\,|\,Q$ or $P \equiv E[\mathsf{connect}\,c\,s\,\{e\}]\,|\,Q$. Then the proof is immediate. Also $P \equiv e\,|\,Q$ with $e,h \longrightarrow e',h'$ is easy, since we get $P,h \longrightarrow e'\,|\,Q,h'$.

The only interesting case is $P \equiv V\,|\,Q$, where V is a parallel of values and Q is a parallel of evaluation contexts containing irreducible session expressions. Note that an irreducible process can only have a receiving expression in the evaluation context. Let $Q \equiv \prod_{1 \leq l \leq n} E_l[e_l]$. Let k_i be the live channel name with the higher index which occurs in P. By Lemma 4.9(1) a receiving expression e_r having k_i^p as subject must then be in evaluation position of some thread $E_r[e_r]$ of P and so there must be a statement $k_i^p:?\varphi\psi \in \Sigma$ by Lemmas 3.5 and A.3. By Lemma 4.7(2) then:

(a) either $h = h' :: [k_i^p \mapsto v : \tilde{v}]$ and $\Gamma;\emptyset \vdash v : \hat{\varphi}$, so the process cannot be stuck on a receiving expression on k_i^p,

(b) or there must be a statement $k_i^{\bar{p}} : !\varphi\overline{\psi} \in \Sigma$. This implies that that there must be a sending subexpression e_s' (sending a value of type $\hat{\varphi}$) of some e_s ($1 \leq s \leq n$) with subject $k_i^{\bar{p}}$ that, by Lemma 4.9, cannot be blocked by any receiving expression, except possibly a receiving expression with subject k_i^p itself preceding e_s' in e_s. This is impossible by Lemma 4.9(1).

Acknowlegments. The authors are indebted to Sophia Drossopoulou who first suggested to explore asynchronous communication rules for sessions in object oriented languages.

References

1. Bierman, G., Parkinson, M., Pitts, A.: MJ: An Imperative Core Calculus for Java and Java with Effects. Technical Report 563, Univ. of Cambridge Computer Laboratory (2003)
2. Bonelli, E., Compagnoni, A., Gunter, E.: Correspondence Assertions for Process Synchronization in Concurrent Communications. Journal of Functional Programming 15(2), 219–248 (2005)
3. Carbone, M., Honda, K., Yoshida, N.: A Theoretical Basis of Communication-centered Concurrent Programming. Web Services Choreography Working Group mailing list, to appear as a WS-CDL working report
4. Carbone, M., Honda, K., Yoshida, N.: Structured Communication-Centred Programming for Web Services. In: ESOP'07. LNCS, Springer, Heidelberg, To appear (2007)
5. Dezani-Ciancaglini, M., Drossopoulou, S., Giachino, E., Yoshida, N.: Bounded Session Types for Object-Oriented Languages. http://www.di.unito.it/ dezani/papers/ ddgy.pdf (2007)
6. Dezani-Ciancaglini, M., Mostrous, D., Yoshida, N., Drossopoulou, S.: Session Types for Object-Oriented Languages. In: Thomas, D. (ed.) ECOOP 2006. LNCS, vol. 4067, pp. 328–352. Springer, Heidelberg (2006)
7. Dezani-Ciancaglini, M., Yoshida, N., Ahern, A., Drossopoulou, S.: A Distributed Object Oriented Language with Session Types. In: Nicola, R.D., Sangiorgi, D. (eds.) TGC 2005. LNCS, vol. 3705, pp. 299–318. Springer, Heidelberg (2005)
8. Drossopoulou, S.: Advanced Issues in Object Oriented Languages Course Notes. http://www.doc.ic.ac.uk/~scd/Teaching/AdvOO.html
9. Fähndrich, M., Aiken, M., Hawblitzel, C., Hodson, O., Hunt, G.C., Larus, J.R., Levi, S.: Language Support for Fast and Reliable Message-based Communication in Singularity OS. In: Zwaenepoel, W. (ed.) EuroSys2006, ACM SIGOPS, pp. 177–190. ACM Press, New York (2006)
10. Garralda, P., Compagnoni, A., Dezani-Ciancaglini, M.: BASS: Boxed Ambients with Safe Sessions. In: Maher, M. (ed.) PPDP'06, pp. 61–72. ACM Press, New York (2006)
11. Gay, S., Hole, M.: Subtyping for Session Types in the Pi-Calculus. Acta Informatica 42(2/3), 191–225 (2005)
12. Gay, S., Vasconcelos, V.T.: A New Approach to Functional Session Types, http://www.di. fc.ul.pt/ vv/papers/gay.vasconcelos:new-functional-sessions.pdf (2006)
13. Gay, S., Vasconcelos, V.T., Ravara, A.: Session Types for Inter-Process Communication. TR 2003–133, Department of Computing, University of Glasgow (2003)
14. Honda, K.: Types for Dyadic Interaction. In: Best, E. (ed.) CONCUR 1993. LNCS, vol. 715, pp. 509–523. Springer, Heidelberg (1993)
15. Honda, K.: Composing Processes. In: Steele, G.L. (ed.) POPL'96, pp. 344–357. ACM Press, New York (1996)
16. Honda, K., Vasconcelos, V.T., Kubo, M.: Language Primitives and Type Disciplines for Structured Communication-based Programming. In: Hankin, C. (ed.) ESOP 1998 and ETAPS 1998. LNCS, vol. 1381, pp. 22–138. Springer, Heidelberg (1998)

17. Honda, K., Yoshida, N., Carbone, M.: Web Services, Mobile Processes and Types. EATCS Bulletin, To appear (2007)
18. Igarashi, A., Pierce, B.C., Wadler, P.: Featherweight Java: a Minimal Core Calculus for Java and GJ. ACM TOPLAS 23(3), 396–450 (2001)
19. S. Microsystems Inc. The Java Tutorial: All About Sockets. http://java.sun.com/docs/books/tutorial/networking/sockets/
20. S. Microsystems Inc. New IO APIs. http://java.sun.com/j2se/1.4.2/docs/guide/nio/index.html
21. Milner, R., Parrow, J., Walker, D.: A Calculus of Mobile Processes, Parts I and II. Information and Computation, vol. 100(1) (1992)
22. Neubauer, M., Thiemann, P.: Session Types for Asynchronous Communication. Universität Freiburg (2004)
23. Pierce, B.C.: Types and Programming Languages. MIT Press, Cambridge, MA (2002)
24. Sparkes, S.: Conversation with Steve Ross-Talbot. ACM Queue 4(2), 14–23 (2006)
25. Takeuchi, K., Honda, K., Kubo, M.: An Interaction-based Language and its Typing System. In: Halatsis, C., Maritsas, D., Philokyprou, G., Theodoridis, S. (eds.) PARLE 1994. LNCS, vol. 817, pp. 398–413. Springer, Heidelberg (1994)
26. Vallecillo, A., Vasconcelos, V.T., Ravara, A.: Typing the Behavior of Objects and Components using Session Types. In: Brogi, A., Jacquet, J.-M. (eds.) FOCLASA'02, ENTCS, vol. 68(3), pp. 439–456. Elsevier, Amsterdam (2002)
27. Vasconcelos, V.T., Gay, S., Ravara, A.: Typechecking a Multithreaded Functional Language with Session Types. Theorical Computer Science 368(1-2), 64–87 (2006)
28. Web Services Choreography Working Group. Web Services Choreography Description Language. http://www.w3.org/2002/ws/chor/
29. Yoshida, N., Vasconcelos, V.T.: Language Primitives and Type Disciplines for Structured Communication-based Programming Revisited. In: SecRet'06, ENTCS, Elsevier, Amsterdam, To appear (2007)

A Proof of Subject Reduction

Lemma A.1. *1.* $\Sigma_1 \preceq \Sigma_1'$, *and* $\Sigma_1' \circ \Sigma_2$ *defined,* *imply* $\Sigma_1 \circ \Sigma_2$ *defined, and* $\Sigma_1 \circ \Sigma_2 \preceq \Sigma_1' \circ \Sigma_2$.
2. $\Sigma \cup \Sigma' \vdash$ ok *and* $\emptyset \preceq \Sigma'$ *imply* $\Sigma \preceq \Sigma \cup \Sigma'$.

Proof. Easy from Definition 3.2.

Lemma A.2. (Generation for Standard Expressions)

1. $\Gamma;\Sigma \vdash x : t$ *implies* $\emptyset \preceq \Sigma$ *and* $x : t' \in \Gamma$ *for some* $t' <: t$.
2. $\Gamma;\Sigma \vdash c : t$ *implies* $\emptyset \preceq \Sigma$ *and* t *is a shared session type.*
3. $\Gamma;\Sigma \vdash$ null $: t$ *implies* $\emptyset \preceq \Sigma$.
4. $\Gamma;\Sigma \vdash v : t$ *with* $v \in \{true, false\}$ *implies* $\emptyset \preceq \Sigma$ *and* $t = $ bool.
5. $\Gamma;\Sigma \vdash o : t$ *implies* $\emptyset \preceq \Sigma$ *and* $o : C \in \Gamma$ *for some* $C <: t$.
6. $\Gamma;\Sigma \vdash$ NullExc $: t$ *implies* $\emptyset \preceq \Sigma$.
7. $\Gamma;\Sigma \vdash$ this $: t$ *implies* $\emptyset \preceq \Sigma$ *and* this $: C \in \Gamma$ *for some* $C <: t$.
8. $\Gamma;\Sigma \vdash e_1; e_2 : t$ *implies* $\Sigma = \Sigma_1 \circ \Sigma_2$, *and* $t = t_2$ *and* $\Gamma;\Sigma_i \vdash e_i : t_i$ *for some* Σ_i, t_i $(i \in \{1,2\})$.
9. $\Gamma;\Sigma \vdash e.f := e' : t$ *implies* $\Sigma = \Sigma_1 \circ \Sigma_2$, *and* $\Gamma;\Sigma_1 \vdash e : C$ *and* $\Gamma;\Sigma_2 \vdash e' : t$ *with* $ft \in$ fields(C) *for some* Σ_1, Σ_2, C.

10. $\Gamma;\Sigma \vdash e.f : t$ *implies* $\Gamma;\Sigma \vdash e : C$ *and* $f t \in$ fields(C) *for some C.*

11. $\Gamma;\Sigma \vdash e.m(e_1,\ldots,e_n,u_1,\ldots,u_m) : t$ $(n,m \geq 0)$, *implies* $\Gamma;\Sigma_0 \vdash e : C$, *and* $\Gamma;\Sigma_i \vdash e_i : t_i$ *for* $1 \leq i \leq n$, *and* $\Sigma_0 \circ \Sigma_1 \ldots \circ \Sigma_n \circ \{u_1 : \rho_1, \ldots, u_m : \rho_m\} \preceq \Sigma$ *and* mtype$(m,C) = t_1,\ldots,t_n,\rho_1,\ldots,\rho_m \to t$, *for some* $\Sigma_0,\Sigma_i,t_i,u_j,\rho_j,C$ $(1 \leq i \leq n, 1 \leq j \leq m)$.

12. $\Gamma;\Sigma \vdash$ new $C : t$ *implies* $\emptyset \preceq \Sigma$ *and* $C <: t$.

13. $\Gamma;\Sigma \vdash$ new $(s,\bar{s}) : t$ *implies* $\emptyset \preceq \Sigma$ *and* $(s,\bar{s}) <: t$.

14. $\Gamma;\Sigma \vdash$ spawn$\{$ e $\} : t$ *implies* $ended(\Sigma')$, $\Sigma' \preceq \Sigma$, $t = Object$ *and* $\Gamma;\Sigma' \vdash e : t'$ *for some* Σ',t'.

Proof. By induction on typing derivations. The inductive step is by case analysis over the shape of the expression being typed, and then over the last rule applied. For all points the proof is non trivial only in the cases in which the last applied rule is a non-structural one. We just show one paradigmatic case of the inductive step.

(14) If the expression being typed has the shape spawn$\{$ e $\}$, let's consider the case in which the last applied rule is **WeakES**, the other cases are similar. Then

$$\frac{\Gamma;\Sigma \vdash \text{spawn}\{\ e\ \} : t}{\Gamma;\Sigma, u : \varepsilon \vdash \text{spawn}\{\ e\ \} : t}$$

By induction hypothesis there exist Σ', t', such that $\Sigma' \preceq \Sigma$, and $ended(\Sigma')$ and $t = Object$ and $\Gamma;\Sigma' \vdash e : t'$. Since $\Sigma \preceq \Sigma, u : \varepsilon$ the property follows immediately by transitivity of $\preceq$.

Lemma A.3. (Generation for Communication Expressions)

1. $\Gamma;\Sigma \vdash$ connect a s $\{e\} : t$ *implies* $s = \text{begin}.\eta$, *and* $\Gamma;\emptyset \vdash a : \text{begin}.\eta$ *and* $\Gamma \setminus a;\Sigma, a : \eta \vdash e : t$, *for some* η.

2. $\Gamma;\Sigma \vdash u.\text{receive} : t$ *implies* $\{u : ?t\} \preceq \Sigma$.

3. $\Gamma;\Sigma \vdash u.\text{send}(e) : t$ *implies* $t = Object$ *and* $\Gamma;\Sigma' \vdash e : t'$ *and* $\Sigma' \circ \{u : !t'\} \preceq \Sigma$ *for some* Σ',t'.

4. $\Gamma;\Sigma \vdash u.\text{receiveS}(x)\{e\} : t$ *implies* $t = Object$ *and* $\Gamma \setminus x ; \Sigma',x : \eta \vdash e : t'$ *and* $ended(\Sigma',x:\eta)$ *and* $\{u : ?(\eta)\} \circ \Sigma' \preceq \Sigma$ *for some* $\Sigma',t',\eta \neq \varepsilon.\text{end}$.

5. $\Gamma;\Sigma \vdash u.\text{sendS}(u') : t$ *implies* $t = Object$ *and* $\{u' : \eta, u :!(\eta)\} \preceq \Sigma$ *for some* $\eta \neq \varepsilon.\text{end}$.

6. $\Gamma;\Sigma \vdash u.\text{receiveIf}\{e_1\}\{e_2\} : t$ *implies* $\Gamma;\Sigma',u : \rho_i \vdash e_i.t$ $(i \in \{1,2\})$ *and* $\Sigma',u : ?\langle\rho_1,\rho_2\rangle \preceq \Sigma$ *for some* Σ',ρ_1,ρ_2.

7. $\Gamma;\Sigma \vdash u.\text{sendIf}(e)\{e_1\}\{e_2\} : t$ *implies* $\Gamma;\Sigma_1 \vdash e : \text{bool}$ *and* $\Gamma;\Sigma_2,u : \rho_i \vdash e_i : t$ $(i \in \{1,2\})$ *and* $\Sigma_1 \circ \Sigma_2, u :!\langle\rho_1,\rho_2\rangle \preceq \Sigma$ *for some* $\Sigma_1,\Sigma_2,\rho_1,\rho_2$.

8. $\Gamma;\Sigma \vdash u.\text{receiveWhile}\{e\} : t$ *implies* $\Gamma;\{u : \pi\} \vdash e : t$ *and* $\{u :?\langle\pi\rangle^*\} \preceq \Sigma$ *for some* π.

9. $\Gamma;\Sigma \vdash u.\text{sendWhile}(e)\{e'\} : t$ *implies* $\Gamma;\emptyset \vdash e : \text{bool}$ *and* $\Gamma;\{u : \pi\} \vdash e' : t$ *and* $\{u :!\langle\pi\rangle^*\} \preceq \Sigma$ *for some* π.

Proof. Similar to that of Lemma A.2.

Lemma A.4. (Generation for Threads)

1. $\Gamma;\Sigma \vdash e : \text{thread}$ *implies* $\Gamma;\Sigma \vdash e : t$ *for some type* t.

2. $\Gamma;\Sigma \vdash P_1 \mid P_2$: thread *implies* $\Sigma = \Sigma_1 \cup \Sigma_2$, *and* $\Gamma;\Sigma_i \vdash P_i$: thread *(i $\in \{1,2\}$) for some* Σ_1, Σ_2 .

Proof. All three cases are trivial.

Lemma 3.4 (Preservation of Typing under Structural Equivalence). *If* $\Gamma;\Sigma \vdash P$: thread *and* $P \equiv P'$, *then* $\Gamma;\Sigma \vdash P'$: thread.

Proof. By induction on the proof of $P \equiv P'$. If the proof is obtained by the commutativity or associativity the property follows by easily by Lemmas A.4(2). The case of composition with a fixed process is trivial. In the case of composition with null, if $\Gamma;\Sigma \vdash P$: thread we have immediately $\Gamma;\Sigma \vdash P \mid$ null : thread.

As for the opposite direction assume $\Gamma;\Sigma \vdash P \mid$ null : thread. Then there are Σ_1, Σ_2 such that $\Sigma = \Sigma_1 \cup \Sigma_2$ and $\Gamma;\Sigma_1 \vdash P$: thread and $\Gamma;\Sigma_2 \vdash$ null : thread. By Lemma A.2(3) we have that $\emptyset \preceq \Sigma_2$ and then, by Lemma A.1(2), $\Sigma_1 \preceq \Sigma_1 \cup \Sigma_2$. By applying Lemma 3.3(2) to $\Gamma;\Sigma_1 \vdash P$: thread we conclude $\Gamma;\Sigma_1 \cup \Sigma_2 \vdash P$: thread.

Lemma A.5 (Preservation of Typing under Substitution)
1. *If* $\Gamma,x:t;\Sigma \vdash e:t'$ *and* $\Gamma;\emptyset \vdash v:t$, *then* $\Gamma;\Sigma \vdash e[v/x]:t'$.
2. *If* $\Gamma\backslash u;\Sigma \vdash e:t$ *and* $k^p \notin \mathrm{dom}(\Sigma)$, *then* $\Gamma;\Sigma[k^p/u] \vdash e[k^p/u]:t$.
3. *If* $\Gamma,\mathrm{this}:C;\Sigma \vdash e:t$ *and* $\Gamma;\emptyset \vdash o:C$, *then* $\Gamma;\Sigma \vdash e[o/\mathrm{this}]:t$.

Proof. (1), (2) and (3) are proven by induction on derivations.

Lemma 3.5 (Subderivations). *If* $\Gamma;\Sigma \vdash E[e]:t$, *then there exist* Σ_1, Σ_2 *and* t' *such that* $\Sigma = \Sigma_1 \circ \Sigma_2$, *and* $\mathrm{dom}(\Sigma_1) = \mathrm{cored}(\Sigma_1)$, *and* $\Gamma;\Sigma_1 \vdash e:t'$ *and* $\Gamma,x:t';\Sigma_2 \vdash E[x]:t$, *where* x *is a fresh variable in* $E[-],\Gamma$.

Proof. By induction on E, and using Generation Lemmas. For example, if $E = [-];e'$, then $\Gamma;\Sigma \vdash e;e':t$ implies $\Sigma = \Sigma_1 \circ \Sigma_2$ and $\Gamma;\Sigma_1 \vdash e:t'$ and $\Gamma;\Sigma_2 \vdash e':t$ by Lemma A.2(8). We conclude $\Gamma,x:t';\Sigma_2 \vdash x;e':t$ by rules **Var** and **Seq**.

Lemma 3.6 (Context Substitution). *If* $\Gamma;\Sigma_1 \vdash e:t'$, *and* $\Gamma,x:t';\Sigma_2 \vdash E[x]:t$, *and* $\Sigma_1 \circ \Sigma_2$ *is defined, then* $\Gamma;\Sigma_1 \circ \Sigma_2 \vdash E[e]:t$.

Lemma A.6. *1. Let* $k^p \notin \mathrm{cored}(\Sigma')$ *and* $\Sigma' \circ \{k^p:\rho\} \preceq \Sigma$. *Then* $\Sigma(k^p) = \rho\psi$ *and* $\Sigma' \preceq \Sigma[k^p \mapsto \psi^\circ]$ *for some light* ψ.
2. *Let* $\{k^p:\rho\} \circ \Sigma' \preceq \Sigma$. *Then* $\Sigma(k^p) = \rho\psi$ *and* $\Sigma' \preceq \Sigma[k^p \mapsto \psi^\circ]$ *for some* ψ.

Proof. All cases are easy. In case (1) note that $\Sigma'(k^p)$ can be either undefined or ε.

Lemma A.7. *Let* $e,h \longrightarrow e',h'$ *via an elementary expression reduction. Then* $\Gamma;\Sigma \vdash e:t$ *and* $\Gamma;\Sigma \vdash h$ *imply* $\Gamma';\Sigma' \vdash e':t$ *and* $\Gamma';\Sigma' \vdash h'$, *where* $\Gamma \subseteq \Gamma'$ *and* $\langle \Sigma';h' \rangle \sqsubseteq \langle \Sigma;h \rangle$.

Proof. The proof is by cases on the kind of expression reduction. We consider two paradigmatic cases.

Rule **SendS**$^{\rightarrow}$.

Let $e = k^p.\mathrm{send}(v)$ and $h = h'' :: [k^{\bar{p}} \mapsto \tilde{v}']$. We have:

$$k^p.\mathrm{send}(v),h'' :: [k^{\bar{p}} \mapsto \tilde{v}'] \longrightarrow \mathrm{null},h'' :: [k^{\bar{p}} \mapsto \tilde{v}':v]$$

By Lemmas A.3(3) and A.2(1)-(4) we have $t = Object$ and for some Σ'', t':

1) $\Gamma; \Sigma'' \vdash v : t'$,
2) $\emptyset \preceq \Sigma''$,
3) $\Sigma'' \circ \{k^p : !t'\} \preceq \Sigma$.

By 2), 3), and Lemma A.6(1) we get:

4) $\Sigma(k^p) = !t'\psi$ with ψ light,
5) $\emptyset \preceq \Sigma[k^p \mapsto \psi^\diamond]$.

Let $\Gamma' = \Gamma$, $\Sigma' = \Sigma[k^p \mapsto \psi^\diamond]$ and $h' = h'' :: [k^{\bar{p}} \mapsto \tilde{v}' : v]$.

By 5), rule **Null** and Lemma 3.3(1):

6) $\Gamma; \Sigma' \vdash \text{null} : t$.

By Definition 3.1 $A(\Sigma'; h')$ trivially holds, since $\text{cored}(\Sigma') = \emptyset$ and $\text{dom}(\Sigma') = \text{dom}(\Sigma)$. Moreover $\Sigma(k^p) = !t'\psi$ and $\Sigma(k^p) = \psi^\diamond$ imply $\langle \Sigma'; h' \rangle \sqsubseteq \langle \Sigma; h \rangle$.

Rule SendSS$^{\rightarrow}$.

Let $e = k^p.\text{send}(k_0^q)$ and $h = h'' :: [k^{\bar{p}} \mapsto \tilde{v}]$. We have:

$$k^p.\text{sendS}(k_0^q), h'' :: [k^{\bar{p}} \mapsto \tilde{v}] \longrightarrow \text{null}, h'' :: [k^{\bar{p}} \mapsto \tilde{v} : k_0^q]$$

By Lemmas A.3(5) we have $t = Object$ and for some $\eta \neq \varepsilon.\text{end}$:

1) $\{k^p : !(\eta), k_0^q : \eta\} \preceq \Sigma$.

By 1), and Lemma A.6(1) (note that η is ended) we get:

2) $\Sigma(k^p) = !(\eta)\psi$ with ψ light,
3) $\Sigma(k_0^q) = \eta$,
4) $\emptyset \preceq \Sigma \setminus k_0^q[k^p \mapsto \psi^\diamond]$.

Let $\Gamma' = \Gamma$, $\Sigma' = \Sigma \setminus k_0^q[k^p \mapsto \psi^\diamond]$ and $h' = h'' :: [k^{\bar{p}} \mapsto \tilde{v} : k_0^q]$.

By 4), rule **Null** and Lemma 3.3(1):

5) $\Gamma; \Sigma' \vdash \text{null} : t$.

By Definition 3.1 $A(\Sigma'; h')$ trivially holds, since $\text{cored}(\Sigma') = \emptyset$ and $k_0^q \notin \text{dom}(\Sigma')$. Lastly we get $\langle \Sigma'; h' \rangle \sqsubseteq \langle \Sigma; h \rangle$ from $\Sigma(k^p) = !t'\psi$ and $\Sigma'(k^p) = \psi^\diamond$ and $k_0^q \in \text{cored}(\Sigma)$ (which implies $k_0^q \notin \text{ran}_c(h)$ by $A(\Sigma; h)$) and $k_0^q \notin \text{cored}(\Sigma')$ and $k_0^q \in \text{ran}_c(h')$.

It is handy to extend to heaps the concatenation operator defined for running session types and session environments at page 10.

Definition A.8 (Heap Concatenation). *The concatenation of two heaps h and h' (notation $h \circ h'$) is the minimal heap such that:*

- $h \circ h'(o) = (C, \tilde{f} : \tilde{v})$ *if* $h(o) = (C, \tilde{f} : \tilde{v})$ *and* $o \notin h'$;
- $h \circ h'(o) = (C, \tilde{f} : \tilde{v})$ *if* $h'(o) = (C, \tilde{f} : \tilde{v})$ *and* $o \notin h$;
- $c \in h \circ h'$ *if* $c \in h$ *and* $c \notin h'$;
- $c \in h \circ h'$ *if* $c \in h'$ *and* $c \notin h$;
- $h \circ h'(k^p) = \tilde{v} : \tilde{v}'$ *if* $h(k^p) = \tilde{v}$ *and* $h'(k^p) = \tilde{v}'$;
- $h \circ h'(k^p) = \tilde{v}$ *if* $h(k^p) = \tilde{v}$ *and* $k^p \notin h'$;
- $h \circ h'(k^p) = \tilde{v}$ *if* $h'(k^p) = \tilde{v}$ *and* $k^p \notin h$.

From Definitions 3.1, 3.7 and A.8 we can easily show:

Lemma A.9. *1. $A(\Sigma_1 \circ \Sigma_2; h)$ implies $h = h_1 \circ h_2$ and $A(\Sigma_1; h_1)$ and $A(\Sigma_2; h_2)$ for some h_1, h_2.*

2. $A(\Sigma_1 \circ \Sigma_2; h_1 \circ h_2)$ and $A(\Sigma_1; h_1)$ and $\langle \Sigma_1; h_1 \rangle \sqsubseteq \langle \Sigma_1'; h_1' \rangle$ imply $A(\Sigma_1' \circ \Sigma_2; h_1' \circ h_2)$ and $\langle \Sigma_1 \circ \Sigma_2; h_1 \circ h_2 \rangle \sqsubseteq \langle \Sigma_1' \circ \Sigma_2; h_1' \circ h_2 \rangle$.

Theorem 3.8. (Subject Reduction)

1. $\Gamma; \Sigma \vdash e : t$ and $\Gamma; \Sigma \vdash h$ and $e, h \longrightarrow e', h'$ via an expression reduction imply $\Gamma'; \Sigma' \vdash e' : t$ and $\Gamma'; \Sigma' \vdash h'$, where $\Gamma \subseteq \Gamma'$ and $\langle \Sigma'; h' \rangle \sqsubseteq \langle \Sigma; h \rangle$.
2. $\Gamma; \Sigma \vdash e : t$ and $\Gamma; \Sigma \vdash h$ and $e, h \longrightarrow e_1 | e_2, h'$ via a thread reduction imply $\Gamma; \Sigma \vdash e_1 | e_2 :$ thread and $\Gamma'; \Sigma' \vdash h'$ where $\langle \Sigma'; h' \rangle \sqsubseteq \langle \Sigma; h \rangle$.
3. $\Gamma; \Sigma \vdash P$:thread and $\Gamma; \Sigma \vdash h$ and $P, h \longrightarrow P', h'$ imply $\Gamma'; \Sigma' \vdash P'$:thread and $\Gamma'; \Sigma' \vdash h'$ where $\Gamma \subseteq \Gamma'$ and $\langle \Sigma'; h' \rangle \sqsubseteq^\flat \langle \Sigma; h \rangle$.

Proof. (1) An arbitrary expression reduction is of the shape $E[e], h \longrightarrow E[e'], h'$ where $e, h \longrightarrow e', h'$ is an elementary expression reduction. The proof follows from Lemmas A.7, 3.5, and 3.6 using Lemma A.9.

(2) We consider the case of rule **ReceiveSS**$^\rightarrow$, in which we have $h = h'' :: [k^p \mapsto k_0^q : \tilde{v}]$ and:

$$E[k^p.\text{receiveS}(x)\{e_1\}], h'' :: [k^p \mapsto k_0^q : \tilde{v}] \longrightarrow e_1[k_0^q/x] \mid E[\text{null}], h'' :: [k^p \mapsto \tilde{v}].$$

By Lemma 3.5 there are Σ_1, Σ_2, t' such that:
1) $\Sigma = \Sigma_1 \circ \Sigma_2$,
2) $\Gamma; \Sigma_1 \vdash k^p.\text{receiveS}(x)\{e_1\} : t'$,
3) $\Gamma, y : t'; \Sigma_2 \vdash E[y] : t$.
By Lemma A.3(4) and 2) we get $t' = Object$ and
4) $\Gamma \setminus x; \Sigma_1', x : \eta \vdash e_1 : t''$,
5) $ended(\Sigma_1', x : \eta)$,
6) $\{k^p :?(\eta)\} \circ \Sigma_1' \preceq \Sigma_1$,
   for some $\Sigma_1', t'', \eta \neq \varepsilon.\text{end}$.
Notice that $A(\Sigma; h)$ implies:
7) $k_0^q \notin dom(\Sigma)$
   and then by 1) and 6) we get:
8) $k_0^q \notin dom(\Sigma_1')$ and $k_0^q \notin dom(\Sigma_2)$.
   1) and 6) imply by Lemma A.1(1)
9) $\{k^p :?(\eta)\} \circ \Sigma_1' \circ \Sigma_2 \preceq \Sigma$
   and then by Lemma A.6(2) for some ψ:
10) $\Sigma(k^p) =?(\eta)\psi$,
11) $\Sigma_1' \circ \Sigma_2 \preceq \Sigma[k^p \mapsto \psi^\diamond]$.
   5) implies by definition of $\circ$:
12) $\Sigma_1' \circ \Sigma_2 = \Sigma_1' \cup \Sigma_2$
   and then using 7), 8) and 11):
13) $\Sigma_1', k_0^q : \eta \cup \Sigma_2 \preceq \Sigma[k^p \mapsto \psi^\diamond], k_0^q : \eta$.
   Let $\Gamma' = \Gamma$, $\Sigma' = \Sigma[k^p \mapsto \psi^\diamond], k_0^q : \eta$ and $h' = h'' :: [k^{\tilde{p}} \mapsto \tilde{v}]$.
   Applying Lemma A.5(2) to 4) and 8) we derive:
14) $\Gamma; \Sigma_1', k_0^q : \eta \vdash e_1[k_0^q/x] : t''$.
   By rule **Null** we have $\Gamma; \emptyset \vdash \text{null} : t'$ and then by 3) and Lemma 3.6 we get:
15) $\Gamma; \Sigma_2 \vdash E[\text{null}] : t$.
   By applying rules **Start** and **Par** to 14) and 15) we derive:

16) $\Gamma; \Sigma_1', k_0^q : \eta \cup \Sigma_2 \vdash e_1[k_0^q/x] \mid E[\mathsf{null}] : \mathsf{thread}$
which implies by 13) and Lemma 3.3(2):

17) $\Gamma; \Sigma' \vdash e_1[k_0^q/x] \mid E[\mathsf{null}] : \mathsf{thread}$.
By Definition 3.1 $A(\Sigma'; h') = A(\Sigma; h)$. Lastly we get $\langle \Sigma'; h' \rangle \sqsubseteq \langle \Sigma; h \rangle$ from $\Sigma(k^p) = ?(\eta)\psi$ and $\Sigma'(k^p) = \psi^\circ$ and $k_0^q \in \mathsf{ran}_c(h)$.

(3) The interesting case is when the reduction is obtained by an application of rule **Connect$^\rightarrow$**:

$$E_1[\mathsf{connect\ a\ s}\{e_1\}] \mid E_2[\mathsf{connect\ a}\ \bar{s}\{e_2\}], h$$
$$\longrightarrow E_1[e_1[k^+/a]] \mid E_2[e_2[k^-/a]], h :: [k^+ \mapsto \varepsilon] :: [k^- \mapsto \varepsilon] \quad k^+, k^- \notin h$$

By Lemma A.4(2) and (1) we have for some Σ_i, t_i:

1) $\Sigma = \Sigma_1 \cup \Sigma_2$,
2) $\Gamma; \Sigma_i \vdash E_i[\mathsf{connect\ u\ s}\{e_i\}] : t_i \quad (i = 1, 2)$.
By Lemma 3.5 there are $\Sigma_i^1, \Sigma_i^2, t_i'$ and fresh $x_i \ (i = 1, 2)$ such that:
3) $\Sigma_i = \Sigma_i^1 \circ \Sigma_i^2$,
4) $\Gamma; \Sigma_i^1 \vdash \mathsf{connect\ a\ s}\{e_i\} : t_i'$,
5) $\Gamma, x_i : t_i'; \Sigma_i^2 \vdash E[x_i] : t_i$.
By Lemma A.3(1) we have for some η:
6) $s = \mathsf{begin}.\eta$,
7) $\Gamma \setminus a; \Sigma_i^1, a : \eta_i \vdash e_i : t_i'$,
where $\eta_1 = \eta$ and $\eta_2 = \bar{\eta}$.
Let $\Gamma' = \Gamma$, $\Sigma' = \Sigma, k^p : \eta, k^{\bar{p}} : \bar{\eta}$ and $h' = h :: [k^+ \mapsto \varepsilon] :: [k^- \mapsto \varepsilon]$.
Let now k^i stand for k^+ if $i = 1$ and for k^- if $i = 2$. Since the k^i are fresh by 7) and Lemma A.5(2) we have:
8) $\Gamma; \Sigma_i^1, k^i : \eta_i \vdash e_i[k^i/a] : t_i'$,
and from 5) and 8), by Lemma 3.6:
9) $\Gamma; \Sigma_i, k^i : \eta_i \vdash E_i[e_i[k^i/a]] : t_i$.
In fact note that $(\Sigma_i^1, k^i : \eta_i) \circ \Sigma_i^2$ must be defined since $\Sigma_i^1 \circ \Sigma_i^2$ is defined and k^i is fresh. For the same reason $(\Sigma_i^1, k^i : \eta_i) \circ \Sigma_i^2 = \Sigma_i, k^i : \eta_i$. From 9) by rules **Start** and **Par** we get:
10) $\Gamma; \Sigma' \vdash E_1[e_1[k^+/a]] \mid E_2[e_2[k^-/a]] : \mathsf{thread}$.
By Definition 3.1 $A(\Sigma; h)$ implies $A(\Sigma'; h')$ since the heaps h and h' only differ for $[k^+ \mapsto \varepsilon] :: [k^- \mapsto \varepsilon]$. Lastly $\langle \Sigma'; h' \rangle \sqsubseteq^\flat \langle \Sigma, h \rangle$ by the last clause of Definition 3.7(3).

KeY: A Formal Method for Object-Oriented Systems

Wolfgang Ahrendt[1], Bernhard Beckert[2], Reiner Hähnle[1], and Peter H. Schmitt[3]

[1] Department of Computer Science and Engineering
Chalmers University of Technology and Göteborg University
{ahrendt,reiner}@chalmers.se
[2] Department of Computer Science
University of Koblenz
beckert@uni-koblenz.de
[3] Department of Theoretical Computer Science
University of Karlsruhe
pschmitt@ira.uka.de

Abstract. This paper gives an overview of the KeY approach and highlights the main features of the KeY system. KeY is an approach (and a system) for the deductive verification of object-oriented software. It aims for integrating design, implementation, formal specification and formal verification as seamlessly as possible. The intention is to provide a platform that allows close collaboration of conventional and formal software development methods.

1   Introduction

The KeY Approach and System. This paper gives an overview of the KeY approach and highlights the main features of the KeY system.

KeY is an approach (and a system) for the deductive verification of object-oriented (OO) software. It aims for integrating design, implementation, formal specification and formal verification as seamlessly as possible. The intention is to provide a platform that allows close collaboration of conventional and formal software development methods.

Recently, version 1.0 of the KeY system has been released in connection with the KeY book [3]. The KeY system is written in Java and runs on all usual architectures. It is available under GPL and can be downloaded from www.key-project.org.

Towards an Integration of Formal Methods in Software Engineering. KeY is primarily not a stand-alone tool, but a plugin to (currently two) well-known CASE tools: Borland Together and the Eclipse IDE. Users can develop a whole software project, comprised of specifications as well as implementations, entirely within either of the mentioned CASE tools. The KeY plugin then offers the *extended functionality* to generate proof obligations from selected parts of

M.M. Bonsangue and E.B. Johnsen (Eds.): FMOODS 2007, LNCS 4468, pp. 32–43, 2007.

specifications and verify them with the KeY prover. The KeY verification component, being the core of the KeY system, can also be used as a stand-alone prover.

KeY supports the OMG standard Object Constraint Language (OCL) [26] for specification as well as the Java Modeling Language (JML) [19], which is increasingly used in industrial contexts [5]. Translation of specifications from OCL and JML into logic, as well as the synthesis of a variety of proof obligations, is completely automatic. The same is true, to a large extent, for proof search. In addition, KeY features a syntax-directed editor for OCL that can render OCL expressions in several natural languages while they are being edited. It is even possible to translate OCL expressions automatically into fragments of English and German. This means that KeY provides a common tool and conceptual base for developers and formal methods specialists. The architecture and interfaces of KeY are depicted in Fig. 1.

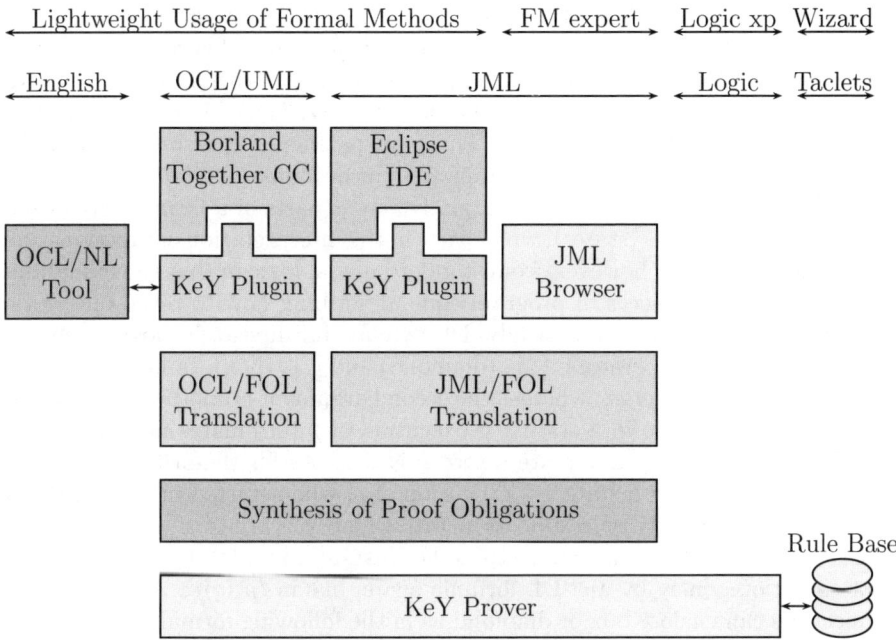

Fig. 1. Architecture and interfaces of the KeY system

2   Full Coverage of a Real World Language

To ensure acceptance among practitioners it is essential to support an industrially relevant programming language as the verification target. We chose Java Card source code [7] because of its importance for security- and safety-critical applications. We refrained from using a home-spun sublanguage of Java, because it is unrealistic to assume that applications are written in it.

The KeY prover and its calculus [3, Chapt. 3] support the full Java Card 2.2.1 language. This includes all object-oriented features, Java Card's transaction mechanism, the (finite) Java integer types, abrupt termination (local jumps and exceptions) and even a formal specification (both in OCL [18] and JML[1]) of the essential parts of the Java Card API. In addition, some Java features that are not part of Java Card are supported as well: multi-dimensional arrays, Java class initialisation semantics, char and String types. In short, if you have a sequential Java program without dynamic class loading and floating point types, then it is (in principle) possible to verify it with KeY.

3   Beyond Hoare Logic

KeY is a *deductive verification* system, meaning that its core is a theorem prover, which proves formulae of a suitable logic. Different deductive verification approaches vary in the choice of the used logic. The KeY approach uses *Dynamic Logic* (DL) [14], which (like Hoare Logic [16]) is transparent with respect to the programs that are subject to verification. Programs are neither abstracted away into a less expressive formalism such as finite-state machines nor are they embedded into a general purpose higher-order logic. Instead, the logic and the calculus "work" directly on the source code. This transparency is extremely helpful for proving problems that require a certain amount of human interaction.

DL is a particular kind of *modal logic*. Different parts of a formula are evaluated in different worlds (states), which vary in the interpretation of functions and predicates. DL differs, however, from standard modal logic in that the modalities are "indexed" with pieces of program code, describing how to reach one world (state) from the other. Syntactically, DL extends full first-order logic with two additional (mix-fix) operators: $\langle\,.\,\rangle\,.$ (diamond) and $[\,.\,]\,.$ (box). In both cases, the first argument is a *program*, whereas the second argument is another DL formula. A formula $\langle p \rangle \varphi$ is true in a state s if execution of p terminates normally when started in s and results in a state where φ is true. As for the other operator, a formula $[p]\varphi$ is true in a state s if execution of p, when started in s, does *either* not terminate normally *or* results in a state where φ is true.[2]

DL is closed under all its connectives. For instance, in a DL formula $\langle p \rangle \varphi$, the post-condition φ may by any DL formula again, like in $\langle p \rangle \langle q \rangle \psi$. Also, arbitrary connectives can enclose box or diamond as in the following formula which states equivalence of p and q w.r.t. the "output", the program variable x.

$$\forall\ val.\quad (\ \langle p \rangle\ \mathtt{x} = val \quad \leftrightarrow \quad \langle q \rangle\ \mathtt{x} = val\ ) \tag{1}$$

A frequent pattern of DL formulae is $\varphi \rightarrow \langle p \rangle \psi$, stating that the program p, when started from a state where φ is true, terminates with ψ being true afterwards. The formula $\varphi \rightarrow [p]\psi$, on the other hand, does not claim termination, and has exactly the same meaning as the Hoare triple $\{\psi\}\ p\ \{\phi\}$.

---

[1] See http://www.cs.ru.nl/~woj/software/software.html

[2] These descriptions have to be generalised when non-deterministic programs are considered, which is not the case here.

Unlike most other variants of DL, KeY DL comprises programs from a real language, namely Java Card. Concretely, p is a sequence of (zero, one, or more) Java Card statements. Accordingly, the logic is called Java Card DL. The following is an example of a Java Card DL formula:

$$\texttt{o1.f} < \texttt{o2.f} \rightarrow \langle\texttt{int t=o1.f; o1.f=o2.f; o2.f=t;}\rangle \texttt{o2.f} < \texttt{o1.f} \quad (2)$$

It says that, when started in any state where the integer field f of o1 has a smaller value than o2.f, the statement sequence "int t=o1.f; o1.f=o2.f; o2.f=t;" terminates, and afterwards o2.f is smaller than o1.f.

The main advantage of DL over Hoare logic is increased expressiveness: one can express not merely program correctness, but also security properties [8,20], correctness of program transformations, or the validity of assignable clauses. Also, a pre- or post-condition can contain programs themselves, for instance to express that a linked structure is acyclic. A full account of Java Card DL is found in the KeY book [3, Chapt. 3].

KeY interfaces with OCL as well as JML specifications, by translating them (and the specified Java code) into *proof obligations* in Java Card DL. Following Fig. 1 from the right to the left, we have essentially four scenarios, varying in the origin of the DL proof obligations (POs):

(i) *Hand-crafted* POs, to be loaded from .key files.
(ii) *Automatically generated* POs
    (a) from JML-augmented Java source files, using
        – the JML browser of the KeY stand-alone system.
        – Eclipse with the KeY plug-in.
    (b) from OCL-augmented UML diagrams and Java source files, using Borland Together with KeY extensions.

4   Symbolic Execution

The actual verification process in KeY can be viewed as *symbolic execution* of source code. Unbounded loops and recursion are handled by induction over data structures occurring in the verification target. Alternatively, partial correctness of loops can also be shown by a rule that uses invariants. Symbolic execution plus induction as a verification paradigm was originally suggested for informal usage by Burstall [6]. The idea to use dynamic logic as a basis for mechanising symbolic execution was first realized in the Karlsruhe Interactive Verifier (KIV) tool [15]. Symbolic execution is extremely suitable for interactive verification, because proof progress corresponds to program execution, which makes it easy to interpret intermediate stages in a proof and failed proof attempts.

Most program logics (e.g., Hoare Logic, wp-calculus) have in common that the state change effected by a program translates, at some point, into substitutions applied to formulae. In the KeY approach to symbolic execution, the application of substitutions is *delayed* as much as possible; instead of using substitutions, the state change effect of a program is made *syntactically explicit* and accumulated in a construct called *updates*. The role of updates is to record the effects of (a certain path in) the execution of a program. Only when symbolic execution has completed are updates turned into substitutions. We omitted updates so far in the discussion of DL and introduce them by example now.

For instance, when proving formula (2), the prover will after some steps construct the following *sequent* as an intermediate goal (slightly adjusted for presentation):[3]

$$\texttt{o1.f} < \texttt{o2.f} \ \vdash \ \{\texttt{t:=o1.f}\}\langle\texttt{o1.f=o2.f; o2.f=t;}\rangle \, \texttt{o2.f} < \texttt{o1.f} \qquad (3)$$

The expression "`t:=o1.f`" is an update, which in this case represents the effect of the symbolically executed initialisation statement. Executing the next Java statement leads to nested (consecutive) updates "`{t:=o1.f}{o1.f:=o2.f}`", which are merged into one *parallel* update:

$$\texttt{o1.f} < \texttt{o2.f} \ \vdash \ \{\texttt{t:=o1.f || o1.f:=o2.f}\}\langle\texttt{o2.f=t;}\rangle \, \texttt{o2.f} < \texttt{o1.f} \qquad (4)$$

Soon after, we have

$$\texttt{o1.f} < \texttt{o2.f} \ \vdash \ \{\texttt{t:=o1.f || o1.f:=o2.f}\}\{\texttt{o2.f:=t}\}\langle\rangle \, \texttt{o2.f} < \texttt{o1.f} \qquad (5)$$

This time, the update merging step results in:

$$\texttt{o1.f} < \texttt{o2.f} \ \vdash \ \{\texttt{o1.f:=o2.f || o2.f:=o1.f}\}\langle\rangle \, \texttt{o2.f} < \texttt{o1.f} \qquad (6)$$

Two things have happened. First, in a parallelisation step, `t:=o1.f` has been *applied* to `o2.f:=t`. Second, `t:=o1.f` has been *simplified away*. This is justified, because `t` does not appear in the post-condition. Finally, the empty modality $\langle\rangle$ is removed. Only thereafter, the parallel update "meets" the post-condition, and is applied as a substitution, leading to a trivially true sequent.

The second component of symbolic execution, next to updates, is *program transformation*. Java (Card) is a complex language, and the calculus for Java Card DL performs program transformations to resolve all the complex constructs of the language, breaking them down to simple effects that can be moved into updates. For instance, in the case of `try-catch` blocks, symbolic execution proceeds on the "active" statement *inside* the `try` block, until normal or abrupt termination of that block triggers different transformations.

Loops can be dealt with by using invariants in the traditional Hoare style. Alternatively, the calculus allows to combine *unwinding* with *induction*, which we come to in the following section.

5 KeY Is Not Merely a VCG

The KeY system is not merely a verification condition generator (VCG), but a theorem prover for program logic that combines a variety of automated reasoning techniques. The KeY prover differs from most other deductive verification

---

[3] KeY uses a sequent style calculus, see below. For now, it is sufficient to read the sequent arrow $\vdash$ as an implication.

systems in that symbolic execution of programs, first-order reasoning, arithmetic simplification, external decision procedures, and symbolic state simplification are *interleaved*. This interleaving takes place on the level of proof strategies, but also on the level of individual rules.

To illustrate the latter point, we discuss a few rules of our *sequent calculus*. Sequents have the form $\phi_1, \ldots, \phi_n \vdash \phi_1', \ldots, \phi_m'$, with two (possibly empty) lists of formulae connected by the sequent arrow $\vdash$. The meaning of a sequent is that at least one of the $\phi_1', \ldots, \phi_m'$ follows from the conjunction of the $\phi_1, \ldots, \phi_n$. An example of a rule in the sequent calculus for Java Card DL is the *induction rule* over natural numbers:

$$\frac{\Gamma \vdash \phi(0), \Delta \qquad \Gamma \vdash \forall n.(\phi(n) \to \phi(n+1)), \Delta}{\Gamma \vdash \forall n.\phi(n), \Delta} \tag{7}$$

The meaning of a sequent calculus rule is that, in order to prove a sequent matching the conclusion of the rule (here "$\Gamma \vdash \forall n.\phi(n), \Delta$"), it is sufficient to prove all premisses (two in this case). As usual, the rules are actually *rule schemas* and appear properly instantiated in the context of a concrete proof.

But what has the induction rule (7) to do with Java Card DL, as it looks like a pure first-order rule? The point is that ϕ matches an arbitrary formula in Java Card DL, possibly containing Java Card code (in a modality). And indeed, this rule can be employed for handling loops in ϕ. After applying (7), one proof branch handles the "loop exit" case. In the other branch, the step case is handled, where the loop is unwound once using the *loop unwind* rule:

$$\frac{\Gamma \vdash \langle \pi \text{ if } (e) \{p \text{ while}(e) \ p\} \ \omega \rangle \phi, \Delta}{\Gamma \vdash \langle \pi \text{ while}(e) \ p \ \omega \rangle \phi, \Delta} \tag{8}$$

This is the interplay of symbolic execution and induction which is best described by the title of Burstall's original paper [6]: "Program proving as hand simulation with a little induction."

6   User-Friendly Graphical User Interface

In spite of a high degree of automation (see Sect. 8), in many cases there are significant, non-trivial tasks left for the user. For that purpose, the KeY system provides a user-friendly graphical user interface (GUI). When proving a property which is too involved to be handled fully automatically, certain rule applications need to be performed in an interactive manner, in dialogue with the system. This is the case when either the automated strategies are exhausted, or else when the user deliberately performs a strategic step (like a case distinction) manually, *before* automated strategies are invoked (again).

In the case of human-guided rule application, the user is asked to solve tasks like: *selecting a proof rule* to be applied, *providing instantiations for* the proof rule's *schema variables*, or *providing instantiations for quantified variables* of the logic. The system, and its advanced GUI, are designed to support these

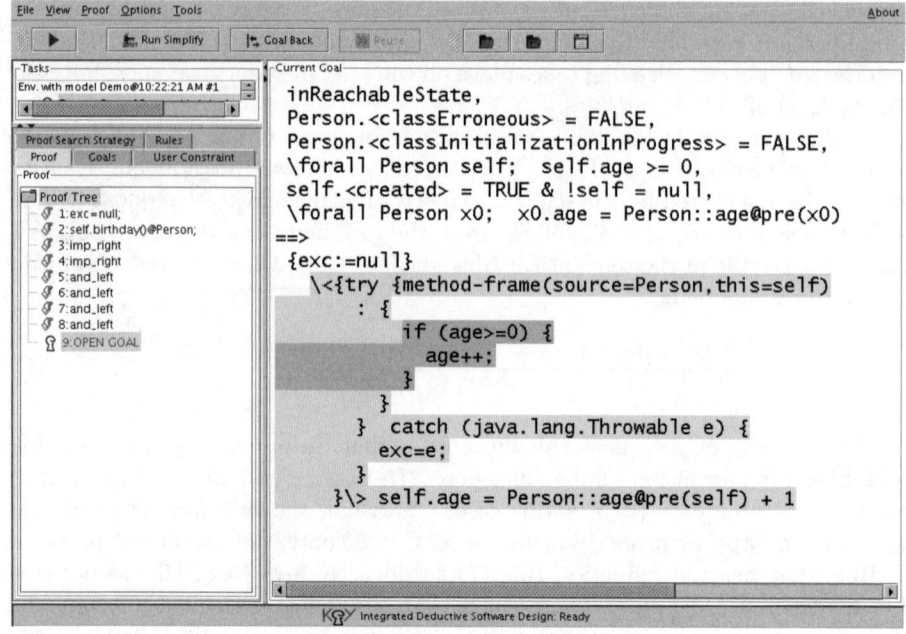

Fig. 2. Screenshot of the GUI of the KeY prover

steps well. For instance, the selection of the right rule, out of over 1500(!), is greatly simplified by allowing the user to highlight any subexpression of the proof goal simply by positioning the mouse. In the screenshot of the GUI of the KeY prover displayed in Fig. 2, a `try-catch` statement is highlighted. The first active statement in it, the `if` statement, appears in grey.

A dynamic context menu will offer only those few rules that apply to this expression, in this case, the rule for a statement within a `try-catch` block that is not a `throw`. Furthermore, the menus provide tooltips for each rule. When it comes to interactive variable instantiation, *drag-and-drop* mechanisms greatly simplify and speed-up the usage of the instantiation dialogues, and in some cases even allow to omit explicit rule selection. For example, if the user drags an equation onto a term, the system will try to rewrite the term with the equation. And if the user drags a term onto a quantifier, the system will try to instantiate the quantifier with this term.

Other supported forms of interaction in the context of proof construction are the inspection of proof trees, the pruning of proof branches, stepwise backtracking, and the triggering of proof reuse.

7   A Simple High-Level Rule Language

The implementation of the sequent proof rules in the KeY prover is closely related to the pragmatics of interaction within the GUI as described in the previous section. The rules are written in a high-level language, called the "taclet language." Each rule is represented as one *taclet*. Besides the conventional declarative semantics, taclets have an operational semantics that defines their pragmatics in automatic and interactive proof search. The following example shows a "modus ponens" rule in textbook notation (left) and as a taclet (right):

$$\frac{\Gamma, \phi, \psi \vdash \Delta}{\Gamma, \phi, \phi \rightarrow \psi \vdash \Delta}$$

```
\find (p -> q ==>)       // implication in antecedent
\assumes (p ==>)          // side condition
\replacewith(q ==>)       // action on focus
\heuristics(simplify)     // strategy information
```

This example taclet consists of four clauses. The arrow "==>", appearing in three of them, is the KeY system's representation of the sequent arrow $\vdash$. Within taclets, "==>" is used to indicate whether a matching formula appears on the left- or right-hand side of the sequent.

The `find` clause specifies the potential application focus. The taclet will be offered to the user when selecting a matching focus and if a formula mentioned in the `assumes` clause is present in the sequent. The action clauses `replacewith` and `add` (not present in this example) allow modifying (or replacing) the formula in focus, as well as adding additional formulae. The `heuristics` clause records information for the parameterised automated proof search strategy.

Taclets are not only used to represent calculus rules, but also lemmata. The latter can be proven correct against the provided taclets [4]. The taclet language is quickly mastered and makes the rule base easy to maintain and extend. A full account of the taclet language is given in the KeY book [3, Chapt. 4].

8 Automated Proof Search

For automated proof search, a number of predefined strategies are available in KeY using different rule sets that are, for example, optimised to symbolically executing loop-free programs or proving pure first-order formulae.

In order to better interleave interactive and automated proof construction, KeY uses a proof confluent sequent calculus, which means that automated proof search does not require backtracking over rule applications. The taclet language and application mechanism are designed in such a way that the user can write only rules with local effects on sequents, and the handling of meta variables, skolemisation, constraints, etc. is taken care of automatically, to reduce the risk of inadvertently introducing rules which damage confluence.

The automated search for quantifier instantiations uses meta variables[4] that are place-holders for terms. Instead of backtracking over meta-variable instantiations, instantiations are postponed to the point where the whole proof can be closed, and an incremental global closure check is used. Rule applications

---

[4] This kind of variables are known in the tableau theorem proving community under the name of "free variables" [10].

requiring particular instantiations (unifications) of meta variables are handled by attaching unification constraints to the resulting formulas [11].

There is a back end to SMT-LIB syntax[5] for proving near-propositional proof goals with external decision procedures.

9 Customisable Verification

The KeY system offers to customise the rule set used for verification. For instance, the user can choose between different semantics of the primitive Java integer types `byte`, `short`, `int`, `long`, and `char`. Options are: the mathematical integers (easy to verify, but not a faithful model of Java and, hence, unsound), mathematical integers with overflow check (sound, reasonably easy to verify, but unable to verify programs that depend on Java's finite ring semantics), and a faithful semantics of Java integers (sound, complete, but difficult to verify). KeY1.0 comes with the mathematical integer semantics chosen as default option, to optimise usability for beginners. However, for a sound treatment of integers, the user should switch to either of the other semantics. Alternatively, one can employ the *proof reuse* feature of KeY, to first construct a proof using the mathematical integer option, and then *replay* the proof with the mathematical overflow semantics selected.

Other examples where one can customise the degree of faithfulness, versus simplicity, are object creation, and null pointer treatment.

10 A Broader Perspective on Verification

One of the most important insights we gained from our work is the realisation that verification technology with symbolic execution can be seen as the base technology of a whole range of applications in software analysis, many of which are more automatic than full verification. In the future we will develop the KeY system into a general software analysis platform where formal verification is only one of many analysis techniques.

For example, in the area of model-based test case generation [2,9] the prover is used to compute path conditions and to identify infeasible paths. Fully automatic white-box unit test generation for Java Card is possible based on approximative attempts at formal verification of the implementation under test [9]. White-box testing can also be done by combining deduction-based specification extraction and black-box testing, i.e., one generates specifications for given programs and then uses these specifications as input for black-box testing tools [2].

Another usage of verification is in security analysis [8], where the absence and presence of secure information flow including information declassification is shown. Since many security analyses are implemented on the basis of type

---

[5] See http://combination.cs.uiowa.edu/smtlib/

systems [23] it is promising to try to combine the advantages of type-based and deduction-based methods. In [13] it is shown that dynamic logic can serve as a common framework where such a combination can be realized.

Most of the time, verification attempts are *not* successful, because the specification or the implementation contains bugs. In this case, it is extremely valuable for the user to obtain information from failed proof attempts without having to wade through large proof trees. Generating counter examples for failed proofs, so-called "disproving" of programs, is only started to being explored [22].

It is also possible to cast symbolic program execution to the user interface and the functionality offered by a symbolic source code debugger. One can then set breakpoints, watches, and inspect the intermediate program state. But in contrast to a conventional debugger, such a truly symbolic debugger is based on a symbolic execution tree and can represent not only one program run, but *all* possible program runs [1]. We expect interesting synergies on both sides from combining verification with debugging.

11 Applications

Among the major achievements in program verification using the KeY system are the treatment of the Demoney case study, an electronic purse application provided by Trusted Logic S.A. [3, Chapt. 14] and the verification of a Java implementation of the Schorr-Waite graph marking algorithm [3, Chapt. 15]. This algorithm, originally developed for garbage collectors, has recently become a popular benchmark for program verification tools. As far as we are aware, the KeY study provides the first verification of an executable Java implementation. A case study [17] performed within the HIJA project[6] included formal verification of the lateral module of a flight management system being part of the on-board control software from Thales Avionics. Recently, for the first time an implementation of the Mondex banking card case study [24] was verified with the KeY prover [25].

The flexibility of KeY w.r.t. the used logic and calculus manifests itself in the fact that the prover has been chosen as a reasoning engine for a variety of other logics. These include the mechanisation of a logic for Abstract State Machines [21] and the implementation of a calculus for simplifying OCL constraints [12]. A version of the KeY prover that supports the C programming language will be released later this year.

KeY is also very useful for teaching logic, deduction, and formal methods. Its graphical user interface makes KeY easy to use for students. They can step through proofs using different degrees of automation (using the full verification calculus or just the first-order core rules). The authors have been successfully teaching courses for several years using the KeY system. An overview and course materials are available at www.key-project.org/teaching.

---

[6] See http://www.hija.info

References

1. Baum, M.: A verifying debugger. Master's thesis, Department of Computer Science, Institute for Theoretical Computer Science, to appear (2007)
2. Beckert, B., Gladisch, C.: White-box testing by combining deduction-based specification extraction and black-box testing. In: Gurevich, Y. (ed.) Proceedings, International Conference on Tests and Proofs (TAP), Zürich, Switzerland. LNCS, Springer, Berlin Heidelberg New York (2007)
3. Beckert, B., Hähnle, R., Schmitt, P.H. (eds.): Verification of Object-Oriented Software: The KeY Approach. LNCS (LNAI), vol. 4334. Springer, Heidelberg (2007)
4. Beckert, B., Klebanov, V.: Must program verification systems and calculi be verified?. In: Proceedings, 3rd International Verification Workshop (VERIFY), Workshop at Federated Logic Conferences (FLoC), Seattle, USA (2006)
5. Burdy, L., Cheon, Y., Cok, D., Ernst, M., Kiniry, J., Leavens, G.T., Leino, K.R.M., Poll, E.: An overview of JML tools and applications. International Journal on Software Tools for Technology Transfer 7(3), 212–232 (2005)
6. Burstall, R.M.: Program proving as hand simulation with a little induction. In: Information Processing, vol. 74, pp. 308–312. Elsevier, Amsterdam, North-Holland (1974)
7. Chen, Z.: Java Card Technology for Smart Cards: Architecture and Programmer's Guide. In: Java Series, June 2000, Addison-Wesley, London, UK (2000)
8. Darvas, Á., Hähnle, R., Sands, D.: A theorem proving approach to analysis of secure information flow. In: Hutter, D., Ullmann, M. (eds.) SPC 2005. LNCS, vol. 3450, pp. 193–209. Springer, Heidelberg (2005)
9. Engel, C., Hähnle, R.: Generating unit tests from formal proofs. In: Gurevich, Y. (ed.) Proceedings, International Conference on Tests and Proofs (TAP), Zürich, Switzerland. LNCS, Springer, Berlin Heidelberg New York (2007)
10. Fitting, M.C.: First-Order Logic and Automated Theorem Proving, 2nd edn. Springer, New York (1996)
11. Giese, M.: Incremental closure of free variable tableaux. In: Goré, R.P., Leitsch, A., Nipkow, T. (eds.) IJCAR 2001. LNCS (LNAI), vol. 2083, pp. 545–560. Springer, Heidelberg (2001)
12. Giese, M., Larsson, D.: Simplifying transformations of OCL constraints. In: Briand, L., Williams, C. (eds.) MoDELS 2005. LNCS, vol. 3713, Springer, Heidelberg (2005)
13. Hähnle, R., Pan, J., Rümmer, P., Walter, D.: Integration of a security type system into a program logic. In: Montanari, U., Sanella, D. (eds.) Proc. Trustworthy Global Computing, Lucca, Italy. LNCS, Springer, Berlin Heidelberg (2007)
14. Harel, D., Kozen, D., Tiuryn, J.: Dynamic Logic. MIT Press, Cambridge (2000)
15. Heisel, M., Reif, W., Stephan, W.: Program verification by symbolic execution and induction. In: Morik, K. (ed.) Informatik Fachberichte. Proceedings, 11th German Workshop on Artificial Intelligence, vol. 152, Springer, Berlin Heidelberg (1987)
16. Hoare, C.A.R.: An axiomatic basis for computer programming. Communications of the ACM 12(10), 576–580, 583 (1969)
17. Hunt, J.J., Jenn, E., Leriche, S., Schmitt, P., Tonin, I., Wonnemann, C.: A case study of specification and verification using JML in an avionics application. In: Rochard-Foy, M., Wellings, A. (eds.) Proceedings, 4th Workshop on Java Technologies for Real-time and Embedded Systems (JTRES). ACM Press, New York (2006)
18. Larsson, D., Mostowski, W.: Specifying Java Card API in OCL. In: Schmitt, P.H. (ed.) OCL 2.0 Workshop at UML 2003, ENTCS, vol. 102C, pp. 3–19. Elsevier, Amsterdam, North-Holland (2004)

19. Leavens, G.T., Poll, E., Clifton, C., Cheon, Y., Ruby, C., Cok, D., Müller, P., Kiniry, J., Chalin, P.: JML Reference Manual. Draft Revision 1.200 (February 2007)
20. Mostowski, W.: Formalisation and verification of Java Card security properties in dynamic logic. In: Cerioli, M. (ed.) FASE 2005. LNCS, vol. 3442, pp. 357–371. Springer, Heidelberg (2005)
21. Nanchen, S., Schmid, H., Schmitt, P., Stärk, R.F.: The ASMKeY prover. Technical Report 436, Department of Computer Science, ETH Zürich (2004)
22. Rümmer, P., Shah, M.A.: Proving programs incorrect using a sequent calculus for Java Dynamic Logic. In: Gurevich, Y. (ed.) Proceedings, International Conference on Tests and Proofs (TAP), Zürich, Switzerland. LNCS, Springer, Berlin Heidelberg (2007)
23. Sabelfeld, A., Myers, A.C.: Language-based information-flow security. IEEE Journal on Selected Areas in Communications 21(1), 5–19 (2003)
24. Stepney, S., Cooper, D., Woodcock, J.: An electronic purse: Specification, refinement, and proof. Technical monograph PRG-126, Oxford University Computing Laboratory (July 2000)
25. Tonin, I.: Verifying the Mondex Case Study: the KeY approach. Technical report, Department of Computer Science, Institute for Theoretical Computer Science (April 2007)
26. Warmer, J., Kleppe, A.: The Object Constraint Language: Getting Your Models Ready for MDA. In: Object Technology Series, August 2003, Addison-Wesley, London, UK (2003)

Verifying Distributed, Event-Based Middleware Applications Using Domain-Specific Software Model Checking*

L. Ruhai Cai, Jeremy S. Bradbury, and Juergen Dingel

School of Computing, Queen's University
Kingston, Ontario, Canada
{cai,bradbury,dingel}@cs.queensu.ca

Abstract. The success of distributed event-based infrastructures such as SIENA and Elvin is partially due to their ease of use. Even novice users of these infrastructures not versed in distributed programming can quickly comprehend the small and intuitive interfaces that these systems typically feature. However, if these users make incorrect assumptions about how the infrastructure services work, a mismatch between the infrastructure and its client applications occurs, which may manifest itself in erroneous client behaviour. We propose a framework for automatically model checking distributed event-based systems in order to discover mismatch between the infrastructure and its clients. Using the SIENA event service as an example, we implemented and evaluated our framework by customizing the Bandera/Bogor tool pipeline. Two realistic Java applications are implemented to test and evaluate the framework.

1 Introduction

The notion of an event has established itself as a successful communication and integration mechanism. In modern, object-oriented systems, events are often present on the language-, component-, and middleware-level. For instance, events are indispensable for GUI programming, allow the easy customization of frameworks such as Eclipse though "plug-ins" that implement some "EventListener" interface, provide the basis for the implementation of many design patterns (e.g., the model-view-controller and observer patterns), and are an important means of communication in many object-oriented middleware infrastructures such as CORBA, Elvin, and Siena. Events even form a central ingredient to the model of computation underlying UML 2 [17].

In this paper, we address the challenge of verifying applications that have been built on top of a distributed, event-based infrastructure. The analysis of these kinds of system is necessary, because clients are often concurrent which increases the complexity and the likelihood of unwanted behaviour. Moreover, an application running on top of an event-based infrastructure will only function

---

* This work was supported by the Natural Sciences and Engineering Research Council of Canada (NSERC).

M.M. Bonsangue and E.B. Johnsen (Eds.): FMOODS 2007, LNCS 4468, pp. 44–58, 2007.

correctly if it uses the services of the infrastructure appropriately and does not make any incorrect assumptions on how the service works. Despite the complexity of their underlying implementation, distributed event-based infrastructures typically have a small and intuitive interface. Unfortunately, the intuitive nature of the interface can be misleading. This observation is supported by one of the authors of the distributed event-based infrastructure SIENA [4]:

> "...people make a lot of assumptions on the order in which they will receive events. In other words, they program their applications with a synchronous communication model in mind, and end up getting weird results when events queue up and get delivered in an unexpected order."

For instance, SIENA clients may assume that events are delivered in the same order in which they have been sent, or that they will never receive an event to which they have unsubscribed. In reality, SIENA is considered a best-effort service and does not maintain the order of events. Therefore, clients using SIENA must be designed and implemented accordingly [5]:

> "...the implementation of SIENA must not introduce unnecessary delays in its processing, but it is not required to prevent race conditions induced by either the external delay or the processing delay. Clients of SIENA must be resilient to such race condition; for instance, they must allow for the possibility of receiving a notification for a canceled subscription."

The goal of our research is to develop a framework to discover if clients make incorrect assumptions about the event service and if a mismatch between the service and its clients has occurred that prevents the overall application from behaving as desired. Unfortunately, it can be very difficult to discover this kind of architectural mismatch and to determine that, for instance, the clients are not robust enough to handle possible race conditions. The main reasons include: First, clients are often concurrent which can render conventional testing methods insufficient. Second, the distributed nature of these systems prevents the straight-forward application of more sophisticated quality assurance techniques such as randomized testing, model checking, or static analysis. For instance, to be able to analyze a single client its environment has to be modeled. However, the construction of a correct and adequate environment model typically is quite difficult. Third, implementations of middleware infrastructures are large and complicated enough that the automatic extraction of a model is not feasible.

Our approach to analyzing distributed event-based systems leverages the system architecture to split the analysis into two smaller tasks. In one task, we summarize the behaviour of the infrastructure services with a manually created finite-state machine model and verify that the clients function correctly when composed with this model. In the resulting system, communication between distributed clients via the event service is replaced by message-passing between parallel threads. Automatic model extraction and optimization are used as much as possible to ensure that the resulting model is accurate and tractable. In the second task, we verify that the implementation of the event infrastructure conforms to the model. In this paper, we focus on the first task and leave the second for future work. In particular, we suggest to accomplish the first task by means of a semi-automatic framework that leverages the increasing power, maturity, availability, and customizability of software model checkers.

To prove the viability of the framework, we implemented it for use with the SIENA event service. A customized version of the Bandera/Bogor tool pipeline is used for model extraction, optimization, and analysis. While the default version of the pipeline provided most of the required functionality, the model extraction phase had to be customized to allow for the automatic integration of different event service/infrastructure models. Moreover, the Indus slicer and the Bogor model checker were customized.

Model checking has already been suggested as an analysis technique for event-based systems using the implicit-invocation architecture [10,1]. However, the scope of this previous work was limited to systems with centralized event services and did not attempt to analyze *realistic distributed* event services. Moreover, the systems analyzed by previous work were idealized examples while our work is applied directly on actual implementations. A third contribution of our work is the application of domain-specific software model checking techniques and a detailed description of the customizations necessary for using a state-of-the-art software model checker.

We will first provide a description of distributed event-based systems and the Bandera/Bogor pipeline in Section 2. In Section 3, we outline our conceptual framework before describing an implementation of the framework for the SIENA event service using the Bandera/Bogor model checking pipeline. In Section 4, we evaluate our implementation using a chat program and a peer-to-peer file sharing system. In Section 5, we discuss related work and in Section 6 we provide conclusions and future work.

2   Background

2.1   Distributed Event-Based Systems

There are two basic kinds of clients in an event-based system: publishers and subscribers. Publishers publish events or notifications, to the event service, and subscribers subscribe with the event service to the type of events they are interested in. When the event service receives a notification from a publisher, it goes through all subscriptions and dispatches the event to those who have subscribed to it. Publishers announce events without knowing the identity of the subscriber components and do not wait for any response from subscribers. Therefore, event-based systems allow for anonymous, asynchronous communication which in turn provides loose coupling between client components and thus ensures maintainability.

There are three main types of distribute event-based systems [15]: *co-located middleware* – the event service is in the same address space as the clients (e.g., mSECO [11]); *single separated middleware* – the event service is located on a single machine while the clients are distributed on other machines (e.g., CORBA);

multiple separated middleware – clients and event service are distributed and execute on different machines or address spaces (e.g., SIENA). While our approach could be applied to all three types of system, we chose SIENA because both the clients and middleware are distributed making it a challenging architecture in which to discover mismatch.

SIENA. In SIENA, the event service is implemented with one or more servers connected in a hierarchical, acyclic peer-to-peer, generic peer-to-peer or hybrid topology. Events in a SIENA system are attribute-value pairs. A client can subscribe to an event by sending a subscription, which contains the filter patterns that specify the types of events it wants to receive. A filter pattern is a set of (attribute, operator, value) triples. The operator is normally a binary comparison operator, such as "=", ">". Each triple specifies the value range for an attribute and all triples in a filter are combined conjunctively. The event message notifications and filters are used in SIENA to publish events, subscribe to a given filter, unsubscribe from a filter, advertise intent to generate events that match a filter and to unadvertise the publishing of events that will match a filter. In our work we are only interested in the publication and subscription of events and do not handle advertisements. As discussed earlier, client application developers often make incorrect assumptions regarding the behaviour of the SIENA event service. The most prominent incorrect assumptions appear to be:

1. *"A client will not receive notifications to which it is not subscribed."*
2. *"Notifications will be delivered in the order in which they have been sent."*
3. *"Notifications are never lost."*

Later in this paper, we will focus on discovering mismatch due to the first two assumptions in our chat program and peer-to-peer file sharing system.

2.2   Domain-Specific Model Checking with Bandera/Bogor

The Bandera/Bogor tool pipeline is a set of tools for automatically extracting finite-state models from Java source code for model checking [7,16]. The pipeline has an open structure and the order of the tools in the pipeline is determined in a configuration file by specifying that the output of one tool forms the input of the next tool in the pipeline. Tools can easily be added to or removed from the pipeline by modifying the configuration file. The main tools in the Bandera/Bogor tool pipeline are:

- *Soot:* translates Java class into Jimple, an intermediate representation suitable for optimization.
- *Indus:* slices the Jimple code.
- *J2B:* transforms the Jimple code into BIR, the input language for the model checker Bogor.
- *Bogor:* model checks the BIR models.

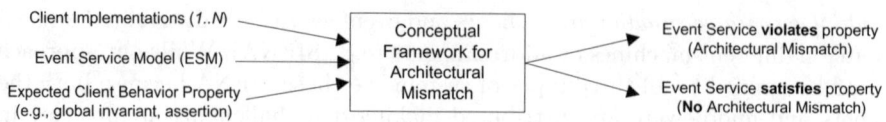

Fig. 1. Conceptual Framework

This pipeline is ideal for our research because both the transformation from Java to BIR and the model checking using Bogor is highly flexible can easily be customized to better support SIENA programs written in Java. The J2B tool, for instance, allows the user to add arbitrary BIR code to the model and to replace portions of the automatically generated BIR code. Bogor, on the other hand, can be extended with new primitive types, expressions and commands to provide better support for the modeling of different domains. Moreover, Bogor has a highly modular, open architecture which allows, for instance, new search algorithms or optimizations to be swapped in. We will discuss our specific customization of the Bandera/Bogor tool pipeline in Section 3.1.

3 Conceptual Framework

The input and output required and produced by our conceptual framework is given in Figure 1. Specifically, our framework requires three input artifacts:

1. *Client implementations:* we use actual implementations of client components written in a program language like Java.
2. *Event service model (ESM):* The ESM is assumed to be formulated in the input language of the model checker employed in the framework. Moreover, the ESM is assumed to correctly capture the behaviour of the event infrastructure from a client's perspective. At the moment, the framework offers no validation to ensure the implementation of the infrastructure actually conforms to the ESM.
3. *Expected client behavior properties:* A formal specification of a property that some or all of the clients need to satisfy. Only incorrect client assumptions that cause this property to fail will lead to mismatch that our framework is able detect. While property specifications could be provided using any formalism that the model checker understands (e.g., LTL, CTL, Buechi Automata), in this paper, we will assume that the specification is given as a global system invariant or an assertion.

The conceptual framework will take the client component implementations and transform them into the input language for model checking. During the transformation, common optimizations include slicing and various abstraction techniques such as data and predicate abstraction are used to reduce the state space. The client component models produced via transformation are integrated with the manually created event service model (ESM). The combined system model (client models + ESM) is input to a model checker that verifies the expected client behavior properties and reports any violations together with a counter example. The conceptual framework allows client applications to be checked for different incorrect assumptions through the use of different ESMs. For instance, to see if the correct behaviour of the clients depends on the preservation of the event order, an ESM is built which does not preserve event order. To determine if a client is resilient to message loss, an ESM is built in which messages can get lost.

It is important to note the advantages and disadvantages of using a manually created ESM. A clear disadvantage is that the conformance of the infrastructure to the ESM is not checked. If the ESM does not reflect the behaviour of the infrastructure, our analysis may provide spurious results. Moreover, user effort is required to construct the ESM. However, despite the availability of automatic model extractors such as Bandera's J2B tool, the automatic extraction of an ESM suitable for model checking from the infrastructure code is currently not an option, due to the size, complexity and typically distributed nature of event infrastructures. A manually created ESM, on the other hand, will be considerably more succinct. Moreover, one ESM could be used for checking several applications so that the cost of building it can be amortized across multiple uses. In conclusion, we feel that a manually created ESM is the best option, and note conformance checking between ESM and the infrastructure implementation as an important direction for future work.

3.1   Example Implementation of Framework Using Bandera/Bogor

In this section, we will describe an implementation of our conceptual framework using a customization of the Bandera/Bogor tool pipeline (see Figure 2). To test the feasibility of the framework, we chose Java client applications that use SIENA as the underlying distributed event-based infrastructure.

Client application transformation and optimization. The Java source code of the client application is translated into a BIR model for model checking using Soot to translate from Java to Jimple, Indus to slice and optimize the Jimple representation, and J2B to translate the sliced Jimple into the BIR modeling language.

Event service model creation. The behaviour of the SIENA event service is captured by manually created BIR models (ESM$_i$). The SIENA ESM (see Figure 3) is quite small (less than 100 LOC of BIR code) and simple. It uses two data structures to handle the events, a communication channel between the client and the service model, and an event set to store the events at the server before they are dispatched. As we discussed in Section 1, SIENA event service does not guarantee the order of dispatching of events. By using an event set, we will be able to exhaustively check all dispatching orders of the events. Since events will be removed from the set in every possible order, a regular FIFO queue is sufficient to simulate the communication channel. Bogor extensions are used to implement the event set and the message queue. The SIENA ESM is developed

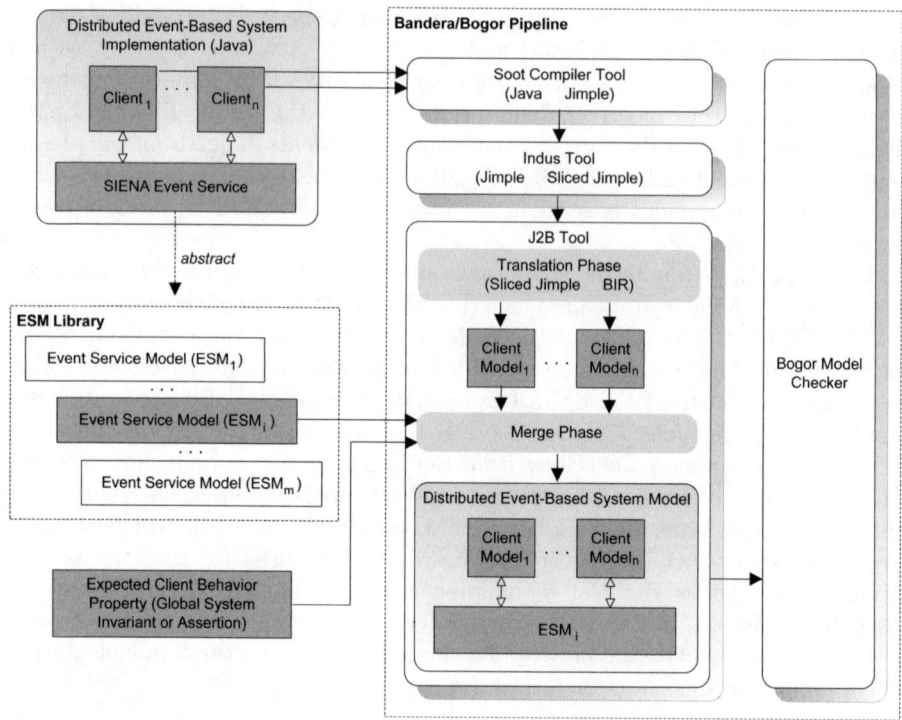

Fig. 2. Software model checking framework for SIENA

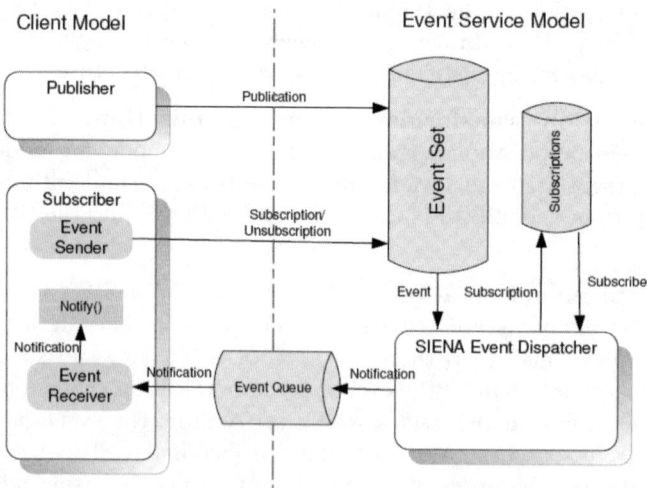

Fig. 3. Event Service Model (ESM) and Client Model Interaction for SIENA

```
function ThinClient.subscribe (Pattern p) {
    loc loc0:    invoke initialize()
                 goto loc1;
    loc loc1:    do invisible {
                     sub := new Event;
                     sub.pattern := p.pattern;
                     sub.type := EVENT_TYPE.SUBSCRIBE;
                     Set.add<Event>(events, sub);
                 } return;
}
```

Fig. 4. Subscribe method in the event service model

as an active thread that waits for the arrival of events and handles them based on their types. The current implementation of the model only supports three types of event operations: subscribe, unsubscribe and publish. Note that in our examples, we do not check if clients are resilient to message loss. To do that, an ESM would have to be created in which message can get lost. Recall that the ESM for SIENA is independent of the client applications so the same ESM can be reused to check for mismatch in all SIENA client applications.

Client model and ESM integration. The integration of the automatically generated client application model and the ESM to form a system model happens in the J2B tool. Recall that that the main function of the J2B tool is to translate Jimple code into BIR models. After the BIR models are generated for the client application, the J2B tool allows the user to replace methods and threads in the models with user specified methods or threads. It also allows the user to add additional BIR extensions, global variables, methods and threads to the existing BIR model. The SIENA ESM is added as a BIR addition. In order to integrate the client and service models, the methods on the client side that handle the communication between the client and the service need to be replaced. The SIENA implementation provides a standard *ThinClient* class as an interface for the SIENA client to exchange events with the SIENA event service. Thus we only need to replace all the methods in the *ThinClient* class. As the *ThinClient* is standard, the replacement can be reused for different client applications with minor customization. Figure 4 shows the *subscribe* method in the ESM that will be invoked instead of the *subscribe* method in SIENA when Bogor carries out its analysis. A large portion of the code of the *ThinClient* class handles low level socket communication. As all methods of the *ThinClient* class will be replaced, there is no need to translate this code into BIR. Thus only method stubs are kept for the *ThinClient* class.

Model and property integration. A property that a client application is expected to satisfy is provided as an assertion or global invariant. On the one hand, an assertion can be inserted manually into the BIR code at the appropriate place. Typically, we want to check if the behaviour carried out in response to the receipt of a notification is correct. Therefore, the assertion is often placed

Table 1. A comparison of the Java source and BIR model sizes for our examples

Example program	# processes	# Java classes	# Java LOC	average # BIR LOC	average # relevant BIR LOC
Chat program	3	11	906	8974	1815
Peer-to-peer file sharing system	3	16	1188	8133	2426

in the notify() method of a client (see Figure 3). which is called whenever the client receives a notification from the event service. On the other hand, a global invariant is inserted into an active monitor thread that is added to the integrated client and service models.

Model checking the system model. The combined client model and ESM is checked by the Bogor model checker with respect to the assertion or global property invariant. We will discuss specific model checking results as well as the relationship between property failures and architectural mismatch in the next section during our evaluation of two real Java applications that use the SIENA event service.

4   Evaluation

To evaluate the effectiveness of our implementation of the framework two realistic examples are provided – a chat example and a peer-to-peer file sharing system. Table 1 indicates the size of each example implementation as well as the size of the BIR models. For each example the average BIR model size is given which correspond to the average of the optimized model sizes for each property. Additionally, the average relevant model size column refers to the average portion of the BIR model that corresponds to actual client source code and excludes the details related to included Java library files.

4.1   Chat Program

Description. In this program, there are an arbitrary number of distributed clients, which can subscribe, unsubscribe, create and close chat rooms, and post messages to and display messages from the chat rooms. The system uses the SIENA event service for message exchange. The basic events in the system are *SubscribeChatRoom*, *UnSubscribeChatRoom*, *CreateChatRoom*, *CloseChatRoom* and *PostMessage*. Each client acts as both a publisher and a subscriber and maintains a list of all active chat rooms.

Our chat program has a GUI interface to display posted messages for each chat room. Unfortunately, the current version of Bandera does not support the Java Swing library, which is used to build the GUI for this program. However, issues of architectural mismatch in SIENA client applications like the chat program require analyzing and model checking the interaction between the client and the SIENA event service not the GUI interface. Therefore, for the purposes of our analysis we separate the GUI from the rest of the application. To facilitate the removal of the GUI code, we assume hat the client has been implemented using the MVC (Model-View-Controller) architecture, which provides a clean separation between the view (GUI) component and the model and control part of the system. Recall that transforming client applications into client BIR models in Bandera requires as input the client application byte code. Thus, the application must compile even with the GUI code removed. A skeleton of the GUI classes needs to be kept with all method body and the Java Swing class names removed. This is a manual preprocessing step that is done prior to using our framework. Additionally, some of the skeleton GUI classes are replaced with BIR code during the model integration to simulate any interaction between the GUI and the controller that is required during model checking.

Analysis. For the chat program we consider the analysis of two properties both of which demonstrates architectural mismatch between chat client applications and the SIENA event service.

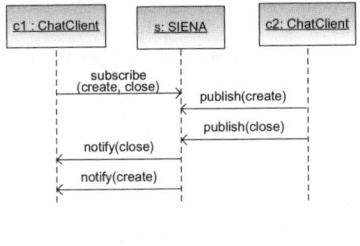

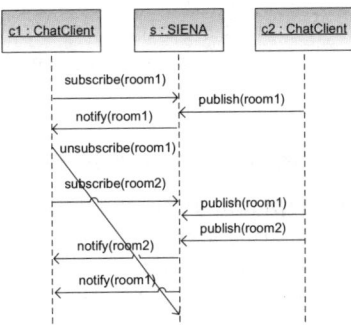

Fig. 5. Counter example for *Chat_Rooms_Close_Correctly*

Fig. 6. Counter example for *Displayed_Msgs_Always_for_Current-_Chat_Room*

Property 1: Chat rooms are always closed properly. In this case, the client creates a chat room and then closes it. We use a set to store the list of chat rooms which the client maintains. When a chat room is created, the chat room number is added to the list, and when it is closed, it is removed from the list. In this example, the room list is empty at the beginning and there is only one chat room being created and closed. Therefore, the set will be empty if the chat room is closed properly. The property is expressed as an assertion, which is inserted into the notify() method of the client:

assert allEventsDelivered -> chatRoomList.isEmpty();

where -> denotes implication. The analysis of the chat program with this assertion using our framework shows that the assertion fails because the event service does not preserve event order. The *CreateChatRoom* and *RemoveChat-Room* events are not commutative. If the events are delivered in the right order, a chat room will be created and closed properly. But if the order is reversed, as shown in Figure 5, the chat room remains open after these two events are delivered. In conclusion, the correct functioning of the operation of closing chat room relies on an implicit assumption (preservation of message order) which is not satisfied by the SIENA event service.

Property 2: Displayed messages are always for the current chat room. There are two steps involved in switching chat rooms: unsubscription from the current chat room and subscription to a new chat room. This property is expressed as an assertion which is again located in the client's notify() method:

assert (PostMessage.roomName == currentRoomName);

This assertion states that the room name of the incoming message is the current room name and is evaluated whenever a message is received. The analysis using our framework shows that this assertion fails with a counter example as shown in Figure 6. Since it is possible in SIENA for the client to receive unsubscribed events, it is possible for the client to receive messages for the previous chat room after switching to a new chat room. If these messages are not processed properly, as is the case in our example, they might be displayed in the wrong chat room.

4.2   Peer-to-Peer File Sharing Example

Description. In the paper [13], the author shows how to use SIENA to implement a file-sharing service similar to Gnutella – a well-known peer-to-peer file sharing service. This example was also used in other research on compositional reasoning of descriptions of architectural middleware [3]. Following the ideas in [13], we have implemented a prototype of a peer-to-peer file sharing service as a client application of SIENA. In this prototype, a client can play two roles: file provider (subscriber) and query originator (publisher). There are three message types, which are mapped to the communication events of the underlying event-based system. First, *Offer* messages are sent out by file providers as a subscription of queries. An offer message describes the files located on a host. Second, *Query* messages are publications that a query originator sends to describe the files it is interested in with patterns. A query message publication will be delivered by the event service to all file providers who offer the files matching the patterns. Third, *Response* messages are generated by the file provider and sent back to the query originator via the event service. A response message is actually a notification that contains the detailed description of the files, which match the query as well as a return address, which will be used by the query originator.

Similar to the chat program, the peer-to-peer file sharing example has a GUI interface, that we have implemented using the MVC pattern. Also, since we are mainly concerned with the mismatch between the client and the SIENA event service, the actual file sharing portion of the program is irrelevant and thus not implemented.

Analysis. We evaluate potential mismatch between SIENA and the peer-to-peer client applications by evaluating two properties.

Property 1: The displayed responses are for the current search. This property is an assertion located in the notify() method of the query originator:

assert (currentQuery.pattern == Notification.pattern);

The model checking result shows that this assertion fails. When the query originator starts a query, it sends out the query and subscribes to the response from the file provider. The user of a query originator may choose to stop receiving responses to the current query and start a new query by unsubscribing the old response and sending out a new query (as shown in Figure 7). With SIENA, a query originator may receive unsubscribed responses. However, due to architectural mismatch, the query originator in this example assumes that no unsubscribed responses will be received and that all received responses will be displayed as the responses for the current query.

Property 3: No queries are received after a file provider revokes the offer. This property is expressed with the following assertion in the notify() method of the file provider:

assert offerRevoked(p) -> (Notification.pattern != p);

Model checking using the framework determines that the assertion is violated with the counter example shown in Figure 8. Consider a file provider that stops sharing certain files by sending a *revokeOffer(pattern)* event (i.e., an unsubscription). In our example the SIENA event service sends out a response every time a query is received assuming no queries for the offer will be received after it is revoked. But since this is not always the case files can still be shared after being revoked.

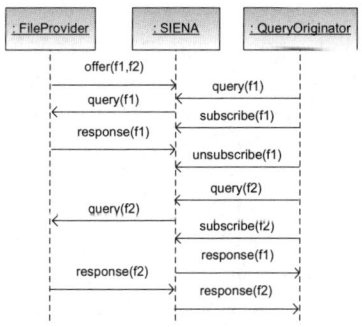

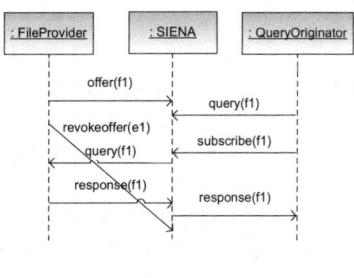

Fig. 7. Counter example for *Displayed_Responses_For_Current_Search*

Fig. 8. Counter example for *No_Queries_After_Revoke_Offer*

Table 2. Anaylsis results for all global system invariants and assertions

Global system invariant or assertion	Result	Time (h:m:s:)	# of states	Reason for mismatch
Chat program				
Chat_Rooms_Close_Correctly	False	00:25:53	67291	Reordering
Displayed_Msgs_Always_For_Curr_Room	False	01:23:23	222566	Unsubscription
Peer-to-peer file sharing system				
Received_Responses_For_Current_Search	False	00:00:43	2379	Unsubscription
No_Queries_After_Revoke_Offer	False	00:01:08	3008	Unsubscription

4.3   Summary

We have successfully used our framework to identify architectural mismatch between two realistic client applications and the SIENA event service. The counter examples produced were used to locate the bugs and correct the programs. Table 2 summarizes the results of our analysis together with some relevant metrics. All of the timing results were achieved on a Linux system with 5 GB of memory and four 3 GHz processors.

One drawback to our current approach is limitations of applying it to GUI-basd event systems. For both of our GUI examples a limited amount of manual modification of either the input Java code or the the generated BIR model was required and we have not considered how to check applications that do not use the MVC pattern. Moreover, our SIENA model does currently not support the *advertise* and *unadvertise* operations and complex filters available in SIENA. Finally, state space explosion only allowed minimal configurations with only 3 processes to be analyzed. Nonetheless, we believe that we have presented a viable approach to the discovery of architectural mismatch in distributed event-based system implementations and that most of the limitations mentioned above can be mitigated or even removed with further research.

5   Related Work

Several existing projects have focused on model checking event-based systems using publish/subscribe architectures [10,1,12,21]. The work started by Garlan, Khersonsky and Kim [10] and later extended by Bradbury and Dingel [1] focuses on model checking systems with a centralized event services, not distributed. Further extensions to this work have allowed for the model checking of event systems written in a special purpose language, IIL [21]. The Cadena project uses an approach to model checking systems that use CORBA [12]. Similar to our project, Cadena uses Bogor as a model checker, however, unlike our work Cadena requires manual specification of component behavior. Another related project by Caporuscio et al. focuses on compositional model checking of middleware specifications but does not consider middleware implementations which is the focus of our paper [3]. Other related work in the area of event-based systems includes a semi-automatic approach to the analysis of GUI systems using

Bandera/Bogor [8], and several approaches to the analysis of distributed Java that use remote method invocation [18,6]. Another related project in the area of model checking software architectures is CHARMY which allows for the specification of UML-like diagrams for system design and verification [14].

Previous work on discovering architectural mismatch has primarily focused on specification-based approaches. For example, discovering mismatch using architecture description languages (ADLs) [19,20]. Our approach differs from this work in that we allow for the discovery of mismatch in existing applications and do not require the manual specification of all component and connector assumptions, instead we require only a global system invariant or assertion. and the manual construction of the ESM. Our approach does not require specification of any of the client applications.

6   Conclusions and Future Work

In this paper, we have proposed an approach for the discovery of architectural mismatch between an event-based system and its clients based on invalid assumptions the client makes about the behaviour of the event service. We have described a proof-of-concept implementation of this approach that targets the Java version of the SIENA event service and uses a customized version of the Bandera/Bogor tool pipeline. Finally, we have demonstrated the viability of the approach by evaluating our implementation on several case studies – a chat program and a file-sharing application.

Our implementation leverages the increasing maturity of software model checking tools in general and the customizability and power of the Bandera/Bogor tool pipeline in particular. The biggest drawback of our approach is its reliance on a manually created event service model that correctly captures the relevant aspects of the behaviour of the event service. Currently, the conformance of the event service to its model is not checked, but it is conceivable that ideas from model-based testing (e.g., [2]) or conformance checking (e.g., [9]) could be used to address this issue. Additional directions for future work include: increase the degree of automation of the framework, and evaluation of the framework on other event-based infrastructures such as CORBA.

Acknowledgments

We would like to thank the members of the SAnToS Laboratory at Kansas State University for support in customizing the Bandera/Bogor tool pipeline.

References

1. Bradbury, J.S., Dingel, J.: Evaluating and improving the automatic analysis of implicit invocation systems. In: Proc. of ESEC/FSE 2003, pp. 78–87 (2003)
2. Campbell, C., Grieskamp, W., Nachmanson, L., Schulte, W., Tillmann, N., Veanes, M.: Model-based testing of object-oriented reactive systems with Spec Explorer. Technical report, Microsoft Research (2005)

3. Caporuscio, M., Inverardi, P., Pelliccione, P.: Compositional verification of middleware-based software architecture descriptions. In: Proc. of ICSE 2004, pp. 221–230 (2004)
4. Carzaniga, A.: Personal e-mail correspondance with J. Dingel. Feb. 9 (2005)
5. Carzaniga, A., Rosenblum, D.S., Wolf, A.L.: Design and evaluation of a wide-area event notification service. ACM Trans. on Comp. Sys. 19(3), 332–383 (2001)
6. Cassidy, T., Cordy, J., Dean, T., Dingel, J.: Source transformation for concurrency analysis. In: Proc. of the Int. Work. on Language Descriptions, Tools and Applications (LDTA 2005) (April 2005)
7. Corbett, J.C., Dwyer, M.B., Hatcliff, J., et al.: Bandera: extracting finite-state models from java source code. In: Proc. of ICSE '00, pp. 439–448 (2000)
8. Dwyer, M.B., Robby, Tkachuk, O., Visser, W.: Analyzing interaction orderings with model checking. In: Proc. of ASE 2004, pp. 154–163 (2004)
9. Fournet, C., Hoare, C., Rajamani, S., Rehof, J.: Stuck-free conformance. In: Alur, R., Peled, D.A. (eds.) CAV 2004. LNCS, vol. 3114, Springer, Heidelberg (2004)
10. Garlan, D., Khersonsky, S., Kim, J.: Model checking publish-subscribe systems. In: Ball, T., Rajamani, S.K. (eds.) The Int. SPIN Work. on Model Checking of Software (SPIN 2003). LNCS, vol. 2648, Springer, Heidelberg (2003)
11. Haahr, M., Meier, R., Nixon, P., Cahill, V., Jul, E.: Filtering and scalability in the ECO distributed event model. In: Proc. of the Int. Symp. on Soft. Eng. for Parallel and Distributed Systems (PDSE '00), p. 83 (2000)
12. Hatcliff, J., Deng, X., Dwyer, M.B., Jung, G., Ranganath, V.P.: Cadena: an integrated development, analysis, and verification environment for component-based systems. In: Proc. of ICSE 2003, pp. 160–173 (May 2003)
13. Heimbigner, D.: Adapting publish/subscribe middleware to achieve Gnutella-like functionality. In: Vaudenay, S., Youssef, A.M. (eds.) SAC 2001. LNCS, vol. 2259, pp. 176–181. Springer, Heidelberg (2001)
14. Inverardi, P., Muccini, H., Pelliccione, P.: Charmy: an extensible tool for architectural analysis. In: Proc. of ESEC/FSE-13, pp. 111–114 (2005)
15. Meier, R., Cahill, V.: Taxonomy of distributed event-based programming systems. The Computer Journal 48(5), 602–626 (2005)
16. Robby, Dwyer, M., Hatcliff, J.: Bogor: an extensible and highly-modular software model checking framework. In: Proc. of ESEC/FSE-11, pp. 267–276 (September 2003)
17. Selic, B.: On the semantic foundations of standard uml 2.0. In: Bernardo, M., Corradini, F. (eds.) Formal Methods for the Design of Real-Time Systems(SFM-RT 2004). LNCS, vol. 3185, pp. 181–199. Springer, Heidelberg (2004)
18. Stoller, S.D., Liu, Y.A.: Transformations for model checking distributed Java programs. In: Dwyer, M.B. (ed.) Model Checking Software. LNCS, vol. 2057, Springer, Heidelberg (2001)
19. Uchitel, S., Yankelevich, D.: Enhancing architectural mismatch detection with assumptions. In: Proc. of the Int. Conf. and Work. on the Engineering of Computer Based Systems, pp. 138–146 (April 2000)
20. Zhang, B., Ding, K., Li, J.: An XML-message based architecture description language and architectural mismatch checking. In: Proc. of Comp. Soft. and Applications Conf. (COMPSAC 2001), pp. 561–566 (October 2001)
21. Zhang, H., Bradbury, J.S., Cordy, J.R., Dingel, J.: Using source transformation to test and model check implicit-invocation systems. Special Issue on Source Code Analysis and Manipulation, Science of Computer Programming 62(3), 209–227 (Oct. 2006)

Model Checking of Extended OCL Constraints on UML Models in SOCLe[*]

John Mullins[1],[**] and Raveca Oarga[2]

[1] INRIA Rhône-Alpes, Domaine Scientifique de la Doua, Bât. Léonard de Vinci,
21, av. Jean Capelle - 69621 Villeurbanne Cedex. France
[2] École Polytechnique de Montréal, Campus de l'U. de Montréal, Pavillon Mackay-Lassonde,
2500, Chemin de Polytechnique - Montréal (Qc) Canada, H3T 1J4

Abstract. We present the first tool that offers dynamic verification of extended OCL constraints on UML models. It translates a UML model into an Abstract State Machine (ASM) which is transformed by an ASM simulator into an abstract structure called *UML-valued OO TransitionSystem* ($OOTS_{UML}$). The *Extended Object Constraints Language* (EOCL) is interpreted on computation trees of this $OOTS_{UML}$ allowing for the statement of both OCL expressions modelling the system and OO primitives binding it to UML on the one hand, and safety or liveness constraints on the computation trees of the UML/OCL model on the other hand. An *on-the-fly* model checking algorithm, which provides the capability to work, at any time, on as small a possible subset of states as necessary, has been integrated into the tool.

1 Introduction

1.1 Motivation

Why use UML/OCL. In recent years, the Unified Modeling Language (UML) has been accepted as a *de facto* standard for object-oriented software design. The UML notation supports designers by allowing them to express both structural and behavioral aspects of their design, through class diagrams and statechart diagrams respectively. Based on mathematical logic, the Object Constraint Language (OCL) is a notation embedded in UML allowing constraint specifications such as well-formedness conditions (e.g. in the definition of UML itself), and contracts between parts of the modeled system (e.g. class invariants or the pre- and post-condition methods).

Why use formal methods in UML/OCL. Furthermore, used alongside formal method-based tools, UML / OCL also offers a unique opportunity for developing complex or critical software systems with high quality standards in an industrial context. Such systems require a high level guarantee that they can cope with their specifications from end to end of the development cycle.

---

[*] The SOCLe project is sponsored by Defence Research and Development Canada (DRDC) (Government of Canada).
[**] Corresponding author. On leave from École Polytechnique de Montréal. Supported by an NSERC individual research grant (Government of Canada).

M.M. Bonsangue and E.B. Johnsen (Eds.): FMOODS 2007, LNCS 4468, pp. 59–75, 2007.
© IFIP International Federation for Information Processing 2007

1.2   Related Work

In this section we describe various proposed tools and promising verification frameworks that integrate UML/OCL in some way. These are divided into the following categories related to the depth of integration. First, tools performing UML model checking of logic where OCL is not embedded. Second, proposals to embed or extend OCL in a clean and systematic way, to take liveness properties into account, which have model checking in mind but where verification issues are not extensively discussed. Finally, UML tools for OCL constraints that support something other than model checking as a validation technique. (Due to space limitations, these are discussed in Appendix A-1).

Model checking of UML without OCL. All these tools are based on translation of UML models into the modeling language of some model checking tool. While some of them opt explicitly for the specification language of the model checker itself to specify properties e.g.([1, 2, 3], others define methods based on the diagrammatic capabilities of UML to specify properties before verification [4, 5, 6].

The tool proposed in [2] maps the static part of a UML model, including OCL expressions on the object diagrams, onto an ASM and offers static verification including syntactic correctness according to the well-formedness constraints of the UML metamodel, and coherence of the object diagram with respect to the class diagram. However, OCL expressions are not integrated in the UML semantics, and are not evaluated as the model evolves. The statecharts modeling the behavior, are mapped onto SMV. Similarly, in [1] a subset of UML statechart diagrams is translated into Promela, the modeling language of the SPIN model checker. Specifications are then expressed in LTL (Linear Temporal Logic), the specification language of SPIN, for checking. UMC (UML *on-the-fly* Model Checking, [3]) is an environment that integrates the JACK model checker into UML. UMC also translates UML statecharts restricted to signals (no method calls or returns), into labeled transition systems, the modeling language of JACK, while properties are specified in ACTL, the specification language for JACK.

In [4], the authors propose an architecture for UML model checking based on a translation of UML models into IF, a language for the modeling and verification of hierarchical extended communicating automata. In IF, properties are specified by means of automata called *observer automata*, that are expressive enough to specify safety properties. Furthermore, an extension of UML, (*observers classes*), has been proposed to verify safety properties, which would then be translated along with the UML model into IF. The resulting IF automata are then translated into the specification language of equivalence-checkers like EVALUATOR. In [5], the authors propose vUML. This tool translates a restricted form of UML statechart diagrams into Promela. To express properties, statechart diagram annotations called *stereotypes* are used. The annotated statechart diagram is then translated into LTL before the model checking is done with SPIN. In HUGO [6], a restricted form of UML statechart diagrams is translated into Promela. *Collaboration diagrams* are used to specify properties. These are more expressive than vUML stereotypes. They allow some sequence patterns between objects and statecharts events to be described, but are not expressive enough to specify more complex properties. Collaboration diagrams are then translated into a Büchi automaton and SPIN solves *on-the-fly* the emptiness problem for the automata resulting from the synchronization of the Promela automata with the Büchi automaton.

Toward model checking OCL and beyond. There are also many logical extensions of OCL with *modalities* [7, 8, 9] or translations of OCL into modal logic [10].

In [10], an object-based version of CTL called BOTL is used. BOTL, in contrast to EOCL does not extend OCL by temporal operators. Instead, it translates a fragment of OCL into BOTL. This means that temporal extensions of OCL could be translated into BOTL as well, but such extensions are not provided. Hence, verification issues for these extensions cannot be addressed. The purpose of BOTL is model checking of existing OCL. A strength of this work is that it provides a clear and precise object-based operational model which we reuse in $OOTS_{UML}$ with minor modifications together with extensions to cope with inheritance.

In [8] $\mathcal{O}_\mu(\text{OCL})$ is presented. Thus extends OCL with temporal constructs using observational μ-calculus, a two-level temporal logic in which temporal features at the higher level interact with the domain specific logic OCL at the lower level. Even though $\mathcal{O}_\mu(\text{OCL})$ was clearly designed with verification in mind, verification issues have not been extensively discussed in the paper. The strength of this work is that it provides a unified framework to design new logics combining the cleanly dynamic power of the μ-calculus with the static expressiveness of OCL (which we reuse in EOCL with minor modifications to cope with $OOTS_{UML}$ and CTL). In [7], the authors present an OCL extension, also based on CTL. This extension concerns system behavior modeled with statecharts, but evolution of attributes is not considered. In [9], an extension of OCL with elements of a bounded linear temporal logic is proposed. The semantics of this extension is given with respect to sequences of states representing the UML model history. However, the authors do not discuss how to compute these sequences from the model's behavioral diagrams.

SOCLe: model checking OCL on UML. Starting from a clean framework drawn from the above second category proposals and taking advantage of lessons learned from the above first category proposals, we present the first UML model checker of EOCL.

1.3   Content of the Paper

The work presented in this paper only addresses tool-related issues: The specification of an extended Object Constraint Language (EOCL) (Sec. 2) i.e. its syntax (Sec. 2.2), and operational semantics (Sec. 2.3) in terms of a transition system extended with state labels denoting UML-typed values ($OOTS_{UML}$) (Sec. 2.1), together with some illustrations of how this language might be used in practice to support a wider range of constraints on OO systems (Sec. 2.4); the sketch of the basic principles of the static (Sec. 3.1) and dynamic (Sec. 3.2) semantics of the modeling language UML on an Abstract State Machine (ASM); and a short overview of the SOCLe tool by itself (Sec. 4). A quick demonstration of the tool is given in Appendix A-2 while Sec. 5 provides the conclusion.

Out of the scope of the paper. Due to space limitations, the *on-the-fly* model checking algorithm of EOCL on $OOTS_{UML}$ that is implemented in the tool is not presented here. The reader is referred to [11] for a systematic presentation of this algorithm, but in summary, it is a version of Vergauven and Lewi's *on-the-fly* linear time CTL model checking algorithm [12] extended to cope with $OOTS_{UML}$ and EOCL. The ASM semantics of UML itself are presented only to the extent necessary for understanding the way a $OOTS_{UML}$ is uniformly generated from an UML/OCL model. For further details on Abstract State Machines, the reader is referred to [13] and [14] for a formal presentation of the ASM semantics of UML as implemented in the tool.

2   Extended OCL

We are now going to design logic that concentrates on the essential features of an object-oriented system (Sec. 2.2). Accordingly, we will define the semantics of this logic (Sec. 3) using a model called *UML-valued Object-Oriented Transition System* ($OOTS_{UML}$), which will be as simple as possible (Sec. 2.1) i.e. containing only the features of UML semantics addressable by the logic and nothing more. The degree of parallelism or the manner of method invocation, for example, need not be parts of $OOTS_{UML}$.

2.1   The Abstract Operational Model

Let us start with some notations that we will use in the paper:

- Σ_c, a finite set of *class names* ranged over by c;
- Σ_m, a finite set of *method names* ranged over by m;
- $\mathcal{V}$, a finite set of variables;
- $\preceq_h$, a partial order over Σ_c called *inheritance relation*;
- $\preceq_o$, a partial order over $\Sigma_c \times \Sigma_m$ called *overriding relation* compatible with $\preceq_h$:
   ($\preceq_h$-**compatibility**), if $(c, m) \preceq_o (c', m')$ then $m = m'$ and $c \preceq_h c'$
       (i.e. an instance of method may only override a homonym in a superclass);
- $\mathcal{N}$, a countable indexing set ranged over by $i, j, \ldots$;
- $\mathcal{C} = \Sigma_c \times \mathcal{N}$, the set of *instances of classes*;
- $\mathcal{M} = \mathcal{C} \times \Sigma_m \times \mathcal{N}$, the set of *instances of methods*;
- $\mathcal{E} = \mathcal{C} + \mathcal{M}$ the set of *UML entities*;

As a first approximation, an $OOTS_{UML}$ can be seen as a transition system whose states are labeled with UML-typed values. A set Type of basic UML types is also defined:

$$\tau \in \text{Type} = \text{Void} \mid \text{Int} \mid \text{Bool} \mid \text{Obj}^c \mid \text{Met}^{c,m} \mid \text{L}(\tau) \tag{1}$$

where types Void, Int and Bool are defined in the usual way and, for every $c \in \Sigma_c$ and $m \in \Sigma_m$,

$$Val^{\text{Obj}^c} = \{c' : c' \preceq_h c\} \times \mathcal{N}$$
$$Val^{\text{Met}^{c,m}} = Val^{\text{Obj}^c} \times \{m' : m' \preceq_o m\} \times \mathcal{N}$$

are respectively the set of all objects of the class c and the set of all instances of the method m of objects of the class c. Finally, $\text{L}(\tau)$ is the type of lists of type τ, with element $[]$ (the empty list) and $h :: w$ (for the list having the element h as head and the list w as tail). We will denote by Val, the universe of values i.e. $Val = \cup_{\tau \in \text{Type}} Val^\tau$, and by $Val_\perp$ its extension with the undefined value ($\perp$). Finally, letting the symbol $\rightharpoonup$ denote a partial function, we define the *class signature* function $C \times M$ in the following way:

$$C \times M : \Sigma_c \rightharpoonup [\mathcal{V} \rightharpoonup \text{Type}] \times [\Sigma_m \rightharpoonup [[\mathcal{V} \rightharpoonup \text{Type}] \rightharpoonup \text{Type}]]$$

which associates to a class c, the declaration $C(c)$ of its attributes, and the declaration $M(c)$ of its methods that is, for each method of the class, the declaration of its formal parameters and the type of its return parameter[1].

Definition 1. *A* UML-*valued Object-Oriented Transition System (OOTS$_{UML}$) is a structure* $\mathcal{OT} = \langle S, \mathcal{R}, s_0 \rangle$ *such that:*

- S *is a set of states. To each state* $s \in S$, *are associated functions* ρ_s, σ_s, γ_s *and* h_s *such that:*
  - $\rho_s : \mathcal{V} \rightharpoonup Val$, *a valuation of attributes and method parameters in* s;
  - $\sigma_s : C \rightharpoonup [\mathcal{V} \rightharpoonup Val]$, *a valuation of objects active in* s *consistent with* $C \times M$ *and* ρ_s *(C_s will denote the domain of* σ_s*);*
  - $\gamma_s : \mathcal{M} \rightharpoonup [[\mathcal{V} \rightharpoonup Val] \rightharpoonup Val_\perp]$, *a valuation of instances of methods active in* s *consistent with* $C \times M$ *and* ρ_s *($\mathcal{M}_s$ will denote the domain of* γ_s *and* $\gamma_s(m).f$, *the value in* s *of the parameter* f *in the instance of method* m*);*
  - $h_s : \mathcal{M} \rightharpoonup S \times \{\circ, \bullet\}$, *a history which associates to each instance of method active in* s, *a pebble and the state where this instance is or has been called. If* s *is the last state for the instance before being returned, the pebble is* $\bullet$ *and otherwise, it is* $\circ$. *The history will provide more particularly a concise and elegant way to define the* OCL *operator* @**pre**. *It has to be consistent with* $\preceq_h$ *and* $\preceq_o$ *i.e.:*
    ($\preceq_h$-**consistency**) *If* $(c, i, m, j) \in \mathcal{M}_s$ *then* $m \in C(c)$ *or* $(m \in C(c')$ *and* $c \preceq_h c')$ *(i.e. an instance of a method can be inherited);*
    ($\preceq_o$-**consistency**) *If* $(c, i, m, j) \in \mathcal{M}_s$ *and* $(c, m) \preceq_o (c', m')$ *then*

    $$\forall_{i, j \in \mathcal{N}} (c, i, m', j) \notin \mathcal{M}_s$$

    (i.e. the instance of an overriding method inhibits any instance of overridden ones);
- $\mathcal{R} \subseteq S \times S$ *is a transition relation*
- $s_0 \in S$ *is the initial state.*

A *computation* or *run* r in an $OOTS_{UML}$ $\mathcal{OT}$ is an infinite sequence of states $r = s_0 s_1 s_2 \cdots$ such that $(s_i, h_i, s_{i+1}, h_{i+1}) \in \mathcal{R}$, for each i. We denote by $r[i]$, the $(i+1)$-th element, s_i, of the path, and by $\mathcal{R}un(\mathcal{OT})$ the set of all computation paths in $\mathcal{OT}$. We denote by $\mathcal{R}un_s(\mathcal{OT})$ the subset of $\mathcal{R}un(\mathcal{OT})$ that comprises the computation paths starting from $s \in S$.

---

[1] Let functions $f_1 : X \rightarrow Y_1$ and $f_2 : X \rightarrow Y_2$. The function $f_1 \times f_2 : X \rightarrow Y_1 \times Y_2$ is the function defined by $f_1 \times f_2(x) = (f_1(x), f_2(x))$.

2.2 Extended OCL Syntax

We propose an extension of OCL (EOCL) working on $OOTS_{UML}$. EOCL is an extension of OCL with CTL temporal operators and some first-order features. It is two-level logic: intuitively, the upper level is CTL extended with quantifiers (the set of *temporal formulae* F_{exp}), and the lower level is a significant fragment of OCL expressions as defined in [15] (the set of *state formulae* P_{exp}). In order to get a clean separation of OCL expressions from purely temporal properties, we restrict OCL expressions to appearances within temporal operators or as atomic formulae of CTL. EOCL is largely inspired by BOTL [10] but is based on an instantiation of the temporal extension framework proposed in [8], and takes into account inheritance and overriding in its semantics. The EOCL syntax is given in Fig. 1.

$$e(\in P_{exp}) ::= x \mid v \mid e.a \mid \omega(e_1, \ldots, e_n) \mid e_1 \rightarrow \textbf{iterate } \{x_1 \; ; \; x_2 = e_2 \mid e_3 \} \mid e \,) \mid$$
$$e \textbf{ @pre} \mid e.\textbf{owner} \mid \textbf{act}(e)$$
$$\varphi(\in F_{exp}) ::= e \mid \neg\phi \mid \phi \wedge \psi \mid \forall z \vdash \tau : \phi \mid \textbf{EX}\phi \mid \textbf{E}[\phi\textbf{U}\psi] \mid \textbf{A}[\phi\textbf{U}\psi]$$

Fig. 1. EOCL syntax

The set of types of OCL expressions is the same one as the UML type set defined in Eq. 1. We write $e \vdash \tau$ to denote that expression $e \in P_{exp}$ has the type τ. We refer the reader to [11] for a complete definition of the typing function $\vdash$. The rest of this section is devoted to an informal description of the meaning of state and temporal formulae. We postpone to Sec. 2.3 the formal description of operational semantics based on $OOTS_{UML}$.

State formulae P_{exp}

- x is a variable in $\mathcal{V}$. These include *self*, a special variable in OCL referring to the current context, fields of objects, parameters of methods and local variables;
- v is a value in $Val_\perp$;
- $e.f$ is a *field/parameter navigation*. If e is an object (resp. a list of objects), then f is a field (resp. a list of fields). If e is a method (resp. a list of methods), then f is a parameter (resp. a list of parameters);
- $\omega(e_1, \ldots e_n)$ stands for the application of any *n*-ary operator on booleans, integers or lists.
- the **iterate** construct is the OCL main collection operator; It lets variable x_1 iterate through values of the collection denoted by e_1, stores successive values of e_3 in variable x_2 (which first evaluates to e_2), and returns the final value of x_2. The **iterate** construct is quite expressive and is used to encode additional collection operators (size, forall, exists, filter), that are also supported by SOCLe.
- **@pre** is a typical OCL operator. It refers to the value of a property at the method call, and may be applied in a postcondition at the method return;
- **act**(e) signifies that the object or method instance e is currently active. An object becomes active when it is created and becomes inactive when it dies, whereas a method becomes active when it is invoked (pushed onto a calling stack) and becomes inactive after it has returned a value (is popped from the calling stack).
- $e.$**owner** denotes the object executing the method e.

Temporal formulae F_{exp}. A formula is built inductively from boolean state formulae ($e \in P_{exp}$ and $e \vdash$ Bool), classical propositional logic operators ($\neg, \wedge$, etc.), CTL temporal operators (AX, EU, etc.), and type domain quantifiers. The temporal operators have the following intuitive meaning:

- **EX**ϕ holds in s if there is a state next to s such that the formula ϕ holds;
- **E**$[\phi\mathbf{U}\psi]$ holds in s if there is a path starting from s such that ϕ holds until ψ holds;
- **A**$[\phi\mathbf{U}\psi]$ holds in s if for every path starting from s, ϕ holds until ψ holds;
- $\forall z \vdash \tau : \phi$ holds in s if ϕ holds for all occurrences z of type $\tau \in$ Type;

The other usual auxilliary operators are obtained by combining these basic operators. It has to be noted that type domains being generally infinite, quantifier scopes are also so.

2.3   Extended OCL Semantics

Let $\mathcal{OT} = \langle \mathcal{S}, \mathcal{R}, s_0 \rangle$, an $OOTS_{UML}$. The semantics of state formulae is defined by the function $[\![\_]\!] : P_{exp} \rightarrow [\mathcal{S} \rightarrow Val_\perp]$ defined as follows:

$$
\begin{aligned}
[\![v]\!]_s &= v \\
[\![x]\!]_s &= \rho_s(x) \\
[\![\omega(e_1, \ldots e_n)]\!]_s &= \omega([\![e_1]\!]_s \ldots [\![e_n]\!]_s) \\
[\![e.f]\!]_s &= \sigma_s((c,i))(f) && \text{if} && [\![e]\!]_s = (c,i) \\
&= \gamma_s((c,i,m,j)).f && \text{if} && [\![e]\!]_s = (c,i,m,j) \\
[\![e.\mathbf{owner}]\!]_s &= (c,i), && \text{where} && [\![e]\!]_s = (c,i,m,j) \\
[\![\mathbf{act}(e)]\!]_s &= \mathsf{True} && \text{iff} && [\![e]\!]_s \in \mathcal{C}_s + \mathcal{M}_s
\end{aligned}
$$

$$
\begin{aligned}
[\![e_1{\rightarrow}\mathbf{iterate}\{x_1; x_2 = e_2 \mid e_3\}]\!]_s \\
= [\![\mathbf{for}\ x_1 \in [\![e_1]\!]_s\ \mathbf{do}\ x_2 := e_3]\!]_{\rho_s[x_2 \mapsto [\![e_2]\!]_s]}
\end{aligned}
$$

where

$$
[\![\mathbf{for}\ x_1 \in [\,]\ \mathbf{do}\ x_2 := e]\!]_s = [\![x_2]\!]_s
$$
$$
[\![\mathbf{for}\ x_1 \in h :: w\ \mathbf{do}\ x_2 := e]\!]_s = [\![\mathbf{for}\ x_1 \in w\ \mathbf{do}\ x_2 := e]\!]_{\rho_s[x_2 \mapsto [\![e]\!]_{\rho_s[x_1 \mapsto h]}]}
$$

and $\rho_s[x \mapsto e]$ stands for the state obtained from s by evaluating x to e in ρ_s. Finally for any instance of method (c, i, m, j):

$$
[\![e@\mathbf{pre}]\!]_s = \begin{cases} [\![e]\!]_{s'} & \text{if } (c,i,m,j) \in dom(\gamma_s) \text{and } h_s(c,i,m,j) = (s', \bullet) \\ \perp & \text{otherwise} \end{cases}
$$

The semantics of temporal formulae (Fig. 2) is given by the relation $\models\ \subseteq \mathcal{S} \times F_{exp}$

2.4   Applying EOCL

Constraints are conditions which have to be fulfilled by the system. An OCL constraint is defined as being in a context. We denote by C_{exp}, the set of constraints defined by the following:

$$s \models e \qquad \Longleftrightarrow \quad [\![e]\!]_s = \text{True}$$
$$s \models \neg\phi_1 \qquad \Longleftrightarrow \quad s \not\models \phi_1$$
$$s \models \phi_1 \wedge \phi_2 \qquad \Longleftrightarrow \quad (s \models \phi_1) \text{ and } (s \models \phi_2)$$
$$s \models \forall z \vdash \tau : \phi_1 \Longleftrightarrow s \models \phi_1[z \mapsto v] \text{ for all } v \in Val^\tau$$
$$s \models EX\phi_1 \qquad \Longleftrightarrow \quad \exists_{r \in \mathcal{R}un_s(OT)} r[1] \models \phi_1$$
$$s \models E[\phi_1 U \phi_2] \quad \Longleftrightarrow \quad \exists_{r \in \mathcal{R}un_s(OT)}$$
$$\exists_{j \geq 0} r[j] \models \phi_2 \wedge \forall_{0 \leq k < j} r[k] \models \phi_1$$
$$s \models A[\phi_1 U \phi_2] \quad \Longleftrightarrow \quad \forall_{r \in \mathcal{R}un_s(OT)}$$
$$\exists_{j \geq 0} r[j] \models \phi_2 \wedge \forall_{0 \leq k < j} r[k] \models \phi_1$$

Fig. 2. Semantics of temporal formulae

$$\kappa(\in C_{exp}) ::= \textbf{context } C \textbf{ inv } e \mid \textbf{context } C :: M \textbf{ pre } e_1 \textbf{ post } e_2$$

where $C \in \Sigma_c$ is the context of an invariant, $M \in \Sigma_m$ is the context of a pre/postcondition and e, e_1, e_2 are boolean OCL expressions. Below, we illustrate how an OCL constraint has its counterpart in EOCL.

Invariant. An invariant is a condition which has to be fulfilled by the system whenever an instance of the context, or of a class inherited from the context is active, and no method of *self* is executing. Since the $OOTS_{UML}$ semantics of EOCL takes into account inheritance, this can be expressed by the following constraint:

context C **inv** $e \equiv$

$$\mathbf{AG}[\forall z \vdash \mathsf{Obj}^C : \mathbf{act}(z) : ((\forall m_1 \in z.M_1 : \ldots \forall m_n \in z.M_k) :$$
$$(\neg\mathbf{act}(m_1) \wedge \ldots \neg\mathbf{act}(m_n)) \Rightarrow e]$$

where

- $\forall m \in z.M : e$ stands for the formula $\forall m \vdash Met^{C,M} : (z.\mathbf{owner} = m) \Rightarrow e$
- z is an active object of the class C;
- $\{M_1, \ldots M_k\}$ is the set of the methods of the class C;
- $\{m_1, \ldots m_n\}$ is the set of instances of the methods of the class C.

Pre/postcondition. A pre/postcondition is verified if for each instance of M of the class C, the post-condition holds when M is returned whenever the pre-condition held when M was called. This can be expressed by the following constraint:

context C :: M **pre** e_1 **post** $e_2 \equiv$

$$\forall z \vdash \mathsf{Obj}^C : \mathbf{act}(z) : \forall m \in z.M :$$
$$\mathbf{AG}[call(m) \Rightarrow \mathbf{AX}[\mathbf{AG}[return(m)] \Rightarrow e_2]]$$

where

- $call(m)$ stands for the formula $\neg act(m) \wedge \mathbf{EX}[act(m) \wedge e_1]$;
- $return(m)$ stands for the formula $act(m) \wedge \mathbf{AX}[\neg act(m)]$;
- z is an object of the class C;
- m is an occurrence of the method M of the object z.

Extended OCL constraints. EOCL allows the expression of liveness properties. For instance a template **after/eventually** could stand for the following property: whenever e_1 is verified during the life of any instance of C then eventually e_2 will also be verified during its life. This could be expressed as the extended constraint:

$$\textbf{context } C \ \ \textbf{after } e_1 \ \textbf{eventually } e_2 \ \equiv$$
$$\textbf{AG}[e_1 \Rightarrow \textbf{A}[\textsf{True } \textbf{U} \ e_2]]$$

3 ASM Semantics of UML

Why use ASM to define UML. While designing semantics of logic requires as simple a model as possible, modeling UML by contrast, requires formalism that, like ASM, has already proved to be a simple and uniform fashion of modeling the operational semantics of models as complex as programming languages. ASM will allow a rich, succinct and understandable operational semantics of UML to be written. In this section, we present UML and its ASM semantics. The UML semantics are presented only to the extent necessary for understanding the way an $OOTS_{UML}$ is uniformly generated from an UML/OCL model. The reader is referred to [13, 14] for a more formal presentation of the ASM semantics of UML and the integration of OCL into this semantics.

An ASM state is a collection of sorts, and a set of enumerated functions for these sorts. ASM evolution is specified by a transition rule built from predicates, control sub-rules and update sub-rules. Predicates are evaluated according to the current interpretation of the ASM state enumerated functions. Control rules supporting non-determinism choose a set of update rules to be applied. Update rules modify the interpretation of the current ASM state functions, yielding successor states.

Basic model elements, such as class or method names, are mapped to sorts. More complex elements, such as method declarations and statechart transitions, are translated into enumerated functions. The object diagram is mapped to a specific subset of these functions, and represents the initial configuration of the UML model (Sec. 3.1). From a configuration, successor configurations are computed by evaluating an ASM rule that captures the dynamic semantics of UML models (Sec. 3.2). Edges are labeled with statechart transitions fired as the UML model evolves.

3.1 Static Semantics of UML

The UML models supported by the tool must contain exactly one class diagram, one statechart diagram for each class, and one object diagram. In this section we illustrate the main features of the static semantics of these three diagrams through the modeling of a simple object-oriented component acting as a small memory cell.

Class Diagram. Fig. 3 presents the supported features of the class diagram. Class *Cell* models a simple memory cell with assignment, retrieval and incrementation. Class *BackupCell* models an extended memory cell with a restore functionality. Notice how class *Client* is tagged with the *thread* stereotype. As a result, a calling stack will be associated with all instances of this class.

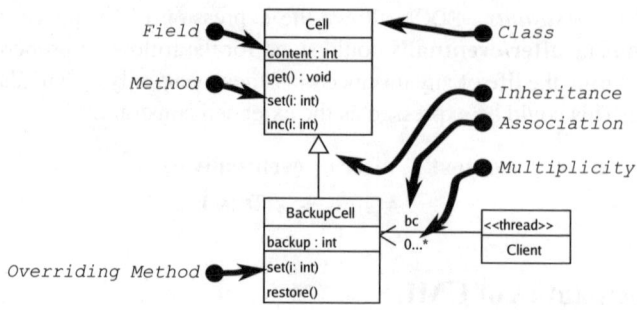

Fig. 3. Example of a class diagram

The first step to create the ASM specification is to map class, method and field names to the following ASM sorts (note that an association is mapped to a field of the owner class), which implement states of the abstract model defined in Sec.2.1. More particularly, *heap* implements σ while *stack* implements γ.

$$\textbf{sort } ClassName = \{Cell, BackupCell, Client\}$$
$$\textbf{sort } FieldName = \{content, backup, bc\} \tag{2}$$
$$\textbf{sort } MethName = \{set, get, inc, restore\}$$

Remaining information, like the inheritance relation $\preceq_h$ and overriding relation $\preceq_o$, is then extracted, and additional functions are implemented. Here are some partially enumerated examples:

$$\textbf{fun } \preceq_h = BackupCell \mapsto Cell, Cell \mapsto Cell, \ldots$$
$$\textbf{fun } \preceq_o = Cell/set \mapsto Cell/set, BackupCell/set \mapsto Cell/set, \ldots$$
$$\textbf{fun } lookup = BackupCell, inc \mapsto Cell, BackupCell, set \mapsto BackupCell, \ldots \tag{3}$$

These functions are then used to define the important *lookup* function indicating whether or not refined or inherited behavior will be executed following a method call.

Statechart Diagrams. Similarly, statechart diagrams are mapped to ASM sorts and functions. Fig. 4 shows supported features for this diagram. Notice how functionalities of the memory cell are modeled by sub-states specifying the behavior of a method. Method *inc*, for example, is modeled in three steps: transition ct_3 retrieves the current value of field *content* by calling method *get*; transition ct_4 increments that current value by calling method *set*; finally, transition ct_5 waits for method *set* to return and terminates method *inc*.

The control flow of a statechart is specified by states and transitions. The basic condition for a transition to be fired is that its source state be active. The basic response to firing a transition is the activation of its target state. In the case of a composite state, the initial states it encompasses are also activated. This control flow of statecharts is

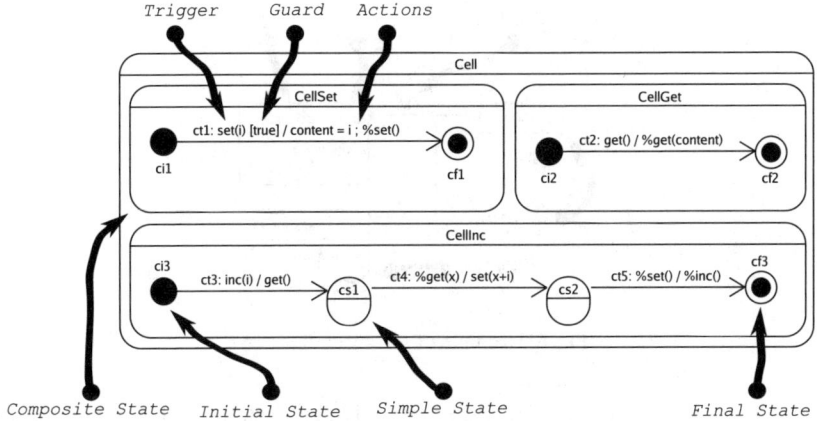

Fig. 4. Example of a statechart diagram

inspired by Harel's statecharts [16] and is statically elaborated and stored in ASM functions. The compiler determines, for example, which states are activated and which deactivated when firing a transition:

$$\textbf{fun} \quad act \ = ct_1 \mapsto \{\}, ct_3 \mapsto \{cs_1\}, \dots$$
$$\textbf{fun} \ deact = ct_1 \mapsto \{CellSet\}, ct_3 \mapsto \{ci_3\}, \dots \tag{4}$$

In addition, transitions are labeled with a trigger, a guard and a list of actions. Triggers refer to signals (atomic events), method calls or method returns. For example, the actions of a transition labeled with trigger *inc*, will model that method's instructions. Guards are boolean OCL expressions. The syntax of OCL expressions used on the UML models is given by Fig. 5, and their semantics are expressed in Sec. 2.2.

$$e(\in E_{exp}) ::= v \mid x \mid \omega(e_1, \dots, e_n) \mid e \, . \, f \mid e_1 \rightarrow \textbf{iterate} \ \{x_1 \ ; \ x_2 = e_2 \mid e_3 \ \}$$

Fig. 5. OCL expressions syntax

The tool supports the following actions: method call/return, field assignment, object creation/deletion, and signal emission. Actions are specified in part by OCL expressions, which enable the designer to model high-level behavior by using non-determinism. In a method call action, for instance, an OCL expression specifies a collection of possible receiver objects, from which the actual receiver is chosen non-deterministically.

Finally, statechart compiling includes a fair amount of static verification: i) statecharts are inspected to ensure they are well-formed, ii) OCL expressions are type-checked to ensure that guards are boolean expressions, that parameters of method calls are well-typed, etc. iii) triggers and actions are analyzed to ensure consistency with the class diagram methods and field declarations.

Object Diagram. An object diagram is mapped to ASM sorts and functions that hold the UML model configuration. Fig. 6 shows such a diagram with all features covered by the tool. It models a simple configuration in which a client accesses two memory cells.

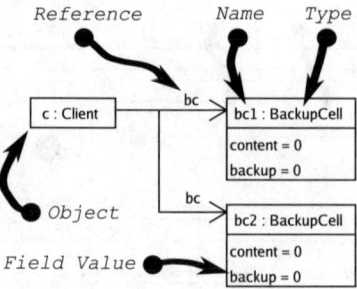

Fig. 6. Example of an object diagram

ASM functions *as*, *class*, *heap* and *stack* hold active states, object types, field environments, and calling stacks, (one for each thread - in this case only object c is a thread), respectively.

$$
\begin{aligned}
\textbf{fun} \quad as &= bc_1 \mapsto \{ci_1, ci_2, \ldots\}, c \mapsto \{cli_1\}, \ldots \\
\textbf{fun} \ class &= bc_1 \mapsto BackupCell, c \mapsto Client, \ldots \\
\textbf{fun} \ heap &= bc_1, content \mapsto 0, bc_1, backup \mapsto 0, \ldots \\
\textbf{fun} \ stack &= c \mapsto \langle (run, \emptyset, \bot, c) \rangle
\end{aligned}
\tag{5}
$$

Note how the calling stack of object c contains method run in the initial configuration to ensure that the thread is active.

3.2 Dynamic Semantics of UML

The ASM transition rule that captures a UML model's dynamic semantics is structured roughly as follows: $i)$ choose the current thread, $ii)$ select the current object and current statechart, $iii)$ choose one of the enabled transitions and $iv)$ fire the transition. It sketches some of the ASM rules that are used to implement the transition relation of the abstract operational model defined in Sec. 2.1.

Sub-rules $i)$ and $iii)$ use a non-deterministic choice to model thread-level and statechart-level concurrency. Sub-rules $i)$ models a simple thread scheduler. The current object $\tilde{o}$ is selected from an active thread's calling stack, i.e. $\tilde{o}$ would be executing a method. Sub-rules $iii)$ computes the transition interleaving of a statechart's concurrent regions.

In sub-rule $ii)$, the current statechart is either the statechart of the current object's class or the statechart of one of its superclasses if inherited behavior is to be executed (this is decided according to the *lookup* function of Eq. 3). This mechanism captures behavioral inheritance, an important feature of object-orientation.

Sub-rule $iii)$ dynamically determines whether a transition is enabled. The basic condition that the source state is active, is checked against the current value of function as (Eq. 5). Moreover, a transition is enabled if $a)$ its trigger corresponds to an active event, $b)$ its guard is satisfied, and $c)$ all of its actions can be fired. An assignment action, for example, will not be fired if it violates the multiplicity requirement (see Fig. 3).

In sub-rule iv), the selected transition $\tilde{t}$ is fired. The basic effect of deactivating and activating states is captured by updating function as using the statically elaborated functions act and $deact$ (Eq. 4): $as(\tilde{o}) := (as(\tilde{o}) \setminus deact(\tilde{t})) \cup act(\tilde{t})$.

Then, the transition's action list is iterated and every action is fired. Objects are created by using the sort extensions mechanism of the ASM formalism, and by updating function $heap$ (Eq. 5) accordingly. If an object creation action a of the form "$\mathbf{new}\ f$" is fired by the current object $\tilde{o}$, for example, the following ASM sub-rule updates the UML model configuration:

$$\mathbf{extend}\ Objects\ \mathbf{with}\ x\ \mathbf{do}$$
$$heap(\tilde{o}, f) := x :: heap(\tilde{o}, f) \tag{6}$$

The assignment action uses the OCL expression evaluation function and updates function $heap$ (Eq. 5) accordingly. For example, if an assignment action a of the form "$content := self.content + i$" is fired by the current object $\tilde{o}$, the following ASM sub-rule updates the UML model configuration: $heap(\tilde{o}, content) := [\![a.e]\!]_\rho$. This sub-rule uses function $[\![\ ]\!]_\rho$ to evaluate $a.e$, the OCL expression of the assignment action (in this case "$self.content + i$"), and updates function $heap$ (Eq. 5). Function $[\![\ ]\!]_\rho$ evaluates an OCL expression by recursively evaluating its sub-expressions relative to the current UML configuration and a variable assignment ρ. The environment always maps the variable $self$ to the current object $\tilde{o}$. In this case it also maps variable i to the value of the formal parameter of method inc as indicated on the calling stack. As the function is external, it uses ASM functions to access the current UML model configuration, but is not enumerated in the ASM state.

4   The Tool SOCLe

The SOCLe tool is divided into three main modules: i) an XmiToAsm compiler, ii) a specialized ASM interpreter and iii) an on-the-fly EOCL model checker. This architecture is depicted in Fig. 7. UML models are expressed in the XML Metadata Interchange format, which is supported by most UML CASE tools.

The verification process has two phases: i) the UML model is translated into an ASM specification according to its UML model static semantics, and ii) an execution graph implementing $OOTS_{UML}$ is generated from the ASM specification while OCL constraints are verified on-the-fly by this execution graph. The model checker implements a version of the Vergauven and Levi's on-the-fly linear time CTL model checking algorithm [12], that is extended to cope with $OOTS_{UML}$ and EOCL, thus improving an earlier version of SOCLe presented in [17], which is based on a naive approach to verification of OCL extended with fixed points to express temporal contracts.

The tool also includes a graphical user interface embedded into ArgoUML, a customizable open-source UML CASE tool developed by Tigris[2]. It allows the designer to visualize verification results and inspect the model's execution graph. A short demonstration of the tool is given in Appendix A-2. It compares the performance of the on-the-fly approach in Fig. 8 with the naive approach in Fig. 9, in the verification of the

---

[2] http://argouml.tigris.org/

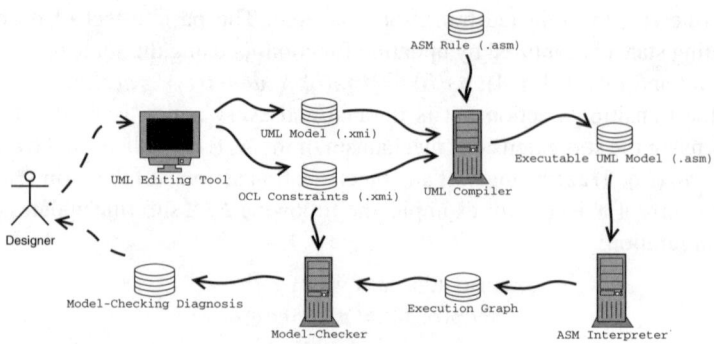

Fig. 7. Tool architecture

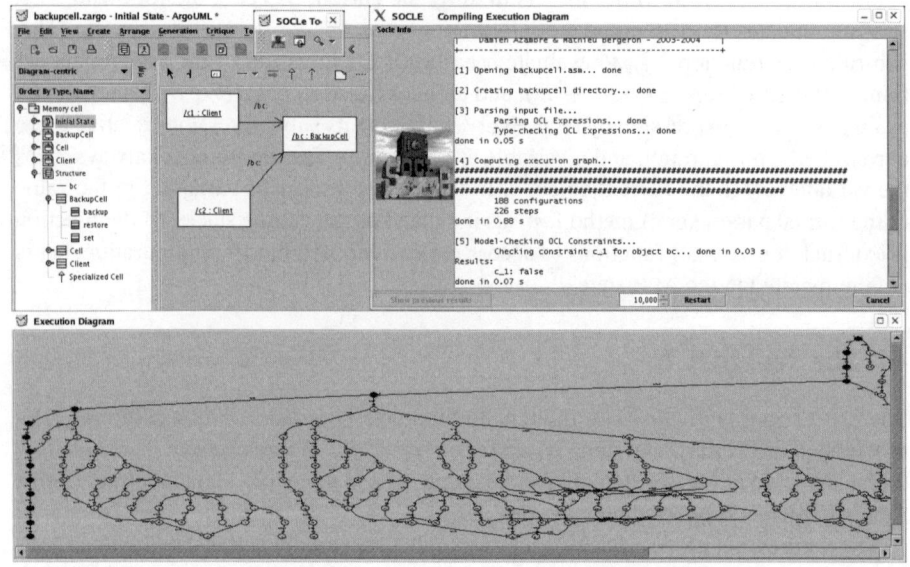

Fig. 8. The SOCLe tool diagnosis - μ-calculus

following invariant stating informally that the backup value of the attribute *backup* is always smaller than or equal to *content*:

> **context:** BackupCell
> **inv:**   *self*.Cell/*content* $<=$ *self*.BackupCell/*backup*

Finally, it should be noted that an extensive case-study on a simplified caveat-separation system has been carried out for Defence Research and Development Canada (DRDC) - Valcartier, as an illustrative example of possible application of SOCLe in the design of secure software. The full case-study has been reported in [18].

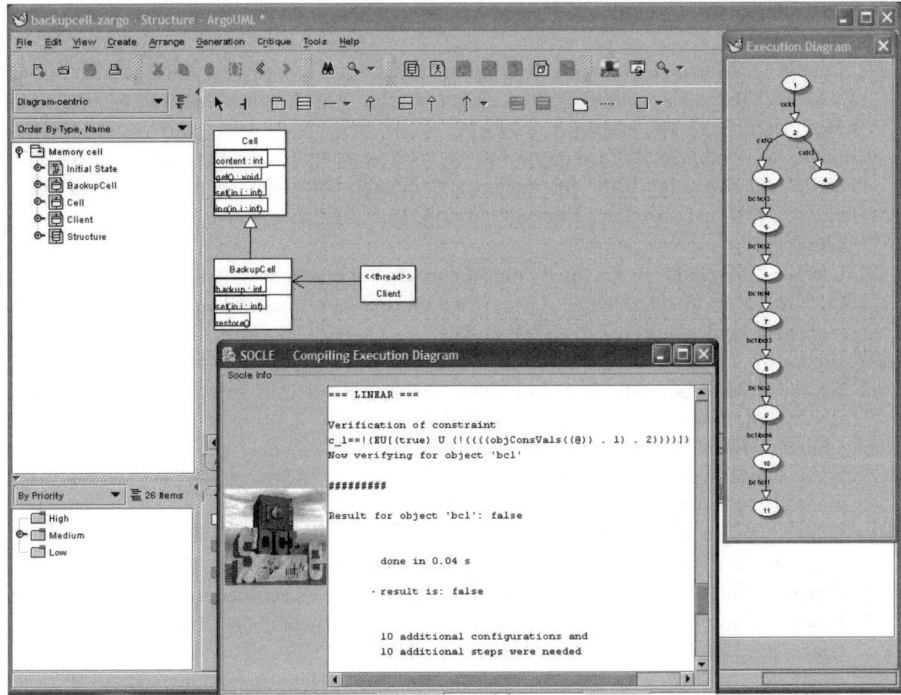

Fig. 9. The SOCLe tool diagnosis - EOCL -logic

5   Conclusion and Future Work

In this paper we have presented the main issues related to SOCLe, an EOCL model-checker of UML models. Firstly, an extension of OCL interpreted into an OO Transition System with UML-type values, in which inheritance and overriding are considered as possibly leading to richer interpretations of extended OCL constraints, where these OO features will have to be taken into account in practice for such things as invariance verification. Secondly, illustrations of how the ASM based semantics of UML models capture complex features of UML such as concurrency, inheritance, overriding, and object creation; and integrate an OCL expression evaluation function that is defined relative to the UML configuration, thus generating an implementation of $OOTS_{UML}$ which includes EOCL models. Finally, the architecture of the tool itself is presented.

We have not extensively discussed the scheme for transformation from ASM to $OOTS_{UML}$ in this paper. Considerable further work is needed to prove the correctness of this transformation. Alongside this, we may directly extract an $OOTS_{UML}$ that represents a UML model saved as XML. Also, abstraction and symbolic techniques to check whether or not the $OOTS_{UML}$ satisfies an EOCL formula have to be developed. Because EOCL incorporates OCL as its lower-level logic, abstraction and symbolic techniques used to check CTL or real-time CTL formulae could be extended to EOCL formulae in a quite simple way.

References

[1] Latella, D., Majzik, I., Massink, M.: Automatic verification of a behavioural subset of UML statechart diagrams using the SPIN model-checker. The International Journal of Formal Methods 11, 637–664 (1999)

[2] Shen, W., Compton, K., Huggins, J.K.: A tool for supporting UML static and dynamic model checking. In: IEEE International Computer Software and Applications Conference (COMPSAC), Oxford, England, pp. 147–152. IEEE Computer Society, Los Alamitos (2002)

[3] Gnesi, S., Mazzanti, F.: On the fly model checking of communication UML state machine. In: Second ACIS International Conference on Software Engineering Research, Management and Applications (SERA2004) (2004)

[4] Bozga, M., Graf, S., Ober, I., Ober, I., Sifakis, J.: Tools and applications II: The if tool. In: Bernardo, M., Corradini, F. (eds.) Formal Methods for the Design of Real-Time Systems. LNCS, vol. 3185, Springer, Heidelberg (2004)

[5] Lilius, J., Paltor, I.P.: vUML: a tool for verifying UML models. In: IEEE/ACM International Conference on Automated Software Engineering (ASE), pp. 255–258. IEEE Computer Society, IEEE Computer Society (1999)

[6] Schäfer, T., Knapp, A., Merz, S.: Model Checking UML State Machines and Collaborations. In: CAV 2001. ENTCS, vol. 55 (3), Springer, Heidelberg (2001)

[7] Flake, S., Mueller, W.: An OCL extension for real-time constraints. In: Clark, T., Warmer, J. (eds.) Object Modeling with the OCL: The Rationale behind the Object Constraint Language, pp. 150–171. Springer, Heidelberg (2002)

[8] Bradfield, J., Filipe, J.K., Stevens, P.: Enriching OCL using observational mu-calculus. In: Kutsche, R.D., Weber, H. (eds.) ETAPS 2002 and FASE 2002. LNCS, vol. 2306, pp. 203–217. Springer, Heidelberg (2002)

[9] Ziemann, P., Gogolla, M.: An OCL extension for formulating temporal constraints. Technical Report 1/03, Universität Bremen (2003)

[10] Distefano, D., Katoen, J.P., Rensink, R.: On a temporal logic for object-based systems. In: Smith, S.F., Talcott, C.L. (eds.) Formal Methods for Open Object-Based Distributed Systems IV - Proc. FMOODS'2000, Kluwer Academic Publishers, Dordrecht (2000)

[11] Oarga, R.: On-the-fly verification of extended OCL constraints over UML models. École Polytechnique de Montréal, Université de Montréal (In French) (2005)

[12] Vergauwen, B., Lewi, J.: A Linear Local Model Checking Algorithm for CTL. In: Best, E. (ed.) CONCUR 1993. LNCS, vol. 715, pp. 447–461. Springer, Heidelberg (1993)

[13] Cavarra, A., Riccobene, E., Scandurra, P.: Mapping UML into abstract state machines: a framework to simulate UML. Studia Informatica Universalis. 3(3), 367–398 (2004)

[14] Bergeron, M.: An ASM semantics for UML/OCL. Master's thesis, École Polytechnique de Montréal, Université de Montréal (2004)

[15] OMG: Response to the UML 2.0 OCL RfP (ad/2000-09-03). Technical Report ad/2002-05-09 (2002)

[16] Harel, D., Naamad, A.: The STATEMATE Semantics of Statecharts. ACM Transactions on Software Engineering and Methodology 5, 293–333 (1996)

[17] Azambre, D., Bergeron, M., Mullins, J.: Validating UML and OCL models in SOCLe by simulation and model checking. In: Lilius, J., et al., (eds.) Proc. of MOMPES'05, 2nd International Workshop on Model Based Methodologies for Pervasive and Embedded Software. Number 39 in General Publications, TUCS, pp. 67–76 (2005)

[18] Painchaud, F., Azambre, D., Bergeron, M., Mullins, J., Oarga, R.: Socle: Integrated design of software applications and security. In: Proceedings of The Tenth International Command and Control Research and Technology Symposium (ICCRTS 2005) (2005)

A-1   UML and OCL Tools for Objectives Other than Model Checking

Some tools support OCL expressions and constraints, but with different objectives in mind (e.g. [1, 2, 3]).

The KeY tool [1] integrates deductive verification techniques within UML/OCL. It translates OCL constraints into dynamic logic for Java CARD, a proper subset of Java for smart-card applications and embedded systems (to specify proof obligations), and provides a state-of-the-art theorem prover to perform verification. The USE tool [2] offers the evaluation of OCL expressions and constraints on manually constructed object models and sequence diagrams. The OCLE tool [3] offers validation of OCL well formedness, profile and methodological rules, defined at the meta-model level on UML models, and i.e., static semantic validation of OCL constraints on UML models.

References

[1] Ahrendt, W., Baar, T., Beckert, B., Bubel, R., Giese, M., Hähnle, R., Menzel, W., Mostowski, W., Roth, A., Schlager, S., Schmitt, P.H.: The KeY tool. Technical Report 2003-05, Department of Computing Science, Chalmers University of Technology and Göteborg University (2003)

[2] Gogolla, M., Richters, M., Bohling, J.: Tool Support for Validating UML and OCL Models Through Automatic Snapshot Generation. In: SAICSIT '03: Proceedings of the 2003 annual research conference of the South African institute of computer scientists and information technologists on Enablement through technology, South African Institute for Computer Scientists and Information Technologists, pp. 248–257 (2003)

[3] Chiorean, D., Pasca, M., Carcu, A., Botiza, C., Moldovan, S.: Ensuring UML Models Consistency Using The OCL Environment. In: UML 2003 - OCL Workshop (2003)

A-2   A Quick Tool Demonstration

As an illustration of the *on-the-fly* approach compared to the naive one, consider the verification of the following invariant stating informally, that the backup value of the attribute *backup* is always smaller than or equal to *content*:

context: BackupCell
inv: *self*.Cell/*content* $<=$ *self*.BackupCell/*backup*

Fig. 8 and 9 provide illustrations of the screen-shots obtained using both approaches for verifying this invariant. With the *on-the-fly* EOCL verification algorithm, a counter-example is found after exploration of only eleven states of the model, while the naive fixed point OCL extension verification algorithm requires exploration of the full state space of the model (4630 states).

Analysis of UML Activities Using Dynamic Meta Modeling

Gregor Engels, Christian Soltenborn, and Heike Wehrheim

Universität Paderborn, Institut für Informatik,
33098 Paderborn, Germany
{engels,christian,wehrheim}@upb.de

Abstract. Dynamic Meta Modeling (DMM) is a universal approach to defining semantics for languages syntactically grounded on meta models. DMM has been designed with the aim of getting highly understandable yet precise semantic models which in particular allow for a formal analysis. In this paper, we exemplify this by showing how DMM can be used to give a semantics to and define an associated analysis technique for UML Activities.

Keywords: UML, semantics, behavior, verification, DMM.

1 Introduction

Dynamic Meta Modeling (DMM) [1,2] has been introduced as a general concept for defining the behavioral semantics of languages syntactically based on *meta models*. Meta models are formalisms for specifying the correct *syntax* of programs (or more generally, models). They allow for a high-level description of syntax abstracting from the concrete way of writing models. This is of particular importance for tool-independent model descriptions and for transformations between models. Meta models have thus become the core instrument in the MDA initiative of the OMG [3]. DMM extends meta models for defining syntax of languages with concepts for describing their dynamic *semantics*. While the primary target of DMM was the UML, the method was designed as to work for any meta model based formalism, thus being universally applicable. The designers set out to define a method which is highly understandable yet formal and precise. The former property was ment for keeping the advantages of visual modeling in the semantics (non-experts should be able to understand semantics); the latter was particularly important for a formal analysis of models.

In this paper, we exemplify the DMM's ability of allowing for a formal analysis by means of defining an automatic analysis technique for UML Activities. For doing so, we first give a DMM semantics to UML Activities following [2]. DMM is conceptually based on *graph transformations* [4], which fits well to the visual appeal of Activities themselves, and more generally of meta models. In contrast to previous approaches to giving semantics for UML Activites [5,6,7], DMM is able to precisely formalise the intricate traverse-to-completion semantics of Activities [8]. The semantic domain for Activities are *transitions systems* whose

M.M. Bonsangue and E.B. Johnsen (Eds.): FMOODS 2007, LNCS 4468, pp. 76–90, 2007.

states are graphs representing the Activities and their current runtime states. The use of the general domain of transition systems allows for a direct application of concepts for comparing models (using notions of equivalence on transition systems) as well as specifying properties of models (e.g. via temporal logics interpreted on transition systems).

The definition of the semantics is the basis for the subsequent development of an automatic analysis technique. Rather than analyzing for individual properties of particular models, we are interested in defining a general quality criterion for Activities. To this end, we identify properties of Activities which characterise "good" models in the main application area of Activities, namely *workflow modeling*. Workflows describe business processes in companies. Activities modeling workflows have to adhere to particular requirements, some of which can be syntactically checked (e.g. whether there is a unique initial and a unique final action) but others referring to the execution of Activities (viz. their semantics). Following an approach of van der Aalst [9] we develop a correctness criterion called *soundness* covering several crucial properties of Activities modeling workflows. Soundness is defined on the particular form of transition systems generated by the DMM semantics for UML Activities.

Our objective is then to get a *fully automatic* check for soundness. Starting from an Activity modeling a workflow, the soundness analysis should essentially be carried out by tools. Instead of building a new tool from scratch, we choose an existing tool (GROOVE [10]) as the basis for our analysis. GROOVE allows for the construction, simulation and verification of transition systems specified via graphs and graph transformations. Verification currently includes CTL model checking [11]. The use of GROOVE thus necessitates a transformation of our soundness criterion into CTL formulas which are then checked on the generated transition systems. We prove correctness of this transformation as to ensure analysis of the correct property.

The paper is structured as follows. The next section gives an introductory example of an UML Activity modeling a workflow. On this we will informally discuss our soundness criterion in general, and already formally define those parts referring to the syntax. Section 3 explains the approach of Dynamic Meta Modeling, and defines the semantics for UML Activities. Section 4 is concerned with the verification of soundness: we give the formal definition of sound Activities by means of their DMM specification. The transformation of soundness into CTL formulas is the main topic of section 5: we show how to perform the transformation and prove its correctness. Additionally, the section explains the usage of tools, in particular GROOVE. The last section concludes and discusses related work.

2   The Idea of Soundness

The purpose of this section is to introduce our notion of workflow modeling using UML Activities, and to discuss the soundness property in the context of that definition. Recall from the introduction that we have chosen soundness as

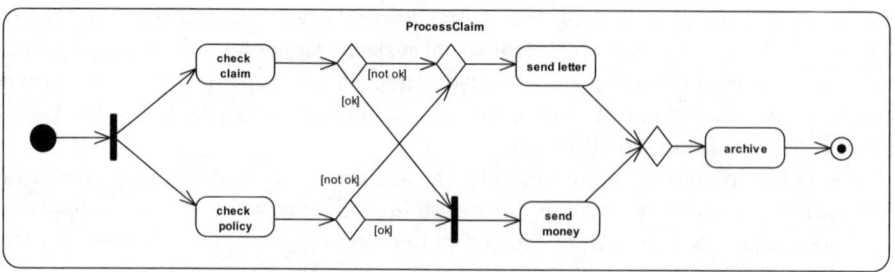

Fig. 1. Workflow "Process claim" as a UML Activity

a generic indication of quality: according to van der Aalst [9,12], every workflow should be sound, regardless of its concrete semantic domain.

We use a workflow which will serve as a running example for the rest of our paper; it describes the processing of an insurance claim in a strongly simplified way and is depicted as a UML Activity in figure 1. The meaning of figure 1 is supposed to be as follows:

> If a claim arrives at an insurance company, two things need to be checked: does the customer have an appropriate policy, and is the claim itself valid? To speed up processing of the claim, the checks are performed in parallel (**check policy** and **check claim**). Only if both checks succeed, money will be sent to the customer (**send money**). If at least one of the checks fails, a letter will be sent to the customer explaining why the claim has been rejected (**send letter**). At the very end, the claim is archived (**archive**).

Before we present our criteria for sound UML Activities, we need to give a basic idea of their semantics (we will look into this in more detail in section 3). The UML specification [13] states that "Activities have a Petri-like semantics", i.e., the semantics is based on token flow. When an Activity is executed, the InitialNode (solid circle) creates a token, which corresponds to a case to be handled by the workflow. That token is then routed through the Activity. Tasks are depicted by rounded rectangles (they are called Actions in the UML terminology). ForkNode and JoinNode (vertical bars) represent parallelity, i.e., they copy respectively join the arriving tokens. DecisionNode and MergeNode (diamonds) are used to route tokens. ActivityFinalNodes (dotted circle) consume arriving tokens.

The reader not familiar with UML Activities should note the ease of understanding figure 1. The expert might notice that we only use a subset of UML Activities, i.e., the FundamentalActivities, BasicActivities and IntermediateActivities packages, since the elements of these packages suffice to model many kinds of workflows.

At first glance the presented workflow seems reasonable. But what about its objective quality? Or, more generally: what properties should an arbitrary workflow at least have to be considered high-quality? In the following, we discuss the soundness property suggested by van der Aalst [9,12]. In his opinion, every workflow should fulfill some basic requirements:

1. The workflow should have well-defined pre- and postconditions.
2. The workflow should not contain any useless elements.
3. If the end condition is reached, no more tasks should be processed.
4. The end condition should finally be reached.

Requirements 1, 2, and 4 are self-explanatory. For requirement 3, assume that tasks are still processed after the end condition has been reached: these tasks obviously do not contribute to the result of the workflow. The work involved in performing these tasks is therefore wasted.

Taking the semantics described above into account, it is straightforward to translate van der Aalst's soundness definition into the world of UML Activities. A UML Activity is considered to be sound if the following conditions hold:

1. The Activity must have exactly one `InitialNode` and `ActivityFinalNode`.
2. Any `Action` must be executed under at least one possible execution of the Activity.
3. If a token arrives at the `ActivityFinalNode`, no more tokens are left in the Activity.
4. A token finally arrives at the `ActivityFinalNode`.

Note that in practice, requirement 1 does not restrict the modeler: more than one `InitialNode` can be modeled equivalently by one `InitialNode` and a `ForkNode` producing the desired number of tokens (`ActivityFinalNode` and `JoinNode` accordingly).

The requirements formulated above put restrictions on both the syntax and the semantics of a sound Activity: requirement 1 restricts the structure, and the other requirements restrict how the Activities must behave to be considered sound.

Since structural restrictions are usually easy to verify, their verification will not be discussed further. The behavioral restrictions are more interesting: to verify them, we need a formal semantics of the behavior of UML Activities. In the next section, we will dicuss the definition of such a semantics by means of Dynamic Meta Modeling (DMM). Section 4 will then show how this semantics can be used to formalize the behavioral restrictions, and section 5 will show how to verify the restrictions in an automatic way.

3 Dynamic Meta Modeling

The most important prerequisite for automatically analyzing the behavior of models is that the behavior is specified formally. Moreover, to allow advanced language users to understand the precise semantics of their models, the specification should be as easily understandable as possible. Dynamic Meta Modeling aims at fulfilling these seemingly contradictory requirements by combining two different approaches into one semantics description technique: *denotational modeling* and *operational rules*.

DMM is targeted at languages having an abstract syntax which is defined by means of a *meta model* as suggested by the OMG, i.e., a model describing the elements the language itself consists of. Sentences of the language must then be consistent with the meta model. Often MOF [14] is used for the specification of meta models, which is basically a subset of UML class diagrams. To follow the OMG layered model, the language's meta model is level M2, the level of the concrete syntax (i.e., an object diagram consistent to the class diagram of level M2) is M1, and the visualization of the concrete syntax (in our case, the picture of the UML Activity) is level M0.

In DMM, the static semantics of a language is specified using *Denotational Meta Modeling*. This means that the semantic domain has its own meta model, to which the meta model describing the Visual Modeling language is mapped. The meta model of the semantic domain often is an enhanced version of the meta model of the language itself. For example, we will see below that the Activity's semantic domain meta model has additional elements like `Token` and `Offer`, which allow to express certain states of execution of the Activity under consideration.

The dynamic semantics is then specified by developing a set of operational rules which describe how instances of the semantic domain meta model change in time. For this, the instances are mapped to *typed graphs* [15], i.e., graphs whose nodes are typed over the semantic domain meta model. The operational rules are then defined as *graph transformation rules*, working on the derived typed graphs.

Since the typed graphs represent states of execution of the Activity, the described specification technique allows for the computation of transition systems representing the precise behavior of the investigated models. The operational rules result in transitions between these states. The resulting transition systems can then be verified for certain properties, as we will see in section 4. The overall concept of DMM is depicted in figure 2.

In the following, we give insight into our DMM semantics specification of UML Activities. Note that we did not specify a semantics for all Activity elements as defined in the UML 2.0 specification [13] yet. We basically implemented the the `FundamentalActivities`, `BasicActivities` and `IntermediateActivities` packages.

Figure 3 shows an excerpt of the semantic domain meta model we have developed to express the behavior of Activities (elements depicted in bold are enhancements to the original meta model). While developing that meta model, we have followed the textual description of the Activity's semantics provided as part of the UML specification [13]. Most importantly, the following concepts have been implemented:

- The execution of an Activity is controlled by the class `ActivityExecution`, which is a composition of the elements needed to describe the states of execution (see below).

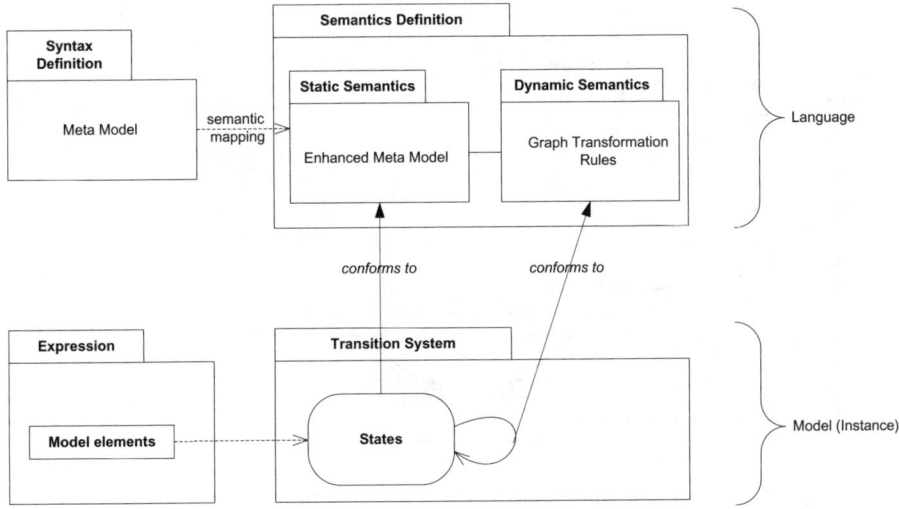

Fig. 2. Overview of the DMM approach

– As expected, the token flow is realized by introducing a `Token` class. Since
according to the UML specification, a token can only rest at a subset of
the Activity elements, an abstract class `BufferNode` is added to the type
hierarchy of those elements.
– The token flow within Activities follows the concept of *traverse-to-completion*. In a nutshell, this means that tokens are only *offered* to edges. An offer
traverses the Activity up to the next `BufferNode`, moving its token only
if such a node is found. In this way, tokens can not get "stuck" within the
Activity in some sense. This behavior is implemented by the `Offer` class and
a couple of other constructs.

Figure 4 shows an example DMM rule implementing the semantics of the
`DecisionNode`. A DMM rule consists of a signature, a number of pre- and post-
conditions and an optional number of invocations of other DMM rules (note
that the presented rule does not have invocations). Slightly simplified, the rule
matches an instance graph if a morphism from the preconditions into the instance graph can be found. If this is the case, the graph will be modified: elements marked {new} are created, and elements marked {destroyed} are deleted.
In our case, the offer on the incoming edge will be deleted, and a new offer will
be created on the outgoing edge, corresponding to the fact that the offer has
passed the `DecisionNode`. Figure 5 illustrates this process: the left part shows a
visualization of the Activity's behavior, the right part shows the matching part
of our example model before and after applying the rule of figure 4.

The derived graph represents the next state of execution. Since a
`DecisionNode` has only one incoming, but several outgoing edges, an arriving
offer will be routed to all of them: the rule matches every combination of the
only incoming and one of the outgoing edges, and produces several new states.

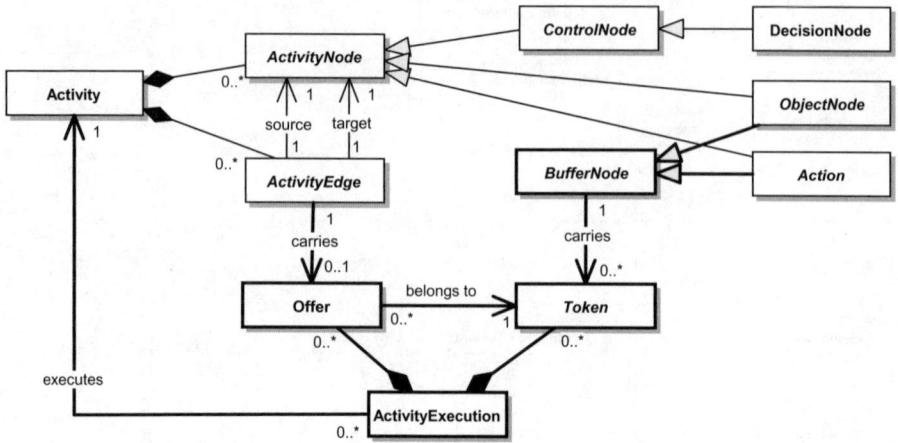

Fig. 3. Enhanced UML Activity meta model

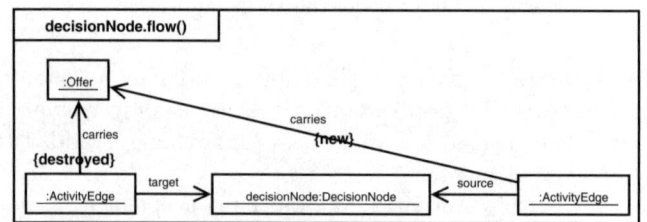

Fig. 4. DMM rule decisionNode.flow()

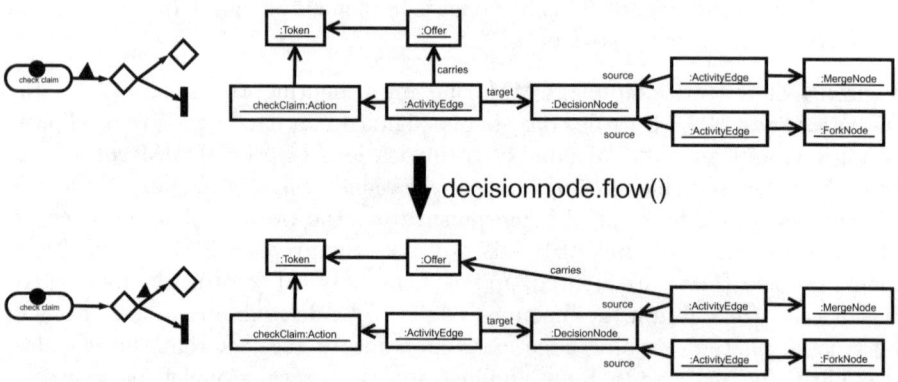

Fig. 5. Application of rule decisionNode.flow()

From the transition system's point of view, the result is a branch, representing all possible executions of the Activity at that point. Figure 5 shows one possible application of rule decisionnode.flow(). In this case, the offer is routed along the top edge of the `DecisionNode`. The right part of that figure shows two consecutive states of the Activity.

The resulting transition system represents the complete behavior of the Activity under consideration. It will be the basis for analysis of the Activity, using standard techniques such as model checking. In the next section, we show how to verify a transition system representing a concrete Activity for soundness.

4   Sound UML Activities

Up to now, we have informally defined soundness for UML Activities in section 2, and we have introduced our formal semantics of Activity's behavior in the last section. In the following, we will use this semantics to formally define soundness, and we will then translate the soundness conditions into CTL formulas in order to be able to verify the formula's validity with a model checker.

Our goal is to be able to make statements about states of execution of the Activity under investigation. We do this in an indirect way: we do not speak about the states themselves, but about rules which match states. As we have seen in the last section, a rule only matches a state (i.e., a graph) if a morphism between the preconditions of the rule and the state can be found. In other words: if a rule matches a state, we know that the preconditions of that rule hold within the state, which means that we have knowledge about the state itself. As we will see in section 5, the model checker provided by GROOVE [16] works exactly this way: it verifies CTL formulas where the atomic propositions are applications of the graph transformation rules used to calculate the transition system under investigation.

Note that the described approach does not restrict the verification process: every property p which can be formulated as a precondition of a rule can be verified by adding a special rule r which has p not only as its pre-, but also as its postcondition (i.e., its application does not change the state). A state s fulfilling p will result in a self-transition (s, s) labeled r. Therefore, if we assume some reasonable kind of *fairness* (see e.g. [17]), checking for the application of r is equivalent to finding a state for which p holds.

Before we present our definition of soundness, we need to introduce the idea of some DMM rules from our semantics definition, and we need to define some predicates. Note that from now on, we slightly simplify our original results (see [18] for a more comprehensive coverage of the content of this section).

First, recall from section 2 that for an Activity to be considered sound, a token must finally arrive at the `ActivityFinalNode`, and at that moment, no other tokens must be left in the Activity. Recall also that `ActivityFinalNodes` consume all arriving tokens. To implement this behavior, we have defined two rules whose task is to destroy arriving tokens as desired: finalnode.destroyToken1() and finalnode.destroyToken2(). Both rules match if a token arrives at an `ActivityFinalNode`; the difference between them is that the former only matches if exactly one token is flowing within the (whole) Activity, and the latter matches if two or more tokens are flowing. We can use this difference to define the desired behavior: an Activity is sound if, under all its possible executions, rule finalnode.destroyToken1() matches at some point in time, and rule finalnode.destroyToken2() never matches. Note that the rules' implementation guarantees that whenever these rules are applied, no other rules can be applied afterwards. This is in compliance with the UML specification which says that a token arriving at an `ActivityFinalNode` immediately ends the Activity.

The other requirement for soundness is that a sound Activity does not contain any useless elements. Since `Actions` are the elements of Activities where actual work is performed, we slightly relax that requirement by only requiring no useless `Actions`. In our semantics, the execution of an `Action` is mainly implemented by the rule N.start(), where N is the name of that `Action` (note that every `Action` has its own rule). We therefore define an Activity to be sound if, under all its possible executions, the rule N.start() matches at some point in time for every `Action` of the Activity.

Having said that, we need to define some predicates which will prove helpful when formalizing our soundness definition:

Definition 1. Let r be a DMM rule, s a state of a UML Activity as described in section 3, i.e., a graph which is typed over the enhanced meta model. Let v be a vertex of that graph.

1. If r matches the state s, then $matches(r, s)$ is true.
2. If v's type is `Action` or a subtype of `Action`, then $isAction(v)$ is true.
3. Let $isAction(v)$ be true. Then $name(v)$ represents the name of the `Action` represented by v.
4. If s is the state derived from an application of rule finalnode.destroyToken1(), then $isFinal(s)$ is true.

Now we are ready to present our formal definition of soundness for UML Activities.

Definition 2 (Sound Activity). Let A be a UML Activity with exactly one `InitialNode` and `ActivityFinalNode`, s_0 the state of A with only a token on the `InitialNode`, and V_{s_0} the vertices of the graph s_0. Let $TS = (S, \rightarrow, s_0)$ be the transition system induced by the DMM rule set as described in section 3 (S contains exactly those states reachable from s_0). A is *sound* if and only if the following conditions hold:

1. $\forall s \in S : (\exists s' \in S : s \rightarrow^* s' \wedge matches(\text{finalnode.destroyToken1}(), s')) \vee isFinal(s)$
2. $\forall s \in S : \neg matches(\text{finalnode.destroyToken2}(), s)$
3. $\forall v \in V_{s_0} : isAction(v) \wedge name(v) = N \Rightarrow \exists s \in S : matches(N.\text{start}(), s)$

Let us briefly discuss the relation between the informal soundness definition from section 2 and definition 2. Condition 1 ensures that from all states s, a state s' is reachable such that rule finalnode.destroyToken1() can be applied to it. If this is the case, we know that a token will finally reach the `ActivityFinalNode`. As rule finalnode.destroyToken2() is never applied, we also know that at this point in time, no other token is left in the Activity. The predicate $isFinal(s)$ of condition 1 takes care of the state derived from applying rule finalnode.destroyToken1(): it is needed because since no other rule can be applied to s (see above), the first part of the condition does not hold. Condition 3 makes sure that for every Action, a state $s \in S$ exists where that Action is executed. Since S contains all states reachable from s_0 (and no more), we know that all Actions are executed under at least one of the possible executions of A.

5   Utilizing the GROOVE Toolset

Our final goal is to have an automatic check for soundness. Hence we need a tool which, given a set of graph transformation rules, can generate the transition system according to our semantics and inspect it with respect to our conditions. For this, we have chosen to use the tool GROOVE. GROOVE is a shortcut for "GRaphs for Object-Oriented VErification" and has been developed by Arend Rensink at the University of Twente [19]. It offers a collection of tools for handling graph transformations: the Generator computes a transition system out of a start graph and a set of graph transformation rules, the Editor allows to edit the graphs and rules, and the Imager visualizes them. The Simulator integrates these tools, and the Model Checker allows for the verification of CTL formulas over the generated transition systems. As expected, we mainly utilize GROOVE's Generator and Model Checker (see figure 6 for the complete workflow).

To use the model checker for checking soundness, we first need to translate the conditions of definition 2 into CTL, i.e., the notion of temporal logic GROOVE understands. Note that the Model Checker works as described in the last section: it verifies CTL formulas over the *application* of graph transformation rules. Before we can translate our soundness definition into the language GROOVE understands, we need some prerequisites. We start by defining the *computations* of a transition system:

Definition 3 (Computations). Let $TS = (S, \rightarrow, s_0)$ be a DMM transition system as defined in definition 2. The set of *computations* $Comp(s_0)$ is defined as follows:

$$Comp(s_0) := \{s_0 s_1 s_2 \ldots : (s_i, s_{i+1}) \in \rightarrow\}$$

$Comp(s_0)$ contains all possible computations starting with state s_0.

Now we briefly define the CTL formulas we will use to express our conditions. Note that this is only a subset of CTL.

Definition 4 (CTL formulas). Let $TS = (S, \rightarrow, s_0)$ be a DMM transition system as defined in definition 2. Let $Comp(s_0)$ be the set of computations as in definition 3, and let p be some atomic proposition. Then

$$TS \models \mathbf{AF}(p) :\Leftrightarrow \forall s_0 s_1 \cdots \in Comp(s_0) \exists k \in \mathbb{N} : p \text{ holds in } s_k$$
$$TS \models \mathbf{AG}(p) :\Leftrightarrow \forall s_0 s_1 \cdots \in Comp(s_0) \forall k \in \mathbb{N} : p \text{ holds in } s_k$$
$$TS \models \mathbf{EF}(p) :\Leftrightarrow \exists s_0 s_1 \cdots \in Comp(s_0) \exists k \in \mathbb{N} : p \text{ holds in } s_k$$

In case of finite computations, k accordingly has to be restricted to the length of the computation. **AF** stands for "On **A**ll paths **F**inally...", **AG** stands for "On **A**ll paths **G**lobally..." and **EF** stands for "There **E**xists a path such that **F**inally...".

We are now ready to formulate our theorem.

Theorem 1. Let A be a UML Activity with exactly one `InitialNode` and `ActivityFinalNode`, s_0 the state of A with only a token on the `InitialNode`. Let $N_1, \ldots, N_k$ be the names of the `Actions` contained in A. Let $TS = (S, \rightarrow, s_0)$ be the transition system induced by the DMM rule set as described in section 3 (S contains exactly those states which are reachable from s_0). A is sound if and only if the following CTL formulas hold for TS:

1. $TS \models \mathbf{AF}(\text{finalnode.destroyToken1}())$
2. $TS \models \mathbf{AG}(\neg\text{finalnode.destroyToken2}())$
3. $TS \models \mathbf{EF}(N_1.\text{start}()) \wedge \cdots \wedge \mathbf{EF}(N_k.\text{start}())$

Proof. We start by showing the equivalence of the first condition of definition 2 and theorem 1. First, we can also write

$$\forall s \in S : (\exists s' \in S : s \rightarrow^* s' \wedge matches(\text{finalnode.destroyToken1}(), s')) \vee isFinal(s)$$

as

$$\forall s \in S : (\exists k \in \mathbb{N} : s \rightarrow s_1 \rightarrow \cdots \rightarrow s_k \wedge matches(\text{finalnode.destroyToken1}(), s_k))$$
$$\vee isFinal(s)$$

Since the above holds for all states $s \in S$, S contains all states reachable from the initial state, and rule flowfinal.destroyToken1() is always the last rule in a computation, we can write this as

$$\forall s_0 s_1 \cdots \in Comp(s_0) \exists k \in \mathbb{N} : matches(\text{finalnode.destroyToken1}(), s_k)$$

Following definition 4, we can now formulate our property as a CTL formula over the application of rule flowfinal.destroyToken1():

$$TS \models \mathbf{AF}(\text{finalnode.destroyToken1}())$$

Now it is easy to see how conditions 2 and 3 of definition 2 can be translated into temporal logic: since condition 2 holds for all states, it must also hold for all computations. We can therefore write the condition as

$$\forall s_0 s_1 \cdots \in Comp(s_0) \forall k \in \mathbb{N} : \neg matches(\text{finalnode.destroyToken2}(), s_k)$$

As above, this can be translated into temporal logic:

$$TS \models \mathbf{AG}(\neg\text{finalnode.destroyToken2}())$$

The last condition of definition 2 states that for all `Actions`, there is some state $s \in S$ such that the start rule of that very `Action` matches. Let $N_1, \ldots, N_k$ be the names of the `Actions`. Since we do not know anything about state s except that it exists, we can only conclude:

$$\exists s_0 s_1 \cdots \in Comp(s_0) \exists k \in \mathbb{N} : matches(N_i.\mathsf{start}(), s_k)$$

$(i = 1, \ldots, k)$. We can again translate this into CTL:

$$TS \models \mathbf{EF}(N_i.\mathsf{start}()) \qquad \qquad \Box$$

Now we have everything needed to verify our running example introduced in section 2 for soundness. As it turns out, the example is not sound: the GROOVE model checker reports that conditions 1 and 2 of theorem 1 do not hold. In other words: there are paths within the transition system where rule finalnode.destroy-Token1() is never applied, and also states where rule finalnode.destroyToken2() matches. Intuitively, this means that there is at least one situation where a token arrives at the `ActivityFinalNode`, but there are more tokens left in the Activity.

A further investigation of the example shows the reasons for this: first, if one of the checks succeeds and the other fails, we end up in a state where a token is stuck at the `JoinNode`. For this situation, both conditions do not hold: the arriving token is consumed by applying rule finalnode.destroyToken2(), and since the other token is stuck, it will not be consumed (in particular not by applying rule finalnode.destroyToken1()).

Second, if both checks fail, two tokens will arrive at the `ActivityFinalNode`, again violating condition 2 of theorem 1. Note that in this case, two letters will be sent to the customer, which is obviously not the desired behavior. Note also that the second token will be consumed by applying rule finalnode.destroyToken1() (i.e., condition 1 is not violated).

It remains to discuss the chain of tools we developed for the automatic verification of Activities. As mentioned in the introduction, DMM has been developed mainly having the UML in mind. This is reflected in figure 6 by using the UML meta model both as input for the semantics editor and the modeling tool: the purpose of the former is to develop operational rules by means of graph transformation rules which are typed over an extension of that meta model (as we have done for UML Activities). The latter utilizes the meta model to verify the syntactical correctness of the models. Note that this might be a typical use of DMM, but basically every meta model can be incorporated into a DMM-based semantics definition.

The semantics editor delivers a complete semantics to the property checker, including a mapping from the original into the enhanced meta model. This mapping is then used to transform a model instance (in our case: a UML Activity) into a start graph typed over the enhanced meta model.

The start graph as well as the graph transformation rules serve as input for the GROOVE generator. As the name suggests, a transition system is generated, having graphs as states and transitions between these states. The transitions are labeled with the name of the applied rule.

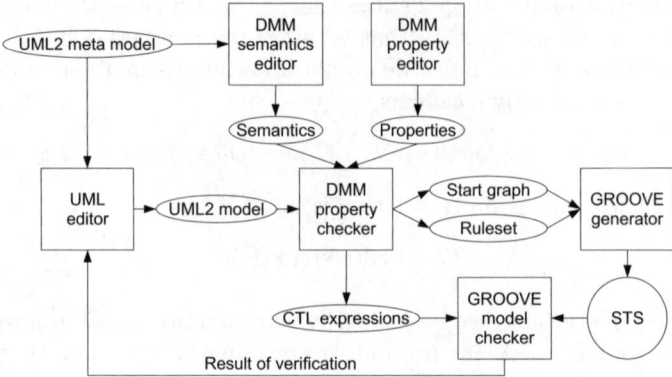

Fig. 6. Tool chain

The generated transition system represents the complete semantics of the input model. It can either be investigated manually by visualizing it with the GROOVE simulator (e.g. to understand the precise semantics of a certain part of a model), or automatic verification techniques can be used.

For the latter, the first step is to identify the properties to be modified, and to formulate them with the help of the DMM property editor. The property checker then generates a set of rules and a start graph, from which the GROOVE generator will compute the transition system. Next, the GROOVE model checker is utilized to verify whether the properties hold on the computed transition system (for the example of figure 1, the whole procedure took 13.7 seconds). The result of the verification process can then be used by the modeler to improve her model.

6   Conclusion

In this paper we have shown how to use dynamic meta modeling for 1) defining a semantics for a modeling formalism based on a given meta model, and 2) carrying out an analysis on the resulting semantics. As application, we used UML Activities which pose a particular challenge for semantics definitions due to their traverse-to-completion behavior introduced in UML 2.0. For the analysis, we have chosen a general quality criterion (soundness) for workflows which are a typical modeling domain for UML Activities. As a result, we now have a tool chain which allows for the automatic analysis of soundness for workflows (using the GROOVE toolset for the generation of the transition system as well as for model checking).

Related work. There have been several apporaches to define a formal semantics for UML Activities. Störrle et al. [20,21,5] try to use Petri nets as the semantic domain for Activities: they conclude that due to the traverse-to-completion semantics introduced in UML 2.0, a mapping from Activities into Petri nets is not possible. Eshuis [22] translates Activity Diagrams from UML 1.5 into the input language of the model checker NuSVM [23], giving Activities a statechart-like semantics as stated by the UML 1.5 specification, and uses that semantics for verification of certain properties. Similarly, [6] and [7] do not treat UML 2.0 Activities, but their 1.5 predecessors.

Our approach is different to the ones described above in two ways: first, we use DMM to define the dynamic semantics of UML Activities. The resulting specification is formal *and* easily understandable and can therefore not only be used for automatic analysis of models at design-time, but also as reference for advanced language users. Note that our specification implements the traverse-to-completion concept for token flow as suggested by the UML 2.0 specification.

Second, our analysis technique for DMM-based semantics allows to easily formulate requirements on the models under consideration: all needed is an understanding of UML object diagrams as well as a basic knowledge in CTL. For instance, to make sure that a certain object structure does never occur when executing a model, that object structure is formulated as an object diagram which serves as the pre- and the postcondition of a DMM rule R (as described in section 4). Using a basic CTL construct, the whole requirement can then be formulated like this: **AG(NOT** R).

Outlook. Since DMM can be used as a semantics specification technique for every visual modeling language based on meta-models, we plan to explore different applications of the described analysis technique. First, the integration of different languages will be explored, e.g. for consistency checks. Second, we are interested in the definition of domain specific languages as extensions of already existing languages. In this area, we plan to use our analysis technique to ensure that extensions of languages describing behavior do not *break* the behavior of the base languages.

References

1. Engels, G., Hausmann, J.H., Heckel, R., Sauer, S.: Dynamic Meta-Modeling: A Graphical Approach to the Operational Semantics of Behavioral Diagrams in UML. In: Evans, A., Kent, S., Selic, B. (eds.) UML 2000 - The Unified Modeling Language. LNCS, vol. 1939, Springer-Verlag, Heidelberg (Oct. 2000)
2. Hausmann, J.H.: Dynamic Meta Modeling. PhD thesis, University of Paderborn (2005)
3. OMG: Model Driven Architecture. http://www.omg.org/mda/
4. Ehrig, H., Engels, G., Kreowski, H.J., Rozenberg, G. (eds.): Handbook of Graph Grammars and Computing by Graph Transformation, Applications, Languages and Tools, vol. 2. World Scientific Publisher, Singapore (1999)
5. Störrle, H.: Semantics of Control-Flow in UML 2.0 Activities. In: VL/HCC, pp. 235–242. IEEE Computer Society Press, Los Alamitos (2004)
6. Bolton, C., Davies, J.: On Giving a Behavioural Semantics to Activity Graphs. In: Evans, A., Kent, S., Selic, B. (eds.) UML 2000. LNCS, vol. 1939, Springer, Heidelberg (2000)

7. Börger, E., Cavarra, A., Riccobene, E.: An ASM Semantics for UML Activity Diagrams. In: Rus, T. (ed.) AMAST 2000. LNCS, vol. 1816, pp. 293–308. Springer, Heidelberg (2000)
8. Hausmann, J.H., Störrle, H.: Towards a Formal Semantics of UML 2.0 Activities. Software Engineering 2005 P-64, 117–128 (2005)
9. van der Aalst, W.: Verification of Workflow Nets. In: Azéma, P., Balbo, G. (eds.) ICATPN 1997. LNCS, vol. 1248, pp. 407–426. Springer, Heidelberg (1997)
10. Rensink, A.: The GROOVE Simulator: A Tool for State Space Generation. In: Pfaltz, J.L., Nagl, M., Böhlen, B. (eds.) AGTIVE 2003. LNCS, vol. 3062, pp. 479–485. Springer, Heidelberg (2003)
11. Clarke, E., Emerson, E., Sistla, A.: Automatic Verification of Finite State Concurrent Systems Using Temporal Logic Specifications: A Practical Approach. In: Conference Record of the Tenth Annual ACM Symposium on Principles of Programming Languages, pp. 117–126. ACM Press, New York (1983)
12. van der Aalst, W., van Hee, K.: Workflow Management - Models, Methods, and Systems. The MIT Press, Cambridge (2002)
13. Object Management Group: UML Specification V2.0. http://www.omg.org/technology/documents/modeling_spec_catalog.htm (2005)
14. Object Management Group: The MOF Specification. http://www.omg.org/cgi-bin/doc?formal/00-04-03 (2004)
15. Corradini, A., Ehrig, H., Löwe, M., Montanari, U., Padberg, J.: The Category of Typed Graph Grammars and its Adjunctions with Categories. In: Cuny, J.E., Ehrig, H., Engels, G., Rozenberg, G. (eds.) Graph Grammars and Their Application to Computer Science. LNCS, vol. 1073, pp. 56–74. Springer, Heidelberg (1994)
16. Kastenberg, H., Rensink, A.: Model checking dynamic states in GROOVE. In: Valmari, A. (ed.) Model Checking Software (SPIN). LNCS, vol. 3925, pp. 299–305. Springer, Heidelberg (2006)
17. Kindler, E., van der Aalst, W.: Liveness, Fairness, and Recurrence in Petri Nets. Inf. Process. Lett. 70(6), 269–270 (1999)
18. Soltenborn, C.: Analysis of UML Workflow Diagrams with Dynamic Meta Modeling techniques. Master's thesis, University of Paderborn (2006)
19. Rensink, A.: GROOVE: A Graph Transformation Tool Set for the Simulation and Analysis of Graph Grammars. Available at http://www.cs.utwente.nl/~groove (2003)
20. Störrle, H., Hausmann, J.H.: Towards a Formal Semantics of UML 2.0 Activities. In: Liggesmeyer, P., Pohl, K., Goedicke, M. (eds) Software Engineering. LNI., GI, vol. 64 pp. 117–128 (2005)
21. Störrle, H.: Semantics and Verification of Data Flow in UML 2.0 Activities. Electr. Notes Theor. Comput. Sci. 127(4), 35–52 (2005)
22. Eshuis, R.: Symbolic model checking of UML Activity diagrams. ACM Trans. Softw. Eng. Methodol. 15(1), 1–38 (2006)
23. Cimatti, A., Clarke, E.M., Giunchiglia, E., Giunchiglia, F., Pistore, M., Roveri, M., Sebastiani, R., Tacchella, A.: NuSMV 2: An Opensource Tool for Symbolic Model Checking. In: Brinksma, E., Larsen, K.G. (eds.) CAV 2002. LNCS, vol. 2404, pp. 359–364. Springer, Heidelberg (2002)

Distributed Applications Implemented in Maude with Parameterized Skeletons*

Adrián Riesco and Alberto Verdejo

Facultad de Informática
Universidad Complutense de Madrid, Spain
ariesco@fdi.ucm.es, alberto@sip.ucm.es

Abstract. Algorithmic skeletons are a well-known approach for implementing parallel and distributed applications. Declarative versions typically use higher-order functions in functional languages. We show here a different approach based on object-oriented parameterized modules in Maude, that receive the operations needed to solve a concrete problem as a parameter. Architectures are conceived separately from the skeletons that are executed on top of them. The object-oriented methodology followed facilitates nesting of skeletons and the combination of architectures. Maude analysis tools allow to check at different abstraction levels properties of the applications built by instantiating a skeleton.

Keywords: Algorithmic skeletons, parameterization, distributed applications, Maude.

1 Introduction

Most interesting computer systems today, as well as those of the future, are distributed in nature, including the Internet, cellular and PDA communications, biological and bio-tech computations, international trade, multi-national corporate databases, and multi-user games. The main goal of a distributed computing system is to connect users and resources in a transparent, open, and scalable way. Ideally this arrangement is drastically more fault tolerant and more powerful than many stand-alone computer systems.

Parallel algorithms divide the problem into subproblems, pass them to many processors and collect the results back together at the end. An *algorithmic skeleton* [3,14] is an abstraction shared by a range of applications which can be executed in a parallel way. The aim is to obtain generic schemes that allow parallel programming where the user does not have to handle low level features like communication and synchronization.

A skeleton can be executed on different architectures/topologies. However, there is often a most suitable architecture for each skeleton that takes advantage of the task distribution specified by it. In our implementation we have opted

* Research supported by MEC Spanish project *DESAFIOS* (TIN2006-15660-C02-01) and Comunidad de Madrid program *PROMESAS* (S0505/TIC/0407).

M.M. Bonsangue and E.B. Johnsen (Eds.): FMOODS 2007, LNCS 4468, pp. 91–106, 2007.

to separate the definition of the architectures from the skeletons, allowing us to combine them in several ways.

Rewriting logic [10] was proposed in the early nineties as a unified model for concurrency in which several well-known models of concurrent and distributed systems can be represented in a common framework. Maude [2] is a high level, general purpose language and high performance system supporting both equational and rewriting logic computations. It can be used to specify in a natural way a wide range of software models and systems, and since (most of) the specifications are directly executable, Maude can also be used to prototype those systems. It has already been used to specify and analyze distributed applications and protocols [4,12]. The recently incorporated support in Maude for communication with external objects makes many other application areas (such as mobile computing and distributed agents) ripe for system development in Maude.

We show here how distributed applications can be implemented in Maude by means of object-oriented parameterized skeletons, that receive the operations needed to solve a concrete problem as a parameter. These operations usually are part of the sequential version of the concrete applications, thus encouraging code reusability. The use of Maude allows us to have the description of the architecture, the definition of the skeleton, and the implementation of the application solving a problem in the same high-level language. Moreover, since Maude has a well-defined semantics, we obtain a good basis for formal reasoning. Tools for doing some kinds of this reasoning in an automatic way and the possibility to define the properties the applications have to fulfill are also provided by Maude.

Typically, declarative implementations of skeletons are based on functional languages (like Eden [9], GpH [16], or PMLS [11]) that naturally represent skeletons as higher-order functions. These languages also allow to prove skeletons correctness [13]. Although rewriting logic is not a higher-order framework, the parameterization features provided by Maude allow to achieve similar results. From a "more practical" world, skeletons have recently been proposed for Java in the JaSkel language [8]. It uses object-oriented features like inheritance and abstract classes to present the skeletons in a hierarchical way that allows the user to instantiate them with concrete applications. We follow a very similar approach which provides an important advantage. The skeletons implemented, analyzed, and proved correct in Maude can then be translated to a language such as JaSkel with little effort.

Below we describe Maude's main features, specially the object-oriented notation used in the rest of the paper. How to implement different architectures is shown in Section 2. Parameterized skeletons are described and instantiated in Section 3. Section 4 shows how to check properties of the architectures and the skeletons. Finally, we present some conclusions and future work. For more detailed explanations of all the topics shown in this paper, see [15].

1.1   Maude

In Maude [2] the state of a system is formally specified as an algebraic data type by means of an equational specification. In this kind of specification we can define new types (by means of keyword $\mathtt{sort(s)}$); subtype relations between types ($\mathtt{subsort}$); operators ($\mathtt{op}$) for building values of these types; and equations ($\mathtt{eq}$) that identify terms built with these operators.

The *dynamic* behavior of such a distributed system is then specified by rewrite rules of the form $t \longrightarrow t'$ *if* C, that describe the local, concurrent transitions of the system. That is, when a part of a system matches the pattern t and satisfies the condition C, it can be transformed into the corresponding instance of the pattern t'.

Regarding object-oriented specifications, *classes* are declared with the syntax $\mathtt{class}\ C\ |\ a_1{:}S_1,\ldots,\ a_n{:}S_n$, where C is the class name, a_i is an attribute identifier, and S_i is the sort of the values this attribute can have. An *object* is represented as a term $<\ O\ :\ C\ |\ a_1\ :\ v_1,\ \ldots,\ a_n\ :\ v_n\ >$ where O is the object's name, belonging to a set $\mathtt{Oid}$ of object identifiers, and the v_i's are the current values of its attributes. *Messages* are defined by the user for each application (introduced with syntax $\mathtt{msg}$).

In a concurrent object-oriented system the concurrent state, which is called a *configuration*, has the structure of a multiset made up of objects and messages that evolves by concurrent rewriting. The rewrite rules specify the behavior associated with the messages. The general form of such rules is

$$M_1 \ldots M_n\ \langle O_1 : F_1 \mid atts_1 \rangle \ldots \langle O_m : F_m \mid atts_m \rangle$$

$$\longrightarrow \langle O_{i_1} : F'_{i_1} \mid atts'_{i_1} \rangle \ldots \langle O_{i_k} : F'_{i_k} \mid atts'_{i_k} \rangle\ \langle Q_1 : D_1 \mid atts''_1 \rangle \ldots \langle Q_p : D_p \mid atts''_p \rangle$$

$$M'_1 \ldots M'_q \quad if\ C$$

where $k, p, q \geq 0$, and the M_s are message expressions. The result of applying a rewrite rule is that the messages $M_1, \ldots, M_n$ disappear; the state and possibly the class of the objects $O_{i_1}, \ldots, O_{i_k}$ may change; all the other objects O_j vanish; new objects $Q_1, \ldots, Q_p$ are created; and new messages $M'_1, \ldots, M'_q$ are sent.

By convention, the only object attributes made explicit in a rule are those relevant for that rule. We use here the Full Maude object-oriented notation [2]. However, the actual implementation of the skeletons is in Core Maude because Full Maude does not support external objects. The complete Maude code can be found in $\mathtt{http://maude.sip.ucm.es/skeletons}$.

Maude modules can be *parametcrizcd* with one or more parameters, each of which is expressed by means of one *theory* that defines the interface of the module, that is, the structure and properties required of an actual parameter. *Views* are used to specify how a particular module is claimed to satisfy a theory.

Maude is *reflective*, that is, it can be represented into itself in such a way that a module in Maude may be data for another Maude module. This functionality has been efficiently implemented in the predefined module $\mathtt{META\text{-}LEVEL}$, where concepts such as reduction or rewriting are reified by means of functions.

2   Different Architectures

In this section we show how *distributed configurations*, made up of located configurations, can be built in Maude, in such a way that the architecture is transparent to the skeletons we will execute on top of it. Thus, the same skeleton can be run over different architectures.

Each located configuration is executed in a Maude process, and they are connected through sockets. Maude supports (bidirectional) sockets as external objects, and offers messages for interacting with them. However, these sockets do not preserve message boundaries, so we have extended their functionality by implementing "buffered sockets" with this feature [15]. In the following sections we present how we use these sockets to define different architectures.

A first approach to really distributed architectures in Maude was shown in [5]. However, those architectures were mixed with the applications. Here, we improve our approach by implementing them in an application-independent way.

2.1   Common Infrastructure

In this section we show the elements that are common to all the architectures we define below. They basically correspond to the way messages are redirected to reach their addresses. The different parts among the architectures correspond to the way the locations are connected.

We assume that each located configuration contains one and only one *router*,[1] plus messages and possibly objects of other classes. The *names* of routers range over the sort Loc (subsort of Oid), and have the form l(IP, N) with the string IP the IP address of the host machine and N a number. We assume global uniqueness of routers names in a distributed configuration. We can communicate the name of a location by using the message new-socket.

Objects situated in a located configuration L must have as identifier a value o(L, N) of sort Oid, where N is a number not used to name other objects in L. All objects can communicate with each other by using the message to_:_, that has as arguments the identifier of the addressee and a term of sort Contents.

```
msg new-socket : Loc -> Msg .
msg to_:_ : Oid Contents -> Msg .
```

Maude sockets can only transmit strings, so we must translate all the messages into strings and convert them back once they are received. To do it in a general way (independently of the concrete application) we use the reflective features of Maude. Concretely, we use a (metarepresented) module with the definition of all the operators used to construct messages that are going to be transmitted. But, since each application (each skeleton, in our case) needs different messages, we define a *parameterized* module, that receives as a parameter the syntax of the transferred data in a module MOD required by the SYNTAX theory.

```
fth SYNTAX is
  inc META-LEVEL .     op MOD : -> Module .
endfth
```

The Router class (that will be specialized in the different architectures) is defined as follows:

---

[1] We identify the router and the location where it is.

```
class Router | state : RouterState, port : Nat,
               neighbors : Map{Loc,Oid}, defNeighbor : Maybe{Oid} .
```

where the predefined parametric sort `Map{Loc,Oid}` represents partial functions from view `Loc` to view `Oid` (that identifies sockets in this case) and `Maybe{Oid}` is a sort that adds a default value `null` to `Oid`. A router may be in states `idle`, `waiting-connection`, or `active`, although other values can be added in concrete architectures. The attribute `port` keeps information about the port through which a server can offer its services or a client can ask for them. To solve the *routing* problem we assume a very general approach consisting in having a routing table in each router, that gives the socket through which a message must be sent if one wants to reach a particular location. The `neighbors` attribute maintains such a routing table as a map associating socket object identifiers to location identifiers. As we will see, each concrete architecture will use the `new-socket` message to update this attribute.

The following rule describes how a message is redirected through the appropriate socket. If a message is sent to an object `o(L, N)` and the message is in a location `L'`, with `L ≠ L'`, that is directly connected to `L` (`LSPF[L] ≠ undefined`), then the message is sent through the socket `LSPF[L]` after converting it to a string with the function `msg2string`, that uses the `MOD` constant from the theory.

```
crl [redirect] :
    to o(L, N) : C
    < L' : Router | state : active, neighbors : LSPF >
 => < L' : Router | > Send(LSPF[L], L', msg2string(to o(L, N) : C))
 if L =/= L' /\ LSPF[L] =/= undefined .
```

In case there is no socket associated to a particular location in the map `neighbors`, there can be a *default socket* stored in the attribute `defNeighbor`. Nevertheless, the value of the `defNeighbor` attribute may also be unspecified.

When a router sees a `Received` message that is not `new-socket`, it extracts the string (by means of the function `string2msg`) putting a new message in the configuration, and keeps listening with a new `Receive` message.

```
crl [Received] :
    Received(L, SOCKET, DATA) < L : Router | >
 => < L : Router | > string2msg(DATA) Receive(SOCKET, L)
 if not new-socket?(DATA) .
```

2.2 Star Architecture

The architecture we present here consists of a location with a *server* router, and several locations with *client* routers. The server is connected to all clients, and each client is connected only to the server. That is, we have a *star network*, with the *center* redirecting the messages between the *nodes*.

We distinguish between the center and the nodes by declaring two subclasses of `Router`: `StarCenter`, with no additional attributes; and `StarNode`, with

an attribute center, that keeps the center's IP address. These classes define
how the locations are connected by filling the neighbors and defNeighbor
attributes.

The center plays the server role from the point of view of the sockets so it
declares itself as a server socket, offering its services on port. Once it receives
a CreatedSocket message, it becomes active and sends a message indicating
that it is ready to accept clients through the server socket. In the rule below, in
addition to sending messages AcceptClient (to continue accepting clients) and
Receive (for receiving messages from the accepted client), the center sends to
the node the message new-socket communicating its identifier.

```
rl [AcceptedClient] :
   AcceptedClient(L, SOCKET, IP, NEW-SOCKET)
   < L : StarCenter | state : active >
=> < L : StarCenter | > AcceptClient(SOCKET, L) Receive(NEW-SOCKET, L)
   Send(NEW-SOCKET, L, msg2string(new-socket(L))) .
```

When a new-socket message is received from a node with its name L', it is
stored in the neighbors attribute.

```
crl [Received] :
   Received(L, SOCKET, DATA)
   < L : StarCenter | state : active, neighbors : LSPF >
=> < L : StarCenter | neighbors : insert(L', SOCKET, LSPF) >
   Receive(SOCKET, L)
if new-socket(L') := string2msg(DATA) .
```

When a StarNode is created, it first tries to establish a connection with the
center by sending a message that uses the IP address and the port of the center,
reaching the state waiting-connection. The response is handled by the following rule connected, where the node also sends the new-socket message right
after the socket is created. Nodes start listening with the Receive message.

```
rl [connected] :
   CreatedSocket(L, SOCKET-MANAGER, SOCKET)
   < L : StarNode | state : waiting-connection >
=> < L : StarNode | state : active > Receive(SOCKET, L)
   Send(SOCKET, L, msg2string(new-socket(L))) .
```

Finally, nodes make the connection with the center the default one.

2.3   Ring Architecture

In a ring topology, each node is connected to two nodes, the previous and the
next one. We show here how to implement a unidirectional ring where each node
receives data from the previous one and sends data to the next one.

In this architecture, each node must be declared as a (Maude) server for the
previous one and as a (Maude) client of the next one. However, to declare a

node as a client it needs another one working as a server, which is impossible for the Maude instance that is first executed. We have decided to distinguish between the *last* Maude instance executed (which knows that all other instances are already running) and the other ones by declaring two subclasses of `Router`:

- `RingNode` defines the behavior of all the nodes but the last one.[2] They first declare themselves as servers and then wait until someone asks to be their client. Once they have accepted a client, they try to be clients themselves of the next node in the ring.
- `RingLast` defines the behavior of the last node, that asks the next one to be its server, and then waits to be a server itself.

Both `RingNode` and `RingLast` will reach the same states, although in different order (thus they need the same attributes), and will declare themselves as servers at start-up, so we define first a superclass `RingRouter` containing the common behavior. It is a subclass of `Router` with attributes `nextIP` and `nextPort` that keep, respectively, the IP address and the port of the next node in the ring. The `port` attribute inherited from class `Router` is the port used by the ring objects to declare themselves as servers and accept clients through it. We also declare new router states `connecting2next` and `waiting4previous`.

When a node is accepted as client, it keeps the socket in the attribute `defNeighbor`, in order to use it to redirect all the messages, and reaches the `active` state. In this architecture the `neighbors` attribute is not used; the ring nodes are just connected by `defNeighbor`, thus obtaining a unidirectional ring.

2.4   Centralized Ring Architecture

We show here a special ring architecture, where in addition to the ring we have a central server connected to each location, so we have a mixture of the two previous architectures. We have tried to reuse them as much as possible. We use the class `StarCenter` from the star architecture for the ring center; and we reuse the classes `RingNode` and `RingLast` described above for the nodes in the ring.

We define a new class `CRingRouter` in charge of connecting to a central server. We will combine the behavior of this new class with the classes `RingNode` and `RingLast` from the ring architecture. This new class has new attributes `centerIP` and `centerPort`, with the IP address and port of the center; new states `connecting2center` and `waiting4center`; and rules for connecting to the central node. When it is in `connecting2center` state, it tries to connect to the center and reaches `waiting4center`. Once the connection has been created, it sends a `new-socket` message and reaches the `active` state.

Now we look for a class that behaves as a `CRingRouter` and as a `RingNode` (or as a `RingLast`, if it is the last node). To obtain it, we define a new class `CRNode`, which is a subclass of both `CRingRouter` and `RingNode` (and a new class `CRLast`, which is a subclass of `CRingRouter` and `RingLast`). These new classes behave

---

[2] Although in a ring there is no "last" node, we refer to the order in which the nodes must be started to be executed.

as the corresponding nodes in the ring, and once they are connected behave as clients of the center. However, we found the problem that all those classes finish in the `active` state, so some of the rules could not be applied. We solve it by renaming the `active` state in the ring nodes to `connecting2center`, so the rules in `CRingRouter` can be applied *after* the ring connections has been established.

```
omod CENTRALIZED-RING-NODE{M :: SYNTAX} is
 pr CENTRALIZED-RING{M} .
 pr RING-NODE{M} * (op active to connecting2center) .
 class CRNode | .    subclass CRNode < CRingRouter RingNode .
endom
```

In the following section we will show how these architectures can be used to execute skeletons on top of them. In [15], we also show how a concrete distributed application can be implemented directly in Maude (without skeletons).

3   Parameterized Skeletons

An important characteristic of skeletons is their *generality*, that is, the possibility of using them in different applications. For this, most skeletons are parameterized by functions and have a polymorphic type. We accomplish this goal by means of parameterized modules whose parameter includes the characterization of the problem. We apply our methodology to three kinds of skeletons [14]:

Data-parallel skeletons: The source of parallelism is the distribution of data between processors and the application of the same operation to all portions of the data. We show the *farm skeleton* with and without *fixed data.*

Systolic skeletons: The systolic skeletons are used in algorithms in which parallel computation and global synchronization steps alternate. We show the *ring* version of the systolic skeleton.

Task-parallel skeletons: The source of parallelism is the decomposition of a task into different subtasks which can be done in parallel. These subtasks need not be identical. We have implemented three task-parallel skeletons: *divide and conquer* (shown here), *branch and bound,* and *pipeline.*

Indications of the most appropriate architecture for each skeleton will be given in the following sections.

3.1   Farm Skeleton

We show here how to implement a skeleton with *replicated workers* and *fixed data.* There is a *master* that initially sends the fixed data and some subproblems to all the *workers.* Each time a task is finished by a worker, the subresult is sent to the master, where it is combined with the partial result already computed, and then new work is given to that worker, reducing the initial problem. Thus, the tasks are delivered on demand, obtaining an even distribution of the work to be done. In order to have a direct communication between the master and the workers the star architecture is the most appropriate one, with the master located in the center and the workers in the nodes.

Each concrete application must define a module fulfilling the RW_FD-PROBLEM theory, that requires the sorts FixData (containing the data common to all the subproblems), Problem (refering to the initial problem), SubProblem (representing the smaller problems solved by the workers), Result (keeping the final result), and SubResult (corresponding to the results obtained by the workers).

The operations required by the theory are: new-work, that extracts a new subproblem from the current problem; reduce, that updates the current problem making it smaller; do-work, that given a subproblem and the fixed data solves the former; combine, that merges the current (partial) result with a new subresult, given the subproblem that was solved (this operation must be commutative[3], in the sense that the final result cannot depend on the order in which the combinations are performed, because the subresults may arrive unordered); and finished?, that checks if the problem has already been solved.

We declare the messages fixData and new-work for sending the fixed data and new tasks to the workers, and finished for communicating the subresults to the master.

The skeleton receives as another parameter the SYNTAX theory, that will be used by the architecture. First, classes for the master and the workers are defined. The workers have the list with unfinished subproblems (nextWorks), the fixed data (fixData), that initially is null, and the master identifier.

```
class RW_FD-Worker | nextWorks : SubProblemList,
                     fixData : Maybe{FixData}, master : Oid.
```

The master stores the fixed data (fixData, that cannot be null), the current unsolved problem, the partial result, the list of idle workers, and the number of initial tasks assigned to each worker (numWorks).[4]

```
class RW_FD-Master | fixData : P$FixData, problem : P$Problem,
                     result : P$Result, workers : OidList, numWorks : Nat.
```

The first action the master must take is to deliver the fixed data and the initial tasks to the workers:

```
rl [new-worker] :
   < O : RW_FD-Master | fixData : FD, problem : P, workers : W OL,
                        numWorks : N >
=> < O : RW_FD-Master | problem : update(P, N), workers : OL  >
   (to W : fixData(FD)) sendTasks(W, P, N).
```

where sendTasks and update are equationally defined operations that generate the messages with the initial tasks and reduce the problem accordingly. While the list of unfinished tasks of a worker is not empty, it must do the following one and send the subresult to the master.

---

[3] This requirement is represented in the theory by means of an equation [15].

[4] P$Sort means that Sort comes from the parameter P.

```
rl [do-work] :
    < W : RW_FD-Worker | fixData : FD, master : O, nextWorks : SP SPL >
 => < W : RW_FD-Worker | nextWorks : SPL >
    to O : finished(W, SP, do-work(SP, FD)).
```

The other tasks of the master are to compose the subresults from the workers and give them more work if it is possible.

Ray tracing instantiation. We can implement this well-known case study by starting from part of the sequential implementation included in module ROWTRACER [15] solving the problem for one row by means of function `traceRow`, and extending it in such a way that it fulfills the requirements from theory RW_FD-PROBLEM. The sort `Pair` is declared to define the initial problem (the highest and the lowest y), while `World` defines the fixed data (the width of the screen, the camera, and the list of figures). A partial function from floats (identifying rows) to colored rows is used to represent the final result. To instantiate the module we create a view [2] and define the mapping between sorts and operators with different names from those in the theory:

```
view RayTracer from RW_FD-PROBLEM to RAYTRACING-PROBLEM is
    sort Problem to Pair.                    sort SubProblem to Float.
    sort Result to Map{Float,ColorRow}.      sort SubResult to ColorRow.
    sort FixData to World.
    op do-work to trace-row.                 op new-work to sub-problem.
    op combine(R:Result, SP:SubProblem, SR:SubResult) to
        term insert(SP:Float, SR:ColorRow, R:Map{Float,ColorRow}).
endv
```

Finally, we instantiate the module RW_FD-SKELETON and use the star architecture. RT-Syntax is a view that encapsulates the syntax of transmitted messages.

```
mod RAYTRACING-SKELETON is
  pr RW_FD-SKELETON{RayTracer, RT-Syntax}.
  pr STAR-ARCH-STAR-CENTER{RT-Syntax}.
  pr STAR-ARCH-STAR-NODE{RT-Syntax}.
endm
```

Euler instantiation. In some problems the fixed data is not needed; we have implemented a slightly modified skeleton to deal with this situation.

The Euler number $\varphi(x)$ is the number of natural numbers smaller than x that are relatively prime to x. We are interested in computing $\sum_{i=1}^{n} \varphi(i)$. We distribute the problem by considering as a single work to calculate each $\varphi(i)$. The only sort involved in this problem is `Nat`, so every sort in the skeleton is mapped to it. The operations are very simple too: a new work of the problem N is just N; we reduce the problem by subtracting 1; the work that must be done is the function `euler` from module EULER; combining two results is just adding them; and we have finished when the number reaches 0.

```
view Euler from RW-PROBLEM to EULER is
  sort Problem to Nat.                          sort SubProblem to Nat.
  sort Result to Nat.                           sort SubResult to Nat.
  op new-work(N:Problem) to term N:Nat.
  op reduce(N:Problem) to term sd(N:Nat, 1).    op do-work to euler.
  op combine(R:Result,S:SubProblem,SR:SubResult) to term R:Nat + SR:Nat.
  op finished?(N:Problem) to term (N:Nat == 0).
endv
```

Calculating $\varphi(x)$ may be quite faster than communicating it, so it is possible that most of the computation time is used in communication. To avoid this problem we can make the granularity of the works coarser by computing more than one Euler number in each step. To do this we only need to make small changes in the instantiation module, while obviously the skeleton remains unmodified. We show here an example where we calculate the sum of 20 Euler numbers in each step with a new function euler20.

```
view Euler20 from RW-PROBLEM to EULER20 is
   ...
  op do-work to euler20.
  op reduce(N:Problem) to term (if N:Nat > 20 then sd(N:Nat, 20)
                                else 0 fi).
endv
```

3.2   Systolic Skeleton

In this skeleton, a master divides the problem among all the workers, that are organized in a circular list because they must share some data through it. When the workers have both initial and shared data (the first shared data is produced by the worker itself), they do their work, combine the partial result, and give the new shared data to the next worker. When a worker finishes all its tasks, it sends its subresult to the master, that will combine them in order.

We define a theory that requires the following sorts: Problem and Result represent the initial and final data; SharedData corresponds to the data that is passed by all the workers; and Pair is a wrapper of Result and SharedData.

The theory defines the following operations: divide splits the initial problem into a list of problems; initialSharedData extracts from the initial data the shared one; do-work computes, given the initial and the shared data, a partial result and the shared data to be communicated to the next worker; combine, used by the workers, merges the current partial result with a new one; combine-all, used by the master, merges all the partial results from the workers; and finished? checks if the worker has finished all its tasks.

We need the following messages: initial-work communicates the initial data to the workers; shared-data delivers the shared data to the next worker; and finished sends a result to the master, once the worker has finished.

This skeleton uses the classes SWorker and SMaster with attributes that allow the workers to keep the partial results and send and receive the shared data in order, and the master to collect and combine the results in order.

The first thing that must be done by the master is to divide the initial problem into a list of problems, that are delivered to all the workers, which first store each problem and extract the initial shared data. Once the worker has shared data it can do a new work and send the updated shared data to the next worker, forgetting its own. When the next shared data arrives, it is checked if the work is not finished, in which case the worker keeps the shared data. Finally, when the master has received all the results, it merges them.

In this case, the centralized ring architecture is the most appropriate one: the workers are located in the ring nodes and the master in the center. Examples can be found in [15].

3.3   Divide and Conquer

Divide and conquer algorithms clearly offer good potential for parallel evaluation. It is not difficult to see that recursively defined subproblems may be evaluated in parallel if sufficient processors are available. The whole execution of a divide and conquer algorithm amounts to the evaluation of a dynamically evolving tree of processes, one for each subproblem generated. However, we show an implementation based on the replicated workers scheme, that allows a balanced distribution of the leaves of the problem tree. This implementation is suitable when decomposition of the problems and the composition of the results are irrelevant compared to the resolution of the subproblems. The master divides the initial problem into subproblems, that are delivered to the workers. The structure of the subproblems is kept in a tree in order to be able to combine their subresults in the appropriate order and get the final result.

We define a theory with operators that allow the skeleton to generate and solve the problem tree. The sorts `Problem` and `Result` define the initial and final data. The function `divide` splits a problem into a list of subproblems, finishing when the problem `isTrivial`. Each trivial task is computed with `solve`. The function `combine` merges a list of subresults into a new subresult.

Only two messages are used: `finished` communicates new results to the master, while `new-work` transmits new tasks to the workers.

This skeleton defines the classes `DCMaster` and `DCWorker`, with attributes that allow the master to keep the tree of results and the workers to transmit the results with their corresponding identifier. First, the master must transform the initial problem into a list of subproblems, and create the initial result tree, that initially has all its nodes without data. Once the list of problems has been calculated, the master must transmit the initial tasks to the workers. Eventually, a task is finished and sent to the server, that inserts it in the result tree, merging the subresults if possible [15].

Since this skeleton is based on replicated workers, the most suitable architecture for the applications that instantiate it (examples are shown in [15]) is the star architecture. When the cost of the composition of the subresults is relevant, a hierarchical architecture with more levels could be more convenient.

4   Formal Analysis of Distributed Applications

Formal verification is the process of checking whether a design satisfies some requirements (properties). In order to formally verify a distributed system, it must first be converted into a simpler "verifiable" format. To do that in Maude, we must be able to represent the whole system in one single term. We have provided an algebraic specification of sockets [15] and represented the processes (hosts in the distributed version) as objects of a class Process identified by the name of the location it represents, and with a single attribute conf keeping the configuration in that host separated from the others. The implementation of the distributed applications can be executed using these "simulated" sockets without changes. By doing this, we can check the properties of a system that is almost equal to the distributed one. However, we can trust some of the components of the whole system, and then abstract them, representing only the "suspicious" elements. These different *abstraction levels* speed up the checking process.

Model checking [1] is used to formally verify finite-state concurrent systems. It has several important advantages over mechanical theorem provers or proof checkers; the most important is that the procedure is completely automatic. The main disadvantage is the *state space explosion*, that can make it unfeasible to model check a system except for very simple cases. For this reason, several state space reduction techniques have been investigated. We use one based on the idea of *invisible transitions* [7], that generalizes a similar notion in partial order reduction techniques. By using this technique we can select a set of rewriting rules that fulfill some properties (such as termination, confluence, and coherence) and convert them into equations, thus reducing the number of states.

Maude's model checker [6] allows us to prove properties on Maude specifications. The properties to be checked are described by using Linear Temporal Logic (LTL) [1]. Then, the model checker can be used to check whether a given initial state, represented by a Maude term, fulfills a given property. To use the model checker we just need to make explicit two things: the intended sort of states (Configuration in our case), and the relevant *state predicates*, that is, the relevant atomic propositions. The latter are defined by means of equations that specify when a configuration C satisfies a property P, $C \mathrel{|=} P$.

Sometimes all the power of model checking is not needed. Another Maude analysis tool is the search command, that allows exploration (following a breadth-first search strategy) of the reachable states in different ways. By using the search command we can check *invariants* [2]. If an invariant holds, then we know that something "bad" can never happen, namely, the negation $\neg I$ of the invariant is impossible. Thus, if the command search init =>* C such that not I(C) has no solution, then I holds.

4.1   Analyzing Architectures

Architectures have been designed independently from the skeletons, and this allows to check properties over them. We show here some simple properties of the centralized ring architecture. Other properties on different architectures can be proved using the same methodology.

Using the model checker. We want to check the behavior of the centralized ring when a node in the ring sends a message to another ring node. To study it we use an initial configuration with one of the nodes in the ring with an object and another with a message for it. Some of the nodes will be traversed by the message and others never will be traversed (at least the center). We define the property has-msg, that checks if a given location contains messages.

```
op has-msg : Loc -> Prop .
eq C < L : Process | conf : C' (to O : CNT) > |= has-msg(L) = true .
eq C |= has-msg(L) = false [owise] .
```

We define the LTL formulas specifying the properties. The formula F(L) below expresses that L receives a message exactly once, and then redirects it, where U represents the *until*, ~ the negation, and [] the *henceforth* LTL operators.

```
eq F(L) = ~ has-msg(L) U (has-msg(L) /\ (has-msg(L) U [] ~ has-msg(L))) .
```

The formula F'(L) states that L never contains a message and F''(L) states that a message reaches L and stays there. They are defined in a similar way as above. We check this property in an example with five nodes in the ring (l(ipi, 0), $i \in 1..5$), and a message from l(ip4, 0) to an object in the location l(ip2, 0), so it must traverse l(ip5, 0) and l(ip1, 0). The center l(ip0, 0) and l(ip3, 0) must receive no message. Therefore we use the following command:

```
red modelCheck(init, F(l(ip4, 0)) /\ F(l(ip5, 0)) /\ F(l(ip1, 0)) /\
               F'(l(ip0, 0)) /\ F'(l(ip3, 0)) /\ F''(l(ip2, 0)) .
result Bool: true
```

Using the search command. We can check now that the connection between each node in the ring and the center is direct. In the configuration above, we place an object in the center and a message for it in the ring node l(ip4, 0). We consider as an invariant (equationally defined) the property messages-invariant, that states that all the nodes in the ring (except the one sending the message) never contain a message in their configuration. The command to check the invariant is:

```
search init2 =>* C such that not messages-invariant(l(ip4, 0), C) .
```

4.2 Analyzing Skeletons

In order to check properties of the skeleton instantiations, we can consider the sequential version of the concrete application as the *specification* of the problem and the distributed, skeleton version as the *implementation*. We use the search command to analyze that in all possible executions of an instantiated skeleton (which introduces nondeterminism) the final result obtained coincides with the result of the deterministic sequential version. We define for each skeleton a getResult operation that, given a final configuration, returns the result kept in the master. We use it to compare the results from the sequential and the distributed implementation, although the comparison can be non trivial [15].

In the Euler example, `getResult` returns a natural number, that we have to compare with the result from the specification. The search command used is:

```
search initial(7) =>! C such that getResult(C) =/= sumEuler(7).
```

In the mergesort application, used to instantiate the divide and conquer skeleton, the postcondition is simple enough to avoid the use of the sequential version to prove the correctness of the skeleton. We can define an `ordered` predicate that checks if a list is sorted and has the same components as another and use it in the `search` command:

```
search init(gen(1000)) =>! C s.t. not ordered(getResult(C), gen(1000)).
```

5   Conclusions

We have presented the implementation of some static architectures using sockets, that Maude supports as external objects. We are currently developing more complex, fault-tolerant architectures, where nodes can join and leave.

We have implemented several skeletons as parameterized modules that receive as parameters the operations solving each concrete problem. This allows us to instantiate the same skeleton for a concrete problem in different ways, for example varying its granularity.

From the Maude side, we show that truly distributed applications can be implemented and that the recently incorporated support for parameterization in Core Maude can be applied to more complex applications. From the point of view of skeleton development, we describe a methodology to specify, prototype, and check skeletons that can be later implemented in other languages such as Java (we plan to study in the near future which is the best way to achieve this).

We have tested the skeletons with some examples, using three 2 GHz PowerPC G5 and two 1.25 GHz PowerPC G4, obtaining a speed-up of 2.5. Although this speed-up is not remarkable, we observed in the executions that all the processors were always busy, so most of the time was wasted in manipulating the transmitted data. We have to study how to improve the efficiency; the profiling feature in Maude allows a detailed analysis of which rules are most expensive to execute in a given application.

Mobile Maude [5], an extension of Maude allowing mobile computation, has also been used to implement skeletons, where the master and the workers were implemented as mobile objects that travelled through the architecture [15]. They had an attribute with the concrete code of the application. Although the same generality as in the work presented in this paper was obtained, the main drawback was lack of efficiency due to the reflection levels introduced.

Finally, we have started to study how our skeletons can be nested by using the object-oriented inheritance features provided by Maude. We are also investigating how to prove properties of the skeletons independently of the instantiations, by means of rule induction.

References

1. Clarke, E.M., Grumberg, O., Peled, D.A.: Model Checking. MIT Press, Cambridge (1999)
2. Clavel, M., Durán, F., Eker, S., Lincoln, P., Martí-Oliet, N., Meseguer, J., Talcott, C.: Maude Manual (Version 2.2), December 2005. http://maude.cs.uiuc.edu/ maude2-manual (2005)
3. Cole, M.: Algorithmic Skeletons: Structure Management of Parallel Computations. MIT Press, Cambridge (1989)
4. Denker, G., Meseguer, J., Talcott, C.: Formal specification and analysis of active networks and communication protocols: The Maude experience. In: Proc. DARPA Information Survivability Conference and Exposition DICEX 2000, Hilton Head, South Carolina, January 2000, vol. 1, pp. 251–265. IEEE, NJ, New York (2000)
5. Durán, F., Riesco, A., Verdejo, A.: A distributed implementation of Mobile Maude. In: Denker, G., Talcott, C. (eds.) Proc. Sixth Int. Workshop on Rewriting Logic and its Applications, WRLA 2006, ENTCS, pp. 35–55. Elsevier, Amsterdam (2006)
6. Eker, S., Meseguer, J., Sridharanarayanan, A.: The Maude LTL model checker. In: Gadducci, F., Montanari, U. (eds.) Proc. Fourth Int. Workshop on Rewriting Logic and its Applications, WRLA 2002, Pisa, Italy, September 19–21, 2002, vol. 71, pp. 115–141. Elsevier, Amsterdam (2002)
7. Farzan, A., Meseguer, J.: State space reduction of rewrite theories using invisible transitions. In: Johnson, M., Vene, V. (eds.) AMAST 2006. LNCS, vol. 4019, pp. 142–157. Springer, Heidelberg (2006)
8. Ferreira, J.F., Sobral, J.L., Proença, A.J.: JaSkel: A Java skeleton-based framework for structured cluster and grid computing. In: CCGRID'06: Proceedings of the Sixth IEEE International Symposium on Cluster Computing and the Grid, pp. 301–304. IEEE Computer Society, Los Alamitos, CA (2006)
9. Loogen, R., Ortega-Mallén, Y., Peña, R., Priebe, S., Rubio, F.: Parallelism abstractions in Eden. In: [14], chapter 4, pp. 95–129
10. Meseguer, J.: Conditional rewriting logic as a unified model of concurrency. Theoretical Computer Science 96(1), 73–155 (1992)
11. Michaelson, G., Scaife, N., Bristow, P., King, P.: Nested algorithmic skeletons from higher order functions. Parallel Algorithms and Applications 16(2-3), 181–206 (2001)
12. Ölveczky, P., Meseguer, J., Talcott, C.: Specification and analysis of the AER/NCA active network protocol suite in Real-Time Maude. Formal Methods in System Design 29, 253–293 (2006)
13. Peña, R., Segura, C.: Reasoning about skeletons in Eden. In: Parallel Computing: Current & Future Issues of High-End Computing, Proceedings of the International Conference ParCo 2005, NIC Series 33, pp. 851–858 (2006)
14. Rabhi, F.A., Gorlatch, S.: Patterns and Skeletons for Parallel and Distributed Computing. Springer, Heidelberg (2002)
15. Riesco, A., Verdejo, A.: Parameterized skeletons in Maude. TR 1/07, Dpto. Sistemas Informáticos y Computación, Universidad Complutense de Madrid http://maude.sip.ucm.es/skeletons/psm.pdf (2007)
16. Trinder, P.W., Loidl, H.W., Pointon, R.F.: Parallel and distributed Haskells. Journal of Functional Programming 12(4-5), 469–510 (2002)

On Formal Analysis of OO Languages Using Rewriting Logic: Designing for Performance

Mark Hills and Grigore Roşu

Department of Computer Science
University of Illinois at Urbana-Champaign, USA
201 N Goodwin Ave, Urbana, IL 61801
{mhills,grosu}@cs.uiuc.edu
http://fsl.cs.uiuc.edu

Abstract. Rewriting logic provides a powerful, flexible mechanism for language definition and analysis. This flexibility in design can lead to problems during analysis, as different designs for the same language feature can cause drastic differences in analysis performance. This paper describes some of these design decisions in the context of KOOL, a concurrent, dynamic, object-oriented language. Also described is a general mechanism used in KOOL to support model checking while still allowing for ongoing, sometimes major, changes to the language definition.

Keywords: object-oriented languages, language design, analysis, model checking, rewriting logic.

1 Introduction

With the increase in multi-core systems, concurrency is becoming a more important topic in programming languages and formal methods research. Rewriting logic [14,13], an extension of equational logic with support for concurrency, provides a computational logic for defining, reasoning about, and executing concurrent systems. While these can be fairly simple systems, entire programming languages, such as object-oriented languages, can be defined as rewrite theories, allowing tools designed to work with generic rewrite specifications to work with the defined programming languages as well.

While there has been much work on analysis and verification techniques with rewriting logic [16,17,5,15], much of this work has not focused on programming languages, or has used simpler, sometimes trivial, languages. Exceptions to this include work on program verification for Java [6], Java bytecode in the JVM [7], and CML [2], a concurrent extension to the ML programming language.

Even with these papers focused on real languages, very little information is given on *why* certain design decisions were made. For the language designer looking to define object-oriented languages using rewriting logic, this is a major shortcoming. Since even small changes to a rewriting logic definition can have major impacts on the ability to analyze programs, making appropriate decisions when defining the language is vitally important. In addition, little information

M.M. Bonsangue and E.B. Johnsen (Eds.): FMOODS 2007, LNCS 4468, pp. 107–121, 2007.

is available about specifically object-oriented definitions; while the work on Java [6] obviously qualifies, the JVM operates at a much lower level, and the model of computation used by CML, based around the strict functional language ML, differs from that used by standard object-oriented languages.

In this paper, we have set out to start filling this gap by providing information on increasing the analysis performance of rewrite logic definitions for object-oriented languages, specifically in the context of Maude [3,4], a high-performance rewriting logic engine. We start in Section 2 by providing a brief introduction to rewriting logic, showing the relationship between rewriting logic and term rewriting and explaining the crucial distinction between equations and rules. Section 3 then provides a brief introduction to KOOL, a concurrent, object-oriented language that will be the focus of the experiments in this paper.

In Section 4, we highlight the search capabilities of Maude by showing some examples of its use. Search provides a breadth-first search over a program's state space, providing an ability to search for program states matching certain conditions (output of a certain value, safety condition violation) that, due to the potentially infinite state space of the program, may not be possible with model checking. Section 5 then discusses model checking of OO programs in rewriting logic, using the classic dining philosophers problem. To improve the performance of search and model checking, Section 6 discusses two potential performance improvements important in the context of object-oriented languages: auto-boxing of scalar values for use in a pure object-oriented language, and optimizing memory access for analysis performance. Section 7 concludes the paper.

2   Rewriting Logic

This section provides a brief introduction to term rewriting and rewriting logic. Term rewriting is a standard computational model supported by many systems; rewriting logic [14,13] organizes term rewriting modulo equations as a complete logic and serves as a foundation for programming language semantics [17,18].

2.1   Term Rewriting

Term rewriting is a method of computation that works by progressively changing (rewriting) a term. This rewriting process is defined by a number of rules – potentially containing variables – which are each of the form: $l \to r$. A rule can apply to the entire term being rewritten or to a subterm of the term. First, a match within the current term is found. This is done by finding a substitution, θ, from variables to terms such that the left-hand side of the rule, l, matches part or all of the current term when the variables in l are replaced according to the substitution. The matched subterm is then replaced by the result of applying the substitution to the right-hand side of the rule, r. Thus, the part of the current term matching $\theta(l)$ is replaced by $\theta(r)$. The rewriting process continues as long as it is possible to find a subterm, rule, and substitution such that $\theta(l)$ matches the subterm. When no matching subterms are found, the rewriting process terminates, with the final term being the result of the computation. Rewriting, like other methods of computation, can continue forever.

There exist a plethora of term rewriting engines, including ASF [21], Elan [1], Maude [3,4], OBJ [8], Stratego [22], and others. Rewriting is also a fundamental part of existing languages and theorem provers. Term rewriting is inherently parallel, since non-overlapping parts of a term can be rewritten at the same time, and thus fits well with current trends in architecture and systems.

2.2 Rewriting Logic

Rewriting logic is a computational logic built upon equational logic which provides support for concurrency. In equational logic, a number of *sorts* (types) and *equations* are defined. The equations specify which terms are considered to be equal. All equal terms can then be seen as members of the same equivalence class of terms, a concept similar to that from the λ calculus with equivalence classes based on α and β equivalence. Rewriting logic provides *rules* in addition to equations, used to transition between equivalence classes of terms. This allows for concurrency, where different orders of evaluation could lead to non-equivalent results, such as in the case of data races. The distinction between rules and equations is crucial for analysis, since terms which are equal according to equational deduction can all be collapsed into the same analysis state. Rewriting logic is connected to term rewriting in that all the equations and rules of rewriting logic, of the form $l = r$ and $l \Rightarrow r$, respectively, can be transformed into term rewriting rules by orienting them properly (necessary because equations can be used for deduction in either direction), transforming both into $l \rightarrow r$. This provides a means of taking a definition in rewriting logic and a term and "executing" it.

In this paper we focus on the use of Maude [3,4], a rewriting logic language and engine. Beyond the ability to execute a program based on a rewriting logic definition, Maude provides several capabilities which make it useful for defining languages and performing formal analysis of programs. Maude allows commutative and associative operations with identity elements, allowing straight-forward definitions of language features which make heavy use of sets and lists, such as sets of classes and methods and lists of computational tasks. Maude's support for rewriting logic provides a natural way to model concurrency, with potentially competing tasks (memory accesses, lock acquisition, etc) defined as rules. Also, Maude provides built-in support for model checking and breadth-first state space exploration, which will be explored further starting in Section 4.

3   KOOL

KOOL is a concurrent, dynamic, object-oriented language, loosely inspired by, but not identical to, the Smalltalk language [9]. KOOL includes support for standard imperative features, such as assignment, conditionals, and loops with break and continue. KOOL also includes support for many familiar object-oriented features: all values are objects; all operations are carried out via message sends;

Program	$P ::=$	$C^* \ E$
Class	$C ::=$	class X is $D^* \ M^*$ end | class X extends X' is $D^* \ M^*$ end
Decl	$D ::=$	var $\{X,\}^+$;
Method	$M ::=$	method X is $D^* \ S$ end | method X ($\{X',\}^+$) is $D^* \ S$ end
Expression	$E ::=$	$X \mid I \mid F \mid B \mid Ch \mid Str \mid (E) \mid$ new $X \mid$ new X ($\{E,\}^+$) $\mid$
		self $\mid E \ X_{op} \ E' \mid E.X(())^? \mid E.X(\{E,\}^+) \mid$ super() $\mid$
		super.$X(())^? \mid$ super.$X(\{E,\}^+) \mid$ super($\{E,\}^+ $)
Statement	$S ::=$	E <- E'; $\mid$ begin $D^* \ S$ end $\mid$ if E then S else S' fi $\mid$
		if E then S fi $\mid$ try S catch $X \ S$ end $\mid$ throw E ; $\mid$
		for X <- E to E' do S od $\mid$ while E do S od $\mid$ break; $\mid$
		continue; $\mid$ return; $\mid$ return E; $\mid S \ S' \mid E$; $\mid$ assert E; $\mid X$: $\mid$ spawn E ; $\mid$
		acquire E ; $\mid$ release E ; $\mid$ typecase E of Cs^+ (else S)$^?$ end
Case	$Cs ::=$	case X of S

$X \in Name, I \in Integer, F \in Float, B \in Boolean, Ch \in Char, Str \in String, X_{op} \in Operator\ Names$

Fig. 1. KOOL Syntax

message sends use dynamic dispatch; single inheritance is used, with a designated root class named `Object`; methods are all public, while fields are all private outside of the owning object; and scoping is static, yet declaration order for classes and methods is unimportant. KOOL allows for the run-time inspection of object types via a typecase construct, and includes support for exceptions with a standard try/catch mechanism.

3.1   KOOL Syntax

The syntax of KOOL is shown in Figure 1. The lexical definitions of literals are not included in the figure to limit clutter, but are standard (for instance, booleans include both true and false, strings are surrounded with double quotes and characters with single quotes, etc). Message sends are specified in a Java-like syntax except for methods named after operators, which are always binary and can be used infix (such as a + b instead of

```
class Factorial is
  method Fact(n) is
    if n = 0 then return 1;
    else return n * self.Fact(n-1);
    fi
  end
end

console << (new Factorial).Fact(200)
```

Fig. 2. Recursive Factorial, KOOL

a.+(b)). Because of this, very few operators are predefined, and operators all have the same precedence and associativity. Finally, semicolons are used as statement terminators, not separators, and are only needed where the end of a statement may be ambiguous – at the end of an assignment, for instance, or at the end of each statement inside a branch of a conditional, but not at the end of the conditional itself, which ends with fi.

To get a feel for the language, a sample program is shown in Figure 2. A new class `Factorial` is defined with a method `Fact` that calculates the factorial of the parameter `n`. After the class definition is the main program expression, which creates a new object of class `Factorial`, invokes method `Fact` with the parameter 200, and then writes the output to the predefined `console` object using the output operation, `<<` (borrowed from C++). This operation invokes the `toString` method on its parameter and returns itself as the method result, allowing chaining of output operations (such as `console << "Value = " << 3`).

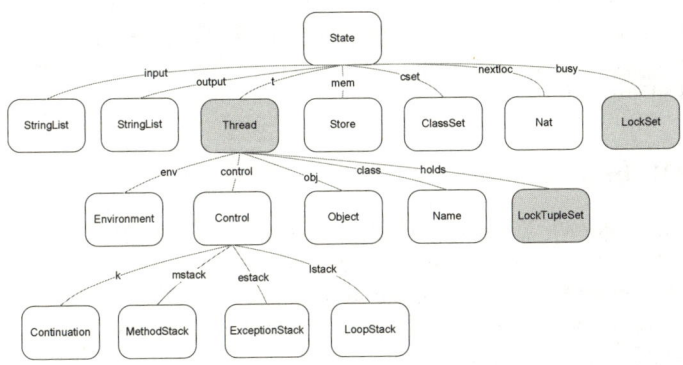

Fig. 3. KOOL State Infrastructure

3.2 KOOL Semantics

The semantics of KOOL is defined using Maude equations and rules, with the current program state represented as a "soup" of sometimes nested terms representing the current computation, memory, the environment, locks held, etc. A visual representation of this term, the state infrastructure, is shown in Figure 3; state components needed specifically for concurrency are shaded.

Figure 4 shows examples of the equations and rules which make up the KOOL semantics. Lists of computations, called continuations, are formed using the `->` operator, with the head of the list to the left. The first three equations (represented with `eq`) process a conditional. The first indicates the value

```
eq stmt(if E then S else S' fi) = exp(E) -> if(S,S') .
eq val(primBool(true)) -> if(S,S') = stmt(S) .
eq val(primBool(false)) -> if(S,S') = stmt(S') .

crl t(control(k(llookup(L) -> K) CS) TS) mem(Mem) =>
   t(control(k(val(V) -> K) CS) TS) mem(Mem)
if V := Mem[L] /\ V =/= undefined .
```

Fig. 4. Sample KOOL Rules

of the guard expression `E` must be computed before a branch is selected. The guard is put at the left end of the list, where it will be computed by rules specific to the type of expression, while the branches `S` and `S'` are saved for later use by putting them into an `if` continuation item. The second and third equations execute the appropriate branch based on whether the guard evaluated to `true` or `false`. The fourth, a conditional rule (represented with `crl`), represents the lookup of a memory location. The rule states that, if the next computation step in this thread is to look up the value at location L, and if that value is V (:= binds V to the result of reducing `Mem[L]`, the memory lookup operation), and if V is not undefined (i.e. L is a properly defined location), the result of the computation is the value V. CS and TS match the unreferenced parts of the control and thread state, respectively, while K represents the rest of the computation in this thread. Note that, since the fourth rule represents a side-effect, it can only be applied when it is the next computation step in the thread (it is at the head of the continuation), while the first three, which don't involve side-effects, can be applied at any time.

3.3 KOOL Implementation

There is an implementation of KOOL available at our website [11], as well as a web-based interface to run and analyze KOOL programs such as those presented here. There is also a companion technical report [10] that explains the syntax and semantics in detail. When run, a KOOL program is first parsed using SDF [21], which we have found better supports the complexities of real programming-language syntax than the parser included with Maude. SDF generates an abstract syntax tree that is then turned into Maude "prefix" form using a custom C program. The `runkool` program coordinates this process and handles the invocation of Maude, running in different modes (execution, search, etc.) based on command-line parameters and returning the program output.

4 Breadth-First Search in KOOL

The thread game is a concurrency problem defined as follows: take a single variable, say x, initialized to 1. In two threads, repeat the assignment x <- x + x forever. In another thread, output the value of x. What values is it possible to output? As has been proved [19], it is possible to output any natural number ≥ 1. In KOOL, spawn is used to execute an arbitrary expression, often a message send, in a new thread. Threads are the main unit of concurrency in KOOL, with each thread containing its own execution context (current class, environment, etc), and all threads accessing a shared store. A KOOL version of the thread game is shown in Figure 5.

```
class ThreadGame is
  var x;

  method ThreadGame is
    x <- 1;
  end

  method Add is
    while true do x <- x + x; od
  end

  method Run is
    spawn(self.Add); spawn(self.Add);
    console << x;
  end
end
(new ThreadGame).Run
```

Fig. 5. Thread Game, KOOL

To check to see if a specific value can be output, one could run the program. Given enough runs, the value of interest may be generated, but this is highly inefficient. Model checking will not help here either, since this is an infinite state system, and the value may not be along the first (depth-first) search path chosen. Maude's search capability can be used, though, either to enumerate possible values (obviously not all possible values here) or to search for a specific value. For instance, searching for 10 yields a result, indicating that 10 is one of the possible values; a sample run showing this is presented in Figure 6.

```
./runkool examples/ThreadGame.kool -t 10
... term omitted ...
Solution 1 (state 2294)
states: 3381  rewrites: 310427 in 14388ms cpu
SL:[StringList] --> "10"
```

Fig. 6. Thread Game Sample Run

Another example of the usefulness of search is illustrated by the program in Figure 7. This program is finite state, so all possible results can be enumerated. When search is used here, requesting all possible final results, three are returned: both 100 and 200 can be output, and an assertion can be thrown if the thread running **Changer** sets the value to 200 between the time the value is set to 100 and the time the next line, with the **assert** statement, is executed.

```
class WrappedInt is
    var wval;

    method WrappedInt(n) is
        wval <- n;
    end

    method setWVal(n) is
        wval <- n;
    end

    method toString is
        return wval.toString();
    end

    method =(n) is
        return wval = n;
    end
end
```

```
class Changer is
    method Run(n) is
        n.setWVal(200);
    end
end

class Main is
    method Run is
        var x;
        x <- new WrappedInt(5);
        spawn ((new Changer).Run(x));
        x.setWVal(100);
        assert(x = 100);
        console << x;
    end
end
```

```
./runkool examples/Spawn7.kool -s
... term and some stats omitted ...
Solution 1 (state 1964)
SL:[StringList] --> "100"

Solution 2 (state 2430)
SL:[StringList] --> "200"

Solution 3 (state 2490)
SL:[StringList] --> "AssertException thrown: Assertion triggered"
```

Fig. 7. Assertions and Search in KOOL

```
class Fork is                      class Main is
end                                  var l1, l2;
                                     var p1, p2;
class Philosopher is
  method Run(id,left,right) is       method Run is
    while (true) do                    l1 <- new Fork;
      hungry:                          l2 <- new Fork;
      acquire left;
      acquire right;                   p1 <- new Philosopher;
                                       p2 <- new Philosopher;
      eating:
      release left;                    spawn(p1.Run(1,l1,l2));
      release right;                   spawn(p2.Run(2,l2,l1));
    od                               end
  end                              end
end
                                   (new Main).Run
```

Fig. 8. Dining Philosophers in KOOL

5   Model Checking KOOL

A canonical example for concurrency is the Dining Philosophers problem. A simple version of this problem, with just two philosophers, is shown written in KOOL in Figure 8. In KOOL, locks can be acquired on any object using `acquire`. Here we create a `Fork` class with no methods or properties; we can create objects of this class and then acquire locks on the objects, representing taking a fork. The `Philosopher` class just contains a single method, `Run`, which enters an infinite loop that cycles through two states: hungry (wants to acquire forks) and eating (has acquired forks). Once a philosopher eats, it releases the locks using `release`, putting down the forks. The `Main` class also contains a `Run` method; this method creates the necessary forks and philosophers, and then uses the `spawn` statement to run each philosopher in its own thread.

We would like to determine if this program can deadlock. Using Maude's model checking capabilities, we can write properties over the program state which can then be used in LTL formulae. For instance, we could create a property named **deadlocked**, and then write a formula like " []∽deadlocked" (it's always the case that we are not deadlocked). A problem with this is that the program state is very complex; it contains all current class definitions, runtime information for each thread, global information for the program (such as memory), and other bookkeeping information. It isn't always obvious how to properly write a property using this information. Here, for instance, we would need to detect when we are trying to acquire a fork by looking into the computation directly, meaning we would need to base the property on the definition of lock acquisition, and formulate this in terms of acquiring a pair of locks. Another problem is that, if we change the state definition as we are modifying the language design, we risk having to change defined properties to match the new state, breaking the modularity of language definitions. A possible solution in this case is to use Maude's search capabilities, described in Section 4, but this is not a general solution, since other properties of interest (starvation, for instance) cannot be checked in this way.

A solution that resolves these problems is to use *label statements*, shown in Figure 8 as identifiers followed by a colon (such as hungry: or eating:), to assist in model checking. This idea is used by other model checkers as well – SPIN [12], for instance, also uses labels. The language semantics then include a rule (not an equation, since this takes us into a non-equivalent state which should be detected during verification) which sets a component of the thread state to the value of the label when the label is encountered. This allows properties to be stated directly in terms of the labels – here, for instance, freedom from deadlock means that upon reaching the hungry label it is always the case that the thread eventually reaches the eating label. This requires much less detailed knowledge about the state, since only label names, included in the program source, need to be known. It also insulates model checking from state changes, as long as the part of the state dealing with labels is not modified. The tradeoff is a potential degradation of performance, since the label semantics are defined in terms of rules, and rule application adds additional states to the state space. In cases where additional performance is needed, it is still possible to write predicates directly against the state, avoiding the use of labels. Again, though, these predicates may be quite complicated, and may require ongoing maintenance as the language evolves.

Using this notion of progress for deadlock freedom, the appropriate LTL formula for the two philosopher problem is then:

$$\text{progress}(2,\text{hungry},\text{eating})\vee\text{progress}(3,\text{hungry},\text{eating})$$

where 2 and 3 are the thread IDs and progress(n,11,12) means that thread n eventually reaches 12 whenever it reaches 11. Thread IDs are needed since LTL lacks quantification – i.e. there is no way to say that, $\forall n.\text{progress}(n,11,12)$. The thread running first has ID 1, and each spawn adds 1 to this.

```
while true do
  hungry:
  if (id % 2 = 0) then
    acquire left;
    acquire right;
  else
    acquire right;
    acquire left;
  fi

  eating:
  release left;
  release right;
od
```

Fig. 9. Dining Philosophers, Deadlock-Free

Running the model checker with this program and formula, we will get a counterexample, since it is in fact possible to deadlock (when the first philosopher grabs the first fork and the second grabs the second). Times for the model checker to find counterexamples, by philosopher count, are given in Figure 12. A fix to the code in the Philosopher class Run method is shown in Figure 9, with "odd" philosophers taking the forks in one order and "even" philosophers in the other. Unfortunately, due to the initial language design, which focused more on executability and less on verification, it is not possible to verify this fix with the model checker – it will run for a time and then crash due to resource exhaustion. This will be addressed in Section 6, where modifications to the design to improve verification performance will be explored. With these modifications in place, the model checker will return true given the LTL formula for deadlock freedom shown above.

6   Tuning the Model

The ability to model check and search programs using language definitions in rewriting logic is very closely tied to the performance of the definition. There are two general classes of performance improvement: improvements that impact execution speed, and improvements that impact analysis speed, which may even slightly reduce typical execution speed. Two examples of improvements are presented here, both of which have appeared in various forms in programming languages but not, to our knowledge, in rewriting logic language specifications. First, auto-boxing is introduced to the language. This allows operations on scalar types, which are represented in KOOL as objects, to be performed directly on the underlying values for many operations (standard arithmetic operations, for instance), while still allowing method calls to be used on an object representation of the scalar where needed. Although mainly useful in dynamic languages like KOOL, this technique can also be used to perform automatic coercions between scalar and object types in statically-typed languages. Second, memory is segregated into two pools, a shared and an unshared pool. Rules are used when accessing or modifying memory in the shared pool, since these changes could lead to data races, while equations are used for equivalent operations on the unshared pool. This follows the intuition that changes to unshared memory locations in a thread cannot cause races. This change may or may not improve execution performance, but has a dramatic impact on analysis performance.

6.1   Auto-boxing

In KOOL, all values, including those typically represented as scalars in languages like Java, are objects. This means that a number like 5 is represented as an object, and an expression like 5 + 7 is represented as a method call. Primitive operations are defined which extract the primitive values "hidden" in the objects (i.e. the actual number 5, versus the object that represents it), perform the operation on these primitive values, and create a new object representing the result. This provides a "pure" object-oriented model, but requires additional overhead, including additional accesses to memory to retrieve the primitive values and create the new object for the result. Since memory accesses are modeled as rules in the definition, this also increases model checking and search time by increasing the number of states that need to be checked.

To improve performance, auto-boxing can be added to KOOL. This allows values such as 5 to be represented as scalars – i.e. directly as the primitive values. A number of operations can then be performed directly on the primitive representation, without having to go through the additional steps described above. For numbers, this includes arithmetic and logical operations, which are some of the most common operations applied to these values. Operations which cannot be performed directly can still be treated as message sends; the scalar value is automatically converted to an object representing the same value, which can then act as a message target to handle the method. Since boxing can occur automatically, by default values, including those generated as the result of primitive operations, are left un-boxed, in scalar form. This all happens behind the scenes, allowing **KOOL** programs to remain unchanged.

```
eq k(exp(f(F)) -> K) = k(newPrimFloat(primFloat(F)) -> K) .
-------------------------------------------------------------------------------
eq k(exp(f(F)) -> K) = k(val(fv(F)) -> K) .
eq k(val(fv(F),fv(F')) -> toInvoke(n('+)) -> K) = k(val(fv(F + F')) -> K) .
eq k(val(fv(F),Vl) -> toInvoke(Xm) -> K) =
   k(newPrimFloat(primFloat(F)) -> boxWList(Vl) -> toInvoke(Xm) -> K) [owise] .
```

Fig. 10. Example Definition Changes, Auto-boxing

An example of the rule changes to enable auto-boxing is found in Figure 10. The first equation is without auto-boxing. Here, when a floating point number F is encountered, a new floating point object of class **Float** is created to represent F using **newPrimFloat**. Any operations on this object, such as adding two floats, will involve a message send. The next three rules are with auto-boxing enabled. In the second equation, instead of creating a new object for F, we return a scalar value. The third equation shows an example of an intercepted method call. When a method is called, the target and all arguments are evaluated, with the method name held in the **toInvoke** continuation item. Here, + has been invoked with a target and argument that both evaluate to scalar float values, so we will use the built-in float + operation instead of requiring a method call. In the fourth equation, the boxing step is shown – here, a method outside of those handled directly on scalars has been called with the floating-point scalar value as the target, in which case a new object will be created just like in the first equation (**[owise]** will ensure that we will try this as a last resort). Once created, the new object, and the values being sent as arguments (held in **boxWList**), will be used to perform a standard method call.

Auto-boxing has a significant impact on performance. Figure 12 shows the updated figures for verification times with this change in place. Not only is this faster than the solution without auto-boxing in all cases, but it is now also possible to verify deadlock freedom for up to 5 philosophers, which was not possible with the prior definition.

6.2   Memory Pools

Memory in the **KOOL** definition is represented using a single global store for an entire program. This is fairly efficient for normal execution, but for model checking and search this can be more expensive than needed. This is because all interactions with the store must use rules, since multiple threads could compete to access the same memory location at the same time. However, many memory accesses don't compete – for instance, when a new thread is started by spawning a method call, the method's instance variables are only seen by this new thread, not by the thread that spawned it. What is needed, then, is a modification to the definition that will allow rules to be used where they are needed – for memory accesses that could compete – while allowing equations to be used for the rest.

To do this, memory in **KOOL** can be split into two pools: a shared memory pool, containing all memory accessible by more than one thread at some point during execution, and a non-shared memory pool, containing memory that is known to be accessed by at most one thread. To add this to the definition, an additional global state component is added to represent the shared memory pool, and the appropriate rules are modified to perform memory operations against the proper memory pool. Correctly moving memory locations between the pools does require care, however, since accidentally leaving memory in the non-shared pool could cause errors during verification.

The strategy we take to move locations to the shared pool is a conservative one: any memory location that *could* be accessed by more than one thread, regardless of whether this *actually* happens during execution, will be moved into the shared pool. There are two scenarios to consider. In the first, the spawn statement executes a message send. In this scenario, locations accessible through the message target (an object), as well as locations accessible through the actual parameters of the call, are all moved into the shared pool. Note that accessible here is transitive – an object passed as a parameter may contain references to other objects, all of which could be reached through the containing object. In many cases this will be more conservative than necessary; however, there are many situations, such as multiple spawns of message sends on the same object, and spawns of message sends on `self`, where this will be needed. The second scenario is where the spawn statement is used to spawn a new thread containing an arbitrary expression. Here, all locations accessible in the current environment need to be moved to the shared pool, including those for instance variables and those accessible through `self`. This covers all cases, including those with message sends embedded in larger expressions (since the target is in scope, either directly or through another object reference, it will be moved to the shared pool).

This strategy leads to a specific style of programming that should improve verification performance: message sends, not arbitrary expressions, should be spawned, and needed information should be passed in the spawn statement to the target, instead of set through setters or in the constructor. This is because the object-level member variables will be shared, while instance variables and formal parameters will not. This brings up a subtle but important distinction – the objects referenced by the formal parameters will be shared, but not the parameters themselves, which are local to the method, meaning that no verification performance penalty is paid until the code needs to "look inside" the referenced objects. Looking inside does not include retrieving a referenced object for use in a lock acquisition statement (however, acquisition itself is a rule).

Figure 11 shows one of the two rules changed to support the memory pools (the other, for assignment, is similar), as well as part of the location reassignment logic. The first rule, which is the original lookup rule, retrieves a value V from a location L in memory Mem. The location must exist, which accounts for the condition – if L does not exist, looking up the current value with Mem[L] will return **undefined**. CS and TS match the rest of the **control** and **thread** states, respectively. The second and third equation and rule replace this first to support

```
crl t(control(k(llookup(L) -> K) CS) TS) mem(Mem) =>
    t(control(k(val(V) -> K) CS) TS) mem(Mem) if V := Mem[L] /\ V =/= undefined .
------------------------------------------------------------------------------------
ceq t(control(k(llookup(L) -> K) CS) TS) mem(Mem) =
    t(control(k(val(V) -> K) CS) TS) mem(Mem) if V := Mem[L] /\ V =/= undefined .

crl t(control(k(llookup(L) -> K) CS) TS) smem(Mem) =>
    t(control(k(val(V) -> K) CS) TS) smem(Mem) if V := Mem[L] /\ V =/= undefined .

ceq t(control(k(reassign(L,L1) -> K) CS) TS) mem(Mem) smem(SMem) =
    t(control(k(reassign(L1,L1') -> K) CS) TS) mem(unset(Mem,L)) smem(SMem[L <- V])
  if V := Mem[L] /\ V =/= undefined /\ L1' := valLocs(V) .

ceq t(control(k(reassign(L,L1) -> K) CS) TS) mem(Mem) smem(SMem) =
    t(control(k(reassign(L1) -> K) CS) TS) mem(Mem) smem(SMem)
  if V := SMem[L] /\ V =/= undefined .

eq k(reassign(empty) -> K) = k(K) .
```

Fig. 11. Example Definition Changes, Memory Pools

Ph	No Optimizations			Auto-boxing			Auto-boxing + Memory Pools		
	States	Counter	DeadFree	States	Counter	DeadFree	States	Counter	DeadFree
2	61	0.645	NA	35	0.64	0.798	7	0.621	0.670
3	1747	0.723	NA	244	0.694	3.610	30	0.637	1.287
4	47737	1.132	NA	1857	1.074	40.279	137	0.782	5.659
5	NA	6.036	NA	14378	4.975	501.749	634	1.629	34.415
6	NA	68.332	NA	111679	49.076	NA	2943	7.395	218.837
7	NA	895.366	NA	867888	555.791	NA	13670	47.428	1478.747
8	NA	NA	NA	NA	NA	NA	63505	325.151	NA

Single 3.40 GHz Pentium 4, 2 GB RAM, OpenSuSE 10.1, kernel 2.6.16.27-0.6-smp, Maude 2.2. Times in seconds, Ph is philosopher count, Counter is time to generate counter-example, DeadFree is time to verify the program is deadlock free, state count based on Maude search results, NA means the process either crashed or was abandoned after consuming most system memory.

Fig. 12. Dining Philosophers Verification Times

the shared and unshared memory pools. The second is now an equation, since the memory under consideration is not shared. The third is a rule, since the memory is shared. This shared pool is represented with a new part of the state, smem. The last three equations represent the reassignment of memory locations from the unshared to the shared pool, triggered on thread creation and assignment to shared memory locations. In the first, the location L and its value are in the unshared pool, and are moved to the shared pool. If the value is an object, all locations it holds references to are also added to the list of locations that must be processed. The second represents the case where the location is already in the shared pool. In this case, nothing is done with the location. The third equation applies only when all locations have been processed, indicating we should continue with the computation (with K).

This strategy could be improved with additional bookkeeping. For instance, no information on which threads share which locations is currently tracked. Tracking this information could potentially allow a finer-grained sharing mechanism, and could also allow memory to be un-shared when threads terminate. However, even with the current strategy, we still see some significant improvements in verification performance. These can be seen in Figure 12. Note that, in every case, adding the shared pool increases performance, in many cases dramatically. It also allows additional verification – checking for a counterexample works for 8 philosophers, and verifying deadlock freedom in the fixed solution can be done for up to 7 philosophers.

7   Conclusions and Future Work

In this paper we have shown how rewriting logic can be used for verification and analysis of a non-trivial concurrent object-oriented language. We have also shown ways in which run-time and verification performance can be improved, in this case by adding auto-boxing of scalar values in a pure object-oriented language and by segregating accesses of shared and non-shared memory locations. We believe the ideas presented here can be used during the design of other rewriting logic definitions of object-oriented languages as a means to improve performance.

There is much future work in this area, some of which was touched on in the paper. Better methods of sharing and un-sharing memory would help in the analysis of longer running programs, and could potentially be used for other purposes as well, such as in the analysis of garbage collection schemes. Also, while we achieve a reduction in the state space by the use of equations to collapse equivalent states, work on techniques like partial order reduction in the context of rewriting logic specifications would help to improve performance further. There has also been some work, in the context of real-time systems, on using different state representations at different points in evaluation to improve analysis performance [20]; it would be interesting to see if similar techniques could be used in language definitions, where the lack of time steps would make it more challenging to determine when the state could be reconfigured. Finally, a method to determine that specification transformations are *semantics preserving* would be valuable, especially if it could be done automatically using the language specifications.

Acknowledgments. We thank the anonymous reviewers for their helpful comments, which have improved the quality of this paper. We also thank the NSF for their support through grants NSF CCF-0448501 and NSF CNS-0509321.

References

1. Borovanský, P., Kirchner, C., Kirchner, H., Moreau, P.-E., Ringeissen, C.: An overview of ELAN. ENTCS, vol. 15 (1998)
2. Chalub, F., Braga, C.: A Modular Rewriting Semantics for CML. In: Proceedings of the 8th. Brazilian Symposium on Programming Languages (May 2004)

3. Clavel, M., Durán, F., Eker, S., Lincoln, P., Martí-Oliet, N., Meseguer, J., Quesada, J.: Maude: specification and programming in rewriting logic. Theoretical Computer Science 285, 187–243 (2002)
4. Clavel, M., Durán, F., Eker, S., Lincoln, P., Martí-Oliet, N., Meseguer, J., Talcott, C.: The Maude 2.0 System. In: Nieuwenhuis, R. (ed.) RTA 2003. LNCS, vol. 2706, pp. 76–87. Springer, Heidelberg (2003)
5. Eker, S., Meseguer, J., Sridharanarayanan, A.: The Maude LTL Model Checker. In: Gadducci, F., Montanari, U. (eds.) Proc. 4th. Intl. Workshop on Rewriting Logic and its Applications. ENTCS, vol. 71, Elsevier, Amsterdam (2002)
6. Farzan, A., Chen, F., Meseguer, J., Roşu, G.: Formal Analysis of Java Programs in JavaFAN. In: Alur, R., Peled, D.A. (eds.) CAV 2004. LNCS, vol. 3114, pp. 501–505. Springer, Heidelberg (2004)
7. Farzan, A., Meseguer, J., Roşu, G.: Formal JVM Code Analysis in JavaFAN. In: Rattray, C., Maharaj, S., Shankland, C. (eds.) AMAST 2004. LNCS, vol. 3116, pp. 132–147. Springer, Heidelberg (2004)
8. Goguen, J., Winkler, T., Meseguer, J., Futatsugi, K., Jouannaud, J.-P.: Introducing OBJ. In: Software Engineering with OBJ: algebraic specification in action, Kluwer Academic Publishers, Dordrecht (2000)
9. Goldberg, A., Robson, D.: Smalltalk-80: the language and its implementation, Boston, MA, USA. Addison-Wesley Longman Publishing Co., Inc., London, UK (1983)
10. Hills, M., Roşu, G.: KOOL: A K-based Object-Oriented Language. Technical Report UIUCDCS-R-2006-2779, University of Illinois at Urbana-Champaign (2006)
11. Hills, M., Rosu, G.: KOOL: Language Homepage. http://fsl.cs.uiuc.edu/KOOL
12. Holzmann, G.J.: The Model Checker SPIN. IEEE Trans. Softw. Eng. 23(5), 279–295 (1997)
13. Martí-Oliet, N., Meseguer, J.: Rewriting logic: roadmap and bibliography. Theoretical Computer Science 285, 121–154 (2002)
14. Meseguer, J.: Conditional Rewriting Logic as a Unified Model of Concurrency. Theoretical Computer Science 96(1), 73–155 (1992)
15. Meseguer, J.: Software Specification and Verification in Rewriting Logic. In: Broy, M., Pizka, M. (eds.) Models, Algebras, and Logic of Engineering Software, Marktoberdorf, Germany, July 30 – August 11, 2002, pp. 133–193. IOS Press, Amsterdam (2003)
16. Meseguer, J., Palomino, M., Martí-Oliet, N.: Equational Abstractions. In: Baader, F. (ed.) Automated Deduction – CADE-19. LNCS (LNAI), vol. 2741, pp. 2–16. Springer, Heidelberg (2003)
17. Meseguer, J., Roşu, G.: Rewriting Logic Semantics: From Language Specifications to Formal Analysis Tools. In: Basin, D., Rusinowitch, M. (eds.) IJCAR 2004. LNCS (LNAI), vol. 3097, pp. 1–44. Springer, Heidelberg (2004)
18. Meseguer, J., Roşu, G.: The rewriting logic semantics project. Theoretical Computer Science, to appear (2006)
19. Moore, J.S.: http://www.cs.utexas.edu/users/moore/publications/thread-game.html
20. Rodríguez, D.E.: On Modelling Sensor Networks in Maude. In: Proceedings of WRLA'06, Elsevier, Amsterdam, to appear (2006)
21. van den Brand, M.G.J., Heering, J., Klint, P., Olivier, P.A.: Compiling language definitions: the ASF+SDF compiler. ACM TOPLAS 24(4), 334–368 (2002)
22. Visser, E.: Program Transf. with Stratego/XT: Rules, Strategies, Tools, and Systems. In: Domain-Specific Program Generation, pp. 216–238 (2003)

Formal Modeling and Analysis of the OGDC Wireless Sensor Network Algorithm in Real-Time Maude

Peter Csaba Ölveczky and Stian Thorvaldsen

Department of Informatics, University of Oslo
peterol@ifi.uio.no, stianth@ifi.uio.no

Abstract. This paper describes the application of Real-Time Maude to the formal specification, simulation, and further formal analysis of the sophisticated state-of-the-art OGDC wireless sensor network algorithm. Wireless sensor networks in general, and the OGDC algorithm in particular, pose many challenges to their formal specification and analysis, including novel communication forms, treatment of geographic areas, time-dependent and probabilistic features, and the need to analyze both correctness and performance. Real-Time Maude extends the rewriting logic tool Maude to support formal specification and analysis of object-based real-time systems. This paper explains how we formally specified OGDC in Real-Time Maude, how we could simulate our specification to perform all the analyses done by the algorithm developers using the network simulation tool ns-2, and how we could perform further formal analyses which are beyond the capabilities of simulation tools. A remarkable result is that our Real-Time Maude simulations seem to provide a much more accurate estimate of the performance of OGDC than the ns-2 simulations. To the best of our knowledge, this is the first time a formal tool has been applied to an advanced wireless sensor network algorithm.

1 Introduction

This paper describes the application of Real-Time Maude [17,15] to the formal specification, simulation, and further formal analysis of the state-of-the-art *optimal geographical density control* (OGDC) wireless sensor network algorithm [22]. To the best of our knowledge, this work represents the first formal modeling and analysis effort of such a complex wireless sensor network system.

A wireless sensor network (WSN) consists of many small, cheap, and low-power sensor nodes that use wireless technology (usually radio) to communicate with each other [2]. Given the increasing sophistication of WSN algorithms—and the difficulty of modifying an algorithm once the sensor network is deployed—there is a clear need to use formal methods to validate system *performance* and *functionality* prior to implementing such algorithms.

In [19] we advocate the use of the language and tool Real-Time Maude [15,17], which extends the rewriting logic-based Maude [3] tool to real-time systems, to formally specify, simulate, and further analyze WSN algorithms. The Real-Time

M.M. Bonsangue and E.B. Johnsen (Eds.): FMOODS 2007, LNCS 4468, pp. 122–140, 2007.

Maude specification language emphasizes expressiveness and ease of specification. The data types of a system are defined by *equational specifications*. Instantaneous transitions are defined by *rewrite rules*, and time elapse is defined by *"tick" rewrite rules*. Real-Time Maude supports the specification of distributed *object-oriented* systems, which is ideal for modeling a network system. The high-performance Real-Time Maude tool provides a range of analysis techniques, including: timed rewriting for simulation purposes; timed search for reachability analysis; and time-bounded linear temporal logic model checking. Real-Time Maude has been used to model and analyze a set of advanced real-time systems, such as large communication protocols [18,8] and scheduling algorithms [13]. Such analysis has found subtle design errors not uncovered during traditional simulation and testing. We argue in [19] that Real-Time Maude's expressive specification formalism, and the ease with which new forms of communication can be defined, should make it ideal to model WSN systems.

Jennifer Hou suggested to us her OGDC algorithm [22] for WSNs as a challenging modeling and analysis task. OGDC is a sophisticated state-of-the-art algorithm that tries to maintain complete sensing coverage of an area for as long as possible by switching nodes on and off. It has been simulated by the algorithm developers Zhang and Hou using the simulation tool ns-2 [12,4].

The OGDC algorithm is an advanced algorithm whose formal specification, simulation, and analysis pose a set of challenges, including:

1. Modeling—and computing with—spatial entities such as coverage areas, angles, and distances.
2. Modeling broadcast communication with transmission delays and limited transmission range.
3. Modeling time-dependent behavior, such as use of timers, transmission delays, and power consumption.
4. Modeling *probabilistic* behaviors. For example, sensor nodes volunteer to start with certain probabilities, and different values are supposed to be "random values, drawn from a uniform distribution."
5. Simulating and analyzing systems with hundreds of sensor nodes.
6. Analyzing both correctness and, in particular, performance.

This is indeed a challenging set of modeling and analysis tasks. This paper shows how Real-Time Maude met these challenges. In particular, during simulations of the algorithm, we are able to do in Real-Time Maude *all* the performance analyses that Zhang and Hou performed using the wireless extension of the network simulation tool ns-2 [12]. In addition, we have subjected the algorithm to *time-bounded* reachability analysis and temporal logic model checking.

By modeling transmission delays (which play a significant role in the definition of the OGDC algorithm), and by comparing our performance measures with the ns-2 simulation results, we found a discrepancy which *could* be explained by a (minor) weakness in the algorithm *if* the ns-2 simulations did not take the transmission delays into account.[1] To test this hypothesis, we also

---

[1] We have not received information of whether the ns-2 simulations actually took the transmission delays into account, only that it is likely that they did not.

performed Real-Time Maude simulations *without* considering transmission delays. The results of these simulations are quite similar to the ns-2 simulations. It is therefore tempting to conjecture that our original simulations provide a much more accurate estimate of the performance of OGDC than the ns-2 simulations.

Related work. Our work represents—to the best of our knowledge—the first formal modeling and analysis of such a sophisticated WSN algorithm as OGDC. Some attempts at using formal methods on WSNs have focused on modeling TinyOS using automaton-based formalisms (see, e.g., [5]), or have considered simple diffusion protocols for discovering routing trees [11]. Our paper [19] explains related work in more detail. That paper also suggests that Real-Time Maude might be a good candidate for formally modeling WSNs, and shows how certain features of such networks, including locations, distances, and communication can be easily modeled in Real-Time Maude. In contrast, this paper focuses on the OGDC case study: It shows how the general techniques suggested in [19] can be applied to specify OGDC; on how advanced features, such as coverage areas, can be modeled in Real-Time Maude; on additional analysis efforts; and on understanding the relationship between the results obtained by Real-Time Maude simulations and by ns-2 simulations. Lately, there has been some initial efforts applying Real-Time Maude to WSNs elsewhere [6,20].

2   Real-Time Maude

A Real-Time Maude *timed module* specifies a *real-time rewrite theory* [14] of the form (Σ, E, IR, TR), where:

- (Σ, E) is a *membership equational logic* [10] theory with Σ a signature[2] and E a set of conditional equations. The theory (Σ, E) specifies the system's state space as an algebraic data type. (Σ, E) must contain a specification of a sort `Time` modeling the time domain (which may be dense or discrete).
- *IR* is a set of *labeled conditional instantaneous rewrite rules* specifying the system's *instantaneous* (i.e., zero-time) local transitions, each of which is written `crl [l] : t => t'` if *cond*, where l is a *label*. Such a rule specifies a *one-step transition* from an instance of t to the corresponding instance of t', *provided* the condition holds. The rules are applied *modulo* the equations E.[3]
- *TR* is a set of *tick (rewrite) rules*, written with syntax

  `crl [l] : {t} => {t'} in time` τ `if` *cond* .

  that model time elapse. `{_}` is a built-in constructor of sort `GlobalSystem`, and τ is a term of sort `Time` that denotes the *duration* of the rewrite.

---

[2] i.e., Σ is a set of declarations of *sorts*, *subsorts*, and *function symbols* (or *operators*).

[3] E is a union $E' \cup A$, where A is a set of equational axioms such as associativity, commutativity, and identity, so that deduction is performed *modulo* A. Operationally, a term is reduced to its E'-normal form modulo A before any rewrite rule is applied.

The initial states must be ground terms of sort `GlobalSystem` and must be reducible to terms of the form $\{t\}$ using the equations in the specifications. The form of the tick rules then ensures uniform time elapse in all parts of the system.

In object-oriented Real-Time Maude modules, a *class* declaration

class C | att_1 : s_1, ... , att_n : s_n .

declares a class C with attributes att_1 to att_n of sorts s_1 to s_n. An *object* of class C in a given state is represented as a term < O : C | att_1 : val_1, ..., att_n : val_n > where O is the object's *identifier*, and where val_1 to val_n are the current values of the attributes att_1 to att_n. In a concurrent object-oriented system, the state, which is usually called a *configuration*, is a term of the built-in sort `Configuration`. It has typically the structure of a *multiset* made up of objects and messages. Multiset union for configurations is denoted by a juxtaposition operator (empty syntax) that is declared associative and commutative, so that rewriting is *multiset rewriting* supported directly in Real-Time Maude. The dynamic behavior of concurrent object systems is axiomatized by specifying each of its concurrent transition patterns by a rewrite rule. For example, the rule

```
rl [1] : m(O,w)  < O : C | a1 : x, a2 : O', a3 : z >   =>
                 < O : C | a1 : x + w, a2 : O', a3 : z >  dly(m'(O'),x) .
```

defines a family of transitions in which a message m, with parameters O and w, is read and consumed by an object O of class C. The transitions have the effect of altering the attribute a1 of the object O and of sending a new message m'(O') *with delay* x (see [17]). "Irrelevant" attributes (such as a3, and the *right-hand side occurrence* of a2) need not be mentioned in a rule.

Timed modules are *executable* under reasonable assumptions, and Real-Time Maude provides a spectrum of analysis capabilities. We summarize below the Real-Time Maude analysis commands used in our case study.

Real-Time Maude's timed *"fair"* rewrite command simulates *one* behavior of the system *up to a certain duration*. It is written with syntax

(tfrew t in time <= τ .)

where t is the initial state and τ is a ground term of sort `Time`.

Real-Time Maude's timed *search* command uses a breadth-first strategy to search for states that are reachable from a given initial state t within time τ, match a *search pattern*, and satisfy a *search condition*. The command which searches for *one* state satisfying the search criteria has syntax

(tsearch [1] t =>* *pattern* such that *cond* in time <= τ .)

Real-Time Maude also extends Maude's *linear temporal logic model checker* [3] to check whether each behavior "up to a certain time," as explained in [17], satisfies a temporal logic formula. *State propositions* are terms of sort `Prop`, and their semantics should be given by (possibly conditional) equations of the form {*statePattern*} |= *prop* = *b*

for *b* a term of sort `Bool`, which defines the state proposition *prop* to hold in all states {*t*} where {*t*} |= *prop* evaluates to `true`. A temporal logic *formula* is constructed by state propositions and temporal logic operators such as `True`, `False`, `˜` (negation), `/\`, `\/`, `->` (implication), `[]` ("always"), `<>` ("eventually"), and `U` ("until"). The time-bounded model checking command has syntax

(mc *t* |=t *formula* in time <= τ .)

for *t* the initial state and *formula* the temporal logic formula.

Finally, the `find latest` command finds how long it takes, in the worst case, to reach a desired state.

3 Overview of the OGDC Algorithm

In a two-dimensional plane, a node with *sensing range* r_s can *sense* events in a circular *coverage area* with radius r_s. It is desirable that the coverage areas of the *active* nodes cover the entire area to be monitored (the "sensing area") for as long as possible. A large number of nodes is often deployed to extend the lifetime of a wireless sensor network, so that some nodes can be intentionally "put to sleep" to save power. A node that is inactive can be switched on when needed. The process of periodically choosing the nodes that can be put to sleep while maintaining coverage (and connectivity) of the sensing area is called the *density control process*. The OGDC algorithm [22] is a state-of-the-art density control algorithm, developed by Zhang and Hou, that tries to select the set of active nodes such that their coverage areas provide the minimum amount of overlap.

The network lifetime is divided into *rounds*, where each round is divided into a *node selection phase* and a *steady state phase*. The node selection phase begins with each node having status "undecided" and *probabilistically* choosing whether or not to volunteer to be a *starting node*. Each node that volunteers sets its *backoff timer* to a small value. The node then becomes *active* when its backoff timer expires, and broadcasts a *power-on* message which contains the location of the node and a *random direction*. When an "undecided" node receives a power-on message, it checks if its entire coverage area is covered by the surrounding active nodes, in which case the node becomes inactive. Otherwise, it sets its backoff timer depending on how close the node is to the *optimal position* w.r.t. the nodes that are currently active. The timer value is set to a gradually larger value as the *distance increases* and the *direction deviates*. When the backoff timer of a node expires, the node becomes active and broadcasts a power-on message that may cause other nodes to reset their backoff timers or to become inactive. The network enters the steady state phase when each node is either active or inactive. When a round is over, the density control process starts over again.

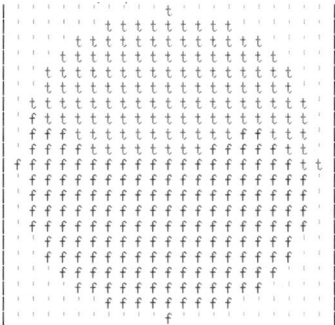

Fig. 1. The bitmap for a node's coverage area

4   The Real-Time Maude Specification of OGDC

This section presents a sample of our specification of the OGDC algorithm.[4]
General techniques for modeling typical WSN features, such as distances and
communication, are described in [19].

4.1   Modeling Locations

We can represent a location in the plane as a term $x.y$, for rational numbers x
and y, of the following sort `Location`:[5]

```
sort Location .
op _._ : Rat Rat -> Location .
```

4.2   Modeling Areas Using Bitmaps

A significant part of the OGDC algorithm consists of checking whether a node's
coverage area is completely covered by the coverage areas of other active nodes,
since this determines whether or not a node can be switched off. Zhang and Hou
suggest in a preliminary version of [22] to use a bitmap to model a node's coverage
area. A coverage area is divided into a *grid*, and each bit in the bitmap represents
the *center* of a grid square. The Real-Time Maude tool is not a graphical tool,
but with proper use of the `format` operator attribute [3], a bitmap can be given
an intuitive appearance as shown in Fig. 1. We define a bitmap as a term of sort
`Bitmap`, which consists of a list of `BitLists`[6], which in itself is a list of `Bits`. A
`Bit` has one of three values: `t` if the location of the bit is covered by at least one

---

[4] Our specification is explained in detail in [21]. The entire executable Real-Time
  Maude specification can be found at http://www.ifi.uio.no/RealTimeMaude/OGDC.

[5] Underbars in the declarations of operators such as _._ denote the places of arguments
  for "mix-fix" function symbols.

[6] Each `BitList` corresponds to a "row" in the bitmap.

other active node, f if the location is not covered, or the bit ' that is used to "pad" the circles as shown in Fig. 1. The sort Bitmap is thus defined as follows:

```
sorts Bitmap BitList Bit .     subsort Bit < BitList .
ops t f ' : -> Bit [ctor] .
op nil : -> BitList [ctor] .
op __ : BitList BitList -> BitList [ctor assoc id: nil format (o s o)] .
op |_| : BitList -> Bitmap [ctor format (ni o o o)] .
op nil : -> Bitmap [ctor] .
op __ : Bitmap Bitmap -> Bitmap [ctor assoc id: nil] .
```

The location of each bit is computed from the location of the node which is the center of the bitmap. A function updateBitmap updates a node's bitmap when the node receives a *power-on* message (see rule recPowerOn1) by setting each bit within the sensing range of the sender to t. The node then also checks whether its (updated) bitmap is completely covered by its neighbors. This is done by the function coverageAreaCovered, which returns false if *some* bit is 'f' and returns true otherwise (owise):

```
vars BITL BITL' : BitList .    vars BM BM' : Bitmap .
op coverageAreaCovered : Bitmap -> Bool .
eq coverageAreaCovered(BM  | BITL f BITL' |  BM') = false .
eq coverageAreaCovered(BM) = true [owise] .
```

We choose to have 1 meter between each bit in a bitmap, which results in bitmaps with 400 bits (including the ' bits) since the sensing range of a node is 10 meters.

4.3   The Definition of Sensor Node Objects

We model sensor nodes as objects of the class WSNode. A sensor node does not have an explicit identifier but can be identified by its *location*. We let locations be object identifiers by giving the subsort declaration subsort Location < Oid .

```
class WSNode | backoffTimer : TimeInf,   coverageArea : Bitmap,
               uncoveredCrossings : CrossingSet,
               remainingPower : Nat,     neighbors : NeighborSet,
               roundTimer : TimeInf,     status : Status,
               volunteerProb : Rat,      hasVolunteered : VolunteerStatus .
```

The attribute names are self-explanatory: backoffTimer denotes the time remaining until the node must perform an action; coverageArea contains the node's coverage area; remainingPower denotes the amount of power the node has left; roundTimer is the time remaining of the round; status denotes the node's status, which is either on, off, or undecided; volunteerProb gives the probability for the node to volunteer as a starting node; and hasVolunteered denotes whether the node has volunteered as a starting node.

4.4 Modeling Time and Time Elapse

We follow the guidelines in [17] for modeling time-dependent behaviors in object-oriented specifications. Time elapse is modeled by the tick rule

```
var C : Configuration .    var T : Time .
crl [tick] : {C} => {δ(C, T)} in time T if T <= mte(C) .
```

The function δ defines the effect of time elapse on a configuration, and the function mte defines the maximum amount of time that can elapse before some action must take place. These functions distribute over the objects and messages in a configuration and must be defined for single objects. The tick rule advances time nondeterministically by *any* amount T less than or equal to mte(C). Before executing the system, a *time sampling strategy* guiding the application of the tick rule must be defined (see Section 5.1). We import the built-in module NAT-TIME-DOMAIN-WITH-INF, which defines the time domain Time to be the natural numbers, with an additional constant INF (for ∞) of a supersort TimeInf.

The function δ is defined on a WSNode object by decreasing its timers and amount of remaining power according to the time that has elapsed:

```
vars L L' : Location .    var T : Time .    vars TI TI' : TimeInf .
var P : NzNat .    var S : Status .    vars M N : Nat .    var D : Int .
var V : VolunteerStatus .    var R : Rat .    var NBS : NeighborSet .

eq δ(< L : WSNode | remainingPower : N, status : S,
                    backoffTimer : TI, roundTimer : TI' >, T)
  =
    < L : WSNode | remainingPower : if S == on then N monus (idlePower * T)
                                    else N monus (sleepPower * T) fi,
                   backoffTimer : TI monus T, roundTimer : TI' monus T > .
```

The constants idlePower and sleepPower denote the amount of power the node consumes per time unit (millisecond) when the node is active and inactive, respectively. The function monus is defined by x monus $y = \max(0, x - y)$.

The function mte is defined so that time cannot advance when a node is in its volunteering process (undecided)—forcing the node to enter this process at the start of each round—and otherwise cannot advance beyond the expiration time of a timer, or beyond the time when the node would run out of power:

```
eq mte(< L : WSNode | backoffTimer : TI, roundTimer : TI', status : S,
                      remainingPower : P, hasVolunteered : V >) =
    if V == undecided then 0 else
       min(TI, TI', if S == on then ceiling(P / idlePower)
                                else ceiling(P / sleepPower) fi) fi .
```

4.5 Modeling Communication

The informal description of the OGDC algorithm says that nodes *broadcast* messages within the radio range. Furthermore, a node does not know its neighbors.

Most time related parameters in OGDC are set according to the *transmission time* of a message, which is assumed to be the same for all broadcast transmissions. This is a clear indication that transmission delays must be captured in the model. In [19] we show how such "area broadcast" with transmission delay Δ can be easily modeled in Real-Time Maude. The idea is that the sender l sends a "broadcast message" `broadcast` m `from` l, where m is the message content, into the configuration. This broadcast message is then defined to be *equivalent* to a set of *single* messages `dly(msg` m `from` l `to` l', Δ`)`, one such message for each sensor node l' within the radio range of l.

Since the description of OGDC does not discuss packet collisions, and only mentions that OGDC also should work in the presence of message losses, we have not modeled problems that are due to packet collisions.

4.6   Probabilistic Behaviors

The OGDC algorithm exhibits probabilistic behaviors in that (i) some actions are performed with probability p, and (ii) some values are supposed to be set to "random values, drawn from a uniform distribution ..." As mentioned, Real-Time Maude does not provide explicit support for specifying probabilistic behavior. Instead, for simulation purposes, we define a function `random`, which generates a sequence of numbers pseudo-randomly and which satisfies Knuth's criteria for a "good" random number generator [7]. The state must then contain an object of a class `RandomNGen` with an attribute `seed` which stores the ever-changing "seed" for `random`. Probabilistic behaviors can then be modeled by "sampling" a value from the given interval using the `random` function. For the purpose of specifying all possible behaviors, we *could have*—but have not, due to the resulting large reachable state spaces that would have made exhaustive analysis unfeasible—modeled probabilistic behavior by nondeterministic behavior by (i) letting a probabilistic action be enabled as long as the probability of it being performed is greater than 0, and (ii) by letting the "random" value be a new variable, only occurring in the *right-hand* side of the rewrite rule, which can be given any value in the desired interval.

4.7   Defining the Dynamic Behavior of the OGDC Algorithm

The dynamic behavior of the OGDC algorithm is modeled in Real-Time Maude by 11 rewrite rules, 3 of which are given below.

At the start of each round of the OGDC algorithm, each node is in state **undecided** and must decide whether or not to volunteer as a *starting node*. This part of the protocol is described as follows in [22]:

> *A node volunteers to be a starting node with probability p if its power exceeds a pre-determined threshold P_t. [...] If a sensor node volunteers, it sets a backoff timer to τ_1 seconds, where τ_1 is uniformly distributed in $[0, T_d]$. When the timer expires, the node changes its state to "ON", and broadcasts a power-on message. [...] The power-on message sent by the starting node contains (i) the*

position of the sender and (ii) the direction α along which the second working node should be located. This direction is randomly generated from a uniform distribution in $[0, 2\pi]$. [...] If the node does not volunteer itself to be a starting node, it sets a timer of T_s seconds. [...]

This part of the OGDC algorithm is probabilistic, since a node decides to volunteer with probability p. We simulate such probabilistic behavior in the following rewrite rules by checking whether the next pseudo-random number generated in the system, modified to a value between 0 and 999 (`randomProb(M)`, defined as `random(M) rem 1000`), is less than R, where R denotes the current volunteering probability multiplied by 1000. The first rule models the start of the "starting node selection" phase when the node's `hasVolunteered` attribute is `undecided`:

```
rl [volunteer] :
   < L : WSNode | remainingPower : P, volunteerProb : R,
                  hasVolunteered : undecided >
   < Random : RandomNGen | seed : M >
  =>
   (if (randomProb(M) < R) and (P > powerThreshold or R == 1000)
    then < L : WSNode | backoffTimer : randomTimer(random(M)),
                        hasVolunteered : true >
    else < L : WSNode | backoffTimer : T_s, hasVolunteered : false,
                        volunteerProb : doubleProb(R) >
    fi)
   < Random : RandomNGen | seed : random(random(M)) > .
```

The node must also have sufficient remaining power (`P > powerThreshold`), or its volunteer probability must have reached 1 (`R == 1000`). If the node volunteers, it sets its backoff timer to a random value between 0 and T_d by the function `randomTimer`. If the node does not volunteer, it sets its backoff timer to T_s. The `seed` is also updated, so that the next application of this (or any other) rule will draw a completely different random number.

A node becomes *active* when its backoff timer expires. If the node volunteered as a starting node, it broadcasts a power-on message that contains the node's location and a *random direction*:

```
rl [startingNodePowerOn] :
   < L : WSNode | remainingPower : P, backoffTimer : 0,
                  hasVolunteered : true >
   < Random : RandomNGen | seed : M >
  =>
   < L : WSNode | remainingPower : P monus transPower,
                  backoffTimer : INF, status : on >
   < Random : RandomNGen | seed : random(M) >
   broadcast (powerOnWithDirection randomDirection(M)) from L .
```

The node consumes `transPower` amount of power when it broadcasts a message.

The actions taken when a node receives a power-on message are described as follows in [22]:

When a sensor node receives a power-on message, if the node is already
"ON", or it is more than $2\,r_s$ away from the sender node, it ignores the mes-
sage; otherwise it adds this node to its neighbor list, and checks whether or not
all its neighbors' coverage disks completely cover its own coverage disk. If so,
the node sets its state to "OFF" and turns itself off. Otherwise [...]

The next rule models the case where the receiver has status `undecided` and its
coverage area becomes entirely covered by its active neighbors (including the
sender of the current power-on message). In this case, the node turns itself `off`:

```
crl [recPowerOn1] :
   (msg (powerOnWithDirection D) from L' to L)
   < L : WSNode | status : undecided, neighbors : NBS, bitmap : BM >
  =>
   < L : WSNode | status : off, neighbors : NBS (L' starting (D >= 0)),
                  bitmap : updateBitmap(L, BM, L'), backoffTimer : INF >
   if (L withinTwiceTheSensingRangeOf L')
      /\ coverageAreaCovered(updateBitmap(L, BM, L')) .
```

5   Simulation and Formal Analysis of OGDC

This section describes how the OGDC algorithm can be subjected to the following kinds of formal analysis in Real-Time Maude:

1. *Monte Carlo simulation*, with probabilistic behavior simulated using our
   pseudo-random number generator, by *timed fair rewriting*. In particular, we
   show how Real-Time Maude can perform *all* the simulations done by Zhang
   and Hou on the wireless extension of the network simulation tool ns-2.
2. Time-bounded *reachability analysis* and *temporal logic model checking* of
   all possible behaviors from some initial state *with respect to the particular
   values generated by the pseudo-random generator*. That is, our analysis is
   incomplete since we do *not* analyze all possible behaviors for a given network topology, but only those that can take place with the specific choice of
   pseudo-random numbers used to simulate the probabilistic behavior. Nevertheless, such analysis covers *many* different behaviors from a given state.

In our experiments, we use the same values for parameters such as sensing range
($10m$), length of a round (1000 seconds), power consumption, transmission times,
etc., as in the ns-2 simulations in [22]. In those simulations, 100 to 1000 nodes
were "uniformly randomly distributed" in a $50m \times 50m$ sensing area.

5.1   Defining Initial States and the Time Sampling Strategy

To easily simulate large sensor networks with different node locations and initial
seeds, we define a function `genInitConf` to generate initial states. The term
`genInitConf`(n, *seed*) defines a configuration with n sensor nodes scattered at
pseudo-random locations within the sensing area, as well as a `RandomNGen` object

with starting seed computed from the initial seed *seed*. (An initial state must also add the operator `{_}`.) We can therefore generate initial states with any number of nodes, and/or place them in different locations, by just changing the parameters *n* and/or *seed* in `genInitConf`.

In the following definition, each generated sensor node location $x . y$ will have $0 \leq x \leq$ `Xsize` and $0 \leq y \leq$ `Ysize` (since `rem` is the remainder function):

```
op genInitConf : Nat Nat -> Configuration .
op genInitConf : Nat Nat Nat -> Configuration .

vars M SEED N : Nat .

eq genInitConf(N, SEED) = genInitConf(N, SEED, N) .

ceq genInitConf(M, SEED, N) =
        if M == 0 then
        --- no more nodes to generate; generate RandomNGen object:
            < Random : RandomNGen | seed : SEED >
        else    --- more nodes to generate:
            < L : WSNode | remainingPower : lifetime, status : undecided,
                           neighbors : none, bitmap : initBitmap(L),
                           uncoveredCrossings : none, backoffTimer : INF,
                           roundTimer : roundTime, volunteerProb : 1000 / N,
                           hasVolunteered : undecided >
            --- and generate the remaining M-1 nodes:
            genInitConf(M - 1, random(random(SEED)), N)
        fi
    if L := random(SEED) rem (Xsize + 1) .          --- x part of L
            random(random(SEED)) rem (Ysize + 1) . --- y part of L
```

Each generated `WSNode` gets the appropriate initial values for its attributes. The third argument to the `genInitConf` in the main equation is needed to store the total number of nodes in the system (`N`) so that the `volunteerProb` attribute gets the correct initial value.

A time sampling strategy guiding the execution of the tick rule must be chosen before any analysis can take place. Since all events in the OGDC algorithm happen at specific times, we have shown in [16] that we can "fast forward" between these events without losing any interesting behaviors. Therefore, in our analysis, we use the *maximal* time sampling strategy declared by the Real-Time Maude command (`set tick max def roundTime .`) which advances time as much as possible, and corresponds to "event-driven simulation."

5.2   The ns-2 Simulations of OGDC in Real-Time Maude

In [22], Zhang and Hou use the network simulation tool *ns-2* [12], with the wireless extension developed by the CMU Monarch group [4], to simulate the OGDC algorithm and measure the following essential *performance metrics*:

- The number of *active* nodes and the percentage of sensing area coverage provided by those nodes at the end of the first round.
- The percentage of sensing area coverage and the total amount of remaining power for the whole system throughout the network's lifetime.
- The total time during which at least α percent of the sensing area is covered. (This can be done in the same way as the first two, and is not treated here.)

We cannot use Real-Time Maude's timed rewrite command *directly* to perform the corresponding analysis, since these performance metrics should be measured at different points in time *throughout* the lifetime of the system, and since the metrics themselves do not appear explicitly in the state. Therefore, we add to the initial state a *record object* that uses a timer to compute a performance metric at the same time (e.g., just before the end of the round) in each round during a simulation of the OGDC algorithm. The computed values are stored in an attribute of the record object as a list n_1 ++ n_2 ++ $\cdots$ ++ n_k, where n_i denotes the value of the metric at the end of round i. Given a sort NatList of lists of natural numbers, with concatenation operator _++_ and empty list nil, we can declare the record object class as follows:

```
class RecActNodes | activeNodes : NatList, timer : TimeInf .
ops r1 r2 r3 : -> Oid [ctor] .    --- names of record objects
```

The following rule applies when the timer of the record object expires. It computes and stores the number of active nodes in the system, and *resets* the timer in order for it to be expire again at the same time in the *next* round:

```
var SYSTEM : Configuration .   var NL : NatList .   var O : Oid .
rl [computeNumActiveNodes]  :
   {< O : RecActNodes | activeNodes : NL, timer : 0 >  SYSTEM}
   =>
   {< O : RecActNodes | activeNodes : NL ++ numActiveNodes(SYSTEM),
                        timer : roundTime >  SYSTEM}  .
```

The function numActiveNodes computes the number of active nodes in a configuration. In the same way, we define record object classes RecCoverage% and RecTotalPower, which compute, respectively, the percentage of the sensing area covered by the active nodes and the total amount of power in the system.

The first simulations in [22] investigate the number of active nodes and the percentage of coverage in the *first* round of the algorithm. The following timed fair rewrite command simulates a system with 600 nodes (in a $50m \times 50m$ sensing area) until the end of the first round of the protocol (in time < roundTime). The initial state contains two record objects, whose metrics will be computed when their timers expire just before the end of the first round (roundTime - 1):

```
Maude> (tfrew {genInitConf(600, 1)
              < r1 : RecActNodes | activeNodes : nil,
                                   timer : roundTime - 1 >
              < r2 : RecCoverage% | cov% : nil, timer : roundTime - 1 >}
          in time < roundTime .)
```

```
Result ClockedSystem :
  {< r1 : RecActNodes | activeNodes : 45, timer : 1000000 >
   < r2 : RecCoverage% | cov% : 100, timer : 1000000 >
   ... }  in time 999999
```

As shown in the analysis messages, 45 of the 600 deployed nodes became
active nodes and together provided 100% coverage of the sensing area.

Zhang and Hou then measure how coverage and total remaining power changes
over time. The following rewrite command simulates 50 rounds of the algorithm
(in time < roundTime * 50) with 200 nodes in the $50m \times 50m$ sensing area:

```
Maude> (tfrew {genInitConf(200, 313)
              < r1 : RecCoverage% | cov% : nil, timer : roundTime - 1 >
              < r2 : RecTotalPower | power : nil, timer : roundTime - 1 >}
          in time < roundTime * 50 .)
```

```
Result ClockedSystem :
  {< r1 : RecCoverage% | cov% : 100 ++ ... ++ 100 ++ 98 ++ ... ++ 100 ++ 94
                          ++ 88 ++ ... ++ 13 ++ 0 ++ ... ++ 0), ... >
   < r2 : RecTotalPower | power : 384639803547 ++ 370475585958 ++ ...
                          ++ 371677818 ++ 0 ++ ... ++ 0), ... >
   ... }  in time 49999999
```

The result shows that the nodes can provide 100% coverage for 19 rounds,
with a decrease of coverage in certain intermediate rounds.

5.3 Comparison with the ns-2 Simulations

The table on the next page compares our simulation results with the ns-2 simulation results in [22]. Our simulations show a higher number of active nodes
(more than twice as many, in fact) and a correspondingly shorter network lifetime. Furthermore, in contrast to the ns-2 simulations, we get more active nodes
when more nodes are deployed in the same area. These differences cannot be explained by us ignoring packet collisions in our simulations, since [22] states that
"the number of working nodes may *increase*" in the presence of message losses.
The most plausible explanation for the different results is instead the following:
In OGDC, if two nodes are close to one another, then the difference between
their backoff timers is smaller than the transmission delay. If transmission delays are ignored during the simulations, potentially because the simulation tool
makes it inconvenient to simulate such delays, then only one of the neighbors will
become active. However, if, as in our case, we capture transmission delays, then
the backoff timer of the "worse" node will expire *before* it receives the power-on
message from the "better" node, and, hence, *both* nodes will become active.

We have, unfortunately, not been able to get an answer to whether or not the ns-2 simulations in [22] actually took the transmission delays into account, although the second author told us it is quite likely that they did not. Therefore, we have also performed the simulations *without* transmission delays (by just removing the dly-part from the single messages created by the broadcast). The following table shows the results of the ns-2 simulations, as well as of the Real-Time Maude simulations both with and without transmission delays, for finding the number of active nodes at the end of the first round for 200, 400, and 600 nodes in the same $50m \times 50m$ area. For the Real-Time Maude simulations, each number represents the average result of five simulations, obtained by using five different initial seeds (and hence getting five different placements of the nodes):

Number of nodes in sensing area	200	400	600
# active nodes in ns-2 simulations	17	18	18
# active nodes in Real-Time Maude simulations *with* trans. delay	34	45	55
# active nodes in Real-Time Maude simulations *without* trans. delay	21	22	22

Indeed, the results of the Real-Time Maude simulations that ignore transmission delays are quite similar to the results of the ns-2 simulations. It is therefore tempting to conjecture that our Real-Time Maude simulations *with* transmission delays give a reasonably accurate estimate of the performance of OGDC in such a setting. In that case, one can conclude that the results of ns-2 simulations are actually quite misleading and that our formal model provides a more accurate simulation setting for OGDC than ns-2 with the wireless extension.

5.4 Further Real-Time Maude Analysis of the OGDC Algorithm

We give some examples of how we can further formally analyze correctness and worst-case performance of the OGDC algorithm by using Real-Time Maude's search and model checking capabilities. Due to the large states involved, we restrict such analyses to systems with 5 to 6 nodes (in a $25m \times 25m$ area), which is much fewer nodes than in a real WSN. Nevertheless, exhaustive analysis with 3 to 4 nodes has uncovered subtle bugs in cryptographic protocols [9] and other kinds of network protocols (e.g., [18]).

The following find latest command finds the *latest* possible time the network enters the steady state phase (such that steadyStatePhase(...)), and thereby also finds out whether this phase is *always* reached in the first round.

```
Maude> (find latest {genInitConf(6, 75)} =>* {C:Configuration}
                    such that steadyStatePhase(C:Configuration)
       in time < roundTime .)

Result: { ... } in time 372
```

That is, the system will reach the steady state phase in *at most* 372 ms. One round of the OGDC algorithm is 1000 *seconds*, which means that the network spends most of its lifetime performing its sensing task.

Another correctness requirement is that the network stays in the steady state phase throughout the first round, once this phase has been reached. We use Real-Time Maude's temporal logic model checker, and define an atomic proposition `steady-state` to hold when the network is in steady state phase:

```
op steady-state : -> Prop [ctor] .
eq {C} |= steady-state = steadyStatePhase(C) .
```

The following command checks whether all states following a state in the steady state phase are also in this phase (*A* => *B* is an abbreviation for [] (*A* -> *B*)).

```
Maude> (mc {genInitConf(5,341)} |=t (steady-state => [] steady-state)
             in time < roundTime .)
```

```
Result Bool : true
```

The most important correctness criterion is that the entire sensing area is covered by the *active* nodes when the system is in the steady state phase (and *all* nodes together cover the entire area and each node has power to last to the end of the round). The following command searches for a state which is in steady state but where the entire $20m \times 20m$ `sensingArea` is *not* covered by the active nodes:

```
Maude> (tsearch [1]
          {genInitConf(5,97)} =>* {C:Configuration}
            such that steadyStatePhase(C:Configuration) /\
                    not coverageAreaCovered(updateArea(sensingArea,
                                                       C:Configuration))
          in time < roundTime .)
```

The function `updateArea` updates the bitmap by changing bits that are covered by the *active* nodes in C to t. The command returned 'No solution.'

Performance figures. The following table shows, for each command presented in this paper, and for the above search command with a different topology (given by seed 1) which does *not* cover the sensing area: the number of sensor nodes; execution time; and memory usage when executed on a 3.6 GHz Intel Xeon:

tfrew 1 rd	tfrew 1 rd	tfrew 1 rd	tfrew 50 rds	find	mc	tsearch	tsearch
200	400	600	200	6	5	6, s=1	5, s=7197
180 sec	1243 sec	5034 sec	4931 sec	4187 sec	26 sec	679 sec	227 sec
85 MB	100 MB	112 MB	93 MB	525 MB	147 MB	1.3 GB	430 MB

The paper [22] does not mention the performance of their ns-2 simulations.

6   Concluding Remarks

Wireless sensor networks are a new kind of network whose modeling, simulation, and/or analysis pose a set of challenges to both network simulation tools and formal tools. OGDC is a state-of-the-art WSN algorithm where new forms of communication and advanced data types must be captured at an appropriate level of abstraction. In this paper we have shown how OGDC was formally specified, simulated, and analyzed using Real-Time Maude. To the best of our knowledge, this is the first formal analysis of an advanced WSN algorithm. Our formal specification captures the behavior of the algorithm at a high level of abstraction and—being precise, intuitive, and operational—could make a good starting point for an implementation of the OGDC algorithm on sensor networks.

We could measure *all* performance metrics measured in the ns-2 simulations in [22] during our "Monte Carlo" simulations. Our simulations showed significantly worse performance of the OGDC algorithm than the ns-2 simulations. Trying to understand why—unlike in the ns-2 simulations—we got more active nodes when more nodes were deployed in the same sensing area, we found that the "tie-breaking" mechanism in OGDC does not break many ties when transmission delays are taken into account. To check this hypothesis, we also simulated OGDC in Real-Time Maude in a setting *without* transmission delays, and got results that were similar to the ns-2 results. It is therefore quite likely that our simulations, which take the delays into account, provide much more accurate performance estimates than the ns-2 simulations that may have ignored such delays. Furthermore, based on communication with Jennifer Hou, it seems that developing the Real-Time Maude specification and performing the Real-Time Maude analysis required much less effort than using a specialized network simulation tool to analyze OGDC.

Our work should continue in different directions. First, we focus on simplicity and elegance when modeling coverage areas and defining functions on such areas. There is a price to pay for this when we have hundreds of nodes, each with a bitmap with 400 "bits." Therefore, more efficient representations of coverage areas should be developed. This would enable us to perform search and model checking on larger networks.

Second, we have not modeled probabilistic behaviors as such, but have used a "sampling" technique for simulation purposes. This means that we cannot reason about probabilistic properties. We should therefore combine Real-Time Maude with methods and tools for probabilistic systems, such as PMaude [1], and should develop methods to fruitfully analyze probabilistic real-time specifications.

Finally, we should also capture message losses due to packet collisions.

Acknowledgments. We are grateful to Jennifer Hou for suggesting the OGDC algorithm as a challenging modeling task, and for discussions on sensor networks, to José Meseguer for discussions on modeling communication in sensor networks, and to the anonymous reviewers for helpful comments on earlier versions of this paper. Support by the Research Council of Norway is also gratefully acknowledged.

References

1. Agha, G., Meseguer, J., Sen, K.: PMaude: Rewrite-based specification language for probabilistic object systems. In: Proc. QAPL'05 (2005)
2. Akyildiz, I.F., Su, W., Sankarasubramaniam, Y., Cayirci, E.: Wireless sensor networks: A survey. Computer Networks 38, 393–422 (2002)
3. Clavel, M., Dúran, F., Eker, S., Lincoln, P., Martí-Oliet, N., Meseguer, J., Talcott, C.: Maude Manual (Version 2.2), December 2005. http://maude.cs.uiuc.edu (2005)
4. CMU monarch extensions to ns. http://www.monarch.cs.cmu.edu/
5. Coleri, S., Ergen, M., Koo, T.J.: Lifetime analysis of a sensor network with hybrid automata modelling. In: WSNA '02, ACM Press, New York (2002)
6. Kim, M., Dutt, N., Venkatasubramanian, N.: Policy construction and validation for energy minimization in cross layered systems: A formal method approach. In: IEEE RTAS'06 Work-in-Progress Session, pp. 25–28. IEEE Computer Society Press, Los Alamitos (2006)
7. Knuth, D.E.: The Art of Computer Programming: Seminumerical Algorithms, 2nd edn., vol. 2. Addison-Wesley, London, UK (1981)
8. Lien, E.: Formal modelling and analysis of the NORM multicast protocol using Real-Time Maude. Master's thesis, Dept. of Linguistics, University of Oslo (2004)
9. Lowe, G.: An attack on the Needham-Schroeder public-key authentication protocol. Information Processing Letters 56, 131–133 (1995)
10. Meseguer, J.: Membership algebra as a logical framework for equational specification. In: Parisi-Presicce, F. (ed.) WADT 1997. LNCS, vol. 1376, Springer, Heidelberg (1998)
11. Nair, S., Cardell-Oliver, R.: Formal specification and analysis of performance variation in sensor network diffusion protocols. In: MSWiM '04, ACM Press, New York (2004)
12. ns-2 network simulator. http://www.isi.edu/nsnam/ns
13. Ölveczky, P.C., Caccamo, M.: Formal simulation and analysis of the CASH scheduling algorithm in Real-Time Maude. In: Baresi, L., Heckel, R. (eds.) FASE 2006 and ETAPS 2006. LNCS, vol. 3922, pp. 357–372. Springer, Heidelberg (2006)
14. Ölveczky, P.C., Meseguer, J.: Specification of real-time and hybrid systems in rewriting logic. Theoretical Computer Science 285, 359–405 (2002)
15. Ölveczky, P.C., Meseguer, J.: Specification and analysis of real-time systems using Real-Time Maude. In: Wermelinger, M., Margaria-Steffen, T. (eds.) FASE 2004. LNCS, vol. 2984, Springer, Heidelberg (2004)
16. Ölveczky, P.C., Meseguer, J.: Abstraction and completeness for Real-Time Maude. In: Proc. WRLA'06 (2006)
17. Ölveczky, P.C., Meseguer, J.: Semantics and pragmatics of Real-Time Maude. Higher-Order and Symbolic Computation, To appear (2007)
18. Ölveczky, P.C., Meseguer, J., Talcott, C.L.: Specification and analysis of the AER/NCA active network protocol suite in Real-Time Maude. Formal Methods in System Design 29, 253–293 (2006)
19. Ölveczky, P.C., Thorvaldsen, S.: Formal modeling and analysis of wireless sensor network algorithms in Real-Time Maude. In: IPDPS 2006, IEEE, NJ, New York (2006)

20. Rodríguez, D.E.: On modelling sensor networks in Maude. In: Proc. WRLA 2006 (2006)
21. Thorvaldsen, S., Ölveczky, P.C.: Formal modeling and analysis of the OGDC wireless sensor network algorithm in Real-Time Maude. Manuscript. http://www.ifi.uio.no/RealTimeMaude/OGDC (Oct. 2005)
22. Zhang, H., Hou, J.C.: Maintaining sensing coverage and connectivity in large sensor networks. Wireless Ad Hoc and Sensor Networks: An International Journal, vol. 1 (2005)

Adaptation of Open Component-Based Systems

Pascal Poizat[1,2] and Gwen Salaün[3]

[1] IBISC FRE 2873 CNRS – University of Evry Val d'Essonne, France
[2] ARLES project, INRIA Rocquencourt, France
`pascal.poizat@inria.fr`
[3] Department of Computer Science, University of Málaga, Spain
`salaun@lcc.uma.es`

Abstract. Software adaptation aims at generating software pieces called adaptors to compensate interface and behavioural mismatch between components or services. This is crucial to foster reuse. So far, adaptation techniques have proceeded by computing *global adaptors for closed systems* made up of a fixed set of components. This is not satisfactory when the systems may evolve, with components entering or leaving it at any time, *e.g.*, for pervasive computing. To enable adaptation on such systems, we propose tool-equipped adaptation techniques for the computation of *open systems adaptors*. Our proposal also support *incremental adaptation* to avoid the computation of global adaptors.

1 Introduction

Compared to hardware components, software components (or services) are seldom reusable *as is* due to possible mismatch that may appear at different levels [10]: signature, behaviour, quality of service and semantics. Once detected, mismatch has to be corrected. However, it is not possible to impact directly on the components source due to their black-box nature. *Software adaptation* [27,10] aims at generating, as automatically as possible, pieces of software called *adaptors* which are used to solve mismatch in a *non intrusive* way. To this purpose, model-based adaptation techniques base upon behavioural component interface descriptions and abstract properties of the adaptation called *adaptation contracts* or *mappings*. Dedicated middleware [2] can be used to put the adaptation process into action once an adaptor model (or implementation) has been obtained, but this is out of scope here.

Existing (global) adaptation approaches [27,21,14,8,11] proceed by generating a *global adaptor* for the whole system which is seen as a *closed* one. First of all this is costly. Moreover, when a component uses a service which does not relate through mapping to the other components' services, then either its use is prevented by adaptation (to avoid deadlock), or it is made internal (related events sent by the component are absorbed by the adaptor). Taking into account that new components, and hence new services, may be available in the future is not possible. Global adaptation approaches suffer from the fact that the adaptor has to be computed each time something changes in the system and are therefore not efficient in contexts such as pervasive systems [20], where services are not

M.M. Bonsangue and E.B. Johnsen (Eds.): FMOODS 2007, LNCS 4468, pp. 141–156, 2007.

fixed or known from scratch. They may evolve, *e.g.*, depending on the mobility of the user –moving around, different services are discovered and may be used, or on connectivity or management issues –some services may be temporary or definitely unavailable. In this paper we address these issues by extending a previous work for the adaptation of closed systems [11] in order to support (i) the *adaptation of open systems* and accordingly, (ii) an *incremental process for the integration and adaptation of open software components*. The definitions and algorithms we present have been implemented in Adaptor [1], our tool for model-based adaptation.

The paper is structured as follows. Section 2 presents our open systems component model and our adaptation techniques for such systems. In Section 3, we present the incremental adaptation of open systems, addressing the addition and the removal of components. Incremental adaptation has an added value at design-time, where the integration of components is known to be a difficult task, which gets worse when components have not been designed altogether from the beginning and therefore when adaptation connectors are needed. This typical use of the incremental adaptation of open systems is illustrated in Section 4. We end with comparison of related work and concluding remarks.

2   Open Systems Adaptation

In this section we address the adaptation of open systems. We first recall a formal model for basic sequential components originating from [11]. Then we define an open composition model on top of it thanks to the definition of (i) compositional vectors, (ii) open synchronous product and (iii) open component-based systems and their semantics. In a second step, our adaptation algorithms are presented.

2.1   Components

Alphabets, the basis for interaction, correspond to an event-based signature. An alphabet A is a set of service names, divided in provided services, $A^?$ (elements denoted as $e?$), required services, $A^!$ (elements denoted as $e!$) and internal actions (denoted with τ). The mirror operation on an alphabet element is defined as $\overline{e?} = e!$, $\overline{e!} = e?$, and $\overline{\tau} = \tau$. Moreover, for an alphabet A, $\overline{A} = \{\overline{e} \mid e \in A\}$.

Component interfaces are given using a signature and a behavioural interface. A *signature* is a set of operation profiles as in usual component IDLs. This set is a disjoint union of *provided* operations and *required* operations. *Behavioural interfaces* are described in a concise way using a sequential process algebra, sequential CCS: P ::= 0 | a?.P | a!.P | τ.P | P1+P2 | A, where 0 denotes termination, a?.P (resp. a!.P) a process which receives a (resp. sends it) and then behaves as P, τ.P a process which evolves with the internal action τ (also denoted using tau in figures) and behaves as P, P1+P2 a process that acts either as P1 or P2, and A the call to a process defined by an equation A = P, enabling recursion. The CSS notation is extended using tags to support the definition of initial ([i]) and final states ([f]). 0 and 0[f] are equivalent. In order to define adaptation algorithms, we use the process algebra operational semantics to retrieve *Labelled Transition Systems* (LTS) from the interfaces, *i.e.*, tuples $\langle A, S, I, F, T \rangle$ where A is the alphabet (set of communication events), S is the set of states, $I \in S$ is the initial state, $F \subseteq S$ is the set of final states, and $T \subseteq S \times A \times S$ are the transitions. The alphabet of a component LTS is built on this component's signature. This means that for each provided operation p in the signature, there is an element $p?$ in the alphabet, and for each required operation r, an element $r!$.

2.2   Open Component Systems

Vectors are an expressive mechanism to denote communication and express correspondences between events in different processes. In this work vectors are extended to take into account open systems and keep track of their structuring. For this purpose, vectors are defined with reference to an (external) alphabet which relates component events to composite systems external interfaces (see Defs. 3 and 4, below).

Definition 1 ((Compositional) Vector). *A compositional vector (or vector for short) v for a set of LTSs $L_i = \langle A_i, S_i, I_i, F_i, T_i \rangle, i \in \{1, \ldots, n\}$ and an (external) alphabet A_{ext} is an element of $A_{\mathrm{ext}} \times (A_1 \cup \{\varepsilon\}) \times \ldots \times (A_n \cup \{\varepsilon\})$. Such a vector is denoted $e : \langle l_1, \ldots, l_n \rangle$ where $e \in A_{\mathrm{ext}}$ and for every i in $\{1, \ldots, n\}$, $l_i \in A_i \cup \{\varepsilon\}$. ε is used in vectors to denote a component which does not participate in a communication.*

The definition of an open synchronous product yields a tree-shaped structure for labels which makes it possible to keep trace of the structuring of composite components. When needed we may restrict to the observable part of labels, defined as $\mathrm{obs}(e : \langle l_1, \ldots, l_n \rangle) = e$. Moreover, labels of simple LTS can be related to composite ones using $l : \langle l \rangle$ for any label l.

Definition 2 (Open Synchronous Product). *The open synchronous product of n LTSs $L_i, i \in \{1, \ldots, n\}$ with reference to a set of vectors V (defined over these LTSs and an external alphabet A_{ext}) is the LTS $\Pi((L_1, \ldots, L_n), A_{\mathrm{ext}}, V) = \langle A, S, I, F, T \rangle$ such that: $A = A_{\mathrm{ext}} \times A_1 \times \ldots \times A_n$, $S = S_1 \times \ldots \times S_n$, $I = (I_1, \ldots, I_n)$, $F = F_1 \times \ldots \times F_n$, and T contains a transition $((s_1, \ldots, s_n), e : \langle a_1, \ldots, a_n \rangle, (s'_1, \ldots, s'_n))$ iff there is a state $(s_1, \ldots, s_n)$ in S, there is a vector $e : \langle l_1, \ldots, l_n \rangle$ in V and for every i in $\{1, \ldots, n\}$:*

- *if $l_i = \varepsilon$ then $s'_i = s_i$ and $a_i = \varepsilon$,*
- *otherwise there is a transition (s_i, a_i, s'_i) with $\mathrm{obs}(a_i) = l_i$ in T_i.*

Remark. In practice, we reduce S (resp. F) to elements of S (resp. F) which are reachable from I using T.

Example 1. Let us suppose we have two LTSs, L_1 and L_2, with one transition each: $(I_1, a?, S_1)$ for L_1 and $(I_2, b!, S_2)$ for L_2. Different sets of vectors may express different communication semantics:

- $\{\tau : \langle a?, b! \rangle\}$ (services $a?$ and $b!$ being synchronised) will produce a product LTS with a single transition: $((I_1, I_2), \tau : \langle a?, b! \rangle, (S_1, S_2))$;

- $\{a? : \langle a?, \varepsilon \rangle, \ b! : \langle \varepsilon, b! \rangle\}$ (services $a?$ and $b!$ left open to the environment)
  will produce a product LTS with four transitions:
  $((I_1, I_2), a? : \langle a?, \varepsilon \rangle, (S_1, I_2)), ((I_1, I_2), b! : \langle \varepsilon, b! \rangle, (I_1, S_2)),$
  $((S_1, I_2), b! : \langle \varepsilon, b! \rangle, (S_1, S_2)), ((I_1, S_2), a? : \langle a?, \varepsilon \rangle, (S_1, S_2)).$

If we take this second case into account and make a product with an LTS L_3
with two transitions, $(I_3, c!, S_3)$ and $(S_3, d?, S_3')$, and vectors $\{\tau : \langle a?, c! \rangle, \ \tau :$
$\langle b!, d? \rangle\}$, we get a product LTS with two transitions:
  $(((I_1, I_2), I_3), \tau : \langle a? : \langle a?, \varepsilon \rangle, c! \rangle, ((S_1, I_2), S_3)),$
  $(((S_1, I_2), S_3), \tau : \langle b! : \langle \varepsilon, b! \rangle, d? \rangle, ((S_1, S_2), S_3')).$

Composites denote sets of hierarchical connected open components.

Definition 3 (Composite (or Open Component System)). *A composite
is a tuple $\langle C, A_{ext}, B_{int}, B_{ext} \rangle$ where:*

- *C is a set of component instances, i.e., an Id-indexed set of LTS $L_i, i \in Id$
  (Id usually corresponds to the integers $\{1, \ldots, n\}$),*
- *A_{ext} is an (external) alphabet,*
- *B_{int} is a set of vectors, with each vector $e : \langle l_1, \ldots, l_n \rangle$ in B_{int} being such that
  $e = \tau$, there is some i in $\{1, \ldots, n\}$ such that $l_i \neq \varepsilon$ and there is at most one
  j in $\{1, \ldots, n\}\backslash\{i\}$ such that $l_j \neq \varepsilon$. B_{int} denotes internal (hidden) bindings
  between the composite sub-components, When clear from the context, such
  vectors can be denoted as couples (l_i, l_j),*
- *B_{ext} is a set of vectors, with each vector $e : \langle l_1, \ldots, l_n \rangle$ in B_{ext} being such
  that $e \neq \tau$, there is some i in $\{1, \ldots, n\}$ such that $l_i \neq \varepsilon$, and for every k in
  $\{1, \ldots, n\}\backslash\{i\}$, $l_k = \varepsilon$. B_{ext} denotes external bindings between the composite sub-components and the composite interface itself. When clear from the
  context, such vectors can be denoted as couples (e, l_i).*

Our structure of composites supports (through model transformation) existing
hierarchical ADLs such as the Fractal one [9] or UML 2.0 component
diagrams [17]. Note that with reference to these models we have an exact correspondence between their notions of component ports and component interfaces
in what we call alphabets. Our model for bindings is more expressive than the
Fractal ADL or UML 2.0 ones as we enable bindings between services with different names, which is mandatory to support adaptation.

Example 2. Let us take a component system described in an ADL (Fig. 1)
where a batch processing client interacts with a database server to perform SQL
requests. Our graphical notation is inspired from Fractal ADL, yet a textual
notation is also supported. This model can be transformed into the following
composite structure:

$\langle$ {Client,SQLServer}, {launch?,exitCode!},
  {(log!,id?), (request!,sqlQuery?), (reply?,sqlValues!), (reply?,sqlError!), (end!,ε)},
  {(launch?,run?), (exitCode!,exitCode!)} $\rangle$.

Open synchronous product is used to give a formal semantics to composites.

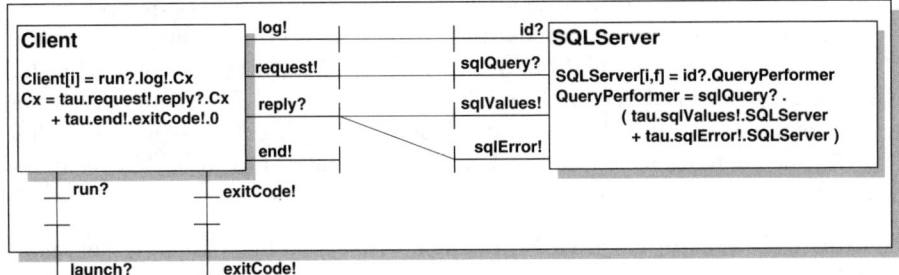

Fig. 1. The Client and SQLServer Example Architecture

Definition 4 (Composite Semantics). *The semantics of a composite $\mathcal{C} = \langle C, A_{\text{ext}}, B_{\text{int}}, B_{\text{ext}} \rangle$ is the LTS $L(\mathcal{C}) = \Pi(C, A_{\text{ext}}, \mathcal{V})$ with $\mathcal{V} = B_{\text{int}} \cup B_{\text{ext}} \cup B_\tau$ where $B_\tau = \bigcup_{i \in \{1, \dots, n\}} \{b_{\tau,i}\}$ and $b_{\tau,i} = \tau : \langle l_1, \dots, l_n \rangle$ where $l_i = \tau$ and $l_k = \varepsilon$ for every k in $\{1, \dots, n\} \setminus \{i\}$.*

In presence of several hierarchical levels (composites of composites), composite sub-components are first translated into LTSs using their semantics (Def. 4), *e.g.*, the semantics of a composite $\mathcal{C} = \langle \{C_1, \dots, C_n\}, A_{\text{ext}}, B_{\text{int}}, B_{\text{ext}} \rangle$ where some C_i is a composite can be obtained replacing C_i by $L(C_i)$ in $\mathcal{C}$.

2.3 Mismatch and Mappings

Composition correctness is defined in the literature [10] either at the composition model level – using deadlock freedom – or at the components' protocols level – using compatibility or substitutability notions. As we want to use compositions in finding ways to correct mismatching components, we rely on the first approach. States without outgoing transitions are legal if they correspond to final states of the composed components. Therefore, we define *deadlock* (and hence mismatch) for a composite with a semantics $\langle A, S, I, F, T \rangle$ as a state $s \in S$ of the composition which has no outgoing transition ($\nexists (s, l, s') \in T$) and is not final ($s \notin F$). A deadlock is a state of the composition in which respective component protocols are incompatible, due to signature and/or behavioural mismatch. Note that if the former one can be solved using correspondences and renaming, the latter one requires more subtle techniques. This is also the case when correspondences evolve over time (*e.g.*, in Example 4 below, id? in SQLServer corresponds first to log! in Client and later on to nothing).

Example 3. Let us get back to the composite presented in Example 2. Mismatch in the example is due first to mismatching names. Moreover, even with an agreement on the service names, the fact that the client works in a connected mode (sending its log only once and disconnecting with end) while the server works in a non connected mode (requiring an id at each request) will also lead to behavioural mismatch after the first request of the client has been processed by the server.

We propose regular expressions of open vectors as the means to express adaptation contracts. A regular expression (or regex for short) over some basic domain $\mathcal{D}$ is the set of all terms build on: d (ATOM), $R1.R2$ (SEQUENCE), $R1 + R2$ (CHOICE), $R1*$ (ITERATION) and N (USE), with $d \in \mathcal{D}$, $R1$ and $R2$ being regular expressions, and N being an identifier referring to a regex definition $N = R$. Such definitions can be used to structure regex but we forbid recursive definitions for operational reasons.

Definition 5 ((Adaptation) Mapping). *An adaptation mapping (or mapping for short) for a composite* $\mathcal{C} = \langle C, A_{\mathrm{ext}}, B_{\mathrm{int}}, B_{\mathrm{ext}} \rangle$ *is a couple* (V, R) *where* V *is a set of (compositional) vectors for the LTSs in* C *and* A_{ext}, *and* R *is a regular expression over* V.

Example 4. To work our system out, one easily guesses that the client has first to be launched, to connect, the system then runs for some time and finally the client disconnects and exits. This is specified for example using the mapping $\mathsf{M}=\mathsf{v}_{\mathsf{launch}}.\mathsf{v}_{\mathsf{cx}}.\mathsf{M}_{\mathsf{run}}.\mathsf{v}_{\mathsf{dx}}.\mathsf{v}_{\mathsf{exit}}$ with vectors $\mathsf{v}_{\mathsf{launch}}=\mathsf{launch}?:<\mathsf{run}?, \varepsilon>$, $\mathsf{v}_{\mathsf{cx}}= \tau :<\mathsf{log}!,\mathsf{id}?>$, $\mathsf{v}_{\mathsf{dx}}= \tau :<\mathsf{end}!, \varepsilon >$, and $\mathsf{v}_{\mathsf{exit}}=\mathsf{exitCode}!:<\mathsf{exitCode}!, \varepsilon >$. Yet, it is more complicated to know what should be done while the system runs ($\mathsf{M}_{\mathsf{run}}$), excepted of course that events are exchanged for requests/results and that somehow a reset (resending the client identification) should be used. Therefore, one may choose to keep this part of the mapping abstract: $\mathsf{M}_{\mathsf{run}}= (\mathsf{v}_{\mathsf{req}}+\mathsf{v}_{\mathsf{res}}+\mathsf{v}_{\mathsf{err}}+\mathsf{v}_{\mathsf{reset}})^*$ with vectors $\mathsf{v}_{\mathsf{req}}= \tau :<\mathsf{request}!,\mathsf{sqlQuery}?>$, $\mathsf{v}_{\mathsf{res}}= \tau :<\mathsf{reply}?,\mathsf{sqlValues}!>$, $\mathsf{v}_{\mathsf{err}}= \tau :<\mathsf{reply}?,\mathsf{sqlError}!>$, and $\mathsf{v}_{\mathsf{reset}}= \tau :< \varepsilon,\mathsf{id}?>$.

Discussion on the mapping notation. Mappings are made up of the definition of possible correspondences (vectors) and a dynamic description over such correspondences (regex). Several behavioural languages may be used to this purpose. We have presented regex for their simplicity. However, the only requirement for the algorithms presented in Section 2.4 to work is to be able to obtain from the mapping an LTS where transitions are labelled by vectors (Algorithm 1, line 13). Currently, Adaptor supports both regex and the direct use of LTS. Message Sequence Charts (MSC) where arrows are labelled by vectors are a user-friendly alternative. LTS can be obtained from MSC using, *e.g.*, [24]. We are also investigating the use of techniques from the composition of Web services [6] in order to get automatically possible correspondences between services (vectors) and ease the user task in the context of end-user composition in pervasive systems.

2.4 Algorithms

Using a mapping and component behavioural interfaces, an adaptor can be generated automatically for a closed system following results from, *e.g.*, [21,14,8,11]. Here, our algorithms (Alg. 1 and 2) enable adaptation on open systems. Algorithm 1, works by translating into a Petri net [16] the constraints of a correct adaptor. This choice is done as Petri nets enable to see messages exchanged between components as resources of the adaptor, to de-synchronise messages and

---

Algorithm 1. build_PetriNet

inputs mapping M, components $C_1, \ldots, C_n$ with each $C_i = \langle A_i, S_i, I_i, F_i, T_i \rangle$
outputs Petri net $\mathcal{N}$

1: $\mathcal{N} := $ empty_PetriNet() // *all remaining actions operate on* $\mathcal{N}$
2: **for all** $C_i = \langle A_i, S_i, I_i, F_i, T_i \rangle, i \in \{1, \ldots, n\}$ **do**
3:     **for all** $s_j \in S_i$ **do** add a place [i@s_j] **end for**
4:     put a token in place [i@I_i] // I_i *is the initial state of* C_i
5:     **for all** $a! \in A_i$ **do** add a place ??a **end for**
6:     **for all** $a? \in A_i$ **do** add a place !!a **end for**
7:     **for all** $(s, e, s') \in T_i$ with $l = \text{obs}(e)$ **do**
8:         add a transition with label $\bar{l}$, an arc from place [i@s] to the transition and an arc from the transition to place [i@s']
9:         **if** l has the form $a!$ **then** add an arc from the transition to place ??a **end if**
10:         **if** l has the form $a?$ **then** add an arc from place !!a to the transition **end if**
11:     **end for**
12: **end for**
13: $L_R = (A_R, S_R, I_R, F_R, T_R) := $ get_LTS_from_regex(R) // *see [13]*
14: **for all** $s_R \in S_R$ **do** add a place [R@s_R] **end for**
15: put a token in place [R@I_R] // I_R *is the initial state of* L_R
16: **for all** $t_R = (s_R, e : \langle e_1, \ldots, e_n \rangle, s'_R) \in T_R$ with $\forall i \in \{1, \ldots, n\}$ $l_i = \text{obs}(e_i)$ **do**
17:     add a transition with label e, an arc from place [R@s_R] to the transition and an arc from the transition to place [R@s'_R]
18:     **for all** l_i **do**
19:         **if** l_i has the form $a!$ **then** add an arc from place ??a to the transition **end if**
20:         **if** l_i has the form $a?$ **then** add an arc from the transition to place !!a **end if**
21:     **end for**
22: **end for**
23: **for all** $(f_r, f_1, \ldots, f_n) \in F_R \times F_1 \times \ldots \times F_n$ **do**
24:     add a (loop) accept transition with arcs from and to each of the tuple elements
25: **end for**
26: **return** $\mathcal{N}$

Algorithm 2. build_adaptor

inputs mapping M, components $C_1, \ldots, C_n$ with each $C_i = \langle A_i, S_i, I_i, F_i, T_i \rangle$
outputs adaptor $Ad = \langle A, S, I, F, T \rangle$

1: $\mathcal{N} := $ build_PetriNet($M, \{C_1, \ldots, C_n\}$) // *see Algorithm 1*
2: **if** bounded($\mathcal{N}$) **then** $L := $ get_marking_graph($\mathcal{N}$)
3: **else** $L := $ add_guards(get_cover_graph($\mathcal{N}$)) **end if**
4: $Ad := $ reduction(remove_paths_to_dead_states(L))
5: **return** Ad

---

therefore support reordering when required. The encoded adaptor constraints are as follows. First, the adaptor must mirror each component interface (places and transitions are generated from component interfaces, lines 2–12). It must also respect the adaptation contract specified in the mapping (places and transitions are generated, lines 14–22, from an LTS description of the mapping obtained in line 13). Algorithm 2 works out the building of the adaptor from this net using several functions. bounded checks if a Petri net is bounded. If so, its marking graph is finite and can be computed (get_marking_graph); if not, then we rely on an abstraction of it, a cover graph (get_cover_graph), where the ω symbol abstracts any token number > 0. Due to the over-approximation of cover graphs, add_guards is used on them to add a guard [#??a>1] (#??a meaning the number of tokens in place ??a) on any a! transition leaving a state where #??a is ω. remove_paths_to_dead_states recursively removes transitions and states yielding deadlocks. The optimising of resulting adaptors is achieved thanks to reduction techniques (reduction). Branching reduction [25] is the most appropriate choice as it does not require a strict matching of τ transitions like strong equivalence. In addition, branching equivalence is the strongest of the weak equivalences, therefore properties restricted to visible actions (*e.g.*, deadlock freedom, but also safety and fair liveness) are preserved by reduction modulo branching equivalence.

Example 5. We present in Figure 2 the Petri net generated for the Client and SQLServer example. To help the reader, we present separately the different parts of the net which are generated for Client (top left), SQLServer (top right) and the mapping (bottom left). The accept transition and the dashed places are used to glue the three subnets. The resulting adaptor is also shown (bottom right). It is more complex than its contract, which demonstrates the need for automatic adaptation processes as presented here.

Our algorithms are supported by Adaptor which relies on ETS [18] for open product computation, TINA [7] for the marking and cover graph computation, and on CADP [12] for adaptor reduction. Due to the computation of marking/cover graphs for the Petri net encodings, this algorithm is in theory exponential in the size of the Petri net, which in turn is related to the sum of the sizes of the component protocols and their alphabets ($\sum_{i \in \{1,...,n+1\}} (|S_i| + |A_i|)$). Yet, in practice, the adapted components are sequential, hence parts of generated Petri nets are 1-bounded which lowers the complexity. The incremental mechanism for adaptation we present in the next section also helps in minimising the complexity of computing adaptors.

3   Incremental Adaptation of Open Component Systems

We may now describe an incremental adaptation approach suitable to open systems. At design-time, it helps in the design and integration of component-based systems, grounding on automatic adaptor-connector generation. At run-time, it avoids the computation of global adaptors and supports evolving systems.

3.1   Architectural Style

The definition of an architectural style is the support for the description, reasoning and implementation of software architectures. As far as design-time incremental adaptation is concerned, resulting design architectural models will

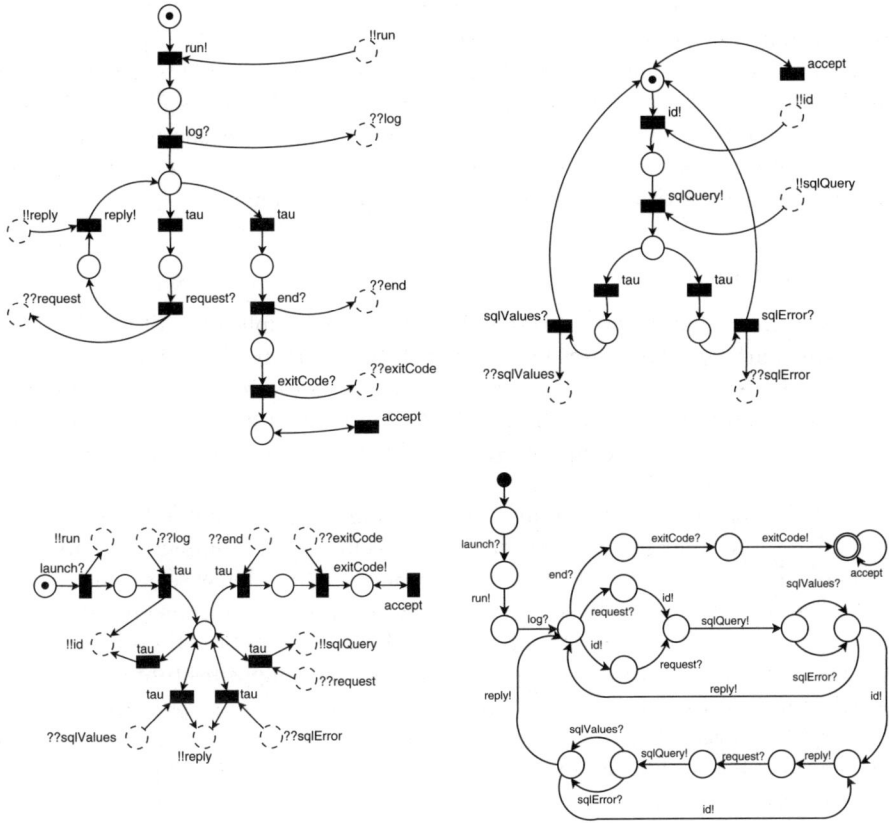

Fig. 2. The Client and Server Example Adaptor Generation

respect our style. As far as run-time incremental adaptation is concerned, communication mechanisms are constrained by it.

Two kinds of entities are distinguished: components and adaptors. Components implement the system's functionalities or services. Adaptors are used as intermediates to avoid deadlock and enforce different coordination policies whose properties are specified in an abstract way in mappings. A component is only connected to its adaptor, and interacts with the rest of the system through it. If the component does not require adaptation, our approach automatically generates a *no-op* adaptor which reproduces from an external point of view exactly the same behaviour as the component. Adaptors can be connected to other adaptors in order to ensure the system's global correctness.

To support implementation or run-time adaptation, two kinds of interactions have to be distinguished at an adaptor level: with its component and with other adaptors. Adaptors have to agree on a common implementation communication protocol to communicate altogether. Mismatch between components which has been solved thanks to adaptors should not be transferred to a mismatch between adaptors which should communicate correctly by construction. *Prefixing* will help there. Communications with the environment are prefixed by the component identifier and communications with other adaptors are prefixed by the identifier of the components these adaptors are in charge of. As far as communication between adaptors and components is concerned, communications are not prefixed as adaptation should be transparent for the adapted component. The use of prefixing is demonstrated in Section 4 on our application.

3.2   Assessment

Adaptors may impose service restriction due to the application of the function removing paths to dead states in the adaptation algorithm (Alg. 2, line 4). These are hard to detect by hand and assessment procedures are therefore required to help the designer (for design-time adaptation) or the end-user (for run-time adaptation). We propose tool-supported procedures based on alphabet comparison and property checking.

Alphabet-based assessment and comparisons may be used either to check the adapted system for services or more specifically to compare the adapted component with reference to the original one. In the first case we may check either successfully synchronised services (obtained hiding in LTSs any transition $e :< l_1, \ldots, l_n >$ where there is only one i such that $l_i \neq \varepsilon$) or actions left open to the environment, possibly new services provided by composites (obtained hiding in LTSs any transition $e :< l_1, \ldots, l_n >$ where there are at least two different $l_i \neq \varepsilon$). Comparison between original and adapted components can be performed on the same basis (internal or external comparison) through difference between their respective alphabets.

Property checking is a finer grained technique and may efficiently be used to detect more subtle architectural flaws. Classical properties such as liveness properties (*e.g.*, *any request will eventually be satisfied*, see Sect. 4 for an application of this) can be easily formalised reusing patterns [15], and then checked against the adapted system model (LTS) using model-checkers. An interesting benefit is that, when the property is unsatisfied, model-checkers return back a counter-example sequence of service calls that may help modifying mappings.

3.3   Addition and Suppression of Components

In this section, we present the algorithms for the addition and for the suppression of components. In the addition algorithm (Alg. 3), a component (C_{n+1}) is adapted and integrated into an existing composite (possibly empty). Adaptation is performed using only the component to be added, a given mapping and adaptors of components referred to in the mapping. Assessment is used to check the result of the integration. It is important to note that, as a preliminary step, automatically built mappings can be proposed. When the system is empty, a no-op mapping, $\left(V, \left(\sum_{v \in V} v\right)*\right)$ with $V = \{(C_{n+1}{:}e, e) \mid e \in A_{C_{n+1}}\}$, simply wraps the added component. When there are already components to communicate with in the system, a trivial mapping, $\left(V, \left(\sum_{v \in V} v\right)*\right)$ with $V =$

Algorithm 3. addition

---

inputs composite $\mathcal{C} = \langle \{C_1, AC_1, \ldots, C_n, AC_n\}, A_{ext}, B_{int}, B_{ext}\rangle$, component C_{n+1}
output new composite $\mathcal{C}^a = \langle \{C_1, AC_1, \ldots, C_n, AC_n, C_{n+1}, AC_{n+1}\}, A^a_{ext}, B^a_{int}, B^a_{ext}\rangle$

1: **repeat**
2:     $M :=$ get_mapping()// *designer or end-user given*
3:     $AC_{n+1} :=$ build_adaptor $(M,$ get_cn'ed_adaptors_from_mapping$(M) \cup \{C_{n+1}\})$
4:     $B'_{ext} :=$ get_externals_from_mapping(M)
5:     $A^a_{ext} := A_{ext} \cup \{e \mid (e, e') \in B'_{ext}\}$
6:     $B^a_{int} := B_{int} \cup$ get_internals_from_mapping(M)
7:     $B^a_{ext} := B_{ext} \cup B'_{ext}$
8:     $\mathcal{C}^a := \langle \{C_1, AC_1, \ldots, C_n, AC_n, C_{n+1}, AC_{n+1}\}, A^a_{ext}, B^a_{int}, B^a_{ext}\rangle$
9: **until** assess_or_stop$(\mathcal{C}^a)$// *human-interaction may stop the process*
10: **return** $\mathcal{C}^a$

Algorithm 4. suppression

---

inputs composite $\mathcal{C} = \langle \{C_1, AC_1, \ldots, C_n, AC_n\}, A_{ext}, B_{int}, B_{ext}\rangle$, $C_{k,k \in \{1,\ldots,n\}}$
output new composite $\mathcal{C}'$

1: $\{C_1, \ldots, C_m\} :=$ reachable$(C_k, \mathcal{C},$added_after$(C_k, \mathcal{C}))$
2: $\mathcal{C}' :=$ build_composite(added_before$(C_k, \mathcal{C}))$
3: **for all** $C_{i, i \in \{1, \ldots, m\}}$ **do** $\mathcal{C}' :=$ addition$(\mathcal{C}', C_i)$ **end for**
4: **return** $\mathcal{C}'$

$\{(C_i{:}e, \overline{e}) \mid C_i{:}e \in A_{ext} \wedge \overline{e} \in A_{C_{n+1}}\}$, can be tested. In this algorithm, function get_cn'ed_adaptors_from_mapping iterates over the set of vectors V of the mapping M. For each v in V, if v respects the form given for B_{int} in Definition 3, we can obtain a couple (l_i, l_j) and then, looking at the n adaptors alphabets, determine the adaptor l_i corresponds to. Function get_externals_from_mapping (resp. get_internals_from_mapping) returns the set of couples (e, l_i) (resp. (l_i, l_j)) from the vectors e : $\langle l_1, \ldots, l_n\rangle$ of the mapping M that respect the form given for B_{ext} (resp. B_{int}) in Definition 3. The suppression algorithm (Alg. 4) first computes all the components that have been added after the component to be removed, and are reachable (in terms of the architectural graph topology) from it. The suppression may impact all these components, therefore their corresponding adaptors are successively updated if needed using the component addition algorithm. In this algorithm we use the following functions. Function added_after (resp. _before) returns the ordered set of all components of the composite $\mathcal{C}$ added after (resp. before) the component C_k. Function reachable returns all components of the composite $\mathcal{C}$ present in a given filtering set (added_after results) which are reachable from the component C_k. Finally, build_composite is used to build a composite applying the addition algorithm on an ordered set of components (result of added_before in the algorithm), and reusing mappings from the former composite construction. Mappings are therefore kept with adaptors while building the system. Removing a component induces the suppression of its adaptor, but also the update of all the adaptors interacting with it. In the worst case, this corresponds to recompute all adaptors which is as costly as the regular case in global adaptation approaches where the adaptor is always recomputed.

4   Application

We have validated our approach on several examples: the dining philosopher problem, a video-on-demand system, a pervasive music player system, and several versions of a library management application. We present here a simplified version of the latter one. The system manages loans in a library. Components were chosen non recursive (this corresponds to the notion of transactional services) to obtain readable resulting adaptors.

The first component, LIB, tests if a book is available in the library or has been borrowed by a user.

```
LIB[i,f] = isBorrowed?. (available!.0 + borrowed!.0)
```

A no-op adaptor, ALIB, is first computed using a no-op mapping generated automatically as presented in Section 3.3. Then, a second component, SUB, is added. It is used as a front-end to the LIB component and checks if a user is a subscriber of the library. If not, SUB replies with the notAvailable! message, otherwise it tests if the requested book is borrowed or available.

```
SUB[i,f] = info?.isRegistered?.(isBorrowed!.SUB_AUX + notAvailable!.0)
SUB_AUX  = (notBorrowed?.available!.0 + borrowed?.notAvailable!.0)
```

It is obvious that the components present both name and protocol mismatch, therefore the trivial mapping fails assessment. We recall that events are prefixed except for those corresponding to interactions between the adaptor and its component (see Section 3.1). To work the mismatch out, a mapping M1= (v1.v2.(v3+v4.(v5.v6+v7.v3)))* is proposed, with vectors

$$
\begin{aligned}
&\text{v1 = SUB:info?} &&: \text{<LIB:ε, info?>} \\
&\text{v2 = SUB:isRegistered?} &&: \text{<LIB:ε, isRegistered?>} \\
&\text{v3 = SUB:notAvailable!} &&: \text{<LIB:ε, notAvailable!>} \\
&\text{v4 = τ} &&: \text{<LIB:isBorrowed?, isBorrowed!>} \\
&\text{v5 = τ} &&: \text{<LIB:available!, notBorrowed?>} \\
&\text{v6 = SUB:available!} &&: \text{<LIB:ε, available!>} \\
&\text{v7 = τ} &&: \text{<LIB:borrowed!, borrowed?>}
\end{aligned}
$$

In Figure 3 we present the architecture resulting from our incremental integration and adaptation process. The left hand part is related to the architecture after the addition of SUB and its adaptor, ASUB. The overall figure corresponds to the final architecture (after all components have been added, see BOR below). The architecture is computed automatically using Algorithm 3.

It was not possible to give all binding names (A_{ext}, B_{int}, B_{ext}) in the figure due to lack of place. However, bindings here are between ports of same name as the architectures are correct by construction using adaptation. The adaptor ASUB generated from M1 is shown in Figure 4.

A third component, BOR, receives requests for loans and checks if the book can be borrowed or not (id! stands for identifiers of the user and book).

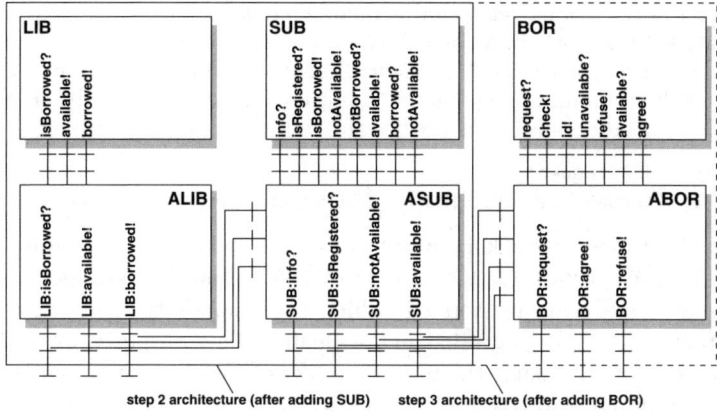

Fig. 3. The Library Example Architecture

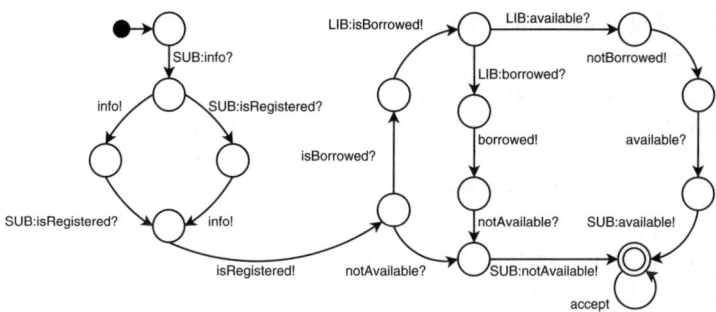

Fig. 4. The Library Example Adaptor

```
BOR[i,f] = request?.check!.id!.
           ( unavailable?.refuse!.0 + available?.agree!.0 )
```

Component BOR can be connected to component SUB using the mapping M2 to make all three components work together. Note in the mapping below that reordering is needed since BOR sends first the check! message and then information about the request id!, whereas SUB accepts first info?, and then the request message isRegistered?. Therefore, the following sequence belongs to the ABOR adaptor: check?.id?.SUB:info!.SUB:isRegistered!.

$$M2 = v1.v2.v3.(v4.v5+v6.v7)*$$

```
v1 = BOR:request?:<SUB:ε,request?>    v5 = BOR:refuse!:<SUB:ε,refuse!>
v2 = τ:<SUB:isRegistered?,check!>      v6 = τ:<SUB:available!,available?>
v3 = τ:<SUB:info?,id!>                 v7 = BOR:agree!:<SUB:ε,agree!>
v4 = τ:<SUB:notAvailable!,unavailable?>
```

Now, let us illustrate assessment procedures on the system made up of the three components, and their corresponding adaptors. This system is quite simple (33 states, 60 transitions, and 25 labels) since the adaptation process has removed all incorrect interactions. External alphabet contains messages `BOR:request?`, `BOR:agree!`, `BOR:refuse!`, and also all the messages left observable in the previous steps, *i.e.*, `LIB:isBorrowed?`, `LIB:available!`, etc. The synchronised alphabet contains all the remaining messages which are connected internally. In addition, the system is deadlock-free and verifies the following liveness property:

```
[true*](["BOR:request?"]
   (mu X. (<true> true and [not ("BOR:agree!" or "BOR:refuse!")]X)))
```

It states that messages `BOR:request!` are always followed after a finite number of steps either by a message `BOR:agree?` or `BOR:refuse?`. Basically, this means that all requests are always replied, which corresponds to the classic pattern "AG request$\Rightarrow$EF reply" encoded in μ-calculus. This property was automatically checked using Evaluator the model-checker of CADP. Consequently, the BOR adaptor is validated, and the final correct architecture is as presented earlier on.

Let us now remove component SUB. This can be done for update purposes or just because the loan check is simplified not to take into account that the user has to be a subscriber. BOR is the only connected component added after SUB. A new mapping is given for component BOR to connect it directly to component LIB, `M2'` = `v1.v2.v3.(v4.v5+v6.v7)*` with vectors

```
v1 = BOR:request?:<LIB:ε,request?>    v5 = BOR:refuse!:<LIB:ε,refuse!>
v2 = τ:<LIB:isBorrowed?,check!>        v6 = τ:<LIB:available!,available?>
v3 = τ:<LIB:ε,id!>                     v7 = BOR:agree!:<LIB:ε,agree!>
v4 = τ:<LIB:borrowed!,unavailable?>
```

The corresponding adaptor is computed, the new system assessed successfully, and we end up with a system made up of components LIB, BOR, and their respective adaptors. To check how the approach integrates in a complete development process, the system has been implemented in COM/DCOM using the adaptor models to obtain their code.

5   Related Work

Since Yellin and Strom's seminal paper [27], adaptation techniques [21,14,8] have been proposed to correct component mismatch building adaptors. In [11] we made significant advances with an approach supporting name mismatch, system-wide adaptation (more than two components) and event reordering. Yet, all these approaches require the computation of a global adaptor, which is costly, and none supports open systems, which prevents application to pervasive systems.

In [22], component wrappers are composed to augment connector behaviour. This has been revisited in [23], providing automation, but still with a centralised global adaptor as starting point, as for [4] where adaptor distribution is addressed. Several theoretical works have focused on the incremental construction of systems and dynamic reconfiguration [5,3,26]. However, these proposals only address syntactic adaptation (via name translation or morphisms) and cannot be used to solve behavioural mismatch. In [19], we have proposed a methodology to help designers in the incremental construction of component-based systems where adaptors are required. The definition of open systems, their composition and related adaptation algorithms were not supported. Incrementality was achieved using implicit vectors exporting in adaptors all the component services in order to make the design process compatible with adaptation as defined in [11]. This limits the application of [19] at design-time where the set of components to be integrated is known.

6 Conclusion

The integration of software components often requires a certain degree of adaptation. Adaptation approaches have addressed closed systems and the distribution of global adaptors but to our knowledge, none supports open systems. Thus, they are not well suited to systems where components or services may enter and leave at any time, such as pervasive ones. To address this issue, we have proposed here (i) a formalising of component-based open systems which thereafter supports, (ii) an extension of software adaptation to open systems, and (iii) an incremental integration process which avoids the computation of global adaptors. The adaptation solutions we propose are supported by a tool, Adaptor. In its current version, Adaptor can deal with both closed systems and open systems. This tool and its set of validation examples (approx. 70 examples, 25,000 lines of XML specifications) are freely available from [1].

Our main perspectives concern the application of our model-based adaptation techniques to service oriented architectures for pervasive computing. First, relations between adaptation models and implementation languages have to be studied. We have done some experiments using COM/DCOM but Web services are more relevant in this area. The combination of adaptation with semantic composition solutions such as [6] is also an interesting perspective to support not only behavioural but also semantic correctness. To end, end-user composition is a crucial issue in pervasive computing. The support in Adaptor for the use of other adaptation contract formalisms, as presented in Section 2.3 is therefore an interesting perspective.

Acknowledgements. This work has been supported by the French National Network for Telecommunication Research. Adaptor has been developed with S. Beauche. We thank M. Tivoli for the COM/DCOM encoding of the case study and C. Canal for fruitful discussions.

References

1. The Adaptor tool (LGPL licence). Available from P. Poizat's Webpage
2. Agha, G.: Special Issue on Adaptive Middleware. CACM 45(6), 30–64 (2002)
3. Aguirre, N., Maibaum, T.: A Logical Basis for the Specification of Reconfigurable Component-Based Systems. In: Pezzé, M. (ed.) FASE 2003. LNCS, vol. 2621, Springer, Heidelberg (2003)
4. Autili, M., Flammini, M., Inverardi, P., Navarra, A., Tivoli, M.: Synthesis of Concurrent and Distributed Adaptors for Component-based Systems. In: Gruhn, V., Oquendo, F. (eds.) EWSA 2006. LNCS, vol. 4344, Springer, Heidelberg (2006)

5. Back, R.J.: Incremental Software Construction with Refinement Diagrams. Technical Report 660, Turku Center for Computer Science (2005)
6. Ben Mokhtar, S., Georgantas, N., Issarny, V.: Ad Hoc Composition of User Tasks in Pervasive Computing Environments. In: Gschwind, T., Aßmann, U., Nierstrasz, O. (eds.) SC 2005. LNCS, vol. 3628, Springer, Heidelberg (2005)
7. Berthomieu, B., Ribet, P.-O., Vernadat, F.: The tool TINA – Construction of Abstract State Spaces for Petri Nets and Time Petri Nets. International Journal of Production Research, vol. 42(14), 2741–2756 (2004)
8. Bracciali, A., Brogi, A., Canal, C.: A Formal Approach to Component Adaptation. Journal of Systems and Software 74(1), 45–54 (2005)
9. Bruneton, E., Coupaye, T., Leclercq, M., Quéma, V., Stefani, J.-B.: The Fractal Component Model and Its Support in Java. Software Practice and Experience, vol. 36(11-12), 1257–1284 (2006)
10. Canal, C., Murillo, J.M., Poizat, P.: Software Adaptation. L'Objet. Special Issue on Software Adaptation 12(1), 9–31 (2006)
11. Canal, C., Poizat, P., Salaün, G.: Synchronizing Behavioural Mismatch in Software Composition. In: Gorrieri, R., Wehrheim, H. (eds.) FMOODS 2006. LNCS, vol. 4037, Springer, Heidelberg (2006)
12. Garavel, H., Lang, F., Mateescu, R.: An Overview of CADP 2001. EASST Newsletter 4, 13–24 (2002)
13. Hopcroft, J.E., Ullman, J.D.: Introduction to Automata Theory, Languages and Computation. Addison Wesley, London, UK (1979)
14. Inverardi, P., Tivoli, M.: Deadlock Free Software Architectures for COM/DCOM Applications. Journal of Systems and Software 65(3), 173–183 (2003)
15. Manna, Z., Pnueli, A.: Temporal Verification of Reactive Systems: Safety. Springer, Heidelberg (1995)
16. Murata, T.: Petri Nets: Properties, Analysis and Applications. Proceedings of the IEEE 77(4), 541–580 (1989)
17. Objet Management Group. Unified Modeling Language: Superstructure. version 2.0, formal/05-07-04 (August 2005)
18. Poizat, P.: Eclipse Transition Systems. RNRT project STACS deliverable (2006)
19. Poizat, P., Salaün, G., Tivoli, M.: An Adaptation-based Approach to Incrementally Build Component Systems. In: Proc. of FACS'06 (2006)
20. Satyanarayanan, M.: Pervasive Computing: Vision and Challenges. IEEE Personal Communications 6(8), 10–17 (2001)
21. Schmidt, H.W., Reussner, R.H.: Generating Adapters for Concurrent Component Protocol Synchronization. In: Proc. of FMOODS'02, Kluwer Academic Publishers, Dordrecht (2002)
22. Spitznagel, B., Garlan, D.: A Compositional Formalization of Connector Wrappers. In: Proc. of ICSE'03, ACM Press, New York (2003)
23. Tivoli, M., Autili, M.: SYNTHESIS, a Tool for Synthesizing Correct and Protocol-Enhanced Adaptors. L'Objet. 12(1), 77–103 (2006)
24. Uchitel, S., Kramer, J., Magee, J.: Synthesis of Behavioural Models from Scenarios. IEEE Transactions on Software Engineering 29(2), 99–115 (2003)
25. van Glabbeek, R.J., Weijland, W.P.: Branching Time and Abstraction in Bisimulation Semantics. Journal of the ACM 43(3), 555–600 (1996)
26. Wermelinger, M., Lopes, A., Fiadeiro, J.L.: A Graph Based Architectural (Re)configuration Language. In: Proc. of ESEC/FSE'01, ACM Press, New York (2001)
27. Yellin, D.M., Strom, R.E.: Protocol Specifications and Components Adaptors. ACM Transactions on Programming Languages and Systems 19(2), 292–333 (1997)

A Representation-Independent Behavioral Semantics for Object-Oriented Components

Arnd Poetzsch-Heffter and Jan Schäfer[*]

University of Kaiserslautern
{poetzsch,jschaefer}@informatik.uni-kl.de

Abstract. Behavioral semantics abstracts from implementation details and allows to describe the behavior of software components in a representation-independent way. In this paper, we develop a formal behavioral semantics for class-based object-oriented languages with aliasing, subclassing, and dynamic dispatch. The code of an object-oriented component consists of a class and the classes used by it. A component instance is realized by a dynamically evolving set of objects with a clear boundary to the environment. The behavioral semantics is expressed in terms of the messages crossing the boundary. It is defined as an abstraction of an operational semantics based on an ownership-structured heap. We show how the semantics can be used to define substitutability in a program independent way.

1 Introduction

The behavior of object systems is often described as a set of loosely coupled objects with encapsulated state that communicate via messages. However, this conceptual view is only partially reflected by existing object-oriented programming languages. Most of them are trimmed for efficient implementation of local computations. Their semantics is usually given in terms of state-transitions based on global heaps. As they do not support clear boundaries between parts of the heap, modular reasoning and abstraction of representation aspects is much more difficult than in a loosely coupled setting.

If runtime components have well-defined boundaries, their behavior can be completely defined in terms of their reaction to incoming message sequences. Considering only the messages that a client sends to a component makes the semantics independent from the representation of the component states. Such *behavioral semantics* has three advantageous properties:

1. Different component implementations can be compared based on the message behavior. Thus, an explicit coupling relation between the states of the implementations as it is needed in state-based approaches (see in particular the seminal paper [3] on representation independence for OO-programs) is

---

[*] Supported by the Deutsche Forschungsgemeinschaft (German Research Foundation).

M.M. Bonsangue and E.B. Johnsen (Eds.): FMOODS 2007, LNCS 4468, pp. 157–173, 2007.

not necessary. This simplifies the notion of behavioral substitutability for components.

2. Behavioral semantics provides a suitable semantical basis for behavioral component specifications, i.e. for specifications that describe component behavior without referring to the implementation.

3. It simplifies modular analysis, because it is easier to abstract from the execution environment of the component. In particular, we can analyze component implementations without knowing their program contexts.

In this paper, we present an approach to behavioral semantics with the above properties for imperative object-oriented languages like Java and C# that support references, aliasing, subclassing, dynamic dispatch, and recursive types and methods. The main technical challenges were (a) to find a simple, yet powerful notion of runtime components, (b) to support callbacks, and (c) to use well-established semantical techniques for the definition of the behavioral semantics.

Approach and Overview. A runtime component in our approach is called a *box*. A box consists of an *owner object* and a set of other objects. A box is created together with its owner by instantiating the class of its owner. Boxes are tree-structured, that is, a box b can have so-called *inner* boxes. We distinguish two kinds of classes, normal classes and box classes (annotated by the keyword box). The instantiation of a normal class creates an object in the *current box*, that is, in the box of the current this-object. The instantiation of a box class creates a new inner box of the current box together with its owner. For simplicity, we do not support the direct creation of objects outside the current box. Such nonlocal creations can only be done by using a method. Note that this is similar to a distributed setting with remote method invocation.

Our approach only uses structural aspects of ownership (similar to [5]). It does not enforce confinement. In particular, our semantical model allows arbitrary references going into and out of a box (In this respect, it is more flexible than that of [3]). For type systems enforcing box confinement, we refer to [21].

The operational semantics for boxes distinguishes between local method calls and calls on objects of other boxes (Sec. 2). From this semantics, we develop a behavioral semantics in two steps (Sec. 3). In the first step, we abstract from box states and consider the concrete message histories at box boundaries. In the second step, we abstract from object identifiers and box environments, getting a semantics that is independent of the program context a component is used in. The remaining sections of the paper show how the semantics can be used to define substitutability (Sec. 4) and contain a discussion of related work and the conclusions.

2   Operational Semantics for Boxes

In this section, we present the operational semantics for our object-oriented core language. Most parts of the semantics follow the reductional style of [13]. The semantics has two new features: (a) It structures the heap into box-local sub-heaps. (b) It handles non-local method invocations by call and return messages crossing the box boundaries. It can express arbitrary sequences of callbacks.

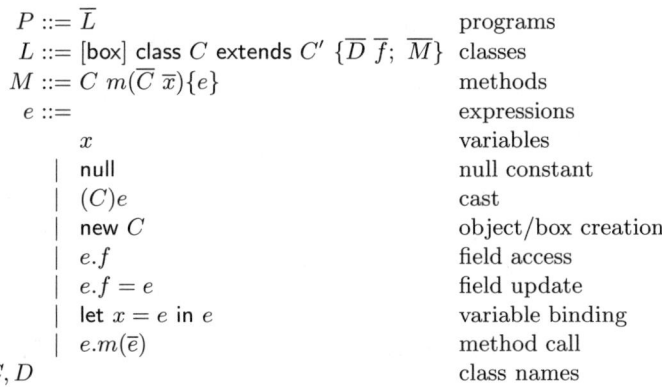

$$P ::= \overline{L} \qquad\qquad\qquad\qquad \text{programs}$$
$$L ::= [\text{box}] \text{ class } C \text{ extends } C' \{\overline{D}\ \overline{f};\ \overline{M}\} \quad \text{classes}$$
$$M ::= C\ m(\overline{C}\ \overline{x})\{e\} \qquad\qquad \text{methods}$$
$$e ::= \qquad\qquad\qquad\qquad\qquad\quad \text{expressions}$$

	x	variables
$\mid$	null	null constant
$\mid$	$(C)e$	cast
$\mid$	new C	object/box creation
$\mid$	$e.f$	field access
$\mid$	$e.f = e$	field update
$\mid$	let $x = e$ in e	variable binding
$\mid$	$e.m(\overline{e})$	method call
C, D		class names

Fig. 1. Abstract syntax

2.1 Syntax and Typing

The abstract syntax of our language is shown in Fig. 1. We use similar notations as Featherweight Java (FJ) [14]. A bar indicates a sequence: $\overline{L} = L_1, L_2, \ldots, L_n$, where the length is defined as $|\overline{L}| = n$. Similar, $\overline{C}\ \overline{f}$; is equal to $C_1\ f_1; \ldots; C_n\ f_n$. If there is some sequence $\overline{x}$, we write x_i for any element of $\overline{x}$. We sometimes write $\overline{x}\cdot x$ for adding x to sequence $\overline{x}$, and $\overline{x} \circ \overline{x}'$ for the concatenation of two sequences. The empty sequence is denoted by $\bullet$. *front* returns a sequence without the last element, and *last* returns the last element of a sequence, i.e. $\overline{x} = front(\overline{x})\cdot last(\overline{x})$. We often apply a function f on a sequence of elements that is only defined on single elements. This means to apply f to each element of the sequence and return the sequence of the results, e.g. $f(x_1, \ldots, x_n) = f(x_1)\cdot f(x_2)\cdots f(x_n)$. We sometimes treat sequences as sets, e.g. if we write $\overline{x}_1 \subseteq \overline{x}_2$, both sequences are implicitly treated as sets.

Our language supports stateful objects, aliasing, inheritance, and dynamic dispatch. It is similar to other core formalizations of Java, namely FJ [14] and CLASSICJAVA [13]. The main difference is the distinction between box and normal classes that provides the structuring of the heap into boxes. A set of classes $\overline{L}$ is called *declaration complete* iff all names used in $\overline{L}$ have a declaration in $\overline{L}$. A program in our language is a declaration complete set of classes $\overline{L}$. The smallest declaration complete program for a class C is called the *code base* of C. In this paper, code bases for the box classes are used as a simple notion of *program components*. In practice, the code base of a box class would be structured by module systems separating the box-local part and the code bases of the inner boxes. We consider this (interesting) aspect beyond the scope of this paper.

Contextual constraints and typing rules are essentially as in Java. The subtype relation will be denoted by $<:$, i.e. $C <: D$ means that C is a subtype of D. We assume that the most general class Object is a normal class without fields and methods. A subclass of a box class has to be as well a box class. We do not support overloading of methods and require that an overriding method has the same signature as the overridden method. We do not consider field hiding, so

$$
\begin{aligned}
b &::= o \mid \mathsf{globox} & \text{boxes} \\
o &::= \langle j, b, C \rangle & \text{objects} \\
v &::= o \mid \mathsf{null} & \text{values} \\
O &::= \overline{v} & \text{object states} \\
B &::= \langle ES, OS, IB \rangle & \text{box states} \\
ES &::= \overline{r} & \text{execution stacks} \\
OS &::= \overline{j} \mapsto \overline{O} & \text{object stores} \\
IB &::= \overline{j} \mapsto \overline{B} & \text{inner boxes} \\
n &::= & \text{messages} \\
& \quad o \rightarrow o'.m(\overline{v}) & \text{call message} \\
& \mid o \leftarrow o'.m{:}v & \text{return message} \\
e &::= \dots \mid \mathsf{result} \mid o & \text{reduction expressions} \\
t &::= n \mid r & \text{terms} \\
r &::= o \rightarrow o'.m\{e\} & \text{call} \\
j & & \text{object identifier}
\end{aligned}
$$

Fig. 2. Dynamic entities and extended expression syntax

all fields declared in a class must have names different from the inherited fields. A method only has a single body expression which is also the return value of the method. Expressions can be variables, the null constant, cast expressions, new-expressions, field accesses, field updates, let-expressions, and method calls. If the class in a new-expression is a box class, a a new box together with its owner object is created; otherwise, a normal object is created in the current box. Let-expressions support local variables and sequential composition.

$$
class(\langle \_, \_, C \rangle) = C \qquad owner(\langle \_, b, \_ \rangle) = b \qquad \frac{\mathsf{box\ class}\ C\ \mathsf{extends}\ C'\ \{\dots\}}{boxClass(C)}
$$

$$
\frac{boxClass(class(o))}{box(o) = o} \qquad \frac{\neg boxClass(class(o))}{box(o) = owner(o)} \qquad \frac{\mathsf{class}\ C\ \mathsf{extends}\ C'\ \{\ \overline{D}\ \overline{f};\ \dots\}}{fields(C) = \overline{D}\ \overline{f} \circ fields(C')}
$$

$$
\frac{\mathsf{class}\ C\ \mathsf{extends}\ \_\{\dots\ D\ m(\overline{D}\ \overline{x})\{e\}\ \dots\}}{method(C,m) = D\ m(\overline{D}\ \overline{x})\{e\}} \qquad \frac{\mathsf{class}\ C\ \mathsf{extends}\ C'\{\dots\ \overline{M}\}\ \ m \notin \overline{M}}{method(C,m) = method(C',m)}
$$

$$
\frac{owner(b) = b'}{b \prec b'} \qquad \frac{b \prec b' \quad b' \prec b''}{b \prec b''} \qquad
\begin{aligned}
address(o \rightarrow o'.m(\overline{v})) &= box(o') \\
address(o \leftarrow o'.m{:}v) &= box(o)
\end{aligned}
$$

Fig. 3. Auxiliary functions

2.2   Operational Semantics

Our operational semantics supports the structuring of the heap into boxes. Its central feature is *box locality*: the rules only refer to the heap parts of the current box and its inner boxes. Box locality is a prerequisite for the abstraction technique in Sec. 3. The semantics is mainly given in reductional small-step style, that is, we represent an evaluation state by a partially evaluated expression over dynamic values and by the states of the created objects. Fig. 2 contains the needed definitions. A box is either represented by its owner object or by the constant `globox` denoting the global box that contains all other boxes. An object is uniquely defined by an identifier j and by its box b. To avoid an extra mapping from objects to their classes, we add the class name as a third component to the object representation. Two objects $\langle j_1, b_1, C_1 \rangle$ and $\langle j_2, b_2, C_2 \rangle$ are different iff $j_1 \neq j_2$ or $b_1 \neq b_2$. Working with identifiers that only need to be unique within the box allows to create new objects in a box without knowing the identifiers of outside objects or objects in inner boxes.

The state of an object is represented by the values for its fields. The state of a box b consists of its execution state, the state of the objects with owner b and the state of the inner boxes. The execution state is a stack of pending method executions. It is used to handle callbacks. For example, if a method executing in box b leads to a call on an object outside of b, this call can call back on b's objects and so forth. Calls to and returns from methods on non-local objects are handled by messages. To represent partially-evaluated expression, the expression syntax of Fig. 2 is extended. An expression can be an object or the keyword `result` indicating that the expression expects the result of a pending call.

Figure 3 shows auxiliary functions needed by our semantics. The *box* function returns the box of an object o. Objects o of box classes represent their own box. Otherwise the box is represented by the object's owner. The relation $b \prec b'$ expresses that b is a direct or indirect inner box of b'. The reflexive closure of $\prec$ is denoted by $\preceq$. An object o is called *box-local* to box b iff $box(o) = b$. In particular, the owner of a box b is box-local to b (see fourth rule in Fig. 3). It *is in* box b iff $box(o) \preceq b$. Otherwise, o *is outside of* b.

Messages. A message $o \rightarrow o'.m(\overline{v})$ contains the sender, o, the receiver, o', the method name m, and the method parameters $\overline{v}$. We distinguish between *call messages* ($\rightarrow$) and *return messages* ($\leftarrow$). Note that for return messages the sender of the message is the object which originally called the message, and the receiver is the receiver of that call, because the original receiver sends the answer back to the original sender. The explicit representation of the sender allows to avoid a stack mechanism. Stacks in combination with callbacks would breach box locality and cause a problem for the abstraction in Sec. 3.

The *address* a of a message n is the box of the object to which the arrow points. A message n that has either the sender or the receiver in a box b is called an *ingoing* message for b if a is in b. and an *outgoing* message otherwise. The receiver object and the method parameters of a message n are called the *parameters, params(n)*, of n. Non-null parameters that are in b are called *inner* parameters of n, the others are called *outer* parameters, denoted by $inner(b, n)$ and $outer(b, n)$ respectively. We say that a return message *matches* a call message if the method names, the sender objects and the receiver objects are the same.

Judgements and Rules. To achieve box locality, we seperate the state of a box from the state of the enclosing boxes and guarantee that execution in a box b only modifies objects in b. The semantical rules specify two different judgements. The outside view to a box is represented by the judgement

$$b \vdash (B, n) \Downarrow (B', n')$$

expressing the fact that sending message n to box b in box state B leads to a terminating execution in b with a reply message n' that has an address outside b. B' is the state of b when n' is sent. For example, the message n could be a call and n' the corresponding return or an intermediate call to an outside object. Analogous to a judgement of big-step operational, the judgement allows to abstract from the execution steps within boxes.

Execution within a box is formalized by a reduction semantics. A triple $b{:}B, t$ is called a *configuration* consisting of a box b, its state B, and a term t representing an execution to be performed in b. A single execution step has the form:

$$b{:}B, t \quad \rightsquigarrow \quad b{:}B', t'$$

We write $\rightsquigarrow^*$ for the transitive, reflexive closure of $\rightsquigarrow$. Note that a reduction step only modifies the state of box b. States of other boxes remain unchanged. In the semantics, so-called *evaluation contexts* represent partially evaluated expressions. An evaluation context $\mathcal{E}$ is an expression with a "hole" $[\,]$ somewhere inside the expression. We write $\mathcal{E}[e]$ to mean that the hole in $\mathcal{E}$ is replaced by expression e. A hole in $\mathcal{E}$ can only appear in certain positions defined as follows:

$$\mathcal{E} ::= [\,] \mid (T)\mathcal{E} \mid \mathcal{E}.f \mid \mathcal{E}.f = e \mid v.f = \mathcal{E} \mid \mathsf{let}\ x = \mathcal{E}\ \mathsf{in}\ e \mid \mathcal{E}.m(\overline{e}) \mid v.m(\overline{v}, \mathcal{E}, \overline{e})$$

Similar to the evaluation context $\mathcal{E}$, we define a context $\mathcal{R}$ as a call with a hole, and we write $\mathcal{R}[\![e]\!]$ to replace that hole by an expression e.

$$\mathcal{R} ::= o \to o'.m\{\mathcal{E}\}$$

The rules for the reduction relation are given in Fig. 4. The upper part describes the evaluation of expressions, the lower part the handling of calls, returns, and messages. Casts are only allowed for box-local objects (R-CAST-OBJ). Thus, casts cannot be used to distinguish outside objects. This property will be used in Sec. 3 for the abstraction of outside objects (cf. the proof of the Abstraction Lemma). A more flexible cast rule would complicate the abstraction. Instantiating a normal class (R-NEW-OBJ) adds a new object to the object state of the box. Instantiating a box class adds a new box and object with an initial box state to the inner boxes. The new object identifier has to be unique with respect to all objects having the same owner. Note that in both cases a new object identifier can be determined based on box-local information. Rules R-FIELD-READ and R-FIELD-WRITE only allow field access on box-local objects. Thus, object creations and field updates only need box-local information and only affect box-local state. All other effects have to achieved via method calls.

R-CAST-NULL

$$\overline{b{:}B, \mathcal{R}[\![(C)\mathsf{null}]\!] \quad \rightsquigarrow \quad b{:}B, \mathcal{R}[\![\mathsf{null}]\!]}$$

R-CAST-OBJ

$$\frac{box(o) = b \qquad class(o) <: C}{b{:}B, \mathcal{R}[\![(C)o]\!] \quad \rightsquigarrow \quad b{:}B, \mathcal{R}[\![o]\!]}$$

R-NEW-OBJ

$$\frac{\neg boxClass(C) \qquad j \notin (dom(OS) \cup dom(IB))}{fields(C) = \overline{D}\ \overline{f} \qquad |\overline{\mathsf{null}}| = |\overline{f}| \qquad o = \langle j, b, C\rangle}{b{:}\langle ES, OS, IB\rangle, \mathcal{R}[\![\mathsf{new}\ C]\!] \quad \rightsquigarrow \quad b{:}\langle ES, OS[j \mapsto \overline{\mathsf{null}}], IB\rangle, \mathcal{R}[\![o]\!]}$$

R-NEW-BOX

$$\frac{boxClass(C) \qquad j \notin (dom(OS) \cup dom(IB))}{fields(C) = \overline{D}\ \overline{f} \qquad |\overline{\mathsf{null}}| = |\overline{f}| \qquad o = \langle j, b, C\rangle \qquad B = \langle \bullet, \{j \mapsto \overline{\mathsf{null}}\}, \varnothing\rangle}{b{:}\langle ES, OS, IB\rangle, \mathcal{R}[\![\mathsf{new}\ C]\!] \quad \rightsquigarrow \quad b{:}\langle ES, OS, IB[j \mapsto B]\rangle, \mathcal{R}[\![o]\!]}$$

R-FIELD-READ

$$\frac{o = \langle j, \_, C\rangle \qquad box(o) = b \qquad fields(C) = \overline{D}\ \overline{f} \qquad OS(j) = \overline{v}}{b{:}\langle ES, OS, IB\rangle, \mathcal{R}[\![o.f_i]\!] \quad \rightsquigarrow \quad b{:}\langle ES, OS, IB\rangle, \mathcal{R}[\![v_i]\!]}$$

R-FIELD-WRITE

$$\frac{o = \langle j, \_, C\rangle \qquad box(o) = b \qquad fields(C) = \overline{D}\ \overline{f} \qquad OS(j) = \overline{v}}{b{:}\langle ES, OS, IB\rangle, \mathcal{R}[\![o.f_i = v]\!] \quad \rightsquigarrow \quad b{:}\langle ES, OS[j \mapsto [v/v_i]\overline{v}], IB\rangle, \mathcal{R}[\![v]\!]}$$

R-LET

$$\overline{b{:}B, \mathcal{R}[\![\mathsf{let}\ x = v\ \mathsf{in}\ e]\!] \quad \rightsquigarrow \quad b{:}B, \mathcal{R}[\![[v/x]e]\!]}$$

R-SEND-CALL-MSG

$$\frac{ES' = o'' \rightarrow o.m\{\mathcal{E}[\mathsf{result}]\} \cdot ES}{b{:}\langle ES, OS, IB\rangle, o'' \rightarrow o.m\{\mathcal{E}[o'.m'(\overline{v})]\} \quad \rightsquigarrow \quad b{:}\langle ES', OS, IB\rangle, o \rightarrow o'.m'(\overline{v})}$$

R-SEND-RTRN-MSG

$$\overline{b{:}B, o \rightarrow o'.m\{v\} \quad \rightsquigarrow \quad b{:}B, o \leftarrow o'.m{:}v}$$

R-EXEC-CALL-MSG

$$\frac{box(o) = b \qquad method(class(o), m) = \_\ m(\_\ \overline{x})\{e\}}{b{:}B, o' \rightarrow o.m(\overline{v}) \quad \rightsquigarrow \quad b{:}B, o' \rightarrow o.m\{[o/this, \overline{v}/\overline{x}]e\}}$$

R-EXEC-RTRN-MSG

$$\frac{box(o) = b \qquad ES = (o'' \rightarrow o.m\{e\}) \cdot ES'}{b{:}\langle ES, OS, IB\rangle, o \leftarrow o'.m'{:}v \quad \rightsquigarrow \quad b{:}\langle ES', OS, IB\rangle, o'' \rightarrow o.m\{[v/\mathsf{result}]e\}}$$

R-FORWARD-INNER

$$\frac{address(n) \preceq b' \qquad b' = \langle j, b, \_\rangle \qquad b' \vdash (IB(b'), n) \Downarrow (B', n')}{b{:}\langle ES, OS, IB\rangle, n \quad \rightsquigarrow \quad b{:}\langle ES, OS, IB[j \mapsto B']\rangle, n'}$$

R-BOX-BIG-STEP

$$\frac{b{:}B, n \quad \rightsquigarrow^* \quad b{:}B', n' \qquad address(n') \npreceq b}{b \vdash (B, n) \Downarrow (B', n')}$$

Fig. 4. Rules of the operational semantics

A method call is treated by sending a message with the current receiver as sender (R-SEND-CALL-MSG). The evaluation state $o'' \to o.m\{\mathcal{E}[\text{result}]\}$ of the current method exection is recorded on the box-local execution stack. The placeholder result marks the position for the result. If the body of a method is fully evaluated, a return message is sent (R-SEND-RTRN-MSG). If the receiver of a call message is in box b (R-EXEC-CALL-MSG), the method is executed with the actual parameters. A return message with address in b pops the pending call from the execution stack, substitutes the result, and continues evaluation (R-EXEC-RTRN-MSG). According to rule R-FORWARD-INNER, a message n with an address in an inner box b' of b is forwarded to b'. If it terminates with a reply message n', the state of b' is updated and n' is handled in b. The last three rules cannot be applied if the address of a message n' is outside b. This is the case in which box-local execution terminates with reply method n' (R-BOX-BIG-STEP).

A program is called *executable* iff it contains a class of the form: class Main extends Object { D main(C p){e}}. It is executed with start configuration $globox{:}\langle\bullet, \{j_p \mapsto input, \dots, j_0 \mapsto \bullet\}, \varnothing\rangle, o_0 \to o_0.main(o_p)$ where $o_0 = \langle j_0, globox, Main\rangle$, $o_p = \langle j_p, globox, C\rangle$, and j_0 and j_p are distinct object identifiers. "*input*" denotes the field values of the parameter object o_p, and the dots indicate the possibility to have additional objects in the start configuration that are referenced by o_p. This allows to encode interesting input in the absence of primitive data types. Program execution can have three *outcomes*:

1. It can terminate normally in a configuration $globox{:}B', o_0 \leftarrow o_0.main{:}v$, i.e. with terminated method main and return value v.
2. It can end up in some configuration different from the above such that no rule is applicable (e.g. a field access on a nonlocal object). We consider this as *abortion*. For space limitation, we do not handle such exceptional cases explicitly.
3. It can diverge.

It is easy to verify that in any configuration at most one rule is applicable. Thus, the semantics is deterministic. Although determinism is not needed in principle for our approach, having a deterministic language simplifies the presentation in the following sections.

3   Behavioral Semantics for Boxes

In the following, we assume that an executable program P is given containing a box class C with code base K. We define a behavioral semantics for C and K, which is independent of the representation of the box states and independent of the environment in which C is used. The latter is not yet achieved because in general the box state encoding still uses identifiers of objects from classes not belonging to C. We reach this goal in three steps. *First*, we define a so-called *interface semantics* which takes a box, a box state, and a message for the box and results in the next state of the box and its answer message. This semantics is directly based on our big-step judgement from above. In a *second* step we abstract from the state of the box by using so-called concrete message histories. A history represents the state of a box without referring to the objects of the box and their field values. The *history semantics* defines how a message n is executed in a box b with a history H. Histories still refer to box and object identifiers. *Third,* we abstract from boxes, their execution environments, and object identifiers by defining *abstract histories*. An abstract history is essentially an equivalence class of concrete histories of boxes with the same box class. Abstract histories are used to define a precise behavioral semantics: Given an abstract history and an abstracted message, it yields the abstract answer of a box class.

The interface semantics *isem* for boxes is defined as a partial function from boxes, box states, and messages to *outcomes*, *oc*, where the outcome is either a pair consisting of a box state and a reply message or one of the constants *ABORT* or *DIVERGE*. More precisely:

Definition 1 (Interface Semantics). *Let b be a box, B a state of b and n an ingoing message for b. We define the interface semantics,* isem, *as*

$$
isem(b, B, n) = \begin{cases} B', n' & \text{if } b \vdash (B, n) \Downarrow (B', n') \\ ABORT & \text{if } b{:}B, n \rightsquigarrow^* b{:}B', n' \text{ and there are} \\ & \text{no } B'', n'' \text{ with } b{:}B', n' \rightsquigarrow b{:}B'', n'' \\ DIVERGE & \text{otherwise} \end{cases}
$$

3.1 History-Based Semantics

To become representation-independent we define a semantics that does not directly refer to the state of a box. The idea is to reconstruct the state from the incoming messages of a box by starting with an empty state and sequentially applying the *isem* semantics:

$$
\begin{aligned}
state(b, \bullet) &= \langle \varnothing, \varnothing, \varnothing \rangle \\
state(b, \overline{n} \cdot n) &= B' && \text{if } state(b, \overline{n}) = B \text{ and } isem(b, B, n) = B', n' \\
state(b, \overline{n} \cdot n) &= undefined && \text{otherwise}
\end{aligned}
$$

It is clear that not every arbitrary sequence of incoming messages for a box, leads to a valid state. In particular, only objects that have been earlier exposed by a method call or return are permitted as parameters and a return message has to match the last callback from the box. Valid sequences of incoming messages are called *concrete histories*.

Definition 2 (Concrete History, Admissible Message). *A concrete history H is a quadruple consisting of a box b, denoted by box(H), a sequence of incoming messages, ims(H), a sequence of pending calls, pcs(H), and a sequence of exposed objects, exp(H). Every concrete history H with box$(H) = b$ satisfies the following conditions:*

- *If ims$(H) = \bullet$, then pcs$(H) = \bullet$ and exp$(H) = \{b\}$.*
- *If ims$(H) = n_1, \ldots, n_z$, then*

1. *there is a concrete history H' with $box(H') = b$ and*
   $ims(H') = n_1, ..., n_{z-1}$.
2. n_z *is* admissible *for H', which means that*
   (a) n_z *is an ingoing message for b*
   (b) $inner(b, n_z) \subseteq exp(H')$
   (c) *if n_z is a return message then n_z matches $last(pcs(H'))$*
3. $isem(b, state(b, ims(H')), n_z) = (B, n)$
4. $exp(H) = exp(H') \circ inner(b, n)$
5. $pcs(H) = \begin{cases} pcs(H') & \text{if } n_z \text{ is a call, and } n \text{ is a return} \\ pcs(H') \cdot n & \text{if } n_z \text{ is a call, and } n \text{ is a call} \\ front(pcs(H')) & \text{if } n_z \text{ is a return and } n \text{ is a return} \\ front(pcs(H')) \cdot n & \text{if } n_z \text{ is a return, and } n \text{ is a call} \end{cases}$

Based on the notions of concrete histories, we define a representation-independent semantics for boxes. The big advantage of a representation independency is that it allows to compare two boxes with different representations without the need to relate their representations (see [3]).

Definition 3 (History-Based Semantics). *Let H be a concrete history with $box(H) = b$. Let n be an admissible message for H. We define the history-based semantics,* hsem, *as*

$$hsem(H, n) = \begin{cases} n' & \text{if } oc = (B, n') \\ oc & \text{otherwise} \end{cases} \quad \text{where } oc = isem(b, state(b, ims(H)), n)$$

3.2   Behavioral Semantics

The incoming message sequence of a concrete history still contains objects and types that depend on the execution environment. In order to abstract from concrete objects we introduce abstract objects $\tilde{o}$. An abstract object is represented by a natural number i, and a subscript indicating whether it is an inner or outer object with respect to a certain box.

$$\tilde{o} ::= i_{in} \mid i_{out}$$

The precise types of the objects are not recorded, as we want to compare histories for implementations with different types. The needed type information can be derived from the method signature in an abstract message, which is defined as follows. Let C be a box class with code base K, and let D be a class in K; *abstract messages* $\tilde{n}$ of C have the form

$$\tilde{n} ::= \tilde{o}.D{::}m(\overline{\tilde{v}}) \mid D{::}m{:}\tilde{v}$$

The left one is a call message and the right one is a return message. A message $\tilde{n}$ is an *ingoing call* if $\tilde{o}$ is an inner object, otherwise it is an *outgoing call*. The method parameters $\tilde{v}$ are abstract objects or null (*abstract values*). The function *inner* on abstract messages returns the set of abstract inner objects occurring as parameters of the message. *params* return the message parameters, i.e. $\tilde{o} \cdot \overline{\tilde{v}}$. $D::m$ denotes method m in class D. This *class qualification* of method names is needed because the receiver type is no longer represented and methods in incomparable classes may have the same name.

Let η be a bijection from concrete objects to abstract objects. We say that a concrete message n *corresponds to* an abstract message $\tilde{n}$, denoted by $n \simeq_\eta \tilde{n}$, if and only if the method names and message kinds are the same, the class qualification of $\tilde{n}$ is the largest supertype of the receiver in which the method is defined, and the parameters are the same under η, i.e. $\eta(params(n)) = params(\tilde{n})$.

Definition 4 (History Abstraction). *Let H be a concrete history. An abstraction G of H consists of a sequence of incoming abstract messages $ims_a(G)$, a sequence of pending abstract calls $pcs_a(G)$, and a sequence of exposed abstract objects $exp_a(G)$ such that the following conditions are satisfied:*

- *There exists a bijection η from concrete objects occurring in H as parameters of messages or as exposed objects, and abstract objects occurring in G, such that*

$$\eta(o) = \begin{cases} i_{in} & \text{if } o \preceq b \\ i_{out} & \text{otherwise} \end{cases}$$

- $\eta(exp(H)) = exp_a(G)$
- $ims(H) \simeq_\eta ims_a(G)$
- $pcs(H) \simeq_\eta pcs_a(G)$

We call G an *abstract history* for a box class C iff G is an abstraction of some concrete history H with $class(box(H)) = C$.

In general, there are many different abstractions of a concrete history, as the object numbers of abstract messages can be arbitrarily chosen. To give every concrete history a unique abstraction, we define a normalization of abstract histories. To normalize an abstract history G we rename all message numbers appearing in G in such a way that the first occurring number is 1 and all following numbers are always advanced by 1. By $absHis(H)$ we denote the *normalized abstraction* of concrete history H and call the resulting history a *normalized abstract history*.

Given a concrete history H and a concrete message n, where all parameters of n already occur in H, we define the function $absMsg(H, n)$ to result in abstract message $\tilde{n}$ as follows: let $G = absHis(H)$ and let η be the bijection of Def. 4; then $\tilde{n}$ is an abstract message that corresponds to n, and the parameters in n are equal to the abstract parameters in $\tilde{n}$ under bijection η. If there are new objects in n which are not in the domain of η, η is extended in a normalized way.

Given a concrete history H and an admissible message n for H. Let $oc = hsem(H, n)$. We denote the abstraction of outcome oc by $absOutcome(oc, H, n)$. If $oc \in \{ABORT, DIVERGE\}$, then $absOutcome(oc, H, n) = oc$. Otherwise, we abstract the message oc w.r.t. H and n in the same way as we defined $absMsg$.

The central property of our abstraction is formulated by the following lemma. It states that abstract histories can express the behavior of a box class and its code base independent of the box instances and of the program in which the box is used. More precisely:

Lemma 1 (Abstraction). *Let C be a box class with code base K, and P_1 and P_2 be two programs containing K. Let b_1 and b_2 be boxes of C in executions of P_1 and P_2 resp.; furthermore let H_1 and H_2 be concrete histories for b_1 and b_2 such that $absHis(H_1) = absHis(H_2)$. If n_1 and n_2 are admissible messages for H_1 and H_2 resp. with $absMsg(H_1, n_1) = absMsg(H_2, n_2)$, then*

$$absOutcome(hsem(H_1, n_1), H_1, n_1) = absOutcome(hsem(H_2, n_2), H_2, n_2) .$$

Proof. A detailed formal proof is beyond the scope of this paper. Here, we give an outline of the central ideas. The proof runs by induction on the length of H_1 (note $|ims(H_1)| = |ims(H_2)|$). Let H_i^k denote the prefix of H_i containing the first k messages.

Induction invariant: For all $k \in \{0, \ldots, |ims(H_1)|\}$ there exists a bijection β^k from the objects and boxes occurring in $state(b_1, ims(H_1^k))$ to the objects and boxes occurring in $state(b_2, ims(H_2^k))$ such that

$$class(o) = class(\beta_k(o)) \quad \text{for the objects in } state(b_1, ims(H_1^k))$$
$$state(b_1, ims(H_1^k)) = state(b_2, ims(H_2^k)) \downarrow \beta^k$$

where $state(b_2, ims(H_2^k)) \downarrow \beta^k$ denotes the box state that is obtained from $state(b_2, ims(H_2^k))$ by replacing all objects o and boxes b by $\beta^k(o)$ and $\beta^k(b)$.

The induction basis follows from rule R-NEW-BOX. Induction step: Because of $absMsg(H_1^k, n_1^k) = absMsg(H_2^k, n_2^k)$, both messages are of the same kind. If they are call messages the receiver has to be an object o_i in b_i. Because the messages n_i^k are admissible, o_i is in $exp(H_i^k)$, thus, o_1 is in the domain of β^k so that $class(o_1) = class(o_2)$. Thus, $absHis(H_1^k) = absHis(H_2^k)$ yields that the methods are the same, in particular, they have the same signature. Thus, the parameter lists have the same length. For parameter objects p_1 of n_1 that already occur in H_1^k, $absHis(H_1^k) = absHis(H_2^k)$ yields that $\beta^k(p_1) = p_2$. Parameter objects not occurring in H_1^k or H_2^k are outside objects (otherwise they are present in $exp(H_i^k)$). Note that they may have different dynamic types. Because of $absHis(H_1^k) = absHis(H_2^k)$, there is a bijection from the parameter objects not occurring in H_1^k to those not occurring in H_2^k that is consistent with the position in the parameter list of n_i^k. By β_+^k we denote the extension of β^k to the object not occurring in H_1^k. A similar construction has to be done, if n_i^k are return messages. In that case, the pending call sequence is used to identify the addressees of the messages.

Now, we have corresponding start states $state(b_1, ims(H_1^k))$ and $state(b_2, ims(H_2^k))$ with corresponding incoming messages. The rules of Fig. 4 keep the correspondence, because none of the rules depend on the concrete object or box identifiers or on the concrete type of outside objects (that is the reason why we do not allow to cast outside objects). Thus, either both executions abort, diverge, or produce corresponding replies, that is replies with the same abstraction. □

Based on the Abstraction Lemma we formulate a behavioral semantics for box classes. Let G be an abstract history. An abstract message $\tilde{n}$ is called *admissible for G* if and only if

- $\tilde{n}$ is an ingoing abstract message, and
- $inner(\tilde{n}) \subseteq exp_a(G)$, and
- if $\tilde{n}$ is a return, i.e. $\tilde{n} = D{::}m{:}\tilde{v}$, then it matches the last pending call, i.e. $last(pcs_a(G)) = i_{out}.D{::}m(\bar{\tilde{v}})$, for some abstract values $\bar{\tilde{v}}$.

Definition 5 (Behavioral Semantics). *Let G be a normalized abstract history and let $\tilde{n}$ be an admissible message for G. We define the behavioral semantics, bsem, as*

$$bsem(G, \tilde{n}) = absOutcome(hsem(H, n), H, n)$$

where H is any concrete history for a box b with $G = absHis(H)$, and n is any admissible concrete message for H with $\tilde{n} = absMsg(H, n)$.

Lemma 2. *bsem is well-defined.*

Proof. Let G be a normalized abstract history and $\tilde{n}$ be an abstract admissible message for G. By definition there exists a concrete history H with $G = absHis(H)$. If we can show that it is possible to choose an admissible message n for H with $\tilde{n} = absMsg(H, n)$, the Abstraction Lemma provides well-definedness, because it guarantees that the abstract outcome does not depend on the choice of H and n.

Let η_G be the bijection of G. If $\tilde{n}$ is an ingoing call, then choose an arbitrary outside sender, and choose arbitrary outside objects for outer parameters not handled by η_G. Use all other objects according to η_G^{-1} given by $ims_a(G)$. Otherwise if $\tilde{n}$ is an ingoing return $D{::}m{:}\tilde{v}$, then let $o \to o'.m(\bar{v}) = last(pcs(H))$ and let $last(ims_a(G)) = i_{out}.D{::}m(\bar{\tilde{v}})$. The compatibility of $pcs(G)$ yields that $o \leftarrow o'.m{:}v$ is an admissible message where $v = \eta_G^{-1}(\tilde{v})$ if $v \in dom(\eta_G)$ or v is some correctly typed object not in $dom(\eta_G)$ otherwise. □

4   Substitutability

In this section, we discuss how our behavioral semantics can be exploited to handle substitutability in object-oriented programming. Central for the exploitation is the representation independency of the semantics based on a well-defined boundary of the runtime components.

A program component K_1 can be substituted by another component K_2 in a program context P if both components have the same behavior in all executions of P. The application of this notion of substitutability to existing OO-languages faces two problems: 1. Beyond classes, there is no suitable standard concept of a program component; and considering only single classes does not scale. 2. Defining "same behavior" without a sufficiently abstract notion of behavior is doable but complex (see [3] and the discussion in Sec. 5).

Our approach gives answers to both problems. A code base of a box class C is a well-defined notion for flexible program components. Having an explicit behavioral semantics makes it straightforward to define substitutability and equivalence for box classes:

Definition 6 (Substitutability, Equivalence). *Let C_1 and C_2 be two box classes with code bases K_1 and K_2 such that $C_1 = C_2$ or C_2 is a subclass of C_1. (C_2, K_2) is called a behavioral substitute of (C_1, K_1) iff*

- *every abstract history G of C_1 is an abstract history of C_2 and*
- *$bsem(C_1, G, \tilde{n}) = bsem(C_2, G, \tilde{n})$ for every abstract history G of C_1 and every admissible abstract message $\tilde{n}$ of G.*

Two code bases K_1 and K_2 for a class C are called equivalent *iff (C, K_1) is a behavioral substitute of (C, K_2) and vice versa.*

Of course, a behavioral substitute can have more behavior. For example, class C_2 or objects exposed by C_2 can have more methods. Thus, they have more admissible messages. However, these messages cannot be used in program contexts in which C_1 is eligible.

Intuitively, a software component SC_2 is substitutable for a component SC_1 if replacing a usage of SC_1 in a program by a usage of SC_2 yields an equivalent program. As we only have a notion of equivalence for box classes, this intuitive meaning gets the following formulation in our setting:

Lemma 3 (Substitution). *Let D, C_1, and C_2 be box classes with code bases K, K_1, and K_2 such that C_1 is used in K and C_2 is a subclass of C_1. Let K' be the code base for D obtained by replacing a creation expression new $C_1()$ by new $C_2()$ in K (as K' is declaration complete it includes K_2). If (C_2, K_2) is a behavioral substitute of (C_1, K_1), then (D, K) and (D, K') are equivalent.*

A proof of the lemma is beyond the scope of this paper. It basically shows that in any context of an executable program an instance of D with code base K can simulate an instance of D with code base K' and vice versa. As in the proof of the Abstraction Lemma, it is crucial that we permit downcasts of an object o only in o's box and that we do not provide an instance-of operator. Consider for example a program context in which (D, K) exposes an owned C_1-object o_1 and (D, K') exposes an owned C_2-object o_2 instead. Casting o_1 and o_2 in this context to C_2 would yield different outcomes and the simulation would fail.

Discussion. The main point of our notion of behavior and substitutability is that the abstraction needed to compare different implementations is given by the behavioral semantics and is independent of the components to be compared and the contexts in which they should execute. Thus, one can do the comparison without component specific coupling relations or specifications.

In one respect, our notion is less flexible than notions of substitutability that are based on classical component specifications. Whereas in our setting admissibility of messages is defined only in terms of the operational semantics, component specifications can and usually do restrict the set of admissible messages by preconditions. Looking at it the other way round, by refining the notion of admissible message, our approach could be used as a semantics for behavioral specifications of program components where a specification defines:

1. The set of possible abstract component states.
2. The admissible messages in a state (using preconditions).
3. The reply to messages and the abstract state in which the reply is sent.

Abstract components states represent and possibly further abstract histories. As a specification can exclude some messages by preconditions, a specification allows less histories than the semantics. The central difference between the classical pre-postcondition approach for behavioral subtyping (see [18]) and a specification technique based on our approach is the treatment of callbacks and effects to the environment. The extensions to the classical approach treat callbacks by supporting controlled dependencies across abstraction boundaries (see e.g. [4]). Our approach suggests to focus on the messages crossing the component boundary. This will simplify the verification of the component and shift part of the burden to the program that connects the components under consideration.

5   Related Work

In [3], Banerjee and Naumann show how confinement properties based on ownership-structures can be exploited to define and verify the equivalence of program components. Like in our approach, they use a semantics-based notion of ownership. Different is the technique to establish the equivalence result. They use relations for coupling execution states and a simulation-based proof technique whereas we abstract the implementations separately and compare the abstractions. The work in [3] and our approach both aim at substitutability for components of scalable size. Other work investigate refinement and inheritance relations on the level of classes (see in particular [2]).

Using message sequences to characterize state and behavior of software components is not a new idea (see e.g. [12] and later [10]). Nierstrasz defines the notion of request substitutability based on request sequences [20]. Broy uses call and return messages to characterize the behavior of methods in a component specification framework ([8]). Abraham et al. investigate interface behavior for a concurrent object calculus in [1]. Like we do, they use call and return messages crossing component boundaries and stacks to handle callback scenarios, but object identifiers are only abstracted with respect to alpha-conversion.

A large core of literature explores behavioral subtyping for object-oriented programming based on class and method specifications. That is, the behavioral subtype relation is not defined in terms of the semantics of the given classes, but in terms of programmer defined specifications that abstract class behavior (see [18]). These techniques build on specification languages for object-oriented programs (e.g. JML for Java [16], Spec# for C# [6]). Leavens and Naumann describe the relation between specification, semantics, and behavioral subtyping in a very concise way [15]. A specification technique with refinement that explicitly handles outgoing messages is developed in [9].

Ownership concepts were originally developed to check confinement properties by type systems: see [11] for an introduction and overview; [7] for a system to check concurrency properties; and [24, 21] for a type system and an type inference technique to check boxes. Boogie [5] and other approaches to modular reasoning (see e.g. [19, 17] use ownership structures to define the semantics of object invariants, to control the dependencies of specification statements, and to partition the heap. The importance to modularize reasoning and analysis based on heap structuring is shown as well by [22], which develops a logic for partial heaps, and by [23] which presents a modular static analysis to identify structural invariants of heap-manipulation programs.

6   Conclusions

We presented a behavioral semantics for flexible object-oriented components with multiple ingoing and outgoing read-write references. The semantics is obtained by a two step abstraction from an extended operational semantics. The semantics formalizes the behavioral aspects that are relevant to a user of the component. We discussed the relation to substitutability and specification-based behavioral subtyping.

A semantics based notion of component behavior has the advantage that it can be used by all language-processing tools and techniques. The abstraction from the execution environment is important for modular static analysis techniques. It guarantees that a "most general client" that generates all admissible message sequences for the component can be used for static analysis. Future work include the refinement of the component model, in particular the transfer of inner boxes from one box to another, the enhancement of our specification and checking techniques, and an extension of the approach to concurrent object-oriented programming.

Acknowledgments. We thank Peter Müller and the anonymous reviewers for their helpful comments.

References

[1] Ábrahám, E., Grüner, A., Steffen, M.: Abstract interface behavior of object-oriented languages with monitors. In: Gorrieri, R., Wehrheim, H. (eds.) FMOODS 2006. LNCS, vol. 4037, pp. 218–232. Springer, Heidelberg (2006)
[2] Back, R.-J., Mikhajlova, A., von Wright, J.: Class refinement as semantics of correct object substitutability. Formal aspects of computing 12(1), 18–40 (2000)
[3] Banerjee, A., Naumann, D.A.: Ownership confinement ensures representation independence for object-oriented programs. Journal of the ACM 52(6), 894–960 (2005)
[4] Barnett, M., Naumann, D.A.: Friends need a bit more: Maintaining invariants over shared state. In: Kozen, D., Shankland, C. (eds.) MPC 2004. LNCS, vol. 3125, pp. 54–84. Springer, Heidelberg (2004)

[5] Barnett, M., DeLine, R., Fähndrich, M., Leino, K.R.M., Schulte, W.: Verification of object-oriented programs with invariants. Journal of Object Technology, vol. 3(6) (2004)

[6] Barnett, M., Leino, K.R.M., Schulte, W.: The Spec# programming system: An overview. In: Barthe, G., Burdy, L., Huisman, M., Lanet, J.-L., Muntean, T. (eds.) CASSIS 2004. LNCS, vol. 3362, Springer, Heidelberg (2004)

[7] Boyapati, C., Lee, R., Rinard, M.: Ownership types for safe programming: Preventing data races and deadlocks. In: Proc. OOPSLA 2002, pp. 211–230. ACM Press, New York (2002)

[8] Broy, M.: A core theory of interfaces and architecture and its impact on object orientation. In: Reussner, R., Stafford, J.A., Szyperski, C.A. (eds.) Architecting Systems with Trustworthy Components. LNCS, vol. 3938, pp. 26–47. Springer, Heidelberg (2006)

[9] Büchi, M.: Safe Language Mechanisms for Modularization and Concurrency. PhD thesis, Turku Centre for Computer Science (May 2000)

[10] Chakrabarti, A., de Alfaro, L., Henzinger, T.A., Jurdzinski, M., Mang, F.Y.C.: Interface compatibility checking for software modules. In: Brinksma, E., Larsen, K.G. (eds.) CAV 2002. LNCS, vol. 2404, pp. 428–441. Springer, Heidelberg (2002)

[11] Clarke, D.: Object Ownership and Containment. PhD thesis, University of New South Wales (July 2001)

[12] de Alfaro, L., Henzinger, T.A.: Interface automata. In: ESEC/FSE-9, pp. 109–120. ACM Press, New York (2001)

[13] Flatt, M., Krishnamurthi, S., Felleisen, M.: A programmer's reduction semantics for classes and mixins. Formal Syntax and Semantics of Java 1523, 241–269 (1999)

[14] Igarashi, A., Pierce, B.C., Wadler, P.: Featherweight Java: A minimal core calculus for Java and GJ. TOPLAS 23(3), 396–450 (May 2001)

[15] Leavens, G.T., Naumann, D.A.: Behavioral subtyping, specification inheritance, and modular reasoning. Technical Report TR06-20a, Computer Science, Iowa State University (2006)

[16] Leavens, G.T., Baker, A.L., Ruby, C.: Preliminary design of JML a behavioral interface specification language for Java. SIGSOFT Softw. Eng. Notes 31(3), 1–38 (2006)

[17] Leino, K.R.M., Müller, P.: Object invariants in dynamic contexts. In: Odersky, M. (ed.) Proc. ECOOP 2004. LNCS, vol. 3086, pp. 491–516. Springer, Heidelberg (2004)

[18] Liskov, B., Wing, J.: A behavioral notion of subtyping. ACM Transactions on Programming Languages and Systems 16(6), 1811–1841 (1994)

[19] Müller, P.: Modular Specification and Verification of Object-Oriented Programs. LNCS, vol. 2262. Springer, Heidelberg (2002)

[20] Nierstrasz, O.: Regular types for active objects. In: Proc. OOPSLA '93, October 1993, pp. 1–15. ACM Press, New York (1993)

[21] Poetzsch-Heffter, A., Geilmann, K., Schäfer, J.: Inferring ownership types for encapsulated object-oriented program components. In: Program Analysis and Compilation, Theory and Practice: Essays Dedicated to Reinhard Wilhelm. LNCS, vol. 4444, Springer, Heidelberg (2007)

[22] Reynolds, J.C.: Separation logic: A logic for shared mutable data structures. In: Proceedings of LICS'02, pp. 55–74 (2002)

[23] Rinetzky, N., Poetzsch-Heffter, A., Ramalingam, G., Sagiv, M., Yahav, E.: Modular shape analysis for dynamically encapsulated programs. In: European Symposium on Programming (ESOP'07), March 2007, Springer, Heidelberg (2007)

[24] Schäfer, J., Poetzsch-Heffter, A.: A parameterized type system for simple loose ownership domains. Journal of Object Technology, June 2007, to appear (2007)

A Formal Language for Electronic Contracts*

Cristian Prisacariu and Gerardo Schneider

Dept. of Informatics – Univ. of Oslo,
P.O. Box 1080 Blindern, N-0316 Oslo, Norway
cristi@ifi.uio.no, gerardo@ifi.uio.no

Abstract. In this paper we propose a formal language for writing electronic contracts, based on the deontic notions of obligation, permission, and prohibition. We take an ought-to-do approach, where deontic operators are applied to actions instead of state-of-affairs. We propose an extension of the μ-calculus in order to capture the intuitive meaning of the deontic notions and to express concurrent actions. We provide a translation of the contract language into the logic, the semantics of which faithfully captures the meaning of obligation, permission and prohibition. We also show how our language captures most of the intuitive desirable properties of electronic contracts, as well as how it avoids most of the classical paradoxes of deontic logic. We finally show its applicability on a contract example.

1 Introduction

With the imminent use of Internet as a means for developing cross-organizational collaborations and virtual communities engaged in business, new challenges arise to guarantee a successful integration and interoperability of such virtual organizations. Service-oriented architectures (SOA) is becoming more and more the trend in this arena. Entities participating in a SOA have no access to complete information, including information for checking the reliability of the service provider and/or service consumer. For instance, a service consumer has no access to the code implementing the service, and is therefore unable to examine, much less verify, the service implementation to have assurance of its compliance with his/her needs. This motivates the need of establishing an agreement before any transaction is performed, through a *contract*, engaging all participants in the transaction under the commitments stipulated in such a document, which must also contain clauses determining penalties in case of contract violations. A service provider may also use a contract template (i.e., a yet-to-be-negotiated contract) to publish the services it is willing to provide. As a service specification, a contract may describe many different *aspects* of a service, including functional properties and also non-functional properties like quality of service (QoS).

In order to advance towards a reliable SOA, we need to be able to write contracts which can be "understood" by the software engaged in the negotiation

---

* Partially supported by the Nordunet3 project "Contract-Oriented Software Development for Internet Services".

M.M. Bonsangue and E.B. Johnsen (Eds.): FMOODS 2007, LNCS 4468, pp. 174–189, 2007.

process, and later may be used by virtual organizations responsible for ensuring that the contract is respected. In other words, contracts should be amenable to formal analysis and thus written in a formal language.

There are currently several different approaches aiming at defining a formal language for contracts, the most promising approach, in our opinion, being the one based on logics. A logic for contracts not necessarily has to be based on, or extend, *deontic logic*, but must contain notions like obligation, permission, and prohibition, and preserve their intuitive properties. Formalizing the usual normative (deontic) notions of obligation, permission and prohibition is not an easy task as witnessed by the extensive research conducted by the deontic community both from the philosophical and the logical point of view, starting as early as 1926 [17].[1] In what follows we discuss some of the problems and challenges that appear when defining *electronic contracts* (e-contracts).

In early papers (e.g. [33]) the approach was to relate the normative notions of obligation, permission and prohibition in a similar way as the quantifiers *all*, *some* and *no*, and the modalities *necessary, possible* and *impossible*. This was the bases of the so-called Standard Deontic Logic (SDL) which builds up on propositional classical logic, leading to a nice formalization but also to many paradoxes which still continue to challenge philosophers, logicians and computer scientists.

Besides avoiding paradoxes, one of the first issues to take into account when formalizing normative notions is whether we want to represent (names of) human actions or (sentences describing) states of affairs, product of a human action. The former is usually known as *ought-to-do* and the latter as *ought-to-be*. For example "Jones ought to pay the money" is an ought-to-do sentence, while "It ought to be the case that Jones pays the money" is an ought-to-be sentence. In general the relationship between both representations is not as obvious as in the above example and the translation from one to the other is much more involved. The discussion among philosophers and logicians is far from an end in what concerns the decision of whether one approach is better than the other, or even if both should coexist in the same reasoning system. In many e-contracts it is more natural to find statements of *ought-to-do* kind; where the *subject* is stated explicitly (the supplier, the client), the *actions* (that are permitted or forbidden) are visible, and also in many cases there might be an *object*. There may also be cases where an ought-to-be approach gives a more concise expression, like in QoS contracts where we may have statements expressing quantitative restrictions like *the average bandwidth should be more than 20kb/s.*

Contracts contain clauses which by definition are violable (if we have the guarantee that nobody will violate them, contracts would be useless). Hence, *contrary-to-duty obligations* (CTD) and *contrary-to-prohibitions* (CTP) are important aspects to be considered. CTDs are statements that represent the fact that obligations might not be respected where CTPs are similar statements which deal with prohibitions that might be violated. Both constructions specify

---

[1] Mally's work is considered a precursor of Deontic Logic, though it is widely accepted that modern Deontic Logic started with the work by G.H. von Wright [33].

the obligation/prohibition to be fulfilled and which is the *reparation/penalty* to be applied in case of violation.

Other problems to be considered when formalizing deontic notions are the study of their interrelation (duality and definition in terms of each other), the understanding of their truth-value (even the discussion whether it is reasonable to talk about the truth-value of such notions), and the difference between "must" and "ought".

Since we are concerned with formal definition of e-contracts we are definitely on a terrain where many of the philosophical problems of the deontic logic are not present. In this paper we take a first step towards the definition of a formal contract language following an ought-to-do approach. Our starting point is [5], where a fix-point characterization of obligation, permission and prohibition is given, based on the modal μ-calculus, allowing the definition of the deontic notions over regular actions.

The main contribution of this paper is the definition of a contract language with the following properties:

1. The language avoids most of the classical paradoxes of deontic logic;
2. It is possible to express in the language obligations, permission and prohibition over concurrent actions keeping their intuitive meaning;
3. Obligation of disjunctive and conjunctive actions is defined compositionally;
4. The definition and semantics of obligation does not contain action negation;
5. It is possible to express CTDs and CTPs;
6. The language has a formal semantics given in a variant of the propositional μ-calculus.

Other side contributions are:

1. We revisit the relations between the deontic notions, providing new insights into how they should be related in the context of e-contracts;
2. We give special attention to the disjunction on obligations, to which we provide a natural and precise interpretation;
3. We extend the propositional μ-calculus with the possibility of expressing concurrent and deterministic actions.

The paper is organized as follows. In Section 2 we start by presenting an example of a partial contract, we then informally discuss some of the desirable properties a contract language should have, and finally present our formal language for writing contracts. In Section 3 we present a variant of the μ-calculus, with its syntax and semantics, and we give a translation of the contract language into the logic. In Section 4 we show that our language avoids many of the paradoxes and that it satisfies most of the desirable properties listed in Section 2. Before concluding, we present in Section 5 the modeling of the example of Section 2 using our contract language.

2   A Formal Language for Contracts

We start by presenting an example, we then list desirable properties for defining a contract language and we describe informally the kind of actions that are needed for our language. In the last subsection we present the syntax of the language for writing e-contracts and the intuition behind it.

2.1 A Contract Example

In what follows we provide part of a contract between a service provider and a client, where the provider gives access to Internet to the client. We consider two parameters of the service: *high* and *low*, which denote the client's Internet traffic. We abstract away from several technical details as how it is measured the Internet traffic. We will consider only the following clauses of the contract:

1. Whenever the Internet traffic is *high* then the client must pay x \$ immediately, or the client must notify the service provider by sending an e-mail specifying that he will pay later.
2. In case the client delays the payment, after notification he must immediately lower the Internet traffic to the *low* level, and pay later $2 * x$ \$.
3. If the client does not lower the Internet traffic immediately, then the client will have to pay $3 * x$ \$.
4. The provider is forbidden to cancel the contract without previous written notification by normal post and by e-mail.
5. The provider is obliged to provide the services as stipulated in the contract, and according to the law regulating Internet services.

A formalization of the above will be presented in Section 5.

2.2 Desirable Properties of a Language for Contracts

In what follows we use $+$ for *choice* among actions, $O(a)$ to denote the obligation of performing a given action a, and similarly for permission $P(a)$ and prohibition $F(a)$. A more precise definition will be given later.

General Requirements: We list first some general intuitive properties we should have, and others we should avoid, when formalizing deontic notions in contracts.

We want to avoid as many logical paradoxes as possible[2], in particular: the Ross paradox (i.e., $O(a) \Rightarrow O(a + b))$[3], and the free choice paradox (i.e., $P(a) \Rightarrow P(a + b)$). Syntactically disallow the classical disjunction between deontic modalities. Obligation should be defined only on actions, not on formulas (which, as argued in the deontic community, would avoid several of the present paradoxes). Conjunction on obligations should imply executing the obliged actions at the same time (not to violate any of the obligations). Obligation of a sequence of actions should imply the obligation of all the subsequent actions. Allow specification of reparations for violations of obligations and prohibitions. Allow the definition of conditional obligations (i.e., $\varphi \Rightarrow O(a)$). Obligation

---

[2] For a list of classical paradoxes see [28].

[3] The symbol " $\Rightarrow$ " is not part of our contract language and we use it informally as a shortcut for "if-then" or "implies".

should imply permission. Do not define permission and obligation in terms of each other (see von Wright's argument [34]). Defining permission in terms of prohibition is natural and desirable.

Properties of Electronic Contracts: In the philosophical and pure logic contexts we find many reasonable discussions related to deontic operators, which we claim can be avoided given that we are restricted to e-contracts. In what follows we provide arguments for restricting syntactically the occurrence in the contract language of certain expressions involving obligation, permission and prohibition applied to actions.

It is not natural to have in contracts statements like *one is NOT obliged to perform an action*, thus $\neg O(a)$ should not occur in a contract. A statement like *one is NOT permitted to do something* can be rewritten as *one is forbidden to do something*; $\neg P(a) \equiv F(a)$. Also *one is NOT forbidden to do an action* can be rewritten as *one is permitted to do the action*; thus we should consider $\neg F(a) \equiv P(a)$. We adhere thus to the usual approach of defining permission and prohibition as one being the negation of the other.

It is not intuitive to have the $+$ under the F operator. Consider for example the following norm: *In Europe it is forbidden one of the following actions (but not both): to drive on the left side of the road (d_l), or to drive on the right side (d_r)* which can be represented as $F(d_l + d_r)$. The problem is that it is not clear under which circumstances each one of the actions can be taken. The natural way to exclusively forbid the choice between two actions is to relate each of the actions with its context. So, the above sentence could be rewritten as: *In the United Kingdom it is forbidden to drive on the right side of the road. In the rest of Europe (except United Kingdom) it is forbidden to drive on the left side of the road.* Which can be formalized as: $\varphi_{UK} \Rightarrow F(d_r)$ and $\varphi_{REU} \Rightarrow F(d_l)$. Where φ_{UK} and φ_{REU} are mutually exclusive. On the other hand, it is possible to forbid two actions a and b simultaneously by imposing $F(a) \wedge F(b)$.

Moreover, we argue that in contracts it is not common to find statements that may be formalized using an exclusive OR operator $\oplus$ between prohibitions. If we take the formula $F(a) \oplus F(b)$ to mean that either is forbidden a or forbidden b but not forbidden both then one case of the statement is $F(a) \wedge \neg F(b)$, which, using the above equivalence between P and $\neg F$ is $F(a) \wedge P(b)$. This means that one has the permission to do b. Similar from the second case, one may conclude that it is permitted to do a. In the end, the formula $F(a) \oplus F(b)$ does not explicitly prohibit anything, making its use completely meaningless and dangerous.

2.3   Actions

Our practical requirements to represent actions found in e-contracts force us to make some changes to the classical dynamic algebra [27]. We first drop the Kleene star (iteration) as it is unnatural to have it under the deontic operators. A second difference involves the inclusion of concurrent actions.

Our action algebra has a set of atomic actions denoted by $\mathcal{L}$, a set $\mathcal{B}$ of formulas in the Boolean algebra, and the action operators which define the compound actions: + for *choice* of two actions[4], · for sequence of actions, & for concurrent execution of two atomic actions. The test operator ? is applied to elements of $\mathcal{B}$ and generates actions of $\mathcal{L}$. For brevity we often drop the sequence operator and instead of $\alpha \cdot \beta$ we just write $\alpha\beta$. We also define *action negation* $\overline{\alpha}$ of a compound action α as the action given by all the immediate traces that *take us outside* the trace of α [5] and is formally defined using a canonic form of the actions.

2.4   The Contract Language

We aim at the definition of a precise syntax of a contract language, with a translation into a logic in order to be able to reason about it. We define the contract language $\mathcal{CL}$, and provide a set of rewriting rules in order to simplify and minimize the number of expressions in the language.

Definition 1 (Contract Language Syntax). *A contract is defined by:*

$$
\begin{aligned}
Contract &:= \mathcal{D} \; ; \; \mathcal{C} \\
\mathcal{C} &:= \phi \mid \mathcal{C}_O \mid \mathcal{C}_P \mid \mathcal{C}_F \mid \mathcal{C} \wedge \mathcal{C} \mid [\alpha]\mathcal{C} \mid \langle\alpha\rangle\mathcal{C} \mid \mathcal{C}\,\mathcal{U}\,\mathcal{C} \mid \bigcirc\mathcal{C} \\
\mathcal{C}_O &:= O(\alpha) \mid \mathcal{C}_O \oplus \mathcal{C}_O \\
\mathcal{C}_P &:= P(\alpha) \mid \mathcal{C}_P \oplus \mathcal{C}_P \\
\mathcal{C}_F &:= F(\delta) \mid \mathcal{C}_F \vee [\delta]\mathcal{C}_F
\end{aligned}
$$

The syntax of $\mathcal{CL}$ closely resembles the syntax of a modal (deontic) logic. Though this similarity is clearly intentional since we are driven by a logic-based approach, $\mathcal{CL}$ is *not* a logic. In what follows we provide an intuitive explanation of the $\mathcal{CL}$ syntax; a more precise meaning will be given later through the translation into an extension of the propositional μ-calculus.

A contract consists of two parts: *definitions* ($\mathcal{D}$) and *clauses* ($\mathcal{C}$). Note that we deliberately let the definitions part underspecified in the syntax above. $\mathcal{D}$ specifies the *assertions* (or conditions) and the atomic actions present in the clauses. ϕ denotes assertions and ranges over Boolean expressions including arithmetic comparisons, like *the budget is more than 200\$*. For now we let the atomic actions underspecified, which for our purposes can be understood as consisting of three parts: the proper action, the subject performing the action, and the target of (or, the object receiving) such an action. Note that, in this way, the partners involved in a contract are encoded in the actions.

$\mathcal{C}$ is the general *contract clause*. $\mathcal{C}_O$, $\mathcal{C}_P$, and $\mathcal{C}_F$ denote respectively *obligation*, *permission*, and *prohibition* clauses. $\wedge$ and $\oplus$ may be thought as the classical conjunction and exclusive disjunction, which may be used to combine obligations and permissions. For prohibition $\mathcal{C}_F$ we have $\vee$, again with the classical meaning of the corresponding operator. α is a compound action with syntax as given in Section 2.3, while δ denotes a compound action not containing any occurrence of +. Operationally, we consider that atomic actions do not require time for their execution, i.e., the atomic actions are *instantaneous*. A concurrent action is also instantaneous, so it can be seen as atomic. Note that syntactically $\oplus$ cannot

---

[4] We do not distinguish between internal (free) choice and external (imposed) choice.

Table 1. Compositional rules

$$
\begin{array}{ll}
(1) & O(\alpha + \beta) \equiv O(\alpha) \oplus O(\beta) \\
(2) & O(a\&b) \equiv O(a) \wedge O(b) \\
(3) & O(\alpha\beta) \equiv O(\alpha) \wedge [\alpha]O(\beta) \\
(4) & P(\alpha + \beta) \equiv P(\alpha) \oplus P(\beta) \\
(5) & P(\alpha\beta) \equiv P(\alpha) \wedge \langle\alpha\rangle P(\beta) \\
(6) & F(\alpha\beta) \equiv F(\alpha) \vee [\alpha]F(\beta)
\end{array}
$$

Table 2. Rewriting rules for obligation O

$$
\begin{array}{ll}
(1) & O(a) \wedge O(b) \rightsquigarrow O(a\&b) \\
(2) & O(a) \wedge O(a\&b) \rightsquigarrow O(a\&b) \\
(3) & O(a) \wedge (O(a) \oplus O(b)) \rightsquigarrow O(a) \\
(4) & O(a) \wedge O(a) \rightsquigarrow O(a) \\
(5) & O(a) \oplus O(a) \rightsquigarrow O(a) \\
(6) & O(c) \wedge (O(a) \oplus O(b)) \rightsquigarrow (O(c) \wedge O(a)) \oplus (O(c) \wedge O(b)) \\
(7) & (\oplus_i O(a_i)) \wedge (\oplus_j O(b_j)) \rightsquigarrow \oplus_{i,j}(O(a_i) \wedge O(b_j)) \quad a_i \neq b_j
\end{array}
$$

appear between prohibitions and $+$ cannot occur under F, as we have discussed in Section 2.2.

We borrow from Propositional Dynamic Logic (PDL) the syntax $[\alpha]\phi$ to represent that after performing α (if it is possible to do so), ϕ must hold. The $[\cdot]$ notation allows having a *test*, where $[\phi?]\mathcal{C}$ must be understood as $\phi \Rightarrow \mathcal{C}$. $\langle\alpha\rangle\phi$ captures the idea that there must be the possibility of executing α, in which case ϕ must hold afterwards. Following temporal logic (TL) [23] notation we have $\mathcal{U}$ (*until*) and $\bigcirc$ (*next*) with intuitive semantics as in TL. Thus $\mathcal{C}_1 \mathcal{U} \mathcal{C}_2$ states that $\mathcal{C}_1$ should hold until $\mathcal{C}_2$ holds. $\bigcirc\mathcal{C}$ intuitively states that the $\mathcal{C}$ should hold in the next moment, usually after something happens. We can define $\Box\mathcal{C}$ (*always*) and $\Diamond\mathcal{C}$ (*eventually*) for expressing that $\mathcal{C}$ holds everywhere and sometimes in the future, respectively.

The rules of Table 1 are guided by common usage in electronic contracts and provides an equivalence relation between different syntactic expressions, which might also be interpreted as a means to define certain constructs compositionally. Note that concurrent actions are compositional only under obligation; there are no similar rules for F and P. Note that F has no rule for $+$ because exclusive choice does not appear under F. For an intuition and examples for these rules we refer to the extensive discussions in the technical report [28].

We give in Table 2 a set of rewriting rules for simplifying $\mathcal{C}_O$ expressions. Rules (1)-(3) are guided by the common examples found in real contracts, rules (4)-(5) are the usual contraction rules, and the rules (6)-(7) basically give the distributivity of conjunction over the exclusive disjunction.

To express CTDs we provide the following notation, $O_\varphi(\alpha)$, which is syntactic sugar for $O(\alpha) \wedge [\overline{\alpha}]\varphi$ stating the obligation to execute α, and the reparation φ in case the obligation is violated, i.e. α is not performed. The reparation may be any contract clause. Similarly, CTP statements $F_\varphi(\alpha)$ can be defined as $F_\varphi(\alpha) = F(\alpha) \wedge [\alpha]\varphi$, where φ is the penalty in case the prohibition is violated. Notice that it is possible to express nested CTDs and CTPs.

In $\mathcal{CL}$, we can write *conditional* obligations, permissions and prohibitions in two different ways. Just as an example let us consider conditional obligations. The first kind is represented as $[\alpha]O(\beta)$, which may be read as "after performing α, one is obliged to do β". The second kind is modeled using the test operator ?: $[\varphi?]O(\alpha)$, representing "If φ holds then one is obliged to perform α". Similarly for permission and prohibition.

3 The Underlying Logic for the Contract Language

3.1 Yet Another Propositional μ-Calculus

We take the classical propositional μ-calculus as defined by Kozen [13] and we extend it with concurrent actions and special propositional constants. We call this extension $\mathcal{C}\mu$. We consider a special set $\mathcal{L}$, which we call *atomic actions* and denote by $a, b, c, \ldots$. We add a set of propositional constants which we denote by P_c. To capture true concurrency we extend the set $\mathcal{L}$ with *concurrent sets* which are *finite subsets of atomic actions* with the intuitive meaning that all the atomic actions inside a concurrent set are executed concurrently (at the same time).

Definition 2 (concurrent sets). *A concurrent action set, denoted by γ (possibly indexed), is a finite subset of the set of atomic actions $\mathcal{L}$, $\gamma = \{a_1, \ldots, a_n\}$ where $a_i \in \mathcal{L}$. The concurrent sets $\gamma \in 2^{\mathcal{L}}$ are the labels of $\mathcal{C}\mu$.*

The *syntax* of $\mathcal{C}\mu$ is given by:

$$\varphi := P \mid Z \mid P_c \mid \top \mid \neg\varphi \mid \varphi \wedge \varphi \mid [\gamma]\varphi \mid \nu Z.\varphi(Z)$$

where P represents *propositional variables*, Z represents *state variables*, $\top$ is the constant proposition denoting true, and $[\gamma]\varphi$ is the formula stating that after executing the concurrent set γ, φ holds. $\nu Z.\varphi(Z)$ is the greatest fix-point, and the other syntactic constructs come from propositional logic. The constant propositions are added in order be able to capture the deontic operators of $\mathcal{CL}$. P_c contains two distinguished kind of constants: *obligation constants* O_a and *prohibition constants* $\mathcal{F}_a$, which are uniquely indexed by the atomic actions $a \in \mathcal{L}$. The constant propositions are interpreted in the same way as the propositional variables of P as a set of states where the constant proposition holds. The intuition of the obligation constants is that when the system is in a state s and by action a it gets to a state t where O_a holds then we may conclude that in the state s the system has the obligation to execute action a. Similarly, $\mathcal{F}_a$ denotes the fact that action a is prohibited.

Note that $\mathcal{C}\mu$ includes the classical μ-calculus because if $\gamma = \{a\}$ then $[\gamma]\varphi \equiv [a]\varphi$, and P_c can be considered as a subset of P. We also have the usual dualities:

$$\varphi \vee \psi \overset{def}{=} \neg(\neg\varphi \wedge \neg\psi)$$
$$\langle\gamma\rangle\varphi \overset{def}{=} \neg[\gamma]\neg\varphi$$
$$\mu Z.\varphi(Z) \overset{def}{=} \neg\nu Z.\neg\varphi(\neg Z)$$

The interpretation of the above syntactic constructs follows the standard set-theoretical approach [13]. The formulas are interpreted over a structure denoted by $\mathcal{T}$. Given a set $Prop = P \cup P_c$ of propositions, and a set of atomic actions $\mathcal{L}$, $\mathcal{T} = (\mathcal{S}, R_{2^{\mathcal{L}}}, \mathcal{V}_{Prop}, \mathcal{V})$, where $\mathcal{S}$ is the set of states (worlds), $R_{2^{\mathcal{L}}} : 2^{\mathcal{L}} \to \mathcal{S} \times \mathcal{S}$ is the function assigning to each concurrent set γ of $2^{\mathcal{L}}$ a relation over $\mathcal{S}$ (i.e., $R_{2^{\mathcal{L}}}(\gamma) \subseteq \mathcal{S} \times \mathcal{S}$, $\gamma \in 2^{\mathcal{L}}$), $\mathcal{V}_{Prop} : Prop \to 2^{\mathcal{S}}$ is the interpretation of the propositions, and $\mathcal{V}$ is a valuation function assigning to each state variable a set of states. The valuation $\mathcal{V}[Z := S]$ maps variable Z to the states set S and in the rest it agrees with $\mathcal{V}$. For the sake of notation instead of $R_{2^{\mathcal{L}}}(\gamma)$ we write R_γ. The semantics of each syntactic construct of $\mathcal{C}\mu$ over a structure $\mathcal{T}$ is:

$$\|\top\|_{\mathcal{V}}^{\mathcal{T}} = \mathcal{S} \quad ; \quad \|P\|_{\mathcal{V}}^{\mathcal{T}} = \mathcal{V}_{Prop}(P) \quad ; \quad \|Z\|_{\mathcal{V}}^{\mathcal{T}} = \mathcal{V}(Z) \quad ; \quad \|P_c\|_{\mathcal{V}}^{\mathcal{T}} = \mathcal{V}_{Prop}(P_c)$$

$$\|\neg\varphi\|_{\mathcal{V}}^{\mathcal{T}} = \mathcal{S} \setminus \|\varphi\|_{\mathcal{V}}^{\mathcal{T}}$$

$$\|\varphi \wedge \psi\|_{\mathcal{V}}^{\mathcal{T}} = \|\varphi\|_{\mathcal{V}}^{\mathcal{T}} \cap \|\psi\|_{\mathcal{V}}^{\mathcal{T}}$$

$$\|[\gamma]\varphi\|_{\mathcal{V}}^{\mathcal{T}} = \{s \mid \forall t \in \mathcal{S}. \ (s,t) \in R_\gamma \Rightarrow t \in \|\varphi\|_{\mathcal{V}}^{\mathcal{T}}\}$$

$$\|\nu Z.\varphi\|_{\mathcal{V}}^{\mathcal{T}} = \bigcup\{S \subseteq \mathcal{S} \mid S \subseteq \|\varphi\|_{\mathcal{V}[Z:=S]}^{\mathcal{T}}\}$$

$$\|\varphi \vee \psi\|_{\mathcal{V}}^{\mathcal{T}} = \|\varphi\|_{\mathcal{V}}^{\mathcal{T}} \cup \|\psi\|_{\mathcal{V}}^{\mathcal{T}}$$

$$\|\langle\gamma\rangle\varphi\|_{\mathcal{V}}^{\mathcal{T}} = \{s \mid \exists t \in \mathcal{S}. \ (s,t) \in R_\gamma \wedge t \in \|\varphi\|_{\mathcal{V}}^{\mathcal{T}}\}$$

$$\|\mu Z.\varphi\|_{\mathcal{V}}^{\mathcal{T}} = \bigcap\{S \subseteq \mathcal{S} \mid S \supseteq \|\varphi\|_{\mathcal{V}[Z:=S]}^{\mathcal{T}}\}$$

Note that $R_{2^{\mathcal{L}}}$ for singleton concurrent sets behaves the same as $R_{\mathcal{L}}$ for actions of μ-calculus. In this case, for the sake of brevity instead of $R_{\{a\}}$ we just write R_a. Also, we often use as shorthand for a concurrent set inside dynamic operators and we write $[a, b]\varphi$ instead of $[\{a, b\}]\varphi$. Furthermore, we have the following restriction for the constant propositions of the form $\mathcal{F}_a$ and O_a: *Constants $\mathcal{F}_a$ and O_a are incompatible, that is their interpretations as sets is disjoint:*

$$\|\mathcal{F}_a\|_{\mathcal{V}}^{\mathcal{T}} \cap \|O_a\|_{\mathcal{V}}^{\mathcal{T}} = \emptyset, \quad \forall a \in \mathcal{L}. \tag{1}$$

The intuition drawn from e-contracts is that it is not possible to be obliged to do something and at the same time be forbidden to do the same thing. The above description gives the following natural result: 1) $O_a \Rightarrow \neg\mathcal{F}_a$ and 2) $\mathcal{F}_a \Rightarrow \neg O_a$.

Action logics like PDL, and consequently propositional μ-calculus, are usually non-deterministic. From the point of view of modeling contracts it is natural to adopt a deterministic variant of an action logic because it does not make sense to specify different outcomes for the same action in a contract. The determinism of $\mathcal{C}\mu$ requires to have only one transition from one state labeled with a concurrent set. Formally we restrict $R_{2^{\mathcal{L}}}$ to assign to each concurrent set only partial

Table 3. The translation function f^T from $\mathcal{CL}$ to $\mathcal{C}\mu$

$$
\begin{aligned}
&(1) && f^T(O(\&_{i=1}^n a_i)) = \langle\{a_1,\ldots,a_n\}\rangle(\wedge_{i=1}^n O_{a_i}) \\
&(2) && f^T(\mathcal{C}_O \oplus \mathcal{C}_O) = f^T(\mathcal{C}_O) \wedge f^T(\mathcal{C}_O) \\
&(3) && f^T(P(\&_{i=1}^n a_i)) = \langle\{a_1,\ldots,a_n\}\rangle(\wedge_{i=1}^n \neg\mathcal{F}_{a_i}) \\
&(4) && f^T(\mathcal{C}_P \oplus \mathcal{C}_P) = f^T(\mathcal{C}_P) \wedge f^T(\mathcal{C}_P) \\
&(5) && f^T(F(\&_{i=1}^n a_i)) = [\{a_1,\ldots,a_n\}](\wedge_{i=1}^n \mathcal{F}_{a_i}) \\
&(6) && f^T(F(\delta) \vee [\beta]F(\delta)) = f^T(F(\delta)) \vee f^T([\beta]F(\delta)) \\
&(7) && f^T(\mathcal{C}_1 \wedge \mathcal{C}_2) = f^T(\mathcal{C}_1) \wedge f^T(\mathcal{C}_2) \\
&(8) && f^T(\bigcirc\mathcal{C}) = [\mathbf{any}]f^T(\mathcal{C}) \\
&(9) && f^T(\mathcal{C}_1 \,\mathcal{U}\, \mathcal{C}_2) = \mu Z.f^T(\mathcal{C}_2) \vee (f^T(\mathcal{C}_1) \wedge [\mathbf{any}]Z \wedge \langle\mathbf{any}\rangle\top) \\
&(10) && f^T([\&_{i=1}^n a_i]\mathcal{C}) = [\{a_1,\ldots,a_n\}]f^T(\mathcal{C}) \\
&(11) && f^T([(\&_{i=1}^n a_i)\alpha]\mathcal{C}) = [\{a_1,\ldots,a_n\}]f^T([\alpha]\mathcal{C}) \\
&(12) && f^T([\alpha + \beta]\mathcal{C}) = f^T([\alpha]\mathcal{C}) \wedge f^T([\beta]\mathcal{C}) \\
&(13) && f^T([\varphi?]\mathcal{C}) = f^T(\varphi) \Rightarrow f^T(\mathcal{C})
\end{aligned}
$$

functions (not relations), i.e., for any $(s,t),(s,t') \in R_\gamma$ then $t = t'$. Naturally a compound action may have several ending worlds, both in the interpretation of the *actions as relations* [9] or the *actions as trajectories* [26]. Note that $(s,t) \in R_a$ and $(s,t') \in R_{\{a,b\}}$ does not introduce non-determinism.

3.2 Translating the Language into the Logic

Because of the special status of the concurrent actions, the compositionality rules of Table 1, and the rewriting rules of Table 2, we choose to translate O, P, and F over both atomic actions a and concurrent actions $a\&b$. We also need to translate the $\oplus$ over obligation and permission as well as the $\vee$ operator over prohibition.

We consider a translation function f^T from expressions of $\mathcal{CL}$ into formulas of $\mathcal{C}\mu$. In Table 3 lines (1)-(6) we give the translation of the basic deontic constructs of $\mathcal{CL}$ ($\mathcal{C}_O, \mathcal{C}_P$ and $\mathcal{C}_F$). Note that the translation of concurrent actions $a\&b$ uses concurrent sets and we use a concise notation which, for example, for atomic actions under O would give $f^T(O(a)) = \langle a\rangle O_a$ —we abuse the notation and denote the atomic actions as conjunction over only one a_i. Lines (7)-(13) show the translation of the other $\mathcal{CL}$ expressions, where **any** is the special action which is interpreted as the union of all actions in $\mathcal{L}$ with the intuition of *doing any action*. The conjunction is translated as the corresponding conjunction operator of $\mathcal{C}\mu$, *next* $\bigcirc$ uses the action **any**, and *until* $\mathcal{U}$ is translated using a fix-point expression as usual. We give separate translations for each compound action inside the *dynamic box* operator of $\mathcal{CL}$. The translation is similar to the translation of PDL into μ-calculus.

Note that with this translation one cannot give a truth value to an obligation $O(a)$ of an action (or a permition or prohibition), because the truth value of its translation $\langle a\rangle O_a$ can be determined only after the execution of the action. This is in accordance with the classical semantics of the deontic modalities [33].

4   Properties of the Contract Language

In this section we show some of the properties $\mathcal{CL}$ enjoys, as well as how the language avoids most of the important deontic paradoxes and the undesirable properties listed in Section 2.2. Most of the proofs are omitted and can be found in [28].

Proposition 1 ensures that it is not needed to use negation on deontic operators, while Proposition 2 establishes the standard relation between obligations and permissions.

Proposition 1. *The following statements are valid in $\mathcal{CL}$:*

a) $P(\alpha) \equiv \neg F(\alpha)$
b) $F(\alpha) \equiv \neg P(\alpha)$.

Proof: The proof follows from the translation of $P(\alpha)$ and $F(\alpha)$ into the logic and the duality between the μ-calculus operators $[\cdot]$ and $\langle \cdot \rangle$.   □

Proposition 2. *The following statement is valid in $\mathcal{CL}$: $O(\alpha) \Rightarrow P(\alpha)$.*

Proof: The proof follows from the translations of $O(\alpha)$ and $P(\alpha)$ into the logic. Moreover, the proof makes use of the equation (1) of the incompatibility of O_a and $\mathcal{F}_a$ constants.   □

The following two results express that $\mathcal{CL}$ does not allow the derivation of certain undesirable properties.

Proposition 3. *The following implications do not hold in $\mathcal{CL}$:*

a) $P(a) \Rightarrow P(a\&b)$
b) $F(a) \Rightarrow F(a\&b)$.

Proof: We give a counter example to show that the implication is not possible, i.e., we give a model in the logic which is a model for the translation of the first $\mathcal{CL}$ formula and is not a model for the translation of the second $\mathcal{CL}$ formula.

For a) consider $(s,t) \in R_a$ and $(s,t') \in R_{\{a,b\}}$ with $t \notin \|\mathcal{F}_a\|_{\mathcal{V}}^{\mathcal{T}}$ and $t' \in \|\mathcal{F}_a\|_{\mathcal{V}}^{\mathcal{T}} \cap \|\mathcal{F}_b\|_{\mathcal{V}}^{\mathcal{T}}$. Consider the model M which has states $\mathcal{S} = \{s, t, t'\}$ and two relations: for action a, $R_a = \{(s,t)\}$ and for action $\{a, b\}$, $R_{\{a,b\}} = \{(s,t')\}$. M is a model for the first formula but is not a model of the second formula.

For b) we change the above model such that $t \in \|\mathcal{F}_a\|_{\mathcal{V}}^{\mathcal{T}}$ and $t' \notin \|\mathcal{F}_a\|_{\mathcal{V}}^{\mathcal{T}}$. M is a model of the first formula but is not a model for the second formula.   □

Proposition 4. *The following implications do not hold in $\mathcal{CL}$:*

a) $F(a\&b) \Rightarrow F(a)$
b) $P(a\&b) \Rightarrow P(a)$.

Proof: The proof is similar to the proposition above.   □

The following proposition expresses that the most important paradoxes of deontic logic are avoided in our contract language, either because there are not expressible in the language or because they are simply excluded by the translation into the underlying logic.

Proposition 5. *The following paradoxes are avoided in* $\mathcal{CL}$:

- *Ross's paradox*
- *The Free Choice Permission paradox*
- *Sartre's dilemma*
- *The Good Samaritan paradox.*
- *Chisholm's paradox*
- *The Gentle Murderer paradox*

5   Example

We formalize here the example introduced in Section 2.1. As part of the formalization of a contract in $\mathcal{CL}$ we first have to define the assertions and actions:

$$\phi = \text{the Internet traffic is high}$$
$$p = \text{client pays } x \ \$$$
$$d = \text{client delays payment}$$
$$n = \text{client notifies by e-mail}$$
$$l = \text{client lowers the Internet traffic}$$
$$s = \text{provider provides the service as stipulated in the contract}$$
$$c = \text{provider cancels the contract}$$
$$e = \text{provider sends a written notification to the client by e-mail}$$
$$w = \text{provider sends a written notification to the client by normal post}$$

The five clauses of the example are written in $\mathcal{CL}$ as follows:

1. $\Box(\phi \Rightarrow O(p + (d \& n)))$
2. $\Box([d, n](O(l) \wedge [l]\Diamond(O(p) \wedge [p]O(p))))$
3. $\Box([\{d, n\} \cdot \bar{l}\,]\Diamond(O(p) \wedge [p]O(p) \wedge [p \cdot p]O(p)))$[5]
4. $\Box(F(c) \wedge [w, e]P(c))$
5. $\Box O(s)$.

Remarks: 1) Formulas 2. and 3. are rather long because we can not represent in $\mathcal{CL}$ quantitative information like *pay two times*. We could use the & operator over actions with the same intuition as in logics of resources (e.g. linear logic [10]) and for *obliged to pay twice* we could write in $\mathcal{CL}$ $O(p\&p)$ instead of $O(p) \wedge [p]O(p)$ which is more concise and natural.

---

[5] The formulas 2 and 3 may be combined in a single formula using CTDs: $\Box([d, n](O_\varphi(l) \wedge [l]\Diamond(O(p) \wedge [p]O(p))$ where $\varphi = O(p) \wedge [p]O(p) \wedge [p \cdot p]O(p)$.

2) Though it is not apparent at first sight the contract allows the client to go from low to high Internet traffic many times and pay the penalty $(2 * x \ \$)$ only once.[6] The problem is that after the client lowers the Internet traffic, he might get a high traffic again and postpone the payment till a future moment. To avoid this situation we should add a clause specifying that "after getting a high Internet traffic, if the client postpones the payment then he can get a high traffic again only after having paid". In $\mathcal{CL}$ this might be expressed by changing formulas 2 and 3 above as:

2' $\Box([d,n](O(l) \wedge [l]\neg\phi\,\mathcal{U}\,(O(p) \wedge [p]O(p)))$
3' $\Box([\{d,n\} \cdot \bar{l}\,](\neg\phi\,\mathcal{U}\,(O(p) \wedge [p]O(p) \wedge [p \cdot p]O(p))).$

This example shows the importance of being able to model check a contract, which may be done only if the contract is written in a formal language, e.g. $\mathcal{CL}$.

3) Notice that our contract language lacks the possibility of expressing time constraints. More involved clauses like *the client must pay within 7 days*, or *the client is forbidden to pass more than 10 times per month from low to high Internet traffic*, can only be expressed here by introducing time, special variables and simulate a counter. For model checking purposes we would like to include the possibility to express these properties directly in the logic and an extension with real-time would be desirable.

6   Conclusion

In this paper we have presented a formal language for writing contracts, and have provided a formal semantics through the translation of the language into a variant of the propositional μ-calculus extended with concurrent actions. The use of a variant of the μ-calculus as a semantic framework for our language is not casual. The logic has nice properties: it is decidable [15], has a complete axiomatic system [32], and a complete Gentzen-style proof system [31]. Our language avoids most of the classical paradoxes, and enjoys all the nice properties listed in Section 2.2. To our knowledge no other work in the field has achieved such goals. Given that our application domain is that of electronic contracts, we have also given arguments for restricting syntactically and semantically certain uses of (and relations between) obligations, permissions and prohibitions, usually considered in philosophical and logical discussions.

Related Work: There are currently several different approaches aiming at defining a formal language for contracts. Some works concentrate on the definition of contract taxonomies [1,2,30], while others look for formalizations based on logics (e.g. classical [8], modal [7], deontic [12,22] and defeasible logic [11,29]). Other formalizations are based on models of computation (e.g. FSMs [21] and Petri Nets [6]). None of the above has reached enough maturity as to be considered

---

[6] See the technical report [28] for a more detailed explanation.

the solution to the problems of formal definition of contracts. Some provide a good framework for monitoring but lack a formal semantics and a reasoning system; others have nice proof systems and model theory, but not mechanism for monitoring or negotiation; many of the deontic-based approaches put too much emphasis on the logical properties and neglect the practical side, including monitoring. None of them captures all the intuitive properties of e-contracts we have described, while avoiding the most important paradoxes.

The idea of using a propositional constant in an action-based logic for giving semantics to the deontic notions was first presented in [19], where the special constant V (corresponding to our $\mathcal{F}_a$) was added to denote an "undesirable state-of-affairs" in the current state. We have, in addition, the constants O_a which are used to define obligation not in terms of action negation but using the diamond modal operator, deviating from other approaches (e.g., [4,19]).

Our work is closely related to those based on logic, and in particular to [5]. Due to lack of space and since part of the motivation of our work is to overcome some of the problems of the approach of Broersen *et al* in [5], we contrast our approach in detail only w.r.t. this paper. Broersen *et al* introduce a very interesting characterization of obligation, permission and prohibition by following an *ought-to-do* approach based on a deontic logic of regular actions. The idea is to use the μ^a-calculus as a basis and then define obligation, permission and prohibition over regular expressions on actions. The main differences w.r.t. our approach are the following. (a) There is no notion of *contract language*, only characterization of obligation, permission and prohibition in the logic. (b) The only deontic primitive is permission over atomic actions; obligation is defined as an infinite conjunction of negation of permission over actions not in the scope of the negation. We avoid this infinite conjunction by defining both prohibition and obligation as primitive (and using the propositional constants O_a and $\mathcal{F}_a$ at the semantic level) and prohibition as negation of permission. (c) All the deontic operators are defined over regular actions, including the Kleene star. We consider it is not natural to have starred actions under the deontic notions, we have thus dropped it. (d) Obligation on the choice of actions is not compositional; it is compositional in our case. (e) There is no conjunction over actions, i.e., it is not possible to express concurrent actions, which is the case in our approach. (f) The approach uses disjunction over actions. We have decided to use the exclusive or instead. (g) Negation on actions (meaning "not performing an action") is defined as a complement of the (infinite) set of actions. In our case the set of actions is finite, at the language level. (h) CTDs cannot be defined unless an extension of the μ^a-calculus is considered. In our setting both CTDs and CTPs are easily defined. (i) The semantics of obligation, permission and prohibition is given in terms of properties over traces, instead of over an extension of the Kripke structure as in our case.

For a nice overview of the history, problems and different approaches on deontic logic see [34]. The chapter of McNamara in the Handbook of the History of Logic contains a general description of the topic, mainly the different paradoxes arising under SDL [20]. For a discussion on CTDs see [24] and references therein.

Future Work: Our work is a first step towards a more ambitious task, and we believe the formalism chosen will allow us to achieve the following goals. The first extension is to add real-time to be able to express and reason about contracts with deadlines. Other immediate extension is the syntactic distinction in the signature of the definition part of $\mathcal{CL}$ between subjects, proper actions and objects. This would permit to make queries (and model check properties) for instance about all the rights and obligations of a given subject, or determine under which conditions somebody is obliged/forbidden to perform something. We have not considered in this paper the problem of negotiation nor monitoring of contracts. We believe these are important features of a contract language which must be taken into account in future work. Concerning actions, we got inspiration from the works on dynamic logics [25]. We would like to deepen the study of the action algebra to make the distinction between the intuitive meaning of conjunction under obligation, permission and prohibition. Further investigation is also needed to characterize negation on actions, both for capturing and distinguishing the ideas of "not doing something" and "doing something but a given action", which are not differentiated in our current approach. We want to explore the proof system of the $\mathcal{C}\mu$ logic, and to extend existing model checkers for μ-calculus [3,18] to analyze contracts as mentioned in the remarks of our example.

References

1. Aagedal, J.: Quality of Service Support in Development of Distributed Systems. PhD thesis, Dept. of Informatics, Faculty of Mathematics and Natural Sciences, University of Oslo (2001)
2. Beugnard, A., Jézéquel, J.M., Plouzeau, N.: Making components contract aware. IEEE 32, 38–45 (1999)
3. Biere, A.: mu-cke - efficient mu-calculus model checking. In: Grumberg, O. (ed.) CAV 1997. LNCS, vol. 1254, pp. 468–471. Springer, Heidelberg (1997)
4. Broersen, J.: Action negation and alternative reductions for dynamic deontic logics. J. Applied Logic 2, 153–168 (2004)
5. Broersen, J., Wieringa, R., Meyer, J.J.C.: A fixed-point characterization of a deontic logic of regular action. Fundam. Inf. 48, 107–128 (2001)
6. Daskalopulu, A.: Model Checking Contractual Protocols. In: Breuker, L.R., Leenes, R., Winkels, R. (eds.) Legal Knowledge and Information Systems, JURIX 2000. Frontiers in Artificial Intelligence and Applications, vol. 48, pp. 35–47. IOS Press, Amsterdam, Trento, Italy (2000)
7. Daskalopulu, A., Maibaum, T.S.E.: Towards Electronic Contract Performance. In: Legal Information Systems Applications, 12th International Conference and Workshop on Database and Expert Systems Applications, pp. 771–777. IEEE, NJ, New York (2001)
8. Davulcu, H., Kifer, M., Ramakrishnan, I.V.: CTR-S: A Logic for Specifying Contracts in Semantic Web Services. In: WWW04. pp. 144–153 (2004)
9. Fischer, M.J., Ladner, R.E.: Propositional modal logic of programs. In: STOC'77, pp. 286–294. ACM Press, New York (1977)
10. Girard, J.Y.: Linear logic. Theor. Compu. Sci. 50, 1–102 (1987)
11. Governatori, G.: Representing business contracts in RuleML. International Journal of Cooperative Information Systems 14, 181–216 (2005)

12. Governatori, G., Rotolo, A.: Logic of violations: A gentzen system for reasoning with contrary-to-duty obligations. Australian Journal of Logic 4, 193–215 (2006)
13. Kozen, D.: Results on the propositional mu-calculus. Theor. Comput. Sci. 27, 333–354 (1983)
14. Kozen, D.: Kleene algebra with tests. ACM Transactions on Programming Languages and Systems (TOPLAS'97) 19, 427–443 (1997)
15. Kozen, D., Parikh, R.: A decision procedure for the propositional μ-calculus. In: Clarke, E.M., Kozen, D. (eds.) 4th Workshop on Logics of Programs. LNCS, vol. 164, pp. 313–325. Springer, Heidelberg (1983)
16. Kozen, D.: On kleene algebras and closed semirings. In: Rovan, B. (ed.) Mathematical Foundations of Computer Science 1990. LNCS, vol. 452, pp. 26–47. Springer, Heidelberg (1990)
17. Mally, E.: Grundgesetze des Sollens. Elemente fer Logik des Willens. Graz: Leuschner & Lubensky (1926)
18. Mateescu, R., Sighireanu, M.: Efficient on-the-fly model-checking for regular alternation-free μ-calculus. Sci. Comp. Program. 46(3), 255–281 (2003)
19. Meyer, J.J.C.: A different approach to deontic logic: Deontic logic viewed as a variant of dynamic logic. Notre Dame Journal of Formal Logic 29, 109–136 (1988)
20. McNamara, P.: Deontic logic. In: Gabbay, D.M., Woods, J. (eds.) Handbook of the History of Logic, vol. 7, pp. 197–289. North-Holland Publishing, Amsterdam (2006)
21. Molina-Jimenez, C., Shrivastava, S., Solaiman, E., Warne, J.: Run-time Monitoring and Enforcement of Electronic Contracts. Electronic Commerce Research and Applications 3, 108–125 (2004)
22. Paschke, A., Dietrich, J., Kuhla, K.: A Logic Based SLA Management Framework. In: Gil, Y., Motta, E., Benjamins, V.R., Musen, M.A. (eds.) ISWC 2005. LNCS, vol. 3729, Springer, Heidelberg (2005)
23. Pnueli, A.: Temporal logic of programs. In: FOCS'77, pp. 46–57. IEEE, NJ, New York (1977)
24. Prakken, H., Sergot, M.: Contrary-to-duty obligations. Studia Logica 57, 91–115 (1996)
25. Pratt, V.R.: Semantical considerations on floyd-hoare logic. In: FOCS'76, pp. 109–121. IEEE, NJ, New York (1976)
26. Pratt, V.R.: A practical decision method for propositional dynamic logic: Preliminary report. In: STOC'78, pp. 326–337. ACM Press, New York (1978)
27. Pratt, V.R.: Dynamic algebras and the nature of induction. In: STOC'80, pp. 22–28. ACM Press, New York (1980)
28. Prisacariu, C., Schneider, G.: Towards a formal definition of electronic contracts. Technical report 348, Department of Informatics, University of Oslo (2007)
29. Song, I., Governatori, G.: Nested rules in defeasible logic. In: Adi, A., Stoutenburg, S., Tabet, S. (eds.) RuleML 2005. LNCS, vol. 3791, pp. 204–208. Springer, Heidelberg (2005)
30. Tosic, V.: On Comprehensive Contractual Descriptions of Web Services. In: IEEE International Conference on e-Technology, e-Commerce, and c Service, pp. 444–449. IEEE, NJ, New York (2005)
31. Walukiewicz, I.: A Complete Deductive System for the μ-Calculus. PhD thesis, Warsaw University (1993)
32. Walukiewicz, I.: Completeness of Kozen's axiomatisation of the propositional μ-calculus. In: LICS'95, pp. 14–24. IEEE, NJ, New York (1995)
33. Wright, G.H.V.: Deontic logic. Mind 60, 1–15 (1951)
34. Wright, G.H.V.: Deontic logic: A personal view. Ratio Juris 12, 26–38 (1999)

A Mechanized Model of the Theory of Objects

Ludovic Henrio and Florian Kammüller

CNRS – I3S – INRIA, Sophia-Antipolis
and
Technische Universität Berlin

Abstract. In this paper we present a formalization of Abadi's and Cardelli's theory of objects in the interactive theorem prover Isabelle/ HOL. Our motivation is to build a mechanized HOL-framework for the analysis of a functional calculus for distributed objects. In particular, we present (a) a formal model of objects and its operational semantics based on de Bruijn indices (b) a parallel reduction relation for objects (c) the proof of confluence for the theory of objects reusing Nipkow's HOL-framework for the lambda calculus. We expect this framework to be highly reusable and allow further development and mechanized proofs of various aspects of object theory, e.g., distribution, aspect orientation, typing.

1 Introduction

"A Theory of Objects" [1] defines the ς-calculus for the abstract and precise characterization of object oriented languages. The ς-calculus is a computation model for object oriented programming in the same way as the λ-calculus models functional programming.

Ever since its creation, the ς-calculus has evolved in many ways. First, [1] already provides a wide range of different extensions for the basic ς-calculus (e.g., [2] and [3]), summarized in the book [1]. The Theory of Objects has also been adopted by many as the *lingua franca* for the theory of object oriented programming and has been taken as a basis for further experimentation and development. For example, Gordon and Hankin extended the ς-calculus towards the paradigm of parallel programming [15]. More recently, the ς-calculus has been incorporated into the ASP calculus that is a theoretical basis for distributed objects [11], and also into higher-level flavors like aspect-orientation [19].

On the mechanized proofs side, a formalization of the imperative variant of the ς-calculus has been defined in Coq [13], this work proves type safety for the imperative ς-calculus, but do not provide any result concerning determinism.

The objective of this paper is to provide a sound foundation and formalization of the ς-calculus. We also expect this work to ground further formalizations of extensions and concepts relying on the ς-calculus, and to impact significantly on the mechanized proofs related to such extensions. We are particularly interested in the design of distributed versions of the ς-calculus, and as such, in proving

M.M. Bonsangue and E.B. Johnsen (Eds.): FMOODS 2007, LNCS 4468, pp. 190–205, 2007.

confluence first for the ς-calculus in order to lift the mechanization to parallelized object calculi. Indeed, in the presence of distributed objects, confluence is recognized as a particularly interesting topic as highlighted in [12,6].

For those projects, and more generally aiming at a wide use of a mechanized theory of objects, we present here a formalization and confluence proof of the untyped ς-calculus. It uses a framework for confluence in Isabelle/HOL [20], and is partially inspired by an earlier attempt on the formalization of the ς-calculus [14]. However, this formalization is quite different from the preceding attempt; and, considering confluence, object-orientation required specific developments in order to adapt the existing confluence framework.

Our contribution in this paper is the following:

- Basically, this article defines a sound formalization of the ς-calculus;
- it provides a confluence proof for the ς-calculus;
- and it demonstrates how Nipkow's framework for confluence in Isabelle/HOL can be adapted in order to support object-orientation.

A first idea could consist in proving confluence in the ς-calculus by relying on its translation into the λ-calculus [2] which is confluent. However, objects are lost in the translation into the λ-calculus, which prevents us from concluding about the confluence in the object world (no function has been defined yet for bringing back a lambda term into an object world – which is a priori impossible). Moreover, a mechanized model adapted to objects allows us to aim at several crucial properties on objects, like typing, confluence of concurrent object languages, etc. We detail some of these perspectives in Section 5.

In this paper we first introduce Isabelle/HOL [21] and the ς-calculus in Section 2 to provide sufficient technical detail for the understanding of the exposition. Then, in Section 3 we present the model as expressed in the input language of Isabelle/HOL. Section 4 introduces confluence proofs, as provided by the framework of Tobias Nipkow [20], and then presents the derivation of confluence for the ς-calculus. The Isabelle/HOL mechanization is available at one of the authors' web page [18].

2   Preliminaries

In this section we introduce Isabelle/HOL and the functional ς-calculus; both with regard to the elements that are relevant for the understanding of the remainder of the paper.

2.1   Isabelle/HOL

The interactive theorem prover Isabelle has foremost been constructed as a generic tool to provide a framework for the creation of specialized theorem provers for various application logics. However, besides Isabelle/ZF, an embedding of Zermel-Fraenkel set theory it is the instantiation to Higher Order Logic (HOL), called Isabelle/HOL, that is nowadays most widely used. In particular for computer science applications, where typing comes in naturally, HOL is well-suited as it provides a logic with types. The following meta-logical formula is an example illustrating the universal quantification with $\bigwedge$, higher order variables P and Q, and implication $\Longrightarrow$ (the square brackets $[\![\,]\!]$ act as a pseudo-conjunction).

```
⋀ P Q x. ⟦ P x; Q x ⟧ ⟹ P x
```

Moreover, the object logic HOL contains the classical logic constructors, like $\longrightarrow$ for implication, $\forall$ and $\exists$ for quantification, $\land$ for conjunction, and $\lor$ for disjunction.

To illustrate Isabelle/HOL syntax, we sketch the definition of a list datatype:

```
datatype α list =    Nil    ("[]")
                |    Cons α (α list)  (infixr "#" 65)
```

The above definition introduces the type `list` over an arbitrary type of elements. The datatype definition introduces two constructors: `Nil` and `Cons`. The code in brackets behind the constructors declares the pretty printing syntax enabling for example the use of `x # l` for a constructed list.

Among the internally generated rules for a datatype specification there are induction rules for recursive types like the above and injectivity rules for the constructors.

Functions over a datatype may be defined as primitive recursive functions. As an illustrative example consider the function that appends two lists to form a new one:

```
consts  append :: [α list, α list] ⇒ α list (infixr "@" 65)
```

Next, the semantics of this function is given by the two classical equations below. Before the colon : optional rule names are specified for later reference.

```
primrec
  append_Nil: [] @ l = l
  append_Cons: (x # l1) @ l2 = x # (l1 @ l2)
```

2.2 Functional ς-Calculus

The Theory of Objects consists in various ς-calculi that are aimed to be as "simple and fruitful as λ-calculi" [2]. Rather than using the λ-calculus to encode objects and their behaviour in a way that is overly complicated, the ς-calculus takes objects as primitive.

The kernel calculus that we model in this paper includes *object definition*, *method invocation*, and *method override*. An object consists of a set of labeled methods. A method is a function with one formal parameter that represents *self*, i.e., the object in which the method is contained. The ς-calculus relies on the following syntax.

$$a, b ::= [l_j = \varsigma(x_j)b_j]^{j \in 1..n} \qquad \text{object definition}$$
$$| \; a.l_j \qquad\qquad (j \in 1..n) \text{ method call}$$
$$| \; a.l_j := \varsigma(x)b \qquad (j \in 1..n) \text{ update}$$

Object fields are not defined as they are considered as degenerate methods not using its self parameter. Therefore selection of a field or invocation (call) of a method are identical. Similarly method override and field update are also interchangeable. We quote next the so-called primitive semantics of objects [2]. For a gentler introduction we refer to the following section where we introduce the ς-calculus step by step in Isabelle/HOL.

Let $o \equiv [l_j = \varsigma(x_j)b_j]^{j \in 1..n}$ (l_j distinct).

o is an object with method names l_j and methods $\varsigma(x_j)b_j$

$o.l_j \qquad \rightarrow_\beta b_j\{x_j \leftarrow o\}$ ($j \in 1..n$) selection / method call

$o.l_j := \varsigma(x)b \rightarrow_\beta [l_j = \varsigma(x)b, l_i = \varsigma(x_i)b_i^{i \in (1..n) - \{j\}}]$ ($j \in 1..n$) update / override

Note that it is possible to encode the ς-calculus into λ-calculus which already features a good formalization and a confluence proof in Isabelle/HOL [20]. However, as stated by Abadi and Cardelli, as soon as one is interested in typing issues for the ς-calculus, the encoding into the λ-calculus is not sufficient. Even more importantly such an encoding is not a good solution because, as objects are lost in the translation, getting properties back to the original object world is generally impossible.

We are also interested in bringing the proof of confluence presented in the following to the parallel and concurrent object world. This is one of the first long-term goals of such a formalization. Moreover, in this context the translation to the λ-calculus is even less adapted than for the classical ς-calculus. For example, in ASP, the notions of objects and concurrency are unified, and as objects are lost in the translation into the λ-calculus, expressing ASP semantics on such a translation is impossible.

3   Isabelle/HOL Model

In this section we introduce the formalization of the ς-calculus with de Bruijn indices [7]. We then show how substitution is formalized on the de Bruijn object terms and how it works technically based on lifting. Finally, we define the reduction relation $\rightarrow_\beta$ and show some first proof results concerning the transitive, reflexive closure $\rightarrow_\beta^*$ of $\rightarrow_\beta$.

The formalization of the ς-calculus by Ehmety [14] in Isabelle/ZF, seems to have followed the earlier formalization of the λ-calculus in Isabelle/HOL [20]. It also uses de Bruijn indices but does not provide any proof. Although, Ehmety's definition of ς-terms, substitution, and the reduction relation has been performed in Isabelle/ZF, they are close enough to Nipkow's λ-formalization in HOL and can be used here. However, we deviate from Ehmety in that we choose lists instead of maps for representing objects.

3.1   Object Terms Using de Bruijn Indices

de Bruijn indices are very useful for implementation of calculi with abstraction as they abstract from variable names. A variable is replaced by a natural number that represents the distance — in terms of nesting depth — of this variable to its binder. Thereby terms contain only numbers, no variable; α-conversion becomes obsolete. This is a considerable advantage as α-conversion is a difficult problem both from a practical point of view and for mechanical proofs. α-conversion has triggered recent research activities on integrating nominal techniques for handling calculi with binders [24,23]. There, classes of terms equivalent by α-conversion are represented by a bijective set; the idea to abandon the somewhat superfluous distinctness created by different variable names is similar to de Bruijn indices. The survey [8] provides a comparison with close regard to theorem proving and shows that de Bruijn indices do still have some advantages when it comes to pragmatics.[1] Moreover, Nipkow's framework for confluence of λ-calculus already uses de Bruijn indices, thus adapting ς-calculus to de Bruijn indices allows us to reuse most of the generic part of Nipkow's framework.

De Bruijn indices are best explained by an example. Consider the following term on the left side in the well known form of λ-calculus with variables and its equivalent on the right side with de Bruijn indices.[2]

$$\lambda x.\lambda y.(\lambda z.\, x\, z)y = Abs(Abs(Abs(Var\, 2)\$(Var\, 0))(Var\, 0))$$

Note that, different variables may be represented by the same number, e.g., z and x both are $Var\, 0$. De Bruijn indices relieves one from having to deal with α-conversion: for example both $\lambda x.x$ and its α-equivalent $\lambda y.y$ are represented by $Abs(Var0)$. The downside of de Bruijn indices is that substitution, crucial for the definition of application, is rather complicated to define: a term has to be "lifted", i.e. his "variables" have to be increased by one, when it moves into the scope of an abstraction in the process of substitution. We will encounter this definition for ς in the next subsection.

In the ς-calculus, abstraction is used to represent the self of an object as a parameter in a method $\varsigma(x)b$ that is replaced by the current enclosing object when this method is called. This abstraction will be represented by de Bruijn indices. Hence, variables are represented as natural numbers. The type dB of ς-terms in Isabelle/HOL is given by the following datatype declaration where Label is just a type synonym for nat, the type of natural numbers.

```
datatype dB =  Var nat
            |  Obj (dB list)
            |  Call dB Label
            |  Upd dB Label dB
```

The constructor Var builds-up a new term dB from a nat representing the de Bruijn index of the variable. The constructor Obj takes a list of fields or methods as parameters; even a method $\varsigma(x)b$ having a formal parameter x is a simple dB term: there is an implicit abstraction for each field of each object, this is due to the fact that each field is a method with a unique parameter. The constructor

---

[1] However, it is planned for future work to experiment with nominal techniques.

[2] We use here the constructors Var, Abs, and $\$$ for variables, abstractions, and application as in Isabelle/HOL .

for invocation Call selects a field given by a label in a dB term representing an object. Field update (method override) Upd replaces a labeled field in an object by another value, i.e., a dB term. This informal semantics will be formally encoded by the definition of the reduction relation $\rightarrow_\beta$ in Section 3.3. In order to define the reduction we need to define substitution on these de Bruijn terms. The fact that we use a list to represent the indexed set of labeled fields in an object will be discussed at the end of this section in 3.4.

3.2 Substitution

As de Bruijn indices discard the use of formal parameters, substitution has to be performed by adapting the numbers representing variables when a term is moved between different layers of the nested scopes of abstraction. This movement occurs precisely when a variable has to be substituted by a term containing a free variable inside the scope of an abstraction. Therefore the notion of substitution is chained with the notion of lifting. We declare the following two constants in Isabelle/HOL.

```
subst ::    [dB, dB, nat] ⇒ dB   ("_[_'/_]" [300, 0, 0] 300)
lift ::     [dB, nat] ⇒ dB
```

Because of the declared mixfix syntax, we can write t[s/n] to express that in a term t the variable represented by n shall be replaced by s. Before defining the semantics of substitution we need to define the lifting of a term. A lifting carries a parameter n representing the *cut* between free and bound variable numbers in the term that shall be lifted. The operation lift is defined by the following set of primitive recursive equations describing the effect of lifting over the various cases of object terms.

```
liftVar:    lift (Var i) k = (if i < k then Var i else Var (i + 1))
liftObj:    lift (Obj f) k = (Obj (map (λ x. lift x (k + 1)) f))
liftCall:   lift (Call a l) k = Call (lift a k) l
liftUpd:    lift (Upd a l b) k = Upd (lift a k) l (lift b (k + 1))
```

A variable is only lifted when it is free, i.e. when its representing number is greater or equal to the "cut" parameter. The "cut" parameter is increased in the recursive call when an abstraction scope is entered. This is the case when the lift function enters inside a method in an object, and when a field is updated by a method. Note that we increase only on the right side of an update because the left side will always be an object seen as a reference whereas the right side is a method.[3]

From the definition of lift, substitution can be defined as follows.

```
subst_Var:   Var i [s/k] =
                if k < i then Var (i - 1) else if i = k then s else Var i
subst_Obj:   Obj f [s/k] = Obj (map (λ x. x[(lift s 0)/(k+1)]) f)
```

---

[3] For clarity, we use here the map function in liftObj. In reality this is rejected by Isabelle/HOL as it violates the primitive recursion scheme. An individual *primitive recursive* function map_lift has to be defined.

```
subst_Call:   Call a l [s/k] = Call (a [s/k]) l
subst_Upd:    Upd a l b [s/k] = Upd (a [s/k]) l (b [lift s 0 / k+1])
```

The idea is that a term s is lifted if it is substituted inside an abstraction scope, i.e., inside an object and at the right side of an update. The lifting is always initiated with "cut" parameter 0 as initially the outermost free variable when entering a scope.[4] The decrementation in the equation for Var in cases of free variables greater than the "cut" parameter is necessary because substitution is only used by the relation $\to_\beta$ that we present next: each time substitution is applied a level of abstraction is lost. In general, defining a substitution outside $\to_\beta$ is not meaningful for a de Bruijn term.

3.3 Reduction Relation

Once substitution is defined the reduction relation can easily be specified. We first declare a relation beta as a set of pairs of terms, and then define $s \to_\beta t$, meaning $(s, t) \in$ beta.

```
consts        beta :: (dB × dB) set
translations
   s →β t == (s, t) ∈ beta
   s →*β t == (s, t) ∈ beta*
```

The relation beta is now defined by an inductive definition. Given a set in Isabelle/HOL, an inductive definition defines a set by inductively specifying its content. Such a definition consists of a set of rules adhering to certain well-formedness criteria. The definition of the set is then implicitly given by the smallest set closed under those rules. As a consequence, induction schemes can be automatically provided by Isabelle/HOL. We profit from the natural style that is defined for lists in Isabelle/HOL: for example to extract the lth method of an object Obj f we can write f ! l. Similarly the update of the lth method by t is Obj (f [l := t]).

```
inductive beta
intros
   beta: l < length f ⟹ Call (Obj f) l →β (f!l)[(Obj f)/0]
   upd : Upd (Obj f) l a →β  Obj (f [l := a])
   sel : s →β t ⟹ Call s l →β Call t l
   updL: s →β t ⟹ Upd s l u →β Upd t l u
   updR: s →β t ⟹ Upd u l s →β Upd u l t
   obj : s →β t ⟹ Obj (f [l := s]) →β Obj (f [l := t])
```

The central and most interesting rule of the reduction is the first rule beta that calls a method on an object. An evaluation of $o.l$ consists in taking the lth field, say $\varsigma(x)b$, of the object o. Evaluation of the method call consist in evaluating b where o substitutes the formal self parameter x. The other rules define the reduction relation beta to be a congruence, i.e., we can reduce terms inside contexts.

---

[4] The problem and solution mentioned in footnote 3 also apply to the map in subst.

For the investigation of the reduction relation, in particular for confluence, we need to investigate the transitive, reflexive closure $\rightarrow_\beta^*$ of $\rightarrow_\beta$. Isabelle/HOL provides sufficient support in its theory database for reasoning about relations. For example, for any relation R of type $(\alpha \times \alpha)$ set the reflexive, transitive closure may be constructed as R^*; corresponding theorems and induction scheme are provided.

Congruence Rules for $\rightarrow_\beta^*$. For the transitive reflexive closure $\rightarrow_\beta^*$ of $\rightarrow_\beta$ the following congruence rules can be derived.

$$
\begin{array}{l}
s \rightarrow_\beta^* s' \implies \texttt{Call s l} \rightarrow_\beta^* \texttt{Call s' l} \\
s \rightarrow_\beta^* s' \implies \texttt{Upd s l u} \rightarrow_\beta^* \texttt{Upd s' l u} \\
s \rightarrow_\beta^* s' \implies \texttt{Upd u l s} \rightarrow_\beta^* \texttt{Upd u l s'} \\
[\![u \rightarrow_\beta^* u'; s \rightarrow_\beta^* s']\!] \implies \texttt{Upd u l s} \rightarrow_\beta^* \texttt{Upd u' l s'} \\
s \rightarrow_\beta^* s' \implies \texttt{Obj(f [l := s])} \rightarrow_\beta^* \texttt{Obj(f [l := s'])}
\end{array}
$$

The last rule is a direct transposition of the rule obj of $\rightarrow_\beta$ to its transitive closure $\rightarrow_\beta^*$. For the use in the confluence proofs however the following derived rule is more suitable because it reflects the stepwise change of an object.

$$[\![\texttt{ n < length f; f ! n} \rightarrow_\beta^* \texttt{x}]\!] \implies \texttt{Obj (f)} \rightarrow_\beta^* \texttt{Obj (f[n := x])}$$

3.4   Extensions for Typing

Evidently, in our HOL model we use lists for the fields of an object where the original Theory of Objects prescribes a sequence of labels mapping to terms. This representation is not quite adequate with respect to typing issues The reasons for this deviation are pragmatic. The type system of classical HOL as encoded in Isabelle/HOL is such that all functions are total. Hence, the type usually used for maps is the Map-type that mimics a partial function type by the total function type $\alpha \Rightarrow (\beta$ option$)$ where β option is the lifting of an arbitrary type β given by the following datatype.

```
datatype α option = None | Some α
```

The option type together with pattern matching enables a smooth treatment of partiality sufficient for many applications.

In the earlier ZF-formalization of ς-calculus [14], this option type had been used to model the map contained in an object. Unfortunately, there is no natural and nicely embedded version of **finite** maps available in Isabelle. It appears that in most proofs, eventually, the finiteness is not necessary to reach the results. Unfortunately, in our case, finiteness is a necessary prerequisite (see for example the lemma of Section 4.4).

Furthermore, lists are well supported, their syntax is very close to maps, and finally using list update, we implicitly respect the "domain" of a map, i.e., an update out of bounds is ignored as described in the following theorem.

$$\bigwedge \texttt{i. length xs} \leq \texttt{i} \implies \texttt{xs[i:=x] = xs}$$

Moreover, there are several inductions on lists available: structural list induction, mutual structural induction, structural induction in reverse form, i.e., over l @ [x], and an induction over the length of lists. Clearly, we could have defined a

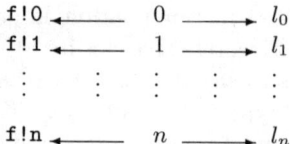

Fig. 1. Extension of object by map to labels for typing

type for finite maps, or a class of finite types and assume maps in that class. In any case, we would have had to construct this infrastructure first, i.e., datatype but also an adequate framework allowing us to reason about this datatype before being able to begin with the formalization of the ς-calculus.

On the other hand, the inadequacy of our model is not irreversible. In fact we can add types later on by extending an object `Obj f` with an additional map from list indices to labels. The principle of this combined mapping is depicted in Figure 1.

As the list selection λ`i`. `l ! i` represents a function, and the map from indices to labels is injective, we can invert it and associate to each label a unique term. In [1], types of objects are defined by their labels, and we can easily provide an extension for typing by integrating labels in our model as explained above. The proof of confluence will not be influenced by such a change. From a general point of view, dealing with natural numbers instead of labels simplifies the handling of the formalization. Currently we build an extension of Isabelle/HOL by finite maps and corresponding induction schemes to represent labels.

4   Confluence Proof

4.1   Nipkow's Framework

Tobias Nipkow provides in [20] a framework for the proof of Church-Rosser properties in Isabelle/HOL. By "framework" we mean that his formalization is in large parts reusable. Although he formalizes only the classical λ-calculus and its operational semantics, the proof of confluence is mainly conducted on a generic level using the polymorphic relation type $(\alpha \times \alpha)$`set`. Therefore, it constitutes a reusable proof enabling the reduction of a confluence proof to central lemmata as shown in this section.

Nipkow follows in his formalization the classical way of proving Church-Rosser as explained in Barendregt's book [4][Chapter 3]. Apparently, it is also this proof method, originated by Tait and Martin-Löf, that is used by Abadi and Cardelli for proving Church-Rosser [2]. Nipkow moreover formalizes an alternative approach of the so-called *complete developments* due to Takahashi, which is shorter and more elegant on paper. Concerning the mechanical proof there is no gain because the classical proof is solved almost automatically by Isabelle.

We give an outline of the main properties of the framework for confluence proofs. The property `square` is a predicate over four relations describing confluence of a relation in its most general from.

```
square :: [(α × α)set, (α × α)set, (α × α)set, (α × α)set] ⇒ bool
square R S T U ==
  ∀ x y. (x, y)∈ R ⟶ (∀ z. (x, z)∈ S ⟶ (∃ u. (y, u)∈ T ∧ (z, u)∈ U))
```

The square predicate is used as a primitive in proofs. Indeed, it enables a reasoning similar to graphical arguments where we express confluence as usually depicted in paper proof.

In general, and also in our case, we want to prove the square with just one relation (the transitive, reflexive closure of the reduction relation) at each edge. Therefore, commute reduces the square to just two relations and diamond to one. Finally confluence is defined as a square over the reflexive transitive closure of a relation.

```
commute   :: [(α × α)set, (α × α)set] ⇒ bool
commute R S == square R S S R
diamond   :: (α × α)set ⇒ bool    diamond R == commute R R
confluent :: (α × α)set ⇒ bool    confluent R == diamond (R*)
```

The original Church-Rosser property describes that any two terms that are connected by the relation or its inverse have a common reduct.

```
Church_Rosser :: (α × α) set ⇒ bool
Church_Rosser R ==
  ∀ x y. (x, y) ∈ (R ∪ R⁻¹)* ⟶ (∃ z. (x, z) ∈ R* ∧ (y, z) ∈ R*)
```

The following general theorem represents the classical equivalence between the Church-Rosser property and confluence, i.e., diamond property of the closure of the reduction relation.

```
Church_Rosser_confluent: Church_Rosser R = confluent R
```

The following theorem provides a further possible way of ensuring confluence of a relation T. Indeed, proving the diamond property of a relation R in between T and its reflexive transitive closure is sufficient to ensure that T is confluent.

```
diamond_to_confluence: ⟦ diamond R; T ⊆ R; R ⊆ T* ⟧ ⟹ confluent T
```

The classical trick already used in the application for the λ-calculus is to use a so-called *parallel reduction* for R for which the diamond property is true. Indeed, in general, the original reduction relation does not verify diamond T, and proving diamond T* directly is very difficult. Thanks to the above theorem, we only have to show the inclusion of the parallel reduction relation in between the original reduction relation T and its transitive, reflexive closure.

4.2 Parallel Reduction

In order to reuse the full extent of Nipkow's framework we have to define a parallel reduction relation for the ς-calculus. In general, a parallel reduction relation is a relation similar to the original reduction relation, but able to reduce several sub-term of the original term: it applies reduction at several possible places at the same time. Hence, the main difficulty is to find such a relation that parallelizes the original relation — and define this relation in such a way that it matches the provisos of Theorem `diamond_to_confluence`, i.e., lies in between the original reduction `beta` and its transitive, reflexive closure `beta*`.

The parallel reduction relation for the ς-calculus that we use is very similar to its equivalent in the λ-calculus: it applies reduction $\rightarrow_\beta$ on any subset of the possible reduction places in parallel. In other words, the parallel reduction applies itself recursively at all possible reduction places, and includes the reflexive relation. It is defined as follows:

```
syntax
  par_beta :: ([dB, dB] => bool)   (infixl "⇒β" 50)
translations
  s ⇒β t == (s, t) ∈ par_beta
inductive par_beta
  intros
    var:  Var n ⇒β Var n
    obj:  ⟦ length s = length s'; ∀ l < length s. s!l ⇒β s'!l ⟧
          ⟹ Obj s ⇒β Obj s'
    upd:  ⟦ s ⇒β s'; t ⇒β t' ⟧ ⟹ Upd s l t ⇒β Upd s' l t'
    upd': ⟦ Obj s ⇒β Obj s'; t ⇒β t' ⟧
          ⟹ (Upd (Obj s) l t) ⇒β (Obj (s' [l := t']))
    sel:  s ⇒β t ⟹ Call s l ⇒β Call t l
    beta: ⟦ Obj f ⇒β Obj f'; l < length f' ⟧
          ⟹ Call (Obj f) l ⇒β (f' ! l)[(Obj f')/0]
```

4.3 Inclusion Lemmata and Diamond Property of `par_beta`

Nipkow's framework provides the general structure for the proof of confluence for a reduction relation on terms. To summarize the preceding section, showing confluence is reduced to showing that the parallel reduction `par_beta` is between `beta` and `beta*` (`beta ⊆ par_beta ⊆ beta*`) and that the diamond property holds for `par_beta`.

We cannot get much more (for free) from the framework. However, we can try to follow the outline of the proofs of these properties in the case of the λ-calculus. In Nipkow's proof all three lemmata are solved almost automatically by Isabelle, but, in the case of the ς-calculus, we need to interact more and to prove some cases manually.

The proof of `beta ⊆ par_beta` is performed using induction and Isabelle's classical reasoner. It needs decisively more guidance than the original proof.

The other inclusion `par_beta ⊆ beta*` is in principle comparable. However, it revealed a lemma that we needed to prove separately (see Section 4.4).

The diamond property `diamond par_beta` finally is rather long and technical in our case. There are a considerable number of combinations between the different constructors leading to numerous cases in the case analysis. Like Nipkow we start the global proof by unfolding the definitions of `diamond`, `commute`, and `square`, and applying `par_beta` induction on the unfolded goal. In contrast to Nipkow, where the rest is done automatically by one application of the classical reasoner, we need to guide the prover on the remaining subgoals. A typical subgoal is the following:

$$\begin{aligned} &\llbracket\ \texttt{length s = length s';} \hfill (1)\\ &\quad \forall\ \texttt{l<length s. s!l} \Rightarrow_\beta \texttt{s'!l} \longrightarrow\\ &\quad (\forall\ \texttt{z. s!l} \Rightarrow_\beta \texttt{z} \longrightarrow (\exists\ \texttt{u. s'!l} \Rightarrow_\beta \texttt{u} \wedge \texttt{z} \Rightarrow_\beta \texttt{u}))\\ &\rrbracket \Longrightarrow \forall\ \texttt{z. Obj s} \Rightarrow_\beta \texttt{z} \longrightarrow \exists\ \texttt{u. Obj s'} \Rightarrow_\beta \texttt{u} \wedge \texttt{z} \Rightarrow_\beta \texttt{u}) \end{aligned}$$

This goal basically means that the diamond property can be lifted to objects, provided it is verified (by recurrence) on all the fields of the object. To solve this goal we use an inversion lemma for objects:

$$\llbracket\ \texttt{Obj s} \Rightarrow_\beta \texttt{z}\ \rrbracket \Longrightarrow \exists\ \texttt{lz. length s = length lz} \wedge \texttt{z = Obj lz}$$

The application of this lemma gives a witness $\texttt{z = Obj lz}$ with $\texttt{Obj s} \Rightarrow_\beta \texttt{Obj z}$. Unfortunately the proviso for the right lower half of the diamond square in the goal (1) ($\forall \texttt{z. s!l} \Rightarrow_\beta \texttt{z} \longrightarrow (\exists \texttt{u. s'!l} \Rightarrow_\beta \texttt{u} \wedge \texttt{z} \Rightarrow_\beta \texttt{u})$) is too fine grained. We need another technical lemma that transforms this proviso into the existence of a list of elements.

$$\begin{aligned} (\exists\ &\texttt{lu. length lu = length s} \wedge\\ &(\forall\ \texttt{l < length s. s'!l} \Rightarrow_\beta \texttt{lu!l} \wedge \texttt{lz!l} \Rightarrow_\beta \texttt{lu!l})) \end{aligned}$$

Using the witness list $\texttt{lu}$ we can then insert $\texttt{Obj lu}$ as the existential witness that represents the lower right corner of the diamond square (u in the goal (1)).

For the remaining two subgoals $\texttt{Obj s'} \Rightarrow_\beta \texttt{Obj lu}$, and $\texttt{Obj lz} \Rightarrow_\beta \texttt{Obj lu}$ we simply apply twice the object reduction lemma that we present in the next section, and has, in fact, already been derived for the proof of $\texttt{par\_beta} \subseteq \texttt{beta}^*$.

4.4 Object Reduction Lemma

In the proof of $\texttt{par\_beta} \subseteq \texttt{beta}^*$ and the diamond property for $\texttt{par\_beta}$ we encounter the following subgoal:

$$\begin{aligned} &\llbracket\ \texttt{length f = length g;}\ \forall\ \texttt{l < length f. f!l} \rightarrow_\beta^* \texttt{g!l}\ \rrbracket \hfill (2)\\ &\Longrightarrow \texttt{Obj f} \rightarrow_\beta^* \texttt{Obj g} \end{aligned}$$

This goal trivially occurs when reduction for objects can be applied; such a reduction reduces simultaneously all fields of an object. Using the recurrence hypothesis, we can infer that each of the field can be obtained by $\texttt{beta}^*$, and we want to prove that this can be lifted to the level of the object (roughly: $\rightarrow_\beta^* \rightarrow_\beta^* \cdots \rightarrow_\beta^* = \rightarrow_\beta^*$).

Although seemingly obvious it is not trivial to prove. We first derive the following lemma that describes the witness of a list that keeps record of all steps in a $\rightarrow_\beta$ step by step transformation from the field map f to the field map g. This transformation is described graphically in Figure 2.

```
lemma rtrancl_beta_obj_lem:
```
$$\begin{aligned} &\llbracket\ \texttt{length f = length g;}\ \forall\ \texttt{l < length f. f!l} \rightarrow_\beta^* \texttt{g!l}\ \rrbracket \Longrightarrow\\ &\quad \forall\ \texttt{k} \le \texttt{length f.}\\ &\quad\quad (\exists\ \texttt{ob. length ob = (k + 1)} \wedge\\ &\quad\quad\quad (\forall\ \texttt{obi. obi mem ob} \longrightarrow \texttt{length obi = length f}) \wedge\\ &\quad\quad\quad (\texttt{ob ! 0 = f}) \wedge (\texttt{Obj (ob ! 0)} \rightarrow_\beta^* \texttt{Obj (ob ! k)}) \wedge\\ &\quad\quad\quad (\texttt{take k (ob ! k) = take k g}) \wedge\\ &\quad\quad\quad (\texttt{drop k (ob ! k) = drop k f})) \end{aligned}$$

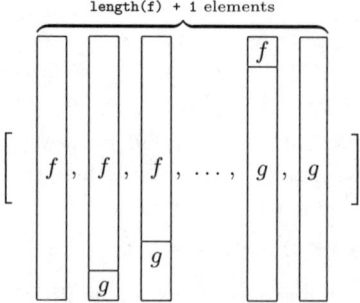

Fig. 2. List of stepwise transformations

The functions `take` and `drop` are predefined list operators. Given a natural number n and a list l the application `take n l` returns the list containing the n first elements of l; `drop n l` returns the rest of l when the first n are dropped. Using the existence of a list `ob` for each n $\leq$ `length f` we can prove the initial subgoal (2) using the lemma `rtrancl_beta_obj_lem` instantiated with `length f`. Having the existence of `ob`, we then only need to infer that its last element is equal to g.

4.5 Confluence

The proof of the confluence property for the ς-calculus is, thanks to Nipkow's framework, simply achieved by proving the theorem `diamond_to_confluence` appropriately instantiated.

⟦ `diamond par_beta`; `beta` $\subseteq$ `par_beta`; `beta` $\subseteq$ `beta`* ⟧ $\Longrightarrow$ `confluent beta`

The provisos of this main theorem, i.e., `diamond par_beta`, `beta` $\subseteq$ `par_beta`, and `par_beta` $\subseteq$ `beta`* are the lemmata described in the penultimate section and just have to be plugged in. Thereby we have shown that the reduction relation $\to_\beta$ for the ς-calculus as defined here is Church-Rosser. This corresponds to the result in the original paper [2][Theorem 2.1-1].

5 Conclusion, Impact and Perspectives

In this paper we have presented the formalization of the ς-calculus in Isabelle/HOL using a de Bruijn notation. We have formalized the syntax and its operational semantics and proved confluence. We did profit from the mechanization of the proof of confluence for the λ-calculus. The latter could be used as a basis for our proofs, but confluence of an object oriented calculus required us additional development compared to the simpler case of λ-calculus, in particular, a particular induction had to be developed for the parallel reduction of fields inside an object. We used a pragmatic representation of lists to contain the fields of an object. Although differing from the original Theory of Objects we argue that no harm is done. Besides a mechanical verification of the ς-calculus the value of our contribution is as a basis for future mechanical models of object oriented languages.

Perspectives and impact of a mechanized ς-calculus. A direct motivation for the mechanization of the ς-calculus is given by the project Ascot [17] for the mechanically supported analysis of aspect-oriented languages. We intend to use the formalization of the ς-calculus as presented in this paper to model and examine type safety of a core aspect calculus.

Another classical extension of this work consists in bringing all the typing theory presented in [1] into the Isabelle/HOL framework for ς-calculus in order to mechanize the proofs of subject reduction and type properties exhibited ten years ago by Abadi and Cardelli.

Finally, a lot of theoretical results have been the objective of previous research on object calculi, e.g., [22,10,9] for concurrency, [5] for mobility, [16] for a bisimilarity relation, etc. Those results generally rely on a calculus very close to the ς-calculus (and sometimes on the ς-calculus itself). Thanks to the mechanized aspect of our model, we think our framework can be used in the future to verify and perhaps improve the properties shown in those various contexts.

Why determinism? ASP calculus as a direct extension of this work. In the presence of distribution, confluence is a particularly interesting question. Therefore we are interested in proving confluence first for the ς-calculus in order to lift the mechanization to distributed object calculi. In practice, this work should first lead to a mechanized version of the ASP calculus [11,12]. This calculus extends the imperative ς-calculus [1] by adding distribution primitives. It mainly relies on the aggregation of objects into so-called activities, and asynchronous method calls between such activities, *futures* acting as promised replies associated to such calls. The ASP-calculus is the theoretical basis for active objects as implemented in the ProActive library. A first step in order to build a mechanized version of ASP could consist in investigating a simpler *functional* version of ASP, for this we plan to rely on the framework presented in this paper.

In this domain, we proved the realizability of such a perspective by designing a functional version of the ASP calculus, realizing a mechanized model for such a calculus, and we provided first proofs such as well-formedness of this calculus. From a practical point of view, this consists in extending the ς-calculus with an *Active* primitive, and the semantics by allowing to: create new activities, perform remote method calls, and retrieve remote results. Our first major and innovative objective is to design and prove the determinism of a functional active object calculus; such a proof will be grounded on the local determinism property proved in this paper. On a longer term point of view we expect to reuse this result to prove new confluence properties, holding on part of the calculus, and based on a distinction between some functional and some imperative services provided by the distributed objects.

Acknowledgment. We would like to thank Larry Paulson for providing us the formalization of the ς-calculus in Isabelle/ZF written by Ehmety.

References

1. Abadi, M., Cardelli, L.: A Theory of Objects. Springer, Heidelberg (1996)
2. Abadi, M., Cardelli, L.: A Theory of Primitive Objects. DEC Research Labs, TR (1995)
3. Abadi, M., Cardelli, L.: An imperative object calculus. In: Mosses, P.D., Schwartzbach, M.I., Nielsen, M. (eds.) CAAP 1995, FASE 1995, and TAPSOFT 1995, LNCS, vol. 915, Springer, Heidelberg (1995)
4. Barendregt, H.P.: The Lambda Calculus, its Syntax and Semantics. North-Holland, 2nd edition (1984)
5. Briais, S., Nestmann, U.: Mobile objects must move safely. Formal Methods for Open Object-Based Distributed Systems IV. In: Proceedings of FMOODS'2002, University of Twente, the Netherlands, Kluwer Academic Publishers, Dordrecht (2002)
6. Niehren, J., Schwinghammer, J., Smolka, G.: A concurrent lambda calculus with futures. Theoretical Computer Science 364(3), 338–356 (Nov. 2006)
7. de Bruijn, N.G.: Lambda calculus notation with nameless dummies, a tool for automatic formula manipulation, with application to the Church-Rosser theorem. Indagationes Mathematicae 34, 381–392 (1972)
8. Berghofer, S., Urban, C.: A Head-to-Head Comparison of de Bruijn Indices and Names. In: Head-to-Head, A. (ed.) Proceedings of the International Workshop on Logical Frameworks and Meta-Languages: Theory and Practice. LFMTP 2006. ENTCS, Elsevier, North-Holland, Amsterdam (2006)
9. Di Blasio, P., Fisher, K.: A calculus for concurrent objects. In: International Conference on Concurrency Theory (1996)
10. Cardelli, L.: A language with distributed scope. In: Conference Record of the 22nd ACM SIGACT-SIGPLAN Symposium on Principles of Programming Languages (POPL'95) (1995)
11. Caromel, D., Henrio, L.: A Theory of Distributed Objects. Springer, Heidelberg (2005)
12. Caromel, D., Henrio, L., Serpette, B.P.: Asynchronous and deterministic objects. In: Proceedings of the 31st ACM SIGACT-SIGPLAN symposium on Principles of programming languages, ACM Press, New York (2004)
13. Ciaffaglione, A., Liquori, L., Miculan, M.: Reasoning about Object-based Calculi in (Co)Inductive Type Theory and the Theory of Contexts. Journal of Automated Reasoning. To appear (2007)
14. Ehmety, S.O.: Theory of objects in Isabelle/ZF. Unpublished theory files (1999)
15. Gordon, A.D., Hankin, P.D.: A concurrent object calculus: reduction and typing. In: concurrent, A. (ed.) Proceedings HLCL'98. ENTCS, 1998, Elsevier, Amsterdam (1998)
16. Gordon, A.D., Rees, G.D.: Bisimilarity for a first-order calculus of objects with subtyping. In: Conference Record of the 23rd ACM SIGACT-SIGPLAN Symposium on Principles of Programming Languages (POPL'96), ACM Press, New York (1996)
17. Jähnichen, S., Kammüller, F.: Ascot: Formal, mechanical foundation of aspect-oriented and collaboration-based languages. Project with the German Research Foundation (DFG) (2006)
18. Kammüller, F.: Author's web-page. http://swt.cs.tu-berlin.de/~flokam (2006)

19. Ligatti, J., Walker, D., Zdancewic, S.: A type-theoretic interpretation of pointcuts and advice. In: Science of Computer Programming: Special Issue on Foundations of Aspect-Oriented Programming, Springer, Heidelberg (2006)
20. Nipkow, T.: More Church Rosser Proofs. Journal of Automated Reasoning 26, 51–66 (2001)
21. Nipkow, T., Paulson, L.C., Wenzel, M.: Isabelle/HOL, LNCS, vol. 2283. Springer, Heidelberg (2002)
22. Pierce, B.C., Turner, D.N.: Concurrent objects in a process calculus. In: Ito, T., Yonezawa, A. (eds.) TPPP 1994, LNCS, vol. 907, Springer, Heidelberg (1995)
23. Urban, C. et al.: Nominal Methods Group. Project funded by the German Research Foundation (DFG) within the Emmy–Noether Programme, Web-page at http://www4.in.tum.de/~urbanc/Nominal/ (2006)
24. Urban, C., Tasson, C.: Nominal Techniques in Isabelle/HOL. In: Nieuwenhuis, R. (ed.) (CADE 2005), LNCS (LNAI), vol. 3632, Springer, Heidelberg (2005)

Pict Correctness Revisited*

Philippe Bidinger[1] and Adriana Compagnoni[2]

[1] VERIMAG, Grenoble, France
[2] Stevens Institute of Technology, Hoboken, NJ, USA

Abstract. The Pict programming language is an implementation of the
π-calculus in which executions of π-calculus terms are specified via an abstract machine. An important property of any concurrent programming
language implementation is the fair execution of threads. After defining
fairness for the π-calculus, we show that Pict abstract machine executions implement fair π-calculus executions. We also give new proofs of
soundness and liveness for the Pict abstract machine.

1 Introduction

The π-calculus [14,17] is a minimal language designed to capture and model key
concepts of communicating concurrent systems in a formal setting. It emphasizes channel-based communication, dynamic channel creation and the ability to
communicate channels as data. Pict [19,16] is a high-level programming language
purely based on π-calculus primitives, as well as to explore the applicability of
theoretical work on type systems. Pict's runtime environment is based on a formal abstract machine specification, but little emphasis has been placed on its
correctness.

The correctness of a programming language runtime is critical since, in order
to be able to reason about programs, we need the guarantee that programs are
executed according to their semantics. Correctness results of implementations
usually relate executions of terms in a high-level language to its implementation in a low-level language. The low-level language can be an existing process
calculus, or like in Pict, an abstract machine specification.

In recent years, many process calculi based on the π-calculus have been introduced to study the dynamics of existing or new paradigms of computation, such
as distributed computing, global computing, or component-based programming.
Much work has been done on the distributed implementation of these calculi
[5,7,22,20,10,8,11,12,1]. On the other hand, since the definition of Pict, there
has been no new insight for the local implementation of these calculi. Therefore, Pict is still a reference implementation of the π-calculus, and we think that
proving its correctness is a first step toward more general proofs of correctness
of implementations of these calculi.

The π-calculus is a concurrent language where concurrency is modeled using
a non-deterministic reduction relation. The Pict Abstract Machine (PAM) implements a particular scheduling strategy that corresponds to a subset of the

---

* This work was funded in part by the US Army under contract W15QKN-05-D-0011.

M.M. Bonsangue and E.B. Johnsen (Eds.): FMOODS 2007, LNCS 4468, pp. 206–220, 2007.
© IFIP International Federation for Information Processing 2007

possible executions in the π-calculus. It is therefore impossible to state an exact correspondence between π-calculus executions and PAM executions. Instead, we will prove the correctness of the abstract machine with three properties:

- A soundness property that states that PAM executions correspond to valid π-calculus executions.
- A liveness property that ensures that the abstract machine is not stuck when its state corresponds to a π-calculus term that can reduce.
- A fairness property that characterizes PAM executions among possible π-calculus executions.

These properties are fairly standard but have not been proven for Pict yet (see section 5 for details). The main contribution of this paper lies in the statement and proof of a fairness property for Pict. To our knowledge, no implementation of a process calculus has been proven fair so far, although fairness is conjectured in [21,19]. Moreover, the technique we propose is general enough to be adapted to similar settings.

Informally, we say that an execution is *weakly fair* if a prefixed process able to communicate *continuously* will eventually do so. An execution is *strongly fair* if a prefixed process able to communicate *infinitely often* will eventually do so. Consider for instance the π-calculus term

$$x!(a) \mid *x?(z).x!(z) \mid y!(0) \mid y?(z).\mathbf{0}$$

where $*P$ represents replicated input. There are valid infinite executions in which the communication on y never takes place even though at any time this communication is possible. Similarly, in the term

$$x!(a) \mid *x?(z).y!(z) \mid *y?(z).x!(z) \mid *x?(z).x!(z)$$

there are infinite executions in which the communication on the last process never takes place, even though such a communication might happen infinitely often (but not continuously). The intuitive expectation of a programmer is that all processes running in parallel will be interleaved *fairly* and so such executions are considered unsatisfactory.

Stating a fairness property for the π-calculus is not immediate. The definition of the π-calculus makes it difficult to identify subprocesses within a process, and in particular, it is difficult to state properties about fair executions of these processes. When considering π-calculus processes, mainly two kinds of confusion can arise.

- Processes are identified up to renaming of bound names and lead to possible confusion of channels. For instance, we have

$$\nu x.\nu y.x!() \mid y!() \mid R \to \nu x.\nu y.x!() \mid R'$$

Because of possible renamings of x and y, we do not know which channel reacted.

- Confusion of structurally equivalent processes.

$$P = x!() \mid x?().x!() \mid *x?().x!()$$
$$P' = x!() \mid x?().x!() \mid x?().x!() \mid *x?().x!()$$

We have $P \equiv P'$ and $P' \to P$, and we do not know which receivers react with $x!()$.

A possible solution is to define an auxiliary calculus in which prefixes are annotated with *labels* in such a way that labels uniquely denote prefixes and that this property is invariant throughout reduction [4,3]. A *live action* of a term is then defined as a couple of labels corresponding to prefixed processes that can react. An infinite labeled execution is strongly fair if there are no labels appearing in an infinity of live actions.

2   Fairness in the π-Calculus

2.1   The π-Calculus

We suppose given a set of names N ranged over by $x, y, \ldots$. We define the set of π-calculus processes P as follows:

$$P, Q, \ldots ::= \mathbf{0} \mid \pi.P \mid \nu x.P \mid P \mid P$$
$$\pi ::= x!(y) \mid x?(y) \mid *x?(y)$$

The π-calculus evaluation contexts are given by:

$$\mathbf{E} ::= \cdot \mid \nu x.\mathbf{E} \mid P \mid \mathbf{E} \mid \mathbf{E} \mid P$$

The operational semantics is defined as the smallest relation such that rules in Figure 2 hold. It makes use of a structural equivalence relation defined as the smallest equivalence relation satisfying the rules in Figure 1. As usual, $\mathtt{fn}(P)$ denotes the set of free names of process P, and $=_\alpha$ equates two processes that differ only by their bound names. We write $\mathbf{E}[P]$ for the context $\mathbf{E}$ in which the hole $.$ has been substituted with P.

$$(P \mid Q) \mid R \equiv P \mid (Q \mid R) \text{ S.Par.Assoc} \qquad P \mid Q \equiv Q \mid P \text{ S.Par.Com}$$

$$P \mid \mathbf{0} \equiv P \text{ S.Par.Nil} \qquad \nu x.\mathbf{0} \equiv \mathbf{0} \text{ S.Nu.Nil} \qquad \nu x.\nu y.P \equiv \nu y.\nu x.P \text{ S.Nu.Com}$$

$$\frac{x \notin \mathtt{fn}(Q)}{(\nu x.P) \mid Q \equiv \nu x.P \mid Q} \text{ S.Nu.Par} \qquad \frac{P =_\alpha Q}{P \equiv Q} \text{ S.}\alpha \qquad \frac{P \equiv Q}{\mathbf{E}[P] \equiv \mathbf{E}[Q]} \text{ S.Ctx}$$

Fig. 1. Structural Equivalence

Without loss of generality, we restrict the usual replication operator to input processes. Rule R.Rep models communication with a replicated input process.

$$\frac{}{x!(y).P \mid x?(z).Q \to P \mid Q\{y/z\}} \ \text{R.Red}$$

$$\frac{}{x!(y).P \mid *x?(z).Q \to P \mid Q\{y/z\} \mid *x?(z).Q} \ \text{R.Rep} \qquad \frac{P \to Q}{\mathbf{E}[P] \to \mathbf{E}[Q]} \ \text{R.Ctx}$$

$$\frac{P \equiv P' \qquad P' \to Q' \qquad Q' \equiv Q}{P \to Q} \ \text{R.Str}$$

Fig. 2. Reduction Relation

2.2   A Labeled π-Calculus

Informally, a fair execution of a process is an execution in which no subprocess is ready to participate in a communication infinitely often. To formalize this statement, we need to identify in a process the subprocesses that can participate in a communication, and keep track of their identities throughout reductions.

To do so, we follow [4,3] and define a labeled version of the π-calculus in which prefixes are annotated with labels. A label has to identify a prefix uniquely in an entire execution of a process. In other words, not only do prefixes have distinct labels in a process, but when new prefixes are created, their labels are new with respect to all the labels in the past execution of the term. We then characterize the labels belonging to prefixes that can participate in a communication. Finally, we give the definition of fairness.

We denote by L a set of labels such that $\mathsf{L} \cap \mathsf{N} = \emptyset$. We use $\mathcal{P}^f(\mathsf{L})$ to denote the finite subsets of L. A labeled process is a pair made of a π-calculus process in which prefixes are labeled, and a finite set of labels. The set of labeled processes LP is generated by the grammar given below.

$$\begin{aligned}
C, D, \dots &::= \overline{P}, \mathcal{L} \\
\overline{P}, \overline{Q}, \dots &::= \mathbf{0} \ \mid \ \pi_l.\overline{P} \ \mid \ \nu x.\overline{P} \ \mid \ \overline{P} \mid \overline{P} \\
& \quad l \in \mathsf{L} \\
& \quad \mathcal{L} \in \mathcal{P}^f(\mathsf{L})
\end{aligned}$$

We also extend contexts with labels and we denote labeled contexts $\overline{\mathbf{E}}$.

We need several auxiliary functions. The function lab returns the set of all labels of a process or a context. The function unl erases all labeling information from a labeled process.

In order to ensure that labels occur uniquely in a process, we define a well-formation predicate wf as the smallest relation on LP such that rules in Figure 3 hold. We write $A \uplus B$ for $A \cup B$ when $A \cap B = \emptyset$. A labeled process C is said to be well-formed if we have $\mathrm{wf}(C)$. We denote by WFP the set of well-formed labeled processes.

The operational semantics is defined in the same way as for the π-calculus via a structural equivalence relation $\equiv$ and a reduction relation $\to$, both binary

$$\frac{}{\text{wf}(\mathbf{0}, \mathcal{L})} \text{ Wf.Nil} \qquad \frac{\text{lab}(\overline{P}) \uplus \text{lab}(\overline{P'}) \subseteq \mathcal{L}}{\text{wf}(\overline{P} \mid \overline{P'}, \mathcal{L})} \text{ Wf.Par} \qquad \frac{\text{wf}(\overline{P}, \mathcal{L})}{\text{wf}(\nu x.\overline{P}, \mathcal{L})} \text{ Wf.New}$$

$$\frac{\text{wf}(\overline{P}, \mathcal{L})}{\text{wf}(\pi_l.\overline{P}, \mathcal{L} \uplus \{l\})} \text{ Wf.Prefix}$$

Fig. 3. Well-Formed Labeled Process

relations over LP. The structural equivalence is defined, as before, as the smallest equivalence relation that verifies rules in Figure 1 (where prefixes are labeled and equivalent processes have the same set of labels). The reduction relation is the smallest relation that verifies the rules in Figure 4. The main difference with the unlabeled reduction relation appears in the rule LR.Rep for replicated input in which fresh labels are generated.

$$\frac{}{x!(y)_l.\overline{P} \mid x?(z)_{l'}.\overline{Q}, \mathcal{L} \to \overline{P} \mid \overline{Q}\{y/z\}, \mathcal{L}} \text{ LR.Red}$$

$$\frac{\alpha \text{ injective and } \mathcal{L}' = \mathcal{L} \uplus \alpha(\mathcal{L})}{x!(y)_l.\overline{P} \mid *x?(z)_{l'}.\overline{Q}, \mathcal{L} \to \overline{P} \mid \overline{Q}\{y/z\} \mid \alpha(*x?(z)_{l'}.\overline{Q}), \mathcal{L}'} \text{ LR.Rep}$$

$$\frac{\overline{P}, \mathcal{L} \to \overline{P'}, \mathcal{L}' \qquad \text{lab}(\overline{\mathbf{E}}) \subseteq \mathcal{L}}{\overline{\mathbf{E}}[\overline{P}], \mathcal{L} \to \overline{\mathbf{E}}[\overline{P'}], \mathcal{L}'} \text{ LR.Ctx} \qquad \frac{D \equiv D' \qquad D' \to C' \qquad C' \equiv C}{D \to C} \text{ LR.Str}$$

Fig. 4. Labeled Reduction Relation

Labeling is stable under reduction and structural equivalence. Hence, in the following, we consider only well-formed processes.

Lemma 1 (Stability of Labeling)

(i) If $C \equiv D$ and $C \in$ WFP, then $D \in$ WFP.
(ii) If $C \to D$ and $C \in$ WFP, then $D \in$ WFP.

The following lemma shows that the labeling system has been designed so that no label can occur more than once in a labeled term, and once a label disappears, it does not reappear in the system.

Lemma 2 (Uniqueness of Labeling)

(i) If $C \in$ WFP then no label l occurs more than once in C.
(ii) If $C \in$ WFP, $C \to^* C' \to^* C''$ and $l \in \text{lab}(C) \cap \text{lab}(C'')$, then $l \in \text{lab}(C')$.

The labeled π-calculus is a conservative extension of the π-calculus. A labeled process has exactly the same reductions as the corresponding unlabeled process. Moreover, we can label any process into a well-formed labeled process.

Proposition 1 (Operational Correspondence). *Let $P \in \mathsf{P}$ and $C \in \mathsf{WFP}$ such that $P = \mathrm{unl}(C)$. We have*

(i) $P \to P'$ implies $\exists C' \in \mathsf{LP}$ such that $C \to C'$ and $\mathrm{unl}(C') = P'$.
(ii) $C \to C'$ implies $P \to \mathrm{unl}(C')$.

Proposition 2 (Existence of a Labeling). *For all $P \in \mathsf{P}$ there exists $C \in \mathsf{WFP}$ such that $\mathrm{unl}(C) = P$.*

We now define the live actions of a labeled process. A live action is a pair of labels corresponding to prefixed processes that can immediately react.

Definition 1 (Live Actions). *The set of live actions of a labeled process $C = \overline{P}, \mathcal{L}$ is defined as*

$$LA(C) = \{\{l, l'\}/C \equiv \nu\widetilde{x}.y!(v)_l.\overline{P_0} \mid y?(z)_{l'}.\overline{P_1} \mid \overline{P_2}, \mathcal{L}$$
$$or\ C \equiv \nu\widetilde{x}.y!(v)_l.\overline{P_0} \mid *y?(z)_{l'}.\overline{P_1} \mid \overline{P_2}, \mathcal{L}\}$$

We also define the set of labels belonging to a live action as

$$L(C) = \{l \in x/x \in LA(C)\}$$

The following lemma states a correspondence between live actions and reductions.

Lemma 3. *$C \to C'$ for some C' if and only if $LA(C) \neq \emptyset$.*

Definition 2 (Execution). *For an arbitrary relation $\to$, an execution is a sequence of terms $T_0, T_1, \ldots$, possibly infinite, such that $T_0 \to \ldots \to T_n \to \ldots$.*

We can now define a strong fairness property for the labeled calculus. An execution is fair if a prefix cannot potentially participate in a reduction infinitely often. According to this definition, we only need to consider infinite executions.

Definition 3 (Strong Fairness in the Labeled π-calculus). *An infinite execution $C_0 \to \ldots \to C_n \to \ldots$ is fair if for any strictly increasing sequence $(u_n)_{n \in \mathbb{N}}$, we have $\bigcap_{n \in \mathbb{N}} L(C_{u_n}) = \emptyset$.*

An execution in the π-calculus is fair if it corresponds to a fair execution in the labeled calculus.

Definition 4 (Strong Fairness in the π-calculus). *An infinite execution $P_0 \to \ldots \to P_n \to \ldots$ is fair if there is a fair execution $C_0 \to \ldots \to C_n \to \ldots$ such that $\forall i \in \mathbb{N}.\mathrm{unl}(C_i) = P_i$.*

3   Abstract Machine

3.1   Syntax and Operational Semantics

The syntax of the Pict abstract machine is given in Figure 5 and follows closely [19] [1]. A machine state, or PAM term, consists of a queue of π-calculus processes $\mathcal{P}$ (the runqueue), a heap $\mathcal{H}$ and a set of names $\mathcal{N}$. A heap is a function that maps channel names to processes queues. We denote by M the set of machine states. We often omit the set of names $\mathcal{N}$ in PAM terms when it is not important, in particular in reduction rules where it remains unchanged. We also write $\mathcal{P} :: \mathcal{Q}$ for the appending of $\mathcal{P}$ and $\mathcal{Q}$. The operational semantics is defined via two reduction

$$\mathcal{M} ::= \langle \mathcal{P}, \mathcal{H}, \mathcal{N} \rangle \qquad\qquad \text{State}$$
$$\mathcal{P}, \mathcal{Q}, \dots ::= [] \mid \mathcal{P} :: \mathcal{P} \qquad\qquad \text{Processes Queue}$$
$$\mathcal{H} ::= \{x \to \mathcal{P}_x\}_{x \in \mathsf{N}} \qquad\qquad \text{Heap}$$

Fig. 5. Syntax of PAM Terms

relations, defined as the smallest binary relations over machine states that satisfy the inference rules given in Figure 6. Intuitively, the relation $\rightsquigarrow$ corresponds to the implementation of $\equiv$, whereas $\mapsto$ implements the actual communication. An actual implementation of this abstract machine does not need to distinguish these relations and would implement $\rightarrow = \rightsquigarrow \uplus \mapsto$, but this distinction will help us to prove correctness properties. In rule AM.NEW, we suppose there is a function freshn : $\mathcal{P}^f(\mathsf{N}) \to \mathsf{N}$ such that freshn$(\mathcal{N}) \notin \mathcal{N}$. We also suppose that names generated by the freshn function never appear in the π-calculus processes in the PAM term (this could be enforced by defining a new syntactic category of names).

We refer the reader to [19,16] for detailed explanations of these rules. We briefly summarize here the main ideas. An execution of the abstract machine starts with an empty heap (we denote it with $\mathcal{H}_{[]}$) that maps all names to empty queues of processes, and a runqueue containing the π-calculus process to be executed. Depending on the form of the process at the top of the runqueue, and the state of the heap, exactly one rule can apply. The execution stops when the runqueue is empty.

A nil process is discarded from the runqueue (rule AM.NIL). Parallel composition of processes is split into two processes that are split in the runqueue (rule AM.PAR). Rule AM.NEW implements name restriction by generating new fresh names. When the first term of the runqueue is a prefixed process willing to communication on a name x, there are two possible cases.If there is no corresponding process in the heap, the process is pushed on the heap queue for x (rules AM.PUSHMESSAGE, AM.PUSHRECEIVER, AM.PUSHREPRECEIVER). If there is a corresponding process in the heap queue (the first element), the communication

---

[1] In particular, this presentation makes use of synchronous communications.

is performed and the continuation of the receiver and sender are placed in the runqueue (rules AM.COM1, AM.RCOM1, AM.COM2, AM.RCOM2).

We can show that processes appearing in an association $x \to \mathcal{P}$ are of the form $\pi.P$, where all prefixes are either output on x, or input (replicated or not) on x. Moreover, this property is invariant by reduction. In the following, we only consider machine states of this form. We also suppose that $\mathcal{H}$ is finite. Moreover, we can notice that the relation $\to$ is deterministic. In particular, generated fresh names are fully determined by the function freshn in rule AM.NEW.

$$\frac{}{\langle \mathbf{0} :: \mathcal{Q}, \mathcal{H} \rangle \rightsquigarrow \langle \mathcal{Q}, \mathcal{H} \rangle} \ \text{AM.NIL} \qquad \frac{}{\langle (P \mid Q) :: \mathcal{Q}, \mathcal{H} \rangle \rightsquigarrow \langle P :: Q :: \mathcal{Q}, \mathcal{H} \rangle} \ \text{AM.PAR}$$

$$\frac{z = \text{freshn}(\mathcal{N})}{\langle \nu x.P :: \mathcal{Q}, \mathcal{H}, \mathcal{N} \rangle \rightsquigarrow \langle P\{z/x\} :: \mathcal{Q}, \mathcal{H}, \mathcal{N} \uplus \{z\} \rangle} \ \text{AM.NEW}$$

$$\frac{\mathcal{P} = [] \vee \mathcal{P} = x?(z).Q :: \mathcal{P}' \vee \mathcal{P} = *x?(z).Q :: \mathcal{Q}}{\langle x?(y).P :: \mathcal{Q}, \mathcal{H} \oplus \{x \to \mathcal{P}\} \rangle \rightsquigarrow \langle \mathcal{Q}, \mathcal{H} \oplus \{x \to \mathcal{P} :: x?(y).P\} \rangle} \ \text{AM.PUSHRECEIVER}$$

$$\frac{\mathcal{P} = [] \vee \mathcal{P} = x!(z).Q :: \mathcal{P}'}{\langle x!(y).P :: \mathcal{Q}, \mathcal{H} \oplus \{x \to \mathcal{P}\} \rangle \rightsquigarrow \langle \mathcal{Q}, \mathcal{H} \oplus \{x \to \mathcal{P} :: x!(y).P\} \rangle} \ \text{AM.PUSHMESSAGE}$$

$$\frac{\mathcal{P} = [] \vee \mathcal{P} = x?(z).Q :: \mathcal{P}' \vee \ \mathcal{P} = *x?(z).Q :: \mathcal{P}'}{\langle *x?(y).P :: \mathcal{Q}, \mathcal{H} \oplus \{x \to \mathcal{P}\} \rangle \rightsquigarrow \langle \mathcal{Q}, \mathcal{H} \oplus \{x \to \mathcal{P} :: *x?(y).P\} \rangle} \ \text{AM.PUSHREPRECEIVER}$$

$$\frac{\mathcal{P} = x!(z).Q :: \mathcal{P}'}{\langle x?(y).P :: \mathcal{Q}, \mathcal{H} \oplus \{x \to \mathcal{P}\} \rangle \mapsto \langle P\{z/y\} :: \mathcal{Q} :: Q, \mathcal{H} \oplus \{x \to \mathcal{P}'\} \rangle} \ \text{AM.COM1}$$

$$\frac{\mathcal{P} = x!(z).Q :: \mathcal{P}'}{\langle *x?(y).P :: \mathcal{Q}, \mathcal{H} \oplus \{x \to \mathcal{P}\} \rangle \mapsto \langle *x?(y).P :: \mathcal{Q} :: P\{z/y\} :: Q, \mathcal{H} \oplus \{x \to \mathcal{P}'\} \rangle} \ \text{AM.RCOM1}$$

$$\frac{\mathcal{P} = x?(z).Q :: \mathcal{P}'}{\langle x!(y).P :: \mathcal{Q}, \mathcal{H} \oplus \{x \to \mathcal{P}\} \rangle \mapsto \langle P :: \mathcal{Q} :: Q\{y/z\}, \mathcal{H} \oplus \{x \to \mathcal{P}'\} \rangle} \ \text{AM.COM2}$$

$$\frac{\mathcal{P} = *x?(z).Q :: \mathcal{P}'}{\langle x!(y).P :: \mathcal{Q}, \mathcal{H} \oplus \{x \to \mathcal{P}\} \rangle \mapsto \langle P :: \mathcal{Q} :: Q\{y/z\}, \mathcal{H} \oplus \{x \to \mathcal{P}' :: *x?(z).Q\} \rangle} \ \text{AM.RCOM2}$$

Fig. 6. PAM Reduction Rules

3.2   Labeled Abstract Machine

We define a labeled version of the Pict abstract machine and essentially follow section 2. This auxiliary calculus is a technical tool, and it is only used for proving the correctness of the abstract machine. Its syntax is defined by adding labels to π-calculus processes appearing in PAM terms. We also extend PAM terms with a finite set of labels. We write LM for the set of labeled PAM terms, and we use $\overline{\mathcal{M}}$ and its variants to range over them.

$$\overline{\mathcal{M}} ::= \langle \overline{\mathcal{P}}, \overline{\mathcal{H}}, \mathcal{N}, \mathcal{L} \rangle \qquad\qquad \text{State}$$

$$\overline{\mathcal{P}}, \overline{\mathcal{Q}}, \dots ::= [] \mid \overline{P} :: \overline{\mathcal{P}} \qquad\qquad \text{Processes Queue}$$

$$\overline{\mathcal{H}} ::= \{x \to \overline{\mathcal{P}}_x\}_{x \in \mathbb{N}} \qquad\qquad \text{Heap}$$

$$\mathcal{L} \in \mathcal{P}^f(\mathsf{L})$$

We define the set of well-formed PAM terms in Figure 7 and call it WFM. Reduction of labeled PAM terms is defined almost exactly as for the unlabeled calculus, apart from the rules AM.RCOM1 and AM.RCOM2. The functions lab and unl extend as expected on processes queues, heaps and machine states.

$$\frac{\mathrm{wf}(\overline{\mathcal{P}}) \qquad \mathrm{wf}(\overline{\mathcal{H}}) \qquad \mathrm{lab}(\overline{\mathcal{P}}) \uplus \mathrm{lab}(\overline{\mathcal{H}}) \subseteq \mathcal{L}}{\mathrm{wf}(\langle \overline{\mathcal{P}}, \overline{\mathcal{H}}, \mathcal{N}, \mathcal{L} \rangle)} \text{ WF.STATE}$$

$$\frac{\mathrm{wf}(\overline{P}) \qquad \mathrm{wf}(\overline{\mathcal{P}}) \qquad \mathrm{lab}(\overline{P}) \cap \mathrm{lab}(\overline{\mathcal{P}}) = \emptyset}{\mathrm{wf}(\overline{P} :: \overline{\mathcal{P}})} \text{ WF.PROCQUEUE}$$

$$\frac{\forall x, y \in \mathbb{N}.x \neq y \implies \mathrm{lab}(\overline{\mathcal{H}}(x)) \cap \mathrm{lab}(\overline{\mathcal{H}}(y)) = \emptyset \qquad \forall x \in \mathbb{N}.\mathrm{wf}(\overline{\mathcal{H}}(x))}{\mathrm{wf}(\overline{\mathcal{H}})} \text{ WF.HEAP}$$

Fig. 7. Well-Formed PAM Term

Lemma 4 (Stability of Labeling)

(i) If $\overline{\mathcal{M}} \equiv \overline{\mathcal{M}}'$ and $\overline{\mathcal{M}} \in \mathsf{WFM}$, then $\overline{\mathcal{M}}' \in \mathsf{WFM}$.
(ii) If $\overline{\mathcal{M}} \to \overline{\mathcal{M}}'$ and $\overline{\mathcal{M}} \in \mathsf{WFM}$, then $\overline{\mathcal{M}}' \in \mathsf{WFM}$.

Proposition 3 (Operational Correspondence). *Let $\mathcal{M} \in \mathsf{M}$ and $\overline{\mathcal{M}} \in \mathsf{WFM}$ such that $\mathcal{M} = \mathrm{unl}(\overline{\mathcal{M}})$. If $\Rightarrow$ denotes either $\mapsto$ or $\rightsquigarrow$, we have*

(i) $\mathcal{M} \Rightarrow \mathcal{M}'$ implies there is $\overline{\mathcal{M}}' \in \mathsf{LM}$ such that $\overline{\mathcal{M}} \Rightarrow \overline{\mathcal{M}}'$ and $\mathrm{unl}(\overline{\mathcal{M}}') = \mathcal{M}'$.
(ii) $\overline{\mathcal{M}} \Rightarrow \overline{\mathcal{M}}'$ implies $\mathcal{M} \Rightarrow \mathrm{unl}(\overline{\mathcal{M}}')$.

We now define the live actions of a labeled PAM term as the live actions of a corresponding π-calculus term. Intuitively, $\{l, l'\}$ is a live action whenever there are two matching prefixed processes somewhere in the PAM term that could *potentially* react.

Definition 5 (Live Actions). *The set of live actions of a labeled PAM term $\overline{\mathcal{M}}$ is defined as*

$$LA(\overline{\mathcal{M}}) = LA(\llbracket \overline{\mathcal{M}} \rrbracket^r)$$

$$\frac{P = x!(z)_{l'}.\overline{Q} :: \overline{P'} \qquad \alpha \text{ injective and } \mathcal{L}' = \mathcal{L} \uplus \alpha(\mathcal{L})}{\langle *x?(y)_l.\overline{P} :: \overline{Q}, \mathcal{H} \oplus \{x \to \overline{P}\}, \mathcal{L}\rangle \mapsto \atop \langle \alpha(*x?(y)_l.\overline{P}) :: \overline{Q} :: \overline{P}\{z/y\} :: \overline{Q}, \mathcal{H} \oplus \{x \to \overline{P'}\}, \mathcal{L}'\rangle} \quad \text{AM.RCOM1}$$

$$\frac{P = *x?(z)_{l'}.\overline{Q} :: \overline{P'} \qquad \alpha \text{ injective and } \mathcal{L}' = \mathcal{L} \uplus \alpha(\mathcal{L})}{\langle x!(y)_l.\overline{P} :: \overline{Q}, \mathcal{H} \oplus \{x \to \overline{P}\}, \mathcal{L}\rangle \mapsto \atop \langle \overline{P} :: \overline{Q} :: \overline{Q}\{y/z\}, \mathcal{H} \oplus \{x \to \overline{P'} :: \alpha(*x?(z)_{l'}.\overline{Q})\}, \mathcal{L}'\rangle} \quad \text{AM.RCOM2}$$

Fig. 8. Labeled PAM Reduction Rules

where $\llbracket . \rrbracket^r$ is defined inductively on the structure of $\overline{\mathcal{M}}$.

$$\llbracket \langle \overline{\mathcal{P}}, \overline{\mathcal{H}}, \mathcal{N}, \mathcal{L} \rangle \rrbracket^r = \nu \mathcal{N}.\llbracket \overline{\mathcal{P}} \rrbracket^r \mid \llbracket \overline{\mathcal{H}} \rrbracket^r, \mathcal{L}$$

$$\llbracket [] \rrbracket^r = \mathbf{0}$$

$$\llbracket \overline{P} :: \overline{\mathcal{P}} \rrbracket^r = \overline{P} \mid \llbracket \overline{\mathcal{P}} \rrbracket^r$$

$$\llbracket \{x \to \overline{\mathcal{P}}_x\}_{x \in \mathsf{N}} \rrbracket^r = \mid_{x \in \mathsf{N}} \llbracket \overline{\mathcal{P}}_x \rrbracket^r$$

We also define the set of labels belonging to a live action as $L(\overline{\mathcal{M}}) = \{l \in x / x \in LA(\overline{\mathcal{M}})\}$.

Lemma 5. *If $LA(\overline{\mathcal{M}}) \neq \emptyset$ then $\exists \overline{\mathcal{M}}'. \overline{\mathcal{M}} \rightsquigarrow^* \mapsto \overline{\mathcal{M}}'$.*

The following theorem can be seen as a fairness property for the labeled abstract machine.

Theorem 1. *If $\overline{\mathcal{M}}_0 \to \ldots \to \overline{\mathcal{M}}_n \to \ldots$ is an infinite execution then for any strictly increasing sequence $(u_n)_{n \in \mathbb{N}}$, we have $\bigcap_{n \in \mathbb{N}} L(\overline{\mathcal{M}}_{u_n}) = \emptyset$*

The proof is technical but it relies on intuitive ideas. Informally, it follows from two key properties of the abstract machine reduction system:

- If a process $\pi_l.\overline{P}$ appears in an evaluation context in the runqueue, it will eventually reach the top of the runqueue.
- The heap queues are organized following a FIFO policy.

4   Correctness

From an operational point of view, the correctness of an abstract machine can be stated by relating abstract machine executions of a process P with π-calculus executions of the same process P executed by the abstract machine. The initial state of an abstract machine running P is $\langle P, \mathcal{H}_{[]} \rangle$, hence we introduce the following translation function.

Definition 6. (Translation from π-calculus to PAM)

$$[\![P]\!] = \langle P :: [], \mathcal{H}_{[]}, \emptyset \rangle \qquad\qquad [\![\overline{P}, \mathcal{L}]\!] = \langle \overline{P} :: [], \mathcal{H}_{[]}, \emptyset, \mathcal{L} \rangle$$

The first property we consider is the soundness of the abstract machine with respect to the calculus. Intuitively, this means that abstract machine executions correspond to valid π-calculus executions. If a machine state $\mathcal{M}$, corresponding to a process state P, reduces to a machine state $\mathcal{M}'$, then $\mathcal{M}'$ must correspond to a process state P' where P reduces to P'. One reduction in the π-calculus may be implemented by several reductions of the abstract machine. In order to model a one-to-one correspondence, we identify two kinds of reductions. Administrative reductions denoted by $\rightsquigarrow$ model structural equivalence. Communication reductions are denoted by $\mapsto$. We will establish a correspondence between the relations $\rightsquigarrow^* \mapsto$ over PAM terms and $\rightarrow$ over π-calculus terms. For that, we define a relation $\mathcal{M} \preceq P$ to mean that P corresponds to $\mathcal{M}$, read $\mathcal{M}$ implements P.

We still need to define the relation $\preceq$. It has to be convincing enough that it effectively relates equivalent process state and machine state. It should at least enjoy the following two properties:

$- [\![P]\!] \preceq P \qquad$ and $\qquad -$ If $\mathcal{M} \rightsquigarrow \mathcal{M}'$ and $\mathcal{M} \preceq P$ then $\mathcal{M}' \preceq P$.

The first property follows the idea that the initial state of an abstract machine executing $[\![P]\!]$ is P. The second property follows the intuition that $\rightsquigarrow$ is a structural, or administrative, reduction and that abstract machine states still implement the same π-calculus process after such reductions. We define $\preceq$ as the smallest relation enjoying these two properties.

Definition 7. $\mathcal{M} \preceq P \iff [\![P]\!] \rightsquigarrow^* \mathcal{M}$.

The definition of $\preceq$ extends naturally to labeled processes.

Note that we do not have a notion of observables, although it would make the correspondence relation $\preceq$ more convincing. However, it should be straightforward to define an observation predicate on π-calculus processes and PAM terms (such as those in [1,7,11]) and show that $\preceq$ preserves the observables.

The following lemma relates the live actions of a labeled PAM term and a labeled process it implements.

Lemma 6. If $\overline{\mathcal{M}} \preceq C$ then $LA(\overline{\mathcal{M}}) = LA(C)$.

To prove the soundness property, we need a translation function from PAM terms to π-calculus processes. This function is very similar to $[\![.]\!]^r$. We do not give its full definition here but the following lemma states the properties needed for the proof of soundness.

Lemma 7. There exists a function $[\![.]\!]^{-1}$ from M to P such that

$- \mathcal{M} \preceq [\![\mathcal{M}]\!]^{-1}$
$- [\![[\![P]\!]]\!]^{-1} \equiv P$

- *if $M \rightsquigarrow M'$ then $[\![M]\!]^{-1} \equiv [\![M']\!]^{-1}$*
- *if $M \mapsto M'$ then $[\![M]\!]^{-1} \mapsto [\![M']\!]^{-1}$.*

Theorem 2 (Soundness). *If $(M \rightsquigarrow^* \mapsto M' \wedge M \preceq P)$ then $(\exists P'.P \rightarrow P' \wedge M' \preceq P')$.*

Proof. The theorem follows from $[\![P]\!] \rightsquigarrow^* \mapsto M \implies (\exists P'.P \rightarrow P' \wedge M \preceq P')$ which is a consequence of Lemma 7 with $P' = [\![M]\!]^{-1}$.

This property is not sufficient to prove the correctness of the abstract machine. Other properties are needed to characterize which executions of the π-calculus are actually implemented. First, a liveness property ensures that a PAM term is never blocked when it corresponds to a π-calculus term that can reduce.

Theorem 3 (Liveness). *If $P \rightarrow P' \wedge M \preceq P$ then $\exists M'.M \rightsquigarrow^* \mapsto M'$.*

Proof. We first prove: $P \rightarrow P' \implies \exists M.[\![P]\!] \rightsquigarrow^* \mapsto M$. If $P \rightarrow P'$, we have $C \rightarrow C'$ with $\mathrm{unl}(C) = P$ and $\mathrm{unl}(C') = P'$, by propositions 2 and 1. Moreover, by Lemma 6, $LA([\![C]\!]) = LA(C)$ with $LA(C) \neq \emptyset$, by Lemma 3. We deduce $[\![C]\!] \rightsquigarrow^* \mapsto \overline{M}'$ for some $\overline{M}'$, by Lemma 5. We conclude, by Proposition 3, that $[\![P]\!] = \mathrm{unl}([\![C]\!]) \rightsquigarrow^* \mapsto \mathrm{unl}(\overline{M}')$.
  We know now that $[\![P]\!] \rightsquigarrow^* M'' \mapsto M'$ for some M'' and M'. Moreover we have $[\![P]\!] \rightsquigarrow^* M$, by definition of $M \preceq P$. Because $\rightarrow$ is deterministic, we conclude $M \rightsquigarrow^* [\![P]\!] \rightsquigarrow^* M'' \mapsto M'$.

Finally, our main result is a fairness theorem.

Theorem 4 (Fairness). *If $M_0 \rightsquigarrow^* \mapsto \ldots \rightsquigarrow^* \mapsto M_n \rightsquigarrow^* \mapsto \ldots$ is an infinite execution then there exists a fair execution $P_0 \rightarrow \ldots \rightarrow P_n \rightarrow \ldots$ such that $M_i \preceq P_i$ for all i.*

Proof. Let $M_0 \rightsquigarrow^* \mapsto \ldots \rightsquigarrow^* \mapsto M_n \rightsquigarrow^* \mapsto \ldots$ be an infinite execution. we have an execution $\overline{M}_0 \rightsquigarrow^* \mapsto \ldots \rightsquigarrow^* \mapsto \overline{M}_n \rightsquigarrow^* \mapsto \ldots$ such that for all i, $\mathrm{unl}(\overline{M}_i) = M_i$, by Proposition 3.
  The soundness theorem (Theorem 2) extends to the labeled calculus and gives us an execution $C_0 \rightarrow \ldots \rightarrow C_n \rightarrow \ldots$ such that

$$
\begin{array}{ccccccc}
\overline{M}_0 & \xrightarrow[\rightsquigarrow^* \mapsto]{} & \overline{M}_1 & \xrightarrow[\rightsquigarrow^* \mapsto]{} & \overline{M}_2 & \xrightarrow[\rightsquigarrow^* \mapsto]{} & \cdots \\
\preceq \Big\downarrow & & \preceq \Big\downarrow & & \preceq \Big\downarrow & & \\
C_0 & \xrightarrow[\rightarrow]{} & C_1 & \xrightarrow[\rightarrow]{} & C_2 & \xrightarrow[\rightarrow]{} & \cdots
\end{array}
$$

From Lemma 6, we have $LA(C_i) = LA(\overline{M}_i)$ for all i. Then we deduce from Theorem 1 that the execution $C_0 \rightarrow \ldots C_n \rightarrow \ldots$ is fair. By erasing the labels in both executions, we deduce the result.

5   Related Work

Comparison with Pict. Correctness results in [19] include a soundness and a liveness property based on the translation function $[\![.]\!]^r$ from PAM terms to π-calculus terms given in Definition 5:

(i) $\mathcal{M} \rightarrow \mathcal{M}' \implies [\![\mathcal{M}]\!]^r \equiv [\![\mathcal{M}']\!]^r \vee [\![\mathcal{M}]\!]^r \rightarrow [\![\mathcal{M}']\!]^r$
(ii) $P \rightarrow P' \implies \exists \mathcal{M}. [\![P]\!] \rightarrow \mathcal{M}$

However, these properties are not sufficient for proving soundness or liveness. The first property means that we can build a π-calculus reduction from a PAM reduction, but does not prove that PAM reductions implement π-calculus reductions. A property relating $\mathcal{M}$ and $[\![[\![\mathcal{M}]\!]^r]\!]$, such as our Lemma 7 is missing. The second property tells us that if P reduces to P', there is a PAM reduction $[\![P]\!] \rightarrow \mathcal{M}$. However, the property cannot be applied on more than the first step of execution, as we do not know if there is P'' such that $P \rightarrow P''$ and $[\![P'']\!] = \mathcal{M}$.

In [18], the Pict abstract machine is proven correct using a notion of testing, and a realistic model of the interactions between the abstract machine and its environment. However, they do not consider fairness issues.

Fairness. Fairness has been defined using labels in CCS [3] and in the π-calculus [4,2]. We essentially followed the same idea but our presentation is simpler as we annotate labeled terms with a set of labels that allow us to generate fresh labels in the replication rules, without relying on a structured labeling language.

In [13], fairness is defined for the π-calculus by considering *normal* reductions where α-equivalence is restricted and tags similar to labels are used to distinguish processes. Fresh tags are generated using the π-calculus name restriction operator.

Correctness of Abstract Machine. There have been several recent papers devoted to the formal description of implementations of process calculi based on the π-calculus or the Ambient calculus. In addition to Pict, one can notably cite the Jocaml distributed implementation of the Join calculus [6,5], the Join calculus implementation of Mobile Ambients [7], Nomadic Pict [22,20], the abstract machine for the M-calculus [10], the Fusion Machine [8], the PAN and GCPAN abstract machines for Safe Ambients [11,12], the CAM abstract machine for Channel Ambients [15] and the abstract machine for the Kell calculus [1]. Most of these works [7,22,20,10,8,11,12,15,1] deal with distributed implementations of calculi, rather than local implementation of concurrent processes like in Pict. They are defined by a translation to a low-level calculus or abstract machine. Their correctness is proven in terms of bisimilary that does not apply to our setting, since Pict implementation makes deterministic choice and PAM reductions do not match all π-calculus reductions. Implementations that consider scheduling of processes are given in [15,10]. In [15], a soundness result is given similar to the one given in Pict. In [10], scheduling of processes is done as in Pict using FIFO lists, but no proof of correctness is given.

6   Conclusion

In this paper, we first defined strong fairness in the π-calculus. We then proved that Pict abstract machine executions are sound with respect to π-calculus executions and that they enjoy fairness and liveness properties. These correctness results for Pict are new and in particular, fairness has not been proven for any implementation of process calculi based on the π-calculus. We believe that these techniques are simple and general enough to be adapted to other calculi.

Very little work has been done on the scheduling of processes in the π-calculus or its variants. For future research, we will investigate alternative scheduling strategies. In particular, we would like to extend Pict and its implementation with priority constraints. Processes could be prioritized in order to allocate more processor time to more important processes. In Pict, even though executions are strongly fair, in a term $P \mid Q$, P can monopolize the processor usage by spawning new subprocesses much faster than Q. One can imagine annotated processes like in $P_h \mid Q_l$ where the annotations are taken into account by the scheduler. Such a scheme would fit naturally in a calculus with hierarchical localities such as [1]. For instance, a term of the form $a[b[P] \mid c[Q]]$ can be interpreted as two (possibly untrusted) agents b and c executed by a site a. The parent site a should be able to control the processor usage of the agents it is executing.

Most correctness results of the implementations of process calculi with localities concern their distributed implementation, but do not deal with the correctness of their local implementation, *i.e.* the scheduling of processes. On the other hand, Pict defines a local implementation. It would be interesting to consider correctness results combining these two approaches. We are currently investigating the proof of a refined abstract machine based on [1].

Acknowledgments. We are grateful to Healfdene Goguen, Benjamin Pierce, Alan Schmitt and Jean-Bernard Stefani, as well as the anonymous reviewers, for their comments on earlier drafts. We thank Pablo Garralda, whose PhD thesis work inspired us to use labeled processes to study fairness [9].

References

1. Bidinger, P., Schmitt, A., Stefani, J.-B.: An abstract machine for the Kell calculus. In: Steffen, M., Zavattaro, G. (eds.) FMOODS 2005, LNCS, vol. 3535, pp. 43–58. Springer, Heidelberg (2005)
2. Cacciagrano, D., Corradini, F., Palamidessi, C.: Fairpi. In: Proceedings of EXPRESS'06, ENTCS (2006)
3. Costa, G., Stirling, C.: Weak and strong fairness in CCS. In: Chytil, M.P., Koubek, V. (eds.) MFCS 1984, LNCS, vol. 176, pp. 245–254, Springer, Heidelberg (1984)
4. Corradini, F., Cacciagrano, D.R.: Fairness in the pi-calculus. Technical report, Dipartimenti di Informatica, Università di L'Aquila, TR 005/2004 (2004)
5. Le Fessant, F.: JoCaml: Conception et Implantation d'un Langage à Agents Mobiles. PhD thesis, Ecole Polytechnique (2001)

6. Fournet, C., Gonthier, G., Levy, J.J., Maranget, L., Remy, D.: A calculus of mobile agents. In: Sassone, V., Montanari, U. (eds.) CONCUR 1996, LNCS, vol. 1119, pp. 406–421. Springer, Heidelberg (1996)
7. Fournet, C., Levy, J.J., Schmitt, A.: An asynchronous distributed implementation of mobile ambients. In: Watanabe, O., Hagiya, M., Ito, T., van Leeuwen, J., Mosses, P.D. (eds.) TCS 2000, LNCS, vol. 1872, pp. 348–364. Springer, Heidelberg (2000)
8. Gardner, P., Laneve, C., Wischik, L.: The fusion machine. In: Brim, L., Jančar, P., Křetínský, M., Kucera, A. (eds.) CONCUR 2002, LNCS, vol. 2421, pp. 418–433. Springer, Heidelberg (2002)
9. Garralda, P.: Boxed Ambients for Global Computing. PhD thesis, Stevens Institute of Technology, New Jersey, USA (2007)
10. Germain, F., Lacoste, M., Stefani, J.B.: An abstract machine for a higher-order distributed process calculus. In: Proceedings of the EACTS Workshop on Foundations of Wide Area Network Computing (F-WAN) (July 2002)
11. Giannini, P., Sangiorgi, D., Valente, A.: Safe ambients: abstract machine and distributed implementation. Sci. Comput. Program. 59(3), 209–249 (2006)
12. Hirschkoff, D., Pous, D., Sangiorgi, D.: A correct abstract machine for safe ambients. In: COORDINATION, pp. 17–32 (2005)
13. Kobayashi, N.: A type system for lock-free processes. Inf. Comput. 177(2), 122–159 (2002)
14. Milner, R., Parrow, J., Walker, D.: A calculus of mobile processes, parts I and II. Inf. Comput. 100(1), 1–78 (1992)
15. Phillips, A., Yoshida, N., Eisenbach, S.: A distributed abstract machine for boxed ambient calculi. In: Schmidt, D. (ed.) ESOP 2004, LNCS, vol. 2986, Springer, Heidelberg (Apr. 2004)
16. Pierce, B.C., Turner, D.N.: Pict: A programming language based on the pi-calculus. In: Plotkin, G., Stirling, C., Tofte, M. (eds.) Proof, Language and Interaction: Essays in Honour of Robin Milner, pp. 455–494. MIT Press, Cambridge (2000)
17. Sangiorgi, D., Walker, D.: The π-calculus: A Theory of Mobile Processes. Cambridge University Press, Cambridge (2001)
18. Sewell, P.: On implementations and semantics of a concurrent programming language. In: Mazurkiewicz, A., Winkowski, J. (eds.) CONCUR 1997, LNCS, vol. 1243, pp. 391–405. Springer, Heidelberg (1997)
19. Turner, D.: The polymorphic π-calculus: Theory and implementation. Technical report, University of Edinburgh, GB (1996)
20. Unyapoth, A., Sewell, P.: Nomadic Pict: Correct Communication Infrastructures for Mobile Computation. In: Proceedings ACM Int. Conf. on Principles of Programming Languages (POPL), pp. 116–127. ACM Press, New York (2001)
21. Wischik, L.: Explicit Fusions: Theory and Implementation. PhD thesis, Computer Laboratory, University of Cambridge, Cambridge (2001)
22. Wojciechowski, P., Sewell, P.: Nomadic Pict: Language and Infrastructure. IEEE Concurrency 8(2), 42–52 (2000)

A Refinement Method for Java Programs

Holger Grandy, Kurt Stenzel, and Wolfgang Reif

Lehrstuhl für Softwaretechnik und Programmiersprachen
Institut für Informatik, Universität Augsburg
86135 Augsburg Germany
{grandy,stenzel,reif}@informatik.uni-augsburg.de

Abstract. We present a refinement method for Java programs which is motivated by the challenge of verifying security protocol implementations. The method can be used for stepwise refinement of abstract specifications down to the level of code running in the real application. The approach is based on a calculus for the verification of Java programs for the concrete level and Abstract State Machines for the abstract level. In this paper we illustrate our method by the verification of a M-Commerce application for buying movie tickets using a mobile phone written in J2ME. For verification we use KIV, our interactive theorem prover [1].

1 Introduction

Refinement is an established method for proving algorithms correct. A concrete specification is a refinement of a more abstract specification if every state change that can be performed on the concrete level is also possible on the abstract level. State based refinement methods (e.g. [8] [30] [3]) have been used in numerous case studies for the verification of algorithmic correctness. The underlying theory and the methods for applying those approaches, also on the level of tool support, are elaborated and widely used.

Much less work has been done on refinement methods for the verification of Java implementations. Although there are many examples of Java [17] program verification, e.g. [16] [5] [6] [22] [15], the authors are not aware of a larger case study of interactive verification using a refinement framework for proving full functional correctness of a Java program respecting an abstract specification.

In the field of security protocol implementations the past has shown that implementation flaws are very common and can be very subtle. In this paper, we present a general refinement method for Java programs inspired by the challenge of verifying security protocol implementations. The method is illustrated by the verification of a Java M-Commerce application, the Cindy[1] case study. The refinement approach is not limited to the field of security protocols. Using the mechanisms described below we can prove functional correctness for all kinds of programs with input, output and state change.

---

[1] Cinema Handy (Handy is the German word for mobile phone).

M.M. Bonsangue and E.B. Johnsen (Eds.): FMOODS 2007, LNCS 4468, pp. 221–235, 2007.

The paper is organized as follows: Section 2 presents the case study, Section 3 illustrates the specifications for refinement and proof obligations. Section 4 describes the mapping of abstract data types to Java classes. Section 5 presents some difficulties the refinement method has to solve stemming from this mapping and Section 6 gives some details on the verification of the case study. Finally, Section 7 compares the approach to related work and Section 8 concludes.

2 The Cindy Case Study

With Cindy users can buy cinema tickets using mobile phones. A user can order a ticket using a Java application running on the device. Payment can be done using the usual phone bill. After having ordered a ticket it is sent to the mobile phone as a MMS (Multimedia Messaging Service) message. The ticket contains the movie

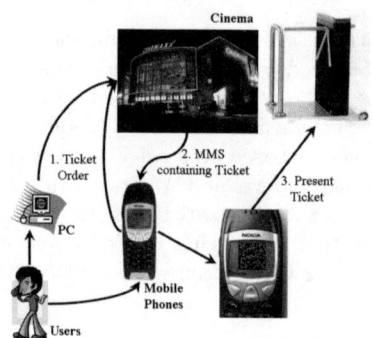

Fig. 1. The Cindy Application

data and an additional unique identifier for the ticket. It can be displayed on the phone using a two-dimensional data matrix barcode and is scanned at the entrance to the cinema directly from the display using a barcode scanner. This kind of application exists e.g. in the Netherlands [2]. Additionally, the German railway company, Deutsche Bahn, has recently implemented a similar service for buying train tickets using a mobile phone.

One important question for the cinema is, of course, how to avoid fraud. The idea is simple: Every ticket contains a nonce, a unique random number that is too long to guess. Therefore it is virtually impossible to 'forge' a ticket.

Full details on the abstract model of Cindy as well as the details on the verification of security properties on this abstract level (which follows our approach for the verification of security protocols called PROSECCO) can be found in [10]. The next section describes the approach for verifying an implementation of Cindy running on a mobile phone written in J2ME.

3 Abstract and Concrete Specification Levels

We assume the reader is roughly familiar with data refinement theory, which in this section we will adopt to Java programs using the notation based on [9].

The abstract level is given as a data type $\mathsf{ADT} = (\mathsf{GS}, \mathsf{AS}, \mathsf{AINIT}, \{\mathsf{AOP}_i\}_{i \in I},$ $\mathsf{AFIN})$ consisting of a set of global states GS and a set of (local) states AS. Total relations $\mathsf{AINIT} \subseteq \mathsf{GS} \times \mathsf{AS}$ and $\mathsf{AFIN} \subseteq \mathsf{AS} \times \mathsf{GS}$ initialize and finalize the data type. $\mathsf{AOP}_i \subseteq \mathsf{AS} \times \mathsf{AS}$ (using an index $i \in \mathsf{I}$) are the operations possible on the data type. In the specification of the Cindy example different agents are involved modelling the different protocol participants. Every **agent** has a type **type(agent)** (the type can be **cellphone**, **cinema**, **user** or **attacker**). The index set I of AOP_i now consists of the different agents, where e.g. $\mathsf{AOP}_{\mathrm{cellphone(n)}}$ denotes the protocol steps of the cellphone agent with number n.

On the conrete level, one agent in the protocol model is replaced by his Java implementation. So the concrete level is given similarly as $\mathsf{CDT} = (\mathsf{GS}, \mathsf{CS}, \mathsf{CINIT}, \{\mathsf{COP}_i\}_{i \in \mathsf{I}}, \mathsf{CFIN})$, where one COP_i is a Java implementation. Details will be given later in Sect. 3.2.

Our operations are total so we use the approach of [13] and a forward simulation $\mathsf{R} \subseteq \mathsf{AS} \times \mathsf{CS}$ leading to the following proof obligations for refinement correctness:

- $\mathsf{CINIT} \subseteq \mathsf{AINIT} \, \S \, \mathsf{R}$ ("initialization")
- $\forall \, i \in \mathsf{I}. \, \mathsf{R} \, \S \, \mathsf{COP}_i \subseteq \mathsf{AOP}_i \, \S \, \mathsf{R}$ ("correctness")
- $\mathsf{R} \, \S \, \mathsf{CFIN} \subseteq \mathsf{AFIN}$ ("finalization")

3.1 The Abstract Level

The state $\mathsf{as} : \mathsf{AS}$ consists of a function $\mathsf{astate} : \mathsf{agent} \to \mathsf{A}_{\mathsf{type(agent)}}$ that maps each **agent** to its internal state in $\mathsf{A}_{\mathsf{type(agent)}}$ For an agent of type **cellphone** this is e.g. the list of current tickets stored on a phone and its phone number. Additionally, as contains the current context $\mathsf{actxt} : \mathsf{context}$ of the communication infrastructure (connections and inputs for every agent that represent the messages that are currently in transit). Together $\mathsf{as} = \mathsf{astate} \times \mathsf{actxt}$. The global state GS contains only the list of tickets of the phones, since we want to show that this list is the same on both levels. GS is ignored in AINIT, AFIN extracts the list of tickets sold so far from GS.

The abstract specification of the functionality of the protocol in Cindy is given as an Abstract State Machine (ASM) [4] consisting of models for all the different agents in the scenario. Although not being used directly by the refinement theory, we use the different rules of this ASM to define the operations $\mathsf{AOP}_{\mathrm{agent}}$. The ASM for Cindy is described in [10], so we only give a slight introduction here.

The interesting part of the abstract ASM specification for this paper is the step of an agent of type **cellphone** because this is the agent that will be refined to Java. An excerpt of the according ASM rule for the cellphone agent which actually loads a ticket on the mobile phone is:

```
APROG_cellphone(agent, tickets, inputs){
  let indoc = first(inputs(agent)) in
        inputs(agent) := rest(inputs(agent))
        if is_load_message(indoc) ∧ #tickets(agent) < MAXTICKETS
        then tickets(agent) := tickets(agent) + getPart(2, indoc)
        else ... // other protocol steps }
```

In this example, astate for the cellphone agent is given by the state function tickets, which stores the list of tickets of every agent. The context actxt is given by the inputs state function, which maps every agent to his current input messages. First an input message indoc is taken from the input ($APROG_{cellphone}$ is only called when the input is non-empty) and the list of input messages is shortened. If the input message has the correct structure of a message to load a ticket (is_load_message(indoc)) and there is space in the list of tickets of the actual agent (#tickets(agent) < MAXTICKETS) then the ticket contained in the input document (getPart(2, indoc)) is added to the list of tickets. For the refinement theory presented in this paper it is sufficient to know that the specification of Cindy consists of ASM rules $APROG_{agent}$ for every agent, which define the input/output behavior and the state changes of agent for every protocol step.

We use the Theorem Prover KIV [1] for our approach. In KIV, Abstract State Machines are modeled using Dynamic Logic (DL). In DL, the formula $\langle \alpha \rangle \, \phi$ states, that ϕ holds after the execution of program α. $APROG_{agent}$ is in fact a DL procedure. To integrate this into the data refinement theory presented above we define the operation AOP_{agent} of ADT using $APROG_{agent}$:

$$AOP_{agent}(astate, actxt, astate', actxt') \leftrightarrow$$
$$\langle APROG_{agent}(astate, actxt) \rangle \, (astate = astate' \wedge actxt = actxt')$$

3.2   The Concrete Level

We now refine our abstract agent specification to Java. This works by stepwise replacement of an agent type and its abstract protocol step specification AOP_{agent} by a Java implementation for agent, preserving every other part of the specification. In this paper, this is illustrated by the refinement of the cellphone agent type. Accordingly, the concrete level is a mixture of steps of agents, that are already replaced by a Java program (cellphone agent here) and other agents (the cinema server or the attacker), that are still preserved as on the concrete level. So the concrete state cs and the concrete operations COP_{agent} are a mixture of Java implementation and abstract specification.

A concrete state cs : CS is defined as cs = cstate × cctxt with cctxt : context and cstate : agent → $B_{type(agent)}$. The context needs to be preserved like in the abstract level because the communication infrastructure is not implementable (it is a model of messages currently in transit). The state of a Java program is stored in an algebraic data type called store in KIV. A store can be seen as the equivalent of the heap of a Java virtual machine (in our case the JVM running on a mobile phone). All the runtime information about pointer structures is contained inside the store. Full details on the store and on the Java Calculus implemented in KIV can be found in [27] [26]. On the concrete level the state of a refined agent is now replaced by a store st : store. The state of non-refined agents remains the same as on the abstract level. This means that $B_{cellphone}$ = store and $B_{agenttype} = A_{agenttype}$ for agenttype ≠ cellphone. Because we now integrate a Java implementation of an agent in our model, we have to do a data transformation step from the abstract data types specifying input and output of the agent into the Java store and vice versa. The inputs of the cellphone agent (given by actxt on the abstract level) need to be mapped to Java data types representing the same input on the programming language level. This is done by a ASM rule called **TOSTORE**. The reverse transformation has to be done for the output, called **FROMSTORE**. More details on this transformation will be discussed later in section 4.

The Java method step() is the protocol implementation of the cellphone agent. For the sake of understandability the implementation itself will be presented later in Sect. 6. Java method calls are written in the Java calculus in KIV as $\langle st;\ step() \rangle\ \phi$, which states that formula ϕ holds after the execution of method $step()$ in the context of store st. Together with **TOSTORE** and **FROMSTORE**, we now define $\mathsf{COP}_{\mathsf{agent}}$ as:

$$\mathsf{COP}_{\mathsf{agent}}(\mathsf{cstate}, \mathsf{cctxt}, \mathsf{cstate}', \mathsf{cctxt}') \leftrightarrow$$
$$\mathbf{if} \neg\ \mathsf{is\_refined}(\mathsf{agent})\ \mathbf{then}$$
$$\mathsf{AOP}_{\mathsf{agent}}(\mathsf{cstate}, \mathsf{cctxt}, \mathsf{cstate}', \mathsf{cctxt}')$$
$$\mathbf{else}\ (\exists\,\mathsf{st}, \mathsf{st}'.\ \mathsf{st} = \mathsf{TOSTORE}(\mathsf{cctxt}, \mathsf{cstate}(\mathsf{agent})) \wedge$$
$$\langle \mathsf{st};\ \mathsf{step}() \rangle\ (\mathsf{st} = \mathsf{st}') \wedge$$
$$\mathsf{cstate}' = \mathsf{cstate}[\mathsf{agent} \mapsto \mathsf{st}'] \wedge$$
$$\mathsf{cctxt}' = \mathsf{FROMSTORE}(\mathsf{st}', \mathsf{cctxt}))$$

$\mathsf{COP}_{\mathsf{agent}}$ is defined to be the same operation as on the abstract level ($\mathsf{AOP}_{\mathsf{agent}}$) for all agents, that are not refined ($\neg\ \mathsf{is\_refined}(\mathsf{agent})$, for example the cinema). When agent is one of the agents, that are refined ($\mathsf{is\_refined}(\mathsf{agent})$, here the cellphone), the $\mathsf{COP}_{\mathsf{agent}}$ is defined using a Java implementation and **TOSTORE** and **FROMSTORE** operations: the inputs are transformed into Java objects in the store ($\mathsf{TOSTORE}(\mathsf{cctxt}, \mathsf{cstate}(\mathsf{agent}))$). Then a Java method call step() implementing the protocol and starting in this store st must result in a store st', which is given by cstate' ($\mathsf{cstate}' = \mathsf{cstate}[\mathsf{agent} \mapsto \mathsf{st}']$). The output of the Java program is extracted from the store using **FROMSTORE** and this output forms the new concrete context cctxt'.

3.3   Proof Obligations for the Example

Fig. 2 gives an overview of the refinement proof obligations in Cindy for initialization, finalization and for the steps of the cinema agent (that is not refined in the example) and of the cellphone agent (which is refined to Java). The circle-like arrows illustrate the refinement proof obligations of commutating sub-diagrams. Fig. 2 also shows the operations **TOSTORE** and **FROMSTORE** before and after the Java method step() of the cellphone implementation is executed.

All together the main proof obligation for the refinement of the cellphone agent now is:

$$\mathsf{R}(\mathsf{astate}, \mathsf{actxt}, \mathsf{cstate}, \mathsf{cctxt})$$
$$\wedge\ \ \mathsf{st} = \mathsf{TOSTORE}(\mathsf{cctxt}, \mathsf{cstate}(\mathsf{agent}))$$
$$\wedge\ \ \langle \mathsf{st};\ \mathsf{step}() \rangle\ (\mathsf{st} = \mathsf{st}')$$
$$\wedge\ \ \mathsf{cstate}' = \mathsf{cstate}[\mathsf{agent} \mapsto \mathsf{st}']$$

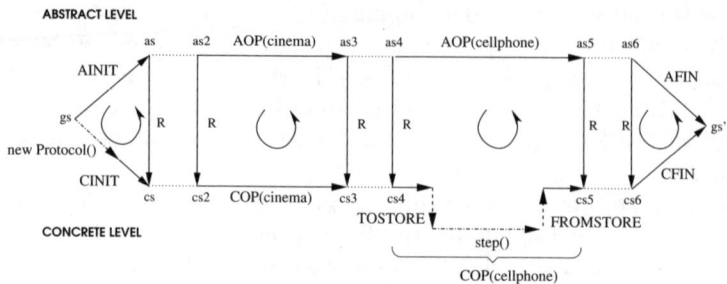

Fig. 2. Refinement diagram

$$\wedge \; \mathsf{cctxt}' = \mathsf{FROMSTORE}(\mathsf{st}', \mathsf{cctxt}) \; \rightarrow$$
$$\exists \, \mathsf{astate}', \mathsf{actxt}'. \; \mathsf{AOP}_{\mathsf{agent}}(\mathsf{astate}, \mathsf{actxt}, \mathsf{astate}', \mathsf{actxt}')$$
$$\wedge \; \mathsf{R}(\mathsf{astate}', \mathsf{actxt}', \mathsf{cstate}', \mathsf{cctxt}')$$

If the retrieve relation holds for two states and the concrete level performs a sequence of **TOSTORE**, the actual protocol step **step()** and **FROMSTORE**, resulting in state $\mathsf{cstate}' \times \mathsf{cctxt}'$, then there must be the possibility to perform a similar step on the abstract level (**AOP**) which leads to a state $\mathsf{astate}' \times \mathsf{actxt}'$ in which the retrieve relation holds again. More details on the proof of this property will be given in Sect. 6.

Fig. 2 also shows the constructor call of the Java class implementing the protocol (**new Protocol()**), which is called during **CINIT**. We have to prove that the constructor call of the Java implementation performs the same initialization steps as **AINIT** for the refined agent type. This proof obligation is omitted here because it is very similar to the main proof obligation above (excepting **TOSTORE** and **FROMSTORE** because there is no input or output for the constructor).

One important point for the proof of our obligations is the definition of the retrieve relation R. It has to express how the state of the Java program and the abstract state of the protocol ASM relate to each other. Since we focus on security protocols, we can give a generic template for this relation. It is:

$$\mathsf{R}(\mathsf{astate}, \mathsf{actxt}, \mathsf{cstate}, \mathsf{cctxt}) \leftrightarrow$$
$$\mathsf{actxt} = \mathsf{cctxt} \wedge \mathsf{AINV}(\mathsf{astate}, \mathsf{actxt}) \wedge \mathsf{CINV}(\mathsf{cstate}, \mathsf{cctxt}) \wedge$$
$$(\forall \, \mathsf{agent}. \mathbf{if} \; \mathsf{is\_refined}(\mathsf{agent}) \; \mathbf{then} \; \mathsf{extract}(\mathsf{cstate}(\mathsf{agent})) = \mathsf{astate}(\mathsf{agent})$$
$$\mathbf{else} \; \mathsf{cstate}(\mathsf{agent}) = \mathsf{astate}(\mathsf{agent}))$$

The relation states the following: The **extract** function gets the state of the agent from the store (more precisely it looks at the fields of the classes implementing the protocol and converts those fields back into an abstract state). The state on the abstract level (**astate(agent)**) must be equal to the corresponding value in the store (**extract(cstate(agent))**), if **agent** is one of the agents that have a Java implementation. For the other agents the state on the concrete level must be exactly equal to the abstract level. The context (like the inputs of the agents) must be equal in every case. Additionally we need an invariant on the abstract state (**AINV**) and an invariant on the concrete state (CINV) that is preserved by every step. The invariants basically state that everything is well-formed and reasonable for our application, e.g. the list of tickets contains only tickets, not other entries.

By proving the refinement, security properties of the abstract ASM specification level now can be transfered to the implementation level via the retrieve relation R. If a property is e.g. invariant for astate(agent) it is also invariant for extract(cstate(agent)) because of the refinement. In general, it is known that not all security properties are preserved under refinement (see e.g. [19]), but those problems arise only when the granularity changes during refinement. This is not the case in our refinement approach, because in our model both the abstract ASM rules and the concrete implementation steps are atomic operations of the same granularity, which last from the receiving of input to the sending of output for every agent. We do not consider attacks on the implementation which take place *during* the execution of a protocol step. This would mean changing of memory contents of the devices during execution and would of course allow a lot more attacks. Also we do not consider problems like power failures of the mobile phone in the middle of a protocol step execution.

4 Data Type Mapping to the Concrete Level

Java programs and Abstract State Machines use different internal types. On the one hand we have the Java class hierarchy (consisting of interfaces and classes) and primitive types, on the other hand we have algebraically specified abstract data types and state functions for the abstract specification level.

For our M-Commerce example same external behavior means sending of the same output messages in reply to the same input messages. On the abstract level input and output are specified using an abstract data type called document. This data type is quite similar to the messages used in [23] or [7]. It is specified algebraically as follows:

```
document = intdoc(.int : int)
         | keydoc(.key : key)
         | noncedoc(.nonce : nonce)
         | secretdoc(.secret : secret)
         | hashdoc(.doc : document)
         | encdoc(.key : key; .doc : document)
         | sigdoc(.key : key; .doc : document)
         | doclist(.list : documentlist)
```

A document can contain an arbitrary large integer (intdoc). The intdoc type is also used to model arbitrary data since every data can be represented as an integer. Documents can also contain a key (keydoc), a nonce (noncedoc) or a secret (secretdoc). Furthermore a document can be the result of a cryptographic hashing operation (hashdoc) or can be an encrypted document with a certain key (encdoc) or a signature of a document with a certain key (sigdoc). To model composition of messages our document type also contains a type doclist containing a list of other documents. In our ASM model the inputs of all agents are represented as an ASM state function inputs : agent → documentlist (which is a part of the context described in section 3).

On the concrete level a natural representation of the abstract document data type is a class hierarchy which is directly implementing our abstract data type. The Cindy application relies on the security of GSM communication which already supports encryption of all sent messages. Therefore the protocol of Cindy only uses the type intdoc for modelling the ticket data or concepts like phone numbers, and noncedoc for modelling the unique identifier of the ticket. Additionally, the doclist type is used for composing those basic documents to MMS messages.

The class hierarchy we use in the implementation of Cindy is shown in Figure 3. We implement every constructor of the abstract data type document by a separate Java class type for exactly that type of document. For our general refinement approach to security protocols the other document types are implemented as well but omitted here.

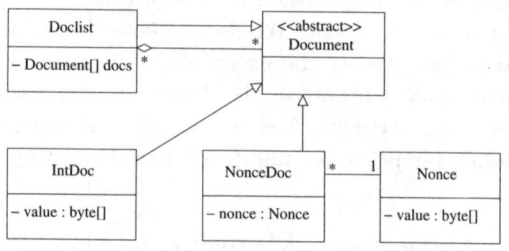

Fig. 3. Document Classes

In addition to input/output behavior we furthermore have to prove that the same state changes are performed on both levels. In the Cindy example the state of the mobile phone consists of a list of documents representing tickets which are currently stored on the phone. This list is specified using the doclist abstract type on the abstract level, respectively implemented by the *Doclist* class for the concrete state. The state function tickets : agent → documentlist specifies this for the abstract level (part of astate(cellphone) as explained in Section 3). In addition the state function inputs : agent → documentlist is relevant for the refinement because it contains the input messages of each agent. Those two functions have to be taken into account for the refinement and have to be transformed to Java data types. Using the abstract data types and the store we define mapping functions for the transformation of the abstract data type into the concrete pointer structure inside the store and vice versa. The store defines a mapping of keys to values. Store keys are a combination of a reference (a memory address) and a class field or a array index. Getting the value for the field f of the instance at reference r is written as st[r.f]. The lookup for static fields can be written as st[.f]. The value can be a primitive value or a reference to another class instance or an array. The operations for the transformation of documents are called addDoc : document × store → reference × store and getDoc : reference ×store → document (all operations below are specified algebraically). addDoc for e.g. the *IntDoc* class type works as follows:

addDoc-intdoc:

$[r_1, r_2] = \mathsf{newrefs}(2, \mathsf{st}) \rightarrow$

$\qquad \mathsf{addDoc}(\mathsf{intdoc}(i), \mathsf{st}) =$

$\qquad\qquad r_1 \times \mathsf{addobj}(r_1, \mathsf{IntDoc}, .\mathsf{value} \times r_2,$

$\qquad\qquad\qquad\qquad \mathsf{addarray}(r_2, \mathsf{byte\_type}, \mathsf{int2bytes}(i), \mathsf{st}))$

Adding an *Intdoc* with value i to the store works by adding an object of class *IntDoc* via the operation $\mathsf{addobj} : \mathsf{reference} \times \mathsf{type} \times \mathsf{fieldvalues} \times \mathsf{store} \rightarrow \mathsf{store}$. The reference r_1 of this new object must not be already contained in the store ($[r_1, r_2] = \mathsf{newrefs}(2, \mathsf{st})$). The actual value i of the *Intdoc* is encoded as an array of bytes. This array must also be added to the store via the operation $\mathsf{addarray} : \mathsf{reference} \times \mathsf{type} \times \mathsf{arrayvalues} \times \mathsf{store} \rightarrow \mathsf{store}$. The reference r_2 of this array must also be a new reference in the store ($\ldots = \mathsf{newrefs}(2, \mathsf{st})$). The array values are obtained by transforming the integer i to a sequence of bytes ($\mathsf{int2bytes}(i)$). The function addDoc additionally returns the reference r_1 of the *IntDoc* instance as well as the store because we have to know where the new instance is placed inside the store.

The getDoc function for the IntDoc type works the other way:

getDoc-intdoc:

$r \neq \mathsf{null} \wedge \mathsf{st}[r.\mathsf{type}] = \mathsf{IntDoc} \rightarrow$

$\qquad \mathsf{getDoc}(r, \mathsf{st}) = \mathsf{intdoc}(\mathsf{bytes2int}(\mathsf{getbytearray}(\mathsf{st}[r.\mathsf{value}], \mathsf{st})))$

Getting the document of type *IntDoc* ($\mathsf{st}[r.\mathsf{type}] = \mathsf{IntDoc}$, where .type is a special field containing the type information of a reference) back from the store is done by first getting the byte array representing the value from the store ($\mathsf{getbytearray}(\mathsf{st}[r.\mathsf{value}])$). The resulting byte sequence is transformed to an integer using the operation $\mathsf{bytes2int}$ and the resulting integer value is used to construct the *Intdoc*.

The operations **TOSTORE** and **FROMSTORE** basically use addDoc and getDoc to transform the input messages of the agents into the Java store. Additionally getDoc implements the extract function described in Section 3 in the retrieve relation of the refinement for the list of tickets of an agent. This works because in Cindy both input/output messages and the state are specified using documents.

5   Additional Attacks on the Concrete Level

An interesting observation is the fact that when implementing the data types by pointer structures there are more possible values on the concrete level than on the abstract level. The reason is that on the concrete level there can be pointer structures that do not have any abstract counterpart. One example for this fact are instances of class *IntDoc* which contain a null pointer in their value field. Since the value field is the counterpart of the abstract value of the integer contained in the *IntDoc* and since null does not represent a number this document has no counterpart. In the following we will call those additional inputs invalid. A refinement respecting only valid inputs would not be correct because in the real world other inputs than the abstract ones may be sent by an attacker and may cause implementation errors or security leaks.

The solution for this problem is to consider the invalid inputs on the concrete level by implementing a check on the input which checks whether the concrete input has an abstract counterpart. We add an additional document type $\perp$ (representing all the invalid inputs) and specify that the abstract level performs an error treatment (e.g. a reset operation on the internal state) when receiving $\perp$. Then the concrete step which receives an invalid input (and discovers this using the input check) has to be a refinement of the abstract error treatment step. With such a refinement nothing bad can happen on the concrete level when receiving invalid inputs. The TOSTORE operation now relates $\perp$ to all invalid documents. An attacker sending $\perp$ on the abstract level is now able to send any invalid document on the concrete level. Formally, the predicate validDoc : reference $\times$ store specifies whether a pointer structure represents an abstract document. The result $r \times st$ of addDoc always satisfies validDoc(r, st). The check for valid inputs is done in the receive() method in the Java implementation. Therefore the implementation of receive() must satisfy:

Receive-correct:
$\dots$ // *reference r is a valid communication interface in st*
$\wedge\ st = st_0 \rightarrow$
$\langle st;\ r_0 = r.\mathsf{receive}();\ \rangle$
$\qquad st = st_0[.\mathsf{input}, \mathsf{null}]\ \wedge$
$\qquad ((\mathsf{validDoc}(st_0[.\mathsf{input}], st_0) \rightarrow r_0 = st_0[.\mathsf{input}])\ \wedge$
$\qquad (\neg\ \mathsf{validDoc}(st_0[.\mathsf{input}], st_0) \rightarrow r_0 = \mathsf{null}))$

If the input is a valid representation (validDoc(...)) of an abstract document, the return value r_0 of receive is the reference which was added in the TOSTORE operation ($st_0[.\mathsf{input}]$). Otherwise null is returned. Additionally receive sets the input buffer to null ($st[.\mathsf{input}, \mathsf{null}]$).

It is not desirable to verify the correctness of a concrete input/output checker again for every single application. E.g. all our security protocol implementations use the document class type as the input type. We have used this type for the implementation of Cindy and also e.g. for the implementation of the Mondex [28] application. Also, a real implementation would not directly send pointer structures but do some kind of encoding (e.g. to byte arrays or XML, which is then sent by MMS). The data checker can be integrated in such a transformation function. We provide an implementation for such a transformation and data check layer which can be verified separately. This enables us to split the refinement proof into two layers. In the first layer the refinement of an abstract specification of the protocol into an implementation working on the document class type is shown using *receive-correct* as an assumption. The second refinement adds the transformation and data check layer. Then TOSTORE has to add an encoding of the input document instead of a pointer structure to the store. The receive method has to check this input and transform it into a pointer structure. Then the property of receive above can be proven using correctness properties of the check and transformation layer.

6   Details on the Cindy Refinement and Implementation

Sect. 3 showed an excerpt of the ASM specification for the cellphone agent, which covers storing of new tickets on the cell phone. The J2ME implementation[2] of this protocol step is:

```
public class Protocol {
 private Doclist tickets; // bought tickets
 ...

 public void step(){
  if(comm.available()){
   Document inmsg = comm.receive();
   phoneStep(inmsg);}}

 private void phoneStep(Document inmsg) {
  Document originator = inmsg.getPart(1);
  inmsg = inmsg.getPart(2);
  Doclist ticket = getTicket(inmsg);
  if(ticket != null && tickets.len() < MAXTICKETLEN){
   tickets = tickets.attach(ticket);}
  ... //other protocol steps}

 private Doclist getTicket(Document indoc) {
  if(indoc != null && indoc.is_comdoc()){
   byte[] ins = indoc.getPart(1).getValue();
   if(ins.length == 1 && ins[0] == LOADTICKET){
    Document indoc2 = indoc.getPart(2);
    if(indoc2 != null && indoc2.len() == 2){
     Document indoc21 = indoc2.getPart(1);
     Document indoc22 = indoc2.getPart(2);
     if(indoc21 != null && indoc21.is_intdoc() &&
        indoc22 != null && indoc22.is_noncedoc()){
      return indoc2;}}}}
  return null;}}
```

The method step() is the top-level method for executing a protocol step. First it tests whether input is available. If there is an input available the receive method is executed and phonestep() is called with the input. This method now tests the structure of the input using getTicket() method. getTicket() returns the data part of the input document if it was a valid representation of a ticket and null otherwise. phonestep() then adds the returned data to the list of actual tickets if the input was valid.

---

[2] This source code is running on any J2ME mobile phone. We have tested it on Nokia 3250 and Sony Ericsson W550i. The receive operation uses the J2ME API to access the MMS messages of the mobile phone.

The proof structure now is the following: Starting with the proof obligation given by the refinement theory in Sect. 3 we first symbolically execute the abstract and the concrete level. The cases for the non-refined agents (such as the attacker) are trivial because they are the same in both specifications. For the refined agent we come to the proof obligation shown in Sect. 3.3. We then formulate theorems for each Java method which relate the behavior of the method to the abstract counterpart of its input. The corresponding theorem for the load-ticket protocol step is for example:

is_load_message(first(inputs(agent))) $\land$ st_1 = store(agent) $\land$
st = TOSTORE(inputs, st_1) $\land$ INV(st_1) $\land$ ...
$\rightarrow$ $\langle$st; Protocol.step(); $\rangle$
     (getDoc(st[Protocol.tickets], st) =
          tickets(agent) + first(inputs(agent))
     $\land$ st[.input] = null $\land$ INV(st))

If the actual input document (first(inputs(agent))) is a correct load message (is_load_message) on the abstract level and if this document is added to the store via TOSTORE then the step method performs the correct state change: It computes the correct ticket list (the new ticket attached to the old tickets). Also the input was deleted (st[.input] = null). Additionally an invariant that holds before the execution of the method (INV(st)) holds again afterwards.

With such theorems the refinement proof obligation is divisible in different proof obligations for every protocol step. After applying those theorems we symbolically execute the corresponding abstract ASM step. This results in an updated abstract state which has to be proven to relate to the Java store which is given by the theorem above via retrieve relation R. Using this technique the whole proof becomes feasible. The whole case study consists of around 1000 lines of code. The implementation of Cindy itself consists of around 350 lines of code. The rest is the implementation of the document classes and some utility classes (e.g. for handling byte arrays). The verification of the refinement starting with the creation of the concrete and abstract specification of the protocol and ending with the refinement proof took around one and a half man months with KIV. The case study consists of 329 theorems which took 11408 proof steps. 4655 of those steps were done by the user. The degree of automation thereby is nearly 60 %. We expect a much higher degree of automation for upcoming case studies because of the high re-usability of the Document implementation and the corresponding library.

7   Related Work

Related work concerning the verification of Java programs was already mentioned in Section 1. Here we focus on related work concerning refinement approaches for security protocols:

[20] describes a similar approach for Java Smart Cards. The authors specify protocols using a high level specification language for proving security properties and a more concrete one which works on the level of byte arrays. They specify

lengths and contents of messages using byte arrays and then use static program analysis on the JavaCard implementation to decide whether the implementation is correct. This approach is limited to the very specific class of protocols the specification language allows while our approach allows any abstract specification using all the possibilities of algebraic specifications on KIV [18]. Additionally, because of the automated analysis and the fact that implementation correctness is undecidable this approach cannot give reliable answers in every case.

[29] uses the Spi Calculus for specifying security protocols and a code generation engine to transform this specification to an implementation, also mapping abstract messages to Java objects. Code generation yields large implementations that are less readable than our code and cannot be optimized without losing correctness guarantees. Their mapping to concrete data types is not formally verified and does not address the problem of invalid inputs on the concrete level.

[14] presents an approach to verify that a JavaCard implementation respects a protocol specification given by a finite state machine. This approach cannot directly transfer security proofs from the abstract specification to the implementation level, because they basically show that the Java program sends certain message types in the right order but do not show that those messages and the internal state of the implementation have the right contents.

The Mondex [21] case study has recently received a lot of attention because its tool supported verification has been set up as a challenge for today's verification tools [31]. The original refinement proofs using Z have been done on a very detailed level by hand [28]. In [25] and [24] we show that the same verification can be done with good tool support and in a short period of time using KIV. An extension of Mondex using our PROSECCO approach can be found in [12]. The Mondex refinement basically splits a world view of an application into components implementing a protocol. But even the lowest level of the Mondex case study is a only an abstract specification of the communication protocol of the involved parties that does not contain cryptographic operations. The approach presented here can be used to do an additional refinement for Mondex adding a real implementation. Details on our implementations of Mondex can be found in [11].

8   Conclusion

We presented a refinement method for Java programs instantiating data refinement. The method is based on a calculus for Java verification and Abstract State Machines using the interactive theorem prover KIV. While the approach is not bounded to KIV only and the method itself could be transfered to other Java verification systems, KIV's strong support for ASM verification, Java verification and algebraic specifications as well as its large library for security protocol verification makes it an efficient tool for this approach.

As discussed in Sect. 3 our approach transfers security properties for the abstract specification down to running Java code. Furthermore, we have shown how to handle invalid inputs that only exist on the concrete level of Java pointer structures. We have demonstrated that the method is suitable for handling case studies of relevant size. Further work includes the incorporation of the method into further verification case studies like Mondex.

References

1. Balser, M., Reif, W., Schellhorn, G., Stenzel, K., Thums, A.: Formal system development with KIV. In: Maibaum, T. (ed.) ETAPS 2000 and FASE 2000, LNCS, vol. 1783, Springer, Heidelberg (2000)
2. Tickets on your Mobile. [last seen 2007-03-16] URL: http://www.beep.nl (2007)
3. Bolton, C., Davies, J., Woodcock, J.C.P.: On the refinement and simulation of data types and processes. In: Araki, K., Galloway, A., Taguchi, K. (eds.) Proceedings of the International conference of Integrated Formal Methods (IFM), pp. 273–292. Springer, Heidelberg (1999)
4. Börger, E., Stärk, R.F.: Abstract State Machines—A Method for High-Level System Design and Analysis. Springer-Verlag, Heidelberg (2003)
5. Breunesse, C., Jacobs, B., van den Berg, J.: Specifying and verifying a decimal representation in Java for smart cards. In: Kirchner, H., Ringeissen, C. (eds.) AMAST 2002, LNCS, vol. 2422, Springer, Heidelberg (2002)
6. Burdy, L., Cheon, Y., Cok, D., Ernst, M., Kiniry, J., Leavens, G.T., Rustan, K., Leino, M., Poll, E.: An overview of jml tools and applications. In: Burdy, L., Arts, T., Fokkink, W. (eds.) (FMICS '03). Eighth International Workshop on Formal Methods for Industrial Critical Systems. Electronic Notes in Theoretical Computer Science, vol. 80, Elsevier, Amsterdam (2003)
7. Burrows, M., Abadi, M., Needham, R.M.: A Logic of Authentication. Technical report, SRC Research Report 39 (1989)
8. de Roever, W., Engelhardt, K.: Data Refinement: Model-Oriented Proof Methods and their Comparison. Cambridge Tracts in Theoretical Computer Science, vol. 47. Cambridge University Press, Cambridge (1998)
9. Derrick, J., Boiten, E.: Refinement in Z and in Object-Z: Foundations and Advanced Applications. FACIT. Springer, Heidelberg (2001)
10. Grandy, H., Haneberg, D., Reif, W., Stenzel, K.: Developing Provably Secure M-Commerce Applications. In: Müller, G. (ed.) ETRICS 2006, LNCS, vol. 3995, pp. 115–129. Springer, Heidelberg (2006)
11. Grandy, H., Moebius, N., Bischof, M., Haneberg, D., Schellhorn, G., Stenzel, K., Reif, W.: The Mondex Case Study: From Specifications to Code. Technical Report 2006-31, University of Augsburg, 2006. URL: http://www.informatik. uni-augsburg.de/lehrstuehle/swt/se/publications/ (2006)
12. Haneberg, D., Schellhorn, G., Grandy, H., Reif, W.: Verification of Mondex Electronic Purses with KIV: From Transactions to a Security Protocol. Technical Report 2006-32, University of Augsburg, 2006. URL: http://www.informatik. uni-augsburg.de/lehrstuehle/swt/se/publications/ (2006)
13. Jifeng, H., Hoare, C.A.R., Sanders, J.W.: Data refinement refined. In: Robinet, B., Wilhelm, R. (eds.) Proc. ESOP 86, LNCS, vol. 213, pp. 187–196. Springer, Heidelberg (1986)
14. Hubbers, E., Oostdijk, M., Poll, E.: Implementing a Formally Verifiable Security Protocol in Java Card. In: Hutter, D., Müller, G., Stephan, W., Ullmann, M. (eds.) Security in Pervasive Computing, LNCS, vol. 2802, Springer, Heidelberg (2004)
15. Huisman, M.: Verification of java's abstractcollection class: a case study. In: Boiten, E.A., Möller, B. (eds.) MPC 2002, LNCS, vol. 2386, Springer, Heidelberg (2002)

16. Jacobs, B., Marche, C., Rauch, N.: Formal verification of a commercial smart card applet with multiple tools. In: Rattray, C., Maharaj, S., Shankland, C. (eds.) AMAST 2004, LNCS, vol. 3116, Springer, Heidelberg (2004)

17. Joy, B., Steele, G., Gosling, J., Bracha, G. (eds.): The Java (tm) Language Specification, 2nd edn. Addison-Wesley, London (2000)

18. KIV homepage. http://www.informatik.uni-augsburg.de/swt/kiv.

19. Mantel, H.: Preserving Information Flow Properties under Refinement. In: Proceedings of the IEEE Symposium on Security and Privacy, Oakland, CA, USA (2001)

20. Marlet, R., Le Metayer, D.: Verification of Cryptographic Protocols Implemented in JavaCard. In: Proceedings of the e-Smart conference (e-Smart 2003), Sophia Antipolis (2003)

21. MasterCard International Inc. Mondex. URL: http://www.mondex.com.

22. Mostowski, W.: Rigorous development of java card applications. In: Clarke, T., Evans, V., Lano, K. (eds), Proceedings, Fourth Workshop on Rigorous Object-Oriented Methods, London, UK (2002)

23. Paulson, L.C.: The Inductive Approach to Verifying Cryptographic Protocols. J. Computer Security 6 (1998)

24. Schellhorn, G., Grandy, H., Haneberg, D., Moebius, N., Reif, W.: A systematic verification Approach for Mondex Electronic Purses using ASMs. Technical Report 2006-27, Universität Augsburg, 2006. URL: http://www.informatik. uni-augsburg.de/lehrstuehle/swt/se/publications/ (2006)

25. Schellhorn, G., Grandy, H., Haneberg, D., Reif, W.: The Mondex Challenge: Machine Checked Proofs for an Electronic Purse. In: Misra, J., Nipkow, T., Sekerinski, E. (eds.) FM 2006, LNCS, vol. 4085, pp. 16–31. Springer, Heidelberg (2006)

26. Stenzel, K.: A formally verified calculus for full Java Card. In: Rattray, C., Maharaj, S., Shankland, C. (eds.) AMAST 2004, LNCS, vol. 3116, Springer, Heidelberg (2004)

27. Stenzel, K.: Verification of Java Card Programs. PhD thesis, Universität Augsburg, Fakultät für Angewandte Informatik, URL: http://www.opus-bayern.de/uni-augsburg/volltexte/2005/122/, or http://www.informatik.uni-augsburg.de/forschung/dissertations/ (2005)

28. Stepney, S., Cooper, D., Woodcock, J.: AN ELECTRONIC PURSE Specification, Refinement, and Proof. Technical monograph PRG-126, Oxford University Computing Laboratory, July 2000. http://www-users.cs. york.ac.uk/~susan/bib/ss/z/monog.htm (2000)

29. Tobler, B., Hutchison, A.: Generating Network Security Protocol Implementations from Formal Specifications. In: CSES 2004 2nd International Workshop on Certification and Security in Inter-Organizational E-Services at IFIPWorldComputer-Congress, Toulouse, France (2004)

30. Woodcock, J.C.P., Davies, J.: Using Z: Specification, Proof and Refinement. Prentice Hall International Series in Computer Science. Prentice-Hall, Englewood Cliffs (1996)

31. Woodcock, J.: First steps in the verified software grand challenge. IEEE Computer 39(10), 57–64 (2006)

Refactoring Object-Oriented Specifications with Data and Processes*

Thomas Ruhroth and Heike Wehrheim

Department of Computer Science
University of Paderborn
33098 Paderborn, Germany
{ruhroth,wehrheim}@uni-paderborn.de

Abstract. Refactoring is a method for improving the structure of programs/specifications as to enhance readability, modularity and reusability. Refactorings are required to be *behaviour-preserving* in that – to an external observer – no difference between the program before and after refactoring is visible. In this paper, we develop refactorings for an object-oriented specification formalism combining a state-based language (Object-Z) with a process algebra (CSP). In contrast to OO-programming languages, refactorings moving methods or attributes up and down the class hierarchy, in addition, need to change *CSP processes*. We formally prove behaviour preservation with respect to the failures-divergences model of CSP.

1 Introduction

Refactoring is a technique which has long been used by programmers to improve the structure of their code once it got unreadable. The word "refactoring" as a general term for frequently occurring clean-up operations on programs has been coined by Fowler [Fow04]. The book [Fow04] collects a large number of refactorings operating on different levels: the level of methods only, those of classes and of the class hierarchy. As Fowler puts it, all these refactorings "should not change the externally visible behaviour of a program". For programs, this type of behaviour preservation is checked via *testing*: there are a number of tests associated with every (part of a) program which are being run before and after the refactoring. An application of a particular refactoring thus does not a priori guarantee behaviour preservation but has to be tested.

This is different for refactorings for formal specifications: the formal semantics allows for a *proof of correctness* of a refactoring, and thus ensures behaviour preservation. Thus, while refactorings for OO-programs are usually stated via an example, refactorings for formal specifications are given by pairs of templates describing before and after state of a refactoring. These template pairs are proven to guarantee behaviour preservation with respect to the formal semantics of

---

* This work was partially funded by the German Research Council DFG under grant WE 2290/6-1.

M.M. Bonsangue and E.B. Johnsen (Eds.): FMOODS 2007, LNCS 4468, pp. 236–251, 2007.

the specification language. Thus, whenever some parts of a specification are an instantiation of a before template, they can be replaced with the proper instantiation of the corresponding after template. Additional constraints might constrain the application of the pattern. An overview of these kind of formal approaches to refactoring can be found in [MT04], in particular [MS04] and [MS06] follow this approach for Object-Z specifications, one of the formalisms we will be interested in here. While a lot of the approaches surveyed in [MT04] show behaviour-preservation only for specific properties (e.g. certain invariants of classes or relationships between objects), the basis for the correctness proof of [MS04] is the notion of *data refinement* [dE98, DB01] in Object-Z. Refinement exactly guarantees the intended substitutability requirement: for an external observer the classes before and after refactoring are not different, and this holds for any kind of (external) observation on the class.

In this paper, we study refactorings for a formal specification language which in addition to state-based descriptions in Object-Z [Smi00] allows for a description of the *dynamic behaviour* via the process algebra CSP [Hoa85, Ros97]. This combination, called CSP-OZ [Fis97], has a semantics defined in terms of the failures-divergences model of CSP. The integration of two orthogonal formalisms gives us a convenient way of modelling both data, methods and the ordering of method executions. For the refactorings, this additional view in our specifications however imposes additional complexity. A change on the Object-Z side most often requires a corresponding change in the process. This in particular applies to refactorings on the level of the class hierarchy where the movement of a method up or down the hierarchy may involve a corresponding move of CSP process parts up or down classes.

As our notion of correctness of refactorings, we use refinement as well as it guarantees the required behaviour preservation. In the combination CSP-OZ, the appropriate notion of refinement is however *process refinement* (failures-divergences refinement), coming from the CSP semantics. Refactorings are only correct if they preserve the failures-divergences semantics of all involved classes, up to refinement. We aim at defining generally usable *templates* for refactorings such that correctness is guaranteed for every concrete instantiation. Here, we present a general proof strategy for CSP-OZ refactorings based on an expansion into CSP_Z given in [Fis00], which in turn is based on a similar semantics for Object-Z [Smi00]. This proves to be a convenient approach since (most of the) refactorings can thus be shown to be correct by syntactical rewritings of schemas only. We, however, also present a correctness proof for a refactoring which involves an explicit construction of a refinement. The whole approach is exemplified with a CSP-OZ specification in which we refactor single classes as well as introduce a class hierarchy via refactoring.

2   Background

We start with a first part of our case study by which we introduce the formalism CSP-OZ, its semantics and the notion of refinement. The following, only partially given class specification is describing one part of a manufacturing system, namely a store. Stores are holding workpieces which can be loaded/deloaded from and to autonomous transportation agents. For this, we first of all need two basic types for workpieces and for names of transportation agents (Hts): $[WP, Hts]$. The class *Store* is a CSP-OZ class consisting of a CSP part describing the dynamic behaviour (ordering of operations) of the class, and an Object-Z part describing the static behaviour (data and operations). Parts not relevant for our refactorings are being omitted (written as ...).

$$
\begin{array}{l}
\hline
\text{Store} \\
\hline
\textbf{chan } load : [wp? : WP] \quad \textbf{chan } deload : [wp! : WP] \\
\textbf{chan } info : \dots \\
\textbf{main} \overset{c}{=} Loading \ |||\ Info \\
Loading \overset{c}{=} load \rightarrow Loading \ \square\ deload \rightarrow Loading \\
Info \overset{c}{=} info \rightarrow Info \\[6pt]
\hline
\end{array}
$$

$$
\begin{array}{ll}
\hline
store : \mathbb{F}\ WP;\ \dots & \text{Init} \\
\hline
\#store \le 100 & store = \varnothing \\
\hline
\end{array}
$$

$$
\begin{array}{ll}
\hline
load & deload \\
\Delta(store) & \Delta(store) \\
wp? : WP & wp! : WP \\
\hline
\#store < 100 & wp! \in store \\
store' = store \cup \{wp?\} & store' = store \setminus \{wp!\} \\
\hline
\end{array}
$$

$info \mathrel{\widehat{=}} \dots$ [Giving information on current state to environment]

The specification consists of a declaration of the *interface* of the class as a number of channels for communication with other classes (viz. objects). Here, channels *load*, *deload* and *info* are declared together with their signatures. After this, a CSP process `main` is given defining the dynamic behaviour of the class (viz. its objects). For class *Store* this is an interleaving ($|||$) of the processes *Loading* and *Info*. Process *Info* just repeatedly executes operation *info* ($\rightarrow$ is the prefix operator describing sequencing), and process *Loading* consists of an external choice ($\square$) over either a *load* or a *deload*.

The remaining part of the specification defines the variables (sometimes also called fields) in the state schema (a variable *store* with an invariant fixing the size of the store), the initial values (in the init schema) and the operations. An operation schema typically consists of a Δ-list, declaring the variables which are allowed to be changed, and input and output variables (denoted by ? and !, respectively) together with a predicate defining constraints on state changes. Here, primed variables denote variables in the after state. For instance, operation *load* is allowed to change variable *store*, has an input variable *wp?* and a predicate stating the precondition of the operation (*store* has not to be full) and the outcome (the workpiece in the input is added to the store). In addition, CSP-OZ allows to specify *inheritance* relationships between classes (not present here), denoted by `inherit` *superclassname*.

Semantics. This combination of CSP and Object-Z has a well-defined semantics in terms of the failures-divergences model of CSP [Fis00]. The semantics is defined by first translating a CSP-OZ specification to CSP_Z (a CSP dialect with Z syntax for expressions and declarations), from which the failures and divergences are then derived. For proving the correctness of our refactorings we only need to go to the level of CSP_Z, thus we will only explain this part. The basic idea is to model the CSP part and the Object-Z part of the CSP-OZ specification in CSP_Z. These two parts can then be combined into a semantics of the whole CSP-OZ specification using the parallel composition operator $(_A\|_B)$ of CSP. More specifically, the semantics of a CSP-OZ class C is

$$proc(C) = procC(C)_{Chans(procC(C))}\|_{Chans(procZ(C))}procZ(C),$$

where $procC(C)$ is the semantics of the CSP part and $procZ(C)$ those of the Object-Z part. The function *Chans* computes the channels used in a process expression, and $_A\|_B$, A, B set of events, is the parallel composition allowing the left process to communicate on events in A and the right in B with synchronisation on events in the intersection. Thus CSP and Object-Z part synchronise on joint operations. The semantics $procC$ is either simply the CSP process `main` (if the class has no superclass), or the parallel composition of `main` with the main process of the superclass S, again synchronising on common operations:

$$procC(C) = \texttt{main}_{Chans(\texttt{main})}\|_{Chans(procC(S))}procC(S)$$

The semantics of the Object-Z part ($procZ$) is defined by first mapping Object-Z constructs to Z and then transforming them to CSP_Z. In this paper we will in particular use the functions **init**() and **state**(), which map Object-Z constructs to pure Z schemas. The function **init**() gives a Z schema representing the initialisation, and **state**() a Z schema representing the state of the class. These and some other functions are used within $procZ$. Due to lack of space, we omit these definitions here, for details and rules see [Smi00, Fis00].

Refinement. Correctness, viz. behaviour preservation of refactorings, is in our setting defined via *refinement* [dE98, DB01]. Refinement guarantees *substitutability*: while internal representations may change, the changes should not be externally visible. Since refactorings are usually applicable in both directions (a method pushed up to a superclass or down to the subclasses), we need refinement in both directions.

For the specification formalism CSP-OZ, two notions of refinement are of importance: *data refinement* from Object-Z and *failures-divergences refinement* from CSP. We start with the former. Data refinement is defined as substitutability of one specification by another, and usually proven by forward and backward simulations. Here, we just need forward simulations and thus give this definition only. It assumes to have two Object-Z classes A and C given (or the Object-Z parts of two CSP-OZ classes), which both consist of a state schema, an initialisation schema and some operation schemas: $A = (AState, AInit, \{AOp_i\}_{i \in I})$ and $C = (CState, CInit, \{COp_i\}_{i \in I})$, where I is some index set for operations.

Definition 1. *C is a* forward simulation *of A, $A \sqsubseteq_D C$, if there is a retrieve relation R between $AState$ and $CState$ such that the following hold:*

1. *Initialisation:* $\forall CState \bullet CInit \Rightarrow (\exists AState \bullet AInit \wedge R)$,
2. *Applicability:* $\forall i \in I, \forall AState, CState \bullet R \Rightarrow (preAOp_i \Leftrightarrow preCOp_i)$,
3. *Correctness:* $\forall i \in I, \forall AState, CState, CState' \bullet$
   $\qquad R \wedge COp_i \Rightarrow \exists AState' \bullet R' \wedge AOp_i$.

Basically, the idea is to find a relation between the variables in A and C such that the operations in C are applicable in a state if and only those in A are applicable in a related state, and the execution of an operation in C can correspondingly be carried out in A leading to related states again. While the definition of variables and operations may have been changed in C, its externally visible behaviour cannot be distinguished from A.

Data refinement, or more specifically forward simulation, is used when we need to look at the Object-Z part of a CSP-OZ specification in isolation. In the combination, the basis for a definition of refinement is the semantics for CSP-OZ, i.e. the failures-divergences model of CSP. Again, we will not actually compute failures and divergences of processes, but work on the level of CSP processes only. For CSP processes P and Q, we write $P \sqsubseteq_{FD} Q$ if Q is a process (failures-divergences) refinement of P.

Finally, we need to know the relationship between these two kinds of refinement. A lot of research has recently been carried out on the comparison of data and process refinement, the relevant result here is the following (from [Fis00]).

Theorem 1. *Let A, C be Object-Z parts of CSP-OZ classes. Then*

$$A \sqsubseteq_D C \Rightarrow procZ(A) \sqsubseteq_{FD} procZ(C) .$$

Furthermore, process refinement is preserved under parallel composition ([Ros97]), which is the operator used for combining the processes of CSP and Object-Z part.

Theorem 2. *Let P_1, P_2, Q_1, Q_2 be CSP processes, A, B sets of events. Then*

$$P_1 \sqsubseteq_{FD} Q_1 \wedge P_2 \sqsubseteq_{FD} Q_2 \Rightarrow P_1{}_A\|_B P_2 \sqsubseteq_{FD} Q_1{}_A\|_B Q_2 .$$

As a consequence, we can separately show a data refinement relationship on the Object-Z parts and a process refinement on the CSP parts, and obtain a process refinement for the combination. Thus refactorings operating on the Object-Z part alone can be proven correct without having to look into the CSP part.

3   Case Study

Next, we continue our example and extend it with another class. These two classes are then the starting point for our refactorings. The second class specifies machines in the manufacturing system. Similar to stores, machines can load and deload workpieces. The machine is furthermore an active entity as it actively seeks to find some transportation agent for a job. The CSP process *Acq* below describes the events carried out for an acquisition of a transportation agent (essentially getting offers from agents, choosing the offer with the smallest cost and ordering this agent), their exact meaning is however not relevant for our aims. In between these operations, loading, processing and deloading of workpieces takes place. The operator ; denotes sequential composition. The variables *orderTo* and *offers* are used for the acquisition of transporation agents.

___ *Machine* _____

  chan $load : [wp? : WP]$ **chan** $deload : [wp! : WP]$
  chan $offer, process, choose, order \ldots$
  main $\overset{c}{=} Acq;\ (load \rightarrow process \rightarrow Acq);\ (deload \rightarrow \textbf{main})$
  $Acq \overset{c}{=} |||_{h:Hts}\ offer.h \rightarrow Skip;\ choose \rightarrow order \rightarrow Skip$

_____   ___ Init _____

$wp : WP$ $offers = \langle\,\rangle$
$orderTo : Hts$
$offers : \text{seq}(Hts \times \mathbb{N})$

___ *load* _____   ___ *deload* _____

$\Delta(wp)$ $wp! : WP$
$wp? : WP$ _____
_____ $wp! = wp$
$wp' = wp?$

There are some obvious similarities between this class and class *Store*: both store workpieces (*Store* up to a hundred, *Machine* only one) and both load and deload workpieces. We could thus think of having a common superclass for both classes describing these common functionalities. This would result in a specification which does not duplicate the description of two operations, and there would be a single point in the specification in which changes to these operations have to be made (for instance during a refinement to code). Our objective is thus now to introduce a common superclass to *Store* and *Machine*, and move common variables and operations to this superclass. This goal is in the following achieved through a number of successive refactorings.

First refactoring. Looking at the two definitions of operations *load* and *deload*, which are candidates for operations of the superclass, we see that they are different. Our first refactoring thus works towards making them similar. In *Machine* we change state, init schema and operations to

$$
\begin{array}{|l}
\hline
\quad\quad\quad\quad\quad\quad\quad\quad\quad\quad\quad \\
store : \mathbb{F}\ WP \\
orderTo : Hts \\
offers : \mathrm{seq}(Hts \times \mathbb{N}) \\
\hline
\#store \leq 1 \\
\hline
\end{array}
\qquad
\begin{array}{|l}
\hline
\text{Init} \quad\quad\quad\quad\quad\quad\quad\quad \\
store = \varnothing \\
offers = \langle\ \rangle \\
\hline
\end{array}
$$

$$
\begin{array}{|l}
\hline
load \quad\quad\quad\quad\quad\quad\quad\quad \\
\Delta(store) \\
wp? : WP \\
\hline
\#store < 1 \\
store' = store \cup \{wp?\} \\
\hline
\end{array}
\qquad
\begin{array}{|l}
\hline
deload \quad\quad\quad\quad\quad\quad \\
\Delta(store) \\
wp! : WP \\
\hline
wp! \in store \\
store' = store \setminus \{wp!\} \\
\hline
\end{array}
$$

Instead of having a variable of type *WP* we now have a set of *WPs* of size one. This looks like a data refinement on the Object-Z side but it is not. The preconditions of *load* and *deload* in the Object-Z part are strengthened: while previously both operations were always enabled, they are now only enabled when *store* is currently empty or filled, respectively. Due to the blocking semantics of Object-Z such a change becomes visible to an observer: operation *load* might sometimes be disabled. Fortunately, in connection with the CSP part it is a correct refinement since the CSP part ensures an alternating execution of *load* and *deload*, thus the blocking has already been present in the previous specification of *Machine*. The correctness of this transformation, i.e. behaviour preservation, can be proven using a technique presented in [DW06]. We thus will not further look at the correctness of this refactoring.

Second refactoring. Our next refactoring tackles the remaining difference between *Store* and *Machine* as far as the field *store* is concerned. We carry out the refactoring "Replace Magic Number with Symbolic Constant" [Fow04] in both classes, replacing the numbers 100 and 1 by a variable *capacity* which is then initially set to the respective value. The relevant part of *Store* looks like this (similarly for *Machine*):

$$
\begin{array}{|l}
\hline
\text{Store} \quad\quad\quad\quad\quad\quad\quad\quad\quad\quad\quad\quad\quad\quad\quad\quad\quad\quad\quad\quad\quad\quad\quad\quad \\
\quad
\begin{array}{|l}
\hline
store : \mathbb{F}\ WP \\
capacity : \mathbb{N} \\
\hline
\#store \leq capacity \\
\hline
\end{array}
\quad
\begin{array}{|l}
\hline
\text{Init} \quad\quad\quad\quad\quad\quad\quad \\
\ldots \\
capacity = 100 \\
\hline
\end{array} \\
\quad \ldots \quad\quad\quad\quad\quad\quad [\text{plus replacing the number in } load] \\
\hline
\end{array}
$$

Third Refactoring. Looking at *Store* and *Machine* we now see that they share similar variables and methods. Hence a superclass can be extracted from them, and variables, part of the initialisation and methods pulled upwards to this class. The next refactoring (called "Extract Superclass") is a combination of four smaller refactorings (all from [Fow04]): "Extract Class" creates an empty class (*Station*) and makes *Store* and *Machine* inherit from this class, "Pull Up Field" moves variables *store* and *capacity* from subclasses to superclass, "Pull Up Init" moves initialisation of *store* to superclass (but not of *capacity* since this is different in the two subclasses) and finally "Pull Up Method" moves methods *load* and *deload* up to *Station* (shown next, omitting interface declaration).

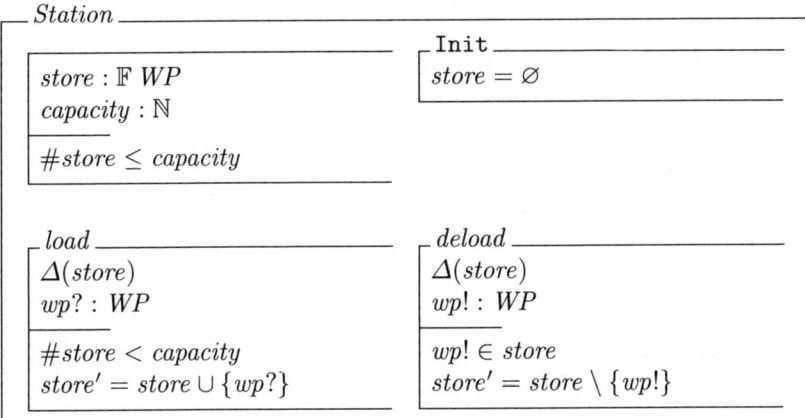

Both *Store* and *Machine* inherit from *Station*, i.e.

```
__Store_____        __Machine_____
  inherit Station                     inherit Station
  ...                                 ...
```

and both do not contain definitions of *load*, *deload*, *store* and *capacity* anymore (being inherited from *Station*), only the initialisation of *capacity* remains in the subclasses as it differs in the two classes.

Fourth Refactoring. Last, we have to look at the CSP part. The two classes have quite different CSP parts, in particular both also refer to operations other than *load* and *deload*. Thus neither the CSP part of *Store* nor that of *Machine* can be completely moved to the superclass. However, one part of *Store* could potentially be moved to *Station*, namely we could define the CSP part in *Station* as

$$\texttt{main} \stackrel{c}{=} Loading$$
$$Loading \stackrel{c}{=} load \rightarrow Loading$$
$$\square \; deload \rightarrow Loading \; ,$$

and change the CSP part of *Store* to $\texttt{main} \stackrel{c}{=} Info$. This refactoring is called "Pull up CSP" (not from [Fow04]); it is moving one part of a parallel composition in a CSP process of a subclass to a superclass. However, due the semantics of inheritance (parallel composition of CSP parts of sub- and superclass) this affects the CSP part of *Machine* as well. We have to make sure that the CSP process obtained by this parallel composition is equivalent to the old CSP process. To this end, we first rephrase the CSP part of *Machine* (refactoring "Rephrase CSP", not from [Fow04]) to a form where this parallel composition is explicitly visible and show behaviour preservation for this transformation. In *Machine* we get

$$\texttt{main} \stackrel{c}{=} Loading_{Chans(Loading)} \|_{Chans(Work)} Work$$
$$Loading \stackrel{c}{=} load \rightarrow Loading \,\Box\, deload \rightarrow Loading$$
$$Work \stackrel{c}{=} Acq;\ (load \rightarrow process \rightarrow Acq);\ (deload \rightarrow Work)$$
$$Acq \stackrel{c}{=} \|\|_{h:Hts}\ offer.h \rightarrow Skip;\ choose \rightarrow order \rightarrow Skip$$

Equivalence, i.e. refinement in both directions, between this new and the old process of *Machine* can be automatically shown using the CSP model checker FDR [FDR97]. Then, *Loading* can be moved upwards to superclass *Station* from both *Store* and *Machine* preserving the overall semantics.

4   Correctness of Refactorings

In the example above we have seen several different refactorings, affecting only the CSP part, only the Object part or both parts.

Object-Z. Refactorings which only affect the classes being changed are called *inner refactorings*. Such inner refactorings of the Object-Z part can be easily derived from the inner refactorings of Object-Z itself (using an approach presented in [Ruh06]), and can - due to Theorem 1 - proven correct by looking at the Object-Z part in isolation. Four refactorings of the example fulfil this condition: "Pull Up Field", "Pull Up Method", "Pull Up Init" and "Replace Magic Number with Symbolic Constant". Here we just prove correctness of "Pull Up Field", the other proofs are similar.

All of our refactorings will be formally described by a template consisting of three parts: A (possibly empty) *condition* stating application conditions for the refactoring, and two patterns of specifications stating the *before* and *after* state of the refactoring. In the patterns we will not have concrete variables, but metavariables which can be instantiated in an arbitrary way. The template for "Pull Up Field" describes how and when a variable v can be moved from (one or more) subclasses to a superclass.

CONDITION:

$v \notin \mathbf{vars}(\mathbf{state}(super_{before})) \land v \notin \mathbf{vars}(\mathbf{state}(sub2_{before}))$

$\exists\, v : T \bullet p_v$

$vars(p_v) \subset \{v\} \cup \mathbf{vars}(\mathbf{state}(super_{before}))$

BEFORE:

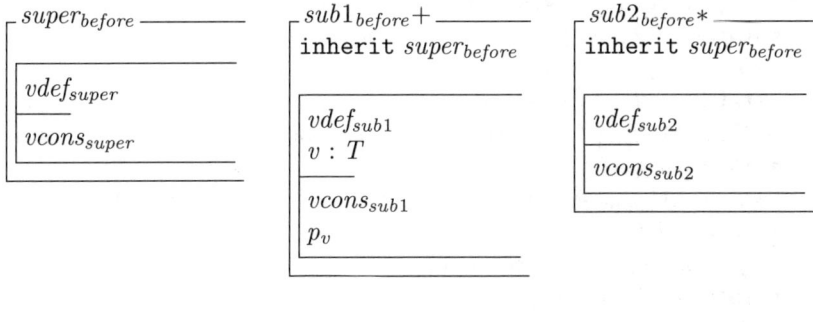

AFTER:

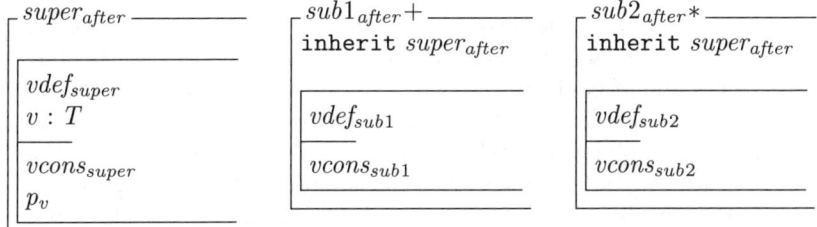

This refactoring assumes that there is a superclass $super_{before}$ with at least one subclass of type $sub1_{before}$ (denoted by +, regular expression) and zero, one or more subclasses of type $sub2_{before}$ (denoted by *). The subclasses of type $sub1_{before}$ all have a field v with the same type T and a predicate p_v constraining the values of v. In addition they may have other (differing) fields (summarised in $vdef_{sub1}$) with predicates $vcons_{sub1}$ over them. Note that the predicate $vcons_{sub1}$ may also constrain variable v. Subclasses of type $sub2_{before}$ and the superclass all do not have the variable v in their state schema. Furthermore, the condition requires that there is at least one possible value for v such that the predicate p_v is fulfilled. The after template describes the specification after the refactoring: field v and its predicate p_v have been pulled upwards into the superclass. Note that when applying this refactoring to our example, we first pull up one variable (e.g. *store*) and an empty predicate (*true*), and in the second step the other variable (here *capacity*) and the predicate $\#store \leq capacity$.

For correctness, we need to prove that the superclass and all subclasses remain equivalent (wrt. refinement) under this transformation. We do this in three steps: first, we show that the classes which previously have included the variable remain the same, second, we prove the same for the classes which have not previously included the variable (i.e. *sub2*), and third, we have to prove equivalence for the superclass. We start with proving equivalence for a class of type *sub1*. The important part is to prove that the semantics of the state does not change, i.e. **state**$(sub1_{before}) = $ **state**$(sub1_{after})$. Using the semantics rules from the language definition (Chapter 4) of [Smi00] we can transform the left part of the equation:

$\mathbf{state}(sub1_{before})$
$= [self : sub1_{before}] \wedge (\mathbf{state}(super_{before})/(self))$
$\quad \bullet \mathbf{state}([v : T;\ vdef_{sub1}\ |\ vcons_{sub1};\ p_v])$
$= [self : sub1_{before}] \wedge (\mathbf{state}(super_{before})/(self))$
$\quad \bullet \mathbf{state}([v : T\ |\ p_v]) \bullet \mathbf{state}([vdef_{sub1}\ |\ vcons_{sub1}])$
$= [self : sub1_{before}] \wedge ((\mathbf{state}(super_{before}) \wedge \mathbf{state}([v : T\ |\ p_v]))/(self))$
$\quad \bullet \mathbf{state}([vdef_{sub1}\ |\ vcons_{sub1})$
$= [self : sub1_{before}] \wedge \mathbf{state}([vdef_{super};\ v : T\ |\ vcons_{super};\ p_v])/(self))$
$\quad \bullet \mathbf{state}([vdef_{sub1}\ |\ vcons_{sub1})$
$= [self : sub1_{after}] \wedge (\mathbf{state}(sub1_{after})/(self))$
$\quad \bullet \mathbf{state}([vdef_{sub1}\ |\ vcons_{sub1})$
$= \mathbf{state}(sub1_{after})$

Essentially, the state of the class, which owns the variable v before applying the refactoring does not change through this refactoring. From this we conclude that the class before and after the refactoring are equivalent (under data refinement).

Next, we prove that classes which did not include the variable, are equivalent before and after applying the refactoring. This is more complicated than the first part because we have to show that the enhanced state does not change the behaviour. Here we have to use another proof technique because the class does not remain equivalent as far as its state is concerned. It is to be proven that the class before and after applying the refactoring are refinements of each other using forward simulation. Here, we only prove that $sub2_{before}$ is a refinement of $sub2_{after}$. We have to show that there is a schema R, which fulfils the conditions of Definition 1. The state of the refactored class is the old state combined with the variable v and some predicates p_v:

$$\mathbf{state}(sub2_{before}) \wedge [v : t\ |\ p_v] \equiv \mathbf{state}(sub2_{after})$$

For this, we choose R to be the identity on the variables of $sub2_{before}$. We immediately get $\mathbf{init}(sub2_{before}) = \mathbf{init}(sub2_{after})$ and $sub2_{before}.Op_i = sub2_{after}.Op_i$, because the definition is not modified and the variable v is not used in any of them. We begin with the initialisation condition from Definition 1:

$\forall\, \mathbf{state}(sub2_{before}) \bullet \mathbf{init}(sub2_{before}) \Rightarrow \exists(\mathbf{state}(sub2_{after}) \bullet \mathbf{init}(sub2_{after}) \wedge R)$
$\equiv$
$\quad \forall\, \mathbf{state}(sub2_{before}) \bullet \mathbf{init}(sub2_{before})$
$\quad\quad \Rightarrow \exists(\mathbf{state}(sub2_{before}) \wedge [v : T\ |\ p_v] \bullet \mathbf{init}(sub2_{before}) \wedge R)$
$\equiv \quad \{sub2_{before}$ and $\mathbf{init}(sub2_{before})$ do not use $v\}$
$\quad \forall\, \mathbf{state}(sub2_{before}) \bullet \mathbf{init}(sub2_{before})$
$\quad\quad \Rightarrow (\mathbf{state}(sub2_{before}) \wedge \mathbf{init}(sub2_{before}) \wedge \exists\, v : T\ |\ p_v \bullet R)$
$\equiv \quad \{$ Definition of $R\}$
$\quad \forall\, \mathbf{state}(sub2_{before}) \bullet \mathbf{init}(sub2_{before})$
$\quad\quad \Rightarrow (\mathbf{state}(sub2_{before}) \wedge \mathbf{init}(sub2_{before}) \wedge \exists\, v : T \bullet p_v)$

$\equiv \exists\, v : T \bullet p_v$

$\equiv$ { Assumption }

   $true$

We omit the simple proof of applicability and go straight to the proof of the correctness condition of forward simulation:

$\forall\, \mathbf{state}(sub2_{after}), \mathbf{state}(sub2_{before}), \mathbf{state}(sub2_{before})' \bullet R \wedge sub2_{before}.Op_i$
   $\Rightarrow \exists\, \mathbf{state}(sub2_{after})' \bullet R' \wedge sub2_{after}.Op_i$

$\equiv$

   $\forall\, \mathbf{state}(sub2_{before} \wedge [v : T \mid p_v]), \mathbf{state}(sub2_{before}), \mathbf{state}(sub2_{before})'$
   $\bullet R \wedge sub2_{before}.Op_i \Rightarrow \exists\, \mathbf{state}(sub2_{before} \wedge [v : T \mid p_v])' \bullet R' \wedge sub2_{after}.Op_i$

$\equiv$

   $\forall\, \mathbf{state}(sub2_{before} \wedge [v : T \mid p_v]), \mathbf{state}(sub2_{before}), \mathbf{state}(sub2_{before})'$
   $\bullet R \wedge sub2_{before}.Op_i \Rightarrow \exists\, \mathbf{state}(sub2_{before} \wedge [v : t \mid p])' \bullet R' \wedge sub2_{before}.Op_i$

$\equiv$ { Definition of R and v is not in Δ }

   $\forall [v : T \mid p_v], \mathbf{state}(sub2_{before}), \mathbf{state}(sub2_{before})' \bullet R \wedge sub2_{before}.Op_i$
   $\Rightarrow \exists [v : t \mid p]' \bullet v = v'$

$\equiv$ { Assumption }

   $\forall [v : T \mid p_v], \mathbf{state}(sub2_{before}), \mathbf{state}(sub2_{before})' \bullet R \wedge sub2_{before}.Op_i$
   $\Rightarrow true$

$\equiv true$

Thus we have proven that the class $sub2_{before}$ is a refinement of $sub2_{after}$. The proof for the common superclass is analogous to the proof of $sub2$. In a similar way we can prove correctness of the other inner refactorings on the Object-Z part, e.g. "Replace magic number with Symbolic Constant", "Pull Up Method" and "Pull Up Init".

CSP. Next we will look at a refactoring only changing the CSP part of a class. This kind of refactoring is used here in two ways. First, we may want to transform the CSP part to an equivalent one within the CSP-OZ class ("Rephrase CSP"). We use "Rephrase CSP" to bring the CSP part into a shape, in which we can apply the second CSP refactoring, namely "Pull Up CSP". Both can be proven by concentrating on the CSP part alone (Theorem 1). Hence, we can simply prove that the CSP part before and after applying the refactoring is the same.

For "Rephrase CSP" there are two possibilities: we have to show that the CSP-part before and after refactoring is equivalent wrt. the failures-divergences semantics of CSP, and this can either be done by using some of the equivalence rules of CSP (see e.g. [Ros97]) or explicitly asking the CSP modelchecker FDR (which we have done for our example). The second CSP refactoring we use in the example is "Pull Up CSP". This refactoring is described by the following template (with empty condition).

BEFORE:

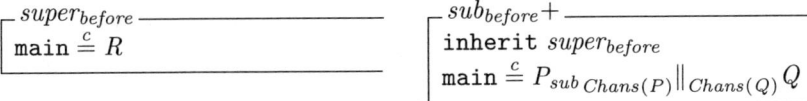

AFTER:

$$\begin{array}{l} \boxed{\begin{array}{l} \rule{0pt}{0pt}\text{— } sub_{after} + \text{—————————}\\ \texttt{inherit } super_{after}\\ \texttt{main} \stackrel{c}{=} P_{sub} \end{array}} \end{array}$$

$$\boxed{\begin{array}{l} \rule{0pt}{0pt}\text{— } super_{after} \text{——————————}\\ \texttt{main} \stackrel{c}{=} Q_{\,Chans(Q)\|Chans(R)}R \end{array}}$$

The template assumes to have a superclass $super_{before}$ and a (nonzero) number of subclasses sub_{before} which all have their CSP processes defined as the parallel composition of some specific process P_{sub} and one joint process Q. The process Q can then be pulled upwards to the superclass.

We can prove the correctness of this refactoring again by looking at the CSP part in isolation. We thus simply prove that the CSP part before and after applying the refactoring is the same. The proof uses the definition of the semantics of inheritance (parallel composition of sub- and superclass).

$$
\begin{aligned}
procC(sub_{before}) &= (P_{\,Chans(P)\|Chans(Q)}Q)_{\,Chans(P\|Q)\|Chans(R)}R\\
&= \quad \{Chans(X_{\,Chans(X)\|Chans(Y)}Y) = Chans(X) \cup Chans(Y)\}\\
&\quad (P_{\,Chans(P)\|Chans(Q)}Q)_{\,Chans(P)\cup Chans(Q)\|Chans(R)}R\\
&= \quad \{_x\|_y - \text{assoc from [Ros97]}\}\\
&\quad P_{\,Chans(P)\|Chans(Q)\cup Chans(R)}(Q_{\,Chans(Q)\|Chans(R)}R)\\
&= \quad \{Chans(X_{\,Chans(X)\|Chans(Y)}Y) = Chans(X) \cup Chans(Y)\}\\
&\quad P_{\,Chans(P)\|Chans(Q\|R)}(Q_{\,Chans(Q)\|Chans(R)}R)\\
&= procC(sub_{after})
\end{aligned}
$$

Extract Superclass. Finally, we show correctness of a refactoring which changes both CSP and Object-Z part of a class. "Extract Superclass" is a complex refactoring. First we introduce an empty superclass, then we use the refactorings "Pull Up Method", "Pull Up Field" and "Pull Up CSP". The latter three are also normal refactorings which we have already treated above. Therefore, we only have to prove correctness of the introduction of a new empty superclass (with template given below).

BEFORE:

$$\boxed{\begin{array}{l} \rule{0pt}{0pt}\text{— } sub_{before} \text{——————————}\\ \texttt{main} \stackrel{c}{=} PE \end{array}}$$

AFTER:

$$\boxed{\begin{array}{l} \rule{0pt}{0pt}\text{— } super_{after} \text{——————}\\ \texttt{main} \stackrel{c}{=} Skip \end{array}}$$
$$\boxed{\begin{array}{l} \rule{0pt}{0pt}\text{— } sub_{after} \text{——————————}\\ \texttt{inherit } super_{after}\\ \texttt{main} \stackrel{c}{=} PE \end{array}}$$

Fortunately, this new superclass does not add new functionality, so we only have to prove that both the CSP and Object-Z part will not be changed. First we prove this for the CSP part:

$$procC(sub_{after}) = PE_{Chans(PE)} \|_{Chans(Skip)} Skip$$
$$= PE_{Chans(PE)} \|_{\{\checkmark\}} Skip$$
$$= PE \equiv procC(sub_{before})$$

For the Object-Z part correctness trivially holds since the superclass does not introduce new constraints on the Object-Z part. Thus we have proven that the introduction of an empty superclass is behaviour preserving as well, which finishes the correctness proofs for the refactorings of our example. These proofs exemplarily show all possible types of correctness proofs for CSP-OZ refactorings: most of them proceed by syntactically rewriting of (state, init or operation) schemas or CSP processes. Some of them, however, explicitly need the construction of a refinement relation.

5   Conclusion

In this paper we have shown how to carry out refactorings in object-oriented specifications involving a state-based as well as a behaviour-oriented part. Refactorings thus concerned either only one of the specification parts (CSP or Object-Z) or both. We have shown correctness of (some of) these refactorings by proving a refinement relationship between before and after specification. This guarantees the desired behaviour preservation.

Related work. Refactoring is a widely used technique in program design and development. An overview over different approaches to refactoring is given in [MT04]. The use of data refinement as a correctness criterion for refactorings is also followed in Cornèlio, Cavalcanti et. al. [Cor04, CCS02] and McComb [MS04, McC04]. Cornèlio defines refactorings and proves their correctness for a refinement-based object-oriented language (ROOL), McComb and Smith use Object-Z. While in particular the latter approach is close to ours, both languages are state based formalisms only and do not include dynamic aspects, like CSP-OZ does. A different approach to correctness of refactorings is taken by Bannwart and Müller [BM06]. They show that particular pre- and post-conditions can be derived from a refactoring and used to ensure correctness by inserting them as assertions into programs. Then they are able to implement a runtime check of the correctness of refactorings.

A frequently used formal approach to refactorings is the application of graph transformations (e.g. [HT04, KHE03, MEDJ05, SD06, BM06a]). Graph transformation rules can be used to describe refactorings when the specification can be seen as a graph (e.g. in case of UML diagrams). They however cannot deal with data-specific conditions, and most often do not treat different views, like the data and process view we have here.

References

[BM06a]   Baar, T., Markovič., S.: A Graphical Approach to Prove the Semantic Preservation of UML/OCL Refactoring Rules. Technical report, Ecole Polytechnique Fédérale de Lausanne (2006)

[BM06]   Bannwart, F., Müller, P.: Changing Programs Correctly: Refactoring with Specifications. In: Misra, J., Nipkow, T., Sekerinski, E. (eds.) FM 2006. LNCS, vol. 4085, pp. 492–507. Springer, Heidelberg (2006)

[CCS02]   Cornélio, M.L., Cavalcanti, A.L.C., Sampaio, A.C.A.: Refactoring by Transformation. In: REFINE'2002. Eletronic Notes in Theoretical Computer Science, vol. 70, Elsevier, Amsterdam (2002)

[Cor04]   Cornélio, M.L.: Refactorings as Formal Refinement. PhD thesis, Universidade Federal de Pernambuco (2004)

[DB01]   Derrick, J., Boiten, E.A.: Refinement in Z and Object-Z. Springer, Heidelberg (2001)

[dE98]   de Roever, W.-P., Engelhardt, K.: Data Refinement: Model-Oriented Proof Methods and their Comparison. CUP (1998)

[DW06]   Derrick, J., Wehrheim, H.: Model Transformations Incorporating Multiple Views. In: Johnson, M., Vene, V. (eds.) AMAST 2006. LNCS, vol. 4019, pp. 111–126. Springer, Heidelberg (2006)

[FDR97]   Formal Systems (Europe) Ltd. Failures-Divergence Refinement: FDR2 User Manual (Oct. 1997)

[Fis97]   Fischer, C.: A combination of Object-Z and CSP. In: FMOODS '97, vol. 2, pp. 423–438. Chapman & Hall, Sydney, Australia (1997)

[Fis00]   Fischer, C.: Combination and Implementation of Processes and Data: from CSP-OZ to Java. PhD thesis, University of Oldenburg (2000)

[Fow04]   Fowler, M.: Refactoring: Improving the Design of Existing Code. Addison-Wesley, London (2004)

[Hoa85]   Hoare, C.A.R.: Communicating sequential processes. Prentice-Hall, Englewood Cliffs (1985)

[HT04]   Heckel, R., Thöne, S.: Behavior-preserving refinement relations between dynamic software architectures. In: 17th Int. Workshop on Algebraic Development Techniques, pp. 1–27 (2004)

[KHE03]   Küster, J., Heckel, R., Engels, G.: Defining and validating transformations of UML models. In: HCC, pp. 145–152. IEEE Computer Society, Los Alamitos (2003)

[McC04]   McComb, T.: Refactoring Object-Z Specifications. In: Wermelinger, M., Margaria-Steffen, T. (eds.) FASE 2004. LNCS, vol. 2984, p. 69. Springer, Heidelberg (2004)

[MEDJ05]   Mens, T., Van Eetvelde, N., Demeyer, S., Janssens, D.: Formalizing refactorings with graph transformations. Journal of Software Maintenance 17(4), 247–276 (2005)

[MS04]   McComb, T., Smith, G.: Architectural Design in Object-Z. In: Australian Software Engineering Conference (ASWEC'04), pp. 77–86. IEEE Computer Society Press, Los Alamitos (2004)

[MS06]   McComb, T., Smith, G.: Refactoring object-oriented specifications: A process for deriving designs. Technical Report SSE-2006-01, University of Queensland, Australia (May 2006)

[MT04]   Mens, T., Tourwé, T.: A survey of software refactoring. IEEE Trans. Software Eng. 30(2), 126–139 (2004)

[Ros97]   Roscoe, W.: The Theory and Practice of Concurrency. Prentice-Hall, En-
           glewood Cliffs (1997)
[Ruh06]   Ruhroth, Th.: Refactoring Object-Z Specifications. In: 18th Nordic Work-
           shop on Programming Theory (2006)
[SD06]   Van Der Straeten, R., D'Hondt, M.: Model refactorings through rule-based
           inconsistency resolution. In: Bézivin, J. (ed.) Proceedings of the 2006 ACM
           Symposium on Applied Computing, pp. 71210–1217. ACM Press, New
           York (2006)
[Smi00]   Smith, G.: The Object-Z Specification Language. KAP (2000)

A Sound and Complete Shared-Variable Concurrency Model for Multi-threaded Java Programs

F.S. de Boer

CWI, Amsterdam, Netherlands
F.S.de.Boer@cwi.nl

Abstract. In this paper we discuss an assertional proof method for multi-threaded Java programs. The method extends the proof theory for sequential Java programs with a generalization of the Owicki/Gries interference freedom test to threads in Java.

1 Introduction

We present a simple proof method which captures the main aspects of the multi-threaded flow of control in Java. In the object-oriented programming language Java instances of thread classes can be dynamically allocated and start their own thread of control. A thread class (defined as an extension of the public built-in Java class 'Thread') defines a run method and a call of the start method creates a new thread of computation initiated by the execution of the run method. The following Java syntax,

```
class MyThread extends Thread {
⋮
public void run() {
··· }
⋮
}
```

specifies a thread class 'MyThread' with a run method. The following code would then create a thread and start it running:

```
MyThread t = new MyThread();
t.start();
```

The thread executing this code continues its own execution, i.e., it does not wait for the start method to return. Operationally, a thread is described by a stack of calls generated by the run method. In this model of computation the different threads share the global object structure which consists of the values of the instances variables of the dynamically allocated objects and the static variables of the classes.

M.M. Bonsangue and E.B. Johnsen (Eds.): FMOODS 2007, LNCS 4468, pp. 252–268, 2007.

Our proof method consists of annotating each class definition of the given program with *assertions* which express certain global properties of the dynamically allocated program variables. Such an annotated class definition is *locally correct* if certain verification conditions hold which characterize the sequential flow of control within one thread. On the other hand, reasoning about the multi-threaded flow of control within an object involves a global *interference freedom test*. This test is modeled after the corresponding test in [13] for concurrent systems consisting of a statically fixed number of processes which interact via shared variables.

The main contribution of this paper is the generalization of the interference freedom test to *dynamic thread creation*. Furthermore, this paper also provides a formal justification of this generalization in terms of soundness and completeness proofs.

Related work. To the best of our knowledge the only other (proven) sound and complete proof method for annotated multi-threaded Java programs is described in [1]. The proof method in [1] combines the Owicki&Gries method for shared variable concurrency with the proof method for Communicating Sequential Processes (CSP) as introduced in [4]. The latter proof method is used to reason about method calls in terms of message passing between objects. By restricting to Java programs that have no static variables and do not allow dereferencing, in [1] objects only interact via message passing. Consequently the interference freedom test in [1] only involves the local state of an object. In contrast, in this paper we extend the proof method for sequential Java programs, which is based on the standard proof theory of recursive procedures (see [2]), with a global interference freedom test. In other words, the main difference is that the proof method in [1] is based on a model of concurrent objects (along the lines of [8]) whereas the proof method in this paper is strictly thread-based. The model of concurrent objects integrates shared-variable concurrency and message passing, whereas the thread-based model integrates shared-variable concurrency with recursive method call. We think the latter integration more faithfully captures the semantics of the Java programming language.

2   Assertions

Assertions are used to annotate the control points of method bodies. In this paper we abstract from the syntax of assertions (we denote by $\neg$, $\wedge$, $\rightarrow$ the logical connectives of negation, conjunction and implication). An assertion P is evaluated in a configuration. A configuration γ consists of an object structure and a local context. For every existing object an object structure assigns values to its instance variables (static variables belong to the object representing their class). A local context assigns values to the the local variables of the method. The local variables of a method include its formal parameters. We view the keyword 'this' as an implicit local variable which denotes the current object. We denote by

$$\gamma \models P$$

that the configuration γ satisfies the assertion P. An assertion is valid, denoted by $\models P$, if $\gamma \models P$, for every configuration γ.

For a (sequential) statement S in Java, we denote by

$$WP(S, P)$$

the weakest precondition which guarantees that every terminating execution of S satisfies P. Formally, this weakest precondition is semantically defined in terms of a structural operational semantics for transitions

$$\langle S, \gamma \rangle \to \gamma'$$

where γ denotes an initial configuration and γ' denotes the resulting configuration of the execution of S. Note that the current object is given by the local context of the initial configuration. Given such an operational semantics, we have the following standard definition

$$\gamma \models WP(S, P) \text{ if and only if } \gamma' \models P, \text{ for } \langle S, \gamma \rangle \to \gamma'$$

We refer to [6] for a weakest precondition calculus which formalizes aliasing and object creation at an abstraction level that coincides with that of the Java programming language.

In this paper, we denote by $P\sigma$ the result of applying the substitution σ to the assertion P. An application of a substitution

$$[e_1/u_1, \ldots, e_n/u_n]$$

simply consists of replacing simultaneously every occurrence of the *local* variable u_i by the corresponding expression e_i.

3   Proof-Outlines

A proof-outline is a correctly annotated program. An annotation of a multi-threaded Java program associates with every sub-statement S (appearing in a method body) a precondition $Pre(S)$ and a postcondition $Post(S)$. Validation of verification conditions establish the correctness of an annotated program. We first discuss the verification condition which establishes that assertions are interference free. Then we discuss the verification conditions which establish that assertions specify correctly the sequential control flow.

Interference Freedom Test

In order to characterize the interference between different threads we assume that each method has a distinguished local variable 'thread' which is used to identify the executing thread. A thread itself is uniquely identified by the initial object executing its run method (in Java calling the start method twice on an object throws the exception ' IllegalThreadStateException').

We define an assertion P to be invariant over the execution of a statement S by a *different* thread if the following verification condition holds:

$$\models (P \wedge Pre(S) \wedge \text{thread!} = \text{thread}') \rightarrow WP(S, P)$$

For notational convenience, we implicitly assume that the local variables of P and $Pre(S)$ are named apart by 'priming' the local variables of P. Note that these local variables include 'this' and 'thread', which are thus renamed in P by 'this''' and 'thread'''. Furthermore, it is important to note that an unqualified instance variable x of the class of the current object denoted by 'this', is transformed by this renaming into 'this$'$.x'.

The above verification condition models the situation that the execution of the thread denoted by the fresh local variable 'thread''' in the object denoted by the fresh local variable 'this''' is interleaved by the execution of the statement S by the thread denoted by the distinguished local variable 'thread' in the object denoted by the distinguished local variable 'this'. That we are dealing with two *different* threads is simply described by the disequality thread! $=$ thread$'$.

Example 1. As a (very) simple example, given a boolean instance variable 'b', the assertion 'thread.b' is invariant over the execution of an assignment 'thread. b=false' by *another* thread. This is captured by the valid verification condition

$$\models (\text{thread}'.\text{b} \wedge \text{thread!} = \text{thread}') \rightarrow WP(\text{thread.b=false}, \text{thread}'.\text{b})$$

Example 2. In example 7 we introduce an instance variable 'lock' to reason about synchronized methods. This variable stores the identity of the thread that owns the lock of the object. That is, for every synchronized method we have the invariant

thread==lock

With this additional information any annotation of a synchronized method is trivially interference free:

$$\models (\text{thread}' == \text{lock} \wedge \text{thread} == \text{lock} \wedge \text{thread!} = \text{thread}') \rightarrow \text{false}$$

Local Correctness

An annotated program is locally correct if the verification conditions hold which characterize the sequential flow of control within one thread. We have the standard verification conditions which characterize control structures like sequential composition, choice, and iteration constructs.

Method invocation and return. Without loss of generality, we restrict discussion to the verification conditions for method calls

$$x = e_0.m(e_1, \ldots, e_n)$$

where x is an instance variable or a local variable, and $e_0, e_1, \ldots, e_n$ are expressions without side-effect and which are not affected by the call itself. Furthermore, we assume that the formal parameters of the method m are read-only. Given such a call we denote by σ the (simultaneous) substitution

$$[e_0, e_1, \ldots, e_n/\text{this}, u_1, \ldots, u_n]$$

This substitution describes the context switch which consists of passing control to the callee, modeled by substituting every occurrence of 'this' by e_0, and initializing the formal parameters $u_1, \ldots, u_n$ of the method m, modeled by substituting every local variable u_i by e_i, $i = 1, \ldots, n$.

Let S denote the body of the method m. We have the following verification condition for the precondition P of the call $x = e_0.m(e_1, \ldots, e_n)$:

$$\models P \rightarrow Pre(S)\sigma$$

Here we assume that the local variables of the precondition $Pre(S)$ of the method body, excluding the formal parameters of the method and the local variables 'thread' and 'this', are named apart from those in P. Note that the distinguished local variable 'thread' thus may occur both in the precondition P of the caller and the precondition $Pre(S)$ of the callee. We do not need to distinguish these different occurrences because the local variable 'thread' in both preconditions denotes the *same* thread executing the method call.

Example 3. Consider the precondition

    account.lock==thread

of a call

    newbalance=account.add(amount)

of a synchronized method. This precondition can be obtained from the precondition

$$\text{lock} == \text{thread}$$

of the body of the method 'add' simply by replacing the (implicit) local variable 'this' by the expression 'account', which transforms the expression 'lock' into the expression 'account.lock'

Furthermore, we have the following verification condition for the postcondition Q of a call $x = e_0.m(e_1, \ldots, e_n)$:

$$\models Post(S)\sigma \rightarrow WP(x = \text{return}, Q)$$

As above, we assume that the local variables of the postcondition $Post(S)$ of the method body, excluding the formal parameters of the method and the local variables 'thread' and 'this', are named apart from those in Q. Note that since the formal parameters are read-only and the actual parameters are not affected by the call itself, we can apply the subsitution σ modeling the context switch and parameter passing. The distinguished local variable 'return' is used to store temporarily the return value. That is, the precondition P and the postcondition Q of a return statement are validated by the verification condition

$$\models P \rightarrow Q[e/\text{return}]$$

where e denotes the return value.

Example 4. Consider the postcondition

$$\text{lock} == \text{thread} \wedge \text{return} == \text{balance} + \text{u}$$

of the body S of the synchronized method 'add' ('u' denotes its formal parameter). Applying the context switch and parameter passing of the call

    newbalance=account.add(amount)

we obtain the assertion

$$\text{account.lock} == \text{thread} \wedge \text{return} == \text{account.balance} + \text{amount}$$

This assertion clearly implies the weakest precondition of the assignment 'newbalance=return' and the postcondition

$$\text{account.lock} == \text{thread} \wedge \text{newbalance} == \text{account.balance} + \text{amount}$$

of the call.

Auxiliary Variables

In general to prove the correctness of a program we need auxiliary variables which are used to describe certain properties of the flow of control.

*Example 5 (**Mutual exclusion**).* Consider the run method defined by

    run(){
    sem.acquire();S;sem.release() }

where sem is a static binary semaphore (initialized to 1). In order to prove that no two threads are executing the critical section S in the body of the run method we introduce a static variable 'in' which stores the set of threads that are in their critical section (it is initialized to the empty set). We extend the run method as follows:

    run(){
    [sem.acquire();in.add(thread)];S;[sem.release();in.remove(thread)] }

The brackets are used to indicate statements which are assumed to be executed atomically, that is without interleaving. Note that without loss of generality we can indeed assume that between acquiring (or releasing) the semaphore and the corresponding update of the auxiliary variable no other threads are interleaved.

Mutual exclusion then can be expressed by the assertion Mutex defined by

$$\text{in.size} == \text{sem} \land 0 <= \text{sem} \land \text{sem} <= 1$$

Note that in the assertion language, the static variable 'sem' is simply an integer variable, which takes the values 0 or 1.

The assertion Mutex is introduced as an invariant of the run method which annotates all its interleaving points, that is, the start and end of the body of the run method itself, and the start and end of the critical section S.

For the proof of the local correctness of the annotation we use the following (standard) characterization of the weakest precondition of a postcondition Q (of the operations for acquiring and releasing the semaphore):

$$WP(\text{sem.acquire}(), Q) = (\text{sem} == 1 \rightarrow Q[0/\text{sem}])$$

and

$$WP(\text{sem.release}(), Q) = (\text{sem} == 0 \rightarrow Q[1/\text{sem}])$$

Local correctness of the invariant Mutex then is expressed by the verification conditions

$$\models \text{Mutex} \rightarrow WP(\text{sem.acquire}(); \text{in.add}(\text{thread}), \text{Mutex})$$

and

$$\models \text{Mutex} \rightarrow WP(\text{sem.release}(); \text{in.remove}(\text{thread}), \text{Mutex})$$

Next we note that these local verification conditions which establish Mutex as an invariant of the run method, (trivially) imply the verification conditions for the interference freedom test:

$$\models (\text{Mutex} \land \text{thread}! = \text{thread}') \rightarrow WP(\text{sem.acquire}(); \text{in.add}(\text{thread}), \text{Mutex})$$

and

$$\models (\text{Mutex} \land \text{thread}! = \text{thread}') \rightarrow WP(\text{sem.release}(); \text{in.remove}(\text{thread}), \text{Mutex})$$

In other words, using a local invariant like Mutex makes the inteference freedom test *redundant*.

Auxiliary variables are also used to describe the semantics of built-in mechanisms in Java. Below we describe the semantics for starting a thread, the execution of synchronized methods, and the semantics of the synchronization mechanism of wait and notify methods.

Start method. In order to describe the specific semantics of the start method, we assume that each thread class has a boolean auxiliary instance variable 'Alive' which indicates that the start method of the object has been called and its run method has not yet terminated. Otherwise it is false. It is initialized to 'false' by the constructor method. Note that in Java starting a running thread throws an exception. Since, for technical convenience only, this paper restricts to invariance properties of normal executions of multi-threaded Java programs, we can describe the semantics of the start method simply by the code

```
if !e.Alive {
  e.Alive=true;e.start }
else { abort }
```

Correspondingly, we append the body of a run method by the assignment 'Alive= false'. We have the following (standard) verification condition of the 'abort' statement: For *arbitrary* postcondition Q

$$\models \text{false} \rightarrow Q$$

Note that this verification condition validates *any* postcondition.

The precondition of a call e.start of the start method is validated like the precondition of an ordinary call, as described above. The postcondition Q of the call e.start is simply validated by the verification condition

$$\models P \rightarrow Q$$

where P denotes its precondition.

Example 6. Clearly we can validate by means of the above verification condition for method calls, for every run method, the precondition

$$\text{thread} = \text{this} \wedge \text{this.Alive}$$

Consequently, every local assertion of a run method is trivially invariant over any local assignment of any run method: For example, the local assertion 'b', where 'b' is an instance variable, is invariant over an assignment b=false in any run method, because

$$\models (\text{this}'.b \wedge \text{thread}' = \text{this}' \wedge \text{thread} = \text{this} \wedge \text{thread!} = \text{thread}') \rightarrow WP(b = \text{false}, \text{this}'.b)$$

trivially holds (note that the antecedent implies this! $=$ this').

*Example 7 (***Synchronized methods***).* In order to describe the specific semantics of synchronized methods in Java, we introduce an auxiliary (instance) variable 'lock' which belongs to the class of the method and which stores the identity of the thread owning the lock. Since a thread releases the lock of an object only when it has finished executing its synchronized methods the thread has called on the object, we also need an auxiliary (instance) variable 'count' which belongs to the class of the thread and which denotes the number of called synchronized methods in the thread. Every method invocation $e_0!m(e_1, \ldots, e_n)$ involving a synchronized method m is prefixed with an *await* statement

```
await e0.lock==thread  || e0.lock==null{
e0.lock=thread;thread.count++ }
```

The boolean condition states that either the thread already owns the lock or the lock is not yet initialized (i.e., is 'free').

On the other hand, every synchronized method ends with the execution of the await statement

```
await true {
thread.count-=1; if thread.count==0 { lock=null}}
```

We extend our notion of proof outlines with the following standard verification condition for await statements

$$\models (P \wedge b) \rightarrow WP(S, Q)$$

where P and Q denote the precondition and the postcondition of the await statement, b denotes its boolean condition and S denotes its main body.

Since the evaluation of the boolean guard of an *await*-statement and the execution of its body are assumed to be atomic we only need to apply the interference freedom test to the pre- and postcondition of the *await*-statement itself.

Example 8 (**Wait and notify**). A thread which owns the lock of an object can release it by calling the wait method on the object. It has to wait until another thread owning the lock calls the 'notify' or 'notifyAll' method on this object. In order to describe the semantics of this mechanism we denote by 'wait' an auxiliary instance variable of the object which is used to store the set of objects waiting for its lock. The semantics of a call

```
e.wait()
```

then is described by the following statement

```
if lock==thread{
u=e;u.lock=null;u.wait.add(thread) }
else { abort };
await u.lock==null & !u.wait.contains(thread) {
u.lock=thread}
```

Here 'u' is a 'fresh' local variable used to keep the identity of the object. This statement first checks whether the thread owns the lock. If so, the thread simply releases the lock and is added to the set of waiting threads. If the thread does not own the lock the execution is aborted because we only consider normal executions (e.g., we abstract from exceptions). The await statement waits for the lock to be free and for the thread to be removed from the set of waiting threads. A call

```
e.notifyAll()
```

of the 'notifyAll' method is modeled by the statement

```
if lock==thread{
e.wait.clear()}
else { abort }
```

which removes all waiting threads (in case the executing thread owns the lock). In order to model a call

e.notify()

which involves an *arbitrary* choice of the thread to be notified, we introduce an (abstract) set operation 'removeAny()' which removes an arbitrary element from a set. We then can model the above call by the statement

```
if lock==thread{
e.wait.removeAny() }
else { abort }
```

Given a precondition P, a postcondition Q of a statement

```
e.wait.removeAny()
```

is validated by the verification condition

$$\models (P \wedge e.\text{wait.contains(any)}) \rightarrow WP(e.\text{wait.remove(any)}, Q)$$

By definition of the validity of assertions the 'fresh' local variable 'any' is here implicitly universally quantified.

In general, auxiliary variables can be introduced as local variables, instance variables and static variables. Assignments to auxiliary variables can be introduced which are side-effect free (e.g., assignments which do not involve methods calls or object creation) and which do not affect the flow of control of the given program. It is important to note that we also allow auxiliary variables as additional formal parameters of method definitions. Such auxiliary variables can be used to reason about invariance properties of method calls.

Example 9 (**Faculty function**). Consider for example the following recursive method for computing the faculty function.

```
fac() {
if x>0 { x-=1;this.fac();x++;y=y*x } else { y=1 }}
```

Here 'x' and 'y' are instance variables. Upon termination 'y' stores the faculty of the value stored by 'x'. In order to prove that the value of 'x' upon termination equals its old value, we introduce as auxiliary variable a formal parameter u and extend the method by

```
fac(u) {
if x>0 { x-=1;this.fac(u-1);x++;y=y*x } else { y=1 }}
```

We then can express the above invariance property by introducing the assertion 'u==x' both as precondition and the postcondition of the method body. This specification of the method body can be validated by introducing 'u-=x+1' as the precondition and the postcondition of the recursive call. We have the following trivial verification conditions for method invocation and return

$$\models u{==}x{+}1 \rightarrow u{-}1{==}x \text{ and } \models u{-}1{==}x \rightarrow u{==}x{+}1$$

where the assertion 'u-1==x' results from replacing the formal parameter 'u' in 'u==x' by the actual parameter 'u-1'.

4 Soundness and Completeness

In this section we sketch soundness and completeness proofs. These proofs are based on a formal semantics of multi-threaded Java programs. This semantics is described in terms of a structural operational semantics which defines a transition relation on global states. A global state Θ of a program consists of a set of threads and an object structure which specifies for every existing object the values of its instance variables. Operationally, a thread is a stack of closures, i.e., pairs (S, τ) consisting of a statement S and a local context τ specifying the values of the local variables of S. For any two closures (S, τ) and (S', τ') belonging to the same thread we have that

$$\tau(\text{thread}) = \tau'(\text{thread})$$

because the local variable 'thread' denotes the initial object (executing its run method). That is, for the bottom closure (S_0, τ_0) of a thread we have that

$$\tau_0(\text{thread}) = \tau_0(\text{this})$$

The thread itself is executing the closure on top of the call stack, which is also called its active closure. All other closures represent pending calls. The details of the definition of the global transition relation

$$\Theta \to \Theta'$$

which represents the execution of an atomic statement by one thread in Θ resulting in the global state Θ', are straightforward and omitted (see also [1]).

For notational convenience only, we assume throughout this section that every interleaving point of the given program is uniquely labeled. Such labels we denote by $l, l', \ldots$. By

$$l : S : l'$$

we denote a statement S with its start and end labeled by l and l', or the label l itself (': $S : l''$ thus being optional). A label on its own marks the termination of a method body. The assertion annotating an interleaving point l we denote by $@l$.

Soundness

Let π be an annotated program. A global state Θ satisfies an annotated program π, denoted by

$$\Theta \models \pi$$

if for every thread in the global state Θ with active closure $(l : S : l', \tau)$, we have

$$\gamma \models @l$$

where γ denotes the configuration consisting of the global object structure of Θ and the local context τ. Roughly, a global state satisfies an annotated program if every thread satisfies the assertion annotating the statement of its active closure. We can now state the following theorem.

Theorem 1 (Soundness). *For any correctly annotated program π (possibly extended with auxiliary variables),*

$$\Theta \models \pi \text{ and } \Theta \to \Theta' \text{ implies } \Theta' \models \pi$$

Roughly, this theorem states the invariance of the assertions of a correctly annotated program. The proof involves a straightforward but tedious case analysis of the computation step.

Completeness

Conversely, we show completeness by proving the correctness of an extended program annotated with so-called reachability predicates. These predicates are introduced in [3] and [12] and adapted to (extended) multi-threaded Java programs as follows: Given a program we define for every interleaving point l the predicate $@l$ by

$\gamma \models @l$
if there exists a reachable global state Θ that realizes the object structure of γ and that contains a thread with an active closure $(l : S : l', \tau)$, where τ is the local context of γ.

A global state Θ is reachable if there exists a partial computation

$$\Theta_0 \to^* \Theta$$

starting from a fixed initial global state Θ_0. Here $\to^*$ denotes the reflexive, transitive closure of $\to$.

Using the encoding techniques of [14] it can be shown that the above reachability predicates can be expressed in the assertion language. Of particular interest to note here is that *pure* methods,. i.e., methods that do not affect the program state, in assertions greatly facilitates such an encoding.

By a straightforward, though tedious, induction on the length of the computation we can prove that a program annotated with the above reachability predicates is locally correct. The main case of interest is a proof of the verification condition

$$\models (@l)\sigma \to WP(x = \text{return}, @l')$$

for validating the postcondition of a method call $x = e_0.m(e_1, \ldots, e_n)$. The label l marks the end of the method body of m and l' the termination of the call. The context switch and parameter passing are modeled by the substitution σ (as described above). In order to validate this verification condition we extend every method definition with an additional formal parameter which stores the local context of the caller and an additional parameter for passing the label identifying the call. The local context of the caller, i.e., the values of its local variables, are stored in an array. These additional formal parameters we denote by 'con' and 'lab' (run methods contain these variables as local variables). In order to initialize the local context of the callee (to be passed in subsequent calls), we add to each method the following initialization:

Objects [ ] mycontext;
mycontext=new Objects[n+1];
mycontext[0]=u_1;

$\vdots$

mycontext[n-1]=u_n;
mycontext[n]=con;
mycontext[n+1]=lab;

Here $u_1, \ldots, u_n$ are the formal parameters of the method (as specified by the given program). A call $x = e_0.m(e_1, \ldots, e_n)$ is extended by

$$x = e_0.m(e_1, \ldots, e_n, \text{mycontext}, l')$$

(the label l' marks its termination). Note that in Java arrays are objects, e.g., the actual parameter 'mycontext' is an object which refers to an array.

The additional parameters ensure that the predicate $(@l)\sigma$ indeed describes the return of the method m to the given call (σ is also extended with these new parameters). To see this, let

$$\gamma \models (@l)\sigma$$

By the usual substitution lemma of the logic underlying the assertion language, this is equivalent to

$$\gamma \models WP(\bar{u} = \bar{e}, @l)$$

where $\bar{u} = \bar{e}$ denotes the sequence of assignments corresponding to the substitution σ. Let

$$\langle \bar{u} = \bar{e}, \gamma \rangle \to \gamma'$$

that is, γ' is the resulting configuration of the execution of the statement $\bar{u} = \bar{e}$ in γ. It follows that

$$\gamma' \models @l$$

Note that the local context τ' of the configuration γ' in fact denotes the result of switching the context from the caller back to the callee.

By the above definition of the reachability predicates it follows that there exists a partial computation

$$\Theta_0 \to^* \Theta'$$

that realizes the object structure of γ' (which equals that of γ) and that contains an active closure (l, τ') which marks the termination of the body of m.
From

$$\langle \bar{u} = \bar{e}, \gamma \rangle \to \gamma'$$

it follows immediately that

$$\tau'(\text{con}) = \tau(\text{mycontext}) \text{ and } \tau'(\text{lab}) = l'$$

So we know that this invocation of m has been called by the given call statement. More specifically, we know that Θ' contains a thread

$$\cdots (x = \text{return}; l' : S : l'', \tau)(l, \tau')$$

Let

$$\Theta' \to \Theta$$

be the computation step which models the context switch from callee to caller. That is, the closure (l, τ') is removed from the above call stack. Since Θ realizes the object structure of γ we conclude that

$$\gamma \models WP(x = \text{return}, @l')$$

Remains to show that the reachability predicates are interference free. More specifically, we have to show that for any interleaving points l and l', with l' marking the start of an atomic statement S, we have

$$\models (@l' \wedge @l \wedge \text{thread!} = \text{thread}') \to WP(S, @l')$$

Roughly, this verification condition states that if one thread reaches l' and if another thread reaches l, then l' is still reachable after the execution of the statement S. This follows trivially if there exists one computation where both threads reach l' and l at the same time. However, in general this is not the case, e.g., the reachability of l' may require a *scheduling* of the threads which is incompatible with the reachability of l.

Example 10 **(Scheduling).** Consider a thread class with the following method

```
run() {
if race() {l₁ : S₁} else {l₂ : S₂}}
```

The labels l_1 and l_2 denote the start of the 'then' and the 'else' branch, respectively. The synchronized method 'race' is defined by

```
race() {
u=b;
if b==true { b=false };
return u }
```

where 'u' is a local variable and 'b' is a static variable. which is initially true. Let the main method of the program initialize 'b' to 'true' and then simply create two instances of the thread class and start their run methods. Let τ be a local context such $\tau(\text{thread})$ and $\tau(\text{thread}')$ are two different instances of the thread class. Let $t = \tau(\text{thread})$ or $t = \tau(\text{thread}')$. Clearly, in both cases there exists a reachable global state Θ in which 'b=false' holds and which contains the active closure $(l_1 : S_1, \tau')$, where $\tau'(\text{thread}) = t$. But there exists no reachable global state in which *both* threads are at l_1 at the same time.

Therefore we introduce a static auxiliary variable 'sched' which records the scheduling of the threads. We introduce this variable as a vector of objects in the class containing the main method. Every read or write operation which involves access to the global object structure is extended with an update which adds the identity of the executing thread.

Example 11. Returning to the above example, we note that this additional scheduling information implies that

$$\models (@l_1' \wedge @l_1 \wedge \text{thread!} = \text{thread}') \rightarrow \text{false}$$

(the predicate $@l_1'$ refers to the thread denoted by the fresh local variable 'thread''). Note that $@l_1'$ implies that 'sched' stores the thread denoted by 'thread'' first, whereas $@l_1$ stores the thread denoted by the distinguished local variable 'thread' first.

Note that the interleaving of the local computations of the threads, i.e., the computations which only access the local context of the active closures and which do not access the global object structures (the static variables and the instance variables of the existing objects), does not affect the global computation. More specifically, the variable 'sched' enforces the following confluence property of the global transition relation.

Lemma 1 (Confluence). *Let π be a multi-threaded Java program extended with the auxiliary variable 'sched' for recording the scheduling of threads, as described above. Furthermore, let the object structures of the global states Θ and Θ' assign the same value to the variable 'sched'. It follows that if*

$$\Theta_0 \rightarrow^* \Theta \text{ and } \Theta_0 \rightarrow^* \Theta'$$

then there exists a global state Θ'' such that

$$\Theta \rightarrow^* \Theta'' \text{ and } \Theta' \rightarrow^* \Theta''$$

Furthermore, these partial compotations only consist of local compouations steps which do not involve (read or write) access to the global object structure.

We can now prove the following theorem which states that the reachability predicates are interference free.

Theorem 2. *For any labeled statements $l : S$ and $l' : S'$ of a program extended with the auxiliary variable 'sched' we have*

$$\models (@l' \wedge @l \wedge \text{thread'!} = \text{thread}) \rightarrow WP(S, @l')$$

Proof. Let

$$\gamma \models @l' \wedge @l \wedge \text{thread!} = \text{thread}'$$

By definition of the reachability predicates $@l'$ and $@l$ there exists partial computations

$$\Theta_0 \rightarrow^* \Theta \text{ and } \Theta_0 \rightarrow^* \Theta'$$

starting from a fixed initial global state Θ_0, such that $(l : S, \tau)$ is the active closure of the thread $\tau(\text{thread})$, whereas the $(l' : S', \tau')$ is the active closure of $\tau(\text{thread}')$. Here τ denotes the local context of the configuration γ and $\tau'(u) = \tau(u')$, for every local variable (remember that primed local variables are introduced in order to avoid name clashes between the local variables of @l and @l'). Furthermore, the global object structure of γ is realized in both the global states Θ and Θ'. The auxiliary variable 'sched' thus has the same value in the global object structures of Θ and Θ'. By the above lemma, there exists a global state Θ'' which can be reached from both Θ and Θ' by local computations only. But then we can also backtrack the local computation steps of the two threads (denoted by $\tau(\text{thread})$ and $\tau(\text{thread}'))$ and obtain a reachable global state in which $\tau(\text{thread})$ is about to execute S and $\tau(\text{thread}')$ the statement S'. Clearly, the thread denoted by $\tau(\text{thread}')$ is still about to execute S' in the global state which results from the execution of S by $\tau(\text{thread})$. It follows by definition of the reachability predicates that

$$\gamma' \models @l'$$

where γ' consists of the object structure resulting from the execution of S' (by $\tau(\text{thread})$) and the initial local context τ' (of $\tau(\text{thread}')$).

5   Conclusion and Future Work

In this paper we presented a sound and complete proof method for multi-threaded Java programs. The proof method distinguishes a local level which is based on a Hoare logic for the sequential flow of control of (recursive) method calls within one thread and a global level which deals with interference between threads. The formal justification of the proof method is based on a formal semantics of Java programs annotated with assertions.

The proof method incorporates the use of auxiliary variables. These variables are used to capture specific aspects of the flow of control. Of particular interest is their use introduced in this paper as additional formal parameters to describe the sequential flow of control of (recursive) method calls within one thread. This use allows a complete characterization of method calls in a multi-threading context. More specifically, in this paper we introduced such a characterization in terms of the reachability predicates instead of the strongest postcondition as is used in the seminal completeness proof of Gorelick ([9]) for recursive procedure calls in a sequential context (see also [2]).

In general, auxiliary variables can be used to extend the proof method in a systematic manner to other mechanisms like synchronized methods, wait and notify methods, and further details of the underlying memory model as described in [10].

Future work. The main challenge is integrated tool support for the annotation of multi-threaded Java programs with assertions (as provided by [11]), the automatic generation of the verification conditions and (semi)automated validation of these conditions using theorem proving (as provided by [7,5]).

References

1. Abraham, E., de Boer, F.S., de Roever, W.P., Steffen, M.: An assertion-based proof system for mutithreaded Java. Theoretical Computer Science vol. 331 (2005)
2. Apt, K.R.: Ten years of Hoare logic: a survey — part I. ACM Transactions on Programming Languages and Systems 3(4), 431–483 (1981)
3. Apt, K.R.: Formal justification of a proof system for Communicating Sequential Processes. Journal of the ACM 30(1), 197–216 (1983)
4. Apt, K.R., Francez, N., de Roever, W.P.: A proof system for Communicating Sequential Processes. ACM Transactions on Programming Languages and Systems 2, 359–385 (1980)
5. Beckert, B., Hähnle, R., Schmitt, P.H. (eds.): Verification of Object-Oriented Software, LNCS (LNAI), vol. 4334. Springer, Heidelberg (2007)
6. de Boer, F.S.: A WP-calculus for OO. In: Thomas, W. (ed.) ETAPS 1999 and FOSSACS 1999. LNCS, vol. 1578, Springer, Heidelberg (1999)
7. The Extended Static Checker for Java (ESC/Java). URL: http://secure.ucd.ie/products/opensource/ESCJava2.
8. Gerth, R.T., de Roever, W.-P.: Proving monitors revisited: A first step towards verifying object oriented systems. Fundamenta informaticae IX, North-Holland, pp. 371–400 (1986)
9. Gorelick, G.A.: A complete axiomatic system for proving assertions about recursive and non-recursive programs. Technical Report 75, Department of Computer Science, University of Toronto (1975)
10. Manson, J., Pugh, W., Adve, S.V.: The Java memory model. In: POPL 2005. Proceedings of the 32nd ACM SIGPLAN-SIGACT Symposium on Principles of Programming Languages, ACM Press, New York (2005)
11. The Java Modeling Language (JML). URL of the JML home page: http://www.cs.iastate.edu/~leavens/JML.
12. Owicki, S.: A consistent and complete deductive system for the verification of parallel programs. Proceedings of the eighth annual ACM symposium on Theory of computing. ACM Press, New York (1976)
13. Owicki, S., Gries, D.: An axiomatic proof technique for parallel programs. Acta Informatika 6, 319–340 (1976)
14. Tucker, J.V., Zucker, J.I. (eds.): Program Correctness over Abstract Data Types, with Error-State Semantics. CWI Monograph Series. Centre for Mathematics and Computer Science, vol. 6. North-Holland, Amsterdam (1988)

Performance-Oriented Comparison of Web Services Via Client-Specific Testing Preorders

Marco Bernardo and Luca Padovani

Università di Urbino – Italy
Istituto di Scienze e Tecnologie dell'Informazione

Abstract. The behavior of a Web service can be described by means of a contract, which is a specification of the legal interactions with the service. Given a repository of Web services, from the client viewpoint a proper service selection should be based on functional as well as non-functional aspects of the interactions. In this paper we provide a technique that enables a client both to discover compatible services and to compare them on the basis of specific performance requirements. Our technique, which is illustrated on a simple probabilistic calculus, relies on two families of client-specific probabilistic testing preorders. These are shown to be precongruences with respect to the operators of the language and not to collapse into equivalences unlike some more general probabilistic testing preorders appeared in the literature.

1 Introduction

The recent trend in Web services is fostering a computing scenario where clients must be able to search at run time services that provide specific capabilities. This scenario requires Web services to publish their capabilities in some known registry and it entails the availability of powerful search operations for capabilities. Possible capabilities that one would like to search concern the format of the exchanged messages, the protocol – or *contract* – required to interact successfully with the service, and, when considering QoS-aware Web services, capabilities describing non-functional aspects of the service.

The Web Service Description Language (WSDL) [11,10,9] and the Web Service Conversation Language (WSCL) [1] are examples of standardized technologies for describing the interface exposed by a service. Such a description includes the service location, the format (or *schema*) of the exchanged messages, the transfer mechanism to be used (e.g. SOAP-RPC, or others), and the contract. Both WSDL and WSCL documents can be published in registries [2,13] so that they can be searched and queried.

This immediately asks for a definition of *compatibility* between different published contracts. It is necessary to define precise notions of contract similarity and compatibility and use them to perform service discovery. Unfortunately, neither WSDL nor WSCL can effectively define these notions, for the very simple reason

M.M. Bonsangue and E.B. Johnsen (Eds.): FMOODS 2007, LNCS 4468, pp. 269–284, 2007.

that they do not provide any formal characterization of their contract languages. This calls for a mathematical foundation of contracts and formal relationships between clients and contracts, which have been investigated in [16,7,8].

With respect to non-functional aspects of Web services, neither WSDL nor WSCL take them into account. In fact, a few extensions have been proposed in the literature [18,15] to enrich service descriptions, in particular WSDL interfaces and UDDI registries, with QoS aspects. In some cases, a "QoS certifier" takes care of certifying the QoS claims of Web services that register themselves with it. Anyway, the QoS aspects are necessarily quantified on the basis of an "average client" interacting with the service, whereas the behavior of each specific client, especially in involved interactions, may result in significant deviations from the declared – possibly certified – quantities.

To overcome this limitation – which may cause many clients to make a wrong service selection – it is first of all necessary that the service contracts are enriched with the description of performance aspects. In fact, to make principled choices a specific client cannot only rely on claims like "the response time is 93 msec", but needs to see in the service contract more low-level performance details, like e.g. an estimate of the probability with which at a certain branching point a service behaves in a given way rather than in a different one.

In this paper we propose a technique by means of which, given a specific client and a repository of Web services whose contracts embody QoS details, the client can detect the presence of compatible services in the repository and, if any, order them on the basis of certain performance requirements that are of interest to the client.

The formal machinery that we develop to implement the technique relies on a basic weighted process calculus to describe client and service contracts. The calculus comprises weighted active and passive actions [6,3] and its only operators are termination, action prefix, and alternative composition. Weights are associated with actions to express performance aspects, with a generative interpretation in the case of active actions and a reactive interpretation in the case of passive actions [17]. As far as active actions are concerned, generative weights can be given a time-abstract interpretation (probabilities) or a continuous-time interpretation (rates of exponentially distributed durations). In the first case, the performance model underlying the interaction of a client with a service is a finite discrete-time Markov chain, while in the second case it is a finite continuous-time Markov chain [19].

A probabilistic variant of testing preorder [14] is then employed both to verify the compatibility of a service with a client and to order compatible services on the basis of client-specific performance properties. Testing preorder is an effective means to achieve the second objective in practice. In fact, a client – suitably enriched with success decorations in the appropriate places – can be viewed as a test that different services pass with different probabilities. Those probabilities precisely characterize the client-specific quality guarantees provided by the various services.

On the theoretical side, the peculiarity of our probabilistic testing preorder, which is shown to be a precongruence with respect to the operators of the basic weighted process calculus, is that of being test specific. In other words, its definition does not exhibit any universal quantification over tests. Therefore we have to do with as many test-specific probabilistic testing preorders as there are tests. An important consequence is that our probabilistic testing preorders do not collapse into equivalences. This happened for instance with the testing preorder for fully generative probabilistic processes of [12], as two processes can be in a certain relation with respect to a test and in the opposite relation with respect to another test. As another example, the testing preorder for continuous-time Markovian processes of [4] suffered from a similar problem, as it is not possible to define it in a way that is consistent with all the reward-based performance measures.

This paper is organized as follows. In Sect. 2 we define the basic weighted process calculus for describing the functional and performance aspects of client and service contracts. In Sect. 3 we define two families of client-specific probabilistic testing preorders, one for the time-abstract case and one for the continuous-time case, and we investigate their precongruence properties. In Sect. 4 we show how to use the two families of client-specific probabilistic testing preorders for compatibility verification. In Sect. 5 we exhibit some examples in which the two families of client-specific probabilistic testing preorders are used to order different services that are compatible with the same client. Finally, in Sect. 6 we provide some concluding remarks.

2 Basic Language for QoS-Aware Contracts

In this section we introduce the syntax and the semantics for a very simple weighted process calculus called WPC, which we shall use to formalize the behavior of client and service contracts in a way that takes performance aspects into account. WPC builds on a set *Name* of action names including τ for invisible actions, which will be ranged over by a, b. Its set of operators is formed only by termination, action prefix, and alternative composition.

Similarly to [6,3], an action of WPC can be either active or passive. An active action represents an activity undertaken by a process, either locally or in cooperation with other processes. By contrast, a passive action models a situation in which a process waits for another process to initiate some activity in which the former is involved as well.

Performance aspects are described by associating a positive real number – which we call weight – with each action and by assuming that the execution probability of each action is proportional to the number associated with it. More precisely, according to the terminology of [17], the choice among active actions is assumed to be generative, i.e. weights are considered across active actions with arbitrary names. By contrast, the choice among passive actions is assumed to be reactive, i.e. weights are considered only within sets of passive actions having the same name. Thus, the choice between two passive actions having different names is nondeterministic.

An active action will be denoted by $<a, w>$ with the generative weight $w \in \mathbf{R}_{>0}$, while a passive action will be denoted by $<a, *_u>$ with the reactive weight $u \in \mathbf{R}_{>0}$. Since in WPC an invisible action can only represent a local activity, it cannot be passive, i.e. it will be of the form $<\tau, w>$. We note that the choice between two observable actions is external – in the sense that it can be influenced by the environment – independently from the fact that the actions are active or passive. Instead, the choice between two invisible actions is internal.

The generative weights associated with the active actions can be given a time-abstract interpretation or a continuous-time interpretation. In the first case, they represent non-normalized probability values and the preselection policy applies. This simply means that the choice among several simultaneously enabled active actions is solved probabilistically on the basis of action weights. In the second case, the weights represent the rates of the exponential distributions quantifying the durations of the actions. In this case the race policy applies, which means that the fastest action among the enabled ones will be executed. It can be shown that also in the second case each enabled action has an execution probability proportional to its weight. Moreover, the average sojourn time for a term turns out to be the inverse of the sum of the weights of the actions enabled by the term.

Definition 1. *The set $\mathcal{P}$ of the process terms of WPC is generated by the following syntax:*

$$\boxed{P ::= \underline{0} \mid <a, w>.P \mid <b, *_u>.P \mid P + P}$$

where $b \neq \tau$. ∎

The semantics for WPC can be defined in the usual operational style, provided that the multiplicity of each transition – corresponding to the number of different proofs for the derivation of the transition – is taken into account. The reason is that the idempotency law $P + P = P$ no longer holds when dealing with probabilistic processes. As an example, in the continuous-time case, a term like $<a, 4.6>.P + <a, 4.6>.P$ is not equivalent to $<a, 4.6>.P$ but to $<a, 9.2>.P$, because the average sojourn time for $<a, 4.6>.P + <a, 4.6>.P$ is $1/9.2$.

As a consequence, the behavior of each WPC term is given by a multitransition system, whose states correspond to process terms and whose transitions are labeled with actions. Observed that the null term $\underline{0}$ cannot execute any action – hence the corresponding labeled multitransition system is just a state with no transitions – we now provide the semantic rules for the other operators of WPC:

– Action prefix: $<a, w>.P$ (resp. $<b, *_u>.P$) can execute an action named a (resp. $b \neq \tau$) and then behaves as P:

$$\boxed{<a, w>.P \xrightarrow{a,w} P \qquad <b, *_u>.P \xrightarrow{b,*_u} P}$$

– Alternative composition: $P_1 + P_2$ behaves as either P_1 or P_2 depending on whether P_1 or P_2 executes an action first:

$$\frac{P_1 \xrightarrow{a,w} P'}{P_1 + P_2 \xrightarrow{a,w} P'} \qquad \frac{P_1 \xrightarrow{b,*_u} P'}{P_1 + P_2 \xrightarrow{b,*_u} P'}$$

$$\frac{P_2 \xrightarrow{a,w} P'}{P_1 + P_2 \xrightarrow{a,w} P'} \qquad \frac{P_2 \xrightarrow{b,*_u} P'}{P_1 + P_2 \xrightarrow{b,*_u} P'}$$

Example 1. Consider a service computing the greatest common divisor and a service computing the square root. Their contracts are described in WPC as follows:

$$S_1(w_1) = \texttt{<gcd,}*_1\texttt{>}.\texttt{<op1,}*_1\texttt{>}.\texttt{<op2,}*_1\texttt{>}.\texttt{<res,}w_1\texttt{>}.\texttt{<end,}1\texttt{>}.\underline{0}$$
$$S_2(w_2) = \texttt{<sqrt,}*_1\texttt{>}.\texttt{<op,}*_1\texttt{>}.(\texttt{<}\tau\texttt{,}1\texttt{>}.\texttt{<res,}w_2\texttt{>}.\texttt{<end,}1\texttt{>}.\underline{0} +$$
$$\texttt{<}\tau\texttt{,}1\texttt{>}.\texttt{<error,}1\texttt{>}.\underline{0})$$

where we use passive actions to model messages that are sent from the client to the service, and we use active actions to model messages that are sent from the service back to the client.

The contract $S_1(w_1)$ describes the behavior of a service that computes the greatest common divisor of two positive integer numbers, with w_1 representing the performance of the service in completing the operation. The service is linear: the conversation is wrapped between actions gcd and end that delimit the actual exchange of information between client and service.

The need for an explicit end action to signal a terminated interaction is not immediately evident. The problem arises when a contract has the form:

$$\texttt{<}\tau\texttt{,}w'\texttt{>}.\underline{0} + \texttt{<}\tau\texttt{,}w''\texttt{>}.\texttt{<}a,w\texttt{>}.P$$

because a client interacting with a service that exposes this contract cannot distinguish a completed interaction where the service has internally decided to behave like $\underline{0}$ from an interaction where the service has internally decided to perform the a action, but it is taking a long time to respond. By providing an explicit end action signaling a completed interaction, the service tells the client not to wait for further messages. This way of modeling a completed interaction is consistent with the WSCL language, which accounts for an explicit termination message called "empty".

The contract $S_2(w_2)$ describes the behavior of a service that computes the square root of a real number, with w_2 representing again the performance of the service in completing the operation. After the number has been sent from the client, the service internally decides whether the operation can be completed successfully, by sending the result back to the client, or if the computation terminates either because the input is invalid (the number is less than zero) or for any other reason (the computational capacity of the service has been exceeded). Invisible actions allow us to model such kind of so-called internal choices.

Finally, we can combine the two contracts and define:

$$S_1(w_1) + S_2(w_2)$$

that describes the behavior of services providing both operations. Because of the actions gcd and sqrt that uniquely determine the kind of operation to carry on, clients can decide which operation to invoke. In other words, this is a so-called external choice.   ∎

3   Client-Specific Probabilistic Testing Preorders

In this section we define two families of client-specific probabilistic testing preorders for WPC and we investigate their precongruence property.

3.1   Interaction System of a Service and a Client

Given a service S and a client C both formalized in WPC, their interaction can be described by means of their parallel composition, which we denote by $S \parallel C$. If we view C as a test and we mark some of its terminal states as successful, then we can talk about the probability with which S passes the test, which corresponds to the QoS guarantee provided by S when interacting with C.

From now on, clients will thus be formalized through the set $\mathcal{P}_s$ of terms generated by the following syntax:

$$P ::= \underline{0} \mid \text{s} \mid \sum_{i \in I} <a_i, \tilde{w}_i>.P_i$$

where the zeroary operator "s" stands for successful termination, I is a finite non-empty set, and $\tilde{w}_i$ stands for a generative or reactive weight (in the second case $a_i \neq \tau$). The use of a guarded alternative composition operator – instead of an action prefix operator and a binary alternative composition operator – is necessary to avoid terms like $\underline{0} + \text{s}$ that are ambiguous for the computation of the probability of passing a test.

The intended meaning of $S \parallel C$ is that S and C have to communicate on any observable action name. If at a certain point the set of observable action names enabled by the current derivative of S is disjoint from the set of observable action names enabled by the current derivative of C, and neither the S derivative nor the C derivative can evolve autonomously by performing an invisible action, then the service requested by C cannot be completed by S.

More precisely, in order for them to be executable, the observable active actions of the current derivative of S (resp. C) must be matched by passive actions of the current derivative of C (resp. S) having the same name. This leads to the generative-reactive synchronization mode described in [6] for time-abstract probabilistic processes and in [3] for continuous-time probabilistic processes. This synchronization mode is defined by the following two operational rules:

$$\frac{S \xrightarrow{b,w} S' \quad C \xrightarrow{b,*_u} C'}{S \parallel C \xrightarrow{b,w \cdot \frac{u}{weight_p(C,b)}} S' \parallel C'} \qquad \frac{S \xrightarrow{b,*_u} S' \quad C \xrightarrow{b,w} C'}{S \parallel C \xrightarrow{b,w \cdot \frac{u}{weight_p(S,b)}} S' \parallel C'}$$

where the weight of $P \in \{S, C\}$ with respect to passive actions of name $b \neq \tau$ is defined as follows:

$$weight_\mathrm{p}(P, b) = \sum \{ u \mid \exists P'. P \xrightarrow{b, *_u} P' \}$$

In addition, we have two operational rules for the autonomous evolution of S (under the constraint that C has not terminated yet) and of C when performing an invisible action:

$$\frac{S \xrightarrow{\tau, w} S' \quad C \notin \{\underline{0}, \mathsf{s}\}}{S \parallel C \xrightarrow{\tau, w} S' \parallel C} \qquad \frac{C \xrightarrow{\tau, w} C'}{S \parallel C \xrightarrow{\tau, w} S \parallel C'}$$

The constraint on the autonomous evolution of S is motivated by the fact that nothing can change from the point of view of passing a test once the test has reached its termination.

Definition 2. *Let $S \in \mathcal{P}$ and $C \in \mathcal{P}_\mathsf{s}$. The interaction system of service S and client C is process term $S \parallel C$, where we say that:*

- *A configuration is a state of the labeled multitransition system underlying $S \parallel C$, which is formed by a service part and a client part.*
- *A configuration is successful iff its client part is "s".* ∎

3.2 Computations: Execution Probability and Average Duration

A computation is a sequence of transitions that can be executed starting from $S \parallel C$. We say that two computations are independent of each other if it is not the case that one of them is a proper prefix of the other one. Moreover we say that a computation is successful if so is its last configuration. We denote by $\mathcal{C}(S, C)$, $\mathcal{IC}(S, C)$, and $\mathcal{SC}(S, C)$ the multisets of the computations, of the independent computations, and of the successful computations of $S \parallel C$, respectively.[1]

Let us define the length of a computation as the number of transitions occurring in it. From the fact that recursion is not allowed and the finitely-branching structure of S and C, it immediately follows that $\mathcal{C}(S, C)$ is finite and all of its computations have finite length. Moreover, $\mathcal{SC}(S, C) \subseteq \mathcal{IC}(S, C)$ because of the maximality of the length of the successful computations.

Two important quantities that can be associated with each computation are its execution probability and – in the continuous-time case – its average duration. Below we provide their inductive definitions.

Definition 3. *Let $S \in \mathcal{P}$, $C \in \mathcal{P}_\mathsf{s}$, and $c \in \mathcal{C}(S, C)$. The probability of executing c is the product of the execution probabilities of the transitions of c, which is defined by induction on the length of c through the following $\mathbf{R}_{]0,1]}$-valued function:*

$$prob(c) = \begin{cases} 1 & \text{if } length(c) = 0 \\ \frac{w}{weight_t(S \parallel C)} \cdot prob(c') & \text{if } c \equiv S \parallel C \xrightarrow{a, w} c' \end{cases}$$

---

[1] Since transitions have multiplicities, computations also have multiplicities.

where the total weight of $S \parallel C$ is defined as follows:

$$weight_t(S \parallel C) = \sum \{\!| \, w \mid \exists a, S', C'. \, S \parallel C \xrightarrow{a,w} S' \parallel C' \, |\!\}$$

We also define the probability of executing a computation of K as:

$$prob(K) = \sum_{c \in K} prob(c)$$

for all $K \subseteq \mathcal{IC}(S,C)$. ∎

Definition 4. *Let $S \in \mathcal{P}$, $C \in \mathcal{P}_s$, and $c \in \mathcal{C}(S,C)$. Assume a continuous-time interpretation for all the generative weights occurring in S and C. The average duration of c is the sequence of the average sojourn times[2] in the states traversed by c, which is defined by induction on the length of c through the following $(\mathbf{R}_{>0})^*$-valued function:*

$$time(c) = \begin{cases} \varepsilon & \text{if } length(c) = 0 \\ \frac{1}{weight_t(S \parallel C)} \circ time(c') & \text{if } c \equiv S \parallel C \xrightarrow{a,w} c' \end{cases}$$

where ε is the empty average duration and $\circ$ is the sequence concatenation operator. We also define the multiset of the computations of K whose average duration is not greater than θ as:

$$K_{\leq \theta} = \{\!| \, c \in K \mid length(c) \leq length(\theta) \, \wedge \\ \forall i = 1, \ldots, length(c). \, time(c)[i] \leq \theta[i] \, |\!\}$$

for all $K \subseteq \mathcal{C}(S,C)$ and $\theta \in (\mathbf{R}_{>0})^*$. ∎

Example 2. Consider three potential clients of the services $S_1(w_1)$ and $S_2(w_2)$ introduced in Ex. 1, whose contracts are described in WPC as follows:

$$C_{1,s} = \text{<gcd, 1>.<op1, 1>.<op2, 1>.<res, }*_1\text{>.<end, }*_1\text{>.s}$$
$$C_{2,s} = \text{<sqrt, 1>.<op, 1>.(<res, }*_1\text{>.<end, }*_1\text{>.s + <error, }*_1\text{>.s)}$$
$$C_{3,s} = \text{<sqrt, 1>.<op, 1>.<res, }*_1\text{>.<end, }*_1\text{>.s}$$

It is easy to see that:

$$\mathcal{SC}(S_1(w_1), C_{1,s}) = \{S_1(w_1) \parallel C_{1,s} \xrightarrow{\text{gcd,1}} \cdot \xrightarrow{\text{op1,1}} \cdot \xrightarrow{\text{op2,1}} \cdot \xrightarrow{\text{res,}w_1} \cdot \xrightarrow{\text{end,1}} \underline{0} \parallel s\}$$

$$\mathcal{SC}(S_2(w_2), C_{2,s}) = \{S_2(w_2) \parallel C_{2,s} \xrightarrow{\text{sqrt,1}} \cdot \xrightarrow{\text{op,1}} \cdot \xrightarrow{\tau,1} \cdot \xrightarrow{\text{res,}w_2} \cdot \xrightarrow{\text{end,1}} \underline{0} \parallel s,$$

$$S_2(w_2) \parallel C_{2,s} \xrightarrow{\text{sqrt,1}} \cdot \xrightarrow{\text{op,1}} \cdot \xrightarrow{\tau,1} \cdot \xrightarrow{\text{error,1}} \underline{0} \parallel s\}$$

$$\mathcal{SC}(S_2(w_2), C_{3,s}) = \{S_2(w_2) \parallel C_{3,s} \xrightarrow{\text{sqrt,1}} \cdot \xrightarrow{\text{op,1}} \cdot \xrightarrow{\tau,1} \cdot \xrightarrow{\text{res,}w_2} \cdot \xrightarrow{\text{end,1}} \underline{0} \parallel s\}$$

from which we derive that $prob(\mathcal{SC}(S_1(w_1), C_{1,s}) = prob(\mathcal{SC}(S_2(w_2), C_{2,s}) = 1$ and $prob(\mathcal{SC}(S_2(w_2), C_{3,s})) = \frac{1}{2}$. ∎

---

[2] The average sojourn time of a term is the inverse of the sum of the weights of the actions enabled by the term.

3.3 Preorder Definition

We are now in a position to define two families of client-specific probabilistic testing preorders – one for the time-abstract case and one for the continuous-time case – which can be used by the clients to order the services on the basis of the QoS levels resulting from the interaction with them. This is helpful from the client viewpoint to select the service providing the best performance guarantees.

Definition 5. *Let $S_1, S_2 \in \mathcal{P}$ and $C \in \mathcal{P}_s$. We say that S_1 is probabilistic testing less than S_2 with respect to C in the time-abstract case, written $S_1 \sqsubseteq^C_{\mathrm{PT,ta}} S_2$, iff:*
$$prob(\mathcal{SC}(S_1, C)) \leq prob(\mathcal{SC}(S_2, C))$$
∎

Definition 6. *Let $S_1, S_2 \in \mathcal{P}$ and $C \in \mathcal{P}_s$. Assume a continuous-time interpretation for all the generative weights occurring in S_1, S_2, and C. We say that S_1 is probabilistic testing less than S_2 with respect to C in the continuous-time case, written $S_1 \sqsubseteq^C_{\mathrm{PT,ct}} S_2$, iff for all $\theta \in (\mathbf{R}_{>0})^*$:*
$$prob(\mathcal{SC}_{\leq\theta}(S_1, C)) \leq prob(\mathcal{SC}_{\leq\theta}(S_2, C))$$
∎

3.4 Precongruence Property

We conclude by proving that the two families of client-specific probabilistic testing preorders are precongruences with respect to the operators of WPC. The result will be presented for the time-abstract case only, as in the continuous-time case it is similar.

As far as action prefix is concerned, the result is formulated in a non-standard way. The reason is that we do not have to do with a standard testing preorder with universal quantification over all tests, but with a family of client-specific testing preorders. Thus, whenever two interaction systems $S_1 \parallel C$ and $S_2 \parallel C$ perform a transition that causes C to evolve to C', the two derivative interaction systems can no longer be compared with respect to C, but have to be compared with respect to C'.

In the following, we denote by $C \stackrel{p}{\Longrightarrow} C'$ the fact that client C can evolve to C' with probability p after executing a finite sequence of zero or more invisible transitions. The probability p is computed as a product of ratios, each of which relates to an invisible transition in the sequence and is given by the weight of the transition itself divided by the sum of the weights of all the invisible transitions departing from the source state of the considered transition. In the case in which $C' = C$, we let $p = 1$.

Theorem 1. *Let $S_1, S_2 \in \mathcal{P}$ and $C \in \mathcal{P}_s$. Whenever for all $C \stackrel{p_i}{\Longrightarrow} C_i \stackrel{b,*u_{i,j}}{\longrightarrow} C_{i,j}$ it holds $S_1 \sqsubseteq^{C_{i,j}}_{\mathrm{PT,ta}} S_2$, then $<b,w>.S_1 \sqsubseteq^C_{\mathrm{PT,ta}} <b,w>.S_2$ for all $b \neq \tau$ and $w \in \mathbf{R}_{>0}$.*
∎

Theorem 2. *Let $S_1, S_2 \in \mathcal{P}$ and $C \in \mathcal{P}_s$. Whenever for all $C \stackrel{p_i}{\Longrightarrow} C_i \stackrel{b,w_{i,j}}{\longrightarrow} C_{i,j}$ it holds $S_1 \sqsubseteq^{C_{i,j}}_{\mathrm{PT,ta}} S_2$, then $<b,*_u>.S_1 \sqsubseteq^C_{\mathrm{PT,ta}} <b,*_u>.S_2$ for all $b \neq \tau$ and $u \in \mathbf{R}_{>0}$.*
∎

Theorem 3. *Let $S_1, S_2 \in \mathcal{P}$ and $C \in \mathcal{P}_s$. Whenever for all $C \xLongrightarrow{p_i} C_i$ it holds $S_1 \sqsubseteq_{PT,ta}^{C_i} S_2$, then $<\tau, w>.S_1 \sqsubseteq_{PT,ta}^{C} <\tau, w>.S_2$ for all $w \in \mathbf{R}_{>0}$.* ∎

In the case of the alternative composition, precongruence is achieved only for pairs of interaction systems satisfying certain weight-related constraints. More precisely, such constraints are concerned with the total active weight of a service S when evolving locally or interacting with a client C:

$$W_s(S, C) = \sum_{S \xrightarrow{a,w} S'} \{\!\vert\, w \mid a = \tau \vee \exists u, C'. C \xrightarrow{a, *_u} C' \,\vert\!\}$$

and with the total active weight of a client C when interacting with a service S alternative to another service R:

$$W_c(C, S, R) = \sum_{C \xrightarrow{b,w} C'} \{\!\vert\, w \cdot \frac{weight_p(S,b)}{weight_p(S,b) + weight_p(R,b)} \mid \exists u, S'. S \xrightarrow{b, *_u} S' \,\vert\!\}$$

Theorem 4. *Let $S_1, S_2 \in \mathcal{P}$ and $C \in \mathcal{P}_s$. Whenever for all $C \xLongrightarrow{p_i} C_i$ it holds $S_1 \sqsubseteq_{PT,ta}^{C_i} S_2$ with $W_s(S_1, C_i) = W_s(S_2, C_i)$ and $weight_p(S_1, b) = weight_p(S_2, b)$ for all $b \neq \tau$ such that C_i enables an active b-action, then $S_1 + S \sqsubseteq_{PT,ta}^{C} S_2 + S$ and $S + S_1 \sqsubseteq_{PT,ta}^{C} S + S_2$ for all $S \in \mathcal{P}$.* ∎

The constraint "$W_s(S_1, C_i) = W_s(S_2, C_i)$" is strictly necessary to achieve precongruence with respect to alternative composition. Consider e.g. the following terms:

$$S_1 = <a, 40>.\underline{0} + <b, 60>.\underline{0}$$
$$S_2 = <a, 5>.\underline{0} + <b, 5>.\underline{0}$$
$$S = <a, 1>.\underline{0} + <b, 9>.\underline{0}$$
$$C = <a, *_1>.s + <b, *_1>.\underline{0}$$

where the only invisible transition sequence of the client is $C \xLongrightarrow{1} C$ with:

$$W_s(S_1, C) = 40 + 60 = 100 \neq 10 = 5 + 5 = W_s(S_2, C)$$

Then we have:

$$prob(\mathcal{SC}(S_1, C)) = \tfrac{40}{100} = 0.4 < 0.5 = \tfrac{5}{10} = prob(\mathcal{SC}(S_2, C))$$

but:

$$prob(\mathcal{SC}(S_1 + S, C)) = \tfrac{40}{110} + \tfrac{1}{110} \approx 0.37 > 0.3 = \tfrac{5}{20} + \tfrac{1}{20} = prob(\mathcal{SC}(S_2 + S, C))$$

Similarly, the constraint "$weight_p(S_1, b) = weight_p(S_2, b)$ for all $b \neq \tau$ such that C_i enables an active b-action" is strictly necessary. Consider e.g. the following terms:

$$S_1 = <a, 4>.\underline{0} + <b, 6>.\underline{0} + <c, *_1>.\underline{0}$$
$$S_2 = <a, 5>.\underline{0} + <b, 5>.\underline{0} + <c, *_{50}>.\underline{0}$$
$$S = <c, *_{55}>.<d, *_1>.\underline{0}$$
$$C = <a, *_1>.s + <b, *_1>.\underline{0} + <c, 10>.<d, 10>.s$$

where the only invisible transition sequence of the client is $C \stackrel{1}{\Longrightarrow} C$ with:

$$W_{\mathrm{s}}(S_1, C) = 4 + 6 = 10 = 5 + 5 = W_{\mathrm{s}}(S_2, C)$$

and:

$$weight_{\mathrm{p}}(S_1, c) = 1 \neq 50 = weight_{\mathrm{p}}(S_2, c)$$

Then we have:

$$prob(\mathcal{SC}(S_1, C)) = \tfrac{4}{20} = 0.2 < 0.25 = \tfrac{5}{20} = prob(\mathcal{SC}(S_2, C))$$

but:

$$prob(\mathcal{SC}(S_1 + S, C)) = \tfrac{4}{20} + \tfrac{10}{20} \cdot \tfrac{55}{56} \approx 0.69 >$$
$$> 0.51 \approx \tfrac{5}{20} + \tfrac{10}{20} \cdot \tfrac{55}{105} = prob(\mathcal{SC}(S_2 + S, C))$$

4 Compatibility Verification

The selection of the service providing the best performance guarantees for a client has to be preceded by a phase during which the client searches the Web service registry for all the services that are compatible with it. Such services are the ones that ensure the complete satisfaction of the client request.

Compatibility is a functional property that can be verified with the time-abstract family of client-specific probabilistic testing preorders. The first step consists of building a canonical service that ensures the termination of the client along each of its branches. The second step consists of searching the Web service registry for all the services that – with respect to a variant of the client in which all of its terminal states are made successful – are not less than the canonical service. In other words, the canonical service is the search key for the Web service registry of the considered client.

The canonical service is formalized as the dual of the client, which is obtained from the client by making passive (resp. active) all of its observable active (resp. passive) actions, by eliminating all of its invisible actions, and by changing to $\underline{0}$ all of its successful terminal states. All the generative and reactive weights occurring in the dual are set to 1, as their values are unimportant for the sake of termination. In the following we denote by $obs(C)$ the fact that at least one observable action occurs inside client C.

Definition 7. *Let $S \in \mathcal{P}$, $C \in \mathcal{P}_{\mathrm{s}}$, and C_{s} be the everywhere-successful variant of C. We say that S is* compatible *with C iff:*

$$prob(\mathcal{SC}(S, C_{\mathrm{s}})) = 1 \qquad\qquad \blacksquare$$

Definition 8. *Let $C \in \mathcal{P}_{\mathrm{s}}$. The* dual *of C is defined by induction on the syntactical structure of C as follows:*

$dual(\underline{0}) = \underline{0}$
$dual(\mathrm{s}) = \underline{0}$
$dual(\sum_{i \in I} <b_i, *_{u_i}>.C_i + \sum_{j \in J} <b_j, w_j>.C_j + \sum_{k \in K} <\tau, w_k>.C_k) =$
$\qquad = \sum_{i \in I} <b_i, 1>.dual(C_i) + \sum_{j \in J} <b_j, *_1>.dual(C_j) + \sum_{k \in K, obs(C_k)} dual(C_k)$

where: $b_j \neq \tau$ for $j \in J$; I, J, and K are pairwise disjoint with $I \cup J \cup K$ finite and non-empty; the term on the right-hand side of the last clause is $\underline{0}$ if all the three index sets are empty. ∎

Lemma 1. *Let $C \in \mathcal{P}_s$. Whenever $dual(C)$ is deterministic, then $dual(C) \parallel C_s$ has as many maximal computations as C_s and all of them are successful.* ∎

Note that the determinism of $dual(C)$ is essential. Consider e.g. the following pair composed of a client and its dual:

$$C = <\tau, 1>.<a, 1>.<b, 1>.\underline{0} + <\tau, 1>.<a, 1>.<c, 1>.\underline{0}$$
$$dual(C) = <a, *_1>.<b, *_1>.\underline{0} + <a, *_1>.<c, *_1>.\underline{0}$$

Then $dual(C) \parallel C_s$ deadlocks after the interaction of the first (resp. second) passive a-action of $dual(C)$ with the second (resp. first) active a-action of C_s.

Theorem 5. *Let $S \in \mathcal{P}$ and $C \in \mathcal{P}_s$. Whenever $dual(C)$ is deterministic and $dual(C) \sqsubseteq_{PT,ta}^{C_s} S$, then S is compatible with C.* ∎

Example 3. Consider the three clients whose everywhere-successful variants are shown in Ex. 2. In order to check the compatibility of these clients with respect to the services defined in Ex. 1 we have to compute their dual contracts:

$$dual(C_1) = <gcd, *_1>.<op1, *_1>.<op2, *_1>.<res, 1>.<end, 1>.\underline{0}$$
$$dual(C_2) = <sqrt, *_1>.<op, *_1>.(<res, 1>.<end, 1>.\underline{0} + <error, 1>.\underline{0})$$
$$dual(C_3) = <sqrt, *_1>.<op, *_1>.<res, 1>.<end, 1>.\underline{0}$$

Now we have that:

$$\mathcal{SC}(dual(C_2), C_{2,s}) = \{ \, dual(C_2) \parallel C_{2,s} \xrightarrow{sqrt,1} \cdot \xrightarrow{op,1} \cdot \xrightarrow{res,1} \cdot \xrightarrow{end,1} \underline{0} \parallel s,$$
$$dual(C_2) \parallel C_{2,s} \xrightarrow{sqrt,1} \cdot \xrightarrow{op,1} \cdot \xrightarrow{error,1} \underline{0} \parallel s\}$$

hence:

$$1 = prob(\mathcal{SC}(dual(C_2), C_{2,s})) \leq prob(\mathcal{SC}(S_2(w_2), C_{2,s}) = 1$$

that is:

$$dual(C_2) \sqsubseteq_{PT,ta}^{C_{2,s}} S_2(w_2)$$

from which we conclude that service $S_2(w_2)$ is compatible with client C_2. On the other hand:

$$\mathcal{SC}(dual(C_3), C_{3,s}) = \{ dual(C_3) \parallel C_{3,s} \xrightarrow{sqrt,1} \cdot \xrightarrow{op,1} \cdot \xrightarrow{res,1} \cdot \xrightarrow{end,1} \underline{0} \parallel s\}$$

and

$$\tfrac{1}{2} = prob(\mathcal{SC}(S_2(w_2), C_{3,s})) < prob(\mathcal{SC}(dual(C_3), C_{3,s})) = 1$$

that is service $S_2(w_2)$ is *not* compatible with client C_3. Indeed, the client C_3 blindly assumes that the service always completes the operation successfully, but this assumption may prove fatal if the service proposes an **error** action. By similar arguments, it is easy to verify that $S_1(w_1)$ is compatible with C_1, and that $S_1(w_1) + S_2(w_2)$ is compatible with both C_1 and C_2. ∎

5 Selecting the Best Compatible Service

While the time-abstract family of client-specific probabilistic testing preorders allows us to reason about the probability that a client interacts with a service following a given computation, the family of continuous-time preorders allows us to reason about the average duration of any of such computations. In this section we present a few examples that show how the continuous-time preorders can be used to sort compatible services according to their performance, and we stress the importance of the client's contract in the selection of the best service.

Example 4. We have seen that $S_1(w_1) + S_2(w_2)$ is compatible with C_2. Consider now the following variant of C_2:

$$C_2' = \texttt{<sqrt,}1\texttt{>.<op,}1\texttt{>.(<res,}*_1\texttt{>.<end,}*_1\texttt{>.s} + \texttt{<error,}*_1\texttt{>.}\underline{0})$$

Then, for all $c \in \mathcal{SC}(S_1(w_1) + S_2(w_2), C_2')$, we have:

$$time(c) = 1 \circ 1 \circ \tfrac{1}{2} \circ \tfrac{1}{w_2} \circ 1$$

from which we notice that greater values for the parameter w_2 guarantee smaller interaction times with the service. ∎

Example 5. Observed that for all $c \in \mathcal{SC}(S_1(w_1) + S_2(w_2), C_{1,s})$ we have:

$$time(c) = 1 \circ 1 \circ 1 \circ \tfrac{1}{w_1} \circ 1$$

it is easy to find w_1', w_2', w_1'', w_2'' such that:

$$S_1(w_1') + S_2(w_2') \sqsubseteq_{\mathrm{PT,ct}}^{C_2'} S_1(w_1'') + S_2(w_2'')$$

and:

$$S_1(w_1'') + S_2(w_2'') \sqsubseteq_{\mathrm{PT,ct}}^{C_{1,s}} S_1(w_1') + S_2(w_2')$$

that is, the relative ordering between services may depend upon clients. This example shows that the usual probabilistic testing preorder, with universal quantification over all the tests, is not suitable to be used in our framework for selecting the best service. ∎

Example 6. In previous work that relate the contracts of different services [7,8,16], services are typically ordered according to their ability of guaranteeing the termination of the client. In our framework such a relation can be roughly stated as follows (recall that C_s is the everywhere-successful variant of C, see Def. 7):

$$S \preceq S' \quad \text{iff} \quad \forall C. prob(\mathcal{SC}(S, C_s)) = 1 \Rightarrow prob(\mathcal{SC}(S', C_s)) = 1$$

meaning that the set of clients that S is compatible with is a subset of the set of clients that S' is compatible with. If we consider a service whose contract is:

$$S_3 = \texttt{<sqrt,}*_1\texttt{>.<real,}*_1\texttt{>.<error,}1\texttt{>.}\underline{0}$$

we can state, for instance, that $S_2(w_2) \preceq S_3$. Indeed, a client that successfully terminates when interacting with $S_2(w_2)$ must take into account *all* of the possible behaviors of $S_2(w_2)$. Since, roughly speaking, contract S_3 is "more deterministic" than $S_2(w_2)$, a client that successfully terminates when interacting with $S_2(w_2)$ does so also when interacting with S_3. However, it is hardly the case that S_3 can be considered "better" than $S_2(w_2)$, as it simply reports a failure regardless of the client's input. While $\preceq$ makes sense from a purely functional point of view (client termination is guaranteed if $S_2(w_2)$ is replaced by S_3) it makes little sense when QoS aspects are taken into account. By appropriately placing the "s" operator in the client's contract, both abstract-time and continuous-time preorder families can be used for sorting services according to the client's expectations (obtaining a result rather than an exception).   ■

6   Conclusion

In this paper we have presented a technique for using a simple weighted process calculus to reason about the compatibility and the performance of services with respect to potential clients. The technique is directly related to and extends previous work on contracts [7,8] and session types [16]. On the practical side, one contribution of the paper is to provide a formal foundation that subsumes and refines existing mechanisms for specifying and assessing QoS aspects of Web services, by associating performance parameters with the single actions occurring during the conversation between a client and a service, rather than with the service as a whole. On the theoretical side, we have provided a motivation for the study of test-specific relations, which do not collapse into equivalences. This allows us to use such relations for ordering services in non-trivial ways according to a specific client's expectations, so as to maximize the client's satisfaction.

There are several directions for further investigations, we mention three of them. First, the weighted process calculus presented in this paper can be extended with a recursion operator, so as to make the language suitable for modeling more realistic scenarios where clients and services perform arbitrarily long interactions adhering to some regular pattern. It is reasonable to expect that this extension does not significantly affect the theory developed so far, and that the results proved in the finite case still hold once the usual annoyances deriving from recursion (such as divergence) have been appropriately taken care of.

Second, the notion of dual contract that we have formalized in Sect. 4 only provides a sufficient condition that guarantees the termination of a client when interacting with a service, however there is strong evidence that this notion can be relaxed. Since the dual contract is used as a search key in a Web service registry, it is desirable to find the *smallest* (or *principal*) key so as to maximize the number of services that are found to be greater than or equal to the key, according to the time-abstract preorder.

Third, we have not taken into account any aspect concerning the *composition* of Web services. Because of their very nature, it is often the case that several Web services have to be assembled together to accomplish a given task. Hence, it is interesting to investigate whether (some variant of) the weighted process calculus presented in this paper is suitable to reason about QoS aspects of compound services. In this respect, the fact that the probabilistic testing pre-orders happen to be precongruences with respect to the operators of the process calculus (action prefix and alternative composition) is particularly important, as this property guarantees that the substitution of a component service with another providing better performance does not compromise the performance of the compound service as a whole.

References

1. Banerji, A., Bartolini, C., Beringer, D., Chopella, V., et al.: Web Services Conversation Language (wscl) 1.0", 2002. http://www.w3.org/TR/2002/NOTE-wscl10-20020314 (2002)
2. Beringer, D., Kuno, H., Lemon, M.: Using wscl in a uddi Registry 1.0, UDDI Working Draft Best Practices Document, 2001. http://xml.coverpages.org/HP-UDDI-wscl-5-16-01.pdf (2001)
3. Bernardo, M., Bravetti, M.: Performance Measure Sensitive Congruences for Markovian Process Algebras". Theoretical Computer Science 290, 117–160 (2003)
4. Bernardo, M., Cleaveland, R.: "A Theory of Testing for Markovian Processes. In: Palamidessi, C. (ed.) CONCUR 2000, LNCS, vol. 1877, pp. 305–319. Springer, Heidelberg (2000)
5. Booth, D., Liu, C.K.: Web Services Description Language wsdl Version 2.0 Part 0: Primer, 2006. http://www.w3.org/TR/2006/CR-wsdl20-primer-20060327 (2006)
6. Bravetti, M., Aldini, A.: Discrete Time Generative-Reactive Probabilistic Processes with Different Advancing Speeds". Theoretical Computer Science 290, 355–406 (2003)
7. Carpineti, S., Castagna, G., Laneve, C., Padovani, L.: "A Formal Account of Contracts for Web Services". In: Bravetti, M., Núñez, M., Zavattaro, G. (eds.) WS-FM 2006, LNCS, vol. 4184, pp. 148–162. Springer, Heidelberg (2006)
8. Castagna, G., Gesbert, N., Padovani, L.: A Theory of Contracts for Web Services. In: Proc. of the 5th ACM SIGPLAN Workshop on Programming Language Technologies for XML (PLAN-X 2007), pp. 37–49. ACM Press, New York (2007)
9. Chinnici, R., Haas, H., Lewis, A.A., Moreau, J.-J., et al.: Web Services Description Language (wsdl) Version 2.0 Part 2: Adjuncts, 2006. http://www.w3.org/TR/2006/CR-wsdl20-adjuncts-20060327 (2006)
10. Chinnici, R., Moreau, J.-J., Ryman, A., Weerawarana, S.: Web Services Description Language (wsdl) Version 2.0 Part 1: Core Language 2006. http://www.w3.org/TR/2006/CR-wsdl20-20060327 (2006)
11. Christensen, E., Curbera, F., Meredith, G., Weerawarana, S.: Web Services Description Language (wsdl) 1.1, 2001. http://www.w3.org/TR/2001/NOTE-wsdl-20010315 (2001)
12. Cleaveland, R., Dayar, Z., Smolka, S.A., Yuen, S.: Testing Preorders for Probabilistic Processes. Information and Computation 154, 93–148 (1999)
13. Colgrave, J., Januszewski, K.: Using wsdl in a uddi Registry, technical note, 2004. http://www.oasis-open.org/committees/uddi-spec/doc/tn/uddi-spec-tc-tn-wsdl-v2.htm (2004)
14. de Nicola, R., Hennessy, M.: Testing Equivalences for Processes. in Theoretical Computer Science 34, 83–133 (1983)
15. Dustdar, S., Schreiner, W.: A Survey on Web Services Composition. International Journal of Web. and Grid Services 1, 1–30 (2005)

16. Gay, S., Hole, M.: Subtyping for Session Types in the π-calculus. Acta Informatica 42, 191–225 (2005)
17. Van Glabbeek, R.J., Smolka, S.A., Steffen, B.: Reactive, Generative and Stratified Models of Probabilistic Processes. Information and Computation 121, 59–80 (1995)
18. Ran, S.: A Model for Web Services Discovery with QoS. ACM SIGecom Exchanges 4, 1–10 (2003)
19. Stewart, W.J.: Introduction to the Numerical Solution of Markov Chains. Princeton University Press, Princeton (1994)

A Probabilistic Formal Analysis Approach to Cross Layer Optimization in Distributed Embedded Systems[*]

Minyoung Kim[1], Mark-Oliver Stehr[2], Carolyn Talcott[2],
Nikil Dutt[1], and Nalini Venkatasubramanian[1]

[1] University of California, Irvine, USA
{minyounk,dutt,nalini}@ics.uci.edu
[2] SRI International, USA
{stehr,clt}@csl.sri.com

Abstract. We present a novel approach, based on probabilistic formal methods, to developing cross-layer resource optimization policies for resource limited distributed systems. One objective of this approach is to enable system designers to analyze designs in order to study design tradeoffs and predict the possible property violations as the system evolves dynamically over time. Specifically, an executable formal specification is developed for each layer under consideration (for example, application, middleware, operating system). The formal specification is then analyzed using statistical model checking and statistical quantitative analysis, to determine the impact of various resource management policies for achieving desired end-to-end QoS properties. We describe how existing statistical approaches have been adapted and improved to provide analyses of given cross-layered optimization policies with quantifiable confidence. The ideas are tested in a multi-mode multi-media case study. Experiments from both theoretical analysis and Monte-Carlo simulation followed by statistical analyses demonstrate the applicability of this approach to the design of resource-limited distributed systems.

Keywords: Probabilistic Formal Methods, Statistical Analysis, Cross-layer Optimization, Resource Management.

1 Introduction

The next generation of distributed applications will be built around massive scale distributed environments with heterogeneous systems (servers, desktops, mobile devices, sensors, wireless access points, routers, etc.) and networks (WLAN, LAN, WAN, etc.). Such networked applications span multiple domains ranging from mission critical applications for military command/control and disaster response to general purpose end-user applications including education, entertainment, and commerce. An overarching characteristic of these applications are that

---

[*] This work was partially supported by NSF award CNS-0615438 and CNS-0615436.

M.M. Bonsangue and E.B. Johnsen (Eds.): FMOODS 2007, LNCS 4468, pp. 285–300, 2007.

they are often data intensive and rich in multimedia content with images, GIS (Geographical Information Systems)-based satellite imagery, video and audio data that is fused together from disparate distributed information sources. The content-rich data are expected to be obtained from, delivered to and processed on resource-constrained devices (sensors, PDAs, cellular handsets) carried by users in the distributed network. The dual goals of ensuring adequate application QoS (expressed as timeliness, reliability and accuracy) and ensuring optimal resource utilization at all levels of the system presents significant challenges in system design.

A holistic approach to understanding timing in such systems is essential for several reasons. Firstly, applications are often confronted with end-to-end hard or soft real-time needs. Secondly, existing techniques for timing analysis do not account for the spectrum of granularities of timing which can vary by orders of magnitude across layers. Thirdly, several system level optimizations for effective utilization of distributed resources can interfere with the timing properties of executing applications. For instance, dynamic voltage scaling mechanisms slow down processors to achieve power-savings but at the cost of increased execution times for tasks. Also, knowledge of timing parameters at the different levels can dramatically improve the performance of applications that often execute in constrained environments where CPU, memory, network and device energy is limited.

Our prior experience developing algorithms for managing QoS/power trade-offs in distributed mobile multimedia applications [1,2] has given us valuable insights into the issues to be addressed. A preliminary study [3] demonstrated the need for integration of formal methods with experimentally based cross-layer optimization methods [1,2]. Systematic analysis based on well-defined models ensures that corner-cases are covered and allows bounds for critical performance parameters to be determined. Our long term goal is to develop a formal methodology to specify and analyze timing constraints at each level, and to correlate timing properties across levels. Furthermore, the formal analyses will be integrated with simulation and experimental methods for developing and adapting system designs. Multimedia applications operated on battery-powered mobile devices are viewed as one of the key application drivers for these next generation distributed systems. Such mobile multimedia applications provide a rich set of QoS/power issues at multiple abstraction levels. Thus, although we intend our approach to be widely applicable, we begin by developing and evaluating formal specification models in the context of distributed multimedia applications.

Our approach is to start with an executable formal model specifying a space of possible behaviors and analyze these possible behaviors using probabilistic/statistical techniques, paying attention to the mathematical meaning of the results. We use the Maude [4] rewriting logic formalism to develop executable specifications that are the basis for subsequent analysis. We have developed two *probabilistic formal* analysis techniques: statistical model checking and statistical quantitative analysis. These analysis results enable policy-based operation and adaptation as well as parameter setting of selected policies.

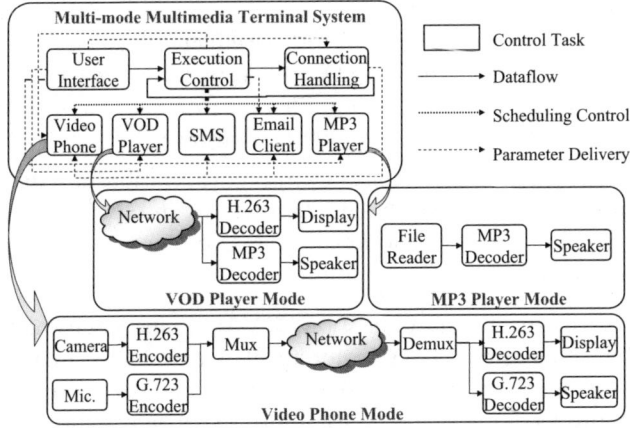

Fig. 1. Case Study: MMMT (Multi-Mode Multimedia Terminal)

This paper contains the following contributions:

- a first attempt to integrate *probabilistic formal* methods with cross-layer optimization;
- adaptation and improvement of existing statistical approaches for statistical model-checking and statistical quantitative analysis;
- modeling, simulation and analysis of a fairly complex system.

The rest of this paper is organized as follows: we start by presenting a multi-mode multimedia communication system as a case study. Next, we describe the modeling effort and specification details of our case study. We then introduce our formal analysis beginning with a brief review of theory, followed by our implementation and experimental results. The last section summarizes our approach and discusses future research directions.

2 Case Study: Multi-Mode Multimedia Terminal

Figure 1 shows an example of a multi-mode multimedia terminal (MMMT) system [5] that we are using as a research vehicle. The figure depicts a hierarchical composition of tasks within the MMMT system. At the top level, three types of hierarchical tasks are defined to specify each mode of operation: soft real-time (a videophone, a VoD player, an MP3 player), event-driven (email client), and time-critical emergency messaging (SMS-Short Message Services). Three other tasks are also specified at the top level for user interface, connection handling, and task execution control. In addition, each mode of operation consists of multiple tasks as shown in the figure. This type of application requires frequent task set changes based on user input and/or node/network conditions (e.g., residual power level, packet drop rate, noise level, etc.). As an example, a high-end videophone mode would be able to better meet its timing constraints at maximum

CPU performance while receiving packets via a reliable channel. However, if residual power level dropped or packet loss rate increased significantly, then we might need to save energy by reducing QoS or suspending some tasks. A user also can explicitly change modes and assign different priorities for each task/mode.

We distinguish between two types of optimizations:

- vertical composition, which depicts QoS/energy relationships in a single task, but across several *vertical* layers of abstraction, and
- horizontal composition, which depicts the QoS/energy relationships across multiple tasks in a dynamic environment

In the context of our driver application (MMMT), vertical composition needs to address the application's QoS requirement across layers in the context of resource management constraints. On the other hand, horizontal composition addresses QoS properties between multiple tasks that may be assigned priorities dynamically based on QoS and resource constraints. In this paper, we restrict our discussion to the videophone mode. Horizontal extension for a complete MMMT system remains a topic of future research.

The resource management policies that are used in the different layers include: a specific video encoding/decoding algorithm at the application layer; network monitoring at the middleware layer; DPM (Dynamic Power Management) and/or DVS (Dynamic Voltage Scaling)[1] at the OS layer [6]. Network traffic shaping and/or trans-coding at the middleware layer can be also utilized. Each policy has parameters that can be used to fine-tune the behavior. In addition, there are hardware parameters that can be set.

For instance, we consider *proactive* PBPAIR (Probability Based Power Aware Intra Refresh) [7] as an application layer policy. The *PBPAIR* scheme inserts intra-coding (i.e., coding without reference to any other frame) to enhance the robustness of the encoded bitstream at the cost of compression efficiency. Intra-coding improves error resilience, but it also contributes to reducing encoding energy consumption since it does not require motion estimation[2] (which is the most power consuming operation in a predictive video compression algorithm). The additional *proactive* feature means that we have a priori information on the user's mobility (e.g., current zone, speed and trajectory, etc.) and network situation (e.g., packet loss rate, delay, etc.) that later will be used for selection among policies and related parameter tuning before the user enters a new zone. If PBPAIR is selected as an application layer policy, then algorithm-specific parameters such as *Intra threshold* value must be chosen for appropriate execution. Note that the parameter selection at one layer affects other layers. For example, PBPAIR increases intra-coding by lowering the *Intra threshold* parameter

---

[1] DPM puts a device into a low power/performance state to save energy when the device is not serving any request during a suitably long time-period determined by the shutdown and wakeup overhead of the device. DVS aims at saving energy by scaling down the supply voltage and frequency when the system is not fully loaded.

[2] In predictive coding, motion estimation eliminates the temporal redundancy due to high correlation between consecutive frames by examining the movement of objects in an image sequence to try to obtain vectors representing the estimated motion.

when there is high network packet loss (monitored at middleware layer), which impacts DVS decision at OS layer since the execution profile of the application is changed.

3 Formal Modeling and Analysis for Cross Layer Optimization

3.1 What to Model

In this subsection, we explain which features of the MMMT case study will be formally modeled at each layer.

- **Application Layer - Proactive PBPAIR:** As an application policy, we utilize proactive PBPAIR. It takes the user's QoS expectation, the network packet loss rate, and raw video sequences as inputs to generate a bitstream robustly encoded against network transmission errors. Therefore, our formal specification needs to generate the execution profile (e.g., when does encoding start/end? how much time is required?). Particularly, we specify an encoding workload profile as a distribution function. For example, we model actual execution time by a uniform distribution between best case execution time (BCET) and worst case execution time (WCET). We also consider a Gaussian distribution with the average and boundary value.
- **Middleware Layer - Network Monitoring:** As briefly mentioned, the middleware layer deals with network status monitoring. We define mobility as a triple *(current zone, speed, trajectory)* to identify the network situation in the current zone and to anticipate the next zone based on user's speed and trajectory. Zone information includes network delay, packet drop rate within the particular zone. Specifically, network transmission delay is modeled as exponential inter-arrival time (Poisson) with mean.
- **OS Layer - Power Management:** Various DPM and DVS power management schemes assuming a worst-case scenario are modeled at the OS layer. The OS layer generates slack time information based on workload from the application layer. This slack time will be used later to reduce energy consumption while guaranteeing QoS requirements for the next frame. Since we are targeting multitask environments, we need to specify various scheduling algorithms (for horizontal composition) like EDF (Earliest Deadline First) and RM (Rate Monotonic).
- **Hardware Layer - Enabling Technology:** To support a DPM and DVS strategy at the OS layer, we assume that the enabling technology (e.g., voltage scalable processor, power-state controllable network card, etc.) is available at hardware layer. In the case of a micro-processor, wakeup/sleep delay and power overhead for a state transition, DVS characteristics (i.e., power consumption for different operating mode/voltage-frequency) should be modeled. As a result of execution, the hardware layer reports residual energy to upper layers.

3.2 Modeling Using Maude

Our formal modeling approach utilizes Maude [8] to formally specify the environmental changes as well as the policies/parameter settings that can be made at each of these levels in isolation and for the combined layers. Maude is a specification language based on rewriting logic with supporting analysis tools. The Maude system has been used in the specification and analysis of a wide range of logics, languages, architectures and distributed systems [9,4].

Rewriting logic [10] is a simple logic well-suited for distributed system specification. The state space of a distributed system is formally specified as an algebraic data type by giving a set of sorts (types), operations, and equations. The dynamics of such a distributed system is then specified by rewrite rules of the form

$$t \to t' \ \text{ if } c$$

where t, t' are terms (patterns) that describe the local, concurrent transitions possible in the system, and c is a condition constraining the application of the rule. Specifically, when a part of the distributed state matches the pattern t, and satisfies c, then this part can change to a new local state t'. Rewriting logic specifications are executable, as proofs in rewriting logic are carried out by applying rewrite rules which can also be viewed as steps of a computation.

The Maude system is based on a very efficient rewriting engine, supporting use of executable models as prototypes. It also provides the capability to search the state space reachable from some initial state by the application of rewrite rules. This can be used to find reachable states satisfying a user-defined property. The system also includes an efficient model-checker for checking properties expressed in linear temporal logic. The Maude system, its documentation, and related papers and applications are available from the Maude website `http://maude.cs.uiuc.edu`.

In the object-oriented specification style supported by Maude, the system state (configuration) is typically represented as a multiset of objects and messages. Passage of time is modeled by functions that update the configuration appropriately, for example decrementing timers or decreasing remaining power. Rules can either be instantaneous or tick rules of the form

$$C \to delta(C, T) \ in \ time \ T \ \ \text{if } T \le mte(C)$$

where C is a term representing the system configuration. This tick rule advances time non-deterministically, according to a chosen time sampling strategy, by a time T less than or equal to $mte(C)$, the maximal time allowed to elapse in one step, in configuration C, and alters the system state, C, using the function $delta$[3]. Both $delta$ and mte are user-defined to capture how time passes in a particular model.

Figure 2 shows a PBPAIR object in the Maude specification for the application layer. In Maude syntax, objects have the general form

$$< ObjectName : ClassName \mid Attribute_1 : Value_1, ..., Attribute_n : Value_n >$$

---

[3] The idea of a tick rule is taken from Real-Time Maude [11].

```
*** Variables
  vars initWCETProfile initBCETProfile : Map .
  vars T T' : Nat .
  vars I I' Q TH miss cm cmc cmm lost lm clc clm : Int .

*** Object
< PBPAIR : Application |
  WCET : initWCETProfile,          *** worst case execution time
  BCET : initBCETProfile,          *** best case execution time
  accEncTime : T,                  *** accumulated encoding time
  seqN : I,                        *** sequence number
  Timer : T',                      *** next frame arrival time
  IntraTh : TH,                    *** intra threshold (parameter)
  Qsize : Q,                       *** encoding queue size
  bufferedReq : I',                *** buffered frame (initialized as ½ × Qsize)
  deadlineMiss : miss,             *** total number of deadline misses
  consecutiveMiss : cm,            *** current consecutive deadline misses
  consecutiveMissCount : cmc,      *** incidence of consecutive deadline miss
  consecutiveMissMax : cmm,        *** maximum consecutive deadline miss
  lostReq : lost,                  *** total number of lost requests
  consecutiveLost : cl,            *** current consecutive lost requests
  consecutiveLostCount : clc,      *** incidence of consecutive lost request
  consecutiveLostMax : clm,        *** maximum consecutive lost request
>
```

Fig. 2. Maude Specification: Application Layer

```
*** Property checker
  op batteryExpires : Configuration → Bool .
  eq batteryExpires(< CPU : HW | residualEnergy : F, atts > C:Configuration)
    = (if (F ≤ 0.0) then true else false fi) .

*** Observer
  msg Obs : Bool → Msg .
  msg EnergyConsumption : Float → Msg .
  msg BatteryExpires : Bool → Msg .

  rl [cpuObs] :
    < CPU : HW | consumedEnergy : F, policy : P, atts >
    ⇒
    EnergyConsumption(F)
    BatteryExpires(batteryExpires(< CPU : HW | consumedEnergy : F, atts >)) .
```

Fig. 3. Maude Specification: Property Checker and Observer

where *ObjectName* is an object identifier, *ClassName* is a class identifier, and each *'Attribute : Value'* pair specifies attribute identifier and its value. The object *PBPAIR* in Figure 2 has attributes like *WCET, BCET* for generating workload profile.

At the end of each execution, we examine the final configuration of a Maude specification that has several objects and messages. From those objects and messages, we need to extract meaningful data – observables. Observables can be

Algorithm 1. Java Foreign Interface for Observables Extraction

```
public static void main (String args[ ])
{
    Maude.initialize("filename.maude");
    mod = Maude.findModule(ModuleName);
    clockedSystem = init(mod, seed);
    conf = extractConfiguration(mod, clockedSystem);
    printObservables(mod, conf);
}
```

properties or values. For example, to check whether the battery expires or not at the end of the execution, we need to check the *residualEnergy* attribute in *CPU* object at hardware layer. If the value for the *residualEnergy* attribute is positive, then the battery does not expire. Otherwise, the *batteryExpires* property returns *true* meaning the system used up the battery. We encode the check of properties into the model so that the result contains *true* or *false* depending on whether a property holds or not. On the other hand, if we want to have the energy consumption rather than the answer for property hold, we can utilize the observer such as the one shown in Figure 3. The observer replaces each object with suitable messages that have data values for the observables. For example, *deadlineMiss* and *lostReq* in Figure 2 are observables for this kind.

Furthermore, we use the Maude API, a foreign language interface to embed the Maude rewriting engine into larger applications, to extract observables from the Maude execution and generate statistics of results. Specifically, we use a Java/Maude interface that calls Maude as a dynamic library. The Algorithm 1 gives a simplified overview of this procedure. At the beginning, the *initialize* function of the API initializes the Maude engine and loads the formal specification. Then *findModule* is used to locate the appropriate module identified by *ModuleName*. Now, the *init* function uses other functions of the Maude API to perform rewriting from a suitable initial configuration until a terminal configuration is reached. A random seed will be embedded in the initial configuration to initialize the random number generator that determines which execution path is selected in the model. The *init* function returns the result of executing the model as a *clockedSystem*. The associated configuration will be used for data extraction by *extractConfiguration*. In summary, the Java interface provides a convenient way to deal with data extraction and subsequent processing.

3.3   Analysis

In this section, we explain two statistical evaluation methods that we implemented: statistical model checking and statistical quantitative analysis. For statistical model checking, probabilistic properties such as "*Probability* that a system can survive with given residual energy in t time units is more than θ %" will be examined. In case of statistical quantitative analysis, we estimate the expected value of certain observables such as "*Average* energy consumption in t time units within confidence interval (δ) and error bound (α)".

Statistical Theory Background and Our Implementation. To evaluate a stochastic system properly, we need to remove non-quantifiable non-determinism [12]. We replace all non-determinism with probabilistic choices and stochastic timed operations in the tick rule[4].

- **Statistical Model Checking:** We use statistical model checking to verify probabilistic properties, more precisely hypothesis testing based on Monte-Carlo simulation results. In hypothesis testing, we test whether the probability p of a property under examination is above or below the threshold θ. We can formulate this as the problem of testing the hypothesis $H : p \geq \theta$ against the alternative hypothesis $K : p < \theta$. Specifically, we implemented two statistical model checking techniques in our framework: *sequential* testing [13] and *black-box* testing [14]. Sequential testing generates sample execution paths until its answer can be guaranteed to be correct within the required error bounds. Black-box testing instead computes a quantitative measure of confidence for given samples. Here, *black-box* means that the system cannot be controlled to generate execution traces, or trajectories, on demand starting from arbitrary states. The implementation of sequential testing and black-box testing can be found as part of the Ymer [15,16] and VeStA [14] tools, respectively.
- **Statistical Quantitative Analysis:** Statistical evaluation can be performed with a large quantity of data that follows a normal distribution, and hence allows the estimation of the expected value and our confidence. To determine the mathematical soundness of the approximation, we perform a Jarque-Bera (JB) normality test [17]. The normality is determined by testing the null hypothesis (that the sample in vector X comes from a normal distribution with unknown mean and variance) against the alternative (that it does not come from a normal distribution). The JB test computes the *p-value* (the smallest level of significance at which a null hypothesis may be rejected) from the JB test statistic and χ^2 (chi-square) distribution. One rejects the null hypothesis if the p-value is smaller than or equal to the significance level α. For example, a p-value=0.05 indicates that the probability of getting a value of test statistics as extreme as or more extreme than that observed is at most 5% if the null hypothesis is actually true. Once normality of the data is ensured with high confidence, for a large enough number of sample traces n, the approximate average falls inside a $(1 - \alpha)100\%$ confidence interval

$$(\bar{x} - Z_{\frac{\alpha}{2},n-1}\frac{s}{\sqrt{n}}, \bar{x} + Z_{\frac{\alpha}{2},n-1}\frac{s}{\sqrt{n}})$$

where $\bar{x}$ is the average of the sample variables, s is samples' standard deviation, and $Z_{\frac{\alpha}{2},n-1}$ is a *standard score* (also called *Z-score* or *normal score*) of normal distribution [18]. To obtain the desired confidence, we want the size of this $(1 - \alpha)100\%$ confidence interval to be less than or equal to δ, that is:

---

[4] Non-determinism that is not probabilistic in nature would require the exploration of all possibilities and is currently not supported in our approach. Hence, we use sufficient conditions similar to those of [12] to guarantee the absence of this form of non-determinism.

Algorithm 2. Statistical Quantitative Analysis

Input: error bound α, confidence interval δ, observable under consideration
Output: Expected value E[observable]
initialize d as a negative number;
while $(d > \delta)$
{
    trace generation until normality test succeeds;
    $d = 2Z_{\frac{\alpha}{2},n-1}\frac{s}{\sqrt{n}}$;
}
return the average of observable;

$$2Z_{\frac{\alpha}{2},n-1}\frac{s}{\sqrt{n}} \leq \delta.$$

Our Focus: Simplified Formulae and On-demand Sample Generation

– **Statistical Model Checking:** We note that both, the Ymer and VeStA tools, target complex properties of stochastic systems. For instance, those tools take properties specified in a temporal logic, namely Continuous Stochastic Logic (CSL), for Continuous Time Markov Chains (CTMC) [19] system specifications. The reason is that they want to support complex property checking, (e.g., nested temporal/probabilistic operators, and also a form of hybrid model checking in-between numerical and statistical methods), even though the idea of hypothesis testing based on Monte-Carlo simulation does not need to be tied to any specific specification model or temporal logic. This can be an overkill when it comes to analyzing practical optimization problems, if we only test simple properties such as *"Probability* that a system can survive with a given residual energy in t time units is more than θ %". Those formulae are essentially a restricted version of CSL without nesting. Indeed we found no need for nested formulae or an exact numerical solution for our application domain.

– **Statistical Quantitative Analysis:** The Pseudocode 2 shows the statistical quantitative analysis algorithm [12]. As we mentioned earlier, to approximate the expected value by the mean of n samples such that the size of (1 - α)100% confidence interval is bounded by δ, the sample data should follow normal distribution [18]. For the normality test, we need to have a sufficiently large data set. Since the trace generation takes most of the evaluation time, we generate sample traces only if more samples are required (i.e., JB test cannot accept or reject the normality of data.)[5]. By generating traces on demand, we can significantly reduce the evaluation time since it is linearly proportional to the trace generation time (i.e., Monte-Carlo simulation time with a different seed).

4   Experiments

To demonstrate the applicability of our framework to the QoS/energy tradeoff management, we are exploring several aspects of the system optimization. Our

---

[5] Besides, we use the average value from the randomly chosen traces. This random selection may affect the normality test. However, we believe the effect is negligible.

formal executable specification (Maude) and evaluation method can serve as a simulation study as well as a statistical guarantee for the design. The outcome of the formal analysis helps us determine the right blend of policies/parameter settings that will enable better QoS and better energy efficiency. The following items are examples of the various facets that we want to address.

- Effect of cross-layer optimization: To evaluate the effect of the cross layer optimization, first we need to quantify the impact of the optimization at each layer and their composition.
- Effect of confidence requirements: Statistical model checking involves errors by its nature (e.g., the probability of false negatives, the probability of false positives, etc.). Likewise, statistical quantitative analysis provides the answer with confidence interval and error bound. Confidence requirements for the answer have an effect on the number of samples needed, which in turn affects the solution quality and the evaluation time.
- Effect of worst case vs. average case analysis: Currently, we model energy optimization policies (e.g., DVS, DPM, etc.) to reduce energy consumption while satisfying the QoS requirements even in the worst case scenario. However, typical multimedia applications finish execution much earlier than the worst case execution time in most of the situations, which allows more aggressive optimization based on an average case execution scenario.
- Effect of constraint relaxation: QoS degradation due to optimization is sometimes not noticeable from the viewpoint of an end user (e.g., a user may not recognize video quality drop from a single deadline miss for the video decoding.). In such a case, we can relax system's QoS constraints to enable further optimization.

In the following subsections, we will explain experimental results that illustrate the effect of cross-layer optimization. We model *PBPAIR* as an application layer policy as well as various power management schemes – *Greedy, Cluster, DVS* – as OS layer policies. In the *Greedy* scheme, the power manager shuts down whenever the device is idle, while the *Cluster* scheme tries to aggregate idle periods to maximize energy efficiency. The *DVS* scheme lowers supply voltage as long as the deadline constraint is satisfied. The arrival of incoming processing requests from the network is modeled as a Poisson process with an average arrival rate. When the processor runs at full speed, the execution times of the tasks are modeled as a normal (Gaussian) distribution with the average of $\frac{(BCET+WCET)}{2}$ and the boundary value of $3 \times \delta$, where δ represents the standard deviation. For other types of distributions, we can simply change the Maude operator for the distribution function. A subset of the MMMT system – video encoder and decoder for videophone mode – is modeled with the workload variation of a PB-PAIR encoder [7] and an H.263 decoder [20]. The network zone information is assumed to be given and the DVS capable hardware implementation is from [21]. The experiments were carried out on a 2.8 GHz Pentium 4 processor running Linux.

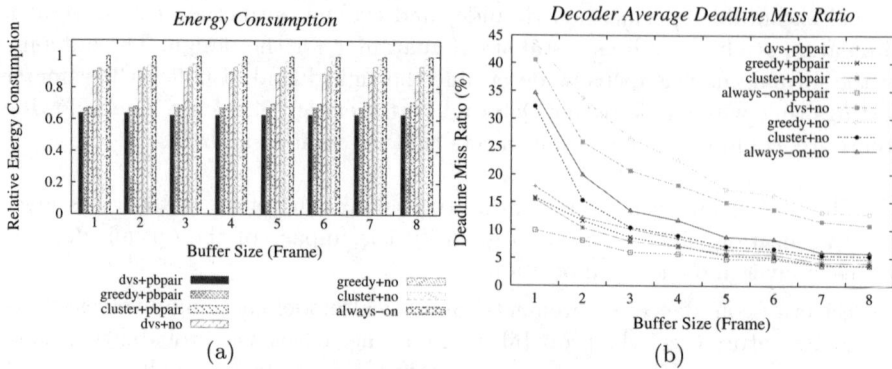

Fig. 4. Monte-Carlo Simulation: Effect of Cross Layer Optimization

4.1   Experimental Results

Monte-Carlo Simulation. Monte-Carlo simulation in Maude is done with the fair rewrite command that generates one possible behavior of the system, starting from a given initial state using a user specified seed for sampling from distributions. Figure 4(a) presents the energy profiles according to the different policies and buffer sizes. *DVS* with *PBPAIR* outperforms other policies from the perspective of relative energy consumption with respect to *Always-on* (i.e., without any policy). QoS measures such as average deadline miss ratio are also examined to evaluate the effect of cross layer optimization. Figure 4(b) shows that *PBPAIR* combined with any OS layer policy delivers more timely decoding than any OS layer policy without *PBPAIR*. Detailed experimental results on QoS aspects are omitted due to space limitations [22]. Note that the number of possible traces depends on the random seed generator and runtime is linearly proportional to the single trace generation time (i.e., Maude rewriting time from initial state). If we consider the rate of 50 frames each (5 frames/sec) for both encoding and decoding, single trace generation takes around 400-500 msecs. Therefore, it is infeasible to produce all possible traces to evaluate policy and parameter changes in dynamic situations. This led us to propose statistical approaches with quantifiable confidence for our evaluation/decision.

Statistical Model Checking. Statistical model checking enables quick detection of problematic situations (e.g., battery expiration) that can arise due to the selection of policy/parameter settings. As an example of sequential testing, we performed statistical model checking of the property

$$Probability \; [\; battery \; expires < 0.1 \;]$$

with arguments $\alpha = 0.05$ (false negative), $\beta = 0.05$ (false positive), $\theta = 0.1$ (threshold), and $\delta = 0.01$ (indifference region), respectively. Sequential testing accepts the hypothesis $H_1: p \ll \theta - \delta$ with 133 traces, that is the *batteryExpires* property checker in Figure 3 gives *false* for all traces. With the same 133 traces

---

(a) Energy Consumption:
 [nSample = 100] Fail to reject Ho (p-value = 0.821)
 E[Energy Consumption] = 3.7121E9 (α = 5.0%, d = 0.036%)

(b) Decoder Average Deadline Miss Ratio:
 [nSample = 100] Reject Ho (p-value = 0.035)
 [nSample = 110] Fail to reject Ho (p-value = 0.194)
 E[Decoder Avg Deadline Miss Ratio] = 0.2032 (α = 5.0%, d = 0.466%)

(c) Decoder Maximum Consecutive Lost:
 [nSample = 100] Fail to reject Ho (p-value = 0.884)
 [nSample = 100] (d = 0.01053) > (δ = 0.01)
 [nSample = 110] (d = 0.01002) > (δ = 0.01)
 [nSample = 121] (d = 0.00958) $\leq$ (δ = 0.01)
 E[Decoder Maximum Consecutive Lost] = 3.2314 (α = 5.0%, d = 0.958%)

Fig. 5. Statistical Quantitative Analysis

that were generated for sequential testing, black-box testing also confirms the formula with error of 8.20E-7. The run time for each statistical model checking is 10-20 msecs in addition to the sample generation, which indicates that this is a feasible proposition for the on-the-fly adaptation.

Statistical Quantitative Analysis. In Section 3.3, we explained the prerequisite and theoretical background for the statistical quantitative analysis and this section provides experimental results on that. Specifically, we test normality of data before we apply the central limit theorem to approximate the expected value by the average of sample mean. We first generate an initial number of sample traces for JB normality test followed by additional trace generation until the normality test succeeds. The p-value should be more than or equal to the error bound (α) to accept normality of given data set (i.e., fail to reject the null hypothesis Ho). If we can not *statistically* limit the confidence interval by δ (*while* loop condition in Pseudocode 2), we produce more samples on-demand.

The Figure 5(a) and 5(b) show our statistical quantitative analysis results with arguments of α (error bound) and δ (confidence interval) as 5% and 1%, respectively. In Figure 5(a), the observable *EnergyConsumption* passes the normality test with 100 initial samples since its p-value (0.821) is more than error bound α (0.05). The resulting confidence interval d (0.036%) is less than the desired value δ (1%). Therefore, we can estimate the expected value for *EnergyConsumption* within error bound and confidence interval. On the other hand, in case of the *DecoderAvgDeadlineMissRatio* observable (Figure 5(b)), we need to generate more samples (10% in this experiment) since the first JB test fails. Even if the sample data follows a normal distribution, we may need more samples for limiting the confidence interval by δ. Figure 5(c) presents such a case. The confidence interval from initial samples (d) is 1.053% and the desired interval (δ) is 1%. Therefore, more samples are generated until d is less than δ.

5   Previous and Related Work

In our previous work (FORGE project [1]), we have identified interaction parameters between the different computational levels that can facilitate effective cross-layer coordination. Specifically, we have studied how to annotate application data with specific information that can be used to improve power efficiency and how to optimize parameters in various layers (e.g., image quality in application layer, the compressed size in network layer, and execution time/power consumption in hardware layer) [2]. We also explored the trade-off between the error resiliency level, compression efficiency, and power consumption for streaming multimedia applications [7]. To leverage our prior effort, we are integrating formal methods with cross-layer optimization in a unified framework.

Previous work on statistical model checking for stochastic systems includes PMaude (Probabilistic Maude) [23,12], a rewriting-based specification language for modeling probabilistic concurrent and distributed systems. The associated tool, VeStA [14], was developed to statistically analyze various quantitative aspects of models such as those specified in PMaude using a query language QuaTEx (Quantitative Temporal Expression) [12] based on CSL (Continuous Stochastic Logic). However, this approach does not provide any procedure by which they can determine the sample size required to achieve normality. Moreover, the authors approximate the expected average by applying *Student's T*-distribution. This is unnecessary since as the sample size n grows, the T-distribution approaches the normal distribution with mean 0 and variance 1. Therefore, we extended their approach by an on-demand sample generation that can compute the sample size sufficient to guarantee the normality of data, and utilize the normal distribution to obtain the error bound and confidence interval.

Ymer [15,16] implements statistical techniques, based on discrete event simulation and sequential acceptance sampling for CSL model checking. The system is modeled by continuous-time Markov chains (CTMCs) and generalized semi-Markov processes (GSMPs). Properties are expressed using Continuous Stochastic Logic (CSL). Ymer also integrates numerical techniques to solve nested CSL queries, by including the hybrid engine of the PRISM [24] tool for CTMC model checking. This, however, limits the modeling power compared with our approach. On the other hand, the expressive power of the Maude language (extended with probability and time) opens a wide spectrum of applications that are beyond the scope of Markovian models.

6   Summary and Future Work

This paper presents the results of the first phase of a project to develop formal analytical methods for understanding cross-layer and end-to-end timing issues in highly distributed systems incorporated resource limited devices, and to integrate these methods into the design and adaptation processes for such systems. We have developed new analysis techniques that combine statistical and formal methods and applied them in a case study treating the videophone mode of a multi-mode multimedia terminal. The results are encouraging, as the underlying formal executable models are moderately simple to develop, and the analyses seem feasible.

Ongoing and future work in this project includes:

- modeling and analysis of the remaining modes of the MMMT (Section 2) as well as scheduling policies and sharing of resources between tasks.
- carrying out a trade-off analysis on the effect of confidence requirements, worst case vs. average case execution models, and constraint relaxation (as discussed in Section 4).
- integration of formal analysis with the simulation framework that includes real system prototypes. This will result in a feedback loop that includes the formal models, simulation, and monitoring of running systems for analysis of system behavior and optimizing choice of policies and parameters.

References

1. Forge Project: http://forge.ics.uci.edu
2. Mohapatra, S., Cornea, R., Oh, H., Lee, K., Kim, M., Dutt, N.D., Gupta, R., Nicolau, A., Shukla, S.K., Venkatasubramanian, N.: A cross-layer approach for power-performance optimization in distributed mobile systems. In: International Parallel and Distributed Processing Symposium (IPDPS '05)
3. Kim, M., Dutt, N., Venkatasubramanian, N.: Policy construction and validation for energy minimization in cross layered systems: A formal method approach. In: Real-Time and Embedded Technology and Applications Symposium (RTAS '06) Work-in-Progress Session. pp. 25–28 (2006)
4. Clavel, M., Durán, F., Eker, S., Lincoln, P., Martí-Oliet, N., Meseguer, J., Talcott, C.: All about maude, a high-performance logical framework. LNCS, vol. 4350. Springer, Berlin Heidelberg New York (2007)
5. Kim, D., Kim, M., Ha, S.: A Case Study of System Level Specification and Software Synthesis of Multimode Multimedia Terminal. In: Embedded Systems for Real-Time Multimedia (ESTImedia '03). pp. 57–64 (2003)
6. Kim, M., Ha, S.: Hybrid Run-time Power Management Technique for Real-time Embedded System with Voltage Scalable Processor. ACM SIGPLAN Notices 36(8), 11–19 (2001)
7. Kim, M., Oh, H., Dutt, N., Nicolau, A., Venkatasubramanian, N.: PBPAIR: an energy-efficient error-resilient encoding using probability based power aware intra refresh. SIGMOBILE Mob. Comput. Commun. Rev. 10(3), 58–69 (2006)
8. Clavel, M., Durán, F., Eker, S., Lincoln, P., Martí-Oliet, N., Meseguer, J., Talcott, C.: The maude 2.0 system. In: Nieuwenhuis, R. (ed.) RTA 2003, LNCS vol. 2706, Springer, Heidelberg (2003)
9. Clavel, M., Durán, F., Eker, S., Lincoln, P., Martí-Oliet, N., Meseguer, J., Quesada, J.F.: Maude: specification and programming in rewriting logic. Theoretical Computer Science 285(2), 187–243 (2002)
10. Meseguer, J.: Conditional Rewriting Logic as a unified model of concurrency. Theoretical Computer Science 96(1), 73–155 (1992)
11. Real-Time Maude 2.2: http://www.ifi.uio.no/RealTimeMaude.
12. Agha, G.A., Meseguer, J., Sen, K.: PMaude: Rewrite-based specification language for probabilistic object systems. Electr. Notes Theor. Comput. Sci. 153(2), 213–239 (2006)

13. Wald, A.: Sequential tests of statistical hypotheses. Annals of Mathematical Statistics 16(2), 117–186 (1945)
14. Sen, K., Viswanathan, M., Agha, G.: Statistical model checking of black-box probabilistic systems. In: Alur, R., Peled, D.A. (eds.) CAV 2004, LNCS, vol. 3114, pp. 202–215. Springer, Heidelberg (2004)
15. Younes, H.: Ymer: A statistical model checker. In: Etessami, K., Rajamani, S.K. (eds.) CAV 2005, LNCS, vol. 3576, pp. 429–433. Springer, Heidelberg (2005)
16. Younes, H., Kwiatkowska, M., Norman, G., Parker, D.: Numerical vs. statistical probabilistic model checking. International Journal on Software Tools for Technology Transfer (STTT) 8(3), 216–228 (2006)
17. Jarque, C., Bera, A.: A test for normality of observations and regression residuals. Internat. Statist. Rev. 55(2), 163–172 (1987)
18. Hogg, R., Craig, A.: Introduction to Mathematical Statistics. 5th edn. (1995)
19. Aziz, A., Sanwal, K., Singhal, V., Brayton, R.: Model-checking continuous-time Markov chains. ACM Trans. Comput. Logic 1(1), 162–170 (2000)
20. Image Process Lab. Univ. British Columbia: TMN 10 (H.263+), ver. 3.2.0 (1998)
21. http://www.intel.com/design/pca/prodbref/252780.htm
22. Kim, M., Stehr, M.O., Talcott, C., Dutt, N., Venkatasubramanian, N.: Modeling and Exploiting Cross-Layer Optimization in Distributed Embedded Systems. Technical Report SRI-CSL-07-02, SRI International (Feb. 2007)
23. Kumar, N., Sen, K., Meseguer, J., Agha, G.: A rewriting based model for probabilistic distributed object systems. In: Najm, E., Nestmann, U., Stevens, P. (eds.) FMOODS 2003, LNCS, vol. 2884, pp. 32–46. Springer, Heidelberg (2003)
24. Hinton, A., Kwiatkowska, M., Norman, G., Parker, D.: PRISM A tool for automatic verification of probabilistic systems. In: Hermanns, H., Palsberg, J. (eds.) TACAS 2006 and ETAPS 2006, LNCS, vol. 3920, pp. 441–444. Springer, Heidelberg (2006)

On Resource-Sensitive Timed Component Connectors*

Sun Meng and Farhad Arbab

CWI, Kruislaan 413, Amsterdam, The Netherlands
{Meng.Sun,Farhad.Arbab}@cwi.nl

Abstract. In this paper we introduce a formal model for reasoning about resource sensitive timed component connectors. We extended the constraint automata model, which is used as the semantic model for the exogenous channel-
based coordination language Reo, through integrating both resource and time information. This model allows to specify both the interactions that take time to
be performed and timeouts. Moreover, the model reflects resource issues, such
as bandwidth or allocated memory, that may affect the time needed for interactions when specifying the timed behavior of connectors. The time duration that
an interaction takes is represented by a function on the available resources. In addition to the formalism, we also discuss compositional reasoning and present two
notions of simulation to relate different connectors from functional and resource-
sensitive temporal perspectives respectively.

Keywords: Coordination, Constraint Automata, Resource-Sensitive Timed
Constraint Automata, Simulation.

1 Introduction

One important challenge of the software engineering field is the so called Service Oriented Computing (SOC) [11]. In SOC, applications are developed by coordinating the
behaviour of autonomous services distributed over an overlay network. Coordination
models and languages provide a formalization of the "glue code" that interconnects the
services and organizes the mutual interactions between them in a distributed processing
environment, and are extremely important to the success of SOC. Several coordination
models have been proposed in the literature. For example, Reo [3,5] offers a powerful
glue language for implementation of coordinating component connectors based on a
calculus of mobile channels. However, most of them were concerned only with functional aspects of the connectors. This means that nothing was said about Quality of
Services [12], e.g., the duration of the interaction. As a consequence, only functional
properties of coordination could be investigated.

Coordination of services requires service consumers to discover service providers
that satisfy both given functional and non-functional requirements, including costs and
QoS requirements such as time that a service takes to perform a certain action. Timing

* The work reported in this paper is supported by a grant from the GLANCE funding program
of the Dutch National Organization for Scientific Research (NWO), through project CooPer
(600.643.000.05N12).

M.M. Bonsangue and E.B. Johnsen (Eds.): FMOODS 2007, LNCS 4468, pp. 301–316, 2007.

constraints are always required to be satisfied in different service oriented applications and the time consumed during the execution of a service falls into one of the following two categories:

- The service consumes time while it performs actions. The time may depend on the availability of resources. For example, the time for downloading a file from a server depends on the bandwidth of the network.
- The time passes while the system waits for a reaction from the environment. In particular, the service can change the system's state if an interaction is not received before a certain amount of time. For example, the connection to some server (like internet banking) might be disconnected if it does not receive any requirement for a long time due to the security reason.

In this paper we consider the temporal issues of Reo which allow the specifier to define how the behavior of channels and component interfaces can be affected by both categories of temporal aspects. Although there are a plethora of timed extensions of classical models [1,16,17], most of them only specify one temporal aspects: Time is either associated with actions or associated with delays/timeouts. We present a formalism based on constraint automata, allowing us to take into account both temporal issues considered before, and specify in a natural way both aspects of temporal properties for connectors. Furthermore, a new contribution in this paper is that resources may influence the timing property of the behavior. Therefore the execution of an interaction may take different time values if the available resources are different.

The choice of Reo as the coordination language (and therefore constraint automata as its operational semantic model) is motivated by the fact that (1) it allows exogenous coordination and arbitrary user defined primitives, and (2) it is unique among other models in allowing arbitrary combination of synchrony and asynchrony in coordination protocols. This, for instance, facilitates multi-party transactions through Reo's inherent propagation of synchrony and exclusion constraints.

We also propose a formal simulation relation allowing to systematically compare connectors given by resource sensitive timed constraint automata. The notion of simulation of ordinary constraint automata has already been studied in the literature [2,4,5]. However, to the best of our knowledge, none of them take resource issues into account. Here, we propose new techniques specifically devoted to resource sensitive timed connectors. Regarding functional simulation we have to consider not only language inclusion as discussed in [5], but also the possible timeouts.

Taking resources and time into account, the simulation relation in our model can be used to check the standard refinement pattern: Having a certain requirement in mind, it is often quite easy to depict a resource sensitive timed constraint automaton A that describes the allowed behavior. In this sense, A can serve as specification for a Reo circuit that is to be designed. A Reo circuit G is viewed to be correct (w.r.t. specification A) iff the resource sensitive timed constraint automaton A_G for G does not show any behavior that is forbidden by the specification, where both functional behavior and temporal behavior are considered.

The rest of the paper is organized as follows: In Section 2 we recall the basic concepts of ordinary constraint automata. Resource sensitive timed constraint automata are introduced in Section 3. In Section 4 we present the simulation relation in our model and provide the congruence result with respect to the composition operators. In Section 5 we consider related research work. We conclude in Section 6 with a brief discussion of some further work.

2 Constraint Automata

Constraint automata (CA) were introduced in [5] as a formalism to capture the operational semantics of channel-based component connectors in Reo. This section summarizes the basis concepts of constraint automata. Constraint automata are variants of labelled transition systems where transitions are augmented with pairs N, g rather than action labels. The states of a constraint automata stand for the network configurations, e.g., the contents of the buffers for FIFO channels. The transition labels N, g can be viewed as sets of I/O-operations that will be performed in parallel. More precisely, N is a set of nodes in the network where data-flow is observed simultaneously, and g is a boolean condition on the observed data items. Transitions going out of a state s represent the possible data-flow in the corresponding configuration and its effect on the configuration.

CA use a finite set $\mathcal{N}$ of nodes. The nodes can play the role of input and output ports of components and connectors, but they can appear outside the interfaces of components as intermediate stations of the network where several channels are glued together and the transmission of data items can be observed. In the sequel, we assume a finite and non-empty set $Data$ consisting of data items that can be transferred through channels. A data assignment denotes a function $\delta : N \rightarrow Data$ where $\emptyset \neq N \subseteq \mathcal{N}$. We write δ_A for the data item assigned to node $A \in N$ under δ and $DA(N)$ for the set of all data assignments for node-set N. CA use a symbolic representation of data assignments by data constraints which mean propositional formulas built from the atoms $d_A = d_B$, $d_A \in P$ or $d_A = d$ where A, B are nodes, d_A and d_B are symbols for the observed data item at node A and $d \in Data$, $P \subseteq Data$ (and the standard boolean connectors $\wedge$, $\vee$, $\neg$, etc.). For a node set N, $DC(N)$ denotes the set of data constraints that only refer to the terms d_A for $A \in N$.

Definition 1. *A* constraint automaton *over the data domain* $Data$ *is a tuple* $\mathcal{A} = (S, S_0, \mathcal{N}, \longrightarrow)$ *where* S *is a set of states, also called configurations,* $S_0 \subset S$ *is the set of its initial state,* $\mathcal{N}$ *is a finite set of nodes,* $\longrightarrow \subseteq \bigcup_{N \subseteq \mathcal{N}} S \times \{N\} \times DC(N) \times S$, *called the transition relation.*

A transition fires if it observes data items in its respective ports/nodes of the component and according to the observed data, the automaton may change its state. We write $s \xrightarrow{N,g} s'$ instead of $(s, N, g, s') \in \longrightarrow$ and refer to N as the node-set and g the guard for the transition. By an instance of $s \xrightarrow{N,g} s'$ we mean a transition of the form $s \xrightarrow{N,\delta} s'$ where δ is a data assignment for the nodes in N with $\delta \models g$. Here the symbol $\models$ stands for the satisfaction relation which results from interpreting data constraints over data assignments.

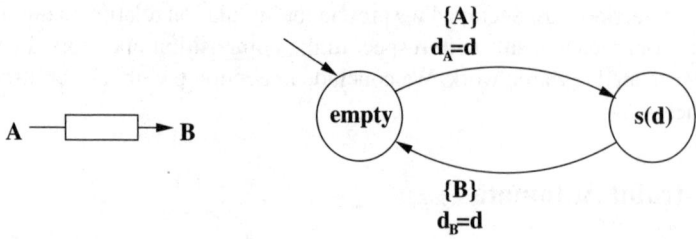

Fig. 1. Constraint Automata for FIFO Channel

The intuitive operational behavior of a constraint automaton can be specified by its *runs*. A run in a constraint automaton is defined as a (finite or infinite) sequence of consecutive transition instances

$$r = s_0 \xrightarrow{N_0, \delta_0} s_1 \xrightarrow{N_1, \delta_1} s_2 \xrightarrow{N_2, \delta_2} \cdots$$

We require that runs are either infinite or finite runs where the last state s_n does not have any outgoing transition where the node set N only consists of mixed nodes. This requirement can be understood as a *maximal progress assumption* for the mixed nodes.

Figure 1 shows a CA for a FIFO1 channel AB in Reo, which is given in the left of the picture. Node A serves as input port where data items can be written into the channel while B can be regarded as output port where the stored data item is taken out and delivered to the environment. State $empty$ represents the configuration in which the buffer is empty, while state $s(d)$ stands for the configuration where data element d is stored in the buffer. The CA given here is a parametric version with meta symbols for data items (Formal definition can be found at [5]).

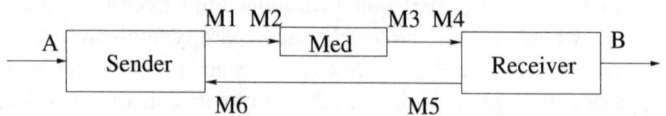

Fig. 2. The Components of Parrow's Protocol

Example 1. As another example, we consider the Parrow's Protocol (PP) [18], which is a simplified version of the well-known Alternating Bit Protocol (ABP). PP provides an error free communication over a medium that might lose messages. Figure 2 shows the components that are involved in this protocol. Data elements from a set Msg are communicated between a Sender and a Receiver. Once the Sender reads a message from its port A, it sends this datum through the communication medium Med to the Receiver, which sends the message out through its port B. The communication medium Med is faulty, thus a message sent through Med can turn up as an error message. Every time the Receiver receives a message via Med, it sends an acknowledgement to the Sender. For simplicity it is assumed that acknowledgements are never lost. We model three components and the three synchronous channels by CA. The pictures are given as in Figure 3.

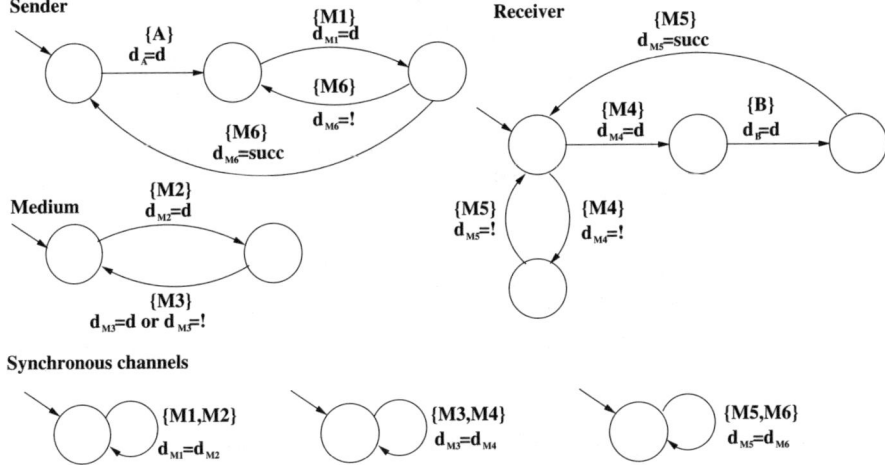

Fig. 3. The Constraint Automata for the Components and Channels in Parrow's Protocol

Constructing complex connectors out of simpler ones is done by the join operation in Reo. Joining two nodes destroys both nodes and produces a new node on which all of their coincident channel ends coincide. Each channel in Reo is mapped to a constraint automaton. We now show how Reo's join operation can be realized by the product construction of constraint automata.

The product for two given constraint automata $\mathscr{A}_1 = (S_1, s_{0,1}, \mathscr{N}_1, \longrightarrow_1)$ and $\mathscr{A}_2 = (S_2, s_{0,2}, \mathscr{N}_2, \longrightarrow_2)$ is defined as a constraint automaton $\mathscr{A}_1 \bowtie \mathscr{A}_2$ with the components

$$(S_1 \times S_2, \langle s_{0,1}, s_{0,2} \rangle, \mathscr{N}_1 \cup \mathscr{N}_2, \longrightarrow)$$

where $\longrightarrow$ is given by the following rules:

- If $s_1 \xrightarrow{N_1, g_1}_1 s_1'$, $s_2 \xrightarrow{N_2, g_2}_2 s_2'$, $N_1 \cap \mathscr{N}_2 = N_2 \cap \mathscr{N}_1 \neq \emptyset$ and $g_1 \wedge g_2$ is satisfiable, then $\langle s_1, s_2 \rangle \xrightarrow{N_1 \cup N_2, g_1 \wedge g_2} \langle s_1', s_2' \rangle$.
- If $s_1 \xrightarrow{N, g}_1 s_1'$, where $N \cap \mathscr{N}_2 = \emptyset$ then $\langle s_1, s_2 \rangle \xrightarrow{N, g} \langle s_1', s_2 \rangle$.
- If $s_2 \xrightarrow{N, g}_2 s_2'$, where $N \cap \mathscr{N}_1 = \emptyset$ then $\langle s_1, s_2 \rangle \xrightarrow{N, g} \langle s_1, s_2' \rangle$.

The first rule is applied when there are two transitions in the automata which can be fired together. This happens only if there is no shared name in the two automata that is present on one of the transitions but not present on the other one. In this case the transition in the resulting automaton has the union of the name sets on both transitions, and the data constraint is the conjunction of the data constraints of the two transitions. The second rule is applied when a transition in one automaton can be fired independently of the other automaton, which happens when the names on the transition are not included in the other automaton. The third rule is symmetric to the second one. A parametric picture for the product of the CA of the Sender, the Receiver, the Medium and the synchronous channels in Example 1 is given in Figure 4.

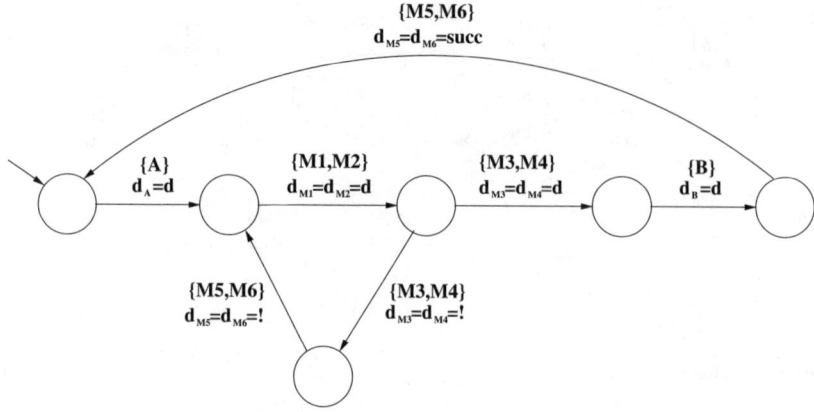

Fig. 4. The Product of Constraint Automata for the Components and Channels in Fig.3

Another operator that is helpful for abstraction purposes and can be used in Reo to build connectors from networks by declaring the internal topology of the network as hidden is the hiding operator. Hiding takes an input a constraint automaton $\mathscr{A} = (S, s_0, \mathscr{N}, \longrightarrow)$ and a non-empty node-set $M \subseteq \mathscr{N}$. The result is a constraint automaton $\mathtt{hide}(\mathscr{A}, M)$ that behaves as $\mathscr{A}$ except that data flow at the nodes $A \in M$ is made invisible. Formally, $\mathtt{hide}(\mathscr{A}, M) = (S, s_0, \mathscr{N} \setminus M, \longrightarrow_M, Q_{0,M})$ where $s \xrightarrow{\bar{N}, \bar{g}}_M s'$ iff there exists a transition $s \xrightarrow{N, g} s'$ such that $\bar{N} = N \setminus M$ and $\bar{g} = \exists M[g]$. Here $\exists M[g]$ stands short for $\bigvee_{\delta \in DA(M)} g[d_A/\delta.A | A \in M]$, where $g[d_A/\delta.A | A \in M]$ denotes the syntactic replacement of all occurrences of d_A in g for $A \in M$ with $\delta.A$. Therefore, $\exists M[g]$ formalizes the set of data assignments for $\bar{N}$ that are obtained from a data assignment δ for N where g holds by dropping the assignments for the nodes in $N \cap M$.

3   Resource-Sensitive Timed Constraint Automata

In this section, we present an extension of the constraint automata model for Reo circuits that yields the basis for reasoning about resources in temporal behavior of channel-based component connectors. *Resource-Sensitive Timed Constraint Automata* (RSTCA for short) rely on the assumption that the execution time of interactions depends on the available resources, while timeout is also permitted. As we have indicated previously, we will add new dimensions to the CA model such that the temporal properties can be properly specified. We consider both timeout behavior and the time being taken when the interactions being executed in the system evolution. The time values will not only depend on the corresponding operation to be performed and the state that the system resides in. Therefore, we have two types of transitions:

- *interactive* transitions where the time needed for the interaction depends on the available resource value, and
- *timeout* transitions where the system can evolve after a given time while no interaction happens.

Before touching the technical details for RSTCA, we first consider a mathematical account of the notion of resource. According to [19], the following properties are reasonable requirements for a model of resource:

- A set $\mathbf{R}$ of resource elements;
- A (partial) combination $\circ : \mathbf{R} \times \mathbf{R} \rightharpoonup \mathbf{R}$ of resource elements;
- A comparison $\sqsubseteq$ of resource elements; and
- A zero resource element e.

which correspond to a preordered partial commutative monoid $(\mathbf{R}, \circ, e, \sqsubseteq)$, subject to the condition that if $r \sqsubseteq s$ and $r' \sqsubseteq s'$ then $r \circ r' \sqsubseteq s \circ s'$. For simplicity, we use $(\mathbb{N}, +, 0, \leq)$ as the model of resource in the following. A resource assignment for resource r is given by $r : n$ which means that n units of resource r is available. In general, a resource assignment is a tuple of resource assignments $\langle r_1 : n_1, r_2 : n_2, \cdots, r_k : n_k \rangle$ for resources $r_1, r_2, \cdots, r_k$. A resource constraint rc for resource $r_1, r_2, \cdots, r_k$ is a conjunction of atoms of the form $r_i \bowtie m$ where $\bowtie \in \{<, \leq, >, \geq, =\}$. RA denotes the set of all resource assignments and RC the set of all resource constraints. We use the symbol $\models$ for the satisfaction relation for resource constraints which results from interpreting resource constraints over resource assignments. The judgement $r : n \models rc$ is read as "resource assignment $r : n$ is sufficient to satisfy rc". We say that a resource constraint rc is satisfiable if there exists a resource assignment x such that $x \models rc$. The monoidal structure allows us to define a multiplicative conjunction $\otimes$ on resource constraints, which is given by

$$r : n \models rc_1 \otimes rc_2 \text{ iff there are two assignments } r : n_1 \text{ and } r : n_2 \text{ such that}$$
$$n_1 \circ n_2 \sqsubseteq n, \text{ and } r : n_1 \models rc_1 \text{ and } r : n_2 \models rc_2$$

The semantics of such a multiplicative conjunction is: the n units of resource r is sufficient to satisfy $rc_1 \otimes rc_2$ just in case that it can be divided into two parts n_1 and n_2 such that n_1 units of r satisfies rc_1 and n_2 units of r satisfies rc_2.

During the rest of the paper we will use the following notation: $\mathbf{T} = \mathbb{R}_{\geq 0} \cup \{\infty\}$ is the domain to define time values. We write $\mathbf{R} \mid_{rc}$ for the subset of $\mathbf{R}$ in which all the elements satisfy the resource constraint rc and $\{\mathbf{R} \to \mathbf{T}\}$ for the function space from $\mathbf{R}$ to $\mathbf{T}$, i.e., the set of possible functions with domain $\mathbf{R}$ and codomain $\mathbf{T}$.

Definition 2 (Resource-Sensitive Timed Constraint Automata). *A RSTCA is defined as a tuple*

$$\mathscr{T} = (S, S_0, \mathscr{N}, R, \longrightarrow)$$

where S is a countable set of control states (also called locations), $S_0 \subseteq S$ is the set of initial states, $\mathscr{N}$ is a finite set of nodes, R is a finite set of resource names, and the edge

$$\longrightarrow \subseteq (S \times \mathbf{T} \times S) \cup (\bigcup_{N \subseteq \mathscr{N}} S \times \{N\} \times DC(N) \times RC \times \{\mathbf{R} \to \mathbf{T}\} \times S)$$

denotes the transitions and we have two types of transitions:

- *timeout transitions: $s \xrightarrow{t} s'$ where $t \in \mathbf{T}$;*

- *interactive transitions: $s \xrightarrow{N,g,rc,C} s'$ where N, g are as in ordinary constraint automata, rc is the resource constraint that should be satisfied to trigger the execution of the transition, and $C : \mathbf{R} \mid_{rc} \to \mathbf{T}$ returns the time value that the transition need to be completed, which depends on the available resource values.*

A configuration in $\mathscr{T}$ is a pair $\langle s, x \rangle$ where $s \in S$ is a state and x is the tuple of resource assignments.

For each state s, the timeout transition $s \xrightarrow{t} s'$ indicates the time that the system can remain at the state s waiting for an interaction to happen and the state to which the system evolves if no interaction happens on time. An interactive transition represents a set of possible interactions given by the transition instances that result by replacing the data constraint g with a data assignment δ where g holds, and replace resource constraint rc with a resource assignment x at state s which satisfies rc respectively. The time duration for executing the such a transition instance will be $C(x)$. Furthermore, available resource values might be changed throughout the computation and communication. Thus, we posit the existence of a modification function μ, in which $\mu(N, \delta, x) = x'$ has the interpretation that the effect of the interaction δ at port N on resource x is to modify it to x'.

We also assume that the interactive transitions always have a higher priority than timeout transitions, and if a RSTCA $\mathscr{T}$ have both an interactive transition and a timeout transition $s \xrightarrow{t} s'$ at a state s, it means that the system will stay at state s for t time units and evolve to state s' if the interactive transition is not enabled in this duration. But at any time point in $[0, t)$, if it can interact with another system by taking the interactive transition, the interaction will happen immediately and the system will move to another state. This idea is represented in Figure 5, where $t_1 \in [0, t)$ and the behavior of the RSTCA on the left side is in fact like on the right side, i.e., the system remembers what it can do at state s in the duration $[0, t)$ and do it whenever it is possible, and forget it at time t, when it arrives at a new state s'.

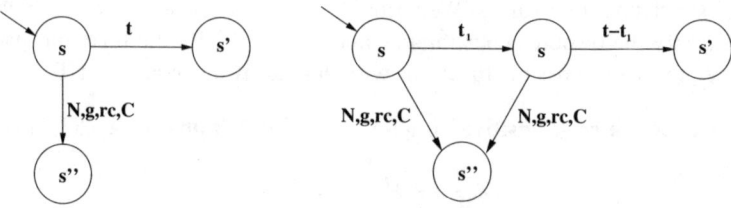

Fig. 5. Timeout and Interactive Transitions

A state is called *terminal* iff it has no outgoing interactive transitions and allows the possibility for unbounded passage of time, i.e., timeout transitions are not allowed in it.

Given a state s and resource assignment x, a transition instance $\langle s, x \rangle \xrightarrow{N,\delta,C(x)} \langle s', x' \rangle$ denotes that if the N-interaction is available, g holds for data assignment δ and the resource assignment x satisfies rc, then the transition happens after $C(x)$ units of time, the new state will be s' and the available resource after the transition is given by x'.

Definition 3. *For a given RSTCA $\mathscr{T}$, suppose s_0 be a state and $c_0 = \langle s_0, x \rangle$ a possible configuration of $\mathscr{T}$. A tuple $(c_0, N, \delta, \bar{t}, t, c)$ is a step of $\mathscr{T}$ for the state s_0 if there exists a configuration $c = \langle s, x' \rangle$ and $k \geq 1$ states $s_1, s_2, \cdots, s_k$ such that for all $1 \leq j \leq k$ we have $s_{j-1} \xrightarrow{t_j} s_j$, and there exists a transition $\langle s_{k-1}, x \rangle \xrightarrow{N, \delta, C(x)} \langle s, x' \rangle$ such that $\bar{t} = [\sum_{j=1}^{k-1} t_j, \sum_{j=1}^{k} t_j)$ and $t = C(x)$. We denote by $\text{Steps}(\mathscr{T}, s)$ the set of steps of $\mathscr{T}$ for the state s.*

We say that a timed s-run of $\mathscr{T}$ is a (finite or infinite) sequence of successive steps of $\mathscr{T}$ starting in state s. Formally, a timed s-run is a sequence of steps as

$$(c_0, N_0, \delta_0, \bar{t}_0, t_0, c_1), (c_1, N_1, \delta_1, \bar{t}_1, t_1, c_2), \cdots \quad (1)$$

where $c_0 = \langle s, x \rangle$ for some possible resource assignment x at state s. We denote by $TR(\mathscr{T}, s)$ the set of timed s-runs of $\mathscr{T}$. In addition, we say that the sequence $(N_0, \delta_0, \bar{t}_0), (N_1, \delta_1, \bar{t}_1), \cdots$ is a functional s-run of $\mathscr{T}$ if there is a timed s-run of $\mathscr{T}$ as given in (1).

Intuitively, a step is an interactive transition proceeded by zero or more timeout transitions. The duration $\bar{t}$ in a step $(c_0, N, \delta, \bar{t}, t, c)$ where $c_0 = \langle s_0, x_0 \rangle$ and $c = \langle s, x \rangle$ indicates the possible time values when an interaction could start. Additionally, timed runs include both time values which inform us about possible timeouts (denoted by the intervals $\bar{t}_i$) and the time consumed to execute the interactive transitions in each step of the run.

For the same timed run in a RSTCA, there may exist different instances which are obtained by instantiating every time interval $\bar{t}_i$ by a concrete time value $\hat{t}_i \in \bar{t}_i$.

Definition 4. *Suppose $(c_0, N_0, \delta_0, \bar{t}_0, t_0, c_1), (c_1, N_1, \delta_1, \bar{t}_1, t_1, c_2), \cdots$ is a timed run for a given RSTCA $\mathscr{T}$, the sequence $(c_0, N_0, \delta_0, \hat{t}_0, t_0, c_1), (c_1, N_1, \delta_1, \hat{t}_1, t_1, c_2), \cdots$ is an instanced timed run if for all i, $\hat{t}_i \in \bar{t}_i$. Additionally, we say that the sequence $(N_0, \delta_0, \hat{t}_0), (N_1, \delta_1, \hat{t}_1), \cdots$ is a instanced functional run of $\mathscr{T}$.*

Example 2. Figure 6 shows a resource-sensitive timed variant for the CA of the components and channels of Parrow's Protocol. Here we assume that the internal computation of Sender takes t_S time units, while the exact time of the Medium and Receiver are t_M and t_R respectively. For all the other interactive transitions of the components, we assume that there is no constraints on the resources and the transitions are performed immediately. For the three synchronous channels, we assume that the communication time depends on the bandwidth, i.e., the amount of data that can be transferred over a certain period of time. In this example, the resource constraint for these channels is that the bandwidth w should be more than $10k/s$, and the duration for the interaction over every synchronous channel is $1/w$ time units.

We now explain how to construct a RSTCA via product and hiding. In the following we assume that the common nodes are those where data flow has to be synchronized.

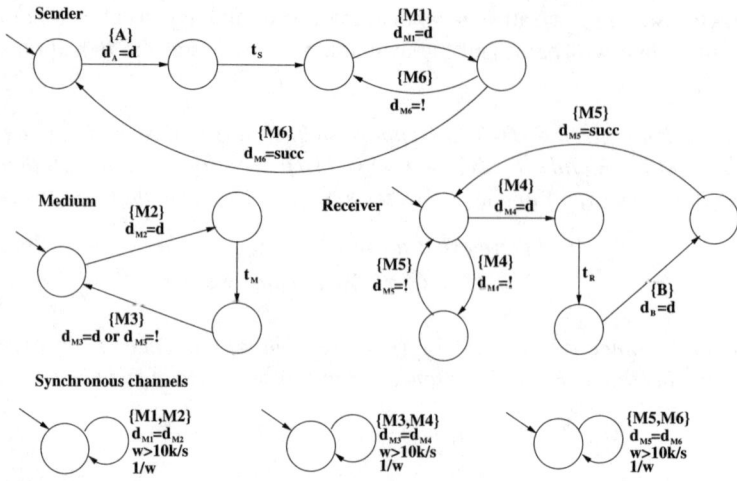

Fig. 6. The RSTCA for the Components and Channels in Fig.3

Definition 5. *Let* $\mathcal{T}_1 = (S_1, S_0^1, \mathcal{N}_1, R, \longrightarrow_1)$ *and* $\mathcal{T}_2 = (S_2, S_0^2, \mathcal{N}_2, R, \longrightarrow_2)$ *be two RSTCA, their product* $\mathcal{T}_1 \bowtie \mathcal{T}_2$ *is the RSTCA* $\mathcal{T} = (S, S_0, \mathcal{N}, R, \longrightarrow)$ *where* $S = S_1 \times S_2$, $S_0 = S_0^1 \times S_0^2$, $\mathcal{N} = \mathcal{N}_1 \cup \mathcal{N}_2$ *and the interactive transitions are defined by the following synchronization and interleaving rule:*

- *If* $s_1 \xrightarrow{N_1, g_1, rc_1, C_1}_1 s_1'$, $s_2 \xrightarrow{N_2, g_2, rc_2, C_2}_2 s_2'$, $N_1 \cap \mathcal{N}_2 = N_2 \cap \mathcal{N}_1 \neq \emptyset$, $g_1 \wedge g_2$ *and* $rc_1 \otimes rc_2$ *are satisfiable, then* $\langle s_1, s_2 \rangle \xrightarrow{N_1 \cup N_2, g_1 \wedge g_2, rc_1 \otimes rc_2, C_1 \odot C_2} \langle s_1', s_2' \rangle$.
- *If* $s_1 \xrightarrow{N, g, rc, C}_1 s_1'$, *where* $N \cap \mathcal{N}_2 = \emptyset$ *then* $\langle s_1, s_2 \rangle \xrightarrow{N, g, rc, C} \langle s_1', s_2 \rangle$.
- *If* $s_2 \xrightarrow{N, g, rc, C}_2 s_2'$, *where* $N \cap \mathcal{N}_1 = \emptyset$ *then* $\langle s_1, s_2 \rangle \xrightarrow{N, g, rc, C} \langle s_1, s_2' \rangle$.

and the following rules for timeout transitions:

$$\frac{s_1 \xrightarrow{t_1} s_1', s_2 \xrightarrow{t_2} s_2', t_1 = t_2 = t}{\langle s_1, s_2 \rangle \xrightarrow{t} \langle s_1', s_2' \rangle}$$

$$\frac{s_1 \xrightarrow{t_1} s_1', s_2 \xrightarrow{t_2} s_2', t_1 < t_2}{\langle s_1, s_2 \rangle \xrightarrow{t_1} \langle s_1', s_2 \rangle, \ s_2 \xrightarrow{t_2 - t_1} s_2'} \qquad \frac{s_1 \xrightarrow{t_1} s_1', s_2 \xrightarrow{t_2} s_2', t_1 > t_2}{\langle s_1, s_2 \rangle \xrightarrow{t_2} \langle s_1, s_2' \rangle, \ s_1 \xrightarrow{t_1 - t_2} s_1'}$$

The interleaving rules are in the style of labelled transition systems. They formalize the case where no synchronization is required since no common nodes are involved. The synchronization rule expresses the synchronization case which means that both automata have to "agree" on the I/O-operations at their common nodes, while the I/O-operations at their individual nodes is arbitrary. In the synchronization, $C_1 \odot C_2$ depends on the allocation of resources: if resource assignment $r : n$ satisfies $rc_1 \otimes rc_2$, then

$C_1 \odot C_2(r : n) = max\{C_1(r : n_1), C_2(r : n_2)\}$ where $n_1 \circ n_2 \sqsubseteq n$ and $r : n_1 \models rc_1$, $r : n_2 \models rc_2$. In general, there may be different allocation strategies that satisfy the condition. Thus, for every such allocation, there is a corresponding value for $C_1 \odot C_2(r : n)$. To decide the exact time value, the concept of scheduler is needed. The details are not of importance here and we will leave the problem of how scheduling can be included in the RSTCA framework as future work.

Note that the definition for this composition operator is an extension of the original product of constraint automata, which has the feature of being neither parallel nor sequential. But it is more powerful than classical sequential and parallel operators and is the source of the expressive power of Reo: not only it does the sequential composition of asynchronous steps, it simultaneously also composes synchronous steps in parallel. More discussions on the reason for this form of composition can be found at [5].

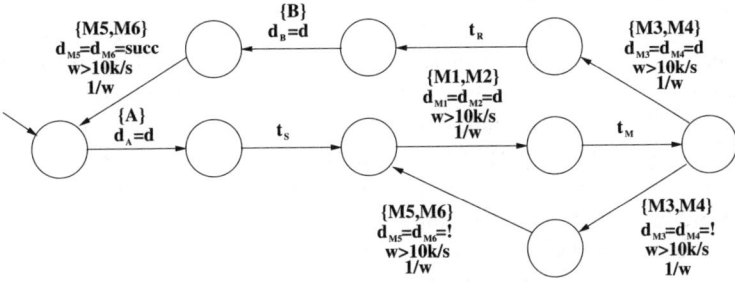

Fig. 7. The Product of the RSTCA for the Components and Channels in Fig.3

Example 3. Consider the RSTCA for the components and channels of Parrow's Protocol as given in Figure 6. Composing them together via the product operator yields the RSTCA as given in Figure 7.

The effect of hiding a node that is internal is that data flow at that node is no longer observable from outside. However, the resource is still consumed and the time being taken should remain the same whether or not the node is hidden.

Definition 6. *The hiding operator takes as input a RSTCA $\mathcal{T} = (S, S_0, \mathcal{N}, R, \longrightarrow)$ and a non-empty node-set $M \subseteq \mathcal{N}$. The result is a RSTCA hide$(\mathcal{T}, M)$ that behaves as $\mathcal{T}$ except that data flow at the nodes $A \in M$ is made invisible. Formally,* hide$(\mathcal{T}, M) = (S, S_0, \mathcal{N} \setminus M, R, \longrightarrow_M)$ *where*

$-\ s \xrightarrow{\bar{N}, \bar{g}, rc, C}_M s'$ *iff there exists a transition $s \xrightarrow{N, g, rc, C} s'$ such that $N \setminus M = \bar{N}$ and $\bar{g} = \exists M[g]$. Here $\exists M[g]$ stands short for $\bigvee_{\delta \in DA(M)} g[d_A/\delta.A | A \subset M]$, where $g[d_A/\delta.A | A \in M]$ denotes the syntactic replacement of all occurrences of d_A in g for $A \in M$ with $\delta.A$.*

and the timeout transition $s \xrightarrow{t}_M s'$ iff there exists a timeout transition $s \xrightarrow{t} s'$.

4 Simulation

Simulation relations were first introduced by Milner in [14] for the purpose of comparing programs, and widely used later to show abstraction and refinement between models and specifications. They provide a sufficient condition for language inclusion that can be established with low complexity, and their precongruence properties are suited for compositional reasoning. In [5] simulation relations for ordinary constraint automata were defined to verify if two automata are language equivalent or the language of one is contained in the language of the other. In this section we propose a notion of *resource sensitive timed simulation* as a way to guarantee not only the inclusion of languages induced by Reo circuits, but also a higher (or at least equal) performance. For example, we may ask a connector implementation to be always faster than what is required by the specification when the same resource is consumed, where both the specification and the implementation are given as RSTCA.

We first consider the non-timed version of simulation for ordinary constraint automata. As discussed in [5], one constraint automaton $\mathscr{T}$ is simulated by another constraint automaton $\mathscr{A}$ if all the languages that are accepted by $\mathscr{T}$ are also accepted by $\mathscr{A}$. In addition to the non-timed simulation, we require some time conditions to hold. For example, we may hope a constraint automata (the implementation) to be always faster than the time constraints imposed by another (the specification) while no more resource is needed. Additionally, we may require that the implementation always complies with the timeouts established by the specification.

We first introduce the functional simulation relation $\lesssim_f$ where only functional aspects of a system are considered while the performance aspects such as the time needed for an interaction are ignored. However, we should note that the time that a system spends waiting for the environment to react has the possibility to affect the behavior of the system. This is because the time may cause a timeout transition and change the system from one state to another. Therefore, a simulation relation focusing on the functional behavior must also take into account the maximal time the system can stay in each state.

Definition 7. *For a given RSTCA $\mathscr{T} = (S, S_0, \mathcal{N}, R, \longrightarrow)$, the functional simulation is defined as the coarsest binary relation $\lesssim_f \subseteq S \times S$, such that for all $s_1, s_2 \in S$ with $s_1 \lesssim_f s_2$ and all $N \subseteq \mathcal{N}, \delta \in DA(N)$, resource assignment x and $t \in \mathbf{T}$,*

- *if $\langle s_1, x \rangle \xrightarrow{N,\delta,t} \langle s_1', \mu(N, \delta, x) \rangle$, then there exists $s_2' \in S$ and $t' \in \mathbf{T}$, such that $\langle s_2, x \rangle \xrightarrow{N,\delta,t'} \langle s_2', \mu(N, \delta, x) \rangle$ and $s_1' \lesssim_f s_2'$,*
- *if $s_1 \xrightarrow{t} s_1'$, then there exists s_2', such that $s_2 \xrightarrow{t} s_2'$ and $s_1' \lesssim_f s_2'$.*

One RSTCA $\mathscr{T}_2$ functionally simulates another RSTCA $\mathscr{T}_1$ (denoted as $\mathscr{T}_1 \lesssim_f \mathscr{T}_2$) iff every initial state of $\mathscr{T}_1$ is functionally simulated by an initial state of $\mathscr{T}_2$ [1].

Note that the idea underlying Definition 7 is that if one RSTCA $\mathscr{T}_2$ functionally simulates $\mathscr{T}_1$, then $\mathscr{T}_1$ does not allow any behavior that is forbidden in $\mathscr{T}_2$. In the following, we introduce another notion of simulation for RSTCA, which focuses on not only functional behavior, but also resource-related timing properties. The simulation establishes

---

[1] Here we assume that $\mathscr{T}_1$ and $\mathscr{T}_2$ rely on the same set of names and resources.

requests over the function from resource values to time values corresponding to the performance of the interactive transitions if they are in the same context of resources.

Definition 8. *For a given RSTCA $\mathcal{T} = (S, S_0, \mathcal{N}, R, \longrightarrow)$, the (strong) simulation is defined as the coarsest binary relation $\lesssim \subseteq S \times S$, such that for all $s_1, s_2 \in S$ with $s_1 \lesssim s_2$ and all $N \subseteq \mathcal{N}, \delta \in DA(N)$, a resource assignment x and $t \in \mathbf{T}$,*

- *if $\langle s_1, x \rangle \xrightarrow{N,\delta,t} \langle s_1', \mu(N, \delta, x) \rangle$, then there exists $s_2' \in S$ and $t' \in \mathbf{T}$, such that $t \leq t'$ and $\langle s_2, x \rangle \xrightarrow{N,\delta,t'} \langle s_2', \mu(N, \delta, x) \rangle$ and $s_1' \lesssim s_2'$,*
- *if $s_1 \xrightarrow{t} s_1'$, then there exists s_2', such that $s_2 \xrightarrow{t} s_2'$ and $s_1' \lesssim s_2'$.*

One RSTCA $\mathcal{T}_2$ simulates another RSTCA $\mathcal{T}_1$ (denoted as $\mathcal{T}_1 \lesssim \mathcal{T}_2$) iff every initial state of $\mathcal{T}_1$ is simulated by an initial state of $\mathcal{T}_2$.

From Definition 7 and 8, we can easily derive the following result:

Corollary 1. *Any strong simulation is also a functional simulation.*

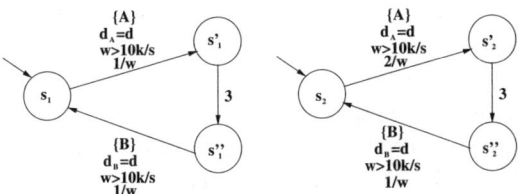

Fig. 8. Simulation

Example 4. We consider the two RSTCA given in Figure 8 for two different implementations of a FIFO channel offered by two providers. Here, state s_1 functionally simulates state s_2 in the same figure, but does not (strongly) simulate it. But on the other direction, we have both $s_1 \lesssim_f s_2$ and $s_1 \lesssim s_2$.

We shall need the familiar property that simulation is a congruence with respect to the product and hiding operators, that is, in our setting, represented by the following theorem:

Theorem 1. *If $\mathcal{T}_1 \lesssim \mathcal{T}_1'$, and $\mathcal{T}_2 \lesssim \mathcal{T}_2'$, then*

(1) $\mathcal{T}_1 \bowtie \mathcal{T}_2 \lesssim \mathcal{T}_1' \bowtie \mathcal{T}_2'$,
(2) $\mathtt{hide}(\mathcal{T}_1, M) \lesssim \mathtt{hide}(\mathcal{T}_1', M)$.

Proof. The proof is carried out by constructing witnessing simulations. We consider the following relation

$$\mathcal{R} = \{((\langle s_1, s_2 \rangle, \langle s_1', s_2' \rangle) : s_1 \lesssim s_1', s_2 \lesssim s_2'\}$$

for (1) and show it to be a simulation.

We only consider the synchronization case. The proof for interleaving and time out transitions are similar. If $\langle\langle s_1, s_2\rangle, x\rangle \xrightarrow{N,\delta,t} \langle\langle \hat{s}_1, \hat{s}_2\rangle, \mu(N, \delta, x)\rangle$ is a transition in $\mathscr{T}_1 \bowtie \mathscr{T}_2$, then according to Definition 5, there exists $N_1, N_2 \subseteq \mathscr{N}$, resource constraints rc_1, rc_2, and some function C_1 and C_2, such that $s_1 \xrightarrow{N_1,g_1,rc_1,C_1}_1 \hat{s}_1$ and $s_2 \xrightarrow{N_2,g_2,rc_2,C_2}_2 \hat{s}_2$ are transitions in $\mathscr{T}_1$ and $\mathscr{T}_2$, respectively, where $N = N_1 \cup N_2$, δ satisfies $g_1 \wedge g_2$, x satisfies $rc_1 \otimes rc_2$, and there exists an allocation of resources such that $C_1 \odot C_2(x) = t$. Since $s_1 \lesssim s_1'$, $s_2 \lesssim s_2'$, it follows that there exist C_1' and C_2', such that $s_1' \xrightarrow{N_1,g_1,rc_1,C_1'}_1 \hat{s}_1'$ and $s_2' \xrightarrow{N_2,g_2,rc_2,C_2'}_2 \hat{s}_2'$ for some $\hat{s}_1'$ and $\hat{s}_2'$ are transitions in $\mathscr{T}_1$ and $\mathscr{T}_2$ respectively, and $\hat{s}_1 \lesssim \hat{s}_1'$, $\hat{s}_2 \lesssim \hat{s}_2'$. Moreover, if we consider the same allocation of resources, then we have $C_1 \leq C_1'$ and $C_2 \leq C_2'$ due to Definition 8. Therefore, $C_1' \odot C_2'(x) \geq t$. Let $t' = C_1' \odot C_2'(x)$, then $\langle\langle s_1', s_2'\rangle, x\rangle \xrightarrow{N,\delta,t'} \langle\langle \hat{s}_1', \hat{s}_2'\rangle, \mu(N, \delta, x)\rangle$ is a transition in $\mathscr{T}_1' \bowtie \mathscr{T}_2'$ and $(\langle s_1, s_2\rangle, \langle s_1', s_2'\rangle) \in \mathscr{R}$.

To prove (2) it suffices to show that given a RSTCA $\mathscr{T} = (S, S_0, \mathscr{N}, R, \longrightarrow)$, any simulation $\lesssim$ for $\mathscr{T}$ is also a simulation for $\text{hide}(\mathscr{T}, M)$. By considering Definition 6, we can obtain the result easily.

5   Related Work

Some timed models have been proposed for coordinating services with real-time properties. For example, Arbab et al. [2] proposed an operational semantics for Reo in terms of Timed Constraint Automata (TCA) and introduced a temporal logic for specifying and verifying real-time properties or connectors. Orthogonally, a Continuous-Time Constraint Automata (CCA) model was proposed in [6], which integrates the features of continuous-time Markov Chains, and introduces a stochastic variant of the constraint automata model where transitions might have a certain delay according to some probability distribution over a continuous time domain. [8] presented an approach for automatic translation from web service choreography description to timed automata. There are also some work on time extensions of finite state machines [17], timed interface automata [7], etc. These models have the implicit assumption that unbounded resources are available. However, in practice, real-time systems are always restricted by resources. To deal with this problem, several approaches have been proposed to integrate real-time models with the scheduling and resource allocation, which aim to facilitate reasoning about systems sensitive to real-time and resource related properties. For example, [10] proposed a compositional model for reasoning about schedulers which allocate resources to tasks, but it is only suitable to analyse asynchronous systems because it is based on an asynchronous language. [9] defined a hierarchy of resource models to handle the resource allocation and reclamation. However, the models are relatively abstract and not compositional. [13] introduced a timed extension of the extended finite state machine model and a testing methodology, taking into account the temporal issues as we discussed in this paper. However, there is no discussion about compositionality for that model.

As in Continuous-Time Constraint Automata model [6], we also have two types of transitions in the RSTCA model describing interactive transitions and timeout transitions. The difference consists of two aspects: On one hand, our model of time-out transitions is not restricted to Markovian transitions, instead we use time variables to describe the time information, which can be more general and satisfy other kinds of distributions. On the other hand, the time that an interactive transition will take is not just a simple time value describing time passage, but depends on the available resources.

6   Conclusion

In this paper we provided an operational model for reasoning about resource and time information related to component connectors under the assumption that the time duration for interactions depends on the available resources. We defined the RSTCA model for this purpose, together with notions of simulation that are preserved under the composition operators product and hiding. Since these are the only operators needed for compositional construction of networks in the channel-based coordination language Reo, our framework fits well in this context and provides the basis for resource-sensitive performance analysis of component connectors.

In terms of future work, what we would like to do in the next step is the integration of our model and the stochastic timed model as in [6]. Another issue we intend to study is to investigate some resource allocation and consumption strategies, like scheduling [15]. Development of special models and logics for reasoning about resource-sensitive timed features in Reo will also be studied.

References

1. Alur, R., Dill, D.: A theory of timed automata. Theoretical Computer Science 126(2), 183–235 (1994)
2. Arbab, F., Baier, C., de Boer, F., Rutten, J.: Models and Temporal Logics for Timed Component Connectors. In: Cuellar, J.R., Liu, Z. (eds.) SEFM2004. 2nd International Conference on Software Engineering and Formal Methods, pp. 198–207. IEEE Computer Society Press, Los Alamitos (2004)
3. Arbab, F.: Reo: A Channel-based Coordination Model for Component Composition. Mathematical Structures in Computer Science 14(3), 329–366 (2004)
4. Arbab, F., Baier, C., Rutten, J., Sirjani, M.: Modeling component connectors in reo by constraint automata (extended abstract). In: Brogi, A., Jacquet, J.-M., Pimentel, E. (eds.) Proceedings of FOCLASA 2003, the Foundations of Coordination Languages and Software Architectures. ENTCS, vol. 97, pp. 25–46. Elsevier, Amsterdam (2003)
5. Baier, C., Sirjani, M., Arbab, F., Rutten, J.: Modeling component connectors in Reo by constraint automata. Science of Computer Programming 61, 75–113 (2006)
6. Baier, C., Wolf, V.: Stochastic Reasoning About Channel-Based Component Connectors. In: Ciancarini, P., Wiklicky, H. (eds.) COORDINATION 2006, LNCS, vol. 4038, pp. 1–15. Springer, Heidelberg (2006)
7. de Alfaro, L., Henzinger, T.A., Stoelinga, M.: Timed interfaces. In: Sangiovanni–Vincentelli, A.L., Sifakis, J. (eds.) EMSOFT 2002, LNCS, vol. 2491, pp. 108–122. Springer, Heidelberg (2002)
8. Diaz, G., Pardo, J.-J., Cambronero, M.-E., Valero, V., Cuartero, F.: Automatic Translation of WS-CDL Choreographies to Timed Automata. In: Bravetti, M., Kloul, L., Zavattaro, G. (eds.) EPEW 2005 and WS-FM 2005, LNCS, vol. 3670, pp. 230–242. Springer, Heidelberg (2005)

9. Jin, N., He, J.: Resource Semantic Models for Programming Languages. Technical Report 277, UNU/IIST (April 2003)

10. Lowe, G.: Scheduling-oriented models for real-time systems. The Computer Journal 38, 443–456 (1995)

11. Papazoglou, M.P., Georgakopoulos, D.: Service Oriented Computing. Comm. ACM 46(10), 25–28 (2003)

12. Menascé, D.A.: Composing Web Services: A QoS View. IEEE Internet Computing 8(6), 88–90 (2004)

13. Merayo, M.G., Núñez, M., Rodríguez, I.: Extending efsms to specify and test timed systems with action durations and timeouts. In: Najm, E., et al. (eds.) FORTE 2006, LNCS, vol. 4229, pp. 372–387. Springer, Heidelberg (2006)

14. Milner, R.: An algebraic definition of simulation between programs. In: Cooper, D.C. (ed.) Proceedings of the 2nd International Joint Conference on Artifiial Intelligence, London, UK. William Kaufmann, British Computer Society (1971)

15. Mousavi, M.R., Reniers, M.A., Basten, T., Chaudron, M.R.V.: PARS: A Process Algebra with Resources and Schedulers. In: Larsen, K.G., Niebert, P. (eds.) FORMATS 2003, LNCS, vol. 2791, pp. 134–150. Springer, Heidelberg (2003)

16. Núñez, M., Rodríguez, I.: Conformance testing relations for timed systems. In: Grieskamp, W., Weise, C. (eds.) FATES 2005, LNCS, vol. 3997, pp. 103–117. Springer, Heidelberg (2006)

17. Park, J.C., Miller, R.E.: Synthesizing protocol specifications from service specifications in timed extended finite state machines. In: Park, J.C., Miller, R.E. (eds.) 17th IEEE International Conference on Distributed Computing Systems, ICDCS'97, pp. 253–260. IEEE Computer Society, Los Alamitos (1997)

18. Parrow, J.: Fairness Properties in Process Algebra. PhD thesis, Uppsala University, Sweden (1985)

19. Pym, D., Tofts, C.: A calculus and logic of resources and processes. Formal Aspects of Computing 18, 495–517 (2006)

Author Index

Printing: Mercedes-Druck, Berlin
Binding: Stein+Lehmann, Berlin

Lecture Notes in Computer Science

For information about Vols. 1–4414

please contact your bookseller or Springer

Vol. 4477: J. Martí, J.M. Benedí, A.M. Mendonça, J. Serrat (Eds.), Pattern Recognition and Image Analysis, Part I. XXVII, 625 pages. 2007.

Vol. 4476: V. Gorodetsky, C. Zhang, V.A. Skormin, L. Cao (Eds.), Autonomous Intelligent Systems: Multi-Agents and Data Mining. XIII, 323 pages. 2007. (Sublibrary LNAI).

Vol. 4475: P. Crescenzi, G. Prencipe, G. Pucci (Eds.), Fun with Algorithms. X, 273 pages. 2007.

Vol. 4472: M. Haindl, J. Kittler, F. Roli (Eds.), Multiple Classifier Systems. XI, 524 pages. 2007.

Vol. 4471: P. Cesar, K. Chorianopoulos, J.F. Jensen (Eds.), Interactive TV: a Shared Experience. XIII, 236 pages. 2007.

Vol. 4470: Q. Wang, D. Pfahl, D.M. Raffo (Eds.), Software Process Dynamics and Agility. XI, 346 pages. 2007.

Vol. 4468: M.M. Bonsangue, E.B. Johnsen (Eds.), Formal Methods for Open Object-Based Distributed Systems. X, 317 pages. 2007.

Vol. 4465: T. Chahed, B. Tuffin (Eds.), Network Control and Optimization. XIII, 305 pages. 2007.

Vol. 4464: E. Dawson, D.S. Wong (Eds.), Information Security Practice and Experience. XIII, 361 pages. 2007.

Vol. 4463: I. Măndoiu, A. Zelikovsky (Eds.), Bioinformatics Research and Applications. XV, 653 pages. 2007. (Sublibrary LNBI).

Vol. 4462: D. Sauveron, K. Markantonakis, A. Bilas, J.-J. Quisquater (Eds.), Information Security Theory and Practices. XII, 255 pages. 2007.

Vol. 4459: C. Cérin, K.-C. Li (Eds.), Advances in Grid and Pervasive Computing. XVI, 759 pages. 2007.

Vol. 4453: T. Speed, H. Huang (Eds.), Research in Computational Molecular Biology. XVI, 550 pages. 2007. (Sublibrary LNBI).

Vol. 4452: M. Fasli, O. Shehory (Eds.), Agent-Mediated Electronic Commerce. VIII, 249 pages. 2007. (Sublibrary LNAI).

Vol. 4451: T.S. Huang, A. Nijholt, M. Pantic, A. Pentland (Eds.), Artifical Intelligence for Human Computing. XVI, 359 pages. 2007. (Sublibrary LNAI).

Vol. 4450: T. Okamoto, X. Wang (Eds.), Public Key Cryptography – PKC 2007. XIII, 491 pages. 2007.

Vol. 4448: M. Giacobini et al. (Ed.), Applications of Evolutionary Computing. XXIII, 755 pages. 2007.

Vol. 4447: E. Marchiori, J.H. Moore, J.C. Rajapakse (Eds.), Evolutionary Computation,Machine Learning and Data Mining in Bioinformatics. XI, 302 pages. 2007.

Vol. 4446: C. Cotta, J. van Hemert (Eds.), Evolutionary Computation in Combinatorial Optimization. XII, 241 pages. 2007.

Vol. 4445: M. Ebner, M. O'Neill, A. Ekárt, L. Vanneschi, A.I. Esparcia-Alcázar (Eds.), Genetic Programming. XI, 382 pages. 2007.

Vol. 4444: T. Reps, M. Sagiv, J. Bauer (Eds.), Program Analysis and Compilation, Theory and Practice. X, 361 pages. 2007.

Vol. 4443: R. Kotagiri, P.R. Krishna, M. Mohania, E. Nantajeewarawat (Eds.), Advances in Databases: Concepts, Systems and Applications. XXI, 1126 pages. 2007.

Vol. 4440: B. Liblit, Cooperative Bug Isolation. XV, 101 pages. 2007.

Vol. 4439: W. Abramowicz (Ed.), Business Information Systems. XV, 654 pages. 2007.

Vol. 4438: L. Maicher, A. Sigel, L.M. Garshol (Eds.), Leveraging the Semantics of Topic Maps. X, 257 pages. 2007. (Sublibrary LNAI).

Vol. 4433: E. Şahin, W.M. Spears, A.F.T. Winfield (Eds.), Swarm Robotics. XII, 221 pages. 2007.

Vol. 4432: B. Beliczynski, A. Dzielinski, M. Iwanowski, B. Ribeiro (Eds.), Adaptive and Natural Computing Algorithms, Part II. XXVI, 761 pages. 2007.

Vol. 4431: B. Beliczynski, A. Dzielinski, M. Iwanowski, B. Ribeiro (Eds.), Adaptive and Natural Computing Algorithms, Part I. XXV, 851 pages. 2007.

Vol. 4430: C.C. Yang, D. Zeng, M. Chau, K. Chang, Q. Yang, X. Cheng, J. Wang, F.-Y. Wang, H. Chen (Eds.), Intelligence and Security Informatics. XII, 330 pages. 2007.

Vol. 4429: R. Lu, J.H. Siekmann, C. Ullrich (Eds.), Cognitive Systems. X, 161 pages. 2007. (Sublibrary LNAI).

Vol. 4427: S. Uhlig, K. Papagiannaki, O. Bonaventure (Eds.), Passive and Active Network Measurement. XI, 274 pages. 2007.

Vol. 4426: Z.-H. Zhou, H. Li, Q. Yang (Eds.), Advances in Knowledge Discovery and Data Mining. XXV, 1161 pages. 2007. (Sublibrary LNAI).

Vol. 4425: G. Amati, C. Carpineto, G. Romano (Eds.), Advances in Information Retrieval. XIX, 759 pages. 2007.

Vol. 4424: O. Grumberg, M. Huth (Eds.), Tools and Algorithms for the Construction and Analysis of Systems. XX, 738 pages. 2007.

Vol. 4423: H. Seidl (Ed.), Foundations of Software Science and Computational Structures. XVI, 379 pages. 2007.

Vol. 4422: M.B. Dwyer, A. Lopes (Eds.), Fundamental Approaches to Software Engineering. XV, 440 pages. 2007.

Vol. 4421: R. De Nicola (Ed.), Programming Languages and Systems. XVII, 538 pages. 2007.

Vol. 4420: S. Krishnamurthi, M. Odersky (Eds.), Compiler Construction. XIV, 233 pages. 2007.

Vol. 4419: P.C. Diniz, E. Marques, K. Bertels, M.M. Fernandes, J.M.P. Cardoso (Eds.), Reconfigurable Computing: Architectures, Tools and Applications. XIV, 391 pages. 2007.

Vol. 4418: A. Gagalowicz, W. Philips (Eds.), Computer Vision/Computer Graphics Collaboration Techniques. XV, 620 pages. 2007.

Vol. 4416: A. Bemporad, A. Bicchi, G. Buttazzo (Eds.), Hybrid Systems: Computation and Control. XVII, 797 pages. 2007.

Vol. 4415: P. Lukowicz, L. Thiele, G. Tröster (Eds.), Architecture of Computing Systems - ARCS 2007. X, 297 pages. 2007.